Christian Origins

By the same author
The Open Heaven (SPCK 1982)

Christopher Rowland

Christian Origins

An Account of the Setting and Character of the most Important Messianic Sect of Judaism

First published in Great Britain 1985
Third impression 1989
SPCK
Holy Trinity Church
Marylebone Road
London NW1 4DU

Unless otherwise stated, biblical quotations are from the
Revised Standard Version of the Bible, copyrighted 1946, 1952, © 1971, 1973,
and are reprinted by permission of the National Council of
the Churches of Christ in the USA.

Extracts from *Jesus' Proclamation of the Kingdom of God* by J. Weiss (1971)
are reprinted by permission of SCM Press.

British Library Cataloguing in Publication Data

Rowland, Christopher
    Christian origins.
    1. Judaism—Relations—Christianity
    2. Christianity and other religions—Judaism
    I. Title
    296   BM535

    ISBN 0-281-04110-5

Photoset by Tradespools Ltd, Frome, Somerset
Printed in Great Britain at the
University Press, Cambridge

For
John O'Neill
and
Ed Sanders

CONTENTS

Contents

ACKNOWLEDGEMENTS

It has been my good fortune to enjoy the advice and support of colleagues and friends during the writing of this book. A period of leave granted by my College enabled me to work on the book during the early part of 1983. While I do not pretend that the book manifests anything other than the tradition of European biblical scholarship, a period in Brazil and Mexico stimulated my exegetical work. I am grateful to the many friends that I made there for the exciting new possibilities for biblical interpretation which they opened up for me. This journey was made possible as a result of grants from Jesus College, the British Academy and the Bethune-Baker Fund of the University of Cambridge. To the members of all these bodies I would like to express my thanks. I am also very grateful to the Cambridge University Press for permission to use material as the basis of the section on apocalyptic.

Judith Longman of SPCK and the anonymous reader of my manuscript have both been of invaluable assistance from the very genesis of the project. I am grateful to Judith for suggesting it to me in the first place, and to Ian Watt for his patience with a large and untidy typescript. William Horbury, Jonathan Knight and Andrew Chester read the manuscript and made helpful suggestions. To two friends I owe a special debt of gratitude. Since I returned to Cambridge four years ago, the friendship and wisdom of John O'Neill have been a great encouragement to me. He read parts of the manuscript and pointed out some of my worst excesses. I appreciate his patience with approaches that he found so diametrically opposed to his own. I have profited from our disagreements. Ed Sanders has not read a word of this book, but during his sabbatical year in Cambridge I found that our discussions on Christian origins clarified innumerable issues.

Finally, I have to thank my family. It was a matter of some frustration to the children that my period of leave did not seem to offer them additional opportunities for playing with their father. They have put up with my hours at my desk with great patience. My wife, Catherine's, support has been an unfailing inspiration and our shared discussions about the wider setting of my interpretative work of fundamental importance for much of what is written here.

None of my friends or advisers should be held responsible for the eccentric positions adopted here or the mistakes which remain. One thing is certain: it would have been a much worse book without their help. I trust that what remains may be of some help to those studying the rise of Christianity and also those who still look to them as a resource for understanding the nature of Christian discipleship in the modern world.

PREFACE

Students in universities and colleges are nowadays being introduced to early Christianity via courses which seek to examine the New Testament documents in the much broader framework of first-century Judaism and the Hellenistic world. It is in order to help the student embarking upon such courses that I have written this book. It is introductory in the sense that it does not include a large amount of technical discussion and exegetical detail but is on a much larger scale than a general introduction to Judaism and early Christianity, because I feel that students need something more substantial than a general introduction, which glances cursorily at a number of topics in a relatively small space. While I make no pretensions to exhaustive coverage, I have attempted to go beyond the passing reference to explore early Christianity and its world in some depth while avoiding detailed exegesis.

Those who set out to write an account of Christian origins face a daunting task. In order to keep such a study within reasonable bounds the presentation inevitably has to cut corners, both in the unravelling of various strands which led to the emergence of Christianity as a dominant religious movement in the later Roman Empire, and in the treatment of the enormous amount of secondary literature which has emerged on the subject in the last century.

I am painfully aware of my own shortcomings as I embark on such an exercise. The perceptive reader will be able to note that my research interests have given a distinct slant to my approach, though I hope they have not distorted it. I have assumed in my presentation that it was the Jewish world which gave Christianity its essential outlines. In saying this, I do not want to suggest for one moment that early Christianity was insulated from Hellenistic culture (how could it have been?), but that its assimilation of Hellenistic ideas and outlook came via Judaism which has to varying extents itself been profoundly influenced by Hellenism. Perhaps if my knowledge of the Roman world were greater, my vision would not have appeared so restricted, but I suspect that my approach would not be significantly different: to understand early Christianity is, first of all, to understand first-century Judaism in all its complexity.

There are two approaches that I could have taken in this study. It would have been possible to offer a student a bird's eye view of scholarship on ancient Judaism and early Christianity, to introduce him or her to the various opinions about the subjects treated here. Such an approach has the merit of giving a degree of objectivity in seeking to present as fairly as possible all sides of the argument and weighing the various possibilities. The other approach is more controversial, though possibly, for the writer, much more interesting; that is, to present a picture of the rise of Christianity, which certainly takes into account the variety of scholarly opinions, but which seeks to test a hypothesis. I have rejected the first approach for several reasons.

First, it would have been difficult to keep a book of this kind within reasonable bounds if I had attempted to offer a history of scholarship on Judaism and Christianity during the last twenty, never mind fifty, years. Secondly, it has become much easier for students to lay their hands on concise summaries of particular approaches, without having to rely on condensations of particular standpoints in student manuals. Thirdly, there is a case to be made for outlining a hypothesis which does not have detailed exegetical support while, of course, seeking to do justice to the main thrust of the early Christian literature. It is often easy to miss the wood for the trees. Fourthly, I have to confess my own reservations about embarking upon a project which seeks, in the main, to offer a history of scholarship. It is not that I do not think that it is unimportant for a student text-book to introduce the gamut of scholarship; of course, that is most necessary. But what is equally important is for a student to learn to read critically and to be aware of the need to assess interpretations of ancient history and ideas which are offered. While I hope that what is written here will enable the reader to gain some insight into the Jewish world of the first century AD and the messianic movement which emerged from it, I would like to think that the book will not be an authoritative source-book, either of material about the ancient world or of modern opinions of it, but a stimulus which provokes both disagreement and further research on the primary sources and the writings of those whose opinions differ from my own. The interpreter of ancient texts acknowledges the very profound limitations of ancient historiography and the restrictions caused by his own interpretative setting. The sooner a student apprehends these very real barriers, the better. Accordingly, I have not set out to write the definitive study of Christian origins; it is a work which arises from a particular exegetical tradition in Europe and evinces certain clear assumptions about the character of Christianity in both its ancient and modern manifestations. This is not to suggest that what is written here stands apart from the mainstream of contemporary scholarship. In its two major theses (the centrality of eschatology and the crucial importance of the Jewish world for the understanding of the New Testament) this book is set very firmly within the mainstream of contemporary scholarly trends. In this sense, the book does not cease to break new ground, though, by going over old ground, it is hoped that it may bring to light matters which have been neglected in the past.

New Testament scholarship is going through a period of transition at present. It is now a little over a decade since James Robinson and Helmut Koester called for new approaches to the study of early Christian literature.[1]

Looking back at their attempt to offer a new approach, it is apparent that what they had to offer did not differ markedly from the well-established methods of New Testament research. In the light of such an assessment, it may be rather premature to speak of another new approach as if it marked a breakthrough, but the growing interest in the socio-economic dimension of religious groups in antiquity promises to introduce us to new insights and to remind us of neglected aspects of scholarly research from the past.

It is a measure of the neglect of this approach that we are still at a very preliminary stage in the utilization of it. This means that we still run the risk of rash generalizations and over-enthusiastic use of tools not adequately fitted to the specific task facing the historian of the early Christian religion. Mistakes in this area have been, and will continue to be, made. Two things are certain. First of all, this dimension of scholarly research has been sadly neglected and has led to certain distortions in the study of Christianity, for example, the preoccupation with the history of ideas, with little or no concern for the social setting of those ideas. Secondly, the inherited wisdom of biblical scholarship is not to be thrown overboard as irrelevant to this approach. Indeed, it may be that some of the more persistent log-jams in scholarly research can be resolved by the introduction of such a different perspective.

I have profited greatly from the studies which have already been written on the social world of the first Christians, and some attempt has been made to take account of it in this study. Nevertheless the indebtedness to this approach has not led me to abandon a traditional method which attributes to certain figures and their lives as much, if not more, importance than the wider religious movements. Thus I have not hesitated to include large sections on Jesus and Paul, though I recognize that the groups which were inheritors of their method and message may have made more impact *in the long run* inside and outside the churches than the two men themselves. Clearly both were part of a much wider complex of social, economic and religious realities, but I do not consider that the new directions which did emerge in the thought and practice of the early Christian groups can be adequately explained by socio-economic forces and group-movements only. The exploration of the contribution of the charismatic leader, in other words, still has its part to play in the portrayal of religious movements. In this respect this study will be regarded by some as being very much in an old-fashioned mould.

I realize that in raising the question of the cultural setting of primitive Christianity, I shall at once provoke expectations which I cannot at present satisfy and as a result disappoint many readers by failing to answer questions such as: what kind of socio-political world produced charismatic figures like Jesus and Paul; what specific features can be gleaned about their social settings from their religious beliefs? That these questions must be asked I have no doubt, but I am also aware that they are not susceptible of easy answers. We cannot glibly assume that utopianism, for example, is the prerogative of the marginalized only. The social context of religious language is a subject which demands detailed examination in the future. To embark upon such an ambitious project in a book of this kind would have needed much more painstaking research than was possible at this stage. I am certain that it is a subject to which I must return in due course.

Let me make some further comments about other assumptions in this study: first, Judaism. It is rare to pick up a text-book on ancient Judaism these days without finding expressed there the conviction that after the fall of Jerusalem in AD 70 significant changes took place in the character of Judaism. Up to that date, it is suggested, there was no such thing as orthodox Judaism (if by that is meant a system of belief and practice to which the majority of Jews subscribed) but a multiplicity of interpretations some of which were mutually exclusive in their understanding of the common traditions. After 70 we find the gradual emergence of a type of Judaism, with close links with Pharisaism, as the dominant expression of Jewish piety. That assumption underlies the whole of this study and makes me cagey about the use of anachronistic terms like Judaism and Christianity as recognizable entities when speaking about pre-70 Judaism.

Secondly, it will be apparent that, like many other students of the New Testament, I have been profoundly influenced by the work of Johannes Weiss and Albert Schweitzer, so that to understand eschatology is to understand early Christianity and its ideology. Few today would dissent from the view that eschatology was central to the earliest Christian proclamation, but a thoroughgoing eschatological interpretation of the early Christian religion has been by no means widely accepted. Perhaps the thesis that the whole of early Christian thought can be explained as a result of the need of Christian thinkers to come to terms with the non-arrival of the kingdom of God is one which makes too many assumptions about the character of early Christian writing and the problems which they may have faced. But the simple fact is that earliest Christian literature has an eschatological foundation not apparent in later manifestations of main-stream Christian belief, and this change requires explanation. Contemporary scholarship has followed the trend of much early Christian doctrinal thinking by concentrating on Christology as the central issue in the earliest phase of Christian theology (as the proliferation of books and articles on this theme makes clear); books on 'the Eschatology of the New Testament' are nothing like as numerous as those on 'the Christology of the New Testament'. We are not often told why it was that the New Testament writers were notably reluctant to engage in christological exposition, despite the attempts of modern interpreters to make them do just that. In addition, the factors which led to the focus of attention becoming the Proclaimer rather than the message he proclaimed continues to be a matter of some importance. Our tendency to offer facile suggestions and the paucity of evidence should not stop us exploring this important ideological development and its related social setting.

Thirdly (and this relates to the two previous considerations), I have assumed that, in early Christianity, we are dealing with a Jewish messianic sect, which continued to be this throughout the bulk of the period we are considering. In making this assumption I cannot agree that there was, from the very start, something novel, which decisively separated the Christians from other Jews. The conviction that the shared Jewish hopes were being fulfilled was not in itself unique, nor was the attempt to interpret Scripture in the light of that conviction. Even if we possess few details of their practice and beliefs, there clearly were individuals and movements who held views similar to those held by many of the early Christians. There is no evidence that there was anything completely novel in its eschatological doctrine, and there are no grounds for seeking to separate it or the study of it from first-century Judaism as a whole. Opposition to it there clearly was, but, as is apparent from a study of our sources, there was nothing unusual in that. To explore the factors which led a Jewish messianic sect to develop into a religion separate from Judaism it is necessary to look at what happened to Judaism. In this exploration I acknowledge that the thesis that Christianity started life as a Jewish sect and finished as the Catholic Church is one that has been given an airing many times before. But the fact that the thesis (and its supporters) are tainted with suspicion of Protestant sympathies and a suspicion of hierarchies should make the thesis none the worse for that!

Finally, I recognize that in my approach to early Christianity I have not only indicated preferences for certain settings and interpretations but have utilized one interpretative method. One of the things that biblical interpreters must face is the complexity of the interpretative task; the historical-critical method which is the method used in this book represents one (albeit dominant) approach to Christian literature. Those of us who use this method need to recognize how easy it is to be trapped into thinking of it as a normative guide to the interpretation of texts. What I have written here does not, of course, imply that the variety of hermeneutical tools used at present (and for that matter throughout history) should be set aside by biblical students. The greater use of such methods in the future can only be of benefit to biblical interpretation.

One of the great difficulties I have found in writing this book has been the need to make a series of judgements about ancient Judaism and early Christianity without detailed argument, particularly where I feel my competence to make those judgements is not what it should be. I am painfully aware of the exegetical shortcomings; detailed discussion of the ancient texts has frequently had to be set on one side. For many readers the way in which assertion has taken the place of reasoned argument and attention to the minutiae of exegesis will be a fatal flaw. In writing of the ministry of Jesus, for example, I recognize that nearly every statement I make could be challenged, and that I have opted for a more positive view of the historicity of the tradition than many would consider appropriate. It is not always possible to appeal to the assured results of scholarship because of the divergence of opinion which exists. I only hope that in avoiding the detailed study I have been able to sketch an outline of Christian origins which reflects the insights offered by modern scholarship, while at the same time being accessible in its scope and treatment to the inquirer into the beginnings of Christianity.

ABBREVIATIONS

Abr	*On Abraham* (Philo)
ANRW	W. Haase ed., *Aufstieg und Niedergang der Römischen Welt*
Ant	*Biblical Antiquities* (Josephus)
ARN	*Aboth de Rabbi Nathan*
b	*Babylonian Talmud*
BJ	*Bellum Judaicum: Jewish War* (Josephus)
BJRL	*Bulletin of the John Rylands Library*
C.Ap.	*Against Apion*
CBQ	*Catholic Biblical Quarterly*
Congr.	*On Preliminary Studies* (Philo)
EH	*Ecclesiastical History* (Eusebius)
EJ	*Encyclopaedia Judaica*
Embassy	*Embassy to Gaius* (Philo)
Enc.Jud.	*Encyclopedia Judaica*
Eng.Hist.Rev.	*English Historical Review*
Exp.T.	*Expository Times*
Fug.	*On Flight and Finding* (Philo)
Gig.	On the Giants (Philo)
Hag.	*Hagigah*
HTR	*Harvard Theological Review*
HUCA	*Hebrew Union College Annual*
IDB	Interpreter's Dictionary of the Bible
j	*Jerusalem Talmud*
JAAR	*Journal of the American Academy of Religion*
JBL	*Journal of Biblical Literature*
JE	*Jewish Encyclopaedia*
JJS	*Journal of Jewish Studies*
JNES	*Journal of Near Eastern Studies*
JQR	*Jewish Quarterly Review*
JSJ	*Journal for the Study of Judaism*

Abbreviations

JSNT	*Journal for the Study of the New Testament*
JSOT	*Journal for the Study of the Old Testament*
JSS	*Journal of Semitic Studies*
JTS	*Journal of Theological Studies*
Jub.	*Jubilees*
Leg. Alleg.	*Legum Allegoriae: Allegorical Interpretation of the Laws* (Philo)
M.	*Mishnah*
Men.	*Menahoth*
Migr.	*On the Migration of Abraham*
Nov.T.	*Novum Testamentum*
NTS	*New Testament Studies*
NTT	J.J. Jeremias, *New Testament Theology*
Post.	*On the Posterity and Exile of Cain* (Philo)
Praem.	*De Praemiis et Poenis: On Rewards and Punishments* (Philo)
Ps.Sol.	*Psalms of Solomon*
RB	*Revue Biblique*
RSR	*Recherches de science religieuse*
Sib.Or.	*Sibylline Oracles*
SJT	*Scottish Journal of Theology*
Spec.Leg.	*Special Laws* (Philo)
SVM	E. Schürer, ed. G. Vermes & F. Miller, *The History of the Jewish People in the Age of Jesus Christ*
T	*Tosefta*
TDNT	*Theological Dictionary of the New Testament*
TLZ	*Theologische Literaturzeitung*
TU	*Texte und Untersuchungen*
Vig.Chr.	*Vigiliae Christiane*
VT	*Vetus Testamentum*
ZAW	*Zeitschrift für alttestamentliche Wissenschaft*
ZNW	*Zeitschrift für neutestamentliche Wissenschaft*
ZPE	*Zeitschrift für Papyrologie und Epigraphik*
ZRGG	*Zeitschrift für Religions- und Geistesgeschichte*

PART I
Introduction

1

The Rock Whence Ye Were Hewn

After nearly two millennia of conflict and persecution, particularly of Jews by Christians, it has become very difficult for adherents of the two religions to acknowledge their common heritage. On both sides there has in the past been antagonism of a most vitriolic kind. A glance at some of the Jewish traditions concerning Jesus reveals the depth of hostility to this wayward offshoot from Judaism.[1] On the other side, the charge of deicide so often laid against Jews and the curse hinted at in Matthew 27.25 have been the cause of appalling violence and cruelty against Jews by Christians. Although the horror of the Nazi persecution of the Jews properly shocked Christians into new assessments of the Churches' relations to Judaism,[2] it should be a matter of considerable concern to Christians that anti-Semitic currents are still not unknown in Europe. Stemming this tide will depend a great deal on the willingness of both Christians and Jews to admit the shame and horror of past treatment (and the spirit of repentance is needed particularly on the Christian side) and to set out to examine the origins of these two outstanding attempts to understand the religious traditions in what Jews call the Tenach, the Hebrew bible comprising the Torah, Nebiim (Prophets) and Kethubim (Writings), and Christians the Old Testament.

From our perspective today, it is rather difficult to be aware of the common heritage. True, the Christian Church shares with the Jews the Hebrew and Aramaic Scriptures, which it includes in its canon of Scripture, but the beliefs of the mainline Christian Churches seem to be far removed from Judaism. Today many Christians, at least subconsciously, agree with the second-century heretic, Marcion, that the Old Testament with its occasional barbarism is the product of some lesser divine being, which has been transcended by a superior revelation initiated by Jesus of Nazareth. Thus the concerns of the Old Testament are really fundamentally different from those of the Christian Churches. In addition, the liturgy[3] and outlook of most Christians seems to be far removed from Judaism. The most obvious difference, of course, is the fact that the Torah, the law of Moses, *as a whole*, has little or no part to play in the ordering of the everyday lives of Christians. Despite the wish of some leading churchmen to see a return to the practice of, say, the Decalogue, the detailed observance which characterizes the Jewish sabbath is totally foreign to most Christians. Likewise the concern with purity and clean and unclean food seems to be alien to the dominant concerns of the Christian gospel. It appears that the rift has grown so wide, as one might expect after such a long period of separation and hostility, that Christianity has almost completely cut loose from its Jewish moorings.

Such a view has received support from many who have written about the emergence of Christianity over the last hundred years or so. While it is admitted that Jesus of Nazareth preached an essentially Jewish message about God and his kingdom,[4] very rapidly, it is argued, the Church turned the one who had proclaimed that message into the central feature of its own proclamation; the Jewish prophet of God's kingdom became the universal saviour.[5] While few today would subscribe to the views of those like Ferdinand Christian Baur and his disciples (the Tübingen school), who affirmed the radical separation between Jewish and Gentile Christianity, elements of this view have not totally vanished from the perspective of many who write on Christian origins.[6] Dominant in the story of the transformation of Judaism into a new religion, it is argued, was Paul. He in particular loosed the bands, which tied the message about Christ, from Judaism and changed it into a religion, which affected the destiny of the whole of humanity, thus initiating a hostile attitude to Judaism. Of course, this role for Paul is given at least superficial support by the often vehement denunciations of the Law of Moses in his own letters (e.g., Gal. 3.10ff.). At his conversion, we are led to believe, Paul turned his back on his Jewish religion in favour of a completely new way of understanding God and his ways.[7] The dominant place which Paul has within the Protestant tradition has doubtless accentuated the dichotomy between the religion of Law and the religion of grace, and as a result has extended the tension between Judaism and Christianity. There can be little doubt that, whatever Paul himself may have believed about the relationship of the Christian gospel to the Jewish tradition, it has all too frequently been the case that his interpreters have understood him to imply a *complete* dichotomy between his life as a Pharisee and his life as an apostle of Jesus Christ, a view we shall want to question later.

There are enormous problems confronting Jews and Christians, as they seek to accept their common heritage and their differing interpretations of that heritage. The time has come to get behind the rigid boundaries imposed by the past, and the bitter controversies which have marked Jewish and Christian relations, to ask what it was that led to that separation and that bitterness. It is worth reflecting that the lines were not so clearly drawn in the second century, even in the midst of so much mutual recrimination and bitterness. We know from early Christian writings that there was a small, though significant, intercourse between Jews and Christians for a considerable period.[8] Despite all its contempt for Judaism, the *Dialogue* of Justin (a Christian who lived in the middle of the second century AD) with the Jew Trypho exhibits a continuing concern among early Christians to justify their interpretation of the Old Testament as the

4

authentic one. There is regret that Christians are excluded from Jewish synagogues (chapters 16, 47f, 93, 95f, 108, 117, 133 and 137), though Justin does not spare his venom on those who have acted in this way, a foretaste of bitter disputes to come.[9] Nevertheless what comes across in the *Dialogue* is the conviction on Justin's part that what the Christians believed was entirely consistent with the Scriptures, which both Jews and Christians shared. The whole of his argument depends on the assumption that belief in Jesus was not an eccentric departure from the traditions but was at least as valid an interpretation as the understanding of those same texts held by Jews.[10]

However much we may cringe at some of Justin's remarks about Judaism and its blindness, a bland rejection of them as inappropriate to our more sensitive and liberal consciences cannot be the way in which such material is handled. It is a fundamental strand in the New Testament that the convictions about Jesus were the authentic fulfilment of the promises of the Jewish Scriptures, the Christian Old Testament. Refusal to accept this fact meant that persistence in an old pattern of religion was tantamount to disobedience to the Most High (e.g., John 14.6; Acts 4.12; Rom. 10.7ff.). A Christian writer cannot deny that this is at the heart of the tradition with which he has to deal, however much he might today want to avoid some of the more excessive interpretations and be more tentative. But to assert the messiahship of Jesus is not to concede that we must simply remain behind battle-lines drawn long ago and the ideologies of centuries' duration. We must cross the divide and attempt to look at the world out of which two conflicting interpretations of the Jewish Scriptures emerged. It may well be that the results of our quest will bring us no nearer to a solution and that the factors which make the two religions what they are prohibit any significant *rapprochement*. But much groundwork needs to be done and dialogue entered into before we can say that we are in a position to understand the factors which led to the separation and the establishment of the ideological divide and mutual hostility. Repentance of the misdeeds of the past is not by itself sufficient to enable us to come to terms with our different histories. Knowledge instead of ignorance of our common origins is the essential preliminary to greater mutual understanding.[11]

Two of the issues separating Judaism and Christianity are the claims made by Christians for Jesus of Nazareth (together with the inevitable consequences of such claims in doctrinal formulation) and the consciousness of being a separate religion. The New Testament material seems to initiate the move to separation and exclusiveness. The problem is, of course, that what we have in the New Testament is a selection of documents, which the Christian Church over the years considered authoritative.[12] The concept of the canon of the New Testament alongside and superior to the

5

Old Testament is one which bears all the hallmarks of a later self-consciously separate religion. The canon gives the impression of a religion, which stresses its separateness, a fact of life for those responsible for the canon. The historian cannot allow the canon to govern his approach to the early Christian movement. The danger is that such an approach will lead to the separation of the Christian writings from Judaism; one runs the risk of misunderstanding primitive Christianity and first-century Judaism if they are viewed as separate entities. The story of primitive Christianity is part of the story of first-century Judaism; to compare primitive Christianity with Judaism is to view the former as if it were a separate religion at this stage. That would be an anachronistic assessment.

Nevertheless the problem remains with us: how are we to treat the New Testament writings? Clearly they do offer a distinctive view among the Jewish texts of antiquity; hence their preservation. This distinctive perspective does compel us to attempt to consider early Christianity in some isolation. That should not be taken to indicate that we are regarding the primitive Christian movement as unique in the history of Judaism: it means only that it should be accorded the same treatment as would be accorded to a sect, such as that which produced the Dead Sea Scrolls.

One of the depressing facts of life for the ancient historian is the paucity of his sources. This may seem a strange assertion to the reader unfamiliar with the period, bewildered by the array of Jewish documents described at the end of this book. Yet the fact remains that today we are confronted in the main with Jewish literature, which bears witness to what in due course became two mutually exclusive interpretations of Jewish tradition, namely rabbinic Judaism and Christianity. But their perspectives form only part of the rich fabric of Jewish life and thought in the first century AD as the non-rabbinic literature indicates. The Dead Sea Scrolls,[13] for example, have allowed us to glimpse the outlook of another sect at the time with many surprising ideas and differences from what had hitherto been supposed to be typical of Judaism.[14] But whatever affinities of outlook we may detect between the early Christian material and the extant ancient Jewish sources,[15] what distinguishes the Christian sources from the bulk of non-Christian Jewish sources is the conviction that something of ultimate importance had taken place in the life, death and resurrection of Jesus of Nazareth and the experience of the first Christians. To put it in theological terms, the Messiah had come and the new age had dawned; the Holy Spirit had been poured out on all flesh and the events had been set in motion for the establishment of God's kingdom on earth. Thus what many of the early Christian texts portray is a movement, which asserted the *fulfilment* of the promises of Israel and the consequences of such a conviction in human existence. It is in this regard that it is surely appropriate to view the Christian sources in some isolation, for by and large they bear witness to the convictions of groups which maintained that the Messiah had come. I do not want to suggest that the early Christians were the only group to have held such beliefs in the first century AD, for there are indications that the writers of the Dead Sea Scrolls may have shared similar beliefs. Messianic movements were common at the time (e.g., *Ant.* 17.254ff.; *BJ* 2.43ff.) and some may well have made similar claims about the fulfilment of the promises and the obsolescence of the Law of Moses as the guiding principle in the religious life of the people of God. What we are left with in our extant Jewish sources, however, tells us little about the beliefs and practices of such movements in first-century Palestine. The one example that we do have (apart from the sect of the Dead Sea Scrolls) is the early Christian movement, the bulk of whose earliest extant literature is to be found in the New Testament. The documents in the New Testament deserve to be considered as evidence of the beliefs and practices of a Jewish messianic movement which moved out from its Palestinian origins to most parts of the Roman world. It deserves to be examined as such, not because it was to form the basis of a separate religion, but because, like the community which produced the Dead Sea Scrolls (and other sectarian movements), it had a high degree of self-awareness from the very beginning, with its own distinctive interpretation of the Jewish Scriptures. But devoting a separate treatment to the nascent Christian movement is not the same as asserting that we are dealing with an outlook which was not very much part of first-century Judaism. To avoid giving the impression that there was a separation between Judaism on the one hand and the Christian movement on the other some consideration will be given throughout the first part of this study, which concentrates on Jewish beliefs and practices, to the early Christian texts as evidence of first-century Jewish outlooks. While these may not always be typical of the totality of Jewish belief and practice, the same may also be said of many rabbinic sources, which in all likelihood represent the views of a small minority within Jewish society; we know precious little about popular belief and practice.

In discussing Christian origins, we must always bear in mind that we should not be concerned to contrast Christianity with Judaism, as if the latter were a uniform body of doctrine and practice. Christianity never conflicted with Judaism as such until well into the second century AD. For the whole of its formative period the hostility which existed between Jews (and others), who believed that Jesus was the Messiah, and those who did not, was spasmodic and lacking in any uniformity.[16] What we can speak of in the first century is a conflict between groups of Jews who rejected Jesus' messiahship and groups which accepted it. We cannot assume that all Jews who did not accept Jesus as such were ranged against Christianity from the very start.

We shall never completely ascertain how the Christian movement adapted to the Roman world, and why it survived the débâcle of the fall of Jerusalem in AD 70 to become (with nascent rabbinic Judaism) the standard-bearer of the Jewish tradition in antiquity. Yet it is a fact that separation between rabbinic Judaism and the Church has been decisive for both religions. A glance at the pages of the New Testament indicates that the kind of Christianity which the later Church regarded as authoritative for its belief and practice[17] differed markedly from the type of Judaism which in due course came to be regarded as authoritative.[18] It is in this respect that the distinctive eschatological outlook of the early Christians and their approach to the Jewish tradition provoked new questions and asserted new priorities. Messianic and other eschatological convictions inevitably presented it with problems, which, while not different in kind from those confronting other Jews in the ancient world, were sufficiently different in degree to elicit unusual answers: for example, the issue of table-fellowship and the problem of circumcision of those Gentiles who confessed Jesus as Messiah.

For all Jews living in the midst of pagans the conflict of two world-views was inevitably awkward and sometimes profoundly difficult. Central precepts like circumcision and sabbath were often viewed with suspicion by pagans,[19] and the observance of the regulations of the Torah, especially those relating to food and idolatry, regularly presented problems of a kind difficult for us to imagine. A similar conflict of ideals confronted the early Christians. They too inherited the Old Testament, and we may suppose that it was some considerable time before all scruples had disappeared, with regard to the observance of food-laws, sabbath and the like (Rom. 14; 1 Cor. 8; 10). In addition to this, early Christianity had at its heart a messianism, which led its adherents to espouse utopian views which ran contrary to the views of society at large. How was it to cope with its convictions about the unity of all believers in Christ when it had to live in a world of class and sexual differentiation? How was it to put into practice its convictions that it represented a new humanity in the midst of an old and fallen order?

An issue which we shall examine in due course is the way in which this messianic movement came to terms with the world in which it lived. It will be suggested that it so adjusted its messianism and utopianism and presented a sufficiently bland façade to the world at large, that its existence would not be threatened too greatly. Clearly it did not manage to do this all the time. Pagan critics of Christianity were fond of pointing to the subversive nature of the religion and its effects on the Roman order.[20]

The problem with this assessment is that it can so easily disguise the extent of the accommodation of Christianity with the world as it was. Arguably this is one of the most important factors which led to its survival. To ignore this issue as one of significance for the emergence of Christianity is to leave out of account one of the most pressing issues confronting Christians in the earliest period.

Thus the issues which this study sets out to explore are as follows:

8

(i) The nature of ancient Judaism before the fall of the Second Temple in AD 70, its practices and beliefs;

(ii) The character of the early Christian movement and its distinctive approach to the Jewish traditions;

(iii) The reasons which led to a clash with other Jews and ultimately to the parting of the ways of the two principal Jewish movements, which survived the Fall of the Second Temple: rabbinic Judaism and the Christian Church;

(iv) How early Christianity accommodated its distinctive beliefs to a world whose outlook was almost completely incongruous with it.

2

An Approach to Ancient Judaism

The last hundred years have seen dramatic steps forward in our understanding of ancient Judaism, as the result of the growing availability of Jewish sources to Christian scholars and the emergence of Jewish studies as a discipline of importance in its own right. One of the problems for any writer on ancient Judaism is to attempt to do justice to the nature of this religion in a short space. To answer the question, what did it mean to be a Jew in the first century AD, is not merely a matter of consulting various sources but also of distilling from those sources some kind of outline of religious practice and belief. But as we are now well aware, excessive dependence on our sources will not lead us to our goal, for we cannot assume that our extant sources give us a complete picture of Judaism. Obviously they give us some indication of the way in which some Jews handled their traditions but we have to be mindful of the fact that they may not enable us to see how all Jews, even a significant minority of Jews, sought to practise their religion. We must beware, therefore, either of assuming that one group should be regarded as typifying 'normative Judaism' or of supposing that the extant sources represent more than a fraction of the Jewish outlook of the first century.

Normative Judaism has been identified with the pharisaic tradition, due in no small part to the substantial contribution this made to the Judaism of the rabbis.[1] The dominance of the corpus of rabbinic literature among the literary remains of ancient Judaism should not, however, lead to the conclusion that the outlook represented in this corpus is either monolithic in itself or representative of a majority view in Judaism before the fall of Jerusalem in AD 70. On the other hand the view which relegates the Judaism of the rabbis to the margins as a source for our understanding of the character of first-century Judaism has rightly been rejected.[2] The tendency evident in some writing on Judaism to polarize the religion of the pharisaic-rabbinic tradition and that reflected in the non-rabbinic Jewish writings should be questioned (if indeed it is possible to reduce to any kind of system the disparate ideas contained in the non-rabbinic literature).[3] Certainly the fall of Jerusalem in AD 70 had the effect of precipitating a change in Judaism which led to the emergence of what we know as rabbinic Judaism.[4] We cannot deny that much of it was in continuity with religious attitudes prevalent during the period of the Second Temple, but its normative character almost certainly did not apply then but results from its emerging dominance in the late first and early second centuries. Nor are we in a position to suppose that the pseudepigrapha are the literary products of the mass of the population.[5] Several of the texts exhibit a sophistication, which suggests a link with the scribal tradition.[6] It is dangerous to elevate any part of our literature to the position of normative guide to first-century Judaism. All that we can say is that it offers evidence of the differing currents flowing throughout Jewish life and thought in our period.

We cannot pierce the veil which shrouds the practice and the belief of those who left us no literary memorial. One thing it is reasonable to suppose, however, is that common to the piety of all Jews was the Torah and, for most, the writings of the Prophets. The obligations laid upon the people of God in the Torah were the common property of all, whatever the level of enthusiasm of the individual or group may have been in the fulfilment of every detail.

In an attempt to understand the character of ancient Judaism we should not forget the most obvious point that the Bible itself offered the framework for religion. Its legal provisions for civil life, diet, cult and family are the basic framework for Jewish existence. The knowledge of the Torah, particularly its legal and cultic provisions, is the beginning of the understanding of Judaism. What we have in the rabbinic literature is the exposition of the ramifications of these biblical provisions. Understanding Judaism in the first or any other century means reading the books of Exodus, Deuteronomy and Leviticus. The weekly sabbath,[7] whatever later accretions of ceremonial may have attached to it, gave a distinctive character to Jewish existence, as did those food laws so clearly enunciated in Scripture (e.g., Deut. 14). Also looming large on the horizon of the first-century Jew was the cult.[8] The bulk of the legislation in the Torah focuses on the cult and the correct procedure for worship. As far as most Jews were concerned, laws concerning tithing and sacrifice necessarily impinged upon them.[9] What is more, Scripture laid down the observance of certain key festivals necessitating pilgrimage to Jerusalem (Lev. 23; Exod. 23.14ff.; Deut. 16).[10]

Such festivals inevitably made Jerusalem an important focus of religious and national attention throughout our period. It was the sole cultic centre (with the exception of the Samaritan shrine on Mount Gerizim and the

Temple at Leontopolis in Egypt),[11] and the place where the Law was studied. Inevitably it had a supremely important place in the affections of Jews, not only as a focus of their religion but also as a centre of religious activity and control which affected every practising Jew.[12]

However devoted a Jew may have been to his religion, Torah and Temple together gave him that essential pattern of existence which distinguished him from his pagan neighbours. But in addition to providing the content of his present religious and social practice the Torah itself offered a vision of the society and the world which God himself wanted for his people. Even if we leave on one side the writings of the Prophets, the Torah itself inspires hope and offers a pattern of existence which is not congruent with what was experienced by most Jews: it promises a land flowing with milk and honey (Deut. 8.7), from which God would clear out all the foreign nations (Deut. 7.22). That was not the inheritance of those who lived in Judaea in the first century AD. Also the Torah itself reflects the messianic hope which looms so large elsewhere in the Bible.[13] The prophet like Moses (Deut. 18.15), the promises concerning the descendant of Jacob in Numbers 24.17, the laws concerning the king in Deut. 17.14ff. and the blessing of Jacob in Genesis 49.9ff. all indicate that present obedience is not the end of the matter; God had something more in store for his people than the round of obedience to the laws in the Torah.

Thus alongside the Torah and the Temple we have to set the emerging eschatological hope of Judaism enshrined as it is in Scripture and reinforced by the disparity which existed between experience and tradition. We might say that on these three foundations the ancient Jewish experience was erected. The superstructure built upon them was by no means monolithic and varied from group to group. But we shall not be far from the mark if we assume that to belong to the covenant people involved the acceptance of these three elements with different emphases and in various guises. Certainly we shall see evidence of intensifications of obedience, practice and hope in different circles but the inspiration derives from these three crucial features of the first-century Jewish outlook.

3

The Jews After the Exile[1]

The situation of the Jews changed with the destruction of Solomon's Temple by Nebuchadnezzar in 587 BC and the exile of leading Judaeans which followed it. When the Jews returned to Jerusalem some fifty or so years later there began a new era of the Jewish religion. The Exile in Babylon had been one of the most productive theological and literary periods in the history of the Jewish nation; the opportunity had been taken to reflect on the ancestral traditions in the light of the experience of destruction and exile. Gone were the days when a king reigned over both the northern kingdom of Israel and the southern kingdom of Judah. It is true that the hopes of the advent of a king like David remained to kindle the embers of religious expectation (cf. Matt. 2), but the Jewish people had once again to come to terms with foreign nations.[2] Babylon, then Persia, Greece and Rome all imposed their lordship on the Jews. Such an imposition was not in every case a threat to the heart of the Jewish religion. Indeed, with the rise of the Persian dynasty Jews found an upsurge of religious tolerance which allowed them to practise their religion under Persian suzerainty (Ezra 6.1ff.; Neh. 2). Persian dominion over Jews continued in one form or another for a very long period. Even after their influence had disappeared from Palestine, Jews in Babylon continued to have to deal with them. It was interrupted in the fourth century BC in Palestine by the conquests of Alexander the Great, under whose remarkable leadership Greek civilization embraced the Near East, including the land of Palestine. As a result of Alexander's early death the vast empire that his conquests had put at his disposal began to split up among his generals, with the establishment of the Ptolemaic dynasty in Egypt and in the region around Syria of the Seleucid dynasty. The position of Palestine centred between the two empires meant that for much of the period 300–200 BC control oscillated between the two. The Seleucids took control in 198 BC, but meanwhile in Egypt the presence of a large number of Jews meant that the Ptolemaic dynasty continued to have dealings with Jews.[3]

The eventual triumph of the Seleucids in Palestine heralded a period of unrest for Jews in the area. A programme of Hellenization was instigated by king Antiochus IV (Epiphanes).[4] His aim was to establish a degree of uniformity in religion and general outlook which would give cohesion to his empire by the inculcation of Greek beliefs and culture. He moved against Jewish religious practices in 167 BC (Dan. 11.30ff.; 1 Macc. 1.1ff.). While there had clearly been a long process of Hellenization going on among certain parts of the population in Jerusalem,[5] the explicit programme of Antiochus provoked a severe backlash against the foreign intrusion into Jewish customs. The attempt to incorporate Judaism into the all-embracing Hellenistic world was resisted and this led to the outbreak of revolt in Judaea,[6] led by the Maccabean family. The outcome of this was a period of independence for Jews in Palestine in 141 BC under Simon, gained by playing off the various pretenders to the throne of Antiochus IV against each other. Simon was made king and high priest and so began the Hasmonean dynasty which was to control Judaea until the advent of the Romans under Pompey in 63 BC.

Certainly these were not easy times for the Jews in Palestine. The period was marked by resentment at the usurpation of the High Priestly office by the Hasmonean kings (as they did not belong to the family from which priests were traditionally drawn), and the growth of sectarian strife. Indeed, it was internal strife which finally brought the Romans into Jerusalem to intervene in the struggle between the two brother Hasmoneans, Hyrcanus and Aristobulus II. Pompey, who was campaigning in Syria, besieged the Temple and in 63 BC entered the Holy of Holies, that part of the Temple where only the High Priest was allowed to go on the day of Atonement (Lev. 16; *Ant.* 14.61ff.). From this time on Rome became the effective overlord, though there continued to be a large degree of religious freedom; the cult and its operation were almost completely unaffected. The advent of the Romans was to have a profound effect on the nature of Jewish attitudes, particularly in Judaea, during the crucial years which saw the rise of the Christian movement with the exception of brief periods in the first century AD. National freedom was at an end after the brief period of autonomy under the Hasmoneans. It is true that between 37 and 4 BC there was independence under the client king Herod the Great, whose Idumean origin did not commend him to Jews. He spent vast amounts of money, for example, on rebuilding the Temple in Jerusalem (*BJ*1.524; 1.401ff.; *Ant.* 15.299ff.; 16.149ff.; 17.302ff.). After Herod's death in 4 BC, his kingdom was split up, and his sons for a brief period reigned over his territory. In AD 6 there was trouble in Judaea, and Archelaus' territory was placed under direct Roman rule, which necessitated a census, while Herod Antipas (Mark 6.17; Luke 23.6f.)[7] and Philip ruled Galilee and Batanaea until AD 39 and 33 respectively. Philip's territory was eventually added to the province of Syria and Herod Antipas' was given to Agrippa I, who ruled Judaea between AD 37 and 44. Later the son of Agrippa I, Agrippa II, was allowed by the Romans to have limited jurisdiction and in 53 was given the former territory of Philip as well as parts of Galilee and Peraea; he was also given the right to nominate the High Priest.

The story of the first century AD in Judaea is one of Roman misunderstanding of Jewish scruples and the inexorable growth of disaffection within the Roman province for social, religious and political reasons. The best known of the procurators of Judaea, Pontius Pilate, is a good example of the lack of sensitivity. He was in Judaea for about ten years (AD 26–36), and during this time he instructed his legions to bring their shields into Jerusalem, a provocative act. This act offended Jewish religious scruples. Stories of his behaviour are told by both Philo (*Embassy* 299ff.) and Josephus (*BJ* 2.175ff.). Indeed, it was his reckless action against the Samaritans on Mount Gerizim which led to his removal from office.[8]

The Jewish historian Josephus has much to say about this period in his account of the origins and course of the Jewish war against Rome in 66–70. His pro-Roman sympathies are well known. While he lays much of the blame for the disastrous revolt against Rome in 66–70 at the door of the Zealots (Jewish freedom fighters, *BJ* 2.254ff.), he does not neglect to note Roman maladministration as a cause of the conflagration (e.g., *BJ* 2.271ff.). The act which finally provoked the revolt of Jews against Rome was the robbery of the Temple by the procurator Florus (*BJ* 2.285ff.). Sacrifice for the emperor was stopped (*BJ* 2.415), and once the revolt had started there was to be no going back, despite the pleas of some of the leading citizens. The revolt itself is a story of fanatical courage, bitter internal strife and suffering on an enormous scale. It dragged on for four years; indeed, the last resistance was not quelled until Flavius Silva finally took the desert fortress of Masada in 73. The reason for the prolonged war was the trouble in the empire at large provoked by the death of Nero (see Tacitus, *Histories* 5).[9] In AD 68 there were no less than four emperors in quick succession. In this political confusion the struggle carried on in Palestine, and was only resolved when Vespasian became emperor, and his son Titus took command of the campaign against the Jews in Palestine which led to the destruction of Jerusalem in 70.

With the end of Temple worship profound changes came upon the Jewish religion. The Temple, focus as it was of so much devotion and a crucial part of the religious practice of Judaism, lay in ruins. The regular payment of half a shekel by all male Jews for the upkeep of the Temple and its worship was diverted by the Romans to the Temple of Jupiter Capitolinus in Rome (*BJ* 7.216ff.). Despite all the difficulties caused for Rome by the Jews, Judaism was not proscribed, and Titus refused the pleas of those who asked him to withdraw privileges (*BJ* 7.110f.). The history of the period following the First Revolt is by no means clear. A Roman procurator was once again in charge and Judaea became an imperial province.

Despite the ravages of the First Revolt, there was a revolt of Jews in North Africa in 115, and in 132 Simeon bar Koseba or Bar Kochba led the Second Revolt of Jews against Rome, provoked by Hadrian's wish to turn Jerusalem into a Greek city, Aelia Capitolina, to plough the Temple land, and build a shrine to Jupiter there.[10] This revolt brought about even greater devastation and loss of life (Dio Cassius, *History* 69.12ff.; Eusebius, *EH* 4.6.1ff.). The fact that another uprising could have taken place within sixty years of the calamitous First Revolt is ample testimony to the Jewish religious spirit and the undying convictions concerning God's promises for his people. The legend of the coins of the Second Revolt, 'for the freedom of Jerusalem', demonstrates the continuing eschatological fervour and how much the yearning for the freedom of God's people from foreign domination still exercised the imaginations of the Jewish nation. Indeed, according to the rabbinic tradition, Simeon bar Koseba was hailed as the one promised in Numbers 24.17 by no less a figure than Rabbi Akiba, the leading Jewish teacher of his generation.

The history of the period is one of political subjection, continued Torah-observance and eschatological fervour. It would be easy to assert that such hope for deliverance was rooted solely in oppression and economic hardship. That there was such cannot be doubted, but it would be wrong to suppose that the whole of Palestine was as a result infected by earnest revolutionary zeal. The evidence suggests, as we shall see, that Judaea was probably worst affected of all, though the vitality of the religious tradition meant that ultimately most Jews could not fail to note the contrast between hope and reality. It was as much religious as socio-economic factors which led to the disturbances throughout the first century. Spurred on the Jews might have been by the poverty of their existence, but it was the religious traditions themselves which fired the flames of dissatisfaction and gave a point of comparison with the inadequacies of the present.

As we have seen, Palestine in the first century AD had become very much part of the Graeco-Roman world. Those who espoused the idiosyncrasies of the Jewish religion had to learn to coexist with the Greek language and Roman law and administration. The conquests of Alexander had brought about a vast dissemination of Greek culture. However much the Jews may have wanted to, they could not entirely isolate themselves from the influence of Greek ideas.[11] Certainly explicit Hellenizers were resisted, but the writings of Philo of Alexandria demonstrate a blend of Greek philosophy and the Jewish traditions, which indicates how far the subtle influence of Hellenism could permeate Judaism, at least in Egypt.[12]

When brought under Roman rule, Judaea experienced politically what it had undergone socially for at least one hundred years: assimilation to a wider framework of life and thought. It was a small part of a large empire, though its strategic importance on the boundary of the empire should not be ignored. The influence of foreign culture was not at all times apparent, nor was the path to complete assimilation a direct one. All the evidence suggests that in Palestine in particular there could well have been pockets which remained to a considerable degree unaffected by the prevailing spirit of the age. Even in the Diaspora, as we shall see, Jews enjoyed some independence and a degree of separation from the surrounding culture. But to say this cannot minimize the insidious effects that this culture continued to have on Jews throughout the Roman world. Even when they retreated to the desert of Judaea, as the Qumran sect did, it was impossible to retain a separation which avoided contact with the outlook of Hellenism.

We have already noted that Jews in Palestine were allowed a significant degree of religious freedom. With the exception of the control over the appointment of the High Priests (*Ant.* 18.26; 93; cf. *BJ* 4.151ff.), Temple worship continued until AD 70, unaffected by Roman restrictions. There was not complete freedom to practise the Jewish law, though the Romans allowed the Sanhedrin as the local law-making body to continue its activities within certain parameters.[13] The Romans continued to allow the death penalty to be carried out on all those who transgressed the line which marked the furthest point to which Gentiles were allowed to go in the Temple.[14] While sacrifice to the emperor would have been anathema to the Jews (cf. Philo, *Embassy* 157), it became customary to offer sacrifice *on behalf of* the emperor.[15]

As far as the religion of the ordinary people was concerned, the pious probably found that there was little to affect their quest for holiness. It has been pointed out that during the first century AD, Pharisaism had undergone quite a significant shift of emphasis from being a movement extensively politically involved during the reign of Alexander Janneus (103–76) and Alexandra (76–67) to one that was primarily pietistic in its orientation, concerned with the inner life.[16] Such a movement corresponds to the growing lack of involvement in political matters at all levels.[17] As most popular piety was focused on the cult in Jerusalem the continuation of its activities, without any significant harassment from outside influences, meant that there was normally little cause for general religious unrest. The storm of protest, which greeted attempts to interfere with the religious activities of the Temple, indicates the level of feeling with regard to the cult.

It is all too easy for us to stop analysis of Palestinian and Diaspora Judaism with a reference to religious difference as the core of the debate within Judaism and to imagine that differing attitudes to the traditions are themselves the sole cause of strife. Such cannot be regarded as an adequate assessment. Rightly we are asked to press behind the religious differences and to ask what these religious ideas also tell us about the social and economic circumstances of those who espoused rival views.[18] While we cannot always say with certainty that the advocates of change were those who had least to lose and most to gain, it is apparent that those who had most to lose were the ones who were, in fact, in charge of centres of religion like the Temple, and resisted any extensive change or any subversive activity, which might destabilize the precarious political situation. Attempts there have been in the past to examine the political and economic situation in Palestine round about the beginning of the Christian era and to assess how much of a contribution this might have made to the emergence of Christianity.[19] The importance of the insights of social and economic history and theory should not necessarily lead to the wooden application of the thesis that religion is merely the product of the interaction of economic forces. Equally, however, the place of economic life in the construction of a religious outlook should not be neglected; religious ideas are no less important for being at least partly explicable by the changes in the socio-economic structure. Of course, one of the problems which confronts total explanations of this kind is the paucity of evidence which would make an adequate socio-economic explanation possible. Nevertheless the contribution which such investigations are going to make to our understanding of Christian origins should not be under-estimated. In recognizing this, we should note the comment of Milan Machovec,[20] who wants to distinguish between the willingness to explain ideas by their socio-economic conditioning and 'an incapacity to explain even the most sublime human ideals by anything other than socio-economic conditioning'. This is an important distinction, for it means that the totality of religious belief is not reduced to the projection of the economic struggle on to the ideological plane. Indeed, we should not neglect to note that even those ideas which are shaped by socio-economic forces can themselves exercise a retroactive influence on the economic circumstances that produced them.[21]

It is a great mistake to suppose that one has sufficiently accounted for the birth of religious movements merely by explaining the developments which have taken place in the history of ideas. An adequate account of Jewish and Christian beliefs and practices must derive as much from the knowledge of the social history of the period as the history of doctrines. The history of Judaism in the first century has been a prime candidate for an interpretation in which the socio-economic factor looms large. After all, as we have seen, it was the culmination of a succession of periods of dominance by foreign overlords, which eventually bubbled over into open revolt in 66. This may well be the consequence as much of economic and social factors as religious enthusiasm. The heart-felt comment of the companion of Jesus on the road to Emmaus illustrates this: 'We thought that he was the one to liberate Israel' (Luke 24.21) may well be a religious expression which includes economic dissatisfaction. It is surely no coincidence that the intensification of acts of insurgency mounted during the period of the Roman procuratorship (*BJ* 2.55ff.; 2.224ff.). While we must not generalize too much about the effect of Roman rule on the whole area,[22] but give due attention to the peculiar factors which led to certain divergences in attitudes in different regions during our period, a deepening awareness of the nature of the Jewish economy and Jewish society cannot but enable us to ascertain more faithfully the circumstances which led to the birth of the early Christian movement.

Two caveats need to be entered here. We have already noted that ideas which reflect social and political conditions themselves take on a life of their own and have an active role in the creation of the kind of society which they outline. There is another dimension to the study of the social history of Judaism, namely the biblical traditions themselves. Whatever the social and economic circumstances which led to the genesis of those traditions, there can be no question that the biblical material was itself a factor in the emergence of attitudes. It may be, as we have noted, that some aspects of the common tradition were given more prominence by one group and other aspects by another, reflecting the social and political status of the individual group. Nevertheless the religious tradition was not itself, of course, the product of the world of the first century. Its interpretation was; but its distinctive message cannot be excluded from any consideration of the social world of Judaism. Its presence as a catalyst was one which could, and clearly did, lead to dangerous and subversive attitudes (e.g., *BJ* 7.255). Resentment would have been there, but it is hard to see that resentment being channelled into such revolutionary attitudes without the contribution made by the Scriptures themselves.

The traditions about the glorious future which God had prepared for his people was itself, therefore, a cause of disaffection. Once the contrast between social and political realities stood in the sharpest possible contrast to the glorious future promised in the Scriptures and echoed in writings of the period, the situation led to disillusionment, a narrowing of religious vision or the conviction that change was needed. That hopes were entertained not merely as articles of faith but also as part of a programme of action is confirmed by the Dead Sea Scrolls. In the War Scroll from Qumran (1QM) we find there the belief that the might of God's enemies would be overthrown in a battle in which the angelic legions would come to the aid of the sons of light. The fantastic detail of the preparations outlined in the War Scroll gives some indication of the frame of mind of some groups as they entertained hopes of participating in an armed struggle against the enemies of Israel (cf. *BJ* 5.459; 388).

While it would be wrong to suppose that an increase in eschatological hopes always accompanies times of political unrest and economic dissatisfaction, there is a strong case to be made for the view that the period when the early Christian movement emerged was one which favoured the utopian dreamer (see *BJ* 2.259ff.; 6.351.; 7.437f.; *Ant.* 20.167ff.). Many of the apocalypses were written during this period, and memories of some autonomy were strong enough to make the present Roman domination seem all the more unsatisfactory. In addition to the visions the presence of pagan soldiers on the soil of Israel[23] made the political situation resemble the era of Antichrist more than almost any earlier period of Jewish history.

If politically the situation in Palestine fitted in ill with Jewish hopes, economically the various attempts to reorganize the country led to a deterioration of the standard of life, particularly for those at the lowest end of the social order. The reorganization of land by Pompey in 63 BC had caused a considerable land shortage[24] and, as a result, a large number of landless peasants, whose impoverishment inevitably contributed to the feelings of dissatisfaction which were experienced at the time.[25] There seem to have been large landowners, upon whose land a great number of the landless rural proletariat would have been called to work as day labourers.[26] Large problems faced the tenant farmer throughout our period.[27] As has often been pointed out, several of Jesus' parables reflect the social situation of first-century Palestine with its unemployment (Matt. 20.3ff.) and large pools of people looking for work (Luke 16.1ff.; Mark 12.1ff.; Luke 17.7; 19.19). In addition, the level of taxation dating from Herod the Great's day proved to be an added burden, which had not afflicted the populace since the time of the Seleucids.[28] The fact that one of the first acts of the rebels in AD 66 when Jerusalem fell to the rebels was to burn the record of debts kept in the Temple (*BJ* 2.427) indicates that the problem posed by the need to borrow money was one causing considerable hardship during this period.[29] The degree of social and class conflict should not be underestimated, as is suggested by the attack of Simeon bar Giora on the houses of the large estate owners.[30] Certainly Judaea was helped by the great influx of capital as the result of the flourishing industry connected with the Temple and the Temple tax, the tax levied on every male (Exod. 30.15; M. Shek. 1.3; *Ant.* 3.196; cf. Neh. 10.32). The needs of the Temple must have helped, at least in Jerusalem and its environs, to create employment (M. Shek. 4.1ff.).[31] Yet it must be remembered that the control of the Temple and its worship was largely in the hands of the High Priestly families, and there was considerable room for exploitation of a source of income (*Ant.* 20.180f.; T. Men. 13.21) whose size and significance can be judged from the covetous glances which successive Roman emperors and officials gave to it (e.g., *BJ* 2.175ff.; *Ant.* 18.60ff.) culminating of course in Vespasian's confiscation of the Temple tax after AD 70.[32]

Thus the economic conditions of the country must have played a significant role in the rise of discontent which ultimately led to the First Revolt. Josephus is in doubt about the impoverishment of the people (*Ant.* 15.121; 299ff.; *BJ* 1.370).[33]

It may be that we have still a very long way to go before we can adequately unravel all the social and economic issues which led to the First Revolt. But it has been all too easy for the student of Christian origins to forget the enormous contribution of economic and social factors in the formation of attitudes in the first century AD.[34] Perhaps we have gone as far as we can with an account of the social and economic history of Judaism in Palestine which depends on Josephus,[35] but the literature of Palestinian Judaism still awaits an assessment. How far do the production of distinctive literary forms and specific religious interests manifest the spiritual disillusionment and deteriorating economic situation in Palestine? All too often we have to rest content to examine the religious ideas in such documents only without seeking to establish what evidence they give us of the social and economic circumstances out of which they were born.

The brief survey of social and economic factors influencing the emergence of religious belief has concentrated on those negative factors in Palestine which helped to precipitate revolt against Rome. The picture given might seem to indicate that the influence of Rome was in fact actually hostile to Judaism and the Christian movement; this would be an inadequate assessment. Popular belief is that the early Church was persecuted by the Romans, but generally speaking, such action that was taken was spasmodic and local, and Jews normally received very favourable treatment from Romans.[36] The positive note sounded by some New Testament writers towards Rome, particularly the writer of Acts but also the authors of 1 Peter and the Pastoral Epistles (e.g., Rom. 13, 1 Tim. 2.1ff.), indicates that the benefits of the *pax Romana* for the spread of the Christian gospel were not to be underestimated. The control by Rome of the area bordering on the Mediterranean not only conditioned the direction which the Christian mission took but also made it possible for Christian missionaries to move reasonably freely throughout the area under Roman jurisdiction. The possibility offered to Paul was one which derived almost entirely from the subjugation of the area of his mission under the control of one authority. Indeed, it is difficult to imagine that Paul would have found it anything like as easy to have embarked on the kind of missionary project he set himself some two hundred years previously.

Paul travelled round a world in which Judaism was by and large firmly established. Not only in the major cities of the Roman empire but also in the Parthian empire Jewish communities of varying sizes were to be found.[37] It is clear that Jews were a significant, and often influential, minority within the Roman world. Their religion and its practice were often guaranteed and not subject to the proscription faced by other alien cults.[38] At times their often extensive rights, which Josephus describes in *Ant.* 14, provoked hostile reactions from pagan neighbours (e.g., *Ant.* 12.125f.; 16.27ff.).[39] In many cases the rights of Jews also extended to the possession of Roman citizenship, a good example, of course, being Paul of Tarsus himself (Acts 16.37; 21.39).[40] They had the right to collect the money for the Temple tax and were exempt in many cities from military service.[41] For a period the early Christians also were able to shelter under the umbrella of Judaism and to avail themselves of many of these privileges.

The meeting place for Jews outside Palestine was the synagogue.[42] Philo speaks of synagogues as places where the ancestral customs of Judaism were taught (*Life of Moses* 2.216), and Josephus similarly speaks of the injunction of Moses to spend one day each week in the study of the Law (*Contra Apionem* 2.175). Archaeological evidence[43] indicates that these places for meeting were to be found all over the Roman world, and in cities like Alexandria where there were large Jewish communities, it would be expected that there would be several synagogues, each with its own distinctive religious outlook (cf. Acts 6.9). As well as being the focal point for Jews the synagogues attracted the attention of many pagans who for various reasons were sympathetic to Judaism but found it impossible to become full converts (proselytes). They took it upon themselves to fulfil certain requirements.[44] This cosmopolitan aspect of synagogue life is stressed by Philo, who calls them 'places open to all as schools of good sense' (*Spec. Leg.* 2.62). Acts furnishes us with several examples of God-fearers being in the synagogue congregations when Paul preached (Acts. 13.26; 13.16).[45] Paul's offer that 'every one that believes is freed from everything from which you could not be freed by the Law of Moses', would have had considerable attractions for those God-fearers who did not wish to go the whole way and accept the requirement of circumcision.[46]

With Paul the Christian gospel not only left the predominantly Jewish atmosphere of Palestine but also underwent other changes. As we shall see later in this study, the mission and work of Jesus started life not in the cities but in the Galilean countryside. The character of discipleship required by him was certainly not geared to urban existence, with his emphasis on the wandering disciples who trusted to God alone for their food and clothing (Luke 10.1–12; Matt. 6.25ff.). With Paul the Christian communities became primarily, if not solely, urban in their make-up. Their concerns and problems differed greatly from the wandering disciples who followed Jesus, the Son of Man, who had nowhere to lay his head. The understanding of this fundamentally important social change goes a long way towards explaining the development of the Christian movement in subsequent centuries.[47]

The importance of such questions is only being recognized again by New Testament scholars, though investigation of such matters has had a long pedigree.[48] We may not always be able to ascertain what precisely were the circumstances in which early Christian literature like the gospels was written. Nevertheless the examination of broader social trends in the period as well as hints in the extant literature will enable us to build up a picture of the problems which would confront the early Christians with their distinctive view of the world.

PART II

Jewish Life and Thought at the Beginning of the Christian Era

1

God and his Covenant with Israel

It is tempting for Christian writers on Jewish religion at the time of Jesus to imagine that the contents of Jewish works like the Mishnah with its vast collection of legal prescriptions represent the sum total of Jewish piety at this time. Such an assessment has been the cause of many views of Judaism, which concentrate on its minute legal detail and contrast it with the religion of grace and liberty manifested in the pages of the New Testament.[1] It should not be forgotten that in the detailed prescriptions of the Mishnah we have reflected the major themes of the Jewish Scriptures. The absence of ideas like covenant, promise, grace and the like from the Mishnah should not blind us to the fact that the same Jews, who sought to observe the minute detail of rabbinic regulation, continued to belaud the God who had brought their ancestors out of Egypt into the land of promise and who would bring his creation to perfection under the dominion of his chosen representative, the scion of David. The celebration of the deliverance from Egypt year by year in the Passover and the praise of God in the liturgy is the necessary framework for our understanding of the detailed minutiae contained in the Mishnah.[2] So a consideration of the tractate dealing with the celebration of the Passover in the Mishnah (tractate *Pesahim*) might lead the unwary to suppose that all that the Jews of the period, who wrote this material, were concerned about was the minutiae of the observance of a particular ritual rather than the great religious themes which undergird it (Exod. 12). A glance at the Passover Haggadah recited at the Passover meal would put the Mishnah in perspective. The great mistake is to suppose that concern with the correct observance of the festivals and other aspects of Jewish life implies that the theology which undergirds the observance has been lost sight of. It is precisely because Jews felt the great debt of obligation to the God of their fathers, to the God of Abraham, Isaac and Jacob, that they concentrated such attention on the minutiae of observance; a God who wrought such a great deliverance was worthy of the utmost devotion.

Ed Sanders has shown how certain stereotypes of Judaism have been widely accepted over the years by Christian scholars.[3] Unfortunately all too often this has been accompanied by the apologetic aim of throwing into sharp relief the bankruptcy of Judaism over against the vitality of nascent Christianity. Sanders has rightly protested against some of the caricatures of Judaism, by showing that the basic concerns which most Jewish writers of our period are accused of ignoring are presupposed by them. Thus the fact that God has chosen the people of Israel and has shown himself in divers ways to them throughout their history are things which are taken for granted by the Jewish authors, particularly those responsible for compiling the legal codes. It is not that this matter is no longer worth discussing but that the obligations of those who have been fortunate enough to be recipients of this salvation need to do all in their power to respond by showing a type of obedience which can in some way express the gratitude appropriate to such a divine act.

It is in this context that the importance of the covenant between God and his people should be mentioned, for, as Sanders has pointed out, the rabbinic collections and other Palestinian literature presuppose the idea of covenantal nomism, as he calls it.[4] By this he means the character of Jewish religion in which the detailed legislation is to be regarded as the consequence of response to the divine initiative. The theme of the covenant is one which is to be found throughout the bulk of the Old Testament[5] and takes different forms. Thus God makes a covenant with Noah not to send another flood to destroy the earth (Gen. 9.9ff.), with Abraham to make of his descendants a great nation (Gen. 15.18) and a promise sealed by circumcision (Gen. 17), with the people of Israel (Exod. 24)[6] and then with the family of David (2 Sam. 7.8ff.). From time to time this covenant is renewed (e.g. Josh. 24; Ezra 10.3ff.). In various ways the notion of covenant has exercised a profound influence on the understanding of God's relationship with his people.

The Qumran community, whose views are preserved in the Dead Sea Scrolls, believed, like the early Christians, that they had entered into a new covenant with God (e.g., *CD* 6.19; cf. Mark 14.24; Heb. 8.7ff.).[7] The covenant was central to the lives of Jews. Outward recognition of belonging to the people of God was marked at the very beginning of the life of every male Jew. On the eighth day after birth every male is circumcised and shown to be a member of the covenant people (Gen. 17. 10ff., Lev. 12.3; cf. Luke 2.21; Phil. 3.5). That is a sign that the God who cared for the ancestors of the Jews now accepted this member of the holy nation, who in his own turn would undertake to observe the demands of God. It is essential to grasp the central importance of this rite as a sign of membership of the covenant people to understand the strength of feeling generated by Paul's decision not to insist on circumcision for his Gentile converts to Christianity.[8]

The gracious act of God is intimately linked with the command of God to his people to keep his statutes and ordinances (Deut. 7.6ff.). The introduction of the Decalogue in Exodus 20.1 is an indication of the balance between divine initiative and human response in the covenant relationship. The God who brought his people out of the house of bondage also summons them to accept the conditions of a continuing relationship with him. The observance of the commandments, together with due care to ensure proper fulfilment, is the only appropriate response to God in his dealings with his people. Thus behind the detailed discussions in the early rabbinic literature about the meaning of various passages there lies the need to make every endeavour to put into practice the precepts of God in the different circumstances of the Graeco-Roman world. The detailed and ongoing interpretation is a witness to the highest priority given to the covenant. Nothing else can explain why it is that Jews of every generation felt the need to go to so much trouble to ascertain the demands of God. To learn from the ways in which past generations have responded to the covenant-demands is the reason for the respect for other tradition, as well as that contained in the Bible. Those who had walked the way before could doubtless cast light on the pilgrimage of those who now had to tread a similar path.

In another area of Jewish life the covenant had a continuing role. One of the biblical passages concerning the covenant speaks of God's promises to David. The remarkable thing about the oracle of Nathan in 2 Samuel 7.8ff. is that, as well as linking the promise with that made to Israel as a whole (v.9), there is a promise made by God to guarantee the dynasty of David for ever (7.13) and to treat his descendants as a father would a son (v.14). The promise that 'the throne of his kingdom' would be for ever is very important for our understanding of the development of later Jewish messianic hopes.[9] Already in the Bible we find that the promise is taken up and examined in very different circumstances. Thus, for example, Psalm 89 contrasts the present plight of Israel (89.38) with the promise given to David (89.28). Similarly in Psalm 132.10 prayer is made to God that he will not abandon his anointed 'for David's sake' (cf. 2 Chron. 6.42). In these psalms the contrast between God's unshakable promise and the present state of affairs is never so bluntly put. Much later, in the Psalms of Solomon 17.5, we find in the context of the fully-fledged messianic picture an allusion to 2 Samuel 7 again, with a lament over the fact that God's promise to David has not been realized.

To be aware of the covenant as a dominant theme in the Jewish religion is a step towards understanding the nature of Judaism. It is when we accept that the underlying theme of a relationship with its obligations is itself dependent on the divine initiative that we shall begin to do justice to Judaism. It was not early Christianity which invented a doctrine of grace and election; these are rooted in the Old Testament. No doubt it may have been possible to find areas of Judaism in the first century, where the obedience to the Law had become an end in itself and had obscured the derivative position as a response to the divine initiative; but it is inconceivable that obedience to the commandments could ever have become separated from the mighty acts of God for his people. While there may have been grounds

27

for various critiques of Jewish piety (after all, Christians were not the only ones to criticize Jews who disagreed with them), the existence of concern with the minutiae of observance indicates neither the emergence of dry legalism nor a radical shift from the perspective of the Old Testament itself.[10]

Central to the covenant was the promise of land.[11] According to Genesis 12.7, when God appeared to Abraham at Moreh, he promised that his descendants would inherit the land, a promise that is confirmed in 15.18 and 17.8 and renewed to the patriarch Jacob (28.13; 35.12). It is a promise, which is repeated in the context of the passover ritual (Exod. 12.25), and lies at the heart of the mission of Moses (Exod. 3.8). The goal of the wanderings of God's people in the wilderness is the Promised Land, and its conquest is told in the books of Numbers and Joshua. At the centre of the covenant renewal in Joshua 24 is the inheritance of land, and it is clear that a major theme of the book of Deuteronomy is the covenant between an obedient people and a God who gives his people land. The land emerged as an issue during the Babylonian crisis in the sixth century BC (cf. Ps. 137). Those left behind in the land of Israel after the deportation to Babylon regarded their position as a sign of divine favour, a matter about which Jeremiah speaks in Jeremiah 24, and the repossession of the land is a dominant theme in some of the oracles preserved in Jeremiah 29 and 32. By the time we get to the first century AD the land of Israel promised to the descendants of the patriarchs was once again inhabited and ruled by Gentiles. Even if in fact the Jews in the land of Israel were allowed to practise their religion much as before, the fact that the rightful inheritance of the covenant people was not entirely theirs was a source of irritation and inspired a zealous hope for restoration.

Since the time of David the promise with regard to the land had become tied up with a particular place (Deut. 12.5): Jerusalem, Zion, the city of the great God. No one can read through the book of Isaiah (e.g., ch. 29), or the Psalter (e.g., Ps. 46ff.) without noticing how prominent a place Zion has within the framework of the divine promise.[12] The restoration after the destruction of the First Temple was to be centred on Zion (Haggai 1–2) and in later Jewish eschatological beliefs the city of David figured prominently (see e.g., Rev. 21.1ff.). In the oracle of Nathan in 2 Samuel 7, the promise of the land and the promise to David are both linked with the building of the house of God in Zion (2 Sam. 7.13), a combination of themes with important implications for later Jewish belief.

2

The God of the Covenant[1]

Theology as an abstract speculative exercise did not form a significant part of the religious reflection of most Jews. While the philosophical tradition of Alexandria helped Philo to articulate a complex theology,[2] the God whom the Jews worshipped was the God of the Covenant, who had made a bond with the ancestors of the Jewish nation and remained faithful to his people through the many vicissitudes of its history. To speak about God was to speak about the experiences of the Jewish nation throughout history. The simple formula in Deuteronomy 26.5ff. encapsulates the central features of Jewish theology:

> A wandering Aramean was my father; and he went down to Egypt and sojourned there, few in number; and there he became a nation, great, mighty and populous. And the Egyptians treated us harshly, and afflicted us, and laid on us harsh bondage. Then we cried to the Lord the God of our fathers, and the Lord heard our voice and saw our affliction, our toil and our oppression; and the Lord brought us out of Egypt with a mighty hand and outstretched arm, with great terror, signs and wonders; and he brought us into this place and gave us this land, a land flowing with milk and honey.[3]

The deliverance from Egypt and the settlement in the land of Canaan were central to the Jewish apprehension of God. The deity was not to be found primarily in the wonders of nature[4] (though such ideas are not entirely lacking in the pages of the Old Testament, as Ps. 19, 104, 148 and Job 38ff. make plain), or in the annual cycle of the seasons, but in the movement of history itself. The Exodus experience became central to Israel's apprehension of God. The redemption from slavery was a gratuitous act of God, who offered a relationship with this oppressed people (Deut. 20.1, cf. 4.37); it was the basis of the bulk of theological recollection and the reason for hope when circumstances seemed to be at their blackest. In the midst of the Exile, the prophet Isaiah of the Exile recalls the deliverance from Egypt as the basis of a new work to be wrought by God (Isa. 52.3–6), and later in early Christian literature the Exodus experience became a paradigm of God's saving act (e.g., Mark 10.45; Heb. 11.27ff.; Rev. 5.9, 15)

These twin features dominate Israel's theology. The God who delivered his people is the God of history as a whole and is to be obeyed. In the biblical tradition we find that these elements condition the way in which people and events are interpreted. Foreign kings and nations become the agents of God's purposes (Isa. 10.5; 45.1ff.). In the aftermath of their direst calamity, the Exile, Jews reflected on that experience in history as an experience of their God; and in the story of their nation, in the books of Samuel and Kings, there is an attempt to reflect on the disasters and disobedience, which culminated in the sack of the city in 586.[5] It is taken for granted that God remains faithful to his people, even when judgement seems to be the only proper course of action in the light of the people's infidelity.[6] God's concern for his people is evident throughout the Old Testament; they were his own possession (Exod. 19.5), in a position of privilege which would be theirs, provided that they obeyed God's voice and kept his covenant. That is not to suggest that the view of God outlined in the Old Testament was thoroughly exclusive. Jewish apologists and the writers of eschatology, despite the fierce nationalism which one often encounters, certainly acknowledged that the God of Israel was the God of every nation. Some indeed looked forward to a time when the nations would join Israel in worshipping the one God (Zech. 8.20; Ps. 72.10f.; Rev. 21.25).[7] In the classic statement of the supreme position of the God of Israel in Isaiah 40ff., a universal significance of Israel's God is clearly enunciated in a context where the worship of other gods is so roundly condemned (Isa. 45.21f.; 44.6–11).

One should not suppose that the road to monotheism was one that was taken easily or unambiguously in the Old Testament. Much of the biblical material is taken up with the need to persuade the people of Israel of the exclusive claims of YHWH, the God of Israel. The settlement in a foreign land, with its own theological traditions, caused the new settlers to consider whether in fact they ought not to add the worship of the indigenous deities to their devotion to Yahweh. The idolatry, which is roundly condemned in the prophecy of Hosea, manifests this kind of espousal of Canaanite religion. It was an understandable development, as a nomad people accommodated itself to the settled urban life of their promised land. The God of the desert wanderings might not have been appropriate or even adequate for new conditions of life. Nevertheless despite the utter repudiation of the Canaanite deities in the pre-exilic prophets, a great debt was owed by Israelite theology to the mythology of Canaanite religion. We can see this particularly in those passages dealing with the heavenly court (Ps. 82.1; Job 1–2; Isa. 6).[8] These beliefs are found in a distinctively Israelite guise; God, the God of Israel is seated as *lord* in the assembly of the gods, 'he is a judge among gods' (Ps. 82.1). Even Isaiah of the Exile with his denunciation of idolatry and promotion of the uniqueness of the God of Israel (Isa. 45.14) works within the framework of this heavenly court mythology (Isa. 40.1).[9] In later times such views must have had their contribution to make to the angelology of Judaism. The attendants in the heavenly court ceased to be lesser divinities, but angels, the servants of God (cf. Heb. 1.14) and the heavenly representatives of people and nations (e.g., 1 Enoch 89.59; Daniel 10.13; 12.1; and the angels of the seven churches in Rev. 1–3).[10] The repudiation of idolatry was not so much a rejection of the existence of the demonic world and the reality of the spiritual entities which stood behind the religious activities of the pagan nations (cf. 1 Cor. 10.14ff.; Col. 2.14; Eph. 1.21) but an emphatic rejection of such religious devotions as *true* religion. The Jews had to accept that there was only one possible way of worship and only one object of their devotion; any concession to syncretism, where worship of other gods was added to the worship of YHWH was a threat to the covenant (Exod. 20.3). In later times, when the world was thought to be populated with legions of spiritual powers, the assertion of the lordship of the God of Israel and his Christ over this demonic world was an important recommendation for the Jewish and Christian tradition. No longer was it necessary to hedge one's bets; complete devotion was required and with it came the conviction that there was no need to be concerned with other gods, for in the God of Israel there was the only living and true god (Wisd. 13ff.; Sib. Or.; 1 Thess. 1.9).[11]

The future hope which is so intimately linked with the historical perspective in Israelite theology is not unusual. Utopian ideas are to be found in a variety of religious traditions; the return to paradise is one which is deeply rooted in the human race.[12] What is much more remarkable in Jewish thought is the consistent streak of self-criticism which is manifest in the prophetic literature. This has much to do with the covenant. It is recognized that the criticisms of Israel and the oracles of doom, which we find in the prophetic literature, have their origin in the knowledge of the covenant demands.[13] The prophets were able to speak out against the abuses within Israelite society, because of their knowledge of the covenant demands and their apprehension of the discrepancy which existed between those demands and the behaviour of the people. The development of the prophetic vocation from frantic dervishes via cultic officials to the divine spokesmen against cultic and social abuses is a fascinating story.[14] Underlying it is the conviction that the fulfilment of the demands of the God of Israel is an integral part of the maintenance of a well-ordered society. The ability of this small nation to reflect on its experiences and to relate them to its traditions in the distinctive way in which we find them in the pages of the Old Testament, is a remarkable phenomenon. Notwithstanding their subordinate position in the political history of our period, the Jews continued to maintain that their religious beliefs alone were authentic and that ultimately they would be shown to be so, when all the earth acknowledged the supremacy of their God. The existence of the Jewish nation and its distinctive way of life are as important as a theological datum as any series of theological propositions. As a holy nation and God's special possession, the Jews themselves were a living testimony to the character of the God whom they worshipped. Their concern for holiness (Lev. 19.2) and their criticism of their past failures to attain to the demands of God reflect the conviction that God and his ways are to be found in the fabric of everyday existence and not in the solitude of the inner life. Holiness was something which could be appreciated and acted out in society, just as God's hand could be seen at work in the deeds of men.

It is often alleged that in the post-Exilic period Jewish theology underwent a profound development. The emergence of an elaborate cosmology in the apocalyptic literature, in which heaven was believed to be populated by a multitude of beings and to consist of a number of different compartments, is supposed to have contributed to an increased emphasis on God's transcendence. Instead of being with his people God was enthroned in the highest heaven, far away from the world and the affairs of men. This transcendent God separate from the flux of human history and glimpsed only occasionally by the fortunate visionary (e.g. Rev. 4) embodied that perfection of the divine will, which was so obviously absent from human affairs. The fact that this view is often to be found should not be taken to indicate that it tells the whole story of post-biblical developments in Jewish theology. The emerging cosmology did not necessarily lead to a belief in the absence of God from history, though on occasion such beliefs are to be found.[15] What we find in later Jewish literature are varieties of ways of speaking about the presence of God with his people, for example, concepts like the *Shekinah* (God's presence) (Aboth 3.2),[16] the divine Wisdom permeating human affairs (Wisd. Sol. 7–9) and Philo's Logos,[17] as well as the Holy Spirit.[18] All these indicate that far from being totally absent in his heavenly dwelling God was still thought of as being present with his people.[19]

As we have already noted, Jewish writers did not speculate much about the nature and the attributes of God. Yet there are indications of the beginning of a speculative theology in Judaism. The belief that no man could see God and live (Exod. 33.20) itself implies a conviction that God *could* be seen. Within the Bible itself mention is made of visions of the all-holy God enthroned above the cherubim (Isa. 6; Ezek. 1; 10). In the later apocalyptic literature, with its more elaborate cosmology, God is enthroned in heaven surrounded by the heavenly host.[20] In such passages God's person and dress are sometimes described (e.g. Dan. 7.9; 1 Enoch 14.20f.). Such anthropomorphism, which has its origin in Ezekiel's call-vision (1.27f.), became a feature of much later Jewish mystical tradition. It would be a mistake to suppose that such speculative extravagance formed part of the piety of a later age only. There is evidence to suggest that from a very early period there was a colourful, and sometimes bizarre, theological speculation, which might have represented currents in popular piety, even if it tended to be frowned on by official organs of Judaism.[21] There was discouragement of speculative activity among the rabbis (M. Hagigah 2.1), though even the rabbinic academies were not totally free from such theological speculation.[22] While the amount of material dealing with such speculative activity forms only a small part of the rabbinic corpus, we must not minimize the central position which it had in the lives of some of the leading rabbis at the beginning of the Christian era. Indeed, the exegetical activity which occupied the attention of the rabbis inevitably brought them face to face with those parts of Scripture most open to theological speculation. As we shall see, passages like the account of Creation in Genesis 1 and the chariot vision of Ezekiel 1 were both subjects on which there was extensive reflection and formed the centre of a visionary and mystical tradition in Judaism.[23]

In the last analysis an introduction to Jewish theology cannot possibly end without stressing the prime conviction that God's attributes were understood by the people of God in the context of their experience throughout history. God was like an earthly father who cared for his children but was not afraid to discipline them also (Deut. 1.31; cf. Prov. 3.11f.). Israel as a nation had experienced God as one who kept his side of the covenant and who remained faithful, even when his people forsook him. It was convictions like these which influenced Jewish theology and lent it the distinctive hue which it has among the religions of antiquity.

3

The Heavenly Host[1]

We have already noted that in Jewish theology there was an ancient tradition, which stressed the importance of God as the Lord of the heavenly host.[2] By the beginning of the Christian era, Judaism had an elaborate angelology and demonology.[3] In the Torah we find references to the Angel of the Lord, who acted as the embodiment of God's presence and purpose (e.g. Gen. 16.7ff.; 22.11ff.).[4] In the later biblical material, particularly the book of Daniel and the contemporary apocalyptic writings, we find an angelology in which God is served by exalted angels like Michael (10.13, 21) and Gabriel (Dan. 8.15f.; 10.5f.). The former was regarded as the guardian angel of the people of Israel and their representative in the heavenly court (Dan. 12.1f.; 1QM 17.5; cf. Rev. 12.7). The archangels acted as emissaries of God, to communicate his will to those chosen to receive it (e.g., Luke 1.11, 26). Just as the development of an elaborate cosmology did not make God more remote from his people, so also the developing angelology did not lead automatically to the separation of God from men by the lower angelic forces and to the need for angelic mediation. That step was taken by the gnostics, whose writings come from the second century AD. They effected a separation between the transcendent god and a lesser divinity. But such a separation between the God of the highest heaven, untainted by any form of ill, and the lower created god, involved with a benighted creation, is contrary to the outlook of the angelic beliefs of Judaism. Nowhere is it suggested that the angelic powers have usurped God's sovereignty.[5]

The development of angelic powers hostile to God is a feature of the post-biblical literature. In affirming that the nations of the world had their representatives in the heavenly court, Jewish writers were admitting that the reign of God was something not yet evident in the affairs of men. While not directly opposed to God, since they acted by divine permission, the angelic powers were thought to be temporarily opposed to God's purposes and would ultimately have to face punishment (1 Enoch 89.59). The growth of angelology to embrace angelic counterparts in heaven to human beings on earth is a mark of the spirituality of the age (Matt. 18.10; Acts 12.15).

More significant is the growth of a belief in a hostile power opposed to God, Satan.[6] In his appearances in the Old Testament, Satan is not an opponent of God but an accuser in the divine court (Job 1; Zech. 3.1), as well as an agent of temptation (1 Chron. 21.1). Elements of this idea persisted into the early Christian period (Rev. 12.9), but dominant was Satan's position as the chief celestial opponent of God and his ways (Mark 1.13; Luke 10.18, cf. 2 Cor. 4.4; Ephes. 2.2). Evil angels came to have a dominant role in the writings of our period.[7] It is no accident that the conquest of the angelic powers is an important feature of the triumph of Christ as it is set out in the New Testament (1 Cor. 15.25ff.; Col. 2.14f.; 1 Pet. 3.22).

Related to the development of a belief in Satan as an evil angel is the way in which the 'sons of God' mentioned in Gen. 6.1 began to assume an important position in the explanation of the origin of evil.[8] This myth has an important position within the early Enochic literature, for example 1 Enoch 6–11. There was obviously a great temptation to place the blame for evil in the world at the door of supernatural forces opposed to God. The transference of blame for evil in the world onto the supernatural plane brought with it a rather fatalistic attitude towards human destiny.[9] If the battle between good and evil was being fought on a cosmic plane, then the puny attempts of mankind to interfere were doomed to disaster, unless an individual was given the resources to cope with the phenomenon. The existence of this superhuman struggle was a fact of life of the world of late antiquity. Its presence within the religious traditions and the resources for dealing with it are testimony enough to that fact. The growth of magic as a way of dealing with this supernatural evil is also a feature of our period.[10]

4

Angelic Mediators

Much discussion has taken place over the years about the growth in the number and character of intermediary figures, not least because of the importance of such figures for the development of beliefs about Christ.[1] There is little doubt that, already in the Old Testament, God's attributes were spoken of in a way which might lead one to suppose that they could be conceived of as separate divine beings participating in the nature of God himself. Thus God's Wisdom in both Ecclesiasticus and the Wisdom of Solomon is spoken of in quasi-angelic terms. She dwells with God (Ecclus. 24.1ff.); sits alongside him (Wisd. 9.4) and comes to the world of men (Ecclus. 24.3f.; Wisd. 9.10). Indeed, even in Proverbs 8.22 Wisdom is spoken of as if she were a divine being. There has been much debate over the significance of such ideas,[2] as well as the similar development, which we may discern in Philo's use of the term Logos, which speaks of God's immanent activity in the world of men. Even if we may be reluctant to suppose that these writers have taken the step of supposing that Wisdom and Logos are intermediary figures who were angelic personalities participating in the divine nature, it is evident that such developments provided at the very least the raw material of later christological reflection.[3]

We find in some of the literature of the period evidence of other heavenly beings, who were regarded as embodiments of the divine presence and will. Much has been written about the figure, the Son of Man. There is still much disagreement over the meaning of the phrase in the seventh chapter of Daniel. There the seer in his vision reports that he sees 'one like a son of man coming with the clouds of heaven' (v. 13). Some scholars prefer to regard this reference merely as a symbol of the persecuted people of God, the Saints of the Most High, and therefore not a reference to a divine being.[4] There is a considerable body of opinion, however, which argues that we should regard the figure described in this verse as an angelic being, whose character resembles other angelic figures mentioned in the book of Daniel (e.g., 3.25; 8.15; 10.5f.).[5] Certainly when we come to examine the later development of the phrase in the Similitudes of Enoch (1 Enoch 37–71), there can be little doubt that this writer had in mind a heavenly being who existed with God and even sat on his glorious throne (61.8; 62.2; 69.29).[6]

One specific development deserves to be mentioned here, namely, an exalted angel described as having divine attributes.[7] There is evidence from the Jewish apocalyptic tradition that there was an aspect of angelology emerging, which spoke of an angelic being, who embodied the divine attributes and appeared as the presence of God himself, similar in many ways to the function of the *mal'ak YHWH* in the early chapters of Genesis. This is most apparent in the angelophany in Apoc. Abraham 10f., where an angel called Jaoel appears to the patriarch and announces that he has the ineffable name of God dwelling in him (cf. Exod. 23.20). Similar ideas may be found in other works, and evidence of similar ideas is to be found in the New Testament, in Revelation 1.13ff.[8] Angelology of such theological sophistication was bound to lead to some confusion, and it may be that some connection exists between it and the earliest forms of gnostic heresy, not to mention the binitarian elements in the earliest Christian theology.

Much attention has been devoted to mediatorial figures in Judaism, because of the possible contribution they may have made to nascent Christology.[9] What is becoming clear is that we cannot blithely assume that there was a clear-cut monotheistic theology which was adhered to by all Jews. The gap between early Christian theology and pre-Christian Jewish theology is not as wide as is sometimes assumed.[10]

Communion between heaven and earth, between man and the angels, was an important feature of the piety of the Dead Sea Scrolls.[11] In discussing the relationship between angels and men, mention must be made of an aspect of Jewish angelology which, while it cannot be regarded as a prominent feature of ideas of our period, is of considerable importance for the evolution of early Christology.[12]

One of the central features of early Christian preaching is the conviction that the God of Abraham has vindicated his servant Jesus and exalted him to his right hand in glory: 'this Jesus whom you have crucified God has made lord and Christ' (Acts 2.36). Certainly for Saul of Tarsus this was a radical claim, but if his letter to the Galatians is anything to go by, the problem was the fact that the man so designated had died the ignominious death of crucifixion (Gal. 3.13; cf. 1 Cor. 1.23) rather than that such claims could be made for a human being. It seems unlikely that Paul would have found any problem at all with the exaltation of a man to the presence of God. Already in the Old Testament we find the account of Elijah's ascent to heaven on the chariots of fire (2 Kings 2.11). The conviction grew that Enoch also had been privileged to ascend to heaven directly without tasting of death. This is based on an enigmatic verse in Genesis 5.24, which states that 'Enoch walked with God and was not, for God took him'. In later Jewish tradition this was interpreted as a reference to the privilege granted to Enoch to go to the Garden of Eden (Jub. 4.21), to be the heavenly scribe (1 Enoch 12.4; Test. Abr. Rec. B 11; Targum Ps. Jon. on Gen. 5.24) and even to be transformed into the heavenly Son of Man (1 Enoch 71.14) and the archangel Metatron (3 Enoch).[13]

Such beliefs, however, are by no means confined to Enoch. The discovery of a fragmentary text in Cave 11 at Qumran has given us evidence that well before the first century AD, similar beliefs were held about Melchizedek.[14]

36

Although the text is very fragmentary it would appear that the first verse of Psalm 82 ('God has taken his seat in the congregation of Gods') has been applied to Melchizedek. The priest of Salem, therefore, is regarded as the heavenly judge in the divine tribunal and is called Elohim (God). In similar vein the proto-martyr Abel is described as the heavenly arbiter seated on a throne of glory in the Testament of Abraham. Like Enoch at the end of the Similitudes of Enoch Abel is seated on God's throne and is attired with the raiment of majesty fitting for God himself. He exercises judgement over the future destiny of men.[15]

Links between heavenly beings and righteous men are found in a rather different form in two works which probably come from Egypt, the Prayer of Joseph and Joseph and Asenath.[16] In the former, which is quoted in fragmentary form by Origen in his commentary on the Fourth Gospel, we find that the patriarch Jacob is none other than the incarnation of an exalted archangel, Israel. In the latter, which has some peculiar elements, a glorious angel who appears to Asenath, Joseph's future wife, is said to resemble Joseph in all things (JA 14). Indeed it seems that the angel is the heavenly counterpart of the patriarch (cf. Acts 12.15).

A figure of central importance for Judaism was, of course, Moses.[17] Like Enoch, he was the subject of extensive speculation in various Jewish works, though his position as the mediator of the divine revelation in the Torah meant that speculation about him was of central importance to the very heart of Judaism. In the book of Jubilees we find that Moses' ascent of Sinai becomes the setting for the communication of divine revelations by the angel of the presence. In this case the content of the revelations is the history as set down in the books of Genesis and Exodus 1–12. Moses' ascent of the mount was regarded in later tradition as an account of an ascent into heaven, though some of the rabbis became a little sensitive about such claims (b. Sukkah 5a). In Philo's eyes Moses became the revealer of supreme importance and able to pierce into the innermost secrets of divinity. The material available to us does not allow us to reconstruct with any degree of certainty the contours of this speculation about Moses at the beginning of the Christian era. Later sources, particularly the samaritan material, certainly allow us to glimpse the way in which the ideas developed. Thus while we may be certain that Moses' ascent to God (Exod. 19.3) was interpreted as an ascent to heaven (an understandable conclusion in the light of the developing cosmology), other aspects of the speculation concerning Moses are for the most part hidden from us. There is, however, one text which should be mentioned. This clearly antedates the rise of Christianity. It is quoted by Eusebius in *Praeparatio Evangelica* and goes under the name of Ezekiel the Tragedian.[18] In it we find an account of Moses' being offered a throne by God. It is an isolated glimpse of ideas about Moses which must have had considerable currency at this time.

In the bulk of these works mentioned here we do not appear to have a doctrine of the pre-existence of the human being concerned. By and large it would appear that a righteous man is merely exalted to heaven and then identified with a heavenly being or given a place of pre-eminence in the heavenly world. With some the situation is a little more complicated. Certainly the Prayer of Joseph seems to suggest that an angelic being (Israel) descended to earth and was incarnate in the person of Jacob. What cannot be doubted is that we have here a form of speculation on the destiny of the righteous individual which is of considerable importance for our understanding of the way in which the first Christians fashioned their beliefs about Jesus. It becomes a little more comprehensible why in so short a time a group of Jews could make such extravagant claims. What seems to be clear from the evidence available to us is that Jewish religion already furnished the framework of ideas to make such claims possible. Indeed, one might go further and say that it would have been surprising if, in the light of the various ideas which existed in Judaism, a sophisticated Christology had not developed.[19]

So recognition of the existence of traditions of this kind should cause us to pause before we suppose that the christological developments of early Christianity necessarily indicate an inventiveness and unique creativity which cannot be paralleled in early Judaism. Recent study of Jewish texts is making it abundantly clear that the whole area of theology and anthropology, particularly in so far as the latter impinges on the former, is an area which has not received sufficient attention in the past. What has emerged is a complex pattern of ideas concerning the heavenly position of righteous men and the equally extensive delegation of divine authority among a multiplicity of heavenly potentates. While this doubtless never infringed monotheistic belief (at least explicitly), the daring character of many of the ideas should make us pause before we confine the boundaries of Jewish beliefs about man and God too narrowly. For a Jew to have called another being 'God' or to have supposed that divine characteristics may have been shared by an exalted man of old seems to have been an accepted part of Jewish thought among some of the groups during this period. While it would be as dangerous to suppose that such views were accepted by all Jewish groups though without minimizing their importance, the theological possibilities which they exhibit demonstrate the panorama of options available to the early Christian exposition of the doctrine of the person of Christ. Contrary to what is often asserted, the categories of Judaism offered many opportunities for a profound expression of the intimacy of the relationship between Jesus and God and to produce a highly developed Christology, albeit in Jewish categories. The claim made by Jesus in John 10.30 that 'I and the Father are one' was certainly one that was considered blasphemous by some. What is not so clear is that such a claim would have been considered completely out of bounds within first-century Judaism. Indeed, it may be the case, as has been suggested recently,[20] that early Christianity may itself offer testimony in its christological reflection more to the theological complexity already inherent within contemporary Jewish religion rather than to the unique inventiveness of its adherents.

5

The Temple[1]

The fact that the Mishnah contains a tractate (*Middoth*) which deals with the measurements of the Temple,[2] despite the fact that the building had long lain in ruins, is testimony enough to the importance of the cult within Jewish life. The growing dominance of the Torah and its interpretation in the years after the fall of Jerusalem in AD 70 could not erase from the memory the tragedy of the Temple's destruction nor the hope for its rebuilding. In an old Jewish prayer dating from the years after the destruction of the Temple (the *Shemoneh Esreh*) there is included a prayer for the rebuilding of the Temple.[3] In the Bible itself there is interest in the legal sections in cultic matters. The regulations for the organization of and building of the Tabernacle in Exodus 25ff. and the details for ritual in Leviticus all manifest the intense concern with the details of cultic activity among collectors of Israel's traditions.

The place of the worship of the Temple within Israelite life before the Exile owed a great deal to the mythology which surrounded Zion as the dwelling place of God and his Messiah, the descendant of David.[4] Although much of this mythological picture ceased to have much influence after the Exile, the preservation of the mythological language in the psalms and the concern felt to rebuild the Temple (backed up by a prophetic vision in Ezekiel 40ff.) indicate that there was a considerable amount of residue from the pre-exilic ideas. In the books of Chronicles, for example, we find a concern with the establishment of the cult on a sure foundation as one of the dominant hopes fulfilled in the return from Exile.[5] The reappearance of some of the mythology in the prophecy of Haggai concerning the rebuilding of the Temple indicates that there was still a great aura attached to the building as the mark of God's presence with his people. The prophet tells the people that a close link existed between the glory of Zion and the emerging prosperity of the nation (1.4), and that neglect of the former had dire consequences for the latter.

In view of the central place which the Temple played in Israelite life it is hardly surprising that it should have loomed large in the piety of emerging Judaism. The centralization of cultic activity, particularly after the Deutero-nomic law (Deut. 12.13), meant that the influence of the Temple worship was very much linked with Jerusalem. That is not to say that there were no departures from this rule, for we have to remember that Onias built a Temple in Leontopolis (*BJ* 7.420ff.; *Ant.* 13.62ff.) and mention is made of cultic activity in the Elephantine papyri.[6] Nevertheless the centralization of the cult meant that worship for most Jews took place only in Jerusalem and, without a local shrine, cultic acts were confined to certain occasions, when journeys were made to Jerusalem. In our period this would have particularly applied to the three pilgrim festivals (Deut. 16.16): Passover (*Pesah*), the Feast of Weeks (*Shavuot*) and the Feast of Tabernacles (*Sukkoth*).[7]

Even if actual participation in the worship carried on in the Temple in Jerusalem was occasional, the influence of the Temple and its requirements was felt by all pious Jews and its position as a focus of devotion and affection was considerable. A tax was levied on all Jews to help with the massive costs incurred by the demands of the Temple and its worship (Neh. 10.33f.; cf. Exod. 30.11ff.).[8] Various decrees were issued outside Palestine to make sure that the dues paid there would in fact reach the Temple (e.g.; *Ant.* xvi, 28). After the destruction of the Temple the emperor decreed that the money should be paid to the temple of Jupiter Capitolinus in Rome;[9] this posed a real problem for Jewish Christians as Matthew 17.24ff. indicates.[10] In addition the Jew was liable to further calls on his resources in connection with the cult. Already in the time of Nehemiah we find that priestly dues were being enforced[11] (Neh. 10.36ff.; cf. Num. 18.8ff.; Lev. 7.30ff.). Many of the sacrificial offerings or a portion of them were given to the Levites. The various sacrifices necessitated by infringements of the Torah and as the demands laid down in the Torah which involved the payment of certain parts of one's estate to the Temple placed a significant demand on all members of the Jewish nation as well as providing a regular source of income for one group within Jewish society, the priests. Whether these enormous privileges were a significant bone of contention within the Second Temple period is not clear, but it is not too difficult to imagine what a burden it must have put upon the righteous Jew, whose circumstances made it so difficult for him to fulfil the laws of tithe or make his contribution towards the elaborate Temple worship. There was a growing number of Jews whose fulfilment of all but the basic laws was spasmodic.[12]

The variety of public and private sacrifices day by day kept the priests on duty in Jerusalem busy. The *tamid*, the daily burnt offering of the people (Exod. 29.38ff.) and the daily grain offering of the High Priest were the regular features of the sacrificial round. In addition the priests were expected to attend the altar of incense. The elaborate procedures for the public sacrificial worship of the Temple were accompanied during the day by the innumerable private acts of piety, which were carried out by the priests on behalf of all those who had come to Jerusalem with their own particular cultic act to make at the place which the Lord had chosen.

There were various demands made upon those responsible for the cult. There was responsibility for the vast amount of wealth owned by the Temple as the result of donations and the wealth accumulated as the result of the payment for sacrificial offerings and the cost of redeeming the firstborn male (Num. 18.15f.). The demands of the cult and its maintenance were an ever present factor in the lives of Jews in the first century. As we shall see, the vision of Pharisaism[13] was the extension of cultic purity into everyday life, yet another indication of the extraordinary influence of this institution.[14] While the financial demands were a regular burden on all Jews, the participation in the Temple's activities was not a frequent part of the life of most Jews. This was especially true of Jews in the Diaspora. Of course the giving of first fruits (Deut. 26) did not normally apply to those who did not live in the Holy Land. Interest in the Temple and participation in its ritual were of great importance to these Jews as well, as the representations of Philo about the setting up of a statue of Caligula in the Temple make clear (*Embassy to Gaius*). The fact is that, as far as regular patterns of religious observance were concerned, the synagogue, with its study of the Torah and the application of that study to everyday life, had in practice far more influence on Jews, particularly those outside Palestine. With hindsight we can see that, already at the beginning of the first century, the cult may have been obsolescent. Few, if any Jews would have admitted as much, but the practice of most only serves to confirm this judgement. Early Christianity and the Qumran community regarded the Temple in high esteem, and yet both found it necessary to spiritualize cultic actions and apply them to the deeds of the respective communities. In the case of the Qumran community there was the expectation of a renewed Temple in the last days;[15] some early Christian writers, however, took a more radical line towards its position in the new age, especially the writers of the Fourth Gospel, Hebrews and Revelation.[16] We may suppose that the end of Temple worship gave the final impetus to trends which had been emerging long before: to concentrate the heart of religion in Torah, the community and the divine presence in the hearts and lives of the pious.

6

Jewish Festivals

In the Jewish calendar there are several festivals, some of which are, prescribed by Torah, namely Passover/*Pesah*; Tabernacles/*Sukkot*; Weeks/*Shavuot* and others such as *Purim* (derived from the book of Esther 9.26ff.) and *Hannukah* (on which the dedication of the Temple after its desecration by Antiochus Epiphanes was celebrated). In addition to the festivals the season of penitence around the Day of Atonement (*Yom Kippur*) and the New Year (*Rosh ha-Shanah*) should also be mentioned.[1]

Whatever the origins of the three major festivals,[2] by the time of Jesus they had become intimately intertwined with Israel's experience of salvation and were occasions when Jews congregated together in the holy city, as they were pilgrim festivals (Exod. 34.23). The Passover festival[3] was the reminder of God's deliverance of his people (Exod. 12; Deut. 16.1–8; cf. M. Pes. 10.5). It lasted seven days, starting on the fifteenth day of the month Nisan and had been merged with the feast of Unleavened Bread (Deut. 16.2). On the eve of the festival (14th Nisan) lambs were offered as a sacrifice and were then eaten in family groups after being roasted whole. There were thus two major parts to the festival: the slaughter of the Passover lambs, which had to take place in the forecourt of the Temple (2 Chron. 30.15ff.; Jub. 49.16, 20); and the meal which, in the time of the Second Temple, had to be eaten in houses in Jerusalem (Mark 14.12; M. Pes. 7.9). During the meal the deliverance was recalled (cf. Exod. 13.8; M. Pes. 10.4) and in the later Passover *seder* or ritual it concludes with a prayer for redemption.[4]

The second pilgrim feast, *Shavuot*[5] (Weeks or Pentecost), took place on the sixth day of Sivan (Exod. 34.22; Deut. 16.10; Num. 28.26; Exod. 23.16; Lev. 23.15ff.). It fell fifty days after the sheaf had been waved on the day after the sabbath on the Feast of Passover (Lev. 23.15). During it, two loaves waved before the Lord, a reminiscence of its agricultural origin as a festival of the firstfruits (cf. Deut. 26.1–11; Jub. 6.21, 22.1), stress its agricultural nature. The festival became an anniversary of the giving of the Law on Sinai (Exod. 19.1; b. Pes. 68b).[6] In Jubilees 6. 1–21 it is seen as a feast of covenant renewal.

The third major festival is *Sukkot* or Tabernacles which took place on the 15th day of Tishri[7] and was the last of the three feasts connected with the agricultural year (Exod. 23.16; 34.22; Lev. 23.34–6; 39–43; *Ant.* 3.245; Deut. 16.13ff; Neh. 8.13ff.). It commemorated the period spent by the children of Israel in the wilderness. The major feature of it was the obligation to dwell in booths (Lev. 23.40) 'that your generations may know that I made the people of Israel dwell in booths when they came out of the land of Egypt' (Lev. 23.43). The booths were made of olive, myrtle and palm (Neh. 8.15), and the Jew had to sleep and eat all his meals in the booth for seven days. During the period of the second Temple, the festival was the occasion of several rites in the Temple, including a water libation (M. Suk. 4.9; John 7.37), during which priests with water from the pool of Siloam processed round the altar before pouring the water. Branches were taken from trees to form the *lulab* (Lev. 23.39ff.; cf. Neh. 8.17). Also during the festival four huge candlesticks illuminated the Temple area[8] (John 8.12) and Psalm 118 was sung. On the seventh day the Hosanna featured prominently in the liturgy. In 1 Kings the Feast of Tabernacles was the occasion of the dedication of Solomon's Temple and, like the Passover, it came to be associated with the eschatological hope (Zech. 14.16ff.; Rev.7).[9]

Finally mention must be made of the solemn day of penitence, the Day of Atonement,[10] whose ritual is set out in Leviticus 16 and Numbers 29.7–11 (cf. M. Yoma and Heb. 9). It fell on the tenth day of Tishri. The purpose of the rite was to cleanse the Temple (Lev. 16.16), priesthood (16.11) and people from sin (16.15, 33). During the rite the High Priest in special vestments (Lev. 16.4) entered the Holy of Holies in the Temple for the only time during the year (16.2), offered incense before the Mercy Seat (16.12ff.) and laid hands upon the scapegoat which was released into the wilderness (16.20ff.).

While the Temple still stood there was a very different pattern of religious activity as compared wih the situation after AD 70. The ritual of the Day of Atonement and the elaborate, Temple-based celebrations connected with the feasts of Tabernacles and Passover all disappeared after the destruction of the Second Temple, though memory of them was kept alive in the disputes, which are recorded in the Mishnah. The importance of this difference should not be underestimated. In so far as the cult looms largest in the pages of the Torah the demands of religion were very much centred on its activity. Obedience as a Jew was therefore tied up with fulfilling that obligation to stand before the Lord three times a year (Exod. 34.22) and to observe what was prescribed in the Torah concerning sacrifice and remedy of uncleanness (see Lev. 11ff.). Even those who lived outside the land of Israel did not neglect to attend these festivals[11] (*BJ* 2.280; *Ant.* 17.26; see also Acts 2). The pressures which were moving towards change had little effect so long as the Temple stood and its round of sacrifices and monopoly provision of religious dues dominated the religious scene.

7

The Synagogue[1]

Few would deny the central importance of the synagogue for the religion of post-exilic Judaism. The place of meeting where the traditions of the fathers were read and expounded was central to the vision of a people trained and able to apply the customs of the fathers. The origins of the synagogue are shrouded in obscurity.[2] Tradition traces it back to Moses himself, but it seems more likely that the origin was much more recent. Positive evidence is not available from primary sources much before the third century BC, though we may suppose that the various places of meeting mentioned in Scripture, for example, Ezekiel 8.1 and Psalm 137.1, may well reflect the beginnings of the process which led to the emergence of the synagogue. Of

43

course, the idea of a local assembly was not in itself new in Israelite religion. Despite the Deuteronomic regulation, which forbade the worship of Yahweh outside Jerusalem (e.g., Deut. 12), Israel had a long history of local shrines administered by the priests from the local area. The abolition (or at least attempted abolition) of these shrines probably caused a large vacuum in the religious practice of the people (2 Kings 18.4; cf. 23.5), and the pressure to continue the worship in this or similar form must have been enormous. While there is nothing to suggest that there was any connection whatsoever between these local high places or shrines and the later synagogues, it can be imagined that the emergence of the synagogue would provide an opportunity for those outside Jerusalem to practise their religion in a regular and frequent way, a problem accelerated by the dispersion of Jews out of close contact with the cult in Jerusalem (Dan. 6.10).

There can be no question of any direct parallel between the form of devotion conducted at the pre-Deuteronomic shrines and the Temple in Jerusalem on the one hand and the synagogues on the other. What evidence has come down to us about early synagogue practice, mainly from Philo and Josephus, indicates that the chief occupation of the synagogue was the study of the Scriptures.[3] The offering of sacrifices and similar cultic activities was, in conformity with the Deuteronomic law, confined to the Temple in Jerusalem. Outside Palestine, and probably in those cities in Palestine with a mixed population of Jews and Gentiles, the synagogue would have been the focus of religious and national identity, with the elders of the synagogue being the leading members of the local community. In Palestine itself synagogues seem to have taken on a more sectarian air (e.g., Acts 6.9), for the synagogue often represented the distinctive viewpoint of a particular sect, rather than being closely identified with the nation's rulers.

As the synagogue was essentially a place for study and devotion rather than for elaborate cultic activity, it will come as no surprise to find that the archaeological remains from the synagogues of the early Christian era reveal a plain style of construction. With the exception of the orientation of the synagogue towards Jerusalem, the place of prominence for the seat of Moses and in later synagogues, a place for the ark of the Torah, the structures were quite simple. The same cannot be said of the decoration of synagogues. Since the discovery of the synagogue at Dura-Europos (third century AD), it has become clear that there was by no means strict adherence to the ban on imagery.[4] Some of the mythology in the Dura paintings indicates the extent to which popular piety had been infiltrated by a vast array of ideas.[5]

As has already been stated, the principal function of the synagogue was the meeting for the study of Scripture. The requisite quorum for worship was ten persons, and the central feature of the worship was the reading from the Torah as well as from the Prophets and Writings. In addition there would have been the recitation of the Shema' ('Hear O Israel, the Lord thy God, the Lord is one.' Deut. 6.4–9; 11.13–21; Num. 15.37–41), the recitation of prayers, and the priestly blessing. The form of the prayers (*Tefillah*) was considerably altered after the fall of Jerusalem by the rabbis at Jamnia with the inclusion of, among other items, the twelfth benediction, so that we cannot be sure what form it took before the destruction of the Temple.[6]

The reading and exposition of the Scriptures were the vital part of the synagogue liturgy, as their correct understanding and interpretation were crucial to the continuation of the Jewish tradition. In the course of time a regular pattern of reading was established, so that the whole of the Pentateuch was read in a three-year cycle and the other parts of the canon ordered in relation to it.[7] Despite various attempts to show that various lectionary patterns antedate the fall of Jerusalem and have influenced various books in the New Testament,[8] there is no evidence to suggest that the three-year cycle was in existence during the Second Temple period. There can be little doubt that portions from the prophets (*haftaroth*) were included in the synagogue liturgy at the time of Jesus, as various passages from the New Testament make plain (e.g., Luke 4.17; Acts 13.15).

By the first century knowledge of Hebrew was not widespread. Thus, while it was still the case that the learned academies still discussed and wrote in Hebrew, the language of the common people in Palestine was Aramaic. As the common tongue of the empire, Greek was spoken and may well have been used even in Aramaic-speaking areas.[9] Thus it was necessary for the readings from the Bible in Hebrew to be translated.[10] This translation or *targum* offered a version of the original in Aramaic, which in due course had a fixed form but almost certainly from a very early period sat fairly loosely to the Hebrew text. Certainly in the form in which we now possess them, the targumim contain much extraneous material, indicating a considerable degree of elaboration of the biblical text.[11]

Among the prayers recited in the synagogue, particular mention should be made of the Tefillah or Shemoneh Esreh which had to be recited three times a day by Jews. Much interest has attached to this prayer, because of supposed links between its developed form, which came into being after the destruction of the Temple, and certain New Testament documents. Most attention has been devoted to the twelfth benediction, the so-called *birkath ha-minim*, which includes a curse of Christians.[12] New Testament scholars are convinced that certain New Testament documents, particularly the Gospels of Matthew and John, reflect the formulation and use of this benediction.[13]

It would be wrong to think of the synagogue and its life as being confined solely to Jews. Evidence from Acts indicates that, on the fringes of the synagogue, there was a large body of pagans sympathetic to Judaism, described as God-fearers (Acts 13.26). Indeed, while it may have been the case that part of Philo's purpose in recommending the activities of the synagogue to his pagan readers was to defend Jews against the taunts of contemporaries, it would not be surprising to find that the attraction of the Jewish life as set out by the Alexandrian Jew was the reason for many participating in the activities of the synagogue and accepting limited portions of the Jewish life as their own (*Life of Moses* 2.216). Indeed, a degree of missionary activity and positive rather than merely negative apologetic work can be found in some of the literary remains of early Judaism (e.g., Sibylline oracles).[14]

8

The Torah[1]

Central to the theology of Judaism was the belief that the law-giver, Moses, had bequeathed to Israel the first five books of the Hebrew Bible, the Torah. Much of this is devoted to law and the history of the origin of the covenant people. For all groups which claimed affinity with Judaism, these five books formed the central pillar of their faith. It must be remembered that in addition to offering an explanation of their origin as an elect people, the Torah sets out the conditions under which this election may be given effect. Israel is a holy nation, and its obedience to God is characterized by distinctive cultic and civic regulations. The mark of the Jew is circumcision (Lev. 12.3; Gen. 17.9ff.). In remembrance of God's rest at the end of creation, the Jew rests on the seventh day (Gen. 2.1f.; cf. Exod. 20.8f.). In his daily life the Jew is expected to observe the laws of cleanness (Lev. 13–15) and to have due regard for what he eats (Lev. 11; Deut. 14.3ff.). Unlike the nations round about, the Jews are not to practise idolatry (Lev. 19.4; Exod. 20.4); blasphemy is excluded (Lev. 24.11), and there are strict laws with regard to sexual behaviour (e.g. Lev. 18; Deut. 27.21ff.). There are the rudiments of civil law set out in the Torah (Exod. 20ff.; Lev. 25.25ff.; Deut. 17; 22) and there is evidence of avoidance of excessive repression in Israelite society (e.g., Lev. 25; Deut. 15). There are strict laws relating to agriculture (Lev. 19.9ff.), which are linked with certain cultic observances, like the tithe (Deut. 26.12). Dominant in the pages of the Torah are the detailed prescriptions with regard to cultic activity, which take up a large part of the books of Exodus and Leviticus.

There is considerable uncertainty about the status of other books which we now class as part of the Jewish canon. The canon as we know it in the Protestant churches[2] was probably formally ratified at the rabbinic gathering at Jamnia, though that is not to suggest that the various groups which existed before this time did not have a fairly clear idea what was and what was not authoritative (Josephus *Contra Ap.* i, 38–41; Ecclus. 49.10; cf. 4 Ezra 14.45). By the time of the first century most Jewish groups would have regarded the prophetic literature as an authoritative continuation of the divine proclamation, which expounded the initial deposit in the Torah. In the introduction to Pirke Aboth, for example, we find a chain of tradition outlined, in which the prophets take their place in the long line of expositors of the tradition of Jewish tradition stemming from Moses himself (Aboth 1.1; cf. Ecclus. 39.12f.). Whether groups like the Pharisees placed the prophetic oracles on the same level as the Torah cannot easily be decided, though that seems likely in the light of their regard for the value of continuing tradition. It has often been thought that the Sadducees, like the Samaritans, denied the authoritative status of the prophetic writings, but it is difficult to substantiate this statement. In the light of their rejection of the doctrine of resurrection, it may be possible to suppose that the status of works like Daniel and those prophetic writings which might seem to point in the direction of resurrection (e.g., Isa. 26.19), was given a subordinate position by them. Josephus tells us that they rejected the tradition of oral interpretation which formed such an important part of the pharisaic-rabbinic approach though all the evidence suggests that they had their own tradition of interpretation.[3] It would not be an exaggeration to say that the Sadducees represented the traditional attitude towards Scripture. Their rejection of belief in the resurrection from the dead, as well as other developed doctrines of angels and demons (Acts 23.8) indicates not so much a group which was unfaithful to the Torah as one which refused to go further than what was written. Sadducees, therefore, in so far as we can reconstruct their beliefs, represented a more literalistic approach to the interpretation of Scripture (*Ant.* 13.297) and their attitude may have been much more widespread than we sometimes suppose.[4] They seem to have been reluctant to accept the need for hermeneutical flexibility and were not exponents of any explicit heretical ideas, despite the attempts of the pharisaic-rabbinic tradition to taint them in this way (M. San. 10.1).

Mention of the interpretation of Scripture brings us face to face with one of the major developments in Jewish religion after the return from Exile: the emergence of a religion of the book. The great burst of literary activity during the Exile, when ancient traditions were codified and reflections on recent experience took place,[5] meant that a significant shift began to take effect in the character of Jewish religion. The vindication of the prophetic message of doom in the sixth century BC and the greater weight given thereby to the hopes of restoration and future bliss meant that the prophetic oracles were treated with great reverence and set alongside the original deposit stemming from Moses as the bedrock of the Jewish faith. It is difficult to know whether the collection of the prophetic oracles was the cause or merely a consequence of the diminution of the living prophetic voice.[6] Whatever may have been the case, the return from Exile saw the gradual waning of the prophetic movement. Possibly it may have been discredited by the fervent support given to the messianic movement centred on Zerubbabel by Haggai and Zechariah, but little is known, apart from a few cryptic passages (e.g., Zech. 13.1ff.) about the fate of the movement. It is difficult to believe that it vanished without trace, and the suggestions of those who think that it was either forced underground during a power struggle in the post-exilic community or be connected to emerging apocalyptic may have some cogency.[7] Nevertheless prophecy became not the living words of the contemporary individual but the written deposit of past sages whose words were looked to as means of ascertaining the divine will in the present.

Direction in the life of the community had before the Exile been given by priest and prophet, and practical guidance on particular problems relating to religious observance continued to be given by priests after the Exile (Hag. 2.11ff.); but there grew up a body, which gradually took their place as expounders of the Torah and guides to the righteous people, the Scribes.[8] Ezra, the great exponent of the centrality of the Torah, the scribe *par excellence* in Jewish tradition, was himself a priest. But such priestly influence did not continue in the face of the rapid growth of the body of Scribes whose task it was to study, write and expound the sacred writings for the use of the people of God. In the days of Jesus ben Sirach the Scribes rank in a position of some importance (Ecclus. 39). The man who spends his time studying the oracles of bygone days is in a position not only to help his companions but also to be of assistance to the mighty (Ecclus. 39.4). In the writer's eyes he is not merely a student of the ancestral writings who, by his study, can make plain that which is difficult to understand, but also a man of prayer, who may be filled with the spirit of intelligence and, as a result, may produce maxims of his own, which may enlighten his hearers.

We do not possess enough information about the nature of this scribal activity in the second century BC. While we would not expect the sophistication of method or exegetical result which is apparent in later texts, it is probably correct to assume that what we have in the Mishnah is the end-product of a process which is already at work in the scribes of Ben Sirach's day and long before, perhaps already evident in the Bible itself.[9] It is evident from Ecclus. 39.3 that detailed exegesis was part of scribal expertise. The Scribes were the custodians of the religious demands of God and as the ones who could understand the intricacies of the Scriptures had great powers over those who would wish to practise the religion as set out in the Torah. They were the ones, who, in Jesus' words, had the key of knowledge (Luke 11.52). Already in Nehemiah 8.8, 13, we see that the importance of a correct knowledge and understanding of the Law is stressed. What emerges in these chapters is the close connection which exists between correct understanding and observance and the fulfilment of the covenant obligation.

The fact that the Torah laid down rules for conduct outside as well as inside the cult meant that scribal influence extended to everyday existence. Such knowledge of the Torah and its application to the *whole* of life and not to specifically 'religious' acts increased the power of those who had the knowledge of what the demands were and could seek to ascertain what areas of life needed to be regulated by them. The expertise which characterized the Scribes was something which was of such importance within the religious life of the nation that steps were taken to ensure the transmission of their knowledge and skill to future generations. We know from texts which relate to the situation after the fall of Jerusalem that considerable care was taken to ensure that the knowledge of previous opinions was passed on to succeeding generations.[10] Part of the task of the later Sages was to teach and to assemble pupils who would be sufficiently well equipped with the exegetical skill and knowledge of earlier ideas to continue the ongoing interpretative process.

In the first century AD, dominant in the interpretation and application of the Torah, particularly in Palestine, was the Sanhedrin.[11] Its composition, the extent of its authority and the character of its religious outlook are unclear. According to the Gospels and Acts, it had a significant role to play in the prosecution of action against Jesus and the first Christians (Mark 14; Acts 3–7) both in Palestine and beyond (Acts 9.2), and in it the priestly element seems to have predominated (Mark 14.61; John 18.19ff.; Acts 4.5f., 5.17). With the fall of Jerusalem in AD 70, it ceased to have such a dominant role and its function was usurped by the rabbis meeting at Jamnia.

At the heart of the Jewish religion there lies the Torah. That collection of history, legend and Law gives the reason for Israel's existence and sets out the means by which that existence can be continued under God. To appreciate the centrality of the Torah is to understand why so much energy is expended in rabbinic commentaries in providing detailed explanations of its demands, not to mention why Paul's peculiar interpretation of it (e.g., Gal. 3.16f.) constituted such a threat to Judaism as widely understood.

9

The Interpretation of Scripture[1]

It has already been stated that by the time we reach the first century AD, the Torah had assumed a position of pre-eminence in Jewish life. Not only was it the major source of information for the ordering of the cult but also it offered the inspiration for all Jews on the character of obedience which God expected of his covenant people. The problem with the Torah, however, was that the statutes and ordinances laid down by God for his people were nothing like as explicit as was necessary in order to ascertain the precise form of the obedience required. Even cultic regulations about which there was far more information in the Torah than on other issues were a source of bitter conflict.[2] The ongoing interpretation of the biblical text produced a tradition of legal principles and enactments, which are designated *halakah*. *Halakah* as opposed to *haggadah*, which is non-legal material, centres on the practice of religion: what is necessary in a particular situation in order to abide by the ordinances of God. In the rabbinic literature as we have it, *halakah* is presented in two forms. On the one hand, guidance is offered on the basis of the elucidation of a particular passage of Scripture. On the other hand, such guidance, while relating in general terms to a particular aspect of Jewish law (cleanness, festivals, sabbath, etc.), is not explicitly linked with a particular passage of Scripture and takes the form of a pronouncement on the appropriate matter by a rabbi. A distinction is made therefore between *halakah* and *halakic midrash*. The latter involves the interpretation of biblical passages in such a way that it relates to conduct; midrash relates to the interpretation of Scripture, whereas the former involves the pronouncement of a teacher either on the basis of tradition and custom or new formulation to meet differing circumstances. Some of the practices which were given the status of *halakah* were not sanctioned in Scripture nor were they the deductions from exegetical activity. Rather they were the practices and customs of the Jewish people sanctified by time and their practical desirability.[3] Such, we may suppose, were some of the practices connected with the sabbath, for example, the lighting of the sabbath light and the various rites connected with the sabbath meal.

Many differences are apparent in the interpretative approaches to the Torah found in the writings of Jewish groups of the period, though we have to admit that our knowledge of non-Christian Jewish interpretation is mainly confined to the pharisaic-rabbinic. It is this tradition which will be outlined first of all.

Underlying the *halakah* of the rabbis was the concern that every precaution was taken to ensure no accidental disobedience of the divine commands: 'Making a fence around the Torah' (*Aboth* 1.1). That meant outlining precautions to be taken to make sure there was no accidental breaking of a biblical law. Then there was the constant attempt to show how the ancient legal code could be made relevant for the changed circumstances of the Hellenistic world. The bulk of the legal material in the Torah concerns cultic activity, with very little impinging directly on civil and commercial life. When Jews were involved in trade and commerce to earn a living for themselves and their families, it became imperative to know how the demands of, say, sabbath or festivals impinged on the regular activity of earning a living.

One of the most famous examples of a pharisaic enactment coined with the specific intention of facilitating the participation of Jews in commercial life was the *prozbul*. This relates to the law prescribed in Deuteronomy 15.1–11, which states that every seven years all debts should be remitted. Obviously this placed a severe obstacle in the way of successful commercial activity. When the year of remission of debts drew near, there would have been considerable reluctance on the part of the lender to lend money for fear that he would never see it again. In direct contradiction to the biblical ruling, though with the intention of facilitating the practice of Judaism and efficient business life, Hillel instituted the *prozbul*. This enabled the creditor to make a declaration (*M. Sheb* 10.4), which effectively enabled him to reclaim his debt. In this and other matters Hillel and his school took a liberal line towards the observance of the Torah, preferring to concentrate on its spirit rather than the letter, ensuring a continued observance of Jewish religion by those for whom the circumstances of life had made such a task either impossible or extraordinarily difficult.

The very nature of Jewish religion meant that the *halakah* was an ongoing process. The situations which had caused the enactment of past decisions changed. There was a need for new thinking and fresh insight. Thus the *halakic* process was never ending, and over the course of time fresh decisions accepted by the majority of the rabbinic academy themselves took their place alongside the other *halakoth*. In rabbinic traditions these ranked alongside the written Torah as part of the revelation given by God to Moses on Sinai (e.g., Ex. Rabbah 47.7).

While much of this legal material has practical relevance, not all of it was formulated to meet the difficulties which confronted Jews in the observance of their religion. Some decisions have their setting not in the actual problems of Jews but in the theoretical discussions of the rabbinic academies (e.g., M. Yad. 4.3f.). Before AD 70 when the rules of the Pharisees were not always binding upon all Israel, the influence of the proposals of the pharisaic Sages had little effect outside the intimate circle of those groups (*haburoth*) who pledged themselves to put their rules into practice.[4]

The scholarly activity on the Torah centred on the conviction that God's revelation was deserving of the most careful study and, what is more, would yield to those who searched carefully enough the insights which would enable man to live according to the divine will. Over the centuries the study of the Scripture had made the scholars aware of the contradictions, similarities and variety within the text. As well as being the cause of problems to be solved Scripture offered new resources as a means of ascertaining new information, as related passages yielded new insights which a similar passage would not necessarily give. Although it is likely that exegetical tools were developed over the years, rabbinic tradition specifically attributes to Hillel the responsibility for formulating seven exegetical rules or *middoth* (see the Aboth de Rabbi Nathan 37a).[5] Two of the best known rules are as follows:

1. *Qal wahomer* : what applies in a less important case will certainly apply in a more important case (e.g., John 7.23).
2. *Gezerah shawah*: similarity of language in two different passages; where the same words are applied to two separate cases it follows that the same considerations apply to both (e.g. Rom. 4.5).

These exegetical rules represented the approach of the Hillelite rabbinic school, but the discovery of the Qumran Scrolls[6] has revealed to us the distinctive approach of this group, which once again has parallels with New Testament exegesis, particularly in the eschatological exegesis (4 Q Test. and 4 Q Flor.). In the scriptural commentaries, particularly the commentaries on the prophetic books of Habakkuk and Nahum, we find that two very distinctive uses of the Old Testament emerge. First of all, in an oft-quoted passage from the Habakkuk commentary (1 QpHab) the writer contrasts the prophetic oracle with the interpretations offered by the Teacher of Righteousness in the following words:

> ... and God told Habakkuk to write down that which would happen to the final generation, but He did not make known to him when time would come to an end. And as for that which he said, that he who reads may read it speedily, interpreted this concerns the Teacher of Righteousness, to whom God made known all the mysteries of the words of his servants the prophets.

It is not unusual in Judaism to find the conviction that an individual is in a position to offer an authoritative interpretation of the text. What makes this particular understanding of authority stand out is that it seems to brook no disagreement whatsoever. What characterizes the rabbinic tradition is the fact that the possibility is allowed of rival interpretations of the same passage, one of which may be opposed by the majority yet may be recorded in the tradition. The unique position given to the Teacher of Righteousness in the tradition by the community reflects the latter's belief that the authentic meaning of the prophetic oracles has been divulged to one man. This man has been given the divine insight and his interpretation is given the force of new revelation akin to the revelations of the apocalyptists.[7] This claim to the authoritative interpretation of Scripture is one which is found in a rather different form in early Christianity. Here both Jesus and Paul claim to know what the true meaning of the Jewish tradition is and push this in the face of opposition from their peers, for example, Matthew 5.20ff.

The other distinctive feature of this interpretative method is what has become known as the *pesher* (Hebrew for interpretation) method of exegesis. This is the method where the words of Scripture are held to apply not to events and persons centuries before but to the particular experience of the righteous community in their struggle to maintain their identity and purity in the face of opposition from the powers of evil. This technique is seen most clearly in the biblical commentaries from Qumran, where events in the life of the community are found predicted in the words of a prophet coined for a very different situation. One of the classic examples of this refers to an incident when the Wicked Priest (mentioned often in these commentaries and variously identified with Jonathan or Simon, the Hasmonean priests) pursued the Teacher of Righteousness to the place of his exile:

> Woe to him who causes his neighbour to drink; who pours out his venom to make them drunk that he may gaze on their feasts.
>
> Interpreted this concerns the Wicked Priest who pursued the Teacher of Righteousness to the house of his exile that he might confuse him with his venomous fury. And at the time appointed for rest, for the Day of Atonement, he appeared before them to confuse them, and to cause them to stumble on the Day of Fasting, their Sabbath of repose.[8]

Here an event which had a significant place within the memory of the community has been explicitly related to biblical prophecy. Such an identification of present historical events with biblical passages is to be found from time to time in the New Testament (cf. Zech. 3.8; 6.12 and the use of older traditions like Isa. 4.2; Jer. 33.15). The obvious examples are the scriptural citations in the Gospel of Matthew.[9] The prophecy of the birth of a son to the Davidic king, the Immanuel oracle (Isa. 7.14) is related by Matthew to the birth of Jesus (1.23). Similarly the story of the entry of Jesus into Jerusalem on an ass is explicitly linked by Matthew with Zechariah 9.9.

Undergirding the use of Scripture in the New Testament[10] is the conviction that the promises found in its pages had been fulfilled (John 5.39; Mark 1.24; 1 Pet. 1.10f.; Mark 1.2f.; Acts 2.16ff.) and that while Jews were the recipients of the oracles of God (Rom. 3.2; 9.4), those who did not accept that Jesus was the promised Messiah had failed to perceive the true significance of the words contained in Scripture (2 Cor. 3.14ff.). Even allowing for the growing exclusivism in the application of Scripture (a feature also evident in the Dead Sea Scrolls), there can be no denying that the Jewish Scriptures provided the Christians with the determinative framework for the establishment of their own identity. There is a wide variety of interpretative methods, for example, typology, where OT figures and events are regarded as types of Christ and the Christian Church (Rom. 5.12ff.; Heb. 7.1ff.; 1 Pet. 3.21ff.; 1 Cor. 10.1ff.), and allegory, where deeper spiritual meaning is read into the text (Gal. 4.24; 1 Cor. 9.8ff.). Some of the rabbinic techniques can be found in the New Testament, for example in John 7.22; Mark 12.35ff.; 2.25f. In addition there is some evidence to suggest that collections of appropriate texts were made similar to those found among the Dead Sea Scrolls (4 Q Test. and 4 Q Flor.), the most popular were Psalms 22; 110.1.[11]

With the formulations of these various exegetical methods, Jewish interpreters were in a position to make the most of the Scriptures at their disposal to obtain further information on disputed points and to justify practices which were not explicitly recommended by the Torah. The sophistication of this work, particularly in the later rabbinic academies, is itself testimony to the conviction that in the Torah there was an eternal supply of spiritual insight waiting for those who would engage themselves patiently and sympathetically in its study (cf. Aboth 6.1, where Rabbi Meir talks of the mysteries of the Torah).

Although the major reason for study of the Torah was the business of ascertaining the import of its words for religious belief and practice, particularly concerned with the correct observance of commands for life and cult, there was also the important task of explaining the Scriptures which did not relate to legal matters.[12] What is loosely referred to as *haggadic midrash* is a rich variety of material dealing with the stories of Israel's past and the supplementing of the sparse accounts with myth and legend. This form of scriptural exposition took many different forms. On the one hand we have texts which explicitly set out to retell the biblical narrative, while there are others, like the apocalypses, which include extended legends about the pseudonymous authors (e.g., Apoc. Abr. 1ff.).

Attempts to retell Israel's history are found in various forms. Hellenistic Jewish historians like Eupolemus and, of course, Josephus, in his *Antiquities*, bear witness to the compulsion to retell Jewish history. In retelling the biblical story, the writers testify to the development of particular stories in their day. Similarly the book of Jubilees, the Genesis Apocryphon (1 Q Gen. Apoc.) from Qumran and the Biblical Antiquities of Pseudo-Philo offer versions of the biblical story of Israel's origins with some very colourful expansions of the biblical text, some of which have little or no basis in Scripture itself.

The most comprehensive of the retelling of the biblical narratives is to be found in the various *targumim*.[13] These are Aramaic-versions of the Bible, in which there is verse by verse translation with considerable augmentation from other material. In their present form the targumim are much later than the New Testament,[14] but few would doubt that they already existed in some form at the time of Jesus. Indeed, evidence from Qumran suggests that the process of translating the Bible into Aramaic for the benefit of Aramaic-speaking Jews in Palestine who knew no Hebrew was already the case in the first century.[15] The most important targumim are those on the Pentateuch and these probably contain the earliest material. There are targumim on other books of the Bible, including the prophets, and in the light of the important use made of the book of Isaiah by the early Christians the careful evaluation of that targum and the extent of its post-Christian reworking is a task of great importance for the understanding of Christian use of this text.[16]

What research on the targumim and the related biblical expositions is teaching us is that we need to be much more sensitive to the various nuances in the material,[17] which might lead us to suppose that one word could give us the clue that a whole wealth of material may stand behind it.[18] Our study of the Jewish exegetical tradition is important because it enables us to build up a picture of the way in which the Bible was expounded and the kind of presuppositions with which Jews would have approached the text. Early Christian exegetes were not functioning with unprecedented methods and traditions of exegesis. The Bible they read was an interpreted Bible. Certainly their own convictions about Jesus would to a great extent colour their own approach but it would be dangerous to suppose that this led them to formulate any novel rules of exegesis. This is a disputed area, and opinion is divided. There are still many who suppose that the insights offered by the study of Jewish literature, and particularly the exegetical literature, will have only a marginal benefit for the study of the New Testament mainly because of problems of dating the material. It is, however, difficult to suppose that, however dramatic and overwhelmingly new the Christian revelation may have been, the early Christians would have completely cast aside the method of study and traditions connected with particular passages which they had inherited from Judaism. The search for signs of the influence of Jewish exegetical traditions on New Testament writers is still in its infancy. It may be that some of the supposed connections have been a little far-fetched, but the development of our methods and the sophistication of our tools for ascertaining the existence of possible links may enable us to throw open the extent of indebtedness to the Jewish exegetical tradition from which the Christian movement emerged.

10

Apocalyptic:
Scripture and the Disclosure of Heavenly Knowledge

There has been renewed interest in recent years in apocalyptic and its place in Jewish and Christian theology. Not that interest in the influence of apocalyptic is anything new, for during the last eighty years or so New Testament commentators have been wrestling with the implications of the work of Johannes Weiss and Albert Schweitzer. Some of the most distinguished New Testament scholars have attempted to deal with the central position which they gave to apocalyptic and eschatology in the teaching of Jesus. It is probably fair to say that much of this discussion has oscillated between using the words apocalyptic and eschatological to describe Jesus' message. This oscillation is a good example of the way in which the treatment of apocalyptic has inevitably ended up as a discussion of eschatology, with well-defined characteristics. Indeed, it is probably fair to say that for many apocalyptic is a type of eschatology which speaks of the imminent end of this world and the introduction from above, amidst cataclysmic disorders, of a transcendent realm.[1]

This eschatological orientation of the understanding of apocalyptic demands a little explanation. While all would recognize that apocalyptic derives from the Greek word *apokalypsis*, a word which is used to describe the disclosure of supernatural persons or secrets, the same word is also used to describe the religious perspective found in a number of writings including Daniel, Revelation, 1 and 2 Enoch, 4 Ezra, Syr. Baruch, Greek Baruch, Apoc. Abraham and Test. Abraham, all of which, with the exception of Revelation, are attributed to a hero of Israel's past. The dominant concern throughout the book of Revelation is with eschatology, expressed in imagery similar to that found in other apocalypses (e.g., Dan. 2.31ff.; 7.1ff.; 8.3ff. and 1 Enoch 85ff.) and with a belief in the imminent irruption of God and the forces of light into the historical process (Revelation 19.11ff.; 22.20). The use of the word apocalyptic to describe this cluster of ideas is widespread, and it is important to recognize this usage, in order to understand how apocalyptic has come to be used virtually as a synonym for eschatology.[2]

It has become very common to find the words apocalypse and apocalyptic used to describe the end of the world. This approach to apocalyptic is so widespread that it inevitably colours the way in which the origins of apocalyptic are outlined. At the heart of apocalyptic, it is argued, is its distinctive expression of the future hope. The belief that this view of the eschatological picture of Revelation is typical of other apocalypses has led to a definition of apocalyptic which concentrates on eschatological features like the doctrine of the two ages, a future realm of a transcendent kind, a divine irruption into history and a pessimistic attitude towards the present age. The origins of these beliefs are traced to several passages in the Old Testament (e.g., Isa. 24–7, Joel, Trito-Isaiah and Zechariah),[3] which seem to provide the antecedents of such an eschatology.

It may seem pointless to question the value of a definition of apocalyptic which stresses mainly eschatological features when the pattern of thought so characterized seems to have sufficiently clear contours to be discerned by all. The fact is that the religious outlook called apocalyptic is by no means as widespread and clear-cut as is often supposed. What is more, the distinction between the apocalypse as a literary genre and apocalyptic as a pattern of thought has led to considerable confusion.[4] Some have rightly questioned whether apocalyptic as usually defined finds its best expression in the apocalypses.[5] When we find that the religious beliefs of the apocalypses cannot be neatly described as eschatological, and, what is more, when the eschatology of the apocalypses only occasionally corresponds to the apocalyptic type, then the time has come to ask whether our understanding of the pattern of eschatological ideas usually identified as apocalyptic may not better be categorized by some other term (for example, transcendent eschatology), thus reserving the word apocalyptic to describe the distinctive religious outlook of the apocalypses themselves.

When we attempt to ascertain the religious outlook of the apocalypses, it becomes increasingly difficult to place such great weight on eschatology as the key to our interpretation of these texts. It is true that interest in the future is prominent in most apocalypses, but the character of this interest and its relationship to other features demand careful consideration.[6] When one investigates the eschatology of the apocalypses, it all too quickly becomes clear that what are often regarded as typical features of apocalyptic are by no means common. What is more, actual teaching about the content of the future hope, for example, the character of the new age, the origin and activity of the Messiah, the organization of the messianic community, etc., are frequently passed over with little explanation. While the apocalyptists may devote much attention to the progress of history leading up to the new age, there is an evident reluctance to speculate about its character. The conviction about a glorious future for the people of God is there, but its character is hardly ever elaborated in detail.

A survey of the contents of the apocalypses would reveal a wide range of topics. Important in many apocalypses is an interest in details of the heavenly world (Dan. 7.9; 1 Enoch 14.8ff.; 71; Apoc. Abraham 18ff.; Test. Levi 2f.;

Greek Baruch; Rev. 4; Ascension of Isa. 6ff.), astronomy (1 Enoch 72ff., Slav. Enoch 23), the course of Jewish history (Dan. 8; 1 Enoch 85ff.; 91.12ff.; 93; Test. Levi 16ff.; 4 Ezra 11f.; Syr. Baruch 35ff.; 53ff.; Apoc. Abraham 27ff.) and man's destiny (Apoc. Abraham 20ff.; 4 Ezra 3.4ff.; Syr. Bar. 48). All these issues correspond roughly with the revealed things which are at the heart of apocalyptic.[7] Of course, all these topics were, for one reason or another, of immense interest to all Jews, and it would be wrong to suppose that interest in history, eschatology, astronomy and cosmology is by any means confined to the apocalypses only. What is distinctive about the use of this material in the apocalypses is that it is offered to the apocalyptic seer as *a revelation direct from God*. It is not the product of human observation or even the application of conventional exegetical techniques to Scripture. What we have expressed in the apocalypses is the conviction that God has spoken directly to the seer, whether by means of vision or angelic pronouncement. As a result the divine truth can be apprehended by the seer and by all those to whom the seer chooses to make known this knowledge.

The fact that there is a lack of detail about the hope for the future, an interest in other subjects and an emphasis on the revelation of divine mysteries suggests that apocalyptic cannot be regarded as merely a science of the end, in which heavenly journeys and other revelations serve only as a convenient back-drop for eschatological information. The evidence from the apocalypses themselves indicates that we should not regard their function as the fanciful speculations of those whose interest was solely in eschatological matters. The emphasis throughout on the revelation of God and the divine purpose for the cosmos as a whole must be seen as an attempt to answer the crisis facing the Jewish tradition at the time of the apocalyptists. While it would be wrong to play down the speculative interest in the descriptions of the heavenly world, the revelation of God enthroned in glory and his ways are an appropriate way of reassuring those whose historical circumstances might indicate that the God of the Israelite tradition no longer cared for his people. Linked to this, the detailed demonstration of divine foreknowledge of Israel's plight and of the divine plan for human history is surely intended to enable a beleaguered religious group to have confidence in its traditional affirmations and hopes. The neglect of detailed eschatological information is partly explained by a much greater need to enable the reader to see the totality of human history from the divine perspective, thereby ensuring that the inevitable preoccupation with the present plight did not detract from belief in God's saving purposes, which according to some apocalypses were on the point of being realized (Dan. 12.6; 4 Ezra 14.10; Syr. Baruch 85.10). The use of apocalyptic provided an authoritative statement of belief which, while rooted in Scripture, avoided the human limitations present in conventional exegesis by recourse to the direct disclosure of heavenly knowledge.

58

It is important to recognize that in considering apocalyptic we are dealing with a religious current in Judaism (and for that matter in the Hellenistic world generally), which spans a long period of time. Even if we date the earliest parts of 1 Enoch to the third century BCE[8] (and they are probably much older) and the latest apocalypses at the end of the first century AD, we are speaking of a period of three hundred years or more. It would be rash to suppose that the interests over this period remained the same and that circumstances did not affect the choice of material for inclusion in the apocalypses. It is in the three apocalypses written in the aftermath of the First Revolt (4 Ezra, Syr. Baruch and Apoc. Abraham), for example, that we find a particular concern for the destiny of Israel together with impassioned pleas for an explanation of the suffering of the people of God.[9] Concern in detail with astronomical data is manifested in the Enochic literature (e.g., 1 Enoch 72ff.), though there is occasional evidence that other apocalyptists may also have been interested in this subject (Syr. Baruch 48.1ff.). Likewise the dominant concern with eschatology in Daniel and Revelation is not typical of other apocalypses. The origin of Daniel in its present form during the religious crisis provoked by the action of Antiochus Epiphanes probably explains the single-minded preoccupation with suffering, martyrdom and eschatological vindication.[10] The dominance given to the revelation of the course of human history leading up to the establishment of the kingdom of God is without parallel in other Jewish apocalypses.[11] Some certainly look forward to imminent deliverance, as we have seen, but this cannot in any sense be regarded as a *Leitmotiv* of all the apocalypses.

One common feature of the Jewish apocalypses is the fact that they are pseudepigrapha (i.e., writings falsely attributed to another person, normally a figure of antiquity). Pseudepigraphy is not peculiar to the apocalypses; the practice probably already had a long history in the prophetic tradition.[12] But while pseudonymity is a common feature of the apocalypses, the figures chosen and the revelations attributed to the various figures show some variation. Whereas Enoch and Abraham, Levi and Isaiah are allowed to ascend to heaven during their lives and return to tell of their experiences, the same cannot be said of Ezra and Baruch in 4 Ezra and Syr. Baruch respectively, though Greek Baruch does speak of Baruch's heavenly ascent. Certainly Ezra and Baruch ascend to heaven at the time of their deaths (Syr. Bar. 13.3; 25.1; 46.7; 76; 4 Ezra 14.9) but not before. Indeed, in 4 Ezra the author seems to go out of his way to play down the heavenly ascent and the disclosures which result from it (4.8).[13] The choice of Baruch and Ezra as recipients of divine revelation is entirely appropriate when one considers that those who had either lived through the catastrophe of the destruction of the First Temple or participated in the rebuilding afterwards appropriately speak for those going through similar experiences after AD 70.

Even if pseudepigraphy was a very common literary convention, we should not exclude the possibility that it served as a means of enhancing the authority of the revelations committed to writing. To see the use of pseudepigraphy in this light leaves open the possibility that the apocalypses are not merely literary creations following a conventional pattern (though this may be true in some cases) but include the relics of actual experiences by unknown visionaries. In suggesting this it is appreciated that one is entering the realm of speculation. The fact remains, however, that study of apocalyptic has not always done justice to the possibility particularly when we remember how significant a part the irrational element played in the religion of antiquity.[14] There is much truth in the assertion of D. S. Russell that, 'it is difficult to see in them [the apocalypses] nothing more than the expression of literary convention; their very nature argues strongly that they reflect the actual experiences of the apocalyptic writers themselves'.[15]

To state the importance of the irrational element in the religion not only of Hellenism but also Judaism is not to say that apocalyptic religion was somehow antithetical to Torah study. There is much in the apocalypses to suggest that there is no fundamental opposition to the Torah (e.g., Jub. 23.26ff.; 4 Ezra 3.19; 7.17ff.; 9.31ff.; 1 Enoch 93.6; 99.14; Syr. Bar. 38.2; 59.2). Rather apocalyptic should be seen as part of Torah study which took its start from precisely those passages which deal with the hidden mysteries of heaven and earth rather than the application of biblical principles to everyday concerns as set out in the Torah.

Frequently it has been asserted that there was a polarization in Judaism between apocalyptic and Pharisaism.[16] Apocalyptic is regarded as the science of the end or an understanding of the whole of history leading up to the kingdom of God, whereas what dominates the study of the scribes and their rabbinic successors is the science of the Torah. The latter is centred on the practical details of everyday existence, not the fanciful speculations of eschatology. Many years ago J. Jeremias challenged this view by asserting that far from being the product of fringe groups in Judaism apocalyptic may well have been the esoteric tradition of the Scribes.[17] In saying this he demonstrated a clear understanding of the nature of apocalyptic religion, with its profound interest in the mysteries of cosmology, astronomy, history as well as eschatology. That such interests did in fact form part of later rabbinic tradition can hardly be doubted, but there seems to be a hint already in the Mishnah that speculative interests, perhaps of an esoteric character, already existed in the Second Temple period.[18] The passage is to be found at M. Hagigah 2.1:

> The forbidden degrees may not be expounded before three persons, nor the Story of Creation before two, nor the Chariot before one alone, unless he is a Sage that understands of his own knowledge. Whosoever gives his mind to four things it were better for him if he had not come into the world – what is above, what is beneath, what was beforetime, and what will be hereafter. And whosoever

takes no thought for the honour of his Maker, it were better for him if he had not come into the world (*The Mishnah*, tr. H. Danby).

In the second part of the Mishnah we find a dire warning against those who would occupy themselves in subjects which, according to Ecclesiasticus 3.21, are difficult for man to comprehend. It hardly needs to be said that the four prohibited topics represent the major concerns of the apocalyptists. The Jewish apocalypses contain speculation about heaven, hell and human destiny, as well as the mysterious workings of human history as it moves towards the New Age. The final threat in the Mishnah is a thinly veiled warning to those whose theological interests led them to speculate in such a way that they would dishonour God.[19]

It is significant that two of the restrictions mentioned in the Mishnah should concern Genesis 1 and Ezekiel 1. Here are two passages from Scripture which inevitably open the door to speculation about the creation of the world and the God who created it. They are passages which the student studied regularly and which pointed him not so much to his obligations and how they could be fulfilled, as to the nature of God and his creation. In the light of the sophistication of the exegetical methods applied to the Scriptures to enable the will of God in specific situations to be discerned, we may well imagine that the hints found in passages like Genesis 1 and Ezekiel 1 would lead the expositor to untold extravagances, as he sought to understand the process of creation and the immediate environs of the Creator. These passages (to which we might add others like Isaiah 6.1ff.) offered the exegete a glimpse into another world, a disclosure of the way things were before the universe existed and the nature of God who sat enthroned in glory on the cherubim chariot above the firmament.

We know from later Jewish texts that cosmogony and theosophy played a very significant part in rabbinic theology. A glance at *b. Hagigah* 12a ff. will indicate that by this time the mystical lore based on Genesis 1 and Ezekiel 1 was fairly extensive. The work of Gershom Scholem has done much to expose the history of Jewish mysticism from its obscure beginnings during the period of the Second Temple through the age of the *hekaloth* texts (which describe the mystical ascent through the heavens via the celestial door-keepers) to the *Kabbalah* itself. While the literary remains are extensive enough to establish the contours of this speculative interest in the fourth and fifth centuries AD, the character of the mystical lore in the age of the Second Temple and just after is unclear. Certainly we find that names like R. Yohanan ben Zakkai (*b. Hag.* 14b) and R. Akiba (e.g., in *b. Hag.* 14b–15b) are linked with it. This suggests at the very least that later interpreters considered that the mystical tradition should be associated with the heart of early rabbinic Judaism rather than be regarded as the interest of a peripheral group. It seems likely, however, that the evidence may allow us to assume that this interest did form part of the religious beliefs of the main academies in the Second Temple period, a fact which seems to be presupposed by the necessity for the regulation in the Mishnah. But even if this be the case, the paucity of information about the mystical involvement of R. Yohanan b. Zakkai and his pupils R. Eleazar b. Arak, R. Joshua and of R. Akiba, and his contemporaries Simeon b. Azzai, Simeon b. Zoma and Elisha b. Abuyah, does not allow us to reconstruct with any degree of certainty the character of this mystical interest. There are certainly hints that visions of Ezekiel's chariot may have been involved (Tos. Megillah 4.28; b. Megillah 24b), though it has to be admitted that the evidence does not allow us to do any more than put this forward as a tentative suggestion.[20]

This interest in passages of Scripture which might enable the expositor to gain further information about God and his ways is not confined to the rabbinic tradition. In several places in apocalyptic literature there is evidence that the apocalyptists were also interested in the first chapter of Ezekiel (Dan. 7.9; 1 Enoch 14.20; Rev. 4; 4Q Serek Širot 'Olah Hassabbat; Apocalypse of Abraham 17f.) and the first chapter of Genesis (*Liber Antiquitatum Biblicarum* 28; 4 Ezra 6.38ff.; Jub. 2.2ff.; Slav. Enoch 25f.).[21] Consideration of the use made of Ezekiel 1 in the apocalypses leads to the suggestion that these passages, one of which (1 Enoch 14) may go back to the beginning of the second century BCE or before, already evince an extensive speculative interest in Ezekiel 1. Here at least is evidence that apocalyptists were not merely interested in eschatology, nor did they regard the throne-vision merely as a convenient back-drop for eschatological teaching. Rather the interest in God's throne is already a matter for study in its own right.

In these cases the basis of the apocalyptic vision is Scripture itself. Thus there is no question here of visionary inspiration independent of Scripture-study, for the vision takes its origin from the insight already communicated in the biblical passage, however further it may take it. Examples of Scripture being the basis for apocalyptic visions and pronouncements can be found elsewhere, for example, Daniel 7 in 1 Enoch 46, 4 Ezra 12–13, Revelation 13, Jeremiah 23 in Daniel 9, Genesis 6 in 1 Enoch 6.1ff. The use of Scripture in the apocalypses is a subject which is only just being investigated in any detail.[22] Preliminary results suggest both that it is a field which demands further study and that many apocalyptic visions may have their origin in the study of Scripture.

When we come to ask about the pseudonymous authorship of the apocalyptic visions and their relationship to biblical antecedents, we have to face the fact that our knowledge of the origin and composition of the apocalypses is very rudimentary. Are we dealing with purely literary compositions, or have we to do on occasion with the relics of actual visionary experiences? Certainly the material occasionally has been subject to later editorial revision; 4 Ezra 11–12 is a good example. Nevertheless the occasional interest in fasting and other preparations for visions (Dan. 10.2f.; Apoc. Abraham 9; 4 Ezra 12.50) suggests that it would be rash to rule out the possibility of some kind of mystical praxis and its results being contained in the apocalypses.[23]

The discovery of the Enoch fragments in Cave 4 at Qumran has pushed back the origin of this work well into the third century BCE. The question arises, therefore, of the relationship between the earliest parts of 1 Enoch and the later biblical traditions. The two important areas for understanding the origin of apocalyptic, prophecy and wisdom, both have considerable affinities with this early apocalypse. It is not just the eschatological teaching of the prophetic literature which is important, but the conviction, inherent in Ezekiel 1 and elsewhere, that God reveals himself and his ways to certain chosen agents of his purposes. The mode of revelation found in the prophetic literature was one, which according to Jewish tradition passed into oblivion with the last of the prophets (Tos. Sotah 13.3). But with Haggai, Zechariah and Malachi did prophecy finish or did it carry on in one form or another? Hints like Zechariah 13.2ff. suggest the latter alternative. What is more, the visionary character of Zechariah 1–8 already points in the direction of later apocalyptic visions.[24] Thus that quest for higher knowledge, so characteristic of apocalyptic, can be grounded in Scripture in the claims of the prophets to direct, visionary experience and to knowledge of the debates in the heavenly court.

To do justice to apocalyptic, however, we cannot ignore that quest for knowledge of things earthly and heavenly, which in part at least is characteristic also of the wisdom tradition.[25] As we have already noted, the links are particularly close in parts of 1 Enoch which gives evidence of a definite interest in the created order, though with the important difference that the information in 1 Enoch comes *through revelation* (e.g., 1 Enoch 72.2). No doubt there *are* significant differences between the apocalypses and the wisdom literature. Nevertheless recent study has pointed out the affinity of certain parts of the apocalypses, particularly parts of Daniel, with mantic wisdom, which was concerned with the interpretation of dreams, divination, mysterious oracles and the movements of the stars.[26] Even within the biblical tradition, however, there is a closer link with the wisdom tradition than is often allowed.[27]

The questioning spirit of the biblical wisdom tradition and the interpretation of dreams and visions are antecedents, which should not be ignored in our attempt to elucidate apocalyptic origins. Thus it would be wrong to assert that apocalyptic has its origin either in prophecy or in wisdom, for both have contributed much to apocalyptic. Rather it is a case of elements of prophecy and wisdom contributing to an outlook which set great store by the need to understand the ways of God. Apocalyptic approaches Scripture with the conviction that the God who revealed himself in the pages of the sacred writings may be known by vision and revelation. Certainly the interpretation of Scripture offered the opportunity to plumb the depths of some of the most profound divine mysteries, often only hinted at darkly in the sacred text. The yearning for this knowledge is akin to some of the passionate searching apparent in the book of Job, though the conviction that God reveals his ways to his chosen agents lies at the heart of the prophetic experience. The apocalyptists were not content with answers to mundane questions and pressed on in search of divine knowledge. Indeed, they were probably the ones castigated in Ecclesiasticus 3.21ff.:

> Do not pry into things too hard for you or examine what is beyond your reach. Meditate upon the commandments you have been given; what the Lord keeps secret is no concern of yours. Do not busy yourself with matters that are beyond you; even what has been shown you is above man's grasp. Many have been led astray by their speculations, and false conjectures have impaired their judgement (cf. 34.1ff. NEB).

In contrast with what we find in the apocalyptic literature, the warning of Ben Sirach is intended to set a limit on the extent to which religious traditions offer opportunities both to seek for and to find answers to the most pressing questions of human existence.

If apocalyptic is first and foremost the knowledge of divine mysteries hinted at in Scripture but manifest fully only through divine revelation, we must ask whether this outlook is to be found in early Christianity. There are many indications that it was a significant component of the early Christian outlook.[28] Visions of a type found in the apocalypses are evident in early Christian literature and serve to initiate the careers of key-figures (Mark 1.10; Gal. 1.12, 16; cf. Acts 9; 26.19). It would not be fair to say that early Christian enthusiasm saw this mystical dimension as the heart of its understanding of God. As we shall argue later, the heart of the early Christian message was in fact eschatological: the coming of the promised Messiah and the pouring out of the prophetic Spirit. But if this is the content of the message, the means by which individuals were enabled to reach this conviction can best be characterized as apocalyptic. Apocalyptic provided the vehicle of eschatological conviction. This may be most clearly seen in the book of Revelation itself. The message of chapters 4–21 is largely to do with the inexorable process whereby the judgement of God is effected and the reign of God established. That eschatological message is communicated by means of an apocalypse, a revelation from Jesus Christ (Rev. 1.1). This is the guarantee of its authenticity (22.15) and authority. Thus what we find in primitive Christianity is apocalyptic functioning as the basis for the eschatological convictions belonging to the key figures in its early history.

11
Jewish Sectarianism

To speak of Jewish sects demands that the commentator explain the way in which he is using a term which has become important in the sociology of religion.[1] We should distinguish between organizations of a more open-ended kind, and the closed group, more readily defined and more exclusive. Certainly there are some advantages in using this categorization. Thus, while it would be possible to argue that a group like the Qumran community manifests all the exclusive characteristics of a sect, the same cannot always be said of rabbinic Judaism. At least as far as the rabbinic sources depict the pharisaic-rabbinic position, there is a degree of flexibility and open-endedness which is absent from the Qumran Scrolls. Some pharisaic groups in the first century AD manifested some of the exclusive features of this social type, but, for example, pharisaic-rabbinic attitudes towards the ordinary people who did not accept pharisaic principles (*'am ha-aretz*), indicates that there was not a widespread rejection of those who refused to espouse the rabbinic position. These people were despised but not rejected from the commonwealth of Israel.[2] In the light of this it would be more accurate to say that the pharisaic-rabbinic group in due course came to manifest some of the characteristics of the group without rigid boundaries. By and large, the earliest Christian communities were exclusive in character, though there was some variety. On the one hand the Johannine writings manifest many of the characteristics of a sect, whereas Paul occasionally manifests some of the uncertainties which characterize the Church-type. This is particularly true of Paul's treatment of Israel in Romans 9–11, where he refuses to deny the possibility of the inclusion of some or even all Jews within the process of salvation despite their rejection of the gospel (11.25ff.). In this respect Paul manifests some of the similar concerns which characterize the rabbinic attitude towards the *'am ha-aretz*.[3]

Unlike those who prefer to reserve the term 'sect' for the group which maintains a fairly strict exclusivism I have decided to use the terms sect and sectarianism to characterize Jewish religion before AD 70.[4] Let it be clear, however, that there are significant differences in outlook between these different groups. Some explicitly seem to arrogate to themselves claims made for the whole of Israel; so that their doctrine involves a rejection of the wider group who refuse to accept particular beliefs and practices. They reject the conviction that the élite would act as a kind of ginger-group to the wider community.[5]

Another caveat needs to be entered at this point, however. It is implicit in the presentation of Judaism in this study that the character of Judaism changed so markedly after the destruction of the Temple that it is impossible to talk of Jewish sectarianism after that date. Such a view needs to be qualified. While there is little doubt that the concerns of the rabbis at Yavneh included a fervent desire to maintain a significant degree of unity,[6] uniformity to any overwhelming degree can hardly be said to characterize the rabbinic traditions. While it may have been the case that most were following a common exegetical method,[7] it is quite apparent that differences of opinion were accepted and after a certain period included in the tradition, so that it would not be unexpected to find two contradictory opinions recorded side by side (e.g., M. Meg. 4.10). Of course, this is certainly not a manifestation of incipient sectarianism, but it should warn us that even in rabbinic Judaism we are not dealing with a monolithic, uniform system but a tradition which was living and changing with room left for a considerable amount of divergence.

The varied character of Jewish religion is something which is hinted by Josephus in his account of the Jewish sects (*haireseis*). In *BJ* 2.119ff. Josephus recounts the beliefs and practices of Sadducees, Pharisees and Essenes, dwelling particularly on the last-mentioned group. In mentioning just three groups Josephus was probably diminishing the variety which existed within Jewish religion for the first century AD. If we take the Pharisees, for example, it is clear from the traditions which have come down to us that, even allowing for a significant editorial process after AD 70,[8] the disputes between the schools of Hillel and Shammai reflect a considerable amount of difference in approach even within a group which is normally given one label. It is this type of divergence which was carried over into early rabbinic Judaism.[9]

What has been stressed again and again in recent years is that we cannot speak of orthodoxy at this period; though with regard to matters like the calendar (date of festivals, etc.) we may expect that there would have been a considerable degree of uniformity.[10] Because of the disappearance of many of the sects and their literary remains after AD 70 we have no means of assessing the extent of the religious variety in Judaism at this time. The problem of sources is a very serious one, especially when one reflects that such an important group as the Sadducees has left virtually nothing. Recent discoveries, including the Dead Sea Scrolls, are confirming that the nature of Judaism was a complex of competing and conflicting opinions and beliefs. Not only the contrast between Diaspora and Palestine but also the contrast within Palestine itself, meant that differences emerged for geographical,[11] and social[12] as well as religious reasons. Consequently diversity of interpretation of the religious traditions was inevitable.

Few would deny that there were common features to most Jewish groups, and one thinks particularly of the Temple and the Torah as two common features which would have united all but the Samaritans, who rejected the shrine in Jerusalem in favour of their own on Mount Gerizim.[13] Even the Qumran covenanters did not reject the Temple outright though they were very disparaging about the way in which the shrine was administered by the priests, who held power.[14] All who claimed allegiance to the faith of Abraham, Isaac and Jacob accepted the centrality of the Torah as the guidance for faith and practice and the source of information about the way in which the cult should be administered. But to say that the Torah and the Temple were in fact central to most Jews is in fact to single out the main reason why there was such variety and the growth of sectarianism. Though the Sanhedrin which met in the Temple area had a significant role[15] in governing the nature of Jewish practice, the kind of control that it exercised was bound to be confined to the official organs of Jewish society which were administered in Jerusalem, such as the Temple and the courts, together with affairs in the immediate environs of the city. They were not in a position to regulate the practice of Jewish individuals and groups, particularly those outside Jerusalem, though we may suppose that they tried to do this (Mark 3.22; Matt. 15.1; Mark 7.1; John 1.19; Acts 9.2). Granted that the Torah laid down what was essential for the observance of the Jew, the nature of the practice of these demands was by no means obvious. God called his people to be holy (Lev. 19.2); but what did this mean in practice? The maintenance of such a religious identity was certainly a possibility, but the means whereby this separation was effected were not always clear in the pages of Scripture. If God had laid down the conditions for a continuing relationship with himself, how did these conditions apply in various situations? The difficulties confronting Jews in the Hellenistic Age were compounded because of the problem of interpretations and the contents of the Torah. The regulations for the administration of the cult were fairly extensive, but in civil and family law the Torah offered woefully inadequate guidance.[16] It is when questions on these issues were put to the Torah that one sees why interpretations and indeed new enactments were necessary and also why differences of the most profound kind emerge, particularly when the traditions of interpretation followed by various groups gave greater degrees of prominence to ancestral customs and beliefs than others.[17]

In a complex political and religious situation where an authoritative Scripture was open to a variety of interpretations, and power politics meant that strictly religious issues might be subordinated to the quest for political influence, it was inevitable that rifts of a profound kind would emerge within Jewish religion, involving a significant degree of hostility between the various factions.

12

An Outline of Jewish Groups in the First Century AD

(a) Sadducees

The Sadducees are frequently regarded as the aristocratic section of Jewish society, amenable to foreign ideas and influence.[1] As the etymology of the word Sadducee indicates, we should not neglect the priestly link implied by the connection with the High Priest Zadok. There is little doubt that during the Maccabean period (c. 170 BC), several of the priests were open to Hellenistic influence,[2] but that should not be taken as the dominant characteristic. In the time of Jesus they had more contact than most Jews with the Roman government, because of their role as religious leaders of the nation, and some supported peaceful co-existence, if not active co-operation, with the Romans, for the sake of peace and security (cf. John 11.48f.).

They appear to have had a very conservative attitude towards the Law of Moses. Their interpretation tended to be literalistic, and they frowned on the more elaborate exegetical enterprises found among other groups. While this could have led them to adopt positions which were unrealistic in the changed circumstances of the Graeco-Roman world, their position had the merit of not extending the domain of the Torah into areas of life which were not explicitly provided for in the Torah. In this respect we may suppose that their attitudes may well have reflected the beliefs of the population at large.[3] It is not easy to reconstruct exactly what the beliefs of the Sadducees were. It used to be thought that Sadducees rejected the authority of all Scriptures, apart from the Torah, as well as the oral tradition (*Ant.* 13.297), but this view has been called into question. According to Paul, the Synoptic Gospels and Josephus (Acts 23.7; Matt. 22.23 and *BJ* 2.165), the Sadducees denied the belief in the resurrection of the dead, because they could find no reference to it in the Torah (cf. *M. Sanhedrin* 10.1).

It would be wrong to assume that all the priestly elements in Judaism could be dubbed Sadducean, at least as far as their beliefs and practices were concerned. We know, for example, that there were many priests who not only sympathized with Pharisaism but classed themselves as part of that movement (there were several priests among the nascent rabbinic group meeting at Jamnia after the Fall of Jerusalem, e.g., R. Jose the Priest). Such priestly sympathy with Pharisaism is not really surprising given the cultic inspiration of the pharisaic ideal. If the rabbinic traditions are to be believed, the Sadducees often found themselves in a position of having to accept pharisaic rulings on matters with which they were intimately concerned, such as the regulation of the Temple worship.

(b) Scribes

In the Gospels we frequently find Scribes and Pharisees lumped together, as if they were part of a united outlook within Judaism.[4] Such an identification would be rather misleading, however. The Scribes were primarily the interpreters of the Torah (Matt. 13.52; 23.2; Luke 11.46), the spiritual descendants of Ezra, who had interpreted the Law in times past (Ezra 7.6). As we have seen, the place of Scripture had become so central, that its accurate transmission and interpretation had become matters of the utmost concern for all Jews. The Pharisees were not the expositors of the Scriptures, though they may have accepted the interpretations offered by some of the Scribes. Likewise the Scribes, as a whole, were not necessarily pharisaic in their outlook. Clearly there were some (perhaps a majority) of Scribes who were Pharisees. As an expositor of the Torah it would have been possible for a Scribe to have espoused a Saducean position with regard to his interpretation of the Scriptures (e.g., Jesus ben Sirach – see ch. 39). When we find in the Gospels Scribes being called 'Scribes of the Pharisees' (Mark 2.16), this is to be regarded as a correct designation[5] and reflects the possibility that Scribes were affiliated to a number of interpretative traditions within first-century Judaism.

(c) Pharisees

Our understanding of the origin of Pharisaism has undergone quite a change in recent years.[6] It used to be said that the Pharisees were the forebears of the rabbis, but it is now apparent that there were other components to rabbinic religion as well as Pharisaism, even if the latter was by far the most important. In the rabbinic literature the rabbis consistently refer to their spiritual forebears not as Pharisees, but sages (*hakamim*) and associates (*haberim*) and reserve the word *perushim* (separatist) for extreme groups.[7] It would be wrong to conclude from this that there is no relationship between the Pharisees of New Testament times and the rabbis, but this fact should warn us that there was probably a very wide spectrum of belief and practice among those to whom the label 'Pharisee' could be applied, so that in interpreting invective against the Pharisees in the New Testament we cannot suppose that one homogeneous group is being addressed all the time.[8]

The pharisaic movement was basically a lay movement which took seriously the obligation laid upon Israel as a whole to be a holy nation before God (Lev. 19.2).[9] There was an element of separation in their religious practice (hence the nickname 'Pharisee', separated one?). The reason for this is stated by Jeremias:

> . . . Pharisaism sought to raise to the level of a general norm the practice of purity laws, even among non-priestly folk, those laws which need only be enforced for priests when they ate the heave-offering.[10]

In other words, what we find in the pharisaic outlook is an extension of cultic purity outside the boundaries of the Temple, into everyday life of family and social intercourse. Pharisaism took seriously the basically cultic Torah and extended it to the everyday life of Jews, so that there were strict regulations with regard to purity and tithes (Matt. 15.1f.; Mark 7.1ff.; Matt. 23.25ff.; Luke 11.42; 18.12).[11]

Pharisaism did not have an overwhelming impact on the lives of most ordinary people, as many working in agriculture and in close proximity to Gentiles, or others not keeping the purity laws strictly, could not possibly guarantee fulfilment of the strict tithing and purity rules. Nevertheless the intention behind the pharisaic vision was far from negative. Pharisees took seriously the need for Israel as a whole to seek holiness, and saw how important it was to make the Law relevant for the contemporary situation. As we have noted, their application of the Law has two characteristics:

(i) the building of a fence around the Torah (*Aboth* 1.1), i.e., enacting cautionary rules to halt a man before he got near breaking the Law;

(ii) by making explicit what the Torah left either implicit or unsaid to enable the Pharisee to know exactly what the divine Law expected of him.

An important feature of Pharisaism was the *haburah* or fellowship. In order to become a member of one of these groups (*haber*), an individual had to undertake certain obligations with regard to tithing and ritual purity. In a sense the pharisaic *haburah* was an enclave of holiness, in which priest and layman alike shared the same degree of holiness. Though the number of Pharisees was probably small, they were distinct groups, with clear-cut demarcation between adherents and outsiders.[12] In this respect they resembled the Essenes, particularly those who, according to Josephus, continued to live in towns and did not separate themselves, as the community at Qumran did.

Josephus hints that the Pharisees attached great significance to eschatology, particularly the belief in the resurrection (*BJ* 2.119ff.; cf. Acts 23.6; *M. Sanhedrin* 10.1). They gave equal weight to other Scriptures as well as the Torah in the emergence of faith and practice, though we cannot be certain that their canon differed from that of other Jews. The use of books like Daniel meant that they could point to a passage such as Daniel 12.2 for an unequivocal statement of their belief in the resurrection, without having to depend solely on the Torah, though we may expect that, like Jesus, they were able to ground the resurrection doctrine in Torah also (cf. Mark 12.26f.).

In addition, they accepted the importance of oral tradition, and in particular that which was passed on by those Scribes who held the pharisaic position.[13] The Torah may have been given by Moses on Sinai, but in succeeding generations pronouncements had been made applying Torah with new insights to each new situation. The *halakah* was eventually codified in the rabbinic corpus, the earliest collections being the *Mishnah* and *Tosefta*,[14] though one must assume that this was but a fraction of the material available and that much more was excluded.

It would be wrong to suppose that the Pharisees played down the centrality of the Temple. The debates between the Pharisees and Sadducees over cultic matters contained in the early rabbinic (tannaitic) sources suggest that the Pharisees (or at the very least their scribes) were very interested in the minutiae of Temple ritual. But as far as the *haburah* was concerned, it was the synagogue which was the main means of communicating the pharisaic ideals.[15] It is likely that even before AD 70, those who met together to study the Torah believed that the divine presence (*shekinah*) was with them (*Aboth* 3.2).[16]

As we have seen, most scholars consider that there is continuity between certain groups of Pharisees and the early rabbis whose teaching is included in the corpus of rabbinic literature. We should not underestimate the vast changes that took place in the years following the débâcle of the First Revolt in 66–70. The outcome, apart form enormous suffering in Judaea and Jerusalem, was almost certainly the cessation of regular Temple worship and the decimation of Judaism as it had been known up to that time. Jewish tradition has it that just before the fall of the city, Rabban Yohanan ben Zakkai, a leading figure of the scribal tradition and possibly a Hillelite Pharisee, escaped from Jerusalem and gained permission from the Romans to move to Yavneh/Jamnia.[17] The effects of this were far-reaching. The fact that this group under Yohanan seized the initiative meant that eventually one faction of first-century Judaism (or to put it another way a faction of a faction, i.e., the Hillelite wing of Pharisaism) gained a decisive voice in the formulation of post-destruction Jewish society.[18] The significance of this was, of course, very far-reaching for the emergence of the hostility between church and synagogue. Instead of Judaism consisting of a variety of groups coexisting with each other amidst varying degrees of mutual hatred and suspicion, one group had become responsible for influencing what the character of Judaism would be.

For reasons which are not too difficult to see, a dominant need of the group at Jamnia was to assert a degree of unity which would enable the struggling religion in Palestine to survive. Even adherents of the pharisaic approach were, according to tradition, given a very rough ride if they refused to accept the decisions of the majority.[19] It was about this time that part of the synagogue prayer, the *Tefillah* was reformulated and the *Shemoneh Esreh* (*Eighteen Benedictions*) came into being. The twelfth of these probably included some kind of formula, which effectively excluded heretics from participation in the liturgy of the synagogue and may even have explicitly cited the Christians (*Nazareans*).[20] While separation between church and synagogue was a long drawn out process stretching over many decades, it is clear that the aftermath of the Jewish War and the decisions taken at Jamnia had a significant part to play.

We need to be very careful indeed in our assessment of Pharisaism. We must not think of it as a monolithic religious system. There was a wide difference of approach between liberals and conservatives.[21] Such differences are well encapsulated in the charming story about the different approaches of Shammai and Hillel towards a proselyte in *b. Shabb.* 31a:

> A Gentile came before Shammai and said to him, 'You can make me a proselyte providing that you teach me the whole Torah while I stand on one leg'. Shammai chased him away with a stick. Then he came before Hillel and asked him the same thing. Hillel replied, 'That which you do not wish men to do to you, do not do to them' (cf. Matt. 7.12). This is the Law and the Prophets. The rest is commentary; go and learn it.

(d) Zealots

Dominant in the story of the First Revolt as it is told by Josephus are the Zealots, some of whom died in the heroic final struggle against the Roman general, Flavius Silva, in the fortress of Masada in 73.[22] From the time of the Maccabees there had been a tradition of militant defence of the faith of the fathers, which involved violent struggle against domination by a foreign power. Such an outlook was given added weight by the stories of the conquest of the Promised Land and the ejection of foreigners in the Torah. Indeed, in the biblical stories such armed struggle is frequently linked with an emphasis on the divine assistance given to the people of God in their struggle (e.g., Judges 6; Josh. 10.10f.; 5.13ff.). When Rome took over Judaea in AD 6 there was resistance to the census from Judas the Galilean,[23] and it was one of his descendants, Menahem, who played an important part in Jerusalem during the First Revolt (*BJ* 2.433). Whether we can speak of a Zealot party as such in existence throughout the whole of the first century AD, from the time of Judas' opposition to the First Revolt, is unclear.[24] What cannot be doubted is the continuous existence of an ideology, which spoke of the need to purify the land of foreign defilement by violent means. Quite probably the War Scroll from Qumran allows us to glimpse something of the mentality of such groups, who believed that, despite all the odds being stacked against them, the people of God could triumph over the forces of darkness with the angelic hosts playing their part alongside.

(e) Essenes

The First Revolt also saw the end of the Essenes (cf. *BJ* 2.152). This group has been the subject of renewed interest ever since the discovery of the Dead Sea Scrolls in the Judaean wilderness just after the Second World War. Much had been known about the Essenes before; Josephus gives a long account of their beliefs and practices in *BJ* 2.119ff. He portrays a closed society with strict rules of admission and conduct. There has been much debate since the discovery of the Dead Sea Scrolls and the excavation of the monastic buildings, which are closely linked with the Scrolls, as to whether in fact the writings are the products of an Essene sect[25] and should be identified with the Essenes mentioned by Josephus, Philo and the Roman writer Pliny.[26] The problem is that the Dead Sea Scrolls never use the word 'Essene' to describe the group. While the similarities between what Josephus has to say and the information from the Scrolls themselves make an identification of the Qumran community as Essene most probable, we should not ignore the significant *priestly* strand within the Scrolls;[27] Zadokite is an apt description of the Scrolls. What the Dead Sea Scrolls have offered the student of first-century Judaism, above all, is a glimpse of another form of Jewish piety, which clearly has links with other groups,[28] but had an extremely hostile attitude towards other Jews and, we may presume, succeeded in existing under the umbrella of Judaism throughout the first century AD.

The origins of the community remain obscure though there are many tantalizing hints in the Scrolls themselves about the reasons which led to the group's formation. Apart from several passages in the biblical commentaries, which refer to significant events in the group's history, we have a passage in the Damascus Document (*CD*), which speaks about the foundation of the community 390 years after the destruction of the Temple by Nebuchadnezzar. For twenty years we are told they were groping for the right way and then the Teacher of Righteousness, a central figure in the Dead Sea Scrolls, appeared, and guided them. There has been much dispute over whether the figure 390 should be taken literally or symbolically. All the indications are that it is approximately right, as the archaeological evidence indicates that the community settlement was built in the second half of the second century BC. A date in the first part of the second century BC would fit in with the growing reaction to the explicit Hellenization, which was taking place in Palestinian Judaism, culminating in the armed reaction against Antiochus Epiphanes recorded in 1 Maccabees and the book of Daniel.

In the accounts of the Essenes and their activities set out in the Dead Sea Scrolls and in the description of their beliefs in the writings of Josephus, we find a description of communities with a strong sense of their separate identity and with a strict organization. There was a stern probationary period and an elaborate initiation process. If the Scrolls are anything to go by, the organization was hierarchical, and the slightest transgression against authority brought about the direst penalties (1 *QS* 7). Holiness was a characteristic of the community, and this affected their view of themselves. It was precisely because they were a well-ordered community reflecting the order of heaven (1 *QS* 2) that they could be an enclave of divine holiness and share the lot of the angels (1 *QS* 11; 1 *QH* 3.20f., 11.10f.).[29]

We need to stress the importance of the priests in the community; they had the leading role in the organization and administration of the community (1*QS* 9). Specifically mention is made of an overseer, who was to be a student of the Torah and who instructed the community (1 *QS* 6). Alongside him, there was a priest who exercised all priestly duties in the community (*CD* 13; 1 *QS* 6).

Entry into the community was seen as the participation in a new covenant (1 *QS* 1, 5, 6; *CD* 15f.). It was the conviction of the community of the Scrolls that they were the faithful remnant of Israel. God had revealed his wisdom to the Teacher of Righteousness and only he knew what was the true will of God. All those who entered the sect had to act in accordance with all that had been revealed of it to the sons of Zadok (1 *QS* 5).

The member of the sect saw himself as a child of light, specially chosen by God (1 *QS* 3). That is not to suggest that there was any unthinking feeling of superiority. Throughout the hymns there is a profound understanding of dependence on God's mercy, which has many affinities with the Pauline understanding of righteousness by faith alone (1 *QH* 19.7; 1 *QS* 11).[30]

In their calendrical observances the sectaries conflicted with the majority practices in Judaism by their observance of a solar calendar. Inevitably this led to a significant disjunction between their own observance of festivals and sabbaths and that of other Jews.[31] Ritual washing was practised in the community (*CD* 11). There also seems to have been some kind of purificatory rite in connection with entry into the community (1 *QS* 3, 5; cf. *CD* 3). There was a hostile attitude to those who managed the Temple in Jerusalem, because it was believed that it had been run by wicked priests. The sectaries were certainly not opposed to the Temple but wished to see the establishment of proper cultic worship, according to the appropriate calendar (*CD* 6, 11). In place of the regular cultic participation we find the same kind of spiritualizing of cultic language as is to be seen in the NT (Rom. 12.1; 1 Cor. 3.16); for example, 1 *QS* 8f.[32] As in other Jewish groups the meal seems to have played a most important part, and a close link seems to have existed between the common meal regularly celebrated and the messianic banquet (1 *QSa*).

The War Scroll indicates a heightened eschatological expectation.[33] This document describes the detailed preparations required of the sons of light in their struggle with the sons of darkness. It breathes a fanatical conviction that, however much the odds may have been stacked against them, the legions of angels would come to the aid of the righteous, as they struggled with the forces of darkness. The archaeological evidence suggests that they probably perished at the hands of the Romans, possibly attempting to put into practice preparations outlined in the War Scroll.

The Scrolls offer us evidence of a community separate from the rest of Israel in the Judaean desert. Due account must be taken of the possibility that its views were entirely eccentric. We should not forget, however, that Josephus tells us that Essenes were to be found in towns (*BJ* 2.124; cf. ii.160), and it would not be fair to suppose that we are dealing with a *totally* aberrant approach to the traditions of Judaism in these documents. Debate about the significance of the Scrolls is still going on. What these documents have indicated is that the world of Judaism in the first century was a complex and confused one in which a variety of different interpretations of the Jewish heritage were being explored and tested in everyday life.

(f) Christianity as a Jewish Sect[34]

Even though we may recognize Jewish influence on early Christianity, we are often unwilling to probe the character of belief and practice before the catastrophe of AD 70, and ask whether our use of the early Christian sources in particular manifests an anachronistic perspective. To put it another way, are we guilty in our characterization of the conflicts mentioned in the Pauline epistles in particular of reading back the later polarization between church and synagogue? Of course, the New Testament writings themselves seem to give credence to the assumption that already in Paul's day the apostle was confronted, as also were his Christian churches, by non-believing Jews, who were easily identified as a group over against the Christians.

Although the evidence is not as great as one would like, it is difficult to believe that the rejection of the messiahship of Jesus was by itself at an early stage a sufficiently unifying theme to unite all those groups which refused to accept the messiahship of Jesus in a common rejection of Christianity. No doubt there were occasions when one Jewish sect manifested its hostility against the Christian group by joining forces with another to deal with the Christians (cf. Mark 3.6), and, if we are to believe Acts 4–7, the Sanhedrin could at times muster enough support to take action against Christians, though even here there may have been dissenters (Acts 5.34ff.). What Paul and the early Christian missionaries were faced with, however, was not a unified stand against them, but a variety of synagogues and Jewish groups with varying degrees of contact with Jerusalem and varied outlooks on the nature of religious observance. So while Acts suggests that attempts may have been made by the High Priest or Sanhedrin to take action against Christians in Damascus (Acts 9.2), the extent to which it was possible at this stage to enforce any kind of unified action must have been limited. Indeed, once again Acts 23 indicates that Paul was able to make use of obvious doctrinal differences between Pharisees and Sadducees in his trial as recorded in Acts 23.6. It is therefore dangerous to assume that the Jewish sects managed to bury their differences and come together to root out Christianity.

Our problem is that we tend to lump together the various groups, Pharisees, Scribes and Sadducees particularly, and assume that from the very start there was a common front against Jesus and his followers. It is not only detailed textual study of the Gospels but also a greater appreciation of the complexity of the religious scene before AD 70 that have compelled us to view the conflict between Jews and Christians in the middle of the first century AD in a new light. We cannot assume that the early Christians ever lost sight of their Jewish heritage, nor were they conscious of being anything other than Jews.[35] Their task was different from that of Justin and those who followed his line. The New Testament writers on the whole are not concerned to show that Christians alone are the true inheritors of the promises, with non-believing Jews being regarded as another race cut off from Israel (though that theme *is* coming to the fore in the Gospel of John). Rather, the New Testament writers seem to be concerned to explain how the Jewish traditions are to be understood in the light of the conviction that Jesus was the Messiah. Of course, it is true that we find some extremely polemical remarks against non-believing Jews, but more often than not these passages occur in situations of extreme conflict when the messianic salvation is at stake (e.g., 2 Cor. 3; Gal. 3–4). This is particularly true of a letter like Galatians. But we have to remember that, in Galatians Paul is not bent on confounding Jews, but persuading those who are already Christians, that their way to God is adequate in itself without recourse to certain rites. It is not that the goal of being a child of Abraham is wrong. Rather it is the *means* whereby that end is achieved by *Gentiles* now that the Messiah has come which so concerns Paul. To understand Paul's indictment of Judaism and his description of it as an inferior religion (e.g., Gal. 4) one must see it in the context of his eschatological perspective. The practices hitherto undertaken by Jews were part of a past aeon and were themselves pointing towards a greater purpose of God which had now been revealed in Christ.[36]

Pauline, like Jewish, studies have not been standing still over the past hundred years. No longer can we treat Paul's letters as a systematic exposition of theology and ethics, for we have to recognize their occasional quality, not to mention the fact that one or two, like Galatians, were written in the heat of the moment. As a result, we shall not now be surprised to find contradictions in them and differing treatments of the same subject.[37] This will help us to explain why it is that in 1 Thessalonians 2.16 Paul seems to speak in frighteningly condemnatory tones about non-believing Jews, whereas in Romans 9–11 the question of Jewish rejection of the gospel is agonized over with considerable courage and, in the end, a considerable degree of optimism. The picture that Paul leaves us with in these chapters is of a Jew whose messianic beliefs have led him to a position which differs significantly from that of many of his Jewish contemporaries, with the result that their rejection of his cherished convictions about the fulfilment of Jewish hopes is a matter of personal sorrow and distress. Nevertheless the debt to the Jewish heritage is so large (look at the way Scripture functions in the argument) and the centrality of the promises made to the Jewish nation so immovable that it is impossible for Paul to conceive of a situation where God finally casts off his people (Rom. 11.25ff.).[38] While in the eyes of some of his Jewish contemporaries Paul may be regarded as a Jewish heretic, his position within the spectrum of Judaism is merely a more extreme form of the various interpretations of the Bible, which were current at the time. What we should remember is that Paul did not reject the validity of the Law (Rom. 7.12). Unlike the Gnostics of the second-century,[39] and Marcion in particular, Paul does not loosen the bonds, which link the new covenant with the old. For him the God of Abraham, Isaac and Jacob is the God and Father of Jesus of Nazareth and those who put their faith in him as the Messiah. What is more, the Law is not the product of some inferior deity (cf. Gal. 4.9). Its subordinate position, since the coming of Christ, is the result of its links with the old aeon. It pointed forward to the completion of God's purposes.

It may with some justice be argued that Paul represents an extreme form of interpretation of Jewish traditions; so extreme, in fact, that he put himself and his churches beyond the boundaries of Judaism. But to speak in these terms presupposes that it was possible to say with any degree of certainty, that a particular individual or group had placed themselves outside these boundaries.[40] What was the test to be which would separate Paul from his contemporaries? Acknowledgement of the validity of the Law? Observance of the Law? Denial of the messiahship of Jesus? Denial and/or acceptance of particular doctrines? While it may be true that in particular instances Paul deviates quite widely from beliefs held by certain Jewish groups in the first century (note Acts 21.2ff., 21.28), the question is whether deviation by itself, however marked it may have been, was enough to deny the position of Paul and his circle within Judaism. After all, Paul could with some conviction argue that he upheld the validity of the Law, that he observed the Law, if that was understood as the Law of the Spirit which, in Paul's view, had replaced the written code (Rom. 8.2f.), and that his doctrines only differed from a group, like the Pharisees, in that he believed that particular Scriptures *had actually been fulfilled* rather than merely being articles of faith. It is thus possible to call Paul a heretic, only if one is working with a pretty clear

77

understanding of what orthodoxy and heresy were in the context of first-century Judaism.[41]

That is not to suggest for one moment that there were no norms by which it was possible to distinguish the Jew from the non-Jew.[42] One thinks immediately of sabbath observance and a rite like circumcision, both of which helped to identify the Jew outside Palestine. In addition, of course, food-laws and the whole apparatus of purity, however that may have been interpreted, inevitably distinguished Jews from the surrounding populace.[43] In the early stages of the Christian movement Jews and Gentile Christians would have appeared outwardly homogeneous to their pagan neighbours. While there may have been rival synagogues (Rev. 2.9), this would have been regarded as the usual internal Jewish strife (Acts 18.14f.). Christians' reputation for the repudiation of idolatry and aloofness from society put them in the same category as Jews.[44] It is possible that Christians may have continued to observe the sabbath,[45] and scruples with regard to food were not immediately abandoned (Acts 15.20; 1 Cor. 8). Pliny seems to have been able to make a distinction between Jews and Christians in his letter to Trajan (*Letters*, x.96f. *c.* AD 112)[46] but in the absence of obvious differences in practice or Jewish hostility (e.g., *Mart. Polycarp* 13) differentiation between Jews and Christians would not have been easy. The situation was different in Palestine itself; especially in those places where Jews predominated. In Judaea, particularly, rather than in the Hellenistic cities on the fringes of the province, the fact that the large majority of the population was Jewish made for a greater degree of homogeneity in practice. Nevertheless the factors, which tended to identify Jews over against their pagan neighbours in the Diaspora, did not apply in Judaea. Thus one of the constraints which brought Jews of differing opinions closer to each other in the face of a common threat no longer applied. In *eretz Israel* the threat to true religion was more likely to come from a fellow Jew than a Gentile, for it was those whose interpretation of the Torah led them into different customs and practices, who seemed to pose the most immediate threat. Of course, this is not to forget the profound disgust at the Roman occupation of Judaea after AD 6, which was a constant bone of contention. But even here there were differing reactions from the complete hostility manifested by the political activists like the Zealots to the resigned acceptance and preference for inward purity favoured by groups like the Pharisees.

It is essential to understand such a background in order to appreciate how the Christian groups could exist as part of Judaism for the first, formative decades of their existence. Belief that the Messiah had already arrived was certainly a profoundly disturbing belief for Judaism. But it was neither eccentric nor was it contrary to the inherited wisdom of Scripture. Indeed, it was none other than the great standard bearer of early rabbinic Judaism, R. Akiba, who himself hailed Simeon Ben Koseba as the Messiah, 'the star of

Jacob' (*Bar Kochba*) (j. *Ta'anith* 68d).[47] Christian eschatological belief seems to have been entirely consistent with that held by other Jewish groups. The fact that they claimed that the beliefs were being fulfilled was certainly unusual, but, even from the limited information available to us, not unique.

The problem about the Christian claims, however, is the authority upon which the claims are based. Herein lies one of the basic issues confronting Judaism. Who is entitled to interpret the ancestral traditions and offer the authentic meaning of them? The issue was posed in the sharpest possible form by early Christianity because of the character of the claims being made. As we shall see in due course, the early Christians were not merely suggesting that they had an alternative explanation of the *halakah* (though they were at times suggesting this e.g., Acts 10–11) but that the perspective, from which they viewed the traditions as a whole, was the conviction that eschatological promises were being fulfilled. Thus the challenge posed by the Christian group did not relate merely to specific issues but to the whole gamut of religious experience. Of course, it was important to know whether a particular sage had the right and the expertise to illuminate the path of righteousness, but the basis on which individuals and groups claimed that Jesus was the Messiah needed to be fully tested, for the obvious reason that such a claim affected the whole fabric of Judaism as then constituted.[48]

The messianic/eschatological character of Christianity did not mean that a split with other Jewish groups, who rejected the Christian beliefs, was inevitable. The reactions of some of Akiba's contemporaries to his support for the messianic claims of Bar Kochba, while very derogatory, do not necessarily imply that such support would have led to exclusion. In this respect the reaction of Gamaliel, as recorded in Acts 5.35ff., is not dissimilar. The test of the authenticity of messianic movements of any kind, despite their disruptive qualities, is, in Gamaliel's view, whether they stand the test of time. Like the test of prophecy in Deuteronomy 13, the validity of such claims depended on whether they actually were fulfilled.[49] Provided that a movement did not attempt to lead people to worship other gods, then it would have to be lived with and tested by its fruits. It may be that some did indeed think that Christianity involved a form of idolatry similar to that hinted at in the book of Deuteronomy. The condemnations of Jesus in Mark 3.22 and John 8.48 point in this direction, and the hostility towards Paul as the result of his attitude to the Law of Moses may well reflect the belief of some that the followers of Jesus were involved in a deception which would ultimately lead Israel astray (John 7.47; cf. *b. San.* 43a).[50]

It is tempting to regard the arrogant claims, which Christian writers made to have found the clue to the Scriptures, as something which was bound to put the Christian movement, particularly in its Pauline form, beyond the pale of Judaism. But this was the presupposition of most, if not all, sects at that time. We know certainly that the Qumran community considered that its understanding of the Scriptures was the only authentic one. While God may have spoken to a prophet like Habakkuk, the true meaning of the words, which the prophet was inspired to utter, did not become apparent until the advent of the Teacher of Righteousness (1 *QpHab* 7). What is more, in later rabbinic haggadah the divine authority of the rabbinic tradition is guaranteed by asserting the essential continuity between the revelation given to Moses, which is found in the written Torah, and the oral Torah which, it was asserted, was also revealed to the Lawgiver on Sinai.[51] Certainly the conviction that God had inspired the particular doctrines of one's own group was something that Christians held in common with others. Coexistence should not be mistaken for religious toleration, however. Our contemporary liberal concern to maintain pluriformity of views as an essential component of human experience is certainly not the basis for the complex religious scene in first-century Judaism. The rise of this particular messianic sect within Judaism must be understood as the consequence of the absence of a strong central religious authority and generally accepted orthopraxy during the last years of the era of the Second Temple.

13

Diaspora Judaism

At least as early as the Exile, the Jewish people had to come to terms with the possibility of permanent dwelling in a land far removed from the holy land of Israel. In the words of the Psalmist, Israel had to learn to sing the Lord's song in a strange land (Ps. 137.4). The dramatic vision of the prophet Ezekiel of the glory of God enthroned on the cherubim-chariot marks a watershed in Jewish theology. God appeared to the prophet in all the glory associated with the Temple of Jerusalem in a pagan land, Babylon by the river Chebar (Ezek. 1). The Second Temple still had to be built, and the next time when the Jews would be without a Temple was six hundred years away, but the vision of the prophet paved the way for a Jewish theology, which allowed for the possibility of acknowledging the presence of God through worship and study outside the land of Israel. From the time of the Exile onwards (sixth century BC), there continued to be a large Jewish community in Babylon, about which we hear occasionally.[1] In time Jews were to be found scattered all around the Eastern Mediterranean. The prophet Obadiah speaks of Jewish communities in Asia Minor (v.20, cf. Isa. 66.19) and Josephus tells us of Jewish immigrants from Babylonia into Phrygia and Lydia at the end of the third century BC (*Ant.* 12.147f.). From the papyri discovered at Elephantine we know of the existence of a Jewish military garrison[2] which maintained close links with Jerusalem and manifested a significant degree of variation in its beliefs and cultic practice.

After the conquests of Alexander the Great, Jews had to come to terms with the ideals of Hellenism.[3] These presented themselves in the establishment of the city (*polis*)[4] as the social unit with its considerable degree of political and economic autonomy and the communal ideal fostered by common principles and divinities. The acceptance of Hellenistic culture enabled the inhabitants of the *polis* to become part of a much larger world. In addition to acquiring a knowledge of Greek literature, it meant accepting the conventional pattern of education[5] and religious practices. Full integration into the life of the *polis* meant acceptance of its gods, unthinkable for a Jew brought up on worship of the one true God and the repudiation of idolatry (e.g., Wisd. 13.17ff., 15.7ff.). Jewish refusal to worship local gods angered pagans (Josephus *C. Ap.* 2.63). Thus total involvement in the *polis* was normally impossible for the Jew, unless he repudiated his religion (as was the case, for example, of Philo's nephew, T. Julius Alexander). There were large Jewish communities in all the major cities, but by far the largest was in Alexandria which had a considerable degree of autonomy.[6] Indeed, according to Philo, the Jewish population of North Africa numbered about one million (*In Flaccum* 43).

There was considerable contact between the Jews in the Diaspora and Jerusalem, a bond which was reinforced by the regular contribution of the half-shekel Temple tax (Philo, *Emb.* 156; Josephus, *Ant.* 14.110; 18.312f.), which after the destruction of the Temple was diverted to the Temple of Jupiter Capitolinus in Rome (*BJ* 7.216f.; Dio Cassius, *Hist.* 66.7). Huge crowds came from all over the Roman world to participate in the major pilgrim festivals in Jerusalem (*BJ* 6.422f.; Acts 2).[7]

Devotion to the Temple in Jerusalem was not uniform throughout all the Jewish communities. We know from Josephus (*BJ* 1.33; *Ant.* 13.62ff.; 12.38; cf. Isa. 19.18, LXX) that Onias, a priestly refugee from Jerusalem received permission to build a Temple at Leontopolis, modelled on the Temple in Jerusalem.[8] Philo has nothing to say about this Temple in Egypt, but it may well have been a focus for popular devotion among the lower classes in Egyptian Jewry, as well as an alternative shrine for Zadokite priesthood. It was considered to be of sufficient importance as a potential focus of revolt after AD 70 that it was closed down by the Romans some years later (*BJ* 7.421ff.).

Jews in the Diaspora enjoyed many privileges.[9] Judaism was respected (Tertullian, *Apol.* 21; Philo *Emb.* 155ff.) and was normally treated well by Greek and Roman authorities (Josephus, *Ant.* 14.306ff.; 16.160ff.). Jewish scruples were respected (*Ant.* 13.251; 14.223ff.; 16.27ff.; 16.162; 12.119), and they were excused participation in the imperial cult (cf. *Ant.* 19.284ff.,

303f.).[10] It would appear that in the first century BC some Jews held Roman citizenship (*Ant.* 14.228, 234ff.; Acts 22.27). It is uncertain whether Jews became citizens of the various cities in which they dwelt (cf. *Ant.* 12.119). Josephus certainly suggests that Jews possessed equal rights with their neighbours, though doubts have been cast on the precision of Josephus' discussion of the matter (*C. Ap.* 2.38ff.; *Ant.* 19.281ff.; 14.188; *BJ* 7.44; *Ant.* 12.119; 16.160). Evidence from Claudius' letter to the Jews of Alexandria would suggest that Alexandrian Jews did not enjoy citizenship rights there (*Ant.* 19.280ff.), though that should not lead us to overlook the enormous rights which were granted to Jews from time to time to organize their religious activities with a great degree of freedom.[11] They certainly administered their own funds and settled their own religious affairs (*Emb.* 156; *Ant.* 16.162). Clearly some Jews may have aspired to and actually achieved citizenship of their city, particularly among those Jews who had accommodated themselves to a considerable degree to the Hellenistic mores.[12] More often than not, however, the basic conflict which existed between the demands of citizenship and the practice of the Jewish religion meant that Jews were quite content with the privileges granted to them to practise their religion.[13] It would appear from Josephus, *Ant.* 14.117 that the Jewish ethnarch in Alexandria had considerable powers to supervise aspects of religious and commercial law as well as settling internal disputes within the community. Titus confirmed the privileges of the Jews in Antioch (*BJ* 7.110; *Ant.* 12.121), even after the costly war which had recently been pursued by the Romans against the Jews in Judaea. The influence of the Jews of Alexandria is seen in the fact that they had the ability to send a delegation to the emperor himself, about which Philo reports in his *Embassy to Gaius.*

In his report about the Jewish community in Sardis, Josephus tells us about the important place which that community had within the life of the city (*Ant.* 14.235, 259ff.). It had a distinct quarter of its own, with rights to import necessary food supplies, thus guaranteeing a certain degree of control on the requisites for obedience to the Law.[14] It also had its own courts and was guaranteed the freedom to send the half-shekel Temple tax to Jerusalem (*Ant.* 16.27 ff.). In addition, archaeological remains indicate that there was a close link between the Jewish synagogue and the gymnasium, suggesting that there was probably a considerable degree of intercourse between Jews and the culture disseminated by such organizations.[15] What is more, Jews were under no obligation to enter Roman military service, which would have necessarily involved them in many religious acts which would have been incompatible with the practice of their religion (*Ant.* 14.228). Such rights did not meet with universal acceptance, however.[16] We have already noted that Titus was put under some pressure to dispense with Jewish rights in Alexandria after the First Revolt, a situation which was paralleled in Antioch (*Ant.* 12.123f; *BJ* 7.110). Yet despite this hostility and the setbacks to Judaism after two revolts, all the evidence suggests that in the earlier Christian era Jewish practice went on unhindered and in some places flourished.[17] Of course, there were isolated incidents, when local Roman officials embarked on violent action against the Jews, such as the incident recorded by Josephus in *BJ* 7.445f. Here Catullus, governor of Libya, moved against the leading Jews of Cyrene after the false declaration of one Jonathan that he had been incited to revolt by them. Even though the charge, according to Josephus, was shown to be false, we are told that three thousand of the leading Jews of the area were put to the sword and their property was confiscated. No doubt unwillingness to be embroiled in seditious activities of any kind had much to do with the decision of the *gerousia* in Alexandria to hand over fellow-Jews, who were also *sicarii*, to the authorities after the fall of Jerusalem (*BJ* 7.407ff.).

Jews in the Greek-speaking Diaspora found themselves in need of a version of the Jewish Scriptures in the language, which most of them spoke. Hebrew became less and less common as the language of Jews outside Palestine. According to Jewish legend in the *Letter of Aristeas*, the response to the presence of large numbers of Jews in Egypt (*Ant.* 12.11ff.) was the commissioning by Ptolemy Philadelphus of seventy-two translators to translate the Hebrew law for his library at Alexandria, hence its title the Septuagint (LXX).[18] The completion of the translation of the books of the Hebrew Bible is clearly the result of many hands over many decades. Its style bears all the hallmarks of the original Hebrew, with several distinctive expressions, which indicate the attempt by the translators to keep as close as possible to the Hebrew original. Yet the changed world of the translators does make its mark in some of the translations. Already we see one of the characteristics of the good translation: interpretation rather than merely the pedantic literalism (e.g., in Gen. 1.1 the Hebrew *tohu wabohu* is translated *aoratos kai akataskeuastos* 'invisible and shapeless').[19]

The order of the books and the content of the LXX differ quite markedly from the Hebrew Bible. In addition to the apocryphal books, which form part of the LXX (e.g., Ecclesiasticus, Tobit, Judith, 1 Esdras and the Maccabean literature, 1 and 2 Maccabees) there was a considerable reordering[20] as compared with the Hebrew Bible. In the latter the last part of the canon is taken up with the Writings: Psalms, Job, other Wisdom literature, the Megilloth (Song of Songs, Lamentations, Ruth, Esther, Ecclesiastes), Daniel and the books of Chronicles. In the former the order finishes with the Latter Prophets as does the Christian Bible, though we must note that we have to rely on versions of the LXX written by Christian scribes.[21]

The textual relationship between the LXX and the Hebrew Bible is complex (some of the Hebrew manuscripts from Qumran coincide with the text and tradition of the LXX). There are many occasions where there are significant differences between the two (e.g., in the books of Kings[22] and in

Chronicles, Ezra, Nehemiah; cf. 1 Esdras[23]). The discovery of biblical manuscripts among the Dead Sea Scrolls has given renewed impetus to the discussion of the history of the text of the Old Testament. It has to be remembered that the Hebrew version used by us (the Massoretic Text: so called because it is the product of Jewish interpreters, the Massoretes, working between the sixth and tenth centuries) is in its present form much later as a recension than the manuscripts of the LXX available to us and the texts available to us from among the Dead Sea Scrolls.

The LXX was of considerable importance as it became the Bible of the nascent Christian community, just as it had been, we may suppose, for Jews in the Diaspora. Throughout the New Testament, we find apologetic and polemic based on this translation, indeed dependent on its version rather than that of the Hebrew Bible (e.g., Acts 15.16f.; Matt. 1.23), though it is possible that early Christian writers were aware of other versions of the Hebrew Bible (e.g., *targums*).[24]

We know little of the Jewish theology of the Diaspora. It cannot be assumed that our main source for Alexandrian Jewish theology, the writings of Philo of Alexandria, is typical of the thought of Judaism outside Egypt. Such hints as are available to us about Judaism in Asia Minor suggest that it was quite different from what we find in the writings of Philo. Attempts to ascertain the background of New Testament documents like the letter to the Colossians have succeeded in offering an outline of Jewish thought in the area.[25] Equally we may not suppose that Philo's thought represents the full range of Jewish theology in Egypt. Other Egyptian documents like the Wisdom of Solomon,[26] the Sibylline Oracles,[27] Joseph and Asenath[28] and Slavonic Enoch[29] indicate a considerably less sophisticated and philosophical approach than what we find in Philo.

The extensive writings of Philo of Alexandria[30] give us some insight into the way in which this part of Diaspora Jewry in the first century dealt with its ancestral traditions.[31] In the extant writings we find an elaborate allegorical exegesis of the Pentateuch in which the contemporary insights of popular philosophy heavily influenced by Platonism have their part to play. Philo was a Jew from the highest echelons of society in Alexandria, and it must be asked whether his sophisticated exposition of Jewish religion actually is indicative of anything but a minority of Jewish adherents in that city. His interpretations of the laws of the Pentateuch indicate an extremely inventive mind with a penchant for extracting the ultimate nuance and meaning from the text, a characteristic he shares with some later rabbinic commentators.

Fundamental to Philo's theology is the distinction between matter of which this world is made and the immaterial world, to which God belongs. God is utterly self-sufficient and is in no way to be identified with the world: 'God is the one who is greater than the good... purer than the one, and apprehensible to himself alone' (*Praem.* 40). Only good, therefore, can come from God, whereas evil things are man's responsibility (*Fug.* 79). The absoluteness of God's divinity and his utter transcendence are guarded by a series of mediatorial figures, most important of which is the Logos (*Cher.* 27f.; *Confus. Ling.* 171f.; *Quaest. Ex.* 2.64ff.). Philo's Logos doctrine shows many affinities with Stoic ideas.[32] Another significant component to Philo's logos doctrine is the wisdom tradition of Judaism, in which personified wisdom is described as a creative and active attribute of God mediating the divine will in creation (cf. *Confus. Ling.* 146f.). The various emanations which separate God from his creation descend in order, so that the last emanation, the *kosmos noetos* (the world of ideas) forms the pattern for the created world (cf. *Confus. Ling.* 171f.).

In the creation of the world unformed matter was given form, according to the ideal plan for the universe (*Op. Mun.* 18, 20, 25). The Logos uses this pattern for the creation of the world. The distinction between the real world of flesh and blood, of change and decay, and the ideal world is best seen in the account of the creation of man in *Alleg. Leg.* 1.31. Here the two accounts of man's creation in Genesis are taken as indications of the type and antetype, the heavenly and the earthly man. The man of Genesis 1.26 is the one corresponding to the divine world, whereas the man whose creation is recounted in Genesis 2 is the man of flesh and blood. In *Op. Mundi* the creation of man, the one who chose evil, is not attributed to God alone (para. 72), an indication that an attempt is made to shield God from evil.[33]

In view of the fact that the created world reflects the pattern of heavenly realities it is the Law of nature which is supreme and not the law of man (*Spec. Leg.* 1.33f.). Human laws cannot be relied upon, except in so far as they are attempts to copy the reflection of heavenly realities to be found in natural law. The Laws of the Torah were concrete applications of the general principles of law expressed in the Decalogue, which in turn were manifestations of the primary Greek virtues.

It is man's destiny to reach beyond the sensible world to the unseen world of God. Man himself is a mixture of the soul and the body (*Cher.* 113f.). The ultimate hope is that the soul would be able to have communion with the eternal world to which it truly belonged. The significance of the biblical narratives for Philo was that, properly understood, they offered the key to the search of man for his true destiny (cf. *Aboth* 3.1). The truth about reality was to be found in these ancient stories which were contained in the Torah. This was why the Torah was so important; it contained within it the route of the soul back to the eternal world. Abraham's journey, for example, from his home in Ur is the story of the movement away from a concentration on material things towards the eternal. His union with Sarah is seen as a union with virtue, preceded by intercourse with Hagar as the use of introductory studies of the material world (*Leg. Alleg.* 3.244; *Congr.* 81, 88). When three men came to visit Abraham at Mamre (*Abr.* 119ff.), it is a revelation of God and his powers. Moses' imprisonment in the ark of bulrushes and his weeping speak of the imprisoned soul yearning for the immaterial. Moses has to have Aaron to speak for him, because he is the Logos, and the divine Logos needs some kind of mediation with the material world (*Migr.* 78f.). The flight from Egypt is naturally enough seen as the flight of the soul from the material world (*Post.* 155). Moses is the one who can save men by leading them out of the sensible world to an apprehension of God (*Gig.* 54f.).

The Torah, therefore, in Philo's thought provides the means of ascertaining how to gain communion with that eternal world. Man needs virtue as a way of existing (*Post.* 132–57), and this has two sides: the theoretical (communion with the eternal) and the practical (human relationships) (*Leg. Alleg.* 1.56–8), though he is in no doubt that the ultimate is communion with the divine. The practical and the theoretical sides of man's existence are well illustrated by his treatment of circumcision, where the benefits of the rite from a practical as well as a spiritual point of view are brought out (*Spec. Leg.* 1.2–12).

It would be wrong to think of Philo merely as an eccentric mystic, concerned solely with escape from the real world.[34] It is clear that he was well-connected in Alexandrian society. Indeed, his nephew was T. Julius Alexander, an apostate Jew, who was Roman procurator of Judaea and later prefect of Egypt. Philo's political concerns are particularly evident in his account of the embassy to the Emperor Gaius (cf. *Ant.* 18.259),[35] and the representations made concerning Gaius' abortive attempt to introduce a statue of himself into the Temple in Jerusalem. It is a work of great importance for our understanding of the delicate balance of relations between Jews and pagans in Egypt, and the extent to which official hostility against the Jews could lead to local anti-Jewish acts (e.g. *Embassy* 132). It also speaks of the various ways in which Romans have lent their support to Jews (276f.) and the respect which Judaism shows to the emperor despite its unwillingness to participate in the cult (157). A similar apologetic motive can be discerned in the work *In Flaccum*, which catalogues the infamy of the prefect of Egypt, Flaccus, and his anti-Jewish activities.

The complexity of Philo's thought and the sophistication of his biblical interpretation make the summary of his thought in small space an unjust reflection of the place of this thinker in the gamut of Jewish thought. While Alexandrian Jewish theology may not have been typical of what was going on elsewhere in the synagogues of the Diaspora, it would be wrong to underestimate the contribution made to the history of religion by Philo and similar thinkers. The Christian Platonists of Alexandria at the end of the second century onwards manifestly stand in a tradition which stems from Philo.[36] Between Philo and Clement and Origen there stand the early gnostic thinkers about whom so little is known. It has been conjectured with some plausibility that the reason for this is that the early second-century form of the religion in Alexandria was gnostic in character.[37] Certainly the gnostic influences on Clement are evident as also is the fact that Egypt has produced one of the foremost testimonies to gnostic religion in the Nag Hammadi library. Philo's own religion already has the seeds within it of some of the main features of gnostic religion.[38] Clearly we are still a considerable distance from the anti-Semitic systems of the mid-second century with their dualistic theologies. But the mediatorial system in Philo and the dualism born from the influence of Platonic philosophy are the seed-bed for those features which were to become so much part of the gnostic religion. The writings of Philo, therefore, not only point us to the vitality of the Jewish mind as it sought to commend its faith in a pagan environment, but also look forward to religious developments in both Christianity and gnosticism for which they were the precursor.

14

The Expression of Hope[1]

(a) An Outline of Jewish Eschatology

The future hope in Judaism and for that matter also in Christianity is often treated as if it were an appendage to other beliefs and practices with the implicit assumption that it is in fact peripheral to an understanding of the religious ideas of the two communities. It may indeed be true that eschatology has become an item which is far from central to the ideas of both religions. But in the first century it would be a gross distortion to imagine that the future hope was peripheral.

It is only when we recognize that when we speak of the future hope we are dealing with something integral to faith that we can properly appreciate its centrality. For Jews the promise of a final vindication of his people and the establishment of a new order in which God's ways would prevail was a belief which had its roots in the covenant relationship itself (2 Sam. 7.8f.). We have already seen that one wing of the covenant promise between God and his people had a messianic component. Thus the prophetic hopes concerning a righteous leader who would act as the agent of God in delivering his people (Isa. 11), many of which were themselves derived from the Davidic covenant promises (Ps. 89, 132; *Ps. Sol.* 17), exercised their own influence on the imagination of the Jewish people. When this was allied to the promise made to the whole nation that they would inherit a land flowing with milk and honey, it becomes easy to see why in the age of Jesus there should have been an intense expectation of redemption. The fact is as we have seen that the promise made to the people was far from being fulfilled.

Two constant features of the eschatological expectation during this period are the belief that a new age would come of peace, righteousness and justice when the faith of the righteous would be vindicated; and the conviction that before this age would come about a period of severe distress, political and cosmic disorder and upheaval of a most cataclysmic kind, would have to be endured.

One of the constant features of Jewish eschatological belief is the 'birth pangs' of the new age, the messianic woes.[2] These are the series of disasters which, it was believed, had to precede the coming of God's kingdom. We find the belief in the New Testament in Mark 13.7ff. (and particularly in Rom. 8.19ff.; Rev. 6, 8 and 9, 16). These disasters included intensified human suffering through wars and natural disasters and disturbances which upset the normal pattern of planetary behaviour. The idea is hinted at briefly in Daniel 12.1 but is clearly evident in the late second century BC in Jubilees 23.11ff. Sometimes, as in Revelation, there is a quota of messianic woes which has to be completed before the kingdom finally comes, (e.g., Syr. Baruch 25ff.). In some pseudepigrapha this series of disasters is regarded as part of the judgement of God. Thus, for example, in Jubilees there is no mention made of a final assize. By means of these events the way is paved for the reign of God to come about; the disasters are the divinely ordained means of removing all that stands in the way of the fulfilment of the divine will.

Belief in the coming of a new age of peace and justice is firmly rooted in the Scriptures (e.g., Isa. 11; Ezek. 40ff.; Zech. 8.20ff., 9–14). It is clear from a study of the pseudepigrapha that passages like Isaiah 11 continued to exercise an important influence. In our earliest texts the detailed character of the new age is hardly discussed. All we have in the book of Daniel, for example, is the conviction that an everlasting kingdom would be established on earth which could not be destroyed, when the saints would reign (2.44, 7.27). This would involve judgement on the nations of the world (7.10f.) and would be preceded by a time of distress (12.1). In the earliest parts of 1 Enoch we find general predictions concerning the renewal of creation, where the flood in the time of Noah has become a type of the destruction and renewal to be undergone at the eschaton (10.17). A much longer eschatological passage is to be found in 1 Enoch 85–90, in which the different persons are represented by animals and birds (hence its name, the Animal Apocalypse). This takes the form of a history of the world from creation to eschaton. The latter is said to take place soon after the Maccabaean period. The rise of the *hasidim* at the beginning of the second century BC is seen as the prelude to a rise of hostile powers against Israel (90.13; cf. *Sib. Or.* 3.663ff.) followed by the triumph of the people of God. Judgement takes place and then the restoration of Zion with the righteous dwelling at peace in the land (cf. Matt. 5.5) and the nations of the world acknowledging the dominion of Israel (90.30ff.). Afterwards the world is transformed into the perfection, which God originally planned (90.37f.; cf. Jub. 23.11ff.; *Sib. Or.* 3.698ff.) and finally the Messiah emerges from the community.

In the Apocalypse of Weeks,[3] which probably dates from a slightly later period, probably round about the end of the second century BC, we have an outline of the history of the world separated into periods of weeks. As in most eschatological passages from Jewish and early Christian literature the hope for the future is centred on this world, albeit one which has been purged of those elements which have rendered it unsuitable for God (1 Enoch 93.9f.; 91.12ff.).

This worldly eschatology is also evident in Jubilees 1.23ff. and 23.11ff. Once again we find that a deterioration in man's condition precedes the coming of a time of great happiness, when there is a return to a study of the Law and to the pattern of existence as it was at the beginning of creation. Similarly in the Syriac Apocalypse of Baruch we find an emphasis on the renewal of the world. The messianic woes are followed by the revelation of the Messiah and the establishment of God's reign on earth, when Behemoth and Leviathan will be food for those who are left (29.3ff.). This time will be marked by periods of great plenty. Here we find, as in 4 Ezra 7.29f., that the reign of the Messiah will be temporary; his departure is followed by the judgement. This passage is typical of eschatological beliefs around the beginning of the Christian era:

> When stupor shall seize the inhabitants of the earth, and they shall fall into many tribulations, and again when they shall fall into great torments. And it will come to pass when they say in their thoughts by reason of their much tribulation: The Mighty One doth no longer remember the earth – yes, it will come to pass when they abandon hope, that the time will then awake ... Into twelve parts is that time divided, and each one of them is reserved for that which is appointed for it. In the first part there shall be the beginning of commotions. And in the second part there shall be slayings of the great ones. And in the third part the fall of many by death. And in the fourth part the sending of the sword. And in the fifth part famine and the withholding of rain. And in the sixth part earthquakes and terrors ... And it shall come to pass in those parts that the Messiah shall then begin to be revealed. And Behemoth shall be revealed from his place and Leviathan shall ascend from the sea, those two great monsters which I created on the fifth day of creation, and shall have kept until that time; and then there shall be food for all that are left. The earth shall yield its fruit ten thousand fold and on each vine there shall be a thousand branches ... And those who have hungered shall rejoice: moreover, also they shall behold marvels every day. For winds shall go forth from before me to bring every morning the fragrance of aromatic fruits, and at the close of the day clouds distilling dews of health. And it shall come to pass that the treasury of manna shall again descend from on high, and they

shall eat of it in those years, because these are they who have come to the consummation of time (Syr. Baruch 24–30).

A periodization of the future age with a temporary messianic kingdom followed by the resurrection and another age seems to have emerged at the end of the first century AD. It is familiar to us from the book of Revelation, where the millennium marks the climax of the eschatological woes but is in its turn followed by the judgement, resurrection and the coming of a new heaven and new earth (21–22; cf. Isa. 65.17; 2 Pet. 3.13; Isa. 66.22). A similar scheme is to be found in 4 Ezra 7.26ff. Ezra is told of the revelation of the new Jerusalem which ushers in a period of bliss of four hundred years. After the death of the Messiah the world returns to primeval silence for seven days (7.30), and then there is the resurrection and the last judgement followed by vindication for the righteous and torment for the wicked (7.38). In this work we find an explicit distinction between two ages, e.g., 7.50: 'For this cause the Most High has made not one age but two' (cf. 6.7). Despite what is often asserted, references to a future world of a transcendent kind are by no means common in the pseudepigrapha. It is certainly true that a distinction is made, albeit implicitly, between the present imperfections and the glorious future, but a radical distinction between this age and the age to come, is by no means common. Indeed, in the contemporary Syr. Baruch, only the expected contrast between the present world of travail and the glorious future is to be found (15.7ff.).[4] Other visions in Syr. Baruch and 4 Ezra do not neglect the traditional eschatological pattern which we have already outlined. It will come as no surprise that, just as in Daniel the overthrow of the regime of Antiochus Epiphanes is of great concern to the writer, it is the imminent demise of the power of Rome which exercises the seer (e.g., 4 Ezra 11–12; Syr. Baruch 36; cf. Rev. 13, 17f.).

Apart from the pseudepigrapha, some eschatological material is found in the writings of Philo and Josephus. It should be remembered that the relative paucity of material in the writings of the latter is due in no small part to his reaction to the way in which eschatological enthusiasm played a part in the revolt against Rome. Indeed, we find Josephus applying those very prophetic oracles, which had provided such a powerful incentive to revolt, to the Emperor Vespasian (*BJ* 6.312).[5] Philo also looks forward to a time when the people of God would assemble together in *eretz Israel* (*Praem.* 164) and the ruined places would be rebuilt. Indeed, the bliss sketched in Isaiah 11 seems to lie behind another passage in *Praem.* (89f.) where the proper relationship of the created world with itself is outlined.

While there are several texts which point to a universal salvation, a belief based on Old Testament texts (Isa. 11.10; 45.22ff; 49.12; 59.19; Zech. 8.20ff.; Mal. 1.11; 1 Enoch 90.35; *Sib. Or.* 3.767f.; Matt. 8.11), the particularity of the salvation is never lost sight of. Thus the centrality of the land of Israel with the life of the cult in Jerusalem at its centre is a feature of some importance (1 Enoch 90.28f.; cf. 4 Ezra 7.26; Syr. Baruch 32.2; *Sib. Or.* 3.767f.).[6] While the position of the Torah within the new age has been an issue over which there has been much discussion, the evidence from the earliest texts seems to indicate its continued validity. Thus in Jubilees a feature of the new age will be the way in which children will once again return to a study of the Torah (23.26).[7]

Another dominant feature of many of the eschatological beliefs in our period is that of the general resurrection.[8] By the first century AD resurrection had become so central to the beliefs of some groups, particularly the Pharisees, that it had become the touchstone of orthodoxy (*M. San.* 10.1). The origins of the resurrection belief are obscure. Certainly the earliest unequivocal reference to the belief in the Old Testament is to be found in Daniel 12.2 (cf. Isa. 26.19; Job 19.25), though we may suspect that earlier passages may have been interpreted in this way before.[9] The centrality of belief in the resurrection of Jesus in early Christianity should not lead us to ignore the important position that the belief enjoyed among the Pharisees, nor, for that matter, the fact that it continued to be a subject of considerable controversy (Acts 23.6). Josephus seems to indicate that the Essenes believed in the immortality of the soul (*BJ* 2.154), but the evidence of the Qumran Scrolls (assuming them to be the product of Essenes) is ambiguous on this question.[10] Nevertheless in the rabbinic literature and the apocalypses, which are now extant, the resurrection is an important component of the eschatological beliefs. Usually this belief takes the form of a general conviction, such as is found in Daniel 12.2, that the dead will be raised, the righteous to eternal life and the impious to torments. Whether the resurrected were thought to be about to participate in a new life in this world or in some transcendent order is by no means clear. If the book of Revelation is anything to go by, both possibilities are reckoned with. Not only do those, who died for their witness to Jesus, participate in the millennium (Rev. 20.4; cf. 1 Cor. 6.2; Matt. 19.28), but subsequently there is a second resurrection and final judgement to ascertain who will participate in the life of the new Jerusalem (20.12).

The fact that there was not complete certainty over the matter can be illustrated by reference to the problem which Paul finds himself confronting in 1 Thessalonians. Here the Christians are perplexed that some of their brethren have died before the age to come has arrived in all its fullness, and the question arises whether the dead would be able to participate in the life of that age. Paul answers by quoting a word of the Lord to the effect that those who were dead would precede those left behind (1 Thess. 4.15). That this was indeed a considerable problem can be illustrated from the two late first-century apocalypses, 4 Ezra and Syr. Baruch. In both these works the references to the resurrection from the dead are to be found *after* the description of the messianic kingdom on earth. Thus, in Syr. Baruch 25ff.

(cf. 4 Ezra 7.26ff.) we find that the sequence of messianic woes is followed immediately by the messianic kingdom itself; nothing whatever is said about the righteous dead participating in that process. Only those who are fortunate enough to be alive at the time will be able to benefit from the blessings of the new age (Syr. Baruch 29.3ff.). It is only after the Messiah has returned in glory (30.1) that the resurrection takes place and perdition comes for the wicked.

In some texts from a Hellenistic Jewish milieu we find clear evidence of a belief in the immortality of the soul (e.g., Wisd. 3.1).[11] Certainly any hard and fast distinction between belief in the resurrection of the body and belief in the immortality of the soul, on the basis of the extent of Hellenistic influence, is a rather clumsy and misleading distinction. Thus Paul, the erstwhile Pharisee, countenances the possibility of some kind of existence with God at death (Phil. 1.23; 2 Cor. 5.1ff.). Even if it may be thought that the apostle to the Gentiles had come under the influence of excessively Hellenistic ideas, the same cannot surely be said of the authors of Revelation 6.9, where we find reference to the souls of the martyrs crying out for vengeance from under the altar. If this passage and 2 Corinthians 5.1ff., are anything to go by, it seems that some Jewish eschatologies had already combined the notion of resurrection with a belief in immortality, particularly as a temporary existence in heaven for the righteous dead, while they awaited the final consummation. In the Testament of Abraham 10f., it is presupposed that judgement takes place at death; it is then that the destiny of each soul is decided.

Other Jewish texts indicate similar kinds of belief. In 1 Enoch 22, mention is made of different places for departed souls (cf. 4 Ezra 7.75ff.) and in later texts there seems to exist a belief that at death there would be a place for souls to exist (e.g. *Ant.* 18.14; Syr. Baruch 30.2; 4 Ezra 4.35; 7.32, 80, 95 and 101). In the Jewish-Christian apocalypse, the Ascension of Isaiah, which probably dates from the last part of the first century AD, we find the belief that the righteous dead have a place in the seventh heaven with God, awaiting the ascent of the Redeemer back to glory, before they can don their garments of glory (Asc. Isa. 9.8ff.). Texts like these make it difficult to draw a distinction between Palestinian texts uninfluenced by the Hellenistic belief in the immortality of the soul and the texts from Hellenistic Judaism where this doctrine is to the fore.[12]

(b) Messianic Belief[13]

As with other areas where the interests of New Testament exegetes have demanded a knowledge of contemporary ideas, the Jewish beliefs about the Messiah have attracted a considerable amount of attention from commentators.[14] The fact is that the material concerning the Messiah, his activity and character is by no means large. Indeed, if we were to confine ourselves solely to those texts which mention the term Messiah (*mashiah, christos*), we would have a small number of texts only to consider. The impression given by the New Testament that the word *christos* had become such a popular technical term to designate the eschatological agent of salvation is misleading. Certainly in the late first-century apocalypses, Syr. Baruch and 4 Ezra, we find references to the Messiah (Syr. Baruch 29.3; 30.1; 39.8; 40.1; 70.9; 72.4; 4 Ezra 7.28f; 12.32). Who this anointed figure is, the texts hardly pause to consider, for little is said about his activity and character. Thus it needs to be pointed out that when we refer to Jewish messianic belief, it is more often than not the case that reference is being made to a large complex of ideas to which the adjective messianic is rather loosely appended. It will be apparent from the following pages that messianic belief covers a much wider spectrum of ideas than merely the belief in the coming of a descendant of David.

However varied Jewish expectation concerning eschatological mediatorial figures may have been, Jewish tradition gave pride of place to the expectation that a descendant of David would arise in the last days to lead the people of God.[15] As we have already seen, such beliefs were intimately linked with the covenant of God with David, which stressed the eternal nature of the promises made to David and his descendants.

With the possible exception of the Similitudes of Enoch and 4 Ezra all the texts which deal with the expectation of a messianic descendant of David indicate the belief that a human descendant of David would arise at the end of the age and by his actions would pave the way for a period of bliss for Israel. He would come from the stock of David and be a man like other men, though anointed with the divine spirit, and pave the way for an era of bliss on earth. The best example of such a belief is to be found in the Psalms of Solomon which offer us one of the most extended descriptions of the Messiah from our period:

> Behold, O God and raise up unto them their king, the son of David. At the time which thou seest, O God, that he may reign over Israel thy servant. And gird him with strength that he may shatter unrighteous rulers, and that he may purge Jerusalem from nations that trample her down to destruction. Wisely, righteously he shall thrust out sinners from the inheritance. He shall destroy the pride of the sinner as a potter's vessel. With a rod of iron he shall break in pieces all their substance; he shall destroy the godless nations with the word of his mouth. At his rebuke the nations shall flee before him, and he shall reprove the sinners for the thoughts of their hearts. And he shall gather together a holy people whom he shall lead in righteousness, and he shall judge the tribes of his people which has been sanctified by the Lord his God. And he shall not suffer unrighteousness to lodge any more in their midst, nor shall there dwell with them any man that knoweth wickedness, for he shall know them that they are all sons of God. And he shall divide them according to their tribes upon the land, and neither sojourner nor alien shall sojourn with them any more. He shall judge peoples and nations in

the wisdom of his righteousness. And he shall have the heathen nations to serve under his yoke; and he shall glorify the Lord in a place to be seen of all the earth; and he shall purge Jerusalem making it holy as of old: so that nations shall come from the ends of the earth to see his glory bringing as gifts her sons who had fainted and to see the glory of the Lord wherewith God had glorified her. And he shall be a righteous king taught of God, over them, and there shall be no unrighteousness in his days in their midst, for all shall be holy and their king the anointed of the Lord. For he shall not put his trust in horse and rider and bow, nor shall he multiply for himself gold and silver for war, nor shall he gather confidence from a multitude for the day of battle. The Lord himself is king, the hope of him that is mighty is through his hope in God. All nations shall be in fear before him, for he will smite the earth with the word of his mouth for ever. He will bless the people of the Lord with wisdom and gladness, and he himself will be pure from sin, so that he may rule a great people. He will rebuke rulers and remove sinners by the might of his word; and relying upon his God throughout his days he will not stumble; for God will make him mighty by means of his holy spirit, and wise by means of the spirit of understanding, with strength and righteousness. And the blessing of the Lord will be upon him; he will be strong and stumble not; his hope will be in the Lord: who then can prevail over him? He will be mighty in his works and strong in the fear of God; he will be shepherding the flock of the Lord faithfully and righteously and will suffer none among them to stumble in their pasture. He will lead them all aright, and there will be no pride among them that any among them should be oppressed (Ps. Solomon 17.33ff.).

This extended quotation from the Psalms of Solomon will enable us to see the main qualities of the descendant of David. There is no doubt about his humanity. Indeed it may be that phrases like 'in his days' and 'throughout his days' indicate that as in 4 Ezra 7.29 the Messiah is an ordinary mortal. There is little doubt that behind the phraseology of this psalm there lies the conviction that the descendant of David would be expected to exercise a military role in purging the land and the holy city of all defilement. He will be supported by the might of God himself (cf. Judg. 7.2ff.), but his dominion over the nations is a theme which has its origins in the biblical hope for the restoration of the idyllic time of Israel's dominion under David. Throughout the quotation allusions to various parts of Scripture are apparent (particularly Isa. 11; 60.6ff.). This passage has, with good reason, been regarded as typical of the central characteristics of messianic belief, with its emphasis on the human descendant of David, the vanquishing of Israel's foes and the establishment of a reign of justice and peace on earth under the direction of the King. In one form or another this belief crops up in most of the different collections of literature from our period, with varying degrees of emphasis being given to the role of the Davidic figure in this process. That its essential features passed on into rabbinic tradition also, albeit much expanded and reflected upon, may be confirmed by reference to the eschatological section in the Babylonian Talmud (*b. San.* 95aff.)[16]

There is not much evidence to suggest that the Messiah was a pre-existent, heavenly figure, though the evidence from 4 Ezra and 1 Enoch 37–71 might seem to suggest that there were moves in this direction, about which something more will be said below. The evidence of 4 Ezra is itself difficult to evaluate. On the one hand we have a passage like 7.29 where there can be little doubt that the Messiah is a mortal figure, whereas ch. 13 implies and 14.9 explicitly suggests that the Messiah was indeed a pre-existent heavenly figure.

Much ink has been spilt over the background and interpretation of the passages in the New Testament which speak of the Son of Man[17] and those Jewish texts (Dan. 7; 1 Enoch 37–71; 4 Ezra 13) which form the background for the interpretation of the New Testament texts. Opinion is still divided over the precise meaning of the various texts. Indeed, some have wondered whether there ever was such a thing as a Son of Man figure among the beliefs of ancient Judaism.[18] In the light of this, it is probably safer to speak not of a belief in the Son of Man, as though it were a widely accepted messianic belief, but merely of diffuse beliefs in heavenly mediators. More will be said on the vexed problem of the Son of Man later. Suffice it to say that the origin of at least one strand of the New Testament doctrine derives from Daniel 7.13 where the figure already is regarded as a heavenly, pre-existent being.[19]

We have already noted that in 4 Ezra there is evidence which suggests that there was emerging a belief in the pre-existence of the Messiah.[20] Such a belief is even more clear in the Similitudes of Enoch (1 Enoch 37–71).[21] In this section we find several passages which speak of the Son of Man (46.1ff.; 48.2ff.; 62.5ff.; 69.26ff. and 71.17) as well as other passages which speak of 'the Elect One' (39.6f.; 40.5; 45.3ff.; 49.2ff; 51.3; 52.6ff.; 53.6; 55.4; 61.5ff; 62.1ff.). The overlap which exists between the characteristics attributed to the two titles suggests that in the Similitudes, as we now have them, the two figures are identified. The references to the Son of Man in 1 Enoch 37–71 derive from Daniel 7.13, and are an extension of the brief reference there in the direction of a presentation of this figure as an angelic being, who sat on his throne and exercised divine judgement in the last days. Despite some recent attempts to discredit the value of this work for New Testament research,[22] it seems difficult to suppose that, whatever the date of the Ethiopic manuscripts now in our possession, the writing of the text can be much later than the first century AD. Indeed, if it is right to suppose, as many commentators would, that the figure of the Son of Man in Daniel 7.13 already has the contours of a heavenly pre-existent figure, then the development which we find in the Similitudes would be nothing out of the ordinary. In what sense the beliefs in heavenly mediatorial figures were linked with messianic belief, has been hotly disputed. It is true that in 1 Enoch 48.10 and 52.4 the Son of Man is explicitly linked with the title Messiah. Whether this involved a confluence of heavenly mediator ideas and the traditional messianic expectation of the descendant of David is unclear, though the use of some traditional Davidic passages lends some support to this theory (e.g., 46.1ff.). The confluence seems to be more apparent in 4 Ezra. In chapter 13, which is clearly dependent on Daniel 7.13, we find that the reference to the eschatological agent is to 'my son' (v.32), kept by God for many ages (13.26, cf. 'Messiah' in 12.32). That these two works are not totally eccentric has been indicated by the discovery of a fragmentary text, which speaks of the activity of Melchizedek in the last days (11 *Q Melch*). In this work it is said that Melchizedek sits in judgement; Psalm 82.1 is applied to him. What is more, he is said to be the one anointed by the spirit (Isa. 61.1f.). This text has indicated the beliefs in a heavenly figure with the appearance of a man which are to be found in some early Jewish texts. The identification of that heavenly figure with a righteous man of Israel's past and the employment of messianic categories to speak of this man all point to a growing fluidity, particularly in texts of a sectarian character, with regard to messianic belief.[23]

Discussion of messianic figures in Judaism inevitably concentrates on the descendant of David as *the* messianic figure. It must be remembered, however, that in the Old Testament various figures are said to be anointed, for example, prophets (Isa. 61) and priests (Lev. 8.12) as well as kings.

The Testaments of the Twelve Patriarchs had for a long time acquainted us with the belief in the coming of a priestly as well as a Davidic Messiah (e.g., Test. Levi 18 and Reuben 6.8). This belief has been strikingly confirmed by the discovery of the Dead Sea Scrolls which speak of Messiahs of Aaron and Israel (1 *QS* 9.11). What is more, in a text which prescribes the regulations for the messianic meal (1 *QSa* 2.1ff.), it is quite apparent that the Messiah of Aaron, the priestly Messiah, takes precedence over the Davidic Messiah. It has been suggested that there was a development in the messianic beliefs of the Qumran community, starting from a priestly messianism based on the expectation that another priestly teacher would arise (CD 20.15).[24]

Another figure mentioned in the Qumran texts is that of the prophet (1 *QS* 9.11, 4 *Q Test.*). The expectation of a prophet who should come in the last days is, like the hope for a descendant of David, firmly rooted in Scripture. In Deuteronomy 18.15ff. (quoted in 4 *Q Test.*) Moses predicts that a prophet should arise like himself who would teach the people of God. This is a belief which is well attested in the New Testament (John 1.31; 6.14) and probably had some influence on the earliest christological formulations.[25] Related to this belief was another rooted in Scripture, namely the expectation that Elijah would come (cf. Mark 6.15; 8.28; 9.11f.).[26] According to Malachi 4.5, the coming of Elijah will be before the great and terrible day of the Lord comes. 'And he will turn the hearts of fathers to their children and the hearts of the children to their fathers.' In other words Elijah's coming reverses the process, which the messianic distress had set in motion, when dissension and strife were the order of the day (*M. Sotah* 9.15; Mark 13.12f.; Jub. 23.9). In addition to this restoring function, Elijah's coming seems to link with the coming of the prophet like Moses in one important way: the interpretation of the Torah. In 1 Maccabees 4.46 we find that the desecrated stones of the Temple are removed to a suitable place, until a prophet should arise who would be able to tell the people exactly what should be done with them. Similarly in the Mishnah (*M. Eduyoth* 8.7) the coming of Elijah will be the time when disputed issues over ritual cleanness and other disputed halakic issues would be settled (*M. Baba Metzia* 3.4f; 1.8; 2.6; *M. Shekalim* 2.5).

The evidence of Philo and the later Samaritan material indicates that the belief in the return of a prophet like Moses was a source of rich and varied speculation of a most extravagant kind. Hints of this Mosaic speculation,[27] albeit confined to the Lawgiver himself and devoid of messianic trappings, are to be found in the rabbinic literature. Particularly important is the belief that Moses' ascent of Sinai was to be regarded as a heavenly ascent (cf. Exod. 24.9). Moses' pre-eminence as the communicator of the definitive divine revelation from God to his people makes him a figure apart from all others. His communion with God and knowledge of heavenly secrets are the basis of a position of special privilege. The prophet who would follow in his steps in the last days, therefore, would be in a peculiarly privileged position to know God (Exod. 33.19f.) and legislate for all those things which were necessary for the proper administration of human affairs.

15

Pragmatism and Utopianism in Ancient Judaism

(a) Zealots and Quietists

The dominant theme in the Old Testament is of God's inspiration of his people to carry all before them as they enter to inherit the land which he had promised to the patriarchs. The stories of the conquest of Canaan in Numbers, Joshua and Judges vindicate the belief that God would raise up men who would lead the hosts of the holy nation in battle to fulfil the divine promises. In Jewish legend these ideas obviously played an important role in conditioning the views of the people of God. So we find that, in the final form of the text of the Pentateuch, the story of the overthrow of Jericho in Joshua 5f. is a great religious occasion, when the might of God is revealed through the obedient response of his people. The heroes of Israel's past like Phineas,[1] whose zeal for God made him violently purge from the community

97

of Israel a man who had yoked himself with a Midianite woman (Num. 25.6ff.), and Gideon (Judg. 6f.) inspired a belief in succeeding generations that the way to achieve the mighty acts of God was by obedient response to God and a readiness to take up arms and fight a holy war for the Lord.[2]

That this was not the only tradition, though it may well have been the more dominant, can be shown by reference to other events in Israel's past. The vanquishing of Pharaoh and his host at the Red Sea is an example of the way in which God with outstretched arm himself slew the enemies of Israel (Exod. 15). In this act the tradition reports that Israel was a passive recipient of the divine mercy and could only look on in wonder as God wrought victory for his people. The divine warrior theme which underlies many of these ideas has received much attention in recent study.[3] It would appear that it could take the form of a direct intervention by God in the affairs of men such as we find, for example, in the Psalms (e.g., 18.7ff.) and in Isaiah 59.15ff. or through the processes of history as in the deliverance from the hand of Sennacherib (Isa. 37.36). It is in the prophecies of Isaiah of Jerusalem that this tradition of dependence on God alone for deliverance for his people reaches its peak. In the crisis over the invasion of Assyria the counsels of the prophet to his nation are clear.[4] The people of Zion are not to resort to alliances with foreign nations (Isa. 30.1ff.) or to force of arms (Isa. 31.1ff; 30.15). Israel has to learn that in the processes of history is the hand of the Lord to be discerned (Isa. 10.5ff.), that quiet trust and faith in God is the key to salvation (Isa. 10.16; 28.14ff.; 29.5ff.; 31.4). This was a tradition which was taken up within the Isaianic tradition by Isaiah of the Exile. In his oracles the people of God are to be witnesses to God's mighty acts in history as a way is prepared for the exiles to return to Zion and the glory of God is revealed before men (Isa. 40.3ff.).

The first century AD saw a considerable increase in the yearning for deliverance of the people of God, such as the fathers had experienced. In the middle of the second century BC the Jews threw off the domination of the Seleucid overlord, who wished to impose Hellenistic ways on Israel by force. The heroic exploits of the Maccabean martyrs,[5] and the success of the tiny nation against the might of the Seleucid empire inevitably fired hopes that similar things could happen again. The situation was made worse because of the possession of the land of Israel by the Romans and the use of its revenue for the profit of an unholy nation. On the death of Herod the Great, who had kept the country under a degree of control, his sons were unable to continue to hold the line, not least because of the feuding which went on between them.[6] The placing of Judaea under direct rule from Rome necessitated a census, which was regarded by many as a horrific encroachment on the rights of the holy land of God. The census involved the assessment of tribute of the land for a pagan, foreign overlord, and the outburst was perhaps to be expected. Judas the Galilean, who instigated the revolt against Rome, said that the census was tantamount to the reduction of the people of God to slavery (*Ant.* 18.4f.) and argued that the Jewish people should accept no one as their master but God alone. Here we have a reflection of the earnest determination found in the ancient traditions to maintain the integrity of the holy nation by force of arms. Despite the disparaging remarks made by Josephus with regard to the Zealots (*BJ* 7.268), it would appear that they did look to the inspiration offered by the biblical zealots as well as to the Maccabees. The incidents, which Josephus relates as examples of their neglect of the law of their fathers, may represent both his attempt to discredit the Zealots and his ignorance of their belief that their actions may have been a *restoration* of the law of their fathers, which had been perverted by the hierarchy in Jerusalem. A glance at their activities will indicate that this was indeed the case. Thus the election of the High Priest by lot during the First Revolt (*BJ* 4.147ff.) was probably an attempt to ascertain, by this age-old method, which member of the priestly family should exercise the office; (e.g., Neh. 10.34). Their execution of collaborators with Rome would be part of an attempt to purge the holy city of all defilement (*BJ* 4.138ff.). Also their abolition of the sacrifice on behalf of Caesar would be the removal of an unnecessary contamination of the cultic activity (*BJ* 2.410). Thus, far from indicating their lawlessness these activities probably reflect their concern to put right abuses in the commonwealth of Israel.

There has been much discussion over whether there was a Zealot party in existence throughout the first century.[7] What cannot be doubted is that there were many groups and individuals, whose intention it was to oppose the presence of Roman power by force. That there was a degree of continuity between the Sicarii, who were active in the middle of the first century AD and during the revolt, is confirmed by the fact that descendants of Judas took a prominent place in the movement. They were led by Menahem and eventually fled to Masada where they committed suicide in the face of capture by the Romans in AD 73 (*BJ* 7.320ff.).

The concern of all these groups, whatever their origin and however loosely they may have been connected, was the redemption of Zion. For the Zealots, Hayward argues as follows:

> ... the census [of AD 6] should be regarded as slavery, and they called on loyal Jews to begin the process of redemption which could not be accomplished without their active assistance [*Ant.* 18.5]. The Bible explicitly states that Israel should not be numbered [2 Sam. 24]: further, the census was a preliminary to taxation, and all adult male Israelites would be required to pay tribute to Caesar with coins bearing Caesar's image. This, in the eyes of Judas, constituted a breach of the Torah, which forbids images, idolatry and worship of other gods. This sharpening of the Torah's demands is evident also in the second tenet of the fourth philosophy, the affirmation that God alone is leader and master, a biblical commonplace which those who fought against Rome were to take *au pied de la lettre*.[8]

At the heart of the Zealot theology, therefore, was the conviction that the freedom of Israel and the redemption of the people of God could not come about unless, as in days of old, the people of God themselves worked actively for this goal. It was no use in their eyes to wait passively for the kingdom of God to come. In this respect the War Scroll (1 *QM*) gives a dramatic insight into the beliefs of those who believed that the establishment of the reign of God on earth would only come about as the result of the participation of the sons of light to eliminate the sons of darkness.

That there were other attitudes towards the way in which salvation would be initiated has already been stressed. Even Josephus, who was later to desert to the Romans, started the revolt as a commander of the Jewish troops. Theologically, there is every reason to suppose that there would have been some hesitation over support for the revolt. Debates recorded between rabbis at the end of the first century reveal that there was a difference of opinion over the conditions, which were necessary for the inauguration of the kingdom of God. On the one side, there were those who thought that the repentance of Israel was a necessary precondition, whereas on the other, there were those who thought that its coming did not depend in any way on human response.[9] We may suspect that those, who believed that it was necessary for Israel to repent before the Messiah came, would have viewed the uprising against Rome with considerable suspicion. Whatever the reason for the escape of Yohanan ben Zakkai from Jerusalem (*ARN* 22f.),[10] it would appear that some of the sages were deeply unhappy with the situation in Jerusalem and sought an opportuniy to start their deliberations elsewhere. Of course, whether or not they gave initial support to the war we are not now in a position to ascertain, though there is every likelihood that at least some of the leading Pharisees supported it.[11]

Leaving aside those who would have objected to the Zealot position, because they considered that the measure of autonomy granted to Jews in Palestine and the daily worship in the Temple were sufficient reasons for supporting Roman rule, we must now consider the views of those who espoused a position which was in the tradition of Isaiah of Jerusalem. On the whole, it would probably be fair to say that the apocalyptic literature evinces an essentially passive attitude. It is true that one or two passages seem to countenance the idea that the people of God will have a part to play in the final struggle (e.g., 1 Enoch 90.19; Syr. Baruch 72.2), but by and large, the picture which emerges of the eschatological events is of a vast struggle in which the people of God are spectators of a drama on a cosmic scale. Thus we may find that the establishment of the kingdom of God comes about after a period of intense distress; God works through human history to bring about his kingdom (Syr. Baruch 25ff.). Otherwise the intervention of a celestial agent, like the heavenly Son of Man in the Similitudes, 'puts down the kings and the mighty from their seats' (1 Enoch 46.1ff.) and establishes a reign of righteousness. At the heart of this approach lies a definite caution with regard to those who claim to be on the point of establishing the kingdom by force of arms (cf. Luke 16.16). The apocalyptic literature is quietist in its approach, preferring to concentrate on urging the righteous to stand firm so that when the kingdom finally does come, they may stand with the elect on Mount Zion (cf. Rev. 14). The apocalypses set out to reveal the totality of the divine plan as a reassurance to the elect and as the basis of their confidence that their obedience to the divine commandments and any suffering that may bring upon them are worthwhile.

(b) Present Response to God and Apocalyptic Fantasy

It is very common to find students of Judaism polarizing Jewish attitudes between rabbinic legalism and eschatological expectation,[12] or priestly, cult-centred religion and the dynamic expectation of the apocalyptists.[13] Such simple summaries of the nature of Judaism have their attractions and the approach has elements of truth in it. The fact is that not enough is done to explore the real nature of such a polarization between various outlooks and the reasons for it.

We have noted that the historical circumstances of Judaism in the Hellenistic and Roman period bred dissatisfaction and hopes for redemption. In so far as the hopes for redemption were themselves the common property of all Jews, we may suspect that the future hope was a feature of the religious and political outlooks of all groups at this time. Nevertheless it would be wrong to minimize the difference in the emphasis placed on eschatology which confronts us in the literature, or to misunderstand the character of the political response, which is involved in it.

One recent commentator on Pharisaism has argued that the first century BCE saw a progressive disengagement of the pharisaic movement from the political arena. In practice this meant involvement with the leading council of the land, the Sanhedrin. It was matched by an increased emphasis on individual piety and by a stress on individual purity through the fulfilment of obligations relating to purity and tithing.[14] What became central was the demand laid upon the individual Jew to reflect the divine holiness. This meant a preoccupation with the minutiae of everyday living and the way in which the circumstances of the day demanded reflection and even modification of the tradition handed down by the fathers. The crucial question now was not, 'Why does God allow circumstances to exist which make true holiness difficult and at times impossible?', but, 'How can the individual best come to terms with the demand of God within the historical framework in which he finds himself?' The decision of the pharisaic-rabbinic tradition to concentrate on the second question rather than the first had several consequences. First of all, it meant that the circumstances in which Jews found themselves were facts of life the changing of which should not normally be of any concern to them (cf. Rom. 13.1). Of course, there were certainly instances where change was urged by Jews, when the circumstances were such that it became impossible for Jews to practise their religion properly, such as Caligula's attempt to erect a statue of himself in the Temple in Jerusalem.[15] Secondly, the concentration of Jews was on the creation of sufficient space for the practice of religion. Once that was achieved, so that purity and ceremonial observance were possible, agitation for change ended. Thirdly, and perhaps most important of all for those who ruled the Jews, this attitude did not conflict too directly with the dominion of the rulers. No doubt there were many instances when the Jews fell foul of the powers that be,[16] but, in fact, this attitude meant that the status quo was accepted; the Jews were to avert their gaze from the wider horizons of the apocalyptic dreams, and turn to the narrower preoccupation with individual and community holiness. That is not to say that there was a repudiation of that wider horizon, for the eschatological hopes of Scripture were retained. Eschatology was something which was left to God alone; he it was who would inaugurate the fulfilment of the promises in his good time. Meanwhile the obligation laid upon the people of God was to present themselves a holy nation of individuals rather than a holy land.

A similar outlook confronts us in the Dead Sea Scrolls. Like the Pharisees, the Qumran community concentrated on holiness, but maintained that its fulfilment depended on *complete* separation. The creation of sufficient space within society itself was not adequate for some of them. They too did not lose their eschatological perspective; the War Scroll indicates how important that was for them. But that preoccupation with universal transformation is subtly undermined in their writings. This is most apparent in those passages which speak of the present communion with heaven enjoyed by members of the community.[17] It has been argued with some conviction that the eschatological bliss reserved for the new age was already believed to be a possibility for the members of the community. As such it provided a diversion from the iniquities of the present age. The closed life of the community in the desert was itself heaven on earth, and as such, the practice of holiness within the community would guarantee the persistence of that compensation for the lack of fulfilment on the cosmic scale of the divine promises.

In contrast to this view, what we know of the Zealots suggests a radically different attitude. As is well known, the Zealots believed that, while the Romans were on the soil of *eretz Israel*, they were defiling the Holy Land, and it became essential to remove them from it by force.[18] For the Zealots personal piety was not enough. Unlike the Pharisees they could not be content with the quest for an answer to the question how God's people might be holy, granted the present political circumstances. For them it was crucial to deal at once with the blight on that quest for holiness which was focused in the Roman presence in the promised land and the compromise of the hierarchy in Jerusalem. The consequences of this outlook were revealed in AD 66, when internecine strife and anarchy followed the departure of the Romans (*BJ* 4.129ff.).

As far as we can ascertain, the hierarchy in Jerusalem itself depended on the continued coexistence with the Romans. If the hint we get from John 11.49 is anything to go by, the priestly-dominated Sanhedrin had reason to fear the possibility of unrest among the populace. They were in danger of losing the focus of their religious supremacy, the Temple, as well as the limited autonomy that they enjoyed. Whatever the dissatisfaction with the Roman hegemony among the priestly aristocracy, by the middle of the first century AD they had become inextricably intertwined with the Romans. The exercise of the High Priestly office depended on the Roman procurator, and the continued running of the Temple and the vast complex of related activities was also dependent on the Roman policy of allowing the religious and political institutions of provinces to continue as far as possible.[19] The fact that the sacrifice prescribed in the Torah could be offered to God in the Temple and that important religious activity centred in the Temple was preserved, meant that the priests had an enormous investment in the continuation of Roman oversight of Judaea.

We have noted what a strong thrust there was towards a pragmatic attitude, both with regard to the maintenance of Roman power and the practical outworking of the faith, granted the continued political and social constraints of the time. The responses of various groups were different, but the majority felt that in practice the biblical idealism had to take second place to a more limited fulfilment of the religious observances within the constraints of a society under foreign domination. But Jews could not escape the reality of their eschatological idealism. We find that the fantasies of the future hope continued to make their appearance. The cosmic concerns of the religion were never allowed to die, despite the factors which compelled some to lay stress on the need for a present, inadequate response. These visions of hope functioned in four ways. First, they demonstrated the way in which the Jewish imagination continually brought to the surface the centrality of that future hope. Secondly, for some they acted as an inspiration to take action in the direction of achieving that utopia which was set out in the visions. Thirdly, they expressed frustration with the socio-economic situation and a longing for divine vengeance and the righting of all wrongs.[20] Fourthly, they offered some an escape from reality, a fantasy of what things might be like and a compensation for the inadequacies of the present, not only for the apocalyptic seer but also for his readers. The reality of the divine world of perfection is established in the visions. A divine dimension to human existence is demonstrated to the readers in the visions of heaven. While it may have had the effect of strengthening adherence to existing religious traditions, that flight into the visionary world often restored support for the status quo by suggesting that while there would be a time of perfection in the future the powers that be (Rom. 13.1) must meanwhile be obeyed as they had been ordained according to God's ordering of the times and seasons.[21]

It would be dangerous to suppose that such dreams of the divine perfection in heaven, the future utopia or the theodicy evident in some apocalyptic communications, were the product of one group or functioned in precisely the same way in all the groups, which made use of this type of thought. We may suppose that the apocalyptic outlook was widely spread within Judaism, but as in every society the dreamers and the pragmatists regarded it in different ways. The pragmatists would not necessarily repudiate it but view it with less sympathy than those who did not have to or did not want to struggle to reach an accommodation with the present order of things. For those who sought to answer the question, 'How shall we be obedient to God, granted the present state of things?' the dreams of redemption and divine glory did not loom so large on the horizon of their everyday practice. Those who found the present state of affairs intolerable, for whatever reason, would have viewed the dreams as a spur to action and a frank rejection of current accommodations. No doubt all shared the same hope; the crucial issue was how that hope coloured the practice of Judaism.

(c) The Crisis for Eschatology

One can only conjecture what the fevered expectation was like in the city of Jerusalem as the siege was intensified by the Roman legions. Josephus gives us a glimpse of the fervent expectation and the insane hopes of deliverance, which circulated among the populace during those tragic days. That the eschatological hopes held in common in different forms by all members of the Jewish religion contributed to the attitudes which brought about the destruction of the city cannot be denied (*BJ* 5.400; 6.285, 364).[22] When one realizes what great suffering such beliefs had caused, and that they brought the Jewish religion to the brink of destruction, it will come as little surprise if it were found that there was a massive reaction against such views in Judaism.

With the destruction of Jerusalem and the cessation of the Temple worship in AD 70, one might have expected a profound shift in the attitudes of the Sages assembled at Jamnia (Yavneh) whose task it was to reorganize the Jewish religion to meet the challenges of an era without the Temple and the long-established institutions of the Jewish faith. It is often suggested that there was a reaction against such eschatological speculations[23] after AD 70 both among Jews and Christians, though for the latter it is assumed that the delay of the parousia was the main reason for a change in eschatological perspective.[24] There is some evidence to suggest that this was indeed the case. Often quoted is a saying of Rabban Yohanan ben Zakkai, the great architect of rabbinic Judaism, which seems to indicate a certain reserve towards eschatological matters:

> If you have a seedling in your hand, and they say to you, Look, here comes the Messiah, Go out and plant the seedling first and then come to meet him (*Aboth de Rabbi Nathan* 31).

But while the saying indicates that messianic claims should be treated with some degree of caution, there is in fact nothing here which indicates a repudiation of eschatology. Indeed, considering what problems it had caused, it seems surprising that there is such a positive piece of advice given by Yohanan. Such an assessment fits in very well with what we know of the attitudes which developed after the Revolt.[25] Included in the Tefillah, a prayer reformulated after the fall of Jerusalem, were several prayers for eschatological fulfilment. Particularly worthy of note are Benedictions 7, 9, 10, 11, 14 and 16:

7   Look on our affliction and plead our cause and redeem us for thy name's sake.

9   Bless this year for us, Lord our God and cause all its produce to prosper. Bring quickly the year of our final redemption; and give dew and rain to the land; and satisfy the world from the treasuries of thy goodness; and bless the work of our hands.

10   Proclaim the liberation with the great trumpet and raise a banner to gather together our dispersed.

11   Restore our judges as in former times and our counsellors as in the beginning; and reign over us, thou alone.

14   Be merciful, Lord our God, with thy great mercies, to Israel thy people and to Jerusalem thy city; and to Zion, the dwelling place of thy glory; and to thy Temple and thy habitation; and to the kingship of David thy righteous Messiah.

16   Be pleased, Lord our God and dwell in Zion; and may thy servants serve thee in Jerusalem.

Nowhere is the continuing strength of the eschatological hope more evident than in these words, which formed a regular part of the worship of Jews. The fervent hope for redemption and the restoration of Israel's fortunes was kept alive in the bleakest days of all for Judaism. That these hopes loomed large on the Jewish horizon during this period is testified by the outbreak of a second revolt against Rome in AD 132.[26] Information about the causes and course of this revolt are scanty in the extreme, but we may be sure that the continuation in so firm a fashion of these beliefs must have had a large part to play in fanning the discontent and the hope of liberation. Indeed, the fact that another leading figure of the early second-century rabbinic Judaism, Rabbi Akiba, identified Simeon ben Koseba, the leader of the revolt as the messiah (*j. Ta'anith* 68d) is another indication of the level of support given to such expectations and their fulfilment by a leader of nascent rabbinic Judaism. The thing which strikes one most about early rabbinic Judaism is not the reserve which is encountered from time to time in these texts about eschatology, but the fact that such hopes continued to linger on; not in some attenuated form but in the full-blooded expectation of an imminent restoration of Israel's fortunes, despite the manifest failure of such eschatological fantasies in the débâcle of the First Revolt.

Even if the case cannot be made for the diminution of eschatological ideas after the fall of the Second Temple, there does seem to be evidence to support the view that there was an increased emphasis in this period on what might be termed the 'vertical' dimension of the relationship with God, communion with the divine, i.e. mysticism. Research into the beginnings of Jewish mysticism has advanced considerably in the last thirty years, thanks largely to the pioneering work of Gershom Scholem. What is now becoming clear is that already, during the period of the Second Temple and extending back considerably into the early Hellenistic period, there was a developed mystical lore based on the study of the first chapter of Ezekiel, the *merkabah*.[27] We have already noted that in the apocalyptic literature there is evidence of this interest, and the suggestion was made that some of these visions may reflect the actual experience of unknown mystics, who preferred to cloak their experience under the garb of some ancient worthy. Interest in the divine throne chariot (*merkabah*) continued in early rabbinic Judaism. If we can assume that the early rabbis continued in the mystical-visionary praxis, then the study of the first chapter of Ezekiel would offer communion with the divine which was bound to give reassurance in times of crisis.[28]

Communion with the divine in the life of the religious community is not something which was confined to mystics. After all, the rabbinic literature is full of evidence to suggest that rabbis believed that the Divine Presence, the *shekinah*, was with rabbis and indeed any group studying the Torah,[29] yet for the élite who were privileged to become part of the tradition of the exponents of the mysteries of theosophy and cosmology the mystical communion with God and his world afforded a glimpse into a world which was cut off from ordinary mortals. The knowledge of the celestial mysteries and the contemplation of them were an effective antidote to the demoralizing effects of oppression and despair in the world of men.

Such a belief that it was possible to taste in the present age the glories of Paradise is attested in the Qumran Scrolls, as we have seen. In the *Hodayoth*, the Hymns, there are several passages which indicate that the community believed that it already participated in the lot of the angels, a belief which is to be found elsewhere in the literature of Judaism, particularly in the apocalypses. Inherent in apocalyptic is an interest in the world above, as it existed above the firmament, quite independent of any future expectation.[30] Not only did the apocalyptists see heaven as the repository of secrets about the world to come but also as a realm, which existed above and in which they could participate, albeit on a temporary basis. In the Qumran texts not only do we find in the War Scroll (12.1ff.) that the community is said to be engaged in a cosmic struggle, but it also thought of itself participating in the life of Paradise, the life of the angels. Geza Vermes has pointed out this particular aspect of the sect's existence and indicated its relationship to the mystical beliefs of the Jewish apocalyptic-mystical tradition:

> The aim of the holy life lived within the covenant was to penetrate the secrets of heaven in this world and to stand before God for ever in the next. Like Isaiah who beheld the Seraphim proclaiming 'Holy, holy, holy' and, like Ezekiel, who in a trance watched the winged Cherubim drawing the divine Throne-Chariot, and like the ancient Jewish mystics who consecrated themselves, despite official disapproval by the rabbis, to the contemplation of the same Throne-Chariot and the heavenly places, the Essenes too strove for a similar mystical knowledge ... The earthly liturgy was intended to be a replica of that sung by the choirs of angels in the heavenly Temple.[31]

In a similar vein we find the writer of the Jewish(-Christian?) hymn book, the Odes of Solomon,[32] which has many affinities with Qumran theology, stressing that it was possible during the worship of his group for its members to participate in the glory of the end-time. In 11.16f. (cf. 20.7) the writer talks about being taken up to Paradise. At the very least, he thinks that, like Paul (2 Corinthians 12.3), he can enjoy the heavenly Paradise in the present rather than having to wait for the coming of the new age for that privilege, as in Revelation 2.7. Elsewhere the writer uses the language of the heavenly ascent to speak of the glories which he experienced in the life of the community:

> I rested on the spirit of the Lord, and she lifted me up to heaven and caused me to stand on my feet in the Lord's high place before his perfection and glory (cf. 1 *QH* 3.20: I walk on limitless level ground, and I know there is hope for him whom thou hast shaped from dust for the everlasting Council).

Many years ago R. M. Grant suggested that we should look for the origin of gnosticism in the frustrated eschatological hopes of groups like that found at Qumran.[33] He pointed out that there is in apocalyptic a vertical dimension which, when loosed from the horizontal-eschatological dimension, quickly becomes a form of spirituality, which is akin to gnosticism.[34] Whether such Jewish theology ever took the path suggested by Grant, we cannot at present be certain. What is clear, however, is that there did exist within Judaism a

ready-made compensation for the crisis over the fulfilment of the eschatological hopes in the apocalyptic tradition itself. It needed only a change of
emphasis for the apocalyptic-mystical tradition to concentrate more on the
vertical dimension of its spirituality than the horizontal, with the latter's
emphasis on the fulfilment of the divine promises in history. The uncertainty
of the times meant that a crisis for eschatological hopes was inevitable, but
the support and sustenance which the mystical element of religion offered to
Jews at this time tempered the worst effects of these disasters.

PART III
The Emergence of a Messianic Sect

Section 1
Introduction

1

Early Christianity: What Kind of Religious Movement?

What were the factors which brought the Christian movement into existence? What kind of people were the early Christians? What were the dominant features of its belief and practice? Answers to questions like these may help us to understand what kind of religious development we are dealing with in the early Church.[1]

From the material which we possess in the New Testament, it is apparent that early Christianity spread rapidly. The stories of the beginnings of Christianity in Jerusalem suggest that we are dealing with an outbreak of religious enthusiasm based on the conviction that Jesus of Nazareth had been raised from the dead, that the promised Spirit had been poured out on all flesh and that therefore the message of Jesus about the imminent reign of God had been confirmed by a mighty act of God. The movement in its initial stages bore all the hallmarks of an enthusiastic group. In the communities which were founded by Paul, there is little evidence of strict control by church officials and the initial enthusiasm of the Jerusalem church seems to have been prevalent (Acts 2), particularly if the Corinthian correspondence is anything to go by. The opportunity for wider participation in religious activity by women as well as men (1 Cor. 11.5), poor as well as rich, was obviously a factor working in favour of the spread of Christianity as a popular movement. When one adds to this the obvious advantage its Pauline form had over other types of Judaism, in not demanding the rite of circumcision as a means of entry into community, it will be seen that Christianity would have offered considerable attractions to a wide group of people.

If Paul is to be believed, the adherents to the new movement were mostly from the lower social classes.[2] The evidence of the infiltration of Christianity into the higher social strata by the end of the first century is not great, though Luke makes every attempt to show what an appreciative attitude was shown to the new movement by Roman officials. According to the traditions in the Gospels, some of the disciples of Jesus themselves came from the lower

111

strata of society and are decribed as uneducated and common men in Acts 4.13 (but cf. Mark 1.16ff.).[3] While one would not want to exclude the possibility that Jesus and the early Church were influenced by pharisaic ideas and practices, particularly in their attitude towards tradition and in the interpretation of Scripture, there is little to suggest that the early Christian movement, either in Jesus' lifetime or after, was characterized by the same outlook as that of the Scribes. The rigid separation between clean and unclean, pious and common people, is hardly evident (Luke 7.34).

One of the main reasons for the enthusiasm of early Christianity lies in its character as what may be loosely termed a millenarian movement.[4] Hope of the reordering of the cosmos by God was a central feature of early Christian experience. Groups, who hold such beliefs, have a clear understanding of their own election and the ultimate character of the message of hope, which they proclaim and to which they exist to bear witness. Inevitably their integration into society at large is considerably affected by the cluster of ideas which they hold. The belief that the present order is passing away and the expectation that a new world will soon come into being means that there is bound to be an uneasy coexistence between the supporters of such a religious outlook and the rest of society. The information at our disposal from early Christian literature does not permit us to know precisely about the nature of this coexistence in the first century of the Church's life. From the pages of the New Testament there is not much indication that early Christians separated themselves from the world and avoided all social intercourse (though note 1 Cor. 5.9; 2 Cor. 6.14.). Monasticism on the Essene model of the group who wrote the Dead Sea Scrolls, was not generally a pattern of life favoured by Christians.[5] But they certainly thought that the present order was about to pass away (1 Cor. 7.26; 29; 31). Thus early Christians had an ideology which conflicted in many respects with those prevailing in society, while at the same time remaining to a considerable extent part of that society, practising trades and, within the limits tolerated by their beliefs, participating in the life of society generally (but note 2 Thess. 3.6).[6] Involvement in the life of the world inevitably brought Christians into contact with pagans, and the reactions to Christians indicate the suspicion with which they were viewed. 'Hated by the populace', Tacitus says of them.[7] Later on we find them despised for their 'atheism' and their contempt for the traditional religion of Rome by their refusal to burn a small piece of incense to the genius of the emperor. However much they wanted to be fully integrated into society (a process which only began with Constantine),[8] there remained the suspicion that at moments of crisis early Christians would be bound to say 'we must obey God rather than men' (Acts 5.29). The problem with millenarian groups is that when fervent hopes become disappointed by events the group which holds such beliefs has to come to terms with disappointment, e.g., 1 Thess. 4.13ff.[9] It is frequently suggested that the delay in the second coming of Christ led to such a disappointment for early Christians that there was a need for reorientation in its attitude. Hope for the future ceased to be the central feature of the early Christian outlook and instead other interests took over.

But what evidence is there that early Christianity was a millenarian, or at least an eschatologically-orientated, movement? To answer that I want to turn now to the issue of the centrality of eschatology in the New Testament.

2

The Centrality of Eschatology in Primitive Christian Belief[1]

All too often eschatology has had the appearance of the final item of Christian doctrine, tacked on as an afterthought, concerned only with the ultimate hopes of Christianity. The reasons for this are manifold. Christian doctrine has tended to settle on the incarnation, atonement and resurrection as paramount. What is more, the eschatological beliefs of the New Testament are not readily appealing to modern believers. Eschatology seems to be an appendage, whose integration within the overall scheme of salvation is not always apparent. Such a view of eschatology seems rather strange, however, to those who have studied the character of biblical scholarship, particularly over the last hundred years.[2] The fact is that there has been a widespread recognition that, whatever the consequences for our theology, we have to grapple with the centrality of eschatology as a controlling and dominant theme in early Christian belief. The meaning of phrases like the Kingdom of God and the Son of Man cannot be disentangled from the eschatological thread which runs through the pages of the New Testament.

The problem is that eschatology is a concept which is not easy to define.[3] Strictly speaking, eschatology is to do with the study of the Last Things, those events which will bring history and this world to its close. Yet we have to recognize that we regularly use the word in a variety of different senses, some of which extend the meaning of the phrase to such an extent that the connection with the original future orientation has virtually disappeared.[4] Thus we can find the term being used to describe the critical nature of human decisions, the fate of the individual believer's soul after death, the termination of this world-order and a setting up of another, events like the Last Judgement and the Resurrection of the Dead and merely as a convenient way of referring to future hopes about the coming of God's kingdom on earth, irrespective of whether in fact they involve an ending of the historical process. It is in this last sense that I want to use it, as a shorthand way of referring to this future hope and its fulfilment.

When we consider Christian doctrine as a whole, it is the cross which is seen by many as the moment of salvation, when the believer is reconciled to God.[5] By concentrating on this, we may lose sight of the fact that for most New Testament writers there is still an unfulfilled element in the process of salvation. Certainly the believer may have tasted of the heavenly gift and participated in the Holy Spirit (Heb. 6.4), but that is not by any means the end of the matter. There is still what is called an 'eschatalogical reservation', a qualification which indicates that the fullness of salvation is still to be experienced by the individual and manifested in the world (Rom. 8.18ff.; 1 John 3.2).[6] It is when we appreciate how pervasive this tension is between what believers have already experienced in Christ *now* and what they still have to wait for (the '*not yet*'), that we can begin to grasp that the early Christian view of salvation has an eschatological dimension, which is often lacking in later Christian schemes and is intimately linked with the understanding of the impact of the death and resurrection of Jesus Christ.

If one pauses to think about the matter, it becomes difficult to see how Jewish writers who believed that Jesus was Messiah, could have conceived of salvation in any other than eschatological terms, the fulfilment of divine promises in history. The bulk of the Jewish literature which has come down to us views salvation in the context of history. Thus the dominion of the God of Abraham, Isaac and Jacob over all flesh is intimately linked with the belief in him as creator and redeemer. Whether the urgency for deliverance was strong or not, the formative experiences of the nation, like the Exodus, spoke of the deliverance and triumph of the people of God, the manifestation of the mighty hand of God in the affairs of men. Thus it is impossible to imagine that salvation could be considered as in any way complete without reference to the fulfilment of that hope for God's kingdom to come on earth.

The eschatological dimensions of salvation are apparent in the early Christian writings. It is instructive to examine some of the most important New Testament concepts, for by so doing, we shall find that it is impossible to understand their significance without taking account of eschatology. Take resurrection, for example. It goes without saying that the resurrection of Jesus has become a cornerstone of the Church's faith, and is already important within the New Testament itself. What we are dealing with, however, is not just a dramatic intervention of God to vindicate his son but a conviction about Jesus, whose meaning is governed entirely by eschatology. What is often lost sight of today is the fact that for Jews and early Christians the resurrection was an essential component of the future hope. To speak of the resurrection of the dead was to speak of the life of the Age to Come.[7] From time to time in the New Testament we have hints that such a close link exists between resurrection and the eschatological events (e.g., 1 Cor. 15.20; Phil. 3.21). The resurrection of Jesus of Nazareth was the firstfruits, a proleptic event, in which a feature of the end-time becomes a reality in the old aeon. Thus in so far as the first Christians spoke of the resurrection of Jesus and made it a cornerstone of their existence as a sect, they were affirming that for them the future hope was already in the process of fulfilment and was not merely an item of faith still to be realized at some point in the future. We cannot, therefore, ignore the fact that, by stressing the centrality of resurrection, the early Christian writers were making eschatology the key to the understanding of their religious outlook.

The New Testament writers looked forward to an imminent manifestation of the righteousness of God, when Jesus returned as Lord to complete the process which had started in the events of his ministry, culminating with the cross and resurrection.[8] The departure of the Son of Man is only a temporary phenomenon, for he would be revealed (1 Cor. 1.7; 1 Pet. 1.7) and would bring about the times of restoration of all things foretold by the prophets (Acts 3.21). Clearly, that was an event not far distant (Rom. 13.11; Rev. 22.20), though the New Testament writers are uniformly unwilling to be too specific about the exact date (Mark 9.1; 13.32; 1 Thess. 5.1; cf. 2 Thess. 2.2f.). What is not in doubt, however, is that the return of Christ on the clouds of heaven was no arbitrary belief, plucked out of the stock of Jewish eschatology. It was intimately linked with the convictions about the resurrection, in that the coming of Christ on the clouds of heaven was the consummation of a promise of which the resurrection of Jesus was the guarantee.

From this it is clear that the early Christians believed that the eschatological salvation was not wholly future, particularly since the New Aeon had broken into the old in the resurrection of Jesus. But the experience of the new age was not confined solely to what had happened to a figure in the recent past, for the experience of the Spirit, such a dominant feature of early Christian religion,[9] cannot be understood apart from the eschatological perspective. In the New Testament the Spirit is frequently linked with prophecy.[10] While it would be wrong to suppose that there was a unified view of the Spirit's activity in contemporary Judaism, there is good evidence to suppose that many Jews thought of the Spirit's activity as part of the past of Israel.[11] Thus the inspiration by the Spirit was confined to the era of the prophets and would only be operative again when new prophets arose, in the Messianic Age. The present aeon was characterized by the absence of the Spirit, and the future glorious aeon would be a time when the Spirit, and therefore prophecy, would return.[12]

Paul certainly seems to hint that experience of the Spirit is closely linked with the eschatological hope. Thus, in outlining the present period of travail in Romans 8.18ff., he speaks of Christians being the ones who have the firstfruits of the Spirit (v.23). The implication is that, despite having already tasted of that glory (cf. Heb. 6.5), even Christians long for a greater redemption still to be made manifest; Christians too, therefore, join in the travail of the messianic woes (cf. 2 Cor. 1.22). Similarly in Acts 2.17, the writer of Acts indicates that the pouring out of the Spirit on the day of Pentecost is a fulfilment of an eschatological promise from the book of Joel. The quotation in Acts interprets the phrase 'afterwards' by the words 'in the last days', an indication that the phenomenon at Pentecost was a fulfilment of the eschatological promise of the return of the Spirit. The experience of the Spirit was seen as the present expression in the life of the individual and the community of that eschatological reality, which had been manifested in the resurrection of Jesus of Nazareth from the dead.

A central feature of Christology in the New Testament is the use in various ways of the title Christ of Jesus of Nazareth. The exploration of the fast-growing doctrine concerning the person of Christ in the earliest period, culminating with the doctrine of the incarnation,[13] should not lead us to ignore the important role the title 'christ' plays in the New Testament writings. Even those documents, like the Fourth Gospel, which want to affirm that Jesus of Nazareth is much more than merely the Messiah, also want to indicate that he is the agent of salvation longed for by Jews (John 20.31; cf. 7.27, 40–4). It is not that Christians were saying that Jesus fulfilled *all* Jewish messianic expectations, which in themselves were many and various,[14] but that he was the agent of eschatological salvation. Even Paul, who is sometimes accused of using the title 'christ' as little more than a proper name,[15] on occasions uses the term as a Jewish technical term to denote the fact that God has acted through Jesus to bring about salvation. As mediator of salvation, it would be only natural for the early Christians to have spoken of Jesus as the Christ. Whatever else it may indicate, the fact that the title has passed into the common usage of the New Testament means that it was a primary category for early Christian expression of their convictions about the eschatological character of the mission of Jesus of Nazareth.

But it would be a mistake to suppose that early Christian reflection on Jesus marks the moment when eschatological categories began to dominate Christian views of Jesus. In this there is surely continuity between the proclamation of Jesus and early Christian reflection upon him. The declaration that Jesus was the Messiah (Acts 2.36) raised from the dead is another way of affirming the reality which Jesus in his own mission and message set out to proclaim. Nearly all commentators are agreed that, whatever the precise background of the phrase 'the kingdom of God', Jesus of Nazareth set out to proclaim its imminence, perhaps even its inauguration. The early Christian kerygma that Jesus was raised from the dead is to be regarded as an alternative way of expressing the conviction which confronts us in the teaching of Jesus: God's kingdom is at hand (Mark 1.15);

in Jesus' resurrection the life of the age to come has drawn near.

In the light of all this it must be said that the book of Revelation, in the view of many an eccentric part of the New Testament canon, is much nearer to the centre of early Christian belief than is often allowed. Not only the thrust of its eschatological message but also its concern with fulfilment (e.g. Rev. 5) indicate how accurately it mirrors, albeit in the imagery of apocalyptic, the central message of the New Testament. The eschatological message of the book of Revelation, therefore, is in essential continuity with those major voices of New Testament theology, Jesus and Paul. To understand the heart of the New Testament is to grapple with the message of hope in the pages of the Apocalypse.[16]

3

The World of Jesus and the First Christians

The Christian religion was born in Palestine, though the majority of the earliest literary witnesses to the Christian faith were not written there. Our earliest Christian sources are written in Greek and are addressed to Christian groups, which were, for the most part, outside Palestine. Yet it was the beliefs and social world of Palestine which gave the Christian movement its distinctive direction. According to our sources, Jerusalem was the place where Jesus of Nazareth finally perished at the hands of the Romans. While Judaea, the Roman province, certainly seems to have been the setting for part of his ministry (more evident in the Fourth Gospel than the Synoptics), a large part of it had been set in Galilee. That distinction is not without its significance, and a consideration of the social and political life in Galilee may help us to get into perspective the character of Jesus' ministry and that of his immediate followers, all of whom, according to our sources, came from this area.

There has been a major study of Galilee in this period by Sean Freyne, and the following paragraphs are indebted to it.[1] Freyne paints a picture of Galilee as a region inhabited by peasants settled in villages, who occupied themselves in farming. The large cities in the area (e.g., Tiberias and Sepphoris) which were Hellenized seem to have exercised little influence on the rural area. There was some tension between the cities and the rural inhabitants.[2] By and large the region fared better than Judaea.[3] The long reign of Herod Antipas may have cushioned the worst effects of Roman rule, and there was a reluctance to interfere with the pattern of life of such a relatively settled society. Freyne points to the growth of a rural proletariat (consisting of day labourers, see Matt. 20.1ff.; 'hired servants' in Mark 1.20; Luke 16.1ff.; cf. Mark 12.1ff.). This rural proletariat had less to lose and, suggests Freyne, had become more conscious of their lot; 'the rural proletariat was likely to have made common cause with the agents of change'.[4] There was injustice in the province, with economic pressures on the small man in both urban and rural settings, as the result of increased taxation, ambitious rulers and foreign exploitation.

Despite this, Freyne is reluctant to agree with the widely held belief that Galilee was a hotbed of revolutionary activity. Although Judas the Galilean led the uprising against Rome in AD 6 (*BJ* 2.118; *Ant.* 18.23f.; also 6–10; cf. *Ant.* 18.118), it should be pointed out that this uprising was based in Judaea. He suggests that the attitude of Jews in Tiberias, who resorted to a peaceful agricultural strike rather than violent resistance in the affair of Caligula's statue, points to a rather different atmosphere in Galilee from that in the more politically inflammable Judaea (*Ant.* 18.274; 284). He does not exclude the existence of such revolutionary ideas, but stresses that Galilee was much less susceptible to revolutionary fervour than Judaea. In Galilee the continued round of farming and the quest for subsistence meant that for a significant part of the rural population there was little incentive to revolt, when the need to stay alive dampened revolutionary ardour (*BJ* 4.84). The scattered Galilean hamlets did not provide the proper political and social environment for the revolutionary movements to flourish. Centuries of political isolation had made those who were able to maintain any kind of stable links with the land, cautious about any large-scale movement that drew its inspiration from the religious and urban conditions of Jerusalem. Certainly Galilee was caught up in the First Revolt in AD 66, but even in this Freyne thinks that it fared marginally better than Judaea.

In its religious attitudes it seems to have been remarkably conservative. The Temple was held in high regard, though there was some antipathy towards tithing (*Ant.* 20.181; *b. Ket.* 105b); God in his Temple provided the fertility and prosperity necessary for subsistence (cf. the prophecy of Haggai). The regular round of pilgrimages to Jerusalem functioned as an emotional outlet for the deeply felt loyalty to the Temple. Pharisaic religion had only a marginal hold in the region in the settlements along Lake Tiberias. It was unlikely that the majority of people were affected by its attitudes. The scribal religion of Jerusalem made little impact. Their religious attitude was, in the words of Freyne, the product of a 'Sadducean ethos'. It was centred on the Temple, and as long as it stood, it continued to be the focus of interest for the Jews there.

Alongside this fairly conservative pattern of religion, Freyne notes the emergence of a tradition of holy men, the *hasidim*.[5] He contrasts their fortunes in Galilee with their fortunes in Judaea. Whereas in the latter they would go to the desert and separate themselves completely from society, the holy men in Galilee tended to live on the fringes of society and highlighted more clearly an alternative life-style. Jesus's life-style as a wandering figure is reflected in his sayings, the preservation of which is indicative of the continuation of that life-style in groups which followed him.[6] According to Freyne, the Jesus-movement was first of all based in rural areas, and when it began to set foot in the urban centres, it began to attract opposition from the more established forms of Judaism (Matt. 23.34ff.). Jesus' condemnation of the Galilean centres of population suggests the rural setting of the original movement (Matt. 11.20ff.; Luke 10.13f.). Certainly Jesus seemed to avoid the Herodian towns. In the light of this, it is interesting to note that, according to Paul, some of Jesus' brothers continued this wandering activity (1 Cor. 9.5; Euseb. *EH* 1.7).

How far we are able to trace the importance of Galilee within the history of Christianity is a much debated issue. Much will depend on the assessment of the traditions now contained in the Fourth Gospel. While a case may be made for the use of this material, it is clear that we are in the realm of speculation in reading too much into it for the reconstruction of Galilean Christianity. Such a task is not as important as noting the character of the region, in which the Christian movement had its origins. While it may be true that, like other areas, Galilee had its fair share of landless poor, it can hardly be said that this had the effect of making it a hotbed of revolution in our period. There is little to suggest that a message of the inauguration of the kingdom of God would have been more welcomed in this area than say, in Judaea, where eschatological fervour was more securely based. A simple explanation of the eschatological message of Jesus merely on the basis of economic and social factors, is, therefore, inadequate.[7] It is true that we know little enough about Jesus' own background and the immediate prelude to his ministry. All the indications are, however, that he did not himself belong to the rural proletariat, among whom the flames of revolution would have been particularly hot. The Gospels portray him as the child of an artisan (Mark 6.3), from humble circumstances to be sure, but not obviously such as to promote an outlook which by itself initiated the demand for change.

While Galilee provided the background for the first seeds of the Christian movement, the ground in which those seeds were to grow was varied in the extreme. Rapidly an important group of Christians was centred in Jerusalem, as both Paul's letters and the Acts of the Apostles testify. The peculiar characteristics of the city, centre as it was of the cult and eschatological hopes (cf. Isa. 2), inevitably produced problems which would have been unparalleled elsewhere. The fact that Jerusalem was the focal point of the devotion of Jews throughout the Mediterranean world necessarily meant that special factors were at work here. What is more, it meant that the church in this city was regarded with a special affection and respect, which was not true of other centres, at least until the growing ascendancy of the church of Rome and other metropolitan centres. Tensions are evident in Acts between Jerusalem and Antioch (Acts 15; cf. Acts 8). Once the Church moved from Palestinian soil, the factors which governed its growth and development differed with the centres in which it was found.[8] What is apparent is that what started life in Galilee as a movement among the rural groups and among itinerant charismatics came to take root in urban centres. What little we can glean about the mission of the Church suggests that it did take root among the urban communities and though not exclusively lower class, it tended to recruit mainly from that echelon of society. There can be little doubt that the more we can place the early Christians within the particular social world of their cities, the more we shall be able to understand of the issues and beliefs which tended to loom largest on their religious horizons.[9]

Some recent sociological studies of early Christianity have enabled further amplification of our knowledge of the social structure of the Christian communities and the problems which confronted them. As may be expected, it has been the Corinthian correspondence which has offered the most obvious opportunity for the development of this method. In several articles on the subject Theissen has argued that it was tension between social groups which caused some of the problems in the Corinthian church.[10] He repudiates the suggestion often made in the light of 1 Corinthians 1.26ff. that the church was entirely made up of the lower classes and mentions as examples of the upper classes Crispus (1.14; cf. Acts 18.8) and Stephanas (1 Cor. 1.14–16; 16.15–18).[11] He has argued that Paul concentrated his work among the artisans and merchant classes, and concludes that the most important members of the congregation were people of some influence and wealth. Indeed, Paul claims only to have baptized those who came from the higher strata: Stephanas, Crispus and Gaius (1 Cor. 1.14–16), who, as God-fearers, were likely to have been of a higher social standing. The church in Corinth, however, expanded with people from the lower end of the social scale. It was the Christians from the upper classes, who were accustomed to eating meat daily; this contrasted with the lower classes, for whom the eating of meat would have been associated with pagan religious festivals (1 Cor. 8). Even when they came together to eat the Lord's Supper, the weak and the strong revealed the different attitudes they had derived from their social background. The rich continued to expect that the differentiation between themselves and the poor in the quantity and quality of the food eaten would have been carried on.

That such research into the class structure of the provincial cities and the earliest Christian communities can be of great benefit to our understanding of the development of the Christian Church cannot be doubted.[12] Even if not all the judgements of Theissen with regard to the problems in Corinth stand up to subsequent examination, he has succeeded in pointing out some important factors in the mission of Christianity which inevitably had their effects on the development of the Church. It is impossible that within the house-church, the patriarchial system of the family would not make its presence felt within the structure of the nascent community. It should be noted that in urging the Corinthian Christians to take note of the admonitions of the earliest converts, Paul is urging them to listen to one who in all probability was himself the head of a household. In this kind of situation, whatever chance there was of the ideals of 1 Corinthians 12.13 being worked out in practice was severely restricted by the social forces at work. If Theissen is right to suppose that part of the problem at Corinth was the social stratification, then we have here one of the earliest examples of the problems of society at large spilling over into the life of the Church. The millenarian movement confronts the cold blast of a stratified society.

Section 2

Jesus

1

The Quest for the Historical Jesus[1]

It hardly needs to be said that Jesus of Nazareth has always been central to the interests of Christians down the centuries. But it is also fair to say that this interest has for the most part been viewed through the lens of the fully-fledged belief in his divinity. His words and deeds on earth were those of the incarnate second person of the Trinity, not the deeds of any ordinary human being. With the rise of historical criticism from the eighteenth century onwards, such an ecclesiastical portrait was not immune from criticism. The renewed interest in history meant that instead of viewing Jesus solely in terms of the history of salvation as told in the Bible, the world in which he lived, both Jewish and Hellenistic, gradually became an important reference for understanding of his mission and message. What is more, the attempt to ascertain what really happened and the tools of secular history inevitably had their effect on the method of New Testament research.

It will come as no surprise, therefore, to find that in the course of time the quest for the historical Jesus manifested a distinct unease, if not downright scepticism, with regard to the stories in the Gospels. The search for what really happened necessitated the use of patient study of the sources to get behind the Church's dogmatic presentation of Jesus to the original man and his message. This meant peeling away the layers of accretion added by early Christians as they sought to express their faith in the one who was seen by them as Lord and God. The nature of this process is discussed in one of the most famous lives of Jesus written by David Friedrich Strauss and translated into English by George Eliot.[2] He speaks as follows about his method:

> When therefore we meet with an account of certain phenomena or events of which it is either expressly stated or implied that they were produced immediately by God himself (divine apparitions, voices from heaven and the like), or by human beings possessed of supernatural powers (miracles and prophecies), such an account is to be considered as not historical. And, inasmuch, in general, the intermingling of the spiritual world with the human is found only in inauthentic

122

records, and is irreconcilable with all just conceptions; so narratives of angels and devils, of their appearing in human shape and interfering with human concerns, cannot possibly be received as historical.

The quest for the historical Jesus went hand in hand with the emerging interest in source criticism. If one wanted to return to the Jesus of history, some attempt had to be made to assess which of the sources offered the nearest in time and content to Jesus himself. This meant in time the establishment of the hypothesis that the Gospel of Mark was the first canonical gospel to be written.[3]

The story of this remarkable period in the study of early Christianity, particularly as it applies to the study of the quest for the historical Jesus, is told in that famous book by Albert Schweitzer, translated into English as *The Quest of the Historical Jesus*. It surveys the nineteenth-century quest from its start in the fragments of the German scholar Reimarus to its later manifestations in the work of the early twentieth-century scholar, Wrede.

The book itself manifests many of the shortcomings of its predecessors, whose views are set out so eloquently, but it also established a fact, which has dominated New Testament study, and in particular the study of the life of Jesus, ever since. In his own reconstruction of the life of Jesus, Schweitzer placed undue reliance on the chronological information of the Gospels, in order to establish Jesus' change of attitude after the disciples had been sent out on their mission (Matt. 10, especially 10.23), so that he believed Jesus expected to suffer and take upon himself the messianic woes. Schweitzer demonstrated for good the shortcomings of the quest, which had taken place hitherto. It was the half-hearted rigour of the quest for Jesus and his historical setting, which really emerged in Schweitzer's presentation. The scholars may have tried hard to get back behind the Church's teachings by stripping away the legendary and Jewish accretions, but the picture that had emerged at the end was of a Jesus, who spoke of the fatherhood of God and a simple moral message of brotherhood and goodwill.[4]

The English Jesuit George Tyrrell said that the nineteenth-century German quest for the historical Jesus resembled the situation where a man looked down a deep well and saw his own reflection in the bottom.[5] The simple moral message of Jesus was not a first-century Jesus at all, but the pale reflection of the values and aspirations of a nineteenth-century liberal outlook. No doubt that there are insights a-plenty in the various attempts to pursue this quest, but the fact was, as Schweitzer's book indicated, that the quest was nothing like radical enough. It had only paid lip-service to the application of the historical method.

While few would want to defend the details of Schweitzer's own reconstruction, the dominant theme of that reconstruction has stood the test of time. That element which Schweitzer demonstrated so painstakingly was the centrality of eschatology in the ministry of Jesus. Not that the insight itself was anything new. In a book which had been published ten years or so before, Johannes Weiss[6] had established the central importance of the Kingdom of God in the message of Jesus and the need to set that concept in the context of first-century Jewish eschatalogical beliefs. This was something which had become more easy to do after the discovery of various non-canonical Jewish works during the previous hundred years (e.g., Ethiopic Enoch) which had broadened the knowledge of contemporary Jewish beliefs.

For many, Schweitzer's solution is an unpalatable one. It offers us a picture of a Jesus whose whole outlook is dominated by a zealous eschatological conviction and who in the end dies a disappointed man. Schweitzer's Jesus is a strange figure and one who does not fit easily into our world. This eschatological Jesus and the strangeness of his life and message have been the lasting contribution of Schweitzer and Weiss, and it is worth recalling those famous words with which Schweitzer started the closing chapters of his book; they are a reminder of the strangeness of the world we are entering:

> The study of the life of Jesus has had a curious history. It set out in quest for the historical Jesus, believing that when it had found him, it could bring him straight back into our time as a teacher and saviour. It loosed the bands by which he had been riveted for centuries to the stony rocks of ecclesiastical doctrine, and rejoiced to see life and movement coming into the figure once more, and the historical Jesus advancing, as it seemed, to meet it. But he does not stay; he passes by our own time and returns to his own. What surprised and dismayed the theology of the last forty years was that, despite all forced and arbitrary interpretations it could not keep him in our own time, but had to let him go.[7]

In many ways Schweitzer's work marked a watershed in research into the life of Jesus. For one thing it placed eschatology at the centre of the stage, from which it has been difficult to dislodge it. Secondly, it was followed with a different and less optimistic theological ethos, the theology of Barth and Bultmann. There is a sense in which the theology of Barth, based as it is on the revealed word of God, is about a God who is unknown and unknowable to man, except through what he has chosen to reveal of himself. The belief that it was man's intellect which could enable him to find out what Jesus was really like was given a severe jolt by Barth. Such an attitude could be regarded as a sign of human arrogance, an unwillingness to submit oneself to the revelation of God in Christ. In the aftermath of the First World War Barth's theology took root.[8] With it there grew up the discipline of Form Criticism in New Testament studies. As practised by Rudolf Bultmann this involved a much more radical scepticism with regard to the gospel tradition.[9] The Gospels were the construction of the Church, and the attempt to get behind our present texts to the kernel of the story was, in many cases, viewed as a forlorn quest, as the origin of many of the stories was within the life of the Church. The disputes and stories were thus more reflections of early Christian controversy than of the life of Jesus. The Gospels were better able to tell us about the Church than about Jesus.

Doubts were expressed about the necessity for the quest. What mattered was not what the historical Jesus said; he, after all, was merely part of the preparation for the gospel and did not preach the gospel.[10] It was Christ crucified and risen again as preached by the early Church and in particular by Paul, which was the heart of the Church's proclamation. In this was the call to decision by mankind to new life in Christ. The quest for the historical Jesus did not serve the elucidation of the gospel. Rather it was an antiquarian quest which would prove relatively fruitless.[11] It should be said at once that Bultmann himself did not believe that it was impossible to find out anything about the historical Jesus. He himself wrote a book on Jesus,[12] and his attitude to the historicity of certain sayings is not as sceptical as is sometimes made out. Nevertheless, of one thing he was not in doubt; there was little point in pursuing this task. All that was needful for the kerygma was the fact that Jesus had died on the cross.

Such an approach was to dominate German New Testament scholarship for the best part of thirty years. Of course, there were exceptions to this approach; Joachim Jeremias continued his patient investigations of the sayings of Jesus and others,[13] like Ethelbert Stauffer,[14] were ready to write stories of Jesus which included a certain amount of chronological ordering. But the main reaction to the Bultmannian position came from within the ranks of Bultmann's own disciples. Ernst Käsemann in a celebrated essay, which is included in his collection *Essays on New Testament Themes*, moved away from the Bultmannian position by affirming that it was indeed necessary to search for information about the historical Jesus as a necessary presupposition of the kerygma about him; it was insufficient merely to assert that he had existed and that he had been crucified under Pontius Pilate.[15] It was Käsemann's essay which paved the way for what has been called the New Quest. In its wake another of Bultmann's pupils, Günther Bornkamm, wrote a book entitled *Jesus of Nazareth*.[16] There is certainly a marked difference about this particular life of Jesus as compared with its nineteenth-century predecessors. The influence of Form Criticism, not to mention the eschatological dimension, is everywhere apparent. There is a reluctance to say too much and to recognize to the full the shortcomings of the material as a basis for writing a history of the life of Jesus. Gone are the days when it was thought possible to trust the order of events in our earliest Gospel as a framework for reconstructing the outline of Jesus' life. There is a widespread recognition that the structure of all the Gospels, with their isolated stories and sayings, rarely reflects the order of events and sayings in Jesus' own life, but is rather the responsibility of the early collectors and transmitters of the gospel tradition. Even those, like Jeremias, who feel that much can be said about Jesus' message and view of his mission, accept without question the basic insights of Form Criticism concerning the make-up of the Gospels. Even allowing for eye-witness testimony in the Gospels and the possibility of a framework for the sayings and stories,[17] few today would want to maintain that we can know the exact relationship of the various pericopes to each other in the setting of Jesus' own life.

Certainly the quest for the historical Jesus has assumed once more an important place in new Testament research, but all who embark on that quest are now convinced of the difficulties of that task.[18] No commentator would underestimate the temptation to portray a Jesus who is acceptable to the modern mind. Perhaps Schweitzer's portrait of the eschatological fanatic is shocking, but it reminds us very clearly that there can be no ignoring Jesus' setting in the confused world of first-century Judaism with its eager longings and frustrated hopes. Any attempt to describe the mission and message of Jesus will refine and build upon that insight.

2

Using the Gospels to Establish the Character of Jesus' Life and Message

Nearly two hundred years of critical study of the Gospels has made many historians of early Christianity extremely wary in their use of the gospel tradition for their reconstruction of the character of Jesus' message. What are the obstacles which hinder our task? Have scholars been too ready to demonstrate their scepticism by raising doubts about the value of the Gospels, where none need exist? Some would answer these questions in the affirmative, but there can be little doubt that the research of the last century or so has rightly cast doubt on the value of the Gospels for our understanding of the course, though not necessarily the character, of the life of Jesus. We live in a questioning age when the miraculous is not regarded as something commonplace.[1] Yet it is not only our scepticism of the miraculous which may impel us to question the authenticity of the Gospels. A glance at the Gospels themselves reveals differences between the accounts, in some cases of a relatively minor kind and in others of a more significant nature.[2] The most obvious discrepancy lies in the relationship between the Gospel of John and the other three Gospels, the Synoptic Gospels, so called because of the similarities which exist between them. The picture of Jesus which emerges in the former differs from that which emerges in the latter. Whereas in Matthew, Mark and Luke Jesus hardly ever speaks about himself and the character of his mission, the recurring theme throughout the Fourth Gospel concerns the identity of Jesus and his mission from the Father. From the very first words of the Prologue the reader is left in no doubt that, as far as the Evangelist is concerned, Jesus of Nazareth is no ordinary man, nor is he merely a prophet; he is the Word become flesh, the emissary from the Father who in his own person makes known the character of the Father (1.18). It is not just the Evangelist who speaks thus; the Johannine Jesus continually bears witness to himself. In the past scholars have explained this discrepancy between the Synoptic Gospels on the one hand and John on the other by supposing that John is a later, theological reflection on the significance of the life and mission of Jesus, what Clement of Alexandria called 'the spiritual gospel'. So it is to the Synoptic Gospels that scholars have gone to find their accounts of the character of Jesus' ministry.

Unfortunately the situation is not so straightforward. For one thing there have been many voices raised in protest over the treatment of John as an unreliable source for the reconstruction of Jesus' life and work. There are those who think that it would be a mistake to consign all the material in this Gospel to the reflections of later thinkers,[3] without taking due account of the instances in the Gospel which may indicate that the Fourth Evangelist has access to tradition which is at least as reliable as that in the Synoptic Gospels and possibly more so. Such an approach to the Gospel has been facilitated by the appreciation of the Jewishness of this Gospel and its themes.[4] What is more, there has been a growing appreciation that we cannot treat the Synoptic Gospels as the biographical accounts, which would be so helpful to modern historians.[5] In their very different ways the traditions in the Synoptic Gospels by their treatment, and in particular by their ordering, may reflect the concerns of the Evangelist and the purpose for which he was writing. Obviously we are no longer in a position to ascertain with any degree of certainty what motivated the Evangelist Luke to write his Gospel and its companion volume, the Acts of the Apostles. That the choice of material does indeed reflect a specific purpose on the part of the Evangelist is evident from various hints throughout both works: the concern to stress the true Jewishness of Jesus and the early Christian movement, his innocence and that of his followers in the eyes of the Roman authorities, the concentration on the activities of Peter and Paul in Acts, and the sudden end to the narrative of Acts when the apostle Paul reaches Rome for the first time. Elaborate theories have been put forward to account for these phenomena.[6] The phenomena are in themselves adequate testimony to the fact that Luke-Acts is a story whose composition betrays the concerns of its writer to present the Christian message of salvation in as attractive a form as possible to his readers. This makes his account less of a history of early Christianity and more of an apology in which historical details are included. Indeed, if we go to Acts looking for information about the acts of the apostles, we shall be disappointed, because attention is concentrated on one whose claim to be an apostle was disputed by many and only rarely recognized by Luke himself (Acts 14.14). The concerns of Luke and for that matter the other Evangelists as well do not allow us easy access to a detailed history of Jesus' life and ministry and the growth of the early Christian movement. The path even to the barest outline of the chronology of his life is one which is beset by many hazards.

The character of the tradition available to us makes it very difficult to reach any satisfactory assessment of this particular episode in the history of Christian origins. Even if an evangelist had wanted to write an ordered, chronological account of the ministry of Jesus, as Luke in his prologue may suggest that he intended (Luke 1.1), it would probably have been impossible for him to do so. The nature of the traditions which he received was such that a chronological account was out of the question. The study of the history of the gospel tradition over the last century or so has shown that what we have in the Gospels is a series of sayings and stories which are often only loosely related to each other with little indication of their chronological relationship.[7] If we were to depend on the Synoptic Gospels alone, we would find that much of Jesus' ministry could be crammed into a very short period. Indeed, most reconstructions of the outline of Jesus' ministry tend to depend on the chronology in the Gospel of John which includes references to various Jewish feasts at various points in the story (e.g., 2.13; 6.4; 7.2; 12.1) and has led scholars to the conclusion that the ministry of Jesus lasted for about three years. Apart from the account of the passion, there are few chronological references in the Gospels and the original setting of the sayings and stories is not readily apparent in the form we have them. Attempts to explore the history of the traditions and explain their development, often called the traditio-historical method, have laid bare the kind of process which went on before the material finally reached its recent form in our Gospels.[8] The comparison between parallel passages in different Gospels allows us to ascertain the extent to the alterations which went on and to assess what may have been the original form of a saying or story. Even well-known passages like the Beatitudes (Matt. 5.1f.; Luke 6.22ff.) and the Lord's Prayer (Matt. 6.9ff.; Luke 11.2ff) reflect the changes which have taken place in the sayings tradition, with minor developments and alterations apparent. These factors have to be taken into account when any assessment of the value of the tradition is carried out.

Books have been written about the method of gospel criticism: form criticism,[9] redaction criticism,[10] criteria for separating authentic from inauthentic sayings and the rest.[11] Knowledge of such tools is important for the student of the Gospels. Yet the central fact of gospel criticism is the

128

phenomenon of the Gospels themselves, with their parallel accounts, variations and differing emphases which confront the student immediately he begins his quest for the historical Jesus. It is when one is confronted with, for example, the two versions of the Beatitudes in the Gospels of Matthew and Luke that it becomes imperative to formulate some kind of method for explaining the relationship between these two versions. This is the heart of the traditio-historical method. It arises from the texts themselves and has not been unnaturally foisted upon them by the excessive attentiveness of scholarly activity.

Let me illustrate the point by referring to a well-known parable found in the Gospels of Matthew and Luke: the parable of the wedding feast (Matt. 22.1–14; Luke 14.15–24).[12] The differences which can be found in these two versions are illustrative of the problems confronting the historian of the gospel traditions. It will be seen that Matthew has a much longer account of this story. Not only does his version contain the addition about the guest, who does not have the appropriate wedding garment (vv.11ff.), but also makes reference to the fact that the host sent his armies to destroy those who refused the initial invitation (v.7). Luke, on the other hand, has a more expanded version of the second instruction to the servant about the guests who would replace those who had been invited initially (14.21). His account tells us a little about the kind of person who was summoned to the feast by the host: the poor, the maimed and the blind. These variations between the two versions may well indicate the concern of the Evangelist (or his tradition) to read into the story a deeper significance than it may have had in the first place. Luke's addition about the character of those invited is consistent with his concern, manifest elsewhere in this Gospel, with the outcasts. The good news of God's salvation comes to the Jewish nation, but it is the tax-collectors and prostitutes who show most enthusiasm and ultimately (in Acts) the Gentiles who are most responsive. We should remember that the story of the mission of the Church in Acts ends with the quotation from Isaiah 6.9f. (Acts 28.26), concerning the rejection of the message by the Jewish people and its acceptance by the Gentile outcasts.

In Matthew the concerns are somewhat different. The addition about the wedding garment, whatever its source (and it may well be a separate parable rather than the creation of the Evangelist or his tradition),[13] demonstrates the enormous concern throughout the Gospel of Matthew to ensure that there is to be no slackening of the understanding of righteousness. Those who are invited to the wedding feast are allowed in on the understanding that 'their righteousness will exceed that of the scribes and Pharisees' (5.20). The addition about the revenge taken by the king upon his ungrateful guests is probably symptomatic of the allegorizing of the parables, which seems to have gone on during the transmission of this material. This has indicated a situation when the parable was interpreted by the Christian community after the fall of Jerusalem in AD 70. So the host at the feast becomes a king who is God himself; those invited to the feast initially are the members of the covenant people. Their rejection of the invitation taken to them by the servants of the king (the prophets) brings upon them the judgement of the king and the destruction of their city (the fall of Jerusalem). Likewise the bad treatment meted out to the servants of the king (v.5f.) is indicative of the rejection of the prophetic ministry alluded to elsewhere in the gospel tradition (e.g., Luke 11.47f.). Thus in Matthew the parable becomes an allegory of the rejection of the offer of God by the Jewish nation, a concise history of salvation, the judgement upon the Jews and the consequences of that action in the Gentile mission.

Several commentators recognize that a process similar to the one just outlined took place in the transmission of this parable. Substantially the Gospel of Luke preserves the original form of the parable, which is to be understood as a picturesque way of speaking about the crisis facing Jesus' hearers, as they listen to his message. Like the guests who were invited initially to the wedding feast (an eschatological image; cf. Isa. 25.6), Jesus' hearers will get no second chance. Now is the time for a decision; it is a time of eschatological crisis; there can be no procrastinating in deciding about the kingdom. Indeed, a refusal in the present will mean that the opportunity will be gone for good.

We are fortunate in having parallel versions of many of the sayings of Jesus and this enables us to assess the degree to which the saying has been subject to change and development in the course of its transmission. Noting the differences which exist between the various versions is a fairly simple task, but it is much more hazardous to move from such a comparison to decisions about priority and about the authenticity of a particular saying or story. It must be admitted that with the investigation of the history of the tradition we are in the realm of possibilities, and the solution which is offered by one interpreter will not be accepted by all. Nevertheless the nature of the gospel material itself compels us to make certain judgements in this area, however provisional. In the reconstructions of Jesus' message there will be as much variation over the sayings which can be used in this exercise as there are scholars and reconstructions.

While we can make some assessment of the relative priority of the traditions contained in the Gospels, the question inevitably arises of the previous history of the earliest form of the saying or story. This has been the subject of considerable controversy and research. Underlying the form-critical method of Bultmann and his disciples was the assumption that the primitive Christian communities were to a large extent responsible for the bulk of the material now contained in the Gospels, so that original sayings of Jesus were subsequently expanded into controversies and stories (so called pronouncement stories).[14] We have to face the fact that we are very much in the dark about the origin and development of the gospel tradition. An attempt was made in the 1960s to argue that early Christian attitudes to the gospel tradition resembled the attitude of the later rabbis to the sayings of the sages.[15] There are shortcomings to this theory as has been pointed out, not least in the evidence from the Gospels themselves of expansion and development in the tradition. There can be no question of the early Christians having treated sayings of Jesus as a holy collection, which was not altered at all in transmission. Nevertheless the consideration of oral transmission in the ancient world, and particularly in Judaism, enables us to take some of the guesswork out of this period, about which we know so little. It seems likely that some kind of oral transmission was practised, and while recent research into rabbinic material has indicated the kinds of development now familiar to us from the Synoptic Gospels,[16] there is every reason to suppose that such patterns may have been operative in the primitive Church and the amount of prophetic creativity was nothing like as large as is often supposed.[17] Hints that we do have suggest that there may well have been more reverence for the sayings of Jesus than some of the earlier form critics allowed for.[18]

3

John the Baptist[1]

According to all our sources, the preaching of John the Baptist played a crucial role in the initial stages of Jesus' ministry. The primitive preaching of the Church, as reported in Acts 10.37 and 13.24, includes reference to him and his teaching, though our earliest sources indicate that the Baptist probably had no personal commitment to Jesus as Messiah (Matt. 11.2 and par. but note John 1.29). The New Testament portrays John as an eschatological prophet who looked forward to the coming of one mightier than himself (Mark 1.7); it is the one mightier than John who would baptize with the Holy Spirit. The baptism with the Holy Spirit is an eschatological judgement (Luke 3.16, cf. the cleansing function of the Spirit in the Dead Sea Scrolls, e.g. 1 *QH* 16).[2] Probably John expected the Messiah; the cleansing function of the one who would baptize with the Holy Spirit is consistent with the view of the purging function of the Messiah as it is found, say, in the Psalms of Solomon 17.24.

At the period water rites were common in a number of religious groups, and occasionally, as in the case with the baptism of converts to Judaism (proselytes) (b. *Yebamoth* 46a) it marked the initiation into a new religious faith.[3] We know that frequent lustrations formed part of the ritual of the

Qumran community (e.g., 1 *QS* 3; *CD* 11; cf. *Ant.* 18.116ff.).[4] There has been much debate about the origins and character of John's baptism. What we need to note is that as far as Jesus is concerned, it was a baptism of repentance, involving a change of life, and had a strong eschatological element. We do not know that those who were baptized felt themselves already to be part of a new age or, as the New Testament implies, underwent baptism as a preparation for the coming kingdom. The evidence from Josephus' account concerning the Baptist (*Ant.* 18.116ff.) suggests that there may well have been a significant eschatological component, as Josephus tells us that John was put into prison because Herod was afraid that his preaching would cause an insurrection;[5] explicable only if we suppose that John's preaching had a subversive element. We cannot be sure that the baptism was performed once only, but the implication of the New Testament writings, supported by the once-only character of Christian baptism, suggests that it may well have been a rite performed once only.

It is the eschatological element in John's message, which is most significant. Mark implicitly (9.12f., though this saying need not imply an identification of John with Elijah) and Matthew explicitly (Matt. 11.14; cf. Luke 7.27) identify John with the Elijah who is to come (Malachi 4.5), and all the Gospels quote the verse in Malachi 3.1. in connection with John the Baptist (Matt. 11.10; Luke 7.27).[6] Certainly the earliest layers of the tradition record that there was a link between John and Jesus after the former had been put into prison. The Baptist sent his disciples to inquire whether Jesus was in fact the one who was to come (Matt. 11.2 and par.). Also if the opening section of the Gospel of John is anything to go by, Jesus' first disciples were themselves disciples of the Baptist. John the Baptist was still revered long after his death,[7] a fact confirmed by the story of the disciples of the Baptist met by Paul in Ephesus (Acts 19.1)[8] and there have been those who would consider that the attitude taken towards the Baptist in the Gospel of John betrays evidence of an attempt to persuade his followers, contemporary with the writer of the Gospel, to accept the messiahship of Jesus.[9]

As far as Jesus himself is concerned, the tradition certainly suggests that he saw a close link between himself and John in his understanding of his ministry. Thus in Luke 7.31ff. he characterizes John and himself as part of the same mission. The little parable quoted in 7.32 is intended to show that two different approaches of God's messengers are both rejected by the people. Indeed, at the end of this little section both John and Jesus are described as children of wisdom.[10] Such a link is unlikely to have been made by the early Church which would have wanted to stress the difference between its Lord and John. The saying probably goes back to Jesus and indicates how closely he saw his ministry being linked with that of the Baptist (John 3.22 cf. 4.1).

The baptism of John was important for Jesus. His own call seems to have depended on it (Mark 1.11 cf. 11.27ff.). But the differences between the two should not be overlooked. Obviously the manner of life of the two differed (Luke 7.33). But while John can be called the greatest among those born of women, the least in the kingdom of God is greater than John.[11] John stands at the fulcrum of the ages; he is the hinge upon which the aeons move. He stands on the brink of the age of fulfilment, but is not himself part of it. In a saying found in Luke 16.16 and Matt. 11.12f., Jesus sees the ministry of John the Baptist as initiating a decisive break with the old order of the Law and the Prophets; but Jesus asserts that the age of fulfilment, to which John bears witness, is inaugurated in his own ministry (Matt. 11.2ff.).

4

The Proclamation of the Kingdom of God

According to the Gospel of Mark Jesus' first words are 'the time is fulfilled; the kingdom of God is at hand; repent and believe in the gospel' (1.15). Few would deny that the phrase, 'the kingdom of God', is a central pillar for our understanding of the message of Jesus.[1] The phrase is not frequent in the contemporary Jewish literature,[2] and for that matter, is not found very often in other parts of the New Testament (e.g., John 3.3; Acts 8.12; Rom. 14.17; 1 Cor. 6.9; cf. 15.24). It is replaced in the Gospel of John by the words, 'eternal life' (the juxtaposition is found in John 3.3, 5).[3] It designates, as most would now agree, a future age of glory, when God's sovereignty would be revealed in the world in the affairs of men. As we have seen, it is a fundamental datum of Jewish eschatology that God would bring about an age of perfection in this world, when the dominance of foreign powers would be overthrown and God's righteousness revealed.[4] The basic characteristics of Jesus' understanding of the kingdom of God have been demonstrated in the celebrated work by the German New Testament scholar, Johannes Weiss, *Jesus' Proclamation of the Kingdom of God.* The conclusions of his investigation of Jesus' proclamation of the kingdom of God still repay consideration:[5]

> 1 Jesus' activity is governed by the strong and unwavering feeling that the messianic time is imminent. Indeed, he even had moments of prophetic vision when he perceived the opposing kingdom of Satan as already overcome and broken (Luke 10.18). At such moments as these he declared with daring faith that the Kingdom of God had actually already dawned.

2   In general, however, the actualizing of the Kingdom of God has yet to take place. In particular, Jesus recognized no preliminary actualization of the rule of God in the form of the new piety of his circle of disciples, as if there were somehow two stages, a preliminary one, and the Kingdom of Completion. In fact, Jesus made no such distinction. The disciples were to pray for the coming of the Kingdom, but men could do nothing to establish it.

3   Not even Jesus can bring, establish, or found the Kingdom of God; only God can do so. God himself must take control. In the meantime, Jesus can only battle against the devil with the power imparted to him by the divine Spirit, and gather a band of followers who, with a new righteousness, with repentance, humility and renunciation, await the Kingdom of God.

4   The messianic consciousness of Jesus consists of the certainty that when God has established the Kingdom, judgement and rule will be transferred to him ...

5   Although Jesus initially hoped to live to see the establishment of the Kingdom, he gradually became certain that before this could happen, he must cross death's threshold, and make his contribution to the establishment of the Kingdom of Israel by his death. After that, he will return upon the clouds of heaven at the establishment of the Kingdom, and do so within the lifetime of the generation which had rejected him ...

6   But when it comes, God will destroy this old world which is ruled and spoiled by the devil, and create a new world ...

7   At the same time, the Judgement will take place, not only over those who are still alive at the coming of the Son of Man ...

8   The land of Palestine will arise in a new and glorious splendour, forming the centre of the new Kingdom ... There will be neither sadness nor sin; instead those who are in God's Kingdom shall behold the living God, and serve him in eternal righteousness, innocence and bliss.

9   Jesus and his faithful ones will rule over this new-born people of the twelve tribes, which will include even the Gentiles.

In general this pattern of interpretation has dominated New Testament scholarship throughout the bulk of this century. Those who want to interpret the meaning of the phrase, the kingdom of God, find themselves interacting with the work of Weiss and Albert Schweitzer, whose presentation of the life and message of Jesus centres on the importance of eschatology for Jesus. Thus even when scholars disagree with Weiss and Schweitzer, it can be said that these two have set the agenda for discussion of the kingdom of God, which has been taken up by all subsequent interpreters.

Since Weiss' day there have been various changes of emphasis in the interpretation of the phrase. C. H. Dodd championed an interpretation which stressed realized eschatology in the ministry of Jesus.[6] Consequently he played down the future elements in Jesus' proclamation, by transposing the future hope of a kingdom of God on to a transcendent plane and minimizing the this-worldly elements. He argued that Jesus preached that the kingdom of God had already arrived. Another position which plays down the eschatological dimension is the view championed by T. W. Manson,[7] dependent as it is on the rabbinic sources rather than the eschatological passages of the pseudepigrapha (e.g. Sifra on Lev. 20.26). He points to the use of the phrase 'taking upon oneself the yoke of the kingdom and setting oneself apart from wrong doing', which is used in rabbinic literature to speak of obedience to the Law in the present by an individual. It thus concerns inward obedience to God and not the cosmic manifestation of the divine sovereignty; the inclination of the heart rather than the renewal of the cosmos. Another group has preferred to follow Schweitzer in regarding the use of the phrase by Jesus as referring entirely to some future entity.[8] Finally, a widely held view stresses that the kingdom of God is an era, which has been inaugurated in Jesus' ministry (Luke 11.20), but still awaits a final consummation when the rule of God would extend over the whole universe and the perfection spoken of in Old Testament passages like Isaiah 11 would be fulfilled.[9] In this interpretation much depends on the interpretation of Luke 11.20 and 17.21. The point is frequently made in discussions of the meaning of the phrase that it is not used in a spatial sense of a particular territory, unlike the kingdom belonging to a king, but means God's sovereignty and rule. Nevertheless it would be wrong to give the impression that the phrase is to be understood in a purely spiritual sense (cf. John 18.36). For God's rule and authority were ultimately to be manifested in the physical world. Salvation for a Jew was not primarily some mystical deliverance for the spirit to enter a private communion with God in the world beyond, but the manifestation on earth of God's authority over the universe and the setting right of all that was wrong. We must not misrepresent the understanding of God's reign in the preaching of Jesus by stressing an individual, otherworldly experience at the expense of the restoration of the community and the physical order. To this extent the Matthaean version of the Lord's Prayer, with its petition that God's kingdom would come and his will be done on earth as in heaven (Matt. 6.10), is an accurate exposition of the essential features of the Jewish (and Jesus') belief concerning the eschatological and this-worldly character of the kingdom.

In conclusion we may say that Jesus inherited from Jewish eschatology a belief in the manifestation of God's reign on earth in the future (Mark 9.1; 13.30 and 14.25). The question is whether, in addition to a purely futuristic hope, there exists in the Gospels evidence of an emphasis on the present as a time of fulfilment. Supporters of the view that Jesus thought of the kingdom as present as well as future point to Luke 16.16 but particularly to sayings like Matthew 11.5f. and to Luke 11.20 and 17.21b.[10] Despite the fact that the consensus of New Testament scholarship accepts that Jesus believed that the kingdom of God had already in some sense arrived in Jesus' words and deeds, the fact has to be faced that the evidence in support of such an assumption is not very substantial. What can be said is that Weiss was on the right lines to stress the importance of the future dimension in Jesus' teaching and the fact that 'Jesus' activity was governed by the strong and unwavering feeling that the messianic time was imminent ... and in moments of prophetic vision perceived the opposing kingdom of Satan as already overcome and broken.'[11]

We turn now to consider some of the different aspects of the teaching of Jesus in the Gospels on the kingdom of God, particularly as they are found in the parables.

5

The Parables[1]

If we examine the teaching of Jesus, we find remarkably little detail about the character of the kingdom, the qualities expected of its members and the style of life which will be enjoyed by those fortunate enough to enter it. That is not to say that we can find out nothing concerning Jesus' expectation and beliefs. His teaching is full of hints of various kinds concerning the fulfilment of the expectation, manifested particularly in the Beatitudes (Matt. 5.1f.; Luke 6.22f.). According to the gospel tradition, when Jesus speaks of the kingdom of God, he uses parables as the mode of communicating his message and the quality of that entity to which he refers. 'The kingdom of God may be compared with ...' (Matt. 13.44) is an introductory phrase which is found frequently in the sayings of Jesus.

The parable was a common teaching device in Judaism and had its origins in the OT (e.g. Isa.5.1ff.; 2 Sam. 12.1ff.). Indeed, some of the later rabbinic expositions of the Scriptures are replete with examples of parables. In the Jewish literature the parable is called a *mashal*: a story which by way of comparison drives home the point which is being made. We must note that the function of a parable is to illustrate and in doing this it usually has only one point to make. The various details of the story are really incidental to the main point of the story. They should not, therefore, usually be given any undue weight in interpretations of the parable. Nor should we feel compelled to give them such attention, however arresting these details may be in adding colour to the parable. Like the similes in English usage the parable attempts to illuminate one particular point by its story. We should no more suppose that every detail of a parable has significance than press a simile like 'he is as stubborn as a mule' into making comparisons between a particular human being and other characteristics of a mule other than its stubborn attitude.

By contrast, an allegory is a story, all of whose details are made to yield points of significance. Evidence of an allegory in the gospel tradition may help to illustrate the point. In the parable of the wheat and the tares an interpretation is offered, which takes the individual components of the original parable and gives to these components a deeper significance (Matt. 13.36ff.).[2] Thus we find that in the interpretation the sower is the Son of Man, the field is the world, the good seed is the sons of the kingdom; the tares are the sons of perdition and the enemy, who comes to sow the tares, is the devil. The final harvest is the close of the age, when the judgement takes place (cf. Rev. 20.10f.) and the separation is parallel to the separation between the sheep and the goats spoken of in the eschatological parable in Matthew 25.31ff. In the critical study of the parables it is often assumed that allegorization is a feature of the process of reinterpretation of the original parables of Jesus by the early Church, as they sought to find new meaning in these texts in the changed circumstances of their day.[3] After a patient attempt to reconstruct the parabolic teaching of Jesus, Jeremias concludes that all 'the parables of Jesus compel his hearers to come to a decision about his person and mission'. Jeremias would want to argue for two major settings for the parables: the life of Jesus and his proclamation of the kingdom of God and the life of the Church. It was the Church, concerned as it was with survival, and issues such as the Gentile mission, which reinterpreted the parables of Jesus in the light of the non-appearance of the kingdom of God.

To acknowledge that the primary method of teaching employed by Jesus is the parable does not exclude the possibility of subsequent private explanation, which in turn may have involved allegorization of parables.[4] It would be dangerous to suppose that all allegory must be inauthentic. After all, the parable of the wicked tenants in Mark 12.1ff. is one which it would have been difficult not to hear allegorically. In addition, in so far as Jesus had disciples it is likely that he offered extra teaching to them (Mark 4.11, cf. Ezra 14.46). Parables can just as easily end up preventing insight as enabling it. So wooden characterizations of the function of parabolic forms in discourse are to be rejected. Hard and fast rules are out of place in investigating the history of tradition at any level. Such uncertainty, however, need not prevent us from ascertaining the main outline of the message contained in the parabolic teaching of Jesus.

The Major Themes of the Parables

In two parables in Mark 2 we find Jesus contrasting the new with the old. The present cannot be a time of fasting and penitence, even though it does mean that Jesus' disciples differ markedly from their contemporaries in their religious practice (2.18ff.). Jesus explains the difference by comparing the situation with a wedding: the bridegroom and his guests do not fast on the wedding day; it is a time of festivity and rejoicing. So it is for the disciples who are tasting the firstfruits of the harvest of the new age. In addition the two parables about the different types of cloth and the wineskins are making a similar point about the break with the past (Mark 2.21f.). There is little point in putting new wine into skins, which are old and unable to carry the wine. New and good wine needs new skins. So it is with the present; a new situation has come about with the ministry of Jesus, which demands new initiatives and patterns of behaviour appropriate for that new situation (cf. Matt. 9.37f.; Mark 13.28f.; Luke 7.22; 10.23).

In Matthew 13.44ff. we find two parables which stress how important it was for those who listened to Jesus' teaching to recognize the significance of that which was confronting them. All other preoccupations and interests should be set aside. Like the merchant who came across a pearl which necessitated his selling all that he had to purchase it, so it must be for those who hear the good news of the kingdom: this is of ultimate value compared with which all else must count as dross. Nothing whatever should come between the would-be disciple and his acceptance of the kingdom of God (cf. Luke 9.59ff.).

In many parables Jesus presents his hearers with a challenge (Matt. 5.25f.; 24.37–39; Luke 12.51; 13.6ff.). In the short parables we have already examined we have noted that the hearers are challenged to recognize the new situation which was before them. Several parables which in their present form are exhortations to believers to be ready for the second coming of Christ have been regarded as originally challenges by Jesus to his contemporaries to take decisive action in the face of the imminent catastrophe which confronts them in his person. Such an interpretation should not lead us to suppose that in Jesus' own teaching there is not an intimate link between his own mission and the coming of the Son of Man (cf. Mark 8.38); the future dimension of the kingdom in Jesus' teaching is more prominent in the tradition than any present realization. Response in the face of God's imminent act is a frequently occurring theme (e.g., Matt. 25.1ff.; also Matt. 24.42–50; 25.14ff.; Mark 13.33ff.; Luke 12.35ff.; 41ff.; 19.12ff.). The point is that the imminence of the kingdom of God demands of men a response which excludes procrastination. It is no use putting off the moment of decision, as the foolish virgins put off the moment of preparation and found themselves left behind when the bridegroom came. It is necessary to prepare now for the imminence of the full breaking in of God's reign. As the first buds on the fig tree show that spring is near, already the signs are present which indicate the coming of a new season of God's activity (Mark 13.28f.; cf. Luke 12.54f.).

The authorities also had to be challenged to stir from their complacency, as parables like Matt. 25.45ff.; 14ff.; Mark 12.1ff.; Luke 12.41ff.; 19.12ff. may indicate.[5] This demands of the hearers a readiness, which does not pedantically stress preconceived ideas of what God's kingdom would involve. Complacency in the face of the coming judgement leads to death (Luke 12.16ff.). There would be no second chance for those who had received the invitation but had refused it (Luke 14.15ff. and par.); it was necessary to take every opportunity available while there was still time (Luke 11.24; 13.6ff.; and 16.1ff.), for the crisis had descended on this generation (cf. Luke 11.29, 50).

One theme which emerges from the parables concerning the growth of seeds (e.g., Mark 4.3ff.; 26ff.; 4.31ff.) is the fact that however small the signs may be at the present that God's reign is on its way, nevertheless it would be revealed in all its glory in due course. The parable of the seed growing secretly (Mark 4.31ff.) is an example of this. The seed grows without the farmer understanding how or even doing much to cultivate it, and yet it is ready for harvest at its due time. In the parable of the mustard seed (Mark 4.30f.; cf. Luke 13.18f.) we have the contrast between the small seed and the large tree: small beginnings leading to a glorious ending. The stress here is on the inexorable growth and the contrast between the inauspicious beginnings and the final outcome (4.26). In both passages the eschatological dimension of the parables is evident, in that both evince influence from Old Testament passages dealing with the coming of the kingdom. At the end of the parable of the seed growing secretly (Mark 4.29), when the harvest is described, there is an allusion to Joel 3.13. At the end of the parable of the mustard seed (Mark 4.32) Daniel 4.11f. and 21 are alluded to. A similar contrast to that found in the parable of the mustard seed is in the parable of the leaven (Luke 13.20f.) in which the difference made by the leaven in the flour is said to be illustrative of the contrast between the present and the glorious future manifestation of the kingdom.

The point is made, therefore, that God's reign has been heralded in the ministry of Jesus. Even if the signs are few, the manifestation of God's sovereignty on earth was sure and imminent. 'Jesus is full of joyful confidence. In spite of every failure and opposition, from hopeless beginnings God brings forth the triumphant end which he promised.'[6] That conclusion comes at harvest when the judgement would come (Matt. 25.31ff., 13.24ff., 47f.).

But if the kingdom is coming, whatever man's response may be and however great the opposition to it, what difference does it make to respond in the present other than to guarantee one's status in the age to come? The theme of the importance of the consequences of the present response is touched on from time to time in Jesus' teaching. The coming of the kingdom in the present is the result of the obedience of Jesus to the will of God. So also the disciple who follows Jesus accepts God's sovereignty, for it means that at the level of the individual God's reign is made manifest in the affairs of men. That is not to suggest that the coming of God's reign is entirely dependent on human response,[7] however; for the bulk of Jewish eschatology the inexorable tide of history was moving under the hand of God ever closer to the establishment of God's reign on earth: the challenge facing Israel was to repent in the face of its advent.

What sort of attitude characterizes this present response? The responsive hearer is like the tax-collector who went up to the Temple to pray, who accepted his sinfulness and humbly cast himself on God's mercy (Luke 18.9ff.; Matt. 21.28). When Jesus compares the disciple with a child, he is referring to the present disposition which will enable entry into the kingdom (Mark 10.13, 16; cf. 9.36). The child-like acceptance of salvation, and the obedience and dependence of the faith is what is demanded by God, not self-righteous assertiveness (cf. Luke 14.7ff.; Matt. 20.28). The disciple who addresses God as his heavenly father, as Jesus taught his disciples to pray (Matt. 6.9ff. and par.) must show the same humility as that of a child (cf. Matt. 18.4). Thus within the overall presentation of the inexorable movement towards God's reign over the whole world, there is room left for the present response.

In his parables Jesus speaks from time to time of God and his relationship with man. This is particularly apparent in the collection of parables in Luke 15 (e.g., vv.4ff., vv.8ff.; cf. Matt. 18.12ff.). It is in the parable of the Prodigal Son in particular that we find a picture of mercy and grace freely shown to the repentant sinner. The God of the kingdom is one who listens to the poor when they call him (Luke 18.2ff.; cf. 11.5ff.), and his offer of mercy is open to all Jews, whatever their present religious affiliations or lack of them (cf. Mark 2.17; Matt. 21.28ff., 22.1ff. and par.; Luke 14.13ff.). In the parable of the Pharisee and the publican we find not a condemnation of Pharisaism, but the use of hyperbole to describe the basis of a relationship with the God of Israel. A relationship with him comes when a man throws himself on his mercy, sorry for what he has done. That is the appropriate response to the divine initiative. Jesus does not see his mission as a threat to the Pharisees (Mark 2.17). Rather he is the eschatological prophet of the final reign of God, proclaiming the love and goodness of the merciful God of all. Yet it is the outcast who eagerly accepts his message (Luke 7.41ff.; cf. 14.13ff.).

One of the characteristic features of Jesus' mission is his consorting with sinners (Matt. 9.11, 13; 11.19; Luke 15.1f.), not just ordinary non-zealous Jews, but those who were regarded as outcasts. These too are called by Jesus, a cause of great offence. What lies behind this call of the sinners is not clear. It may reflect a belief that in the last days *all* the twelve tribes of Israel would be summoned to participate in it, including the outcasts of Israel (Isa. 11.12; 60.4, 9; 27.13; Ps. Sol. 17.26; 4 Ezra 13.40ff.).[8] It is not just those who are not as pious as the Pharisees, who are called, but those who according to the

Law are sinners – called to participate in the kingdom *without* prior repentance.[9]

To be effective in the individual, response to the kingdom has to involve repentance, sorrow and obligation on the part of man, whoever he may be (Luke 19.1ff.).[10] The equality of opportunity offered by God is stressed most clearly in the parable of the labourers in the vineyard (Matt. 20.1ff.). The nearness of the kingdom means that past religious affiliations do not count for anything (cf. Luke 13.28). Like the workers in the vineyard who are given the same wage, however long they have laboured there, those who enter the kingdom enter on the same basis. Past devotion and self-esteem count for nothing. The terms of entry into the kingdom may be clear and uncompromising but the offer is open to all who are ready to follow the path of child-like obedience and trust.

6

Other Teaching

Several of Jesus' parables deal with the quality of life expected of the disciple. In the parable of the sheep and the goats which comes at the end of the eschatological teaching in the Gospel of Matthew (25.31ff.), discipleship is made to depend on the concern for Jesus' brethren in this age rather than any specific religious action or confession (cf. Matt. 6.21ff.). In the parable of the unmerciful servant (Matt. 18.21ff.) the disciple is taught that the kind of mercy shown to him by God is expected of him in dealing with others (cf. Luke 6.36). Absence of it can only lead to judgement. The extreme demands laid upon the disciple are illustrated by the sayings in Luke 13.23ff. cf. Mark 10.25 and par.; Luke 6.20; 9.59; 12.16ff.; 14.26f.; 16.19ff.). Response to Jesus must be met by a whole-hearted desire to follow him, else the last state of that man will be worse than the first (Matt. 12.43ff.; Luke 11.24ff.). To be a disciple cannot mean turning back (Luke 9.62); the cost of discipleship must be counted before embarking on it (Luke 14.28ff.). There can be no dual allegiance (Matt. 6.24; Luke 16.13), for the demands of God must take over the whole person.

The wandering, homeless life of Jesus, as it is reported in the Gospels, is itself a paradigm of discipleship (Luke 9.57f.).[1] It is those like him, who inherit the kingdom of God (Luke 6.22). The rich will find it impossible (Mark 10.24; cf. Luke 16.19), because the accumulation of riches is symptomatic of an alternative devotion and undermines that attitude of dependence and trust, which is so central for the child of God (Matt.

6.19ff.). Wealth can lead to complacency (cf. Luke 12.16ff.); the man, who amasses great wealth, pulls down his barns and builds even larger ones, is in no position to benefit from them when his life is forfeit (cf. Mark 8.35).[2] Jesus apparently allied himself with the poor and the outcast (Luke 4.16ff.).[3] It is not that the good things of the world were evil, for in the age to come the oppressed would be satisfied with those things (Luke 6.22ff.; Mark 10.29ff.). The poor would tend to look to God as their redeemer rather than money. Jesus' good news for the poor was consistent with the Old Testament emphasis on God's vindication of the underprivileged.

Jesus commands his disciples to be perfect as God is perfect (Matt. 5.48; cf. Luke 6.36). This means that there is no end to the obligation laid upon the disciple; he can never sit back and say that he has done God's will, because that suggests a state of self-satisfied righteousness, which can never be the response of man to God (Luke 18.14; cf. 17.10). It is this message which emerges from the parable of the good Samaritan which, in its present context, sets out to show what love of neighbour involves (Luke 10.29ff.; 12.29 and par.).[4]

The main points of the story are well known, but, like the dramatic tale of the Pharisee and the publican, the effect that it must have had is not easy for us to imagine. It is only when we begin to recognize the implacable hostility between Jews and Samaritans stretching back centuries (cf. John 4.9),[5] that the impact of the parable can be seen in a new light. In addition to the fact that the man who came to the aid of the traveller who had been robbed and left for dead is a Samaritan, the actions of the two priestly figures calls for some attention. We have to remember that for the Jew contact with a corpse would have involved ritual uncleanness (Num. 19.11). Thus he would avoid any unnecessary contact, particularly so if he were to be engaged on any divine service, which would have been true of the priest and Levite if they had been travelling in the direction of Jerusalem, for the likelihood is that they would have been going there to participate in the Temple service.

If we take these factors into account, we can begin to understand what it is that Jesus is saying in this parable. First of all, responsibility to one's neighbour does not depend on racial or religious ties, for there can be no limit made on the extent of the demand made by those in need.[6] The fact that the Samaritan in the story did not stop to ascertain whether the man whom he had found half-dead was his co-religionist or a hated Jew, indicates the pattern of response of the disciple. Concern for one in need transcends such divisions.

Secondly, we have an implicit criticism of any religion, which places obedience to the letter of the Law above the demands of those in need (cf. the Qorban controversy in Mark 7.9ff.). To some extent the decision of the priest and the Levite to walk by without going near the man, *in case* it was a corpse and they were defiled by contact with it, is understandable. According to the letter of the Law, any contact with a corpse would have disqualified them from immediate participation in the cult. Thus they were acting within the bounds of what was permissible when they walked past the man. But Jesus, like the rabbinic Sages, considered that some obligations of the Law were more important than others (cf. Luke 11.42) and demanded supersession of the less weighty matters of the Law (e.g., see Mishnah Nazir 7.1; cf. Mekilta Shabb. 1). The problem with any religion which interprets its regulations literally is that, while one knows exactly where one stands with regard to correct behaviour, action outside a prescribed limit is excluded, even when the situation demands it. Jesus in the parable of the Good Samaritan shows that his understanding of true love for one's neighbour can never be fully prescribed, and the demand upon the obedient child of God will continually take him beyond the limits of what is set down. This is the point which is being made in Jesus' interpretation of the Mosaic law in the Sermon on the Mount. It is no use, for example, thinking that avoidance of adultery and fornication will be enough to satisfy God's demands (Matt. 5.27), for love of one's neighbour demands that one is never going to be in the self-satisfied position of asserting that one has fulfilled the demands of God.

What we find in the ethical teaching of Jesus is a refusal to make the outward fulfilment the only basis of ethical rectitude. In the interpretation of the Law contained in the Sermon on the Mount we find both a stricter stance and an inclusion in the regulations of an inward disposition which inevitably makes the line between performance and negligence very blurred indeed. It is probably fair to say that Paul's statement that love is the fulfilling of the Law (Rom. 13.10) and the practical outworking of this injunction in 1 Cor. 8 are a logical corollary of Jesus' teaching. Indeed, there is a case to be made for regarding Jesus' teaching as a kind of eschatological Torah, whose emphasis on the inward motives may find its antecedent in the prophetic hope of the new Law written on the heart[7] (Jer. 31.31; cf. Ezek. 36.27f.; Gal. 5.22ff.).

The ethical teaching of Jesus was not a replacement of the Law.[8] Indeed, we find few legal or halakic statements in the Jesus tradition (Mark 10.11 is an exception). The teaching which is to be found in the Gospels, therefore, is neither the minute regulations of the lawyer nor the ethical maxims of the sage. Jesus seems to set his interpretation of the Law at a level which verges on the impossible. As Anthony Harvey has said,[9] 'The key to understanding it is that he does not regard the circumstances in which he gives it as normal. He comes as a prophet announcing that a decisive stage of history has arrived ... only a fresh return to the basic commandments will enable [the disciple] to discover the response which is demanded of him.'

One of the most striking facts about the teaching of Jesus of Nazareth is its uncompromising, indeed idealistic tone. As a result, the Sermon on the

Mount has served as a criterion of current action and an incentive to renewed moral endeavour throughout the centuries. A pressing question confronts the student of Christian origins, however: where does Jesus stand with regard to the issue of accommodation of his ideals to the old aeon, which did not accept the norms of the kingdom of God? An answer to this is by no means easy. We know so little about Jesus' own background and circumstances that judgements on this issue are bound to be provisional and partial.

In his words about wealth Jesus leaves his hearers in no doubt about wealth (Luke 6.24ff.) and the need for the disciple to sit very lightly to it (Mark 10.17ff.). The disciples themselves in the mission-charge are instructed to carry only what is absolutely necessary (Mark 6.8f.; cf. Luke 10.4). Likewise the call of the first disciples (Mark 1.16ff.) indicates that following Jesus was an extraordinary affair in which there was the expectation that there would be a radical reversal of the former style of life. Those who espouse this alternative pattern of living are the blessed ones (Luke 6.20ff.; Matt. 5.2ff.).

What we have in the teaching of Jesus is not a set of ideals which are unrelated to the practice of Jesus and his group. All the evidence in the Gospels indicates that Jesus was not merely a social reformer, who set before his hearers an ethical standard which he himself did not practise; the teaching that he offers is firmly grounded in the practice of himself and his circle. The evidence of the itinerant ministry of Jesus is well known (Luke 9.58). The harsh saying to repudiate an important religious obligation (to bury a corpse, *M. Nazir* 7.1) is evidence of the challenge to established patterns of existence which Jesus both practised and preached (Luke 9.59). The challenge of the hour is so great that established patterns of behaviour and social relationships are called into question. As Martin Hengel has put it:

> Jesus' call is uttered with an eye to the dawning rule of God and he brings the individual person who is called by him into a community of life and destiny with him, involving an absolute break with all ties, thus at the same time initiating him into service for the cause of the kingdom.[10]

The question is whether Jesus allowed there to be any compromise of this radical ethic. Two passages in particular call for comment. First of all, there is the first occasion when he is confronted with the issue of the relationship between the kingdom and the State (Mark 12.13ff. ; Matt. 22.15ff.; Luke 20.20ff.). What did Jesus mean when he uttered the famous saying 'Render to Caesar the things which are Caesar's and to God the things which are God's' (Mark 12.17)? It is tempting to argue in the light of Romans 13.7 where the saying of Jesus is probably presupposed, and Matthew 22.15, that Jesus intended his hearers to understand that he wanted the tax to be paid and all due obedience given to Caesar as far as was consistent with obedience to God. In the light of the fact that this was the way in which it was interpreted by Paul we may rest content with this explanation, until we recall that, according to Luke 23.2, this reply of Jesus was a reason for taking Jesus to Pilate. This divergence of response indicates the problems confronting the interpreter of the saying. If Jesus was setting some kind of division between God and Caesar, where was the line to be drawn?[11] Yet if we bring into the picture the perspective of the kingdom, we may certainly agree with Cullman that 'Jesus does not regard the State as a final institution, to be equated somehow with the kingdom of God. The State belongs to the age which still exists, but which will definitely vanish as soon as the kingdom of God comes'.[12] The problem is that importing this overall perspective does not allow us to assess whether in fact at some point in his career Jesus was prepared to come to some kind of accommodation with the old order as a temporary expedient until the new age finally dawned.

There are signs of such an attitude elsewhere, particularly in Luke 22.35f. This passage reverses instructions which have been previously given earlier in the Gospel (Luke 10.4f.). Although several commentators have suggested that the passage is a creation by Luke,[13] it could be argued that its creation does reflect a moment in the life of the Church, when it became necessary, through different circumstances, to reverse the rules of Luke 10, which after all relate in their present context to Jesus' ministry only. Also, it may offer some justification for the presence of a sword in the hands of Jesus' disciples in the garden. Whether we can take the saying back to Jesus or not, it indicates that, within the tradition of Jesus' sayings, some problem was felt at some point with regard to the missionary commands of Jesus, with the result that an attempt was made to make them more realistic for changed circumstances.[14]

Finally, mention may be made of Jesus' attitude at the time of his arrest and death. In assessing these accounts, we find ourselves up against the problem of their historicity, yet it has to be said that a constant feature of this is the lack of evidence of any resistance by Jesus (at least) to his arrest and subsequent execution. It may be argued that such evidence of an armed reaction has been edited out of the accounts,[15] but while it may be dangerous to attempt to say too much about Jesus' expectation at this time,[16] the cry of dereliction (Mark 15.33) suggests a disappointment which would be entirely comprehensible if Jesus believed that, even at the last, God may have brought in the kingdom. On the other hand, it may be argued that the evidence suggesting that Jesus expected to die indicates that he had begun to reckon with an interval before the arrival of the kingdom, and a consequent necessity for some accommodation with the aeon which was passing away.

7

The Signs of the Coming Kingdom[1]

If we stress the fact that Jesus looked forward to a reversal of the fortunes of this age and a return to the harmony of the original creation, due attention should be paid to the miracle-stories in the Gospels and the part which they play in stressing the outward manifestation of God's rule.

Much has been written on the mythological and symbolic significance of these stories, and one would not want to deny the important part which this approach can play in helping the modern reader to find meaning in stories which for him seem to be incredible.[2] Yet one has to come to terms with the fact that all strands of the New Testament bear witness to the fact that not only Jesus but also the early Church experienced events of supernatural might. Thus Paul is in no doubt that events of divine power happened in his ministry which he classed as marks of apostolic authority (2 Cor. 12.12; 1 Cor. 2.4; cf. Romans 15.19). In the story of the origins of the Church in Acts miraculous events are reported as signs that the followers of Jesus had tasted of the glories of the new age (cf. Acts 2.17ff.). Throughout the Gospels we find accounts of Jesus' miraculous deeds:[3] the casting out of demons (Mark 3.23; 5.2ff.), the healing of various types of malaise (e.g., Mark 5.25), and miracles affecting the natural order (e.g., Mark 6.45ff.). Jesus' opponents do not deny that he performed miracles; they were suspicious of the origin of his power (Luke 11.15). In the Gospel of John these miraculous events are called signs. The Gospel writers see them as signs of divine activity in the world. An understanding of the miraculous deeds in these terms probably goes back to Jesus himself, who linked the casting out of demons and divine sovereignty (Luke 11.20).

To eliminate the miraculous evidence in the Gospels merely because it offends our modern understanding[4] of the way in which the universe functions, is to be like the interpreters of the last century, who supposed that all miraculous material was to be consigned to the mythological embroidery of the early Church; it is to ignore the weight of the New Testament evidence, not to mention that from an abundance of secular sources.[5] That is not to suggest that we should credulously accept all the material of this kind in the Gospels without question. Rather we should exercise the same careful and critical approach to the miracle traditions, as we would to the tradition of Jesus' sayings, fully recognizing the varied theological presuppositions of our own, which may predispose us either to accept the possibility of the miraculous or have severe doubts about its theological viability. Not only that, but we should also recall that in Jewish tradition Jesus was remembered as a magician, a sorcerer who practised magical deeds and led Israel astray, a feature also of pagan polemic against Jesus.[6]

Miracle-working and magic were very common in the ancient world.[7] The study of the history of religions has revealed many parallels between the gospel accounts and Hellenistic and Jewish material.[8] It is impossible to relegate all this material to the untutored minds of the ancients who tended to attribute anything out of the ordinary to the intervention of the divine into their world. Certainly there was a tendency, evident in the Gospels themselves, to increase the dramatic nature of the supernatural acts described (the coin in the fish's mouth in Matthew 17.24ff.[9] could be a good example of a development in legend of the miraculous character of Jesus' deeds[10]), but abnormal phenomena which are not completely explicable on modern scientific grounds should not be immediately excluded as legend. We know that the Hellenistic world was one of growing irrational beliefs,[11] with a mushrooming belief in the demonic world as well as mystery cults and practices. Thus the exclusion of the miraculous element in the Gospels extracts Jesus from his own age where the performing of miraculous deeds would have been an important authentication of his right to speak and act on God's behalf (Luke 11.29; cf. Matt. 12.38ff.).

As far as Jesus himself was concerned, it is frequently suggested this activity is an important indication that he was the one ordained by God to initiate the kingdom.[12] In this interpretation Luke 11.20 plays a crucial role, but alternative interpretations which deny the preserve of inaugurated eschatology in this saying should be noted.[13] In Matthew 11.1ff. we find that the reply to John the Baptist's question whether he was the one to come involves a reference to the mighty acts performed by him as fulfilment of the scriptural promises (Isa. 35.5f.). As we have noted, even Jesus' enemies did not question the fact that he performed certain spectacular acts (cf. b. San. 43a), though the tradition also reports a refusal by Jesus to perform authenticating signs to order (e.g., Matt. 12.38ff.; cf. John 2.18). Jesus' power to do mighty acts is, however, explained as being the result of a power derived not from God but from the powers of darkness, as Jesus' controversy with his opponents about the origin of his power makes clear (Mark 3.21ff. and par.; cf. John 8.48).

The point needs to be stressed, therefore, that the miraculous element in the Gospels is an important element in the case made for Jesus' proclamation of the nearness of the kingdom. Without it there would have been little doubt that his claim would have seemed an empty one. The refusal by Jesus to perform signs clearly caused problems (Matt. 12.38ff.; Mark 8.11; Luke 11.16; 11.29). The miracle in the desert (Mark 6.30ff. and par.) and the reports of healings all helped to convince his contemporaries that he was either the agent of God or a charlatan whose wonder-working threatened to undermine the order and stability of the Jewish nation just as the warning of the book of Deuteronomy 13 had foretold (cf. John 11.47f.; Balaam in Num. 22ff.):[14] 'If a prophet arises among you, or a dreamer of dreams, and gives you a sign or wonder, and the sign or wonder comes to pass, and if he says, "Let us go after other gods" which you have not known, "and let us serve them" you shall not listen to the words of that prophet or to that dreamer of dreams' (Deut. 13.1f.; 18.20). The problem of true and false prophecy was a difficulty in Jewish life (e.g., Zech. 13.2f.; *CD* 12.2ff.; 1 *QH* 4.15f.; 2 Pet. 2.1; 1 John 2.22f.; Didache 11.5; 16.3 and Justin *Dialogue* 7). Jesus' activity presented all the familiar features of prophecy: claim to direct inspiration and authenticating miracles,[15] neither of which had achieved acceptance of the prophet in the past.

To exclude the miracles from the gospel tradition makes it impossible to see why Jesus should have posed anything like the threat that he seemed to have done to the religious leaders in Jerusalem. The evidence suggests that they were not dealing merely with a deviant teacher (though there were elements of that in the reaction to him) but a claimant to divine power who had in various ways authenticated his right to be the prophet of God by his mighty acts.

8

Jesus and the Future[1]

Despite the attempts of various scholars to play down the future element in Jesus' teaching there seems to be strong evidence in it that he thought that the kingdom of God, which was beginning to draw near in his own ministry, would finally come in the not too distant future. It has already been noted that several sayings indicate that Jesus expected the final demonstration of God's sovereignty in the world (e.g., Mark 9.1), even if its precise date was unknown (Mark 13.32ff.; Matt. 24.42ff.). Even a fairly conservative exegete like W. G. Kümmel is compelled to conclude that Jesus may have been mistaken about the date of the coming of the kingdom.[2] Attempts have been made to explain verses like Mark 9.1 in terms which would avoid the most obvious implication of the text, namely that it refers to the imminent consummation of the kingdom.[3] Indeed, the place of the saying in the Gospel of Mark indicates that the Evangelist may have understood the verse as referring to the demonstration of the glory of Jesus in the transfiguration which follows the saying (Mark 9.2ff.). One can understand why Jesus may have drawn the conclusion that the kingdom might not be long delayed in its final consummation, granted that he believed that already in his own ministry the signs leading to the ultimate reign of God were being realized. After all, in Jewish eschatology, the events leading up to the establishment of the kingdom of God were determined by God and of limited duration (cf. Mark 13.20; 13.29).

But what did Jesus expect to take place in the future? There are several approaches to this question. First of all, we find that Jesus speaks on several occasions about the coming of the Son of Man. Certainly the Evangelists believed that Jesus was speaking of himself. Of course, such an identification between Jesus and the Son of Man, who would come, has been denied by some commentators.[4] Others argue that originally the coming of the Son of Man meant a coming of the Son of Man to God, as part of his exaltation (as in Dan. 7.13), rather than a coming of the Son of Man from heaven to earth, to vindicate the elect (Mark 13.26) and to exercise judgement (Matt. 25.31ff.).[5] This is an area of considerable difficulty and complexity, and one states particular interpretations with the full consciousness of what a minefield this subject is. But it seems likely that Jesus would have considered that he would have had a part to play in the consummation of the kingdom, granted the link between himself and the reign of God. As a result, he would have considered that he would have returned after the death which he sooner or later knew he would have had to suffer (Luke 13.33). Thus the return of the Son of Man may well reflect part of Jesus' own beliefs about his future role in the kingdom of God.[6]

Elsewhere in the gospel tradition we find that Jesus does not speak directly about the life in the future kingdom of God. This contrasts with some of the beliefs of Jewish-Christians in the later part of the Christian century, like Cerinthus (Eusebius, *EH* iii, 28) and John of Patmos (Rev. 20), where explicit millenarian beliefs are to be found. Indeed, in a saying attributed to Jesus which Irenaeus reports to us from the writings of Papias, we find the belief that the whole of creation would be restored to its pristine condition and would even be in a more glorious situation than it had been at the beginning (*Adv. Har.* v.33.3f.).

Some of these themes, albeit in an attenuated form, are to be found in the Beatitudes,[7] where promises are made to the poor, the hungry and the oppressed that their position would be reversed in the future, when the kingdom of God came (Luke 6.22ff.; Matt. 5.3ff.). One picture which Jesus uses to speak of the kingdom is that of a banquet, a familiar figure in Jewish views about the future, going back to Isaiah 25.6ff. and reflected in Luke 13.28f.; 14.15–24 (cf. 1 Enoch 62.14; Syr. Bar. 29.5f.). The meal formed part of Jewish life and was central to Jewish rites like Sabbath and Passover. Close groups used to meet together in fellowships like the pharisaic *haburoth* or the Qumran community, both of which had communal meals as a central part of their common life. The picture which Acts gives us of the life of the early Church is rather similar (Acts 2.46). It is not surprising that a banquet should be used by Jesus to depict the end-time, when barriers are broken between man and God and both exist together in close fellowship (Rev. 21.4; 1 Enoch 62.14). Some of his last words on the night before his death indicate that Jesus looked forward to participating with his disciples in that messianic banquet which was to come, when he would drink of the fruit of the vine from which he had vowed to abstain at the Last Supper.[8] This vow indicates the hope on his part that there would be some great consummation of God's promises on earth (Mark 14.25 and par.), a hope which has a central place in the Lord's Prayer (Matt. 6.10).[9]

One area, which must be considered here, is Jesus' reaction to the Gentile mission, which was to become such an important part of the life of the early Church.[10] Clearly, as the gospel tradition indicates, Jesus' own ministry was centred on Jews and Judaism.[11] The traditions are unequivocal in their emphasis on Jesus' message to Judaism (Matt. 10.5; 15.24). In Jesus' confrontation with the Syro-Phoenician woman in Mark 7.24ff. and par., we see that he was unwilling to let his presence be made known while in predominantly Gentile territory, and the little parable about the children's bread ('it is wrong to take the children's bread and give it to dogs') points to the fact that Jesus saw his ministry as primarily directed to Jews. Only in exceptional circumstances, where the faith of a Gentile was great, do we find him healing or having dealings with them. The case of the centurion's servant is a good example (Luke 7.1ff.). Jesus' final commendation ('I have not found such great faith, even in Israel') and the fact that in Luke Jesus deals entirely with emissaries from the centurion's house rather than with the Gentile solider himself (Luke 7.6f.) suggests that what we are probably dealing with here are exceptional circumstances in the ministry of Jesus.

Nevertheless it is not as though Jesus thought that Gentiles would have no part to play in God's kingdom, merely that his ministry and message on the kingdom were to be directed to the Jewish nation and their call to repentance.[12] The use of the parable in Mark 7.24f suggests that the participation of Gentiles in the kingdom of God was to take place *after* the children of Israel had been given their chance (cf. Matt. 28.18ff.; Mark 13.10; Rom. 11.25). In line with the later prophetic literature (Isa. 2; 45.22; Zech. 8.20) and the views of the writers of some Jewish eschatology of the period (e.g., 1 Enoch 90.30),[13] Gentiles would be given a share in the age to come, a hope which is just as apparent in the Jewish-Christian Revelation of John (21.24f.; 7.9f.) as it is in the writings of Paul, the apostle to the Gentiles. Thus when Jesus speaks of people streaming from all directions to sit and eat at table in the kingdom of God (Luke 13.28f.), there is an indication that, in line with the eschatological teaching of his contemporaries, Jesus looked forward to a time when the Gentiles would share in the glory of the age to come.[14] Just as the offer of participation in the kingdom of God had been thrown open to all Jews, including the outcasts (cf. Isa. 11.12),[15] so also some Gentiles would in due course be allowed to enter the kingdom of God and so fulfil the divine promises.

As Jesus preached the imminence of the kingdom of God, it has often been supposed that he would not, therefore, have had any reason to found an ecclesiastical organization.[16] As A. Loisy put it, 'Jesus foretold the coming of the kingdom of God, but it was the Church that came'.[17] This statement implies two things:

(i) Jesus regarded the kingdom of God coming in fullness as being so near that there was no need for any religious organization of any kind; and

(ii) The ecclesiastical organization was a way of coping with the non-arrival of the kingdom, so that eschatological enthusiasm was channelled into the establishment of the Catholic Church.

If Schweitzer was right to suppose that Jesus believed that the kingdom would come in all its fullness during his ministry (Matt. 10.23) or at his death in Jerusalem, what would happen to his followers after his departure from the scene would not have been an issue for him. There are, however, good reasons for supposing that Jesus did reckon with a period when his followers would carry on his work. Mark 9.1 implies a period, however short, before the kingdom will come in power. Also the predictions of persecution for his followers in Mark 13 cannot all be relegated to the creation of the Church. There is no evidence that Jesus went to his death in Jerusalem believing that the kingdom of God was bound to come at that Passover.[18] Indeed, if the words at the Last Supper are any guide, particularly in the version in which we have them in 1 Corinthians 11.24f., then Jesus interpreted the significance of his death and gave instructions for the repetition of the rite by his followers.[19] Even if we feel bound to leave to one side the Farewell Discourses in John (ch. 14–16), where Jesus speaks of the time after his departure and the work of the Spirit, it seems likely that Jesus would have promised his disciples a share in the eschatological spirit which he himself had experienced (e.g., Mark 13.11; cf. Luke 10.17).[20]

Some of Jesus' sayings and parables probably refer to the group, which followed him, and are not later sayings of the Church, which originally had no applicability to Jesus' followers. Thus we find Jesus using the imagery of the shepherd and his flock (Luke 12.32; cf. Mark 14.27 and par.; Matt. 26.31f.) and he compares the disciples with the throng of guests at a wedding (Mark 2.19f.). Other parables may indicate that he saw the disciples as a distinct group around him (Matt. 13.47; 5.13f.; Mark 10.29f.; Matt. 23.9; Mark 3.34; Matt. 11.25, 25.40). The disciples regarded themselves as a well-defined fellowship with a particular style of prayer (Luke 11.1). Jesus himself thinks that it is important to share his own authority with those who had given up all to follow him (Luke 10.1ff.; Mark 6.7ff.). All these sayings are hints that Jesus saw his group not as an amorphous band of followers but as a body with an emerging identity of its own within first-century Judaism.[21]

All our sources tell us that Jesus, like other teachers, attracted disciples (Mark 2.23; Luke 11.1), though the recruitment of the disciples was different from that of other groups (Luke 5.1ff.); this need not exclude the possibility of Jesus training his disciples.[22] The disciples are regarded as the emissaries of Jesus with power similar to that which Jesus himself possessed (Luke 10.19). Indeed, Jesus explicitly links the task of the disciples with his own mission (Luke 10.16f.; John 20.21). Though the use of the word apostle is rare on the lips of Jesus (Luke 11.49; John 13.16), he does *send* his followers out before him.[23] Luke 10.16 is an important saying in this respect.

The question remains whether the disciples were only appointed by Jesus as emissaries to act on his behalf during his own life or whether they had some continuing role after his death. Certainly Paul has interpreted Jesus' teaching as applying to the life of the community of his followers after his death (Gal. 1–2). The indications from the gospel tradition are few, but it seems that Jesus did see a role for a community of his followers after his departure (Luke 12.35ff.; Mark 10.39), though there may be possible hints in the predictions in Mark 13. Indeed, he promises to his disciples that they will have a share in the final assize (Matt. 19.28; cf. Luke 22.29). If the Luke version of this saying is original,[24] there may be an indication that already the twelve exercise an authority delegated to them by Jesus, something which is set out very clearly in John 20.21 and Luke 10.16f.

This saying indicates the importance of the number twelve. Questions have been raised about the authenticity of this number (and the fact must be faced that they play little part in the Fourth Gospel: two mentions only in John: 6.70; 20.24). Nevertheless they are referred to in ancient tradition in 1 Corinthians 15.5 and Matthew 19.28. It should not surprise us that Jesus called twelve. After all, we have seen that Jesus saw himself as a prophet to the Jewish nation (Matt. 10.6f.), calling it back from the brink before it was too late (Luke 11.32f, 50; 13.1f.), and thus it would be perfectly understandable if, in a situation where his message was rejected by the majority, he should have bestowed upon those around him a group of representative significance: the twelve were the faithful remnant of the twelve tribes, the firstfruits of the people of God called to be part of the dawning kingdom of God.

Of course, any discussion of Jesus and the Church must pause to consider the saying of Jesus contained in this version of Peter's confession in Matthew 16.17ff. Many have doubted the authenticity of the saying, not only because it is found only in Matthew's Gospel, but also because the saying concerning the primacy of Peter includes one of only two references to the word 'church' (*ekklesia*) in the Gospels. Nevertheless it has to be said (and on this most commentators are agreed) that behind the saying there lies a very ancient saying which betrays signs of its original semitic form, particularly in the promise to bind and loose.[25]

The possibility that the saying may in one form or other go back to Jesus should not be lightly dismissed.[26] If it does, it should be pointed out that the use of the word 'church' in this context is to be understood in the light of contemporary usage, particularly in the Dead Sea Scrolls, where the word '*edah* describes the eschatological community of Israel,[27] and we should not necessarily suppose that any extensive hierarchical organization is presupposed here (though this was certainly not excluded at Qumran). What the saying stresses is the blessedness of the one who confesses Jesus as the Messiah, as this is an indication of divinely bestowed insight (16.17). Certainly Jesus intended his authority to pass to those who had persevered in their discipleship (Luke 22.29). It is not impossible that Peter is singled out for special attention as a cornerstone of the community, based on Jesus' call, to share in the life of the kingdom of God. In the light of other passages dealing with the nature of the authority of Jesus' disciples (Luke 22.25f.; Matt. 18.18) we should not assume that Jesus intended the prominence of Peter to exceed that of his companions (Luke 22.31; cf. John 21.15ff.). What evidence is available from other parts of the New Testament (Gal. 1.18, 2.9) suggests that Peter did in fact have a prominent role in the life of the primitive community, though it is very difficult to speak of his primacy over the other apostles (Acts 10–11; 15; Gal. 2.11ff.);[28] James, the brother of Jesus achieves the position of primacy in the Jerusalem church (Acts 15; *Ant.* 20.200).

As far as one can ascertain, Jesus did not envisage a religious system independent of Judaism. He may have prepared for the existence of a sect within Judaism as a temporary measure during the short period before the kingdom of God came, by delegating his authority to preach and act on God's behalf to his followers. Their task would be to bear witness to the message, which he had preached, after his departure. Jesus' proclamation of the kingdom did not exclude a community nor for that matter plans on Jesus' part for one. This group had its identity through the sharing of a common meal (cf. 1 Cor. 11.23ff.) and the preservation of Jesus' sayings and deeds which were the basis for their continued witness to the kingdom of God. Probably there was a rite of initiation derived from John's baptism, for hints like John 3.26 and 4.1 (cf. Acts 2.38) indicate that John's practice was taken up by Jesus and his disciples. But while it may have certain distinctive beliefs and practices, there is nothing which would separate this group from Judaism. Its beliefs may have been peculiar to it, but that was true of all the sects at this period. To an outside observer, however, the group of followers of Jesus was another Jewish sect, committed to the belief that the hopes for the future were being realized but in no way conscious of being outside the boundaries of Judaism.

9

Jesus and Contemporary Judaism[1]

(a) The Basis of Jesus' Authority

Like any charismatic figure Jesus of Nazareth elicited a variety of responses from his contemporaries. On the one hand, according to the Gospels, we find disciples being convinced that he was the Messiah (Mark 8.29) and after his death, that he had been raised from the dead by God and exalted to his right hand (e.g., Acts 2.33ff.). On the other hand, we find many being very hostile to him (though it would be a mistake to suppose that such hostility was typical of all Jews). The Gospel of John may be correct to suggest that, even during his life, there were leading Jews, who were sympathetic and even disciples of Jesus (e.g., John 3.1ff.; 7.50; 12.42; cf. Acts 5.34ff.). There was, of course, growing hostility in some quarters to Jesus and his followers which led to a situation later, in which Christians were excluded from the synagogues of non-Christian Jews, after the fall of Jerusalem, and Jesus became the epitome of all that was evil for emerging orthodox Judaism.[2]

As we have already noted, the religious scene in Palestine (and we may suspect that it was true of the Diaspora as well) was one in which no particular group could be said to have had complete control over the beliefs and practices of the Jewish people. At different times differing interpretations of the Torah achieved ascendancy. Groups like the Pharisees and Sadducees were all competing for the acceptance of their views as authoritative, though the forum in which these debates took place varied enormously. While the Sadducees confined themselves to the manipulation of political power in Jerusalem, their relationships with the Roman procurator, and their activities in the Sanhedrin, the Pharisees, despite their growing introversion, were slightly more involved with the religious and social issues of the people at large.[3]

Within the Judaism of Jesus' day there were many different interpretations of what constituted obedience to God; the only common factor between the groups was the acceptance of the authority of the Torah, which led to bitter animosity between the different groups over the conflicting interpretations of the sacred text. The justification offered for the various interpretations continued to be a source of conflict. The question of authority was thus a pressing one in first-century Judaism.

According to Mark 1.22 (cf. 11.28) Jesus' teaching differed from that of the Scribes,[4] and the distinctive feature about it was its authority. How did Jesus' teaching with authority differ from that of some of his contemporaries? The answer to this question brings us to a consideration of one of the most important issues in the study of the early Christian movement: its attitude to authority. Understanding of the implications of this issue will help us to perceive why Jesus appeared to be such a threat to some of the Scribes – and what is more – to introduce us to an issue, which persistently recurred in the history of the Christian movement. The career of Paul is further evidence of a similar issue (see Gal. 1–2).

At the heart of the scribal and rabbinic religion was the belief that their interpretation of the Torah was no novelty but could be traced back in its essentials to the prophets and ultimately to Moses himself (Pirke Aboth 1.1): 'Moses received the Law from Sinai and committed it to Joshua, and Joshua to the elders and the elders to the prophets and the prophets committed it to the men of the great synagogue,' (cf. later tradition that Moses received the oral Torah on Sinai, Exodus Rabbah 47.7). This concern for tradition and the application of insights from the past to the needs of the present is manifestly absent from Jesus' teaching, which is marked by an authority which must have seemed arrogant to some of his contemporaries. It is to be found, as we have already seen, in the interpretations of the Law of Moses in the Sermon on the Mount (Matt. 5.21ff.; cf. Mark 2.6), where no reference is made to previous doctrinal authorities, but instead the interpretations are introduced with the emphatic 'I', indicating that Jesus considered himself to be an interpreter at least on a par with the doctrinal authorities of his own day.[5]

As far as we can ascertain, Jesus based his authority to speak in this way on an inner conviction, probably (if Mark 11.28 is anything to go by) based on the baptismal experience at Jordan. With this prophetic-type call, Jesus felt no need to submit his message to any other doctrinal authority for confirmation, for he believed that he had been commissioned by God himself to speak and act in the way he did.[6] As such, he was a challenge to the law-making body of Judaism, the Sanhedrin, not to mention all those groups who believed that in their praxis was to be found the authentic interpretation of the Law of Moses. What is more, his assertion that the final revelation of God's kingdom was either already effective or was imminent, was an interpretation of the traditions of Judaism of such importance that its authenticity was bound to be questioned by those who did not share his methods and interpretations. Perhaps we may see the significance of the saying against the Temple in Mark 14.58 in a new light if we realize that what Jesus presented in himself was a threat to the authority of the Sanhedrin and the Temple: the former as the place whence the Torah went forth to the whole of Israel (*M. San.* 11.2) and the latter the place where God's presence was said to dwell.[7] While Jesus may not have explicitly challenged the latter assertion, by his message he was asserting that a more definitive understanding and experience of God was imminent.[8]

The question of Jesus' authority lies behind the Beelzebub controversy (Mark 3.22ff.; Luke 11.14ff.). In this story the independence of Jesus from the recognized channels of authority leads some of the religious groups to suspect that his miraculous powers showed the influence of the powers of darkness. The problem lay in the interpretation of the significance of these mighty works. His opponents considered that, because Jesus was not recognized as an authoritative teacher, his power could not have been from the God of Abraham, Isaac and Jacob, whose religion was preserved by the Scribes. This was a charge which continued to be of importance in Jewish traditions about Jesus (e.g., in *b. Sanhedrin* 43a, 'Jesus practised magic' – with the implication that he was possessed by an alien supernatural power – 'and led Israel astray').[9] The issue of authority is one which comes up in the Fourth Gospel. Throughout the book Jesus claims the authority to speak of the things of God because of his direct experience of God. He speaks what he has seen and heard with the Father (e.g. John 7.16ff.).

(b) Jesus and the Torah[10]

If we are right to suppose that Jesus believed that he had a commission direct from God himself, it is necessary to ask whether he considered the Law of Moses, the Torah, redundant. Sayings like Luke 16.16 ('the law and the prophets were until John') may indicate that he did, but a consideration of the disputes about the Law indicates that he did not differ too greatly from some of the contemporary teachers. Certainly Jesus may have taken a more lax attitude towards certain practices than many, but it would be wrong to mistake his radical interpretations of the Law as a complete rejection of the Law; we find him from time to time going out of his way to uphold it (Mark 1.44).

One of the issues to which the traditions point as an item of conflict between Jesus and his contemporaries was sabbath observance.[11] Sabbath observance was something of a problem within Judaism in any case.[12] There were many different approaches, and with the possible exception of unanimity over the day of the week on which the sabbath occurred, the nature of the observance required varied enormously within the different Jewish groups.

There is evidence to suggest that some Pharisees were more willing than others to be flexible over the character of sabbath observance, though even within this group there was much divergence. Certainly by no means all the Pharisees of the period would have taken a hard line about healing on the sabbath. In Luke 13.10 ff. Jesus himself quotes an example of current practice (v.15) as a justification for his healing. Elsewhere in the tradition, however, we note that according to Mark 3.1ff., it is *Pharisees* who ally themselves with the Herodians, because of Jesus' activities on the sabbath. It may be that we are dealing here with Pharisees with a more strict outlook.[13] It is by no means clear in his healings that Jesus is *obviously* guilty of any proscribed activity (cf. *M. Shabbath* 7.2). We note that no action is reported of Jesus apart from the word of command in Mark 3.1ff., though in Luke 13.13 Jesus lays his hands on the woman. The healing may have been taken as an indication that Jesus believed that God was at work on the sabbath (cf. John 5.17), contrary to some current assumptions (Jub. 2.30). In this respect the Marcan healing narrative differs from the healing on the sabbath in John 9, where an act of Jesus is reported (v.6f.).

More controversial, however, is the account of the disciples of Jesus plucking grain on the sabbath (Mark 2.23ff.). Though it is not stated in the account, the assumption is that they were plucking grain in order to grind it to make flour, an activity which is explicitly forbidden by the Mishnah (*Shabbat* 7.2). A teacher was bound to take some responsibility for the teaching and activities of his disciples, a fact which is recognized in the disputes in Mark 2, e.g., 2.18.[14] But Jesus justifies the activities of his disciples by reference to Scripture. By reference to the act of David, Jesus sets out to justify the activity of his disciples (2.25ff.), by indicating that when man is in need, there is justification for breaking the strict sabbath code. This is a point with which certain pharisaic groups would have had some sympathy, even if there is no evidence that they would have agreed with him in the detail of his interpretation. In a saying, which has some marked similarities with Jesus' saying at the conclusion of this debate, R. Simeon b. Menasiah (mid-second century AD) said: 'The sabbath is given to you, but you are not surrendered to the sabbath' (*Mek. Shabb* 1; cf. Mark 2.27). Clearly Jesus went further than most liberal Pharisees, whose concern was mainly the preservation of life, which is hardly the case here. Yet this controversy makes plain that we do not have an instance of antinomian behaviour here.[15] As Mark 2.27 makes plain,[16] it is man who is important, not the keeping of a regulation at any price.[17] The sabbath controversies show Jesus unwilling at any point to deny the validity of sabbath observance, but, as with liberal Pharisees of his day, more than willing to interpret sabbath observance in such a way that it did not become a bondage for man. The opposition to his views probably came from those who took a rather rigid and literalistic view of sabbath observance.

Elsewhere in the gospel tradition, the saying of Jesus about divorce has been held to be an example of his complete opposition to the Law of Moses. It is true that Jesus takes the Mosaic injunction about divorce (Deut. 24.1ff.) and criticizes it. But it would be wrong to suppose that there is a rejection of the Torah implied in this passage. What we have to remember is that, as far as Jesus was concerned, the *whole* of the Pentateuch was the product of Moses' pen. When we realize this, we see that his reference to the story in Genesis 1.27 and 2.24 is a reference to another part of the Torah and acceptance of that in preference to the law in Deuteronomy. It should not surprise us that Jesus prefers a part of the Torah dealing with the situation as it was at creation. After all, the perfection of the universe at creation is often a paradigm in Jewish texts for the character of the world in the kingdom of God.[18] Thus the ethics of the kingdom of God require a return to that perfect state which God had always intended for his creation.

The debate over what had priority in the Torah is an issue to which we find allusion in the rabbinic literature. Indeed, it is something which we have already had reason to mention in connection with the burial of a corpse (*Mishnah Nazir* 7.1). Elsewhere in the gospel tradition, we find the issue coming up, particularly in the saying in Luke 11.42 ('But woe to you Pharisees for you tithe mint and rue and every herb, and neglect justice and the love of God; these you ought to have done, without neglecting the others.'). In this respect Jesus is in line with the prophetic challenge to the covenant people, drawing their attention to aspects of the Torah which their contemporary practice has managed to submerge.

It is in a similar vein that we should treat the Qorban controversy in Mark 7.9ff. It is often said that this story, in which Jesus rejects a contemporary practice, whereby a gift devoted to the Temple takes precedence over concern for one's parents, is a rejection of the oral tradition of pharisaic Judaism. Now it would be wrong to suppose that Jesus did not have some harsh words to say about particular details of the tradition of interpretation (Luke 11.42; 11.46f.), not only in this story but also in the collection of sayings against the Pharisees collected in Matthew 23. Nevertheless it would be a mistake to suppose that this criticism necessarily involves rejection of the oral tradition or the attitude to Scripture it presupposes.[19] The gospel tradition indicates that Jesus was no literalist in his interpretation of Scripture (Mark 2.25; 12.26). What this story asserts is that when there is a conflict of interest between the written words of Scripture and the oral tradition, it must be Scripture which is allowed to have precedence. When the oral tradition is allowed to take precedence, it means 'making void the word of God' (Mark 7.13). A saying like Matthew 23.2 (if authentic)[20] confirms the impression that Jesus did not reject out of hand the oral Torah. Indeed, his own method of interpretation of the Torah indicates that he too saw the importance of the need for interpretation of the word of God which a mere literalism would leave ineffective.

In one area of his activity, however, Jesus did seem to sit loosely to contemporary practice, and also to the laws of the Torah. This was in the area of uncleanness.[21] Mark 7.14 comes nearest of all to a threat to the Torah, by asserting that nothing from outside a man can defile a man. If taken at its face value, this appears to threaten the importance of the food laws in the Torah (e.g., Deut. 14.3ff.) by saying that nothing which a man can eat can cause him any defilement. It may well be, as Vermes has suggested, that Jesus, like other charismatic figures, sat rather loosely to some inherited customs, unlike the more rigid scribal authorities; but rather more seems to be at stake in Mark 7.14. A comparison of the Marcan version with its Matthaean parallel may indicate a rather different emphasis in the latter. In the Matthaean version it would appear that Jesus thought the issue of external cleanness trivial compared with the moral uncleanness.[22] If this emphasis is the original one (which has been lost in Mark's Gospel because of concern for the Gentile Christians and their rejection of the food laws, see Mark 7.19), then what we have is an emphasis by Jesus on the words and deeds of an individual as being the important evidence of his character rather than that which he receives from outside himself. The Matthaean version is not so much a rejection of the food laws as a statement about the supreme importance of man's behaviour and his inner motives and desires as a test of his character.

It may be said, in conclusion, that the evidence of the Gospels does not allow us to conclude that Jesus was against the Law of Moses. The tradition shows him interpreting the Torah, even though he frequently comes to very different conclusions from those which were commonly held. Even so, these conclusions are more often than not based on the words of Scripture and follow the traditional pattern of argument and exegesis.[23] The real point at issue with other Jewish interpreters was Jesus' right to interpret the Law of Moses rather than the way he did perhaps and the conclusions he came to. As we have seen, he did not possess that validating authority to speak and interpret. With justification, he was asked by his contemporaries, 'By what authority do you do this?' (Mark 11.28). The fact that he did deviate in several respects, even if not radically, over his interpretation of the Torah, meant that his position and teaching were bound to be a matter of dispute. But it was his assertion that he had the right to proclaim the imminence, perhaps even the dawning, of the new age, which proved to be a stumbling block. It was not that his teaching about the new age differed, as far as one can ascertain, from the bulk of his contemporaries, nor for that matter his outlook on Torah. Rather it was the fact that stated that the promised new age was imminent and himself the herald of it. To assert this without so much as the nod of approval from any recognized authority other than his own conviction was a potential cause of hostility.

(c) Jesus and Other Jewish Groups[24]

In Luke 11.39ff. and Matthew 23.1ff. we find a collection of sayings in which Jesus criticizes Scribes (lawyers) and Pharisees. There is not much evidence to suggest that he totally rejected pharisaic piety.[25] Indeed, in Mark 2.16f. we find Jesus taking an eirenic attitude towards Pharisaism: his and their approaches should not be seen as mutually exclusive. Jesus has come as a physician for the sick; the healthy need no medical treatment, though such an attitude presupposes mutual acceptance for its success. The problem with Pharisaism (and for that matter, the outlook of the other sects in Judaism) was that no room at all was found for the common people ('*am ha-aretz*), not to mention sinners and outcasts, who constituted the vast majority of Jews in Palestine. The initial thrust of the pharisaic movement was to democratize the religion of the cult and lay upon the people the obligation to be a holy nation. Religious activity, therefore, was seen to encompass the whole of existence and not just the specifically cultic acts within the Temple. The democratizing process, however, had ground to a halt. There is a sense in which Jesus' offer of salvation to *all* the nation is an attempt to take up once again the torch of Pharisaism: to challenge the people of God once again with the demands of the righteous God laid before them in the crisis which is overcoming them as the kingdom draws near.

In the light of this, Jesus' criticism of the preoccupation of the Scribes and Pharisees with the minutiae of the Torah must be understood (Luke 11.37f.). The problem is that the Pharisees fail to see that the coming of the kingdom has cast their own religious behaviour in a completely new light. Not only in this but also in the prophetic tradition he condemns the outward behaviour, which masquerades as piety. He criticizes a concern for the outward show of religion, when the intentions are so manifestly unholy (cf. Isa. 1.12ff.). Hence in Luke 11.44 Jesus describes the Pharisees as whitewashed tombs. Because tombs contain corpses, they are unclean, but since people do not know that they are tombs, they come into contact with defilement unawares. This is the rebuke of a teacher, who sees outward acts being a sign of a false piety, when inward thoughts and motives leave so much to be desired.

The Scribes are rebuked for their unwillingness to practise what they preach (Luke 11.46). They work out interpretations of the Torah but, according to Jesus, are unwilling themselves to accept such practices. This may be a criticism of some of the hypothetical character of Jewish halakah (laws), which emanated from the academies. Also their activity in building memorials to the prophets is in stark contrast to their attitude to the prophet who stands in their midst: one who is greater than all who had gone before (Luke 11.32). It is only when the prophets are dead that they are revered and men listen to their voices. The problem is that, for this generation, it may be too late (Luke 11.50). The Scribes do indeed have authority as expositors (Matt. 23.2), but they steadfastly refuse to use their knowledge of the ancestral religion to pierce to the mysteries of God's ways and thereby allow others to follow them (Luke 11.52).

160

Very little is said in the gospel tradition about the relationship of Jesus of Nazareth to the Jewish fight for freedom from Roman domination. Even if the Zealots[26] as a specific faction within Judaism had not emerged in Jesus' own day, it is certain that there were already Jews who believed that the road to the kingdom of God lay in the superhuman struggle with the powers of darkness, which would rid the holy land of Israel of the defilement of a pagan overlord (cf. Ps. Sol. 17.24). The absence of explicit mention of this theme in the Gospels should not be taken to indicate that (a) it did not exist; (b) Jesus sympathized with it and therefore did not criticize it, as he did contemporary scribal and pharisaic religion; (c) he ignored it completely. At several points in the Gospels incidents are mentioned, which suggest that the link between the mission of Jesus and the Jewish struggle for freedom from Rome was a critical issue.[27]

Pre-eminently, the discussion has centred on the question about tribute money (Mark 12.13ff. and par.), the triumphal entry and the cleansing of the Temple (Mark 11.1–18), but mention might also be made of the saying concerning conflict (Matt. 10.34f.; cf. Luke 12.51), Jesus' reply to his disciples over the possession of swords in the garden at the time of his arrest (Luke 22.36f.; cf. 22.49) and the enigmatic saying in Luke 16.16.[28]

There is little to suggest here that the gospel tradition supports the view that Jesus actively supported the Jewish fight for freedom.[29] It would, however, be a mistake to suppose that there is an unambiguous repudiation of the goal of the freedom fighters, namely, the establishment of God's kingdom on earth. Indeed, according to Luke 23.2, one of the charges laid against Jesus was that he had *prevented* the payment of tribute to Caesar, a typical Zealot act because it denies the dominion of Caesar.[30] Nevertheless in the light of his exhortations to non-violence (Matt. 5.39ff.), elsewhere in the Gospels, we may suppose that Jesus would not have condoned the *methods* of the Zealots and their predecessors, namely a violent overthrow of the existing order initiated by the people of God. That is not to suggest that he did not expect the violent overthrow of that order, however. We may suppose that, in order that the age to come might be realized in all its fullness, when the poor would inherit the kingdom and the hungry would be fed, the might of Rome would have to be overthrown. We must suppose that Jesus' views resembled those of the apocalyptists who expected God's purposes in history to be worked out and a kingdom of righteousness to be set up without human hand (cf. Dan. 2.34; 4 Ezra 13.38f.). Nevertheless Jesus' proclamation of the kingdom of God inevitably raised hopes of deliverance for the people of God and must have attracted support from those who expected to find in Jesus a leader of the national liberation (cf. John 6.15; Luke 24.21). It should occasion little surprise, therefore, that a freedom fighter was to be found among Jesus' disciples (if that is what the word Zealot means in Luke 6.15; cf. Mark 3.18).

According to the Gospel of Mark, Jesus' dealings with the Sadducees are confined to the time spent in Jerusalem immediately before his arrest and death (12.18ff.).[31] Even if we are unwilling to follow Mark's chronology in its entirety, it is probably right to suppose that Jesus would only have come into contact with the priestly aristocracy in Jerusalem. It should be noted, however, that members of the priestly tribe were scattered throughout the land, and it is likely that the Sadducean understanding of Scripture probably was much closer to the actual practice of the majority of Jews.[32] It is also no accident that they assume a significant role in the last days of Jesus' life, and, as we shall see, probably took the major role in bringing about his death. Like the Herodians, with whom Jesus is reported to have come into contact earlier in his ministry (Mark 3.6), one of their prime concerns was with relations with the occupying power. Indeed their continued hegemony depended on adequate relations with the Roman procurator (John 11.47ff.).[33]

In the debates recorded between Jesus and the Sadducees in the Gospels the issue centres on the question of resurrection. In it Jesus shows how close he is to the pharisaic belief in the resurrection of the dead which was denied by the Sadducees. As is well known,[34] the Old Testament has very little to say explicitly on the belief in the resurrection. Only in Daniel 12.2 do we have it stated unambiguously. To this extent the Sadducees were on strong ground to deny the validity of the resurrection doctrine. What we find in Mark 12.18ff. is Jesus justifying the doctrine on the basis of the Torah (12.26), a fact which would have endeared him to the Pharisees (*M. San.* 10.1) and also arguing for a belief, which spoke of the transformation of the body rather than participation by the resurrected in the kind of life that they had known before (cf. 1 Cor. 15.35ff.).

(d) Jesus' Attitude to the Temple

At the centre of the religious life of Judaism before the First Revolt in AD 66 was the Temple in Jerusalem. The vast complex of cultic activity carried on there in fulfilment of the cultic regulations of the Torah was a focus of devotion for Jews from all over the world. Because of its importance (for all Jews) Jesus' actions and statements about the Temple require some consideration.

All the Gospels record the fact that Jesus entered the Temple and drove out the traders from the outer court (Mark 11.15ff. and par.). In the Gospel of John the incident is said to have taken place at the beginning of the ministry (John 2.13ff.), though it may well have been placed here as part of the structure of argument of the Gospel as a whole (cf. John 4.22).[35] The cleansing of the Temple was not a protest against the Temple as such, though the emphasis on it as a house of prayer (Mark 11.17) may well indicate a preference for the synagogue worship rather than the sacrificial system. The act itself is reminiscent of the dramatic prophetic acts in the Old Testament (e.g., 1 Sam. 15.27).

There has been much debate over the meaning of this story.[36] In interpreting it, much depends on the weight one attaches to the quotations from Scripture (Isa. 56.7; Jer. 7.11). Several commentators regard them as later interpretations, because there seems to be no obvious connection between the acts and the scriptural passages. It is true that the Hebrew of Isaiah 56.7 has a rather different flavour from the Greek ('These foreigners I will bring to my holy mountain and make them joyful in my house of prayer'), but even in this form the words are not inconsistent with the act performed by Jesus: the imminent end of the old Temple, symbolized by Jesus' action, paves the way for a new Temple, to which the Gentiles would come, as predicted in Scripture (Isa. 2.3; Mic. 4.1ff.). It is possible that Jesus saw himself fulfilling the eschatological prophecy in Zechariah 14.21. The quotation from Jeremiah 7.11 is more difficult to explain. Jeremias thinks that it refers to the greed of the High Priestly family which profited from the lucrative Temple trade.[37]

The eschatological setting of Jesus' ministry recalls the belief found in some eschatological material that the new age would see a new Temple (e.g., 1 Enoch 90.29, if it is a reference to the Temple rather than the city as a whole). It is possible that this dramatic act may have symbolized the belief expressed in words elsewhere in the tradition (Mark 14.58; cf. John 2.17) that the old Temple had first to be destroyed to make way for the eschatological Temple. Even the cult had to be purified and renewed for the arrival of the kingdom of God.

There may be a hint in John's version of the cleansing that it was a protest against the sacrificial system, for in this version of the story Jesus ejects the sacrificial animals from the Temple also (2.15). If, however, the Last Supper was a Passover meal, we may suppose that Jesus did accept the sacrificial system (Luke 22.15).[38] Like the prophets before him (cf. Hos. 6.6; Matt. 9.13; 12.7), Jesus condemns the perverted sense of religious obligation which lays such great weight on formal religious devotion embodied in cultic acts and neglects the important aspects of the demand of God's righteousness (cf. Luke 11.42).

There is evidence to suggest that Jesus did predict the downfall of the Temple.[39] At the beginning of the eschatological discourse in Mark 13.2 we find him telling his disciples that there will not be left one stone of the Temple on top of another. But this is clearly the pronouncement of the prophet similar to Jeremiah's prediction in Jeremiah 7 rather than a rejection of all that the Temple stood for.

At the account of his questioning by the High Priest in Mark witnesses report a saying of Jesus, otherwise not reported on the lips of Jesus in the Gospels, to the effect that Jesus would destroy the Temple and in three days build a Temple not made with hands (Mark 14.58; cf. Matt. 26.61). There is a version of this saying on the lips of Jesus in the Gospel of John (2.19), but it takes a rather different form.[40]

The action against the Temple and the words, which Jesus may have spoken about its destruction, must have been regarded as deeply offensive (so Mark 11.18). The Temple in Jerusalem was the place above all where God had caused his presence to dwell (Deut. 12.5). How could a prophet from God speak of its destruction? According to Mark 15.29, Jesus was reproached with this prediction in the last moments of his life. While it is not easy to see how it could be regarded as blasphemy, except in an indirect sense, it was the kind of comment which was bound to cause, at the very least, deep suspicion (e.g., John 11.47ff.; cf. *BJ* 2.397). An action against the Temple may have been misconstrued, but a word against it would have been likely to have brought dire consequences for the one who uttered. We know of another Jesus who predicted the destruction of the Temple and suffered for his pains (*BJ* 6.300f.):

> One Jesus, son of Ananias, a rude peasant, suddenly began to cry out, 'A voice from the east, a voice from the west, a voice from the four winds; a voice against Jerusalem and the sanctuary' ... The magistrates supposing, as was indeed the case, that the man was under some supernatural impulse, brought him before the Roman governor; there, although flayed to the bone with scourges, he neither sued for mercy nor shed a tear, but, merely introducing the most mournful of variations into his ejaculation, responded to each stroke with 'Woe to Jerusalem!' (Translation from the Loeb edition.)

10

The Arrest and Trial of Jesus[1]

According to all our sources, Jesus was crucified by the Romans. Why did a Jewish teacher end up on a Roman gallows? Why was he not punished by the Jews instead? Can we trust the gospel accounts?

According to the Gospels, hostility towards Jesus arose very soon after the beginning of his ministry, and it would be a mistake to suppose that the investigation into his activity was confined only to the last hours of his life (cf. Mark 3.6f.; John 5.18; 8.58; 10.39; 11.47ff.).[2] Indeed, from the charges which are brought against Jesus according to Luke 23.2, it is apparent that words of Jesus uttered earlier in his ministry form a part of the case made against him (the reference to the debate about the tribute money). Such an ongoing investigation about Jesus' teaching, the basis of his authority and his conduct probably continued throughout his activity as a preacher, and what is described in the accounts in the Gospels is a continuation of that process, in which the main participants are those based in Jerusalem.

It was the plot against Jesus when he travelled to Jerusalem (not for the first time during his ministry, if the Gospel of John is to be believed; see also Luke 13.34) which led to his arrest and death. According to our sources Jesus went up to Jerusalem as a prophetic act (Luke 13.33; cf. John 7.3f.) to challenge his nation at the centre of its religious activity. This probably coincided with Passover, and his arrival in Jerusalem was marked by a messianic demonstration on the part of his supporters and a prophetic act in the Temple (Mark 11.15ff. and par.), if the Synoptic chronology is to be believed. While it is true that in the earlier plots to destroy Jesus mentioned in the Gospels (e.g., Mark 3.6; cf. Matt. 22.15), the Pharisees may have had an important part to play, they are not mentioned in the traditions concerned with Jesus' death (except two late references in Matt. 27.62; John 18.3).[3] It would appear from the Gospel accounts that the initiative to remove Jesus was taken by the priestly group (cf. Mark 11.18). At the Sanhedrin trial in the Gospels, the main questioning comes from the High Priest, Caiaphas. It is likely that at this stage, at least, the plot to get rid of Jesus was in the main the responsibility of the priestly faction (Mark 15.11). The activity of Jesus in the Temple, his claim to proclaim the imminence of the kingdom of God and his presence in Jerusalem at Passover, when hopes for a national deliverance ran high, made him a natural target for the priestly and aristocratic faction. After all, it had most to lose if relationships with Rome deteriorated to any significant degree through the outbreak of insurrection (cf. Mark 15.7).

Before embarking on a consideration of the difficulties connected with the accounts of the trial and death of Jesus in the Gospels, let us look in a little more detail at the three versions of the arrest and Jewish trial of Jesus, which we have in the New Testament: the accounts in the Gospels of Mark (Matthew is probably substantially dependent on Mark), Luke,[4] and the Gospel of John.[5]

According to the Gospel of Mark, after Jesus' arrest (14.43ff.) he is taken to the High Priest, Caiaphas, where the chief priests, elders and scribes assembled; it appears to have been a meeting of the Sanhedrin (14.55). In the hearing there was much inconsistent testimony, including the quotation of a saying of Jesus against the Temple (14.58; cf. Mark 13.2; John 2.19ff.). Jesus does not reply until the High Priest asks him if he is the Messiah, the Son of the Blessed. Jesus replies, 'I am, and you will see the Son of Man sitting at the right hand of power' (14.62). On hearing this the High Priest tears his mantle, speaks of Jesus' blasphemy, and the Council finds him to be guilty of a crime deserving of the death penalty (14.64). Jesus is then mocked and asked to prophesy (14.65). This is followed by Peter's denial of Jesus, a story which Mark has already begun to tell before recounting the Sanhedrin trial (14.54ff.). When it is day, the Sanhedrin discuss the matter and resolve to take Jesus to Pilate, presumably on the charge that Jesus has tried to make himself a king (though this is not explicitly stated); hence Pilate's question in 15.2. Jesus is interrogated by Pilate, who offers to release Jesus (15.6ff.). To satisfy the crowd, Pilate releases Barabbas and sends Jesus to be crucified (15.15ff.).

According to Luke, after his arrest Jesus is taken to Caiaphas' house, and at this point Luke relates Peter's denial (22.55ff.), which takes a slightly different and more poignant form in this Gospel: Jesus turns to look at Peter after the denial takes place (22.61). Then Jesus is mocked and asked to prophesy (22.63). At daybreak the assembly of elders, Chief Priest and scribes meets (22.66); they lead Jesus to the Sanhedrin. At this Jesus is asked whether he is the Messiah (22.67). Jesus' reply is evasive (22.67b–8) but is then followed by a variant of the Son of Man saying we find in Mark's Gospel ('But from now on the Son of Man shall be seated at the right hand of the power of God' (22.69; cf. Mark 14.62)). After this, Jesus is asked whether he is the Son of God, and Jesus replies 'You say that I am' (cf. Matt. 26.64). This is enough to convince the Council of his pretensions. Arising out of this, they take Jesus to Pilate and accuse him of three offences: perverting the nation; forbidding the payment of tribute to Caesar; and saying that he is Christ a king (Luke 23.2); only the last of these has been ascertained at the recently completed hearing.[6]

Pilate interrogates Jesus but finds no fault in him (23.4). The charge is repeated that Jesus was stirring up the people (23.5). When he finds that Jesus is from Galilee, Pilate sends Jesus to Herod Antipas, who after questioning him, sends Jesus back to Pilate (23.11). Pilate then calls together the chief priests and rulers of the people and states that he finds no fault in Jesus (23.15). The response is a request for the release of Barabbas and for the crucifixion of Jesus (vv.18ff.).

The Fourth Gospel is most explicit of all about the plots and attempts to kill Jesus throughout his ministry (e.g., 5.18; 8.59; 10.31; 11.8) and includes a discussion of a meeting of the Sanhedrin convened for the purpose of discussing Jesus' ministry before the fateful events surrounding the last Passover (11.49). This meeting discusses the threat to the community posed by the activity of Jesus and by the possibility that the Romans would remove the essential privileges of their religion if he was allowed to continue unhindered. In the Gospel of John, the arrest of Jesus is conducted by a band of soldiers and officers from the chief priests (18.3). Jesus is then taken to the house of Annas, the father-in-law of Caiaphas, himself once a High Priest (18.13). At this point there follows the first part of Peter's denial. Meanwhile Annas asks Jesus about his disciples and his teaching: in other words, it is his position as a teacher rather than a messianic claimant which concerns Annas (18.19). Jesus' reply stresses the openness of his teaching (cf. John 3.1ff.).

He is struck because of his apparent arrogance in answering the High Priest. After this, Annas sends Jesus to Caiaphas (nothing is said about this hearing), and then the rest of the account of Peter's denial is completed (vv.25ff.). Jesus is taken to the praetorium from Caiaphas' house at daybreak, but the Jews are unwilling to enter because they did not want to be defiled (v.28) and so be debarred from eating the passover that same day. The events in John take place twenty-four hours earlier than the chronology of Mark's Gospel suggests (cf. 19.14; though 19.31 may reflect the Synoptic chronology).[7] Pilate asks why the Jews have brought Jesus to him and is told that Jesus is considered an evil-doer (v.31). Pilate tells the Jews to judge Jesus by their own laws. It is then pointed out that the main reason for the Jews' inability to carry out the just demands of their own law is because it is not lawful for them to put any man to death (18.31ff.). The Fourth Gospel implies (18.33), as Mark does, that the Jews had brought a charge against Jesus of making himself a king and therefore a threat to Rome, but there is definitely an implication in John that if the Jews *did* have the right to carry out a capital punishment, they would have used it. Pilate interrogates Jesus (vv.33ff.). Discussion centres on the nature of Jesus' kingship (v.36). Pilate finds no fault in Jesus and wants to release him; the Jews ask for Barabbas.

A comparison between these three different accounts reveals the following points of interest:

(i) Only Mark mentions the charge of blasphemy and an official judgement by the Sanhedrin against Jesus on a capital charge (Mark 14.64);

(ii) Only Mark has Jesus give an unequivocal response to the High Priest's question (14.62). Even in Matthew (26.64), who follows Mark's account quite closely, there is a more ambiguous response;[8]

(iii) In John's account of the Jewish hearing (nothing is said about what happened before Caiaphas), there is no mention of an official Sanhedrin hearing and the emphasis in the interrogation is on Jesus' teaching rather than his messianic pretensions. It is possible that the meeting which took place in Luke 22.66ff. could be construed as an unofficial hearing rather than a full meeting of the Sanhedrin.[9]

(iv) Only John tells us that the main reason for taking Jesus to the Romans was the lack of right to carry out the death sentence (18.31).

Over the years, the accounts of the arrest and trial of Jesus, particularly that which took place before the Jewish authorities, have been subjected to a great deal of critical examination.[10] There is little doubt that, as they stand, the Gospel accounts do present us with certain problems particularly when they are considered in the light of Jewish sources, which discuss the procedure for the trial of capital cases. In addition (though this is a matter which will not be examined in great detail here), some of the aspects of the story concerning the Romans have not found parallels in contemporary provincial legal procedure. Among the major problems in reconciling the Gospel accounts with the external sources the following points may be noted:

(i) According to the earliest codification of Jewish law concerning the procedure of the Sanhedrin (*Mishnah San.* 4.1) cases concerned with capital offences could not be tried at night, on the eve of a festival, nor could a verdict of condemnation be reached on the same day that the trial was started. Thus the account of the Jewish trial in the Gospel of Mark betrays several major discrepancies with Jewish legal procedure.

(ii) According to the Mishnah, a charge of blasphemy could only be upheld against an individual if the divine name (the *tetragrammaton* YHWH) was pronounced (*M. San.* 7.5). It is by no means obvious from our sources that Jesus was guilty of pronouncing the divine name.

(iii) The correctness of the assertion in John 18.31 that the Jews did not have the right to put anyone to death has been challenged by reference to several episodes in the New Testament and contemporary Jewish sources. Thus the stoning of Stephen (Acts 7.57ff.), attempts to stone Jesus (e.g., John 8.59), the killing of James, the brother of Jesus (*Ant.* 20.200 and Hegesippus in Eusebius *EH* 2.23), the stoning of the adulteress (John 8.1ff.), the execution of the priest's daughter related in *M. Sanhedrin* 7.2 and the right to put to death a non-Jew apprehended in the Temple (Joseph *BJ* 5.194) have all been brought forward as evidence that the Jews did in fact have the right to execute those guilty of religious offences at this period.[11]

(iv) The release of Barabbas to the crowd by Pilate, recounted in all four Gospels, has caused surprise to those familiar with Roman provincial legal procedure.[12] There is not much evidence from secular sources which would confirm the occurrence of this practice.

(v) The character of Pilate as it is portrayed in the Gospels, weak and vacillating, and easily swayed by the leaders of an alien nation, is said to contrast greatly with what we know of him from elsewhere. Philo in particular (*Emb.* 299ff.) presents a picture of a determined and ruthless individual, who did not go out of his way to do any favours for the Jews.

(vi) If John 18.12 is to be understood as a reference to Roman soldiers participating in the arrest of Jesus in the garden, the question must be asked why there should have been any need for Jesus to have been taken to the Jewish authorities, as the Romans would already have been involved at this early stage and could well have dealt with him themselves.

These issues have persuaded many scholars that the accounts of Jesus' arrest and trial in the New Testament Gospels cannot be regarded as being in any way accurate accounts of those events. Critics of the Gospel accounts have questioned in particular the historicity of the Sanhedrin trial and the inability of the Jewish authorities to put offenders to death. Certainly the problems raised by the night-trial conducted by the Sanhedrin, as recounted in the Synoptic Gospels, are enormous. But if John 18.31 is incorrect, and the Jews did have the right to execute those convicted on capital charges, why was Jesus crucified by a decision of the Roman procurator? Could it be that it was not a religious offence on which Jesus was found guilty but a political offence; hence his Roman execution?[13] If so, then the Gospels would be seen as an attempt to play down the political nature of Jesus' activity. Their attempt to get round the problem was to place the blame for Jesus' death on the Jews and remove as much blame as possible from the Romans. This would have been done by inventing a Sanhedrin trial, which, it is said, is proved by the way in which the account in the Gospels contradicts Jewish procedure. Certainly, if the Acts of the Apostles is anything to go by, one early Christian apologist wanted to show how little hostility there had been towards the Christian cult from Roman administrators (e.g., Acts 13.12). This was probably partly evangelistic (to show that any person could avail himself of the salvation brought by Jesus of Nazareth),[14] but was also to persuade the Romans that, despite the fact that the founder of the religion had been put to death on a Roman gallows, there was no political offence involved in Jesus' ministry.

In the light of these considerations it is probably not surprising to find that over the years there have been attempts to show that Jesus' death by crucifixion was his penalty for his part in treasonable activity against the Roman overlords as a result of his complicity in the Jewish fight for freedom against Rome. The Gospels are therefore to be regarded as later fabrications by the Church to cover up this embarrassing fact, by stressing the Jewish responsibility for the death of Jesus.

Despite the problems posed for the Jewish trial, as it is set out in the Gospels, by a comparison with other sources, the matter is not as easily resolved as is sometimes supposed. Several comments must be passed on the criticisms made of the Gospel accounts in the light of the external sources:

(i) It is uncertain whether the regulations governing the procedure for a capital trial, as laid out in the *Mishnah*,[15] were in force at the time of Jesus. In the first place, the *Mishnah* was only written in its present form at the end of the second century AD, and while it certainly contains much material going back to the time of Jesus and before, we cannot be sure that the procedures outlined in the *Mishnah* reflect actual regulations from the early part of the first century and are rather the idealized picture of later legal codifiers.

(ii) Even if we could be sure that the regulations were in force in Jesus' day, we have had reason to suggest that the forerunners of the rabbis, whose laws are found in the *Mishnah*, may not have been intimately involved in the final hearings, which preceded the taking of Jesus to Pilate. It must be asked whether the regulations, which we find in the *Mishnah*, would have been accepted as the basis for the procedure accepted by the group, which was responsible for the arrest of Jesus. If, as seems likely, it was dominated by a priestly or Sadducean group, there is little reason to suppose that *pharisaic* laws would have been accepted as the basis for the procedure of this court (if such it was).[16]

(iii) We assume that the hearing before the High Priest was in fact a formal trial. Such a supposition can only be gleaned from the Marcan account (though it is hinted at in Luke), for that alone records the charge of blasphemy made against Jesus and a judicial condemnation. In the versions in Luke and John there seems to be evidence that we are not dealing with a formal *trial* of Jesus, but an informal hearing,[17] which would precede a deputation to Pilate. Indeed, a consideration of the Johannine version with its continued process of inquiry throughout the Gospel, would lead us to the conclusion that what we have on the night before Jesus' death was an informal gathering, whose task it was to carry out the final process of a much longer attempt to incriminate Jesus and take action against him.

(iv) Although we do not have any statement in the Synoptic Gospels, where Jesus pronounces the divine name, Mark (14.62) has Jesus say, 'I am', the great statement of divine revelation familiar to us from the Old Testament. Indeed, it is on the basis of a similar saying in John 8.58 that Jesus is almost stoned to death (cf. 18.6). How much weight we attach to this usage in Mark and to the profound *Ego Eimi* Christology in the Fourth Gospel as the basis for Jesus' condemnation is uncertain.[18] It seems preferable to suppose that the ambiguous response to the messianic question in Matthew and Luke reflects Jesus' own words and the more explicit response found in Mark is a later explication by the Evangelist.

(v) If indeed we are to look for any evidence of Jesus' being guilty of blasphemy (though once more we cannot suppose that the precise regulation for blasphemy, which we found in the *Mishnah*, was in force in Jesus' day, cf. Mark 2.7), then it is probably to be found in the saying about the Son of Man. Once again there has been much discussion about the authenticity of this saying, not to mention about the relationship between the variant forms in Mark and Luke, an issue which cannot be pursued here. If, however, we suppose that all that Jesus was claiming was the messianic office, then it seems unlikely that he would be guilty of blasphemy. Even the arrogance in claiming to be the Messiah would not be regarded as blasphemy. Whatever Jesus may have been saying about himself in this saying the point which

170

comes across in it to his hearers is that another figure will sit at God's right hand. There is no *necessary* self-identification here, unless the phrase Son of Man was *widely* accepted as a means whereby the speaker could refer to himself. Thus it may not be the identification of himself with the heavenly Son of Man, which is the point at issue in this saying, but the theology of Jesus' statement itself. Jesus asserts that there are *two* figures sitting side by side in the heavenly world: God and a man. This could well have been taken as a threat to Jewish monotheism, and, therefore, as a form of blasphemy. This can be illustrated by reference to a story in the Babylonian Talmud, where the distinguished Jewish Rabbi Akiba interprets the two thrones in Daniel 7.9 as being thrones for God and David, an interpretation which earns for him a rebuke from his contemporary R. Jose the Galilean (*b. Hagigah* 14a).[19]

(vi) More attention should be paid to the fact that an issue which preoccupied the authorities was Jesus' right to be a teacher. It has been suggested, for example, that Jesus was on trial as a rebellious elder (Deut. 17.2).[20] Jesus' silence during his trial may indicate a rebellious attitude and defiance to the legally constituted court of law though the motif of silence may be indebted to Isaiah 53.7. In the light of the doubts which have been expressed about the formal nature of the trial we have to ask whether the evidence is strong enough to bear the weight of this interpretation. This suggestion points us to the importance of the character of Jesus' teaching, particularly in the light of the problem of authority and eschatological fulfilment, as a feature of the investigations carried on. Indeed, they help us to understand better the question about the Temple raised at the hearing in Mark (14.58) and our suggestion about the heterodox character of the theological statement in Mark 14.62 may fall into this category.

(vii) An interesting suggestion has been put forward by John O'Neill,[21] namely that it would have been blasphemy had he called himself Messiah, and when the Sanhedrin was convinced that he had in fact done so, it condemned him to death. If such were a live issue in Jesus' day, it would coincide with the issue of authority already discussed: what right did a person have to proclaim the ultimate rule of God and claim a central place in it?

(viii) Discussion of the correctness of John 18.31 has obviously been very important for those who want to support the historicity of the Sanhedrin trial.[22] There is some valuable external material which seems to confirm John's statement (cf., *j. San.* 1.1; *b. San.* 41a; *b. Abod. Zar.* 8b). One example is a Jewish source called the *Megillat Ta'anit*.[23] In chapter 6 of that work we find a list of days on which it was not lawful to fast. The text mentions two dates in the month of Elul: one when the Romans withdrew from Judaea and

Jerusalem and the five days following when Jews once again were permitted to kill the malefactors. This source seems to indicate that during the Roman rule, before the withdrawal, Jews did not have the right to kill those guilty. In addition, in the Jerusalem Talmud (*j. Sanhedrin* 1.1 and 7.2), there is a reference to the fact that the right of Jews to put to death offenders had been taken away forty years before the destruction of Jerusalem, another indication that there was a recollection in the Jewish sources that the right to punish offenders with death had disappeared for a time.

As far as the other examples are concerned, it has to be said that the death of Stephen, while taking place in the context of an official trial (Acts 6.12), does not come as the result of an official decision by the Sanhedrin but a spontaneous reaction to Stephen's speech (7.54). The death of James, the brother of Jesus reported in Josephus, takes place during an interregnum between the procuratorships of Festus and Albinus. Indeed, Josephus himself actually comments on the fact that Annas had acted illegally in the eyes of some of his contemporaries. Finally, the reference to the execution of the priest's daughter in *M. San.* 7.2, while certainly taking place before AD 66, possibly occurred during the period AD 41–4 when Agrippa was king of Judaea.[24]

(ix) Finally, the alleged inconsistency of the picture of Pilate in the Gospels as compared with other sources is probably not great. Indeed, even Philo (*Embassy* 304) indicates that after the incident with the shields, when Pilate deliberately provoked Jewish wrath by flouting Roman insignia in the city, Pilate's position was by no means strong. The unrest which that had caused made him suspicious, and, what is more, made it difficult for him to ignore the pressure of the Jewish authorities, however much he may have hated having to give in to them.[25] Pilate thus could not risk another incident like that of the shields, and we may suppose that such an insecure position was known also to the Jewish leaders.

As far as the release of Barabbas is concerned, the odd piece of evidence may be mentioned which suggests that the practice is by no means as outlandish as was once thought. A passage in the *Mishnah* (*Pesahim* 8.6) speaks of the release of a prisoner at Passover time, though nothing is said about a Roman procurator being involved in this, and Josephus (*Ant.* 20.215) refers to the action of another Roman procurator, Albinus, who brought out of prison those who were imprisoned for trifling offences and released them. Josephus comments: 'The land was infested with brigands.'[26]

It will be seen from this that many of the problems connected with the trial of Jesus can be dealt with if we give more attention than has been done in the past to the accounts in the Gospels of John and Luke. What is more, it seems likely that the pattern of informal hearings hinted at in Luke and found explicitly in John corresponds more nearly with the situation than the formal trial we have in Mark. We may say, therefore, that Mark is wrong in the impression he gives of a formal legal process confined to the last fateful Passover leading to an official condemnation, *though the possibility should not be excluded that some sort of official legal inquiry had been in action over a much longer period of Jesus' ministry.*

The reference to Jesus' saying against the Temple (Mark 14.58 and par.), Annas' inquiry about the nature of Jesus' teaching (John 18.19), as well as the possibly heterodox implications of Jesus' saying found in variant forms in Mark 14.62 and Luke 22.69 should remind us that one of the features of any inquiry instituted against Jesus concerned the nature of his teaching and the authority which he claimed to teach as he did. His claim to speak on behalf of God was a threat against the Temple and the Sanhedrin, which met there to enact laws binding on the whole of Israel.[27] A word against the Temple would be a word against its place in Jewish life and a contumacious attempt to usurp its authority.

Thus there is sufficient evidence for us to suppose that the Gospel accounts concerning a Jewish hearing, though not a trial, on the night before Jesus' death, should not be written off. Indeed, such Jewish sources as mention Jesus at all indicate that Jesus was in fact condemned by Jews, a fact which is often missed in those attempts to play down the Jewish involvement in the death of Jesus. To say this, however, is not to deny that there may well have been some later retouching of the account of Jesus' trial in the Gospels, in order to exculpate Jesus as far as possible from political involvement. Such factors would have been particularly necessary when Jewish and Christian relations were becoming strained; there was a need for Christians to loosen the ties which linked them too closely to the deeds of the hated Jewish nation, and an accommodation with society became more pressing.

But however much we stress the importance of a Jewish hearing as part of the process which led to Jesus' death, and stress the interest in Jesus' teaching, it must be said that it is likely that Jesus said or did something which enabled the priestly section to take Jesus to the procurator on a political charge. Probably Jesus' refusal to deny messianic pretensions, even if we suppose that the Marcan form of the response to the High Priest is secondary, may have confirmed the impression which his preaching, entry into Jerusalem, and action in the Temple had already given, namely that he was a dangerous threat to the interests of the priestly group just as much by his (implicitly) anti-Roman sentiments as his action against the Temple. Satisfactory coexistence with the procurator was of great importance to the aristocracy and the priesthood in Jerusalem, not only because it enabled the High Priest to perform his duties but also because the continued Roman presence guaranteed their livelihood and privileges.[28]

As we have seen, the political implications of the message of Jesus are well brought out in the discussion in John 11.49f. It must be said that Jesus' teaching *did* have implicit political consequences, in so far as it was through and through eschatological. Even if we must reject the assertion that Jesus was himself a Zealot, there can be little doubt that his message was understood in this way by some of his followers. The fact is that the coming of the kingdom of God was seen by Jesus to involve the overthrow of the existing order of God. Thus even if Jesus renounced the methods of the Zealots, his goal of a new age was deeply disturbing to those who preferred the compromises of the present age to the uncertainties of the new.[29]

11

Jesus' Personal Claim[1]

There can be little doubt that, assuming that Jesus did indeed claim that in his ministry the kingdom of God was imminent, there is an implicit claim about the importance of his person in the divine economy. Thus even if we consider that the titles which are used of Jesus in the Gospels reflect the beliefs of the early Church rather than the mind of Jesus himself, it should not cause us surprise that the character of his preaching caused his followers to make such claims about him. Even the most sceptical of gospel critics would want to assert that a Christology is already implicit within the sayings of Jesus in the Gospels. Thus, for example, Hans Conzelmann says:

> How then did Jesus regard himself? The answer cannot be given by a christological concept [i.e., Messiah, Son of God, Son of Man]. It must come through a demonstration of how Jesus associated the announcement of the Kingdom of God with himself as its sign. Of course, a Christology is implied here. It will have to be developed after Easter.[2]

Conzelmann is right to point out the importance of the implicit Christology in the gospel traditions. Jesus' activities in claiming to forgive sins (Mark 2.6f.), his teaching with authority (Mark 1.22), his conviction that God had sent him (Luke 10.16; cf. John 7.16 and the many parallels to this sending formula in this Gospel[3]) all point to a claim of ultimate significance. Indeed, the whole association of Jesus with the kingdom of God is by itself sufficient to make a christological claim of great weight without any recourse to the titles.

Yet it would be wrong to suppose that the titles as a whole do not go back in any shape or form to Jesus. Some consideration of the more important will reveal that there is a likelihood that some further indication of the character of Jesus' personal claim may be gleaned from a survey of their use.

(a) The Prophet[4]

We have already noted the great importance which the baptism had for the beginning of his proclamation of the kingdom of God. Its importance for Jesus is confirmed in sayings, such as Luke 12.50; Mark 11.30. Whatever our views on the historicity of the baptismal account, its Jewish flavour and central place in the gospel tradition provide a convincing explanation of Jesus' ministry, and his immediate relationship with God made possible without any dependence on traditional channels of authority.[5] The baptism account has affinities with the call-experiences of prophets like Isaiah, Ezekiel and Second Isaiah (Isa. 6.1; 42.1; Ezek. 1.1). Mark's version presents it as a personal experience, in which a vision of the Spirit and a divine voice proclaim the nature of his relationship with God.[6] We can probably say that, during this experience, Jesus came to a new understanding of his relationship with God and, if our accounts are to be believed, received the prophetic Spirit. Despite the suspicion which surrounds the references to the Spirit in the gospel tradition,[7] there seems to be no good reason why Jesus should not have believed that he had been filled with the Spirit of God.[8] Support for this position comes from rabbinic sources, where we know that the return of the Holy Spirit to the people of God was considered to be a mark that the new age had in fact dawned. Indeed, in a much-quoted saying in *Tosefta Sotah* 13.3 we read that the prophetic Spirit had departed from Israel with the last of the prophets to return in the last days (cf. Acts 2.17). Such a belief was based on passages like Deuteronomy 18.15 and Malachi 4.5 (cf. Mark 8.28). We have already seen that there was a close link between the coming kingdom and Jesus' own ministry, and it is therefore not impossible that one of the indications of this link was the return of the prophetic spirit.

There are parts of the tradition, which seem to suggest that inspiration by the Spirit was important for Jesus, for example, Mark 3.28 and Matthew 12.28 (though the Luke parallel does not mention the Spirit; cf. Acts 10.38).[9] The account peculiar to Luke of Jesus' preaching in the synagogue in Capernaum (4.16ff.) is based on the fulfilment of Isaiah 61, and the temptation narrative, whatever its original form may have been, is typical of the religiously impelled man undergoing the testing of his vocation.[10]

But it is other material in the Gospels, which seems to indicate that Jesus thought of himself as a prophet and which lends greatest weight to the view that he was inspired by the Spirit (Matt. 13.57; 12.39; Luke 13.33f.). Certainly he was thought to be a prophet by his contemporaries, as certain reports about reaction to Jesus indicate (Matt. 21.11; 26; Luke 7.16; John 6.14). Indeed, it is significant that at his trial Jesus is asked to prophesy by the soldiers, as if there was a view abroad that he was an inspired man who thought of himself as having a divine commission (Mark 14.65).[11]

Like the prophets of old, Jesus comes to condemn his generation for their unbelief and places himself in the long line of prophets who have done the same (Luke 11.49ff.). He comes from rural Galilee, crying woes on the towns (Luke 10.13ff.; 13.34; 22.27ff.).[12] Like them, he is rejected by his contemporaries (Mark 6.4; cf. Jer. 15.10; 20). Like them, his criticisms are directed at the people who have made obedience to God a sham (Luke 11.46). Like them, he preaches doom on the unrepentant (Matt. 11.20ff.). Also he speaks with authority (Mark 1.22); his speech resembles the authoritative divine pronouncement of the prophets, 'Thus says the Lord', prefaced as it is with the solemn 'Truly, truly I say to you'.

It is the conviction that he has to speak God's word to the people, particularly at the heart of the Jewish religion, which takes him up to Jerusalem (Luke 13.31ff.). In doing this, he expects suffering and death as the prophets had suffered before him (Luke 11.49). Suggestions that Jesus could not have spoken about his death seem to be wide of the mark, particularly if the prophetic element is authentic. It is true that the bulk of the sayings, dealing with Jesus' suffering, death and vindication, in their present form reflect the beliefs of the Church and the detail of the historical events; but the sayings concerning the continuation of the prophetic line by Jesus indicate that he reckoned with the possibility of rejection and suffering, like the prophets before him. Indeed, a saying like Luke 9.44 may well contain the original form of Jesus' conviction that he must die, which was later reformulated in the extended passion predictions, which we find in Mark 8.31; 9.31; 10.33ff..[13] But in addition to the fact that they show Jesus facing the possibility of suffering, as the prophets had before him, the Gospels indicate that he also may have interpreted the significance of this suffering. All the Synoptic Gospels, as well as 1 Corinthians 11.23ff. and John 6.51b, preserve sayings of Jesus where he interprets his imminent death as a vicarious suffering sealing the new covenant (cf. Exod. 24).[14] Like the unknown figure of Isaiah 53, whose suffering was regarded as a sin-offering having benefit for others, so Jesus' blood would seal the new covenant (Mark 14.24). Whether Jesus regarded himself as the suffering servant of Isaiah 53 has been much discussed. With the exception of Luke 22.37, there is no explicit quotation from Isaiah 53 on the lips of Jesus, though scholars have pointed to passages like Mark 10.45 as one possible example of an implicit influence.[15] While it may be true that the influence of Isaiah 53 is nothing like as prominent in the New Testament as one might expect (see, e.g., Acts 8.32; 1 Pet. 2.24f.), it is hard to believe that somewhere in the background Isaiah 53 has not influenced the ideas of vicarious suffering found in the Gospels. It is possible that Jesus may have been influenced by Jewish martyrology (e.g., Wisd. 2–3; 4 Macc. 6.28f.),[16] though it is likely that the belief that the death of the righteous would be vicarious did owe something to Isaiah 53.[17] What is clear, however, is that on the night before his death Jesus explained the significance of his death as the sealing of a new covenant. It is important to note that the significance he attached to his passion was the sealing of a covenant and not a sacrifice dealing with sin. As such, it has been rightly suggested that Jesus saw his death not as a new dimension to his life but as the culmination of something which had already been initiated in his life with the inauguration of the kingdom. His death sealed a new relationship already started: the new aeon of the kingdom of God, a point well made by Kümmel:

> It has often been thought that in this context Jesus' death is understood as an atoning death; but the saying about the cup in its earliest form suggests nothing of this. . What is said is merely that Jesus' death initiates this covenant and, according to all that we know from elsewhere of Jesus' preaching, it is highly unlikely that Jesus' death here is to be evaluated and interpreted as a single isolated event and not rather as the consummation of the totality of God's actions in this man. Hence the most obvious assumption – we cannot be entirely certain – is that with the word about the cup Jesus means to say that his dying completes the making of God's new eschatological covenant with men which his entire activity and teaching have set in motion, and thus that through his death the dawning of God's kingdom in his person has finally become effective.[18]

One other theme which should be considered under the heading of Jesus the prophet is a concept, which makes only an isolated appearance in the Synoptic Gospels, but is very frequent in the Gospel of John: Jesus as the emissary of God. In Luke 10.16 (cf. Matt. 11.25ff.) Jesus speaks of himself as the one sent by God. This is a dominant theme in the Fourth Gospel, and its Jewish background and the isolated parallel in the other Gospels demand that we consider the possibility that this theme may indeed express Jesus' own conviction about his role as God's agent.

The basic principle of the Jewish institution of agency, the situation where an individual is sent by another to act on his behalf, is that an agent is like the one who sent him (*Mekilta* Ex. 12.3; cf. M. *Berakoth* 5.5). Thus to deal with the agent is to deal with the sender himself, for example *Sifre* on Numbers 12.8:

> With what is the matter to be compared? With a king of flesh and blood who has an agent in the country. The inhabitants spoke before him. Then said the king to them, You have not spoken concerning my servant but concerning me.[19]

The close links between the activity of Jesus and the divine purposes is brought out in the Fourth Gospel by means of the agency formula (e.g., 12.44; 13.20; 5.23; 7.16; 12.45; 14.9; 15.23). The fact that exactly the same formula makes its appearance in the Synoptic tradition (Luke 10.16; Matt. 10.40ff.; cf. Matt. 18.20) demands that we reckon with the possibility that it may go back in some form to Jesus himself. Such an understanding of his role would coincide with his belief that he was the herald of God's eschatological kingdom, and would also reflect the directness, which is evident in the prophetic type of call, which we find in the baptismal narrative. In the light of the eschatology of his message, it would come as no surprise to find that Jesus spoke of himself as the one sent by God for a mission of ultimate significance for Israel and mankind as a whole.

The complex of traditions associated with the prophet, rooted as it is in the Torah (Deut. 18.15ff.) and in prophetic pronouncements, is an area of great importance for understanding Jesus' ministry.[20] The direct revelation as the basis of authority, the tradition of rejection and suffering, the hints that this suffering might be vicarious and above all the eschatological character of both Spirit and prophecy in some Jewish circles, indicate how many themes of central importance for the ministry of Jesus are covered by this term. This complex of ideas continued to exercise a profound influence on New Testament Christology and ministry as recent studies of the Fourth Gospel and Paul's letters have shown.

(b) Son of God[21]

Because the phrase, 'son of God', has become such a central part of Christian confession, considerable suspicion has been aroused, when suggestions have been made that Jesus may have thought of his own relationship with God in these terms. Since the work of Jeremias, however, it has been possible to see how Jesus may have used the idea of sonship. Jeremias investigated the background and usage in the Gospels of the Aramaic word 'Abba'.[22] He characterizes the use of this word in the Gospels as a distinctive mark of the voice of Jesus of Nazareth. It is, he argues, the word which a small child would use to speak of his earthly father and indicates that degree of trust and dependence which are so characteristic of Jesus' relationship with God.[23]

The possibility that Jesus may have used this word in his address to God is given added credence, when we remember that in the Old Testament the father/son image is used occasionally to speak of the relationship between a human being or a group of human beings and the God of Israel.[24] Thus we find that the relationship between Israel and God is compared to the relationship between a father and a son (Deut. 8.5 and Hosea 11.1). The same is true of the relationship between God and the king (2 Sam.; 7.14f. ; cf. 4 Ezra 13.32). The point to note about this usage is that the image is primarily *descriptive* and does not speak of the nature of the one designated the son of God. It points out God's care and protection for his 'son', and the obligation to obedience and faith on the part of the latter. It is surely in this sense primarily that we are to comprehend Jesus' understanding of the term.

Undoubtedly Jesus *did* stand in a special relationship with God. After all, he was the agent of the coming of the kingdom of God, and his teachings had the authority of God himself. Nevertheless it has to be admitted that the idea of sonship used by Jesus of his relationship with God is not common in the gospel tradition. While the phrase, 'son of God', is found occasionally, 'son' by itself is not so common.[25] Even in the Fourth Gospel, examples of the use are not very frequent. Two examples must suffice: One of them is the 'Johannine thunderbolt' (Matt. 11.25ff. and par. so-called, because it is a saying which resembles some in the Gospel of John and yet is to be found in one of the oldest layers of the Synoptic tradition), and the other is the small section in John 5.19f., where Jesus speaks of his relationship with God. Both of these sections have a similar phraseology and meaning and can thus be treated together. We can best understand them both, if we take the meaning of the father/son relationship in a descriptive sense. Thus it is not a question of the eternal son of God, coeternal with the Father, but a way of speaking about the intimacy of relationship, which enables such a unity of will between Jesus and God in the fulfilment of the divine purposes. Jeremias has characterized the background to the idea of divine sonship in the Gospels aptly in the following section from his treatment of the theme:

> Thus in interpreting the theme 'the Father has transmitted all things to me' with the aid of the father-son comparison, what Jesus wants to convey in the guise of an everyday simile is this: Like a father who personally devotes himself to explaining the letters of the Torah to his son, like a father who initiates a son into the well-preserved secrets of his craft, so God has transmitted to me the revelation of himself, and therefore I alone can pass on to others the real knowledge of God.[26]

One should note the Jewish flavour of Matthew 11.25ff.;[27] it would be rash to reject too quickly its authenticity.[28] The claim to intimate knowledge of the things of God is typical of apocalyptic (Rev.; 2 Cor 12.2ff.; Rom. 11.25; 1 Cor. 15.51).[29] If we are right to suppose that Jesus claimed authority from God to proclaim the imminence of the kingdom, that presupposes a knowledge of God's purposes of a special kind. It is in the light of this Jewish apocalyptic background that support for the authenticity of the saying may be given.

(c) Messiah[30]

Messiah or Christ is perhaps the most familiar of all titles applied to Jesus. It has its background in contemporary Jewish eschatological expectation.[31] We know from contemporary Judaism that such hopes were very diffuse. Indeed, it could be argued that the dominant eschatological expectation centred on the conviction concerning a new age rather than the agent of its arrival. Yet some groups in Judaism looked forward to the coming of some kind of messianic agent, usually human (but not always, e.g., 1 Enoch 37–71), who would help to inaugurate the new age. Perhaps the most typical example of contemporary expectation is that which is found in the Psalms of Solomon 17 and 18, which look forward to the coming of a descendant of David, who would purge the land of Israel of all defilement and overthrow the enemies of God. Elsewhere, for example in the Dead Sea Scrolls, we can see some of the variety in contemporary expectation, when we note that this community expected not only a Davidic messiah but also a priestly messiah and eschatological prophet.[32]

Thus if Jesus claimed to be Messiah, we may suppose that there would have been many who would have understood, at least in general terms, the kind of claim that was being made. In popular belief, however, we may suppose that it was the hope of a descendant of David which was dominant, the coming of one who would free Israel from all her oppressors (cf. Luke 24.21). But evidence of Jesus accepting the title is very rare in the Gospels.[33]

There are three passages in the Synoptic Gospels which we shall examine briefly, to see whether Jesus saw himself as Messiah: Peter's confession, the triumphal entry, and the confession before the High Priest.

In Mark's version (8.27ff.; cf. Matt. 16.13ff.; Luke 9.18ff.; John 6.66ff.), Peter responds to Jesus' question about his person by stating quite simply that Jesus was the Messiah (v.28).[34] According to Mark this is not met with a great deal of enthusiasm by Jesus, who goes on to talk about the suffering which the Son of Man would have to endure (vv.31ff.). Peter is unwilling to accept that Jesus must suffer, and he is rebuked by Jesus and called Satan (v.33). This version of the confession contrasts with Matthew's, where Jesus greets Peter's confession with enthusiasm and promises that Peter will be the rock on which the Church will be built (16.16f.).

If we concentrate on the Marcan version, we are faced with the two possibilities: either Jesus refused to accept Peter's confession of him as the Messiah and, as a result, implicitly denied that he was the Messiah, or he accepted it but, by his reference to suffering, subtly qualified the meaning that he wanted to give to the title. One of the problems of putting too much weight on this episode in its totality is that we cannot be sure that the sequence of sayings in Mark reflects the situation in the life of Jesus and is not an artificial construction by the Evangelist.[35] What we can say is that there is no enthusiasm manifested in Mark for the title messiah without qualification. If we attach some weight to the variant form of the confession in Matthew, it is apparent that we cannot think of Jesus rejecting the title.

In the Synoptic accounts of the triumphal entry into Jerusalem just before Jesus' passion (Mark 11.1ff.; Matt. 21.1ff.; Luke 19.29ff.),[36] it is Jesus who takes the initiative in sending his disciples to find the animal(s) and engineering the spectacle to which the crowd responded in the appropriate manner with *hoshiana*, hailing Jesus as the one who was to come. The crowd quotes from Psalm 118.25, a Psalm which was used at passover and which speaks of salvation and deliverance. The link with Zechariah 9.9 is made explicit in Matthew 21.5 and John 12.15. It has been suggested that Jesus was here trying to interpret his messiahship in the light of this verse, rejecting the warrior messiahship of contemporary expectation and preferring the humble Messiah (cf. Mark 8.31ff.). Such a symbolic act would be of the same kind as that performed by Jesus in the Temple.

Unlike the Synoptic version, however, the version in John (12.12ff.) gives a rather different impression of the event. In this the crowds respond to Jesus and hail him as the one to come, *before* he begins to ride upon the ass. In John the spectacle of Jesus riding on an ass is seen as a reaction to the cries of the crowd rather than a deliberate premeditated act on his part. Thus the account is represented as being an attempt by Jesus to defuse the inflammatory expectation of the people by seeking to fulfil Zechariah 9.9.

It is difficult to be sure which of these two versions is more original. Certainly the version in John helps us to understand the event, without our having to explain why Jesus should have initiated a potentially inflammatory act, though on the other hand the version in Mark does not explicitly quote the text from Zechariah 9.9 and it could be that it was an event which was given added messianic significance only subsequently. But to evacuate the event of all messianic or eschatological significance would be to ignore the eschatological context of Jesus' proclamation and the importance of his visit to Jerusalem (Luke 13.33f.).

Mark records Jesus as explicitly accepting the title Messiah at his trial before the Sanhedrin (14.62; cf. Matt. 26.64; Luke 22.69). Despite the fact that the versions of the saying in Matthew and Luke retain a more ambiguous reply, it is unlikely that they imply a rejection of the title.[37] It seems likely that Jesus did utter some kind of statement, which led his accusers to suppose that he had accepted that he was a messianic pretender; otherwise we could not explain the charge against Jesus of being king of the Jews (Mark 15.26; 32; Luke 23.2). It is likely that the more equivocal version of Jesus' reply to the High Priest is original. Even in Mark acceptance of the title Messiah is once again qualified by reference to the enigmatic 'son of man'.

It seems most unlikely, however, in the light of all that we know about Jesus' attitudes to violence that he accepted the current Davidic messianic categories without qualification, as they would have pointed mainly in the direction of a warrior Messiah, a view which the tradition gives us no warrant for accepting. That Jesus accepted a qualified view of messiahship, seems to be suggested by the discussion of the Davidic sonship in Mark 12.35f. Here messiahship, which is tied closely with the Davidic hope, is questioned by reference to an interpretation of Psalm 110. The point which is being made

181

here is that because David, who was believed to have written Psalm 110, called the Messiah 'Lord' in this psalm, he could not have been referring to one of his descendants but one mightier than himself. It is an implicit denial of the close link-up between messiahship and Davidic descent which may cast light on Jesus' own understanding.

It is inconceivable, in the light of the eschatological character of Jesus' message, that the messianic issue would not have come up either for Jesus or his contemporaries. At the very least we must say that Jesus' claim to be the agent of the coming of the kingdom of God placed him on the same level as the Messiah of Jewish hope, whose task it was to be the agent of God's reign of righteousness. We may suspect, however, that the reluctance of Jesus to accept the title 'son of David', or to use the title Messiah of himself may lie with the bellicose connotations of that title and its related concepts in current usage. That Jesus was the anointed one, to be the agent of the good news of the kingdom of God, is suggested by Luke 4.16ff. and confirmed in early Christian preaching (Acts 10.38). Like Anthony Harvey, I would want to look for Jesus' messianic consciousness in that group of passages which speak of Jesus as the one anointed with the Spirit,[38] whose mission heralded the kingdom (Luke 4.16f.; Matt. 11.2ff. and par.; cf. Isa. 35.5f.; 61.1f.). It is probably in this sense that we may say that Jesus saw himself as the anointed one. Thus the early Church was correct to use the title so freely after Jesus' death to speak of the one who through his life, death and resurrection had begun to initiate the eschatological salvation of God.

(d) The Son of Man[39]

One of the most pressing problems in contemporary study of the Christology of the New Testament is the origin and meaning of the phrase 'the son of man', found so frequently in the Gospels but hardly at all in other parts of early Christian literature (but see Acts 7.56). Opinions about the significance of this phrase have varied widely. On the one hand there are those who think that it offers the key to Jesus' messianic consciousness as the only title frequently found on his lips in the pages of the Gospels and hence the foundation of the Christian doctrine of the person of Christ. On the other hand there are those who consider that it is a mistake to suppose that the phrase is ever used as a messianic title by Jesus (even if it was used in this way for a short time by the early Church) and even in those cases where its dominical usage can be established, it should be regarded as a form of speech devoid of any significant theological content. In the light of the many different approaches to the problem it is hardly possible to cover the whole gamut of scholarly debate or to evaluate all the different interpretations offered. What will be attempted in this section is a brief survey of possible approaches.

The sayings in the Synoptic Gospels have been divided into three categories: sayings dealing with the present situation of the son of man on earth (e.g., Luke 7.33; 9.58; Mark 2.10); references to the suffering of the son of man (e.g., Mark 14.21; 8.31; Luke 9.44); sayings, which speak of a future role for the son of man in vindication, glory and judgement (e.g., Mark 8.38; Matt. 25.31; Mark 14.62).

The Johannine sayings have to be categorized differently, as they cover rather different themes. They can be classified in the following way:[40] exaltation, 3.14; pre-existence, 3.13; 6.62; eschatological, 5.27; 6.27 (the last two probably referring to the role of the son of man in providing eschatological food for the elect) and confessional statement (one only, 9.35). What is clear is that the pattern of the Johannine sayings coincides most closely with the third category of the Synoptic sayings, namely, that dealing with the glorious son of man, though it is apparent in the understanding of exaltation and glory in the Fourth Gospel that the cross plays an important role (cf. 3.14). Indeed, it seems likely that there may be some influence from the Suffering Servant passage of Isaiah 53.[41]

In its present form the Greek phrase 'the son of man' (*ho huios tou anthropou*) looks like a christological title, and yet, the evidence that it was a messianic title, whether well known or not, is not very great. Much has been written about the Aramaic phrases which might lie behind this phrase.[42]

Our concern now will be to examine some of the different ways in which this phrase has been understood. First let us set out some of the various approaches under two major headings:

1 NON-TITULAR USAGE

(i) The phrase in the Gospels is a poetic way of referring to man (cf. Ezek. 2.1; Ps. 8.4) common in the Old Testament, and the usage in the Gospels is a continuation of this.[43]

(ii) The phrase is a well-known circumlocution in Palestinian Aramaic for the first person singular, in which a speaker refers to himself.[44]

2 TITULAR, CHRISTOLOGICAL INTERPRETATIONS

(i) Identification of Jesus with the 'one like a son of man' of Daniel 7.13 interpreted as a symbol of suffering Israel, vindicated by God;

(ii) Identification of Jesus with the 'one like a son of man' of Daniel 7.13 interpreted as a heavenly being;[45]

(iii) Jesus used the phrase 'the son of man' of a heavenly figure different from himself, but who would come to vindicate his own ministry (Mark 8.38);[46]

(iv) Jesus identified himself with the glorious heavenly figure spoken of in Daniel 7[47] but by it referred to his future glory.

Turning to the different understandings of the phrase in the Gospels let us start with the non-christological view. Clearly there is much to commend this, particularly because it is by no means easy to offer a unified theological explanation of all the sayings in the Gospels in the light of a particular Jewish messianic title. Of the two solutions suggested, the more attractive is that which finds in the references to the son of man a circumlocution for the first person.[48] The view which sees the reference to the son of man merely as another way of speaking about mankind in general hardly does justice to the self-reference clearly implied in a saying like Luke 9.58. The explanation of the phrase in the Gospels by reference to a familiar idiom, whereby a speaker referred to himself by using this phrase, is not without its difficulties,[49] but Maurice Casey has suggested with some plausibility that in Aramaic a speaker could use a general statement, in which the expression for a man was 'son of man' in order to say something about himself.[50]

Those who resort to explanations of this type find it easy to explain those sayings dealing with the present role of the son of man and his suffering. The problem comes with the sayings concerning the future glorious role of the son of man, particularly those where there is an explicit or implicit allusion to Daniel 7.13 (e.g., Mark 13.26; 14.62; cf. Luke 22.69). These are regarded as secondary formulations by the Church,[51] so that the reference to Daniel 7 is the result of interpretative activity within the Church.[52] While those scholars are correct to point out how little use is made of Daniel 7.13 in the son of man sayings, the arguments against the authenticity of sayings like Mark 14.62 do not seem to be strong enough to deny the possibility of the influence of Daniel 7.13 on the mind of Jesus. It is inconceivable that Jesus would have denied any part in the establishment of the kingdom of God, particularly if he was its inaugurator. If the twelve were to sit on thrones judging the twelve tribes of Israel (Matt. 19.28), Jesus the Messiah would have been there too.

When we turn to the interpretations where theological content begins to play an important part, it will be apparent that much attention is devoted to a consideration of the Jewish background to the sayings in the Gospels. Daniel 7 is the object of most attention, as opinions are divided about the value of passages like 1 Enoch 37–71 and to a lesser extent 4 Ezra 13, because of uncertainty concerning the date of these passages and hence their value for a study of the New Testament. Even if 1 Enoch 37–71, where the son of man is without doubt a glorious heavenly figure and, if pre-Christian (as I think is likely), gives evidence of a belief in a heavenly Messiah described as a man, Daniel 7 has provided problems enough for the interpreters, as a consideration of the two different approaches to the son of man sayings based on Daniel 7 will show.

The first interpretation. In Daniel 7, it is argued, the figure 'one like a son of man' in v.13 is merely a symbol of the saints of the Most High mentioned in the interpretation of the vision (vv.18, 21f., 25, 27) and has no independent existence in the heavenly world. As a symbol of the righteous of Israel the human figure suffers at the hands of the beasts, just as the righteous suffer at the hands of the kings (vv.20ff.) (though in fact nothing is said about the suffering of the son of man in the vision itself). The vision, therefore, is said to be a graphic way of asserting that suffering and humiliation of the righteous will be followed by vindication and glory for the faithful.[53]

Jesus chose this picture, it is argued, to describe his ministry of suffering, rejection and humiliation as a prelude to glory, because he thought of himself as the embodiment of the righteous of Israel. Thus there is no such thing as a heavenly son of man who comes with the clouds of heaven, for this is merely a pictorial way of referring to the vindication of the suffering righteous.[54]

The significance of looking at Daniel 7 in this way and applying it to the Gospels should not be missed. It enables those who espouse this interpretation to suppose that all the son of man sayings in the Synoptic Gospels can be understood in the light of this background, because the pattern of suffering followed by vindication and the bestowal of authority neatly cover all the material contained within the son of man sayings.

The second interpretation. By contrast the other group of scholars would argue that Daniel 7 fits into a pattern of belief testified to in other sources, including the section from 1 Enoch (37–71) which speaks of a heavenly figure who is compared with a man. Daniel 7.13 is a reference to a heavenly, angelic being who acts as God's vice-regent and the heavenly representative of the people of God, and is probably to be identified with the archangel Michael.[55] That is not to suggest that the son of man was a messianic title familiar to Jesus' hearers, merely to say that there is in Daniel 7 a belief in a heavenly figure, who functions as a representative of the saints of the Most High.

But if we suppose that this interpretation of Daniel 7.13 is correct, when we apply it to the Gospels, we have to accept that its relevance is limited only to those sayings which speak of the son of man and his glorious heavenly activity. It is not easy to explain the humiliation and suffering of the son of man, and possibly also his present activity, in the light of this background. Accordingly, other ways of explaining these groups of sayings are needed.

A passage like Mark 8.38 and parallels, shows us that there was certainly a close link between Jesus in his earthly life and the glorious son of man ('Whoever is ashamed of me and of my words in this adulterous and sinful generation, of him will the son of man also be ashamed, when he comes in the glory of his father and of his holy angels'). I would not want to interpret the apparent separation between Jesus and the son of man as a reference to different figures. Rather, we should see this separation as a way of speaking of the differentiation between Jesus' earthly existence and the glorious role he was destined to occupy in the future. The explanation offered by R. H. Fuller helps to explain the relationship.[56]

> Jesus speaks of the Son of Man as an office which he is destined to enter upon as a result of his earthly activity, but an office which he is proleptically engaged in already . . . during the earthly ministry the kingdom is dawning, though it has not yet come. It is active proleptically and in advance. So also Jesus is not yet the son of man (which is essentially a triumphant figure). But he acts as the one destined to be triumphant Son of Man already during his ministry and humiliation. The Kingdom and the Son of Man 'spill over' or 'jut out' as it were, on to this side of the cross . . .

If one accepts this interpretation, it must, of course, be recognized that sayings from the other groups, particularly those dealing with the suffering and rejection of the son of man are not covered by this background. Certainly in their present form the sayings dealing with suffering are church formulations, showing that they reflect the details of Jesus' passion (e.g., Mark 10.33f.). The earliest form of the prediction concerning the suffering of the son of man is probably to be found in Luke 9.44. There is probably no christological significance in the use of the phrase 'son of man' in sayings dealing with suffering and in some of those which speak of the present activity of the son of man (Luke 7.34). It is probable that these sayings may contain a reference to the son of man, which is a general statement by which the speaker refers to himself in these sayings. The context gives us no warrant to assume any link with Daniel 7 despite the reference to the son of man, but certainly implies a self-reference. So unless there is reason to see any link with Daniel 7 or the tradition concerning the heavenly man from the context in the Gospels, it seems that we must ask whether there is necessarily a deeper christological significance, but only a circumlocution for the first person.

Whatever else may be said about the son of man sayings in the Gospels, it is apparent that they have been accorded an interpretative importance out of all proportion to their place in the gospel tradition. Surely there is some sense in the appeal to release our understanding of Jesus from our preoccupation with the son of man? It is not that the son of man investigation is necessarily a blind alley, but it must be seen as part of the complex of ideas associated with the establishment of the kingdom of God which is so central to the message of Jesus of Nazareth. The problem comes when the dominant thrust of the message of Jesus as it appears in the Gospels, dominated as it is by the proclamation of the kingdom, and the teaching about the new age, is subordinated to the interpretation of a christological title, whose origin and meaning is surrounded by so much uncertainty. When there is more clarity elsewhere in the study of the Jesus tradition, it is rather surprising to find that this phrase has assumed so much importance as an interpretative key to open the door to the solution of other problems.[57]

What we are left with is the use of a phrase, in some of whose authentic occurrences there is a reference to a figure who will come in glory though in the majority of cases it has no christological significance. In identifying himself with this figure, albeit in a veiled way, Jesus asserted the conviction that the vital role which he played in the proclamation of the kingdom of God would continue in the final consummation. Thus the teacher of Nazareth who heralded the reign of God would be present at its final consummation. In using this phrase, therefore, Jesus wanted to speak of himself and his suffering and rejection. On occasion he linked this use with the reference to 'one like a son of man' in Daniel 7.13 to speak of his future glorious role in God's kingdom.[58]

12

The Resurrection Narratives[1]

Modern discussions of the resurrection have perhaps inevitably concentrated on the historicity of the events described in the Gospels and the propriety of speaking of the resurrection as an event in history. From our perspective, this is clearly a most important part (perhaps the most important part) of the discussion concerning the resurrection. It would not be correct, however, to assume that the problems, which we have with belief in the resurrection necessarily loomed so large on the horizon of the first Christians. Obviously it was of central importance for the first Christians that Jesus had risen from the dead, and that there was sufficient evidence to convince themselves and their hearers that this was the case. It was not just a spectacular act on behalf of Jesus that they were concerned with, a validating miracle which enabled them to say something about him, but also it was an event which had profound ramifications for the way in which those first Christians understood themselves and the world in which they lived.

It has been stressed in considering the teaching of Jesus that the eschatological dimension of his message is of central significance. What is more, we noted that the future hope of the restoration of the created order was regarded by Jesus not merely as hope but as also near to fulfilment. The early Christian belief in the resurrection of Jesus confirmed this belief. He was considered to be 'the firstfruits of the harvest of the dead' (1 Cor. 15.20); his resurrection was a sign that the last days had indeed arrived (Acts 4.2). Thus the future hope of Judaism was even more firmly linked to his person. Through Jesus' resurrection the inexorable process towards the new age had indeed made its start (Rev. 5; Rom. 8.11).

The resurrection faith is not just a question of what happened to Jesus.

The new start which Jesus' resurrection signalled, was confirmed in the experience of the first Christians themselves. 'If any one is in Christ, there is a new creation' (2 Cor. 5.17; Gal. 6.15). The life of the new creation (Rev. 21), of which the resurrection of Jesus was a sign, was in addition known to be true by the Christians themselves. They also had tasted of the firstfruits of the new age, the pledge of something more to come (Rom. 8.23; 2 Cor. 1.22) through the Holy Spirit. The Spirit itself was a sign that the last days had finally come (Acts 2.17), and the first Christians linked the experience of the Spirit very closely with the resurrection (Acts 2.35ff.; John 7.39). Linked with the experience of the Spirit was the rebirth of the prophetic gift, a new experience of communal life appropriate to a new age (Acts 2.42; cf. 1 Cor. 12.13) and a conviction that the prophetic community (cf. Rev. 11) had the task of carrying on Jesus' mission: the risen Christ's work was continuing in his followers (Matt. 28.18f.; John 20.21).

Of course, the resurrection said something about Jesus as well. It confirmed the claim that he had made that the kingdom of God, the life of the age to come, was imminent. The first Christians expressed this conviction by affirming that the resurrection proved Jesus' messiahship (Acts 2.36; Rom. 1.3) and vindicated his message (Acts 2.24). It was Jesus who was the key to the eschatological salvation of God (Rom. 10.9), and 'there was no other name under heaven by which men could be saved' (Acts 4.12). While it would not be true to say that the resurrection marked the start of christological reflection, for, as we have seen, that process had made its hidden start in the ministry of Jesus itself, it gave christological reflection an impetus which took up the essential theme of Jesus' own ministry and necessitated the explicit formulation of the character and work of the eschatological agent of God.[2] The assertion that in Jesus was the firstfruits of the harvest of the dead was an alternative expression of his own conviction that in his work the kingdom of God had already drawn near (Mark 1.15; Luke 11.20).

It is essential for us that we appreciate the thoroughly eschatological character of the resurrection language used by the first Christians. We are not just talking about the reversal by God of human error, the bringing back to life again of someone who should never have been executed, though vindication *is* an important theme in the New Testament, particularly in Acts. Resurrection is about the life of the age to come. We can understand this, if we remind ourselves briefly about the character of the resurrection language in contemporary Judaism. As far as we can ascertain, it was only in the last few centuries of the pre-Christian era that a positive belief about life after death emerged in Judaism, probably in response to the problem of innocent suffering.[3] Indeed, the only explicit reference to this belief is found in the late Daniel 12.2, though several other passages are often cited as examples also (e.g., Isa. 26.19; Job 19.25).

It is the eschatological character of the resurrection faith, which is so important for us to grasp. For the early Christians to have asserted that Jesus had been raised from the dead was to make an assertion also about God's ultimate purposes for his creation. This fact is hinted at by the early Christian writers themselves, when they speak of the resurrection of Jesus as a sign of the new age (1 Cor. 15.20; Col. 1.18; Rev. 1.5). To fail to appreciate this is to fail to penetrate the significance of the assertion that Jesus has been raised from the dead. The hope of a similar glory for believers (1 Cor. 15.51ff.) is based on the event of Easter, and the ramifications of that belief extended far and wide into the doctrine and practices of the primitive communities.[4]

Because the resurrection of Jesus stands at the heart of the New Testament gospel it is hardly surprising that the narratives concerning the first Easter, the discovery of the empty tomb and appearances of Jesus to his disciples have received so much critical attention over the past two hundred years. Nearly all modern treatments of the resurrection tradition start with the account in 1 Corinthians 15, which gives a list of witnesses to the resurrection.[5] The chapter was written in the mid-fifties, and it refers to a list of witnesses as being part of a tradition, which Paul himself had received. Inclusion of James the brother of Jesus (cf. Gal. 1.19; Acts 15) may point to the fact that the list may have had its original in the Jerusalem church. In its present form the passage antedates our earliest Gospel by about ten years, and its formulation may well take us back to the early years of the Jerusalem church; it is, therefore, very valuable evidence indeed.

No mention is made explicitly in this passage about the empty tomb (15.4) and, most important of all, Paul seems to place the appearance of the risen Lord to himself on the same level as that to the other apostles. Exactly the same Greek word is used to describe the appearances (*ophthe*) suggesting that, in Paul's view, the character of the resurrection appearances to the first disciples was of the same kind as his own. But this would not seem to be Paul's view only, as it is possible that the tradition, which he had received, also used the same Greek word, which Paul used of his vision on the Damascus road. Like Paul, therefore, who saw the risen Christ in a vision (Gal. 1.12, 16; cf. Acts 26.19), this account seems to suggest that *all* the resurrection appearances were of a similar kind.

From the argument of 1 Corinthians 15 and other places in Paul's letters it is apparent that Paul thought of the resurrection not as the resuscitation of a corpse of flesh and blood (cf. 1 Cor. 15.50) but as the transformation into a new realm of being (1 Cor. 15.42; Phil. 3.21). What Paul saw in his resurrection appearance, therefore, and what by implication all those mentioned in the tradition of witnesses in 1 Corinthians 15 saw, was the risen Christ in a vision transformed into a body of glory.

189

On the basis of this passage, commentators have argued that the earliest stratum of tradition dealing with the resurrection asserts that Jesus appeared alive to his disciples (1 Cor. 9.1). The fact that Paul puts all the appearances, including his own, on the same level indicates that these appearances were likely to be *visions* of the glorified Christ. In addition, absence of any reference to the empty tomb tradition, such as we have it in the Gospels, has suggested that this was a later development invented to explain the conviction of the first Christians that Jesus was really alive and they had seen more than merely a vision of him. This means that the earliest tradition consisted of appearances of Jesus *alive* to the disciples, which were reflected upon, so that the conclusion was reached that the resurrection of the dead must have occurred in the case of Jesus. Once this had taken place, it was a natural development to assume that Jesus' body could not have remained in the tomb. To put it another way: the disciples had been convinced that they had seen Jesus alive, and the only appropriate terminology available to them to express this conviction was that he had been raised from the dead, even if his body had still remained in the tomb.

There are several problems confronting this particular interpretation. Some argue that it would have made sense for Paul to have included an explicit reference to the empty tomb, particularly in the light of 1 Cor. 15.12. But a careful reading of 1 Corinthians 15 seems to make the evidence for the empty tomb tradition, in this section, irresistible,[6] particularly in v.4 where the references to burial and being raised only make sense if it is presupposed. A mere vision of Jesus would not have justified the technical verb 'raise' (*egeiro*).[7] Certainly appearances of Jesus alive after the resurrection need not have necessarily suggested that Jesus had been raised. After all, the tradition of exaltation to heaven (Enoch in Gen. 5.24; Elijah in 2 Kings 2.10 and Moses *after* death),[8] was a well-known one in Judaism. It may be right to say that the original experience was that Jesus was alive,[9] but it does not follow that the subsequent reflection on this experience *necessarily* led to the conviction that Jesus had been raised from the dead. There can be little doubt that when Paul talks of the resurrection of Jesus elsewhere, he presupposes that the tomb was empty (how else can we understand the words in Rom. 6.4, 'Christ was raised from among the corpses'?).

There is a second factor which needs to be considered when using 1 Corinthians 15 as primary evidence, namely, the character of Paul's presentation. Paul himself has an apologetic purpose, whenever he speaks of his relationship with those who were apostles before him. Even a superficial acquaintance with Paul's letters will show that throughout his ministry Paul felt acutely the difference between his apostolic office and those who had been followers of Jesus during the latter's lifetime; hence his attempts to place himself on the same level as the Twelve (e.g., Gal. 1.1f.). Paul would never want to confess too readily that he was inferior to the other apostles, especially as far as the commissioning call-vision was concerned (cf. Gal. 1.12). Paul is likely to have insisted that the appearance of the risen Christ to himself did not differ from those to other apostles, though even he is forced to admit that in some sense at least the appearance of Christ *did* differ (1 Cor. 15.8 'last of all, as to one untimely born'...).[10] While this tells us nothing about the difference in the mode of appearing, it recognizes that there was something unusual about Paul's call, which did in some way set him apart from those who were apostles before him, however painful it may have been for Paul to have admitted this fact. This is the picture which is brought out for us in the Acts of the Apostles, where the call to Paul comes *after* Jesus has ascended into heaven and is only seen by his followers through visions. Similarly when Paul speaks of his conversion in Galatians 1.12; 16, he describes it as the unveiling of a being hidden from human gaze, the revelation of a glorious heavenly being.

Consideration of 1 Corinthians 15, therefore, does not allow us to conclude with any certainty that the character of the resurrection appearance to Paul was exactly the same kind as those to the other witnesses, despite the similarity of language. The possibility should not be excluded that the particular formulation of the resurrection-tradition received by Paul is the result of the Apostle's own reflection. Also it seems most unlikely that Paul did not presuppose the empty tomb tradition, or something very like it, when he spoke of Jesus being raised from the dead.

Let us turn now to the gospel material.[11] As we have seen, in most recent discussions of the evidence for the resurrection, the material in the Gospels fares badly compared with 1 Corinthians, but it seems to me to be an error of some consequence to suppose that because, in its written form, the material in the Gospels is later than that in 1 Corinthians, its authenticity is therefore suspect. We know that the traditions included in the Gospels were formulated long before their written form, and it would be wrong to reject them too quickly.

In the Gospels we find two types of material: that concerned with the empty tomb and that concerned with the resurrection appearances. The reasons for denying the substantial historicity of the former, even leaving out of consideration the angelophanies, seem to be unconvincing, particularly if doubts are expressed about the use of 1 Corinthians 15 for this end. The narratives as they stand are hardly the invention of a community wanting them to be the cornerstone of its faith, particularly as all our accounts have women coming to the tomb and finding it empty (Mark 16.1ff.; cf. Luke 24.2ff.; John 20.1ff.). The value of women as witnesses (*M. Shebu.* 4.1; *Sif. Deut.* 19.17; *b. Bab. Kam* 88a; *Ant.* 4.219) was negligible,[12] and so it would seem that any one wanting to create material to validate the resurrection belief would not have had such insubstantial witnesses.

Significantly also the Gospels maintain a discreet silence about the resurrection itself and other supernatural phenomena. Although Matthew has a legend about the glorious angel, who comes down and rolls the stone away from the tomb (Matt. 28.2), the other Gospels say nothing at all, a deficiency which is remedied by the second-century Gospel of Peter (ch. 10). By the time that Matthew was written, there was obviously a need being felt to counteract rumours that the disciples had stolen the body of Jesus; hence the addition of the story about the guards at the tomb and the bribery of the guards (Matt. 27.62ff.; 28.11ff.).

When we turn to examine the resurrection appearances themselves we find that, with the exception of the sudden appearing and disappearing of Jesus, there is nothing remarkable about the appearances of Jesus, and the conversations differ very little from conversations which had taken place during his earthly life. Instead of the glorious heavenly being spoken of by Paul (cf. Rev. 1.13ff.) we have an ordinary figure. Indeed, it is not without significance that the one narrative which might have been most appropriate as a christophany, the transfiguration, is not included among the appearances of the risen Christ in the Gospels.[13] The differences between it and the appearances of the risen Christ are quite marked.[14]

It has been usual to explain those excessively materialistic passages, which speak of Jesus eating (e.g., Luke 24.42f.) as the latest stratum of the tradition, when it became necessary to stress as unambiguously as possible the physical character of the resurrection in the face of heretical doctrine and external threats to the veracity of the accounts. But the fact remains that such passages would be moving in the *contrary* direction to what we find happening in other parts of the New Testament: a tendency to play down the material in favour of the spiritual (e.g., 1 Cor. 15.35ff.). Thus if we suppose that Paul's doctrine of the resurrection in 1 Corinthians 15 marks a step in the direction of a more spiritual belief, whatever the problems it presents for us today, it is likely that these excessively materialistic passages fit in much better to a Palestinian milieu of Jewish eschatological expectation than some of the other developments which were taking place in the resurrection belief.[15] Accordingly, due consideration should be given to the possibility that they represent an earlier rather than a later part of the resurrection tradition.[16]

Perhaps it is rash to attempt to reconstruct the events of the first Easter. Nevertheless the drift of the remarks made in the previous pages will indicate that the explanation of the emergence of the doctrine and a particular interpretation of it on the basis of the primacy of 1 Corinthians 15 cannot be accepted. I would want to argue that the empty tomb material is part of the oldest stratum of tradition. It should not be the appearances of the risen Christ which should be the starting place for examination of the resurrection faith but the stories of the empty tomb. This does not mean, of course, that we are bound to assume that the body of Jesus was raised; there may be other explanations of the phenomenon of the empty tomb. Nevertheless the finding of the tomb empty on the first Easter morning may have been one of those 'signals of transcendence', as Peter Berger has called them. We cannot know what effect such a discovery would have had on the disciples. It is not impossible that it may have led to the conviction that Jesus had been raised and provoked visions of him. As Rowan Williams has suggested:

> Something must have provided a first stimulus, and, more importantly, a structure of presuppositions within which subsequent experiences could be organised. The empty tomb tradition proposes just such a stimulus and structure. . .[17]

What cannot be in doubt is that the first disciples were convinced that Jesus had been raised, and that the eschatological events, whose fulfilment had started in his ministry, received dramatic confirmation at the first Easter. Obviously our explanations of the phenomenon of the first Easter will depend very much on our own theological pre-understanding, but due consideration should be given to the historicity of the empty tomb and the centrality of this tradition in the formation of the complex we describe as the resurrection faith. From the perspective of the historian of early Christianity the tradition of the empty tomb deserves more careful consideration, something stressed by the distinguished historian of ancient Judaism, Geza Vermes:

> When every argument has been considered and weighed, the only conclusion acceptable to the historian must be that the opinions of the orthodox, the liberal sympathizer and the critical agnostic alike – and even perhaps of the disciples themselves – are simply interpretations of the one disconcerting fact: namely that the women who set out to pay their last respects to Jesus found to their consternation, not a body, but an empty tomb.[18]

Section 3
Paul

1
Introduction

For many Paul is the central figure of early Christianity, the pioneering apostle, who took the gospel of the Jewish Messiah to the ends of the earth. Despite the fact that Paul has been the focus for religious renewal in the history of Christianity, the extent of his influence on Christian thought has been overestimated.[1] This not only applies to the influence of Pauline theology on the life of the Church today but also on the primitive Christian communities. While it may be true that Paul's writings take up a large part of the canon of the New Testament, it would be a mistake to suppose that Paul was the only or even the dominant voice in early Christian theology. As many have pointed out, there was a great variety in the doctrinal exploration of the early Christians.[2] By the same token there is a danger in supposing that Pauline thought was one extreme within the early Christian movement and that other (perhaps dominant) streams of thought were fundamentally opposed to the Pauline interpretation of the Christ event.[3] The assumption that Paul differed *radically* from his Christian contemporaries is questionable, for the amount of innovative thought attributed to Paul has at times been overestimated; the dominance of his voice in the New Testament canon has been mistakenly taken to indicate that he was the *only* voice making the points which we find in his epistles. Paul's concern for tradition and the inherited pattern of belief and practice, which undergirds his thought,[4] should warn us not to assume that Paul was a lone voice and that the doctrine of justification by faith alone, or its equivalent, was a dangerously new interpretation of the Jewish inheritance.[5]

This brings us to Paul's relationship with Judaism. Because of his outspoken statements concerning the Law, Paul has been regarded as the villain of the piece and the one who forsook his Jewish heritage for a new religion.[6] But the attempt to cut Paul the Christian off from Judaism is something which is open to question. For one thing we cannot suppose any more that Paul's conversion involved him in the transference from one

194

religion to another. Such language is anachronistic; yet, implicit in much thinking about Paul, there lurks this belief or something similar. Rather we should interpret the event on the Damascus road, not so much as the transference from one religion to another, but the transference of an individual from one Jewish *sect* to another, from the pharisaic sect to the Christian sect.[7] It was a change *within* Judaism, parallel to the change which might have taken place when an adherent of the Essene group became a Pharisee.[8]

The two major differences which characterized Paul's change of sect, centred on Jesus of Nazareth and the Jewish hope for the future.[9] If the accounts of Paul's life in Acts are to be believed (and they receive some confirmation from Paul himself, e.g. Gal. 1.13; Phil. 3.6; cf. Acts 8.3), Paul's attitude towards Jesus before his conversion was extremely negative (Acts 9.2; 22.4; 26.10f.). Thus the dramatic vision on the road to Damascus meant that the original pattern of beliefs in which Jesus had been an object of contempt and his followers subject to hostility had to be completely reorientated. Perhaps Paul gives some hint of the sort of process which went on when he speaks of the sacrifices he had to make in Philippians 3.7f. and the radical transformation in assessment in Galatians 3.13. Under the Law, Christ was accursed.[10] If Galatians 3.13 is anything to go by, it would appear that Paul's new view of Jesus of Nazareth caused him to assess the place of the Law in the divine economy.[11]

It might be assumed that such a reappraisal is itself the mark of Paul's departure from the Jewish inheritance. How could any Jew in any circumstances possibly countenance a belief which asserted that the Law of Moses was obsolescent? Surely this indicates that Paul had replaced the Jewish Law by devotion to an individual? Of course, in Paul's thought Christ had replaced the Law as the key to God's dealings with man in the present, but the reason for this lies at the heart of the Jewish religious tradition.

It is apparent that Paul believed that Jesus was the Messiah. It is no accident that Christ is Paul's favourite christological term and even if at times his use of it may resemble a proper name, there are occasions when he does indicate its Jewish background and speaks of the eschatological agent of salvation.[12] Indeed, it is when we take full account of Paul's eschatology that we can see that Paul did not replace devotion to the Law by devotion to Jesus. His convictions about Jesus were intimately linked with the fact that he now believed that the pattern of beliefs concerning the future, to which the Scriptures bore witness, was not simply a matter of belief but also of fulfilment; the present time had become the age of eschatological fulfilment. Thus his transference from one Jewish sect to another had involved him in moving from a group which still accepted beliefs concerning the future as an article of faith, to one which claimed that those promises were already a matter of fulfilment. The transference itself was bound up with the meaning of the shared Scriptures.[13] As Galatians 3–4 indicate, Paul's understanding of the Jewish tradition was firmly rooted in his interpretation of Scripture.

Even if we would be wrong to suppose that Paul's position in the life of the primitive Church was not as central as is sometimes supposed, there is little doubt that the problems which he wrestles with in his letters were probably typical of many which were facing the Christian sect during this period: the position of the Law of Moses now that the age to come had dawned; the exposition of the significance of the agent of salvation and the consequences of the experience of the new age for the life and practice of the Christian groups.

Of course, to view Paul as the erstwhile Pharisee who has transferred to another Jewish sect is to take one particular side in contemporary Pauline studies. It is the great contribution of W. D. Davies to modern New Testament scholarship to have rescued Paul from the position of the Hellenizer and de-Judaizer of Christianity and to have offered an interpretation of his thought, which does full justice to the essential Jewishness of his Christian perspective.[14] While this view has received limited acceptance,[15] it would be wrong to suppose that it is everywhere accepted. Of course, there are many reasons why this should be the case. After all, Paul seems to have abandoned the practice of Judaism as we find it expounded in rabbinic and non-rabbinic texts alike (1 Cor. 9.20). Interpretation of the Law and the application of it to the everyday situations which confront the individual is not Paul's method[16] and the difference which emerges between Judaism and Christianity in his letters seems so large that it is difficult to resist the conclusion that Paul *has* in fact helped to give birth to a very different religion, with different concepts and concerns from those of most Jews.

The most obvious point at which Pauline Christianity and the bulk of contemporary Judiasm parted company was over the precise place of the Law of Moses: was it possible to have an interpretation of Judaism which claims to remain a part of that religious tradition without accepting the primacy of that lawcode for matters of belief and practice? The question is a valid one, and those who would argue for the greater degree of continuity between Judaism and Pauline Christianity must face up to the problem which the supersession of the Law presents.

W. D. Davies suggested that it was because Paul had identified Christ with the Torah that the continuity between the new and the old obedience could be asserted.[17] There is certainly some evidence of this, particularly in passages like Romans 10.4 and Colossians 1.15, but it seems likely that the answer to our questions lies elsewhere. As we have already stressed, the conviction that Jesus was the Messiah and that in him the resurrection of the dead had already taken place meant that the possibility of a transfer from

196

one (old) age to another, new age, was already a reality: the cross and resurrection had been the hinge upon which the fulcrum of the ages had swung (cf. 1 Cor. 10.11). Thus what Paul was experiencing and trying to articulate was a new situation, uncharted territory, to which the Jewish traditions had borne witness as a promise, but few, if any, had dared to speak of as a promise fulfilled. Accordingly, it becomes appropriate for him to ask: what now becomes of the Law of Moses, given that the age to come has already dawned? Where do the Gentiles fit into the divine economy, if the last days have come upon all flesh? These questions are ones to which it would have been nice to have answers in Jewish sources. But such speculations are not evident in our extant sources. Certainly there is no clear evidence that any of Paul's rabbinic contemporaries considered the possibility that the Law may have been superseded in the age to come.[18] Nevertheless, while not wanting to depend too much on the argument from silence, we have to face the fact that in the Pauline correspondence we have the articulations of a man who is attempting to probe the significance of his traditions and their meaning within a situation where few had been able to offer any guidance. As such, the fact that Paul felt that within the age to come the written Law of Moses was no longer obligatory should not be taken as an indication of his abandonment of Judaism. All that it tells us is that he had forsaken an interpretation of the Law which was common within *non-eschatological* Jewish groups, for one which is to be understood in the light of the conviction that the age to come is part of the present experience of humanity. In such a situation it need not surprise us that he should have considered a new attitude appropriate, which still retained the essential obligation typical of the old. Whether that was an acceptable attitude is another matter. For our present purposes it is only necessary to show that such a belief was not totally incompatible with the traditions of Judaism, whatever the attitude of those who differed from him. This framework for an interpretation of Paul must be explored in more detail.

197

2

The Gospel Before and Apart from Paul

The canon of the New Testament predisposes us to concentrate on Jesus and Paul. Nevertheless, as we have noted, we should not allow that particular collection to lead us to suppose that the only significant Christian growth came about through the work of Paul and his followers, nor that the sole interpreters of the Jesus tradition were the canonical Evangelists. From what we can see in the New Testament itself, Christianity in Antioch and Rome emerged before Paul had any contact with either city.[1] The problem is that we are not in a position to say much about Christianity apart from Paul. It is true that in the last twenty years or so commentators on the Gospels have attempted to demonstrate the way in which the traditions were used and moulded at the pre-canonical stage, but we often have to resort to patient and imaginative reconstruction to say much that is substantial about the Christian faith and practice of the communities from which and to which the New Testament documents were written. There are several areas which need to be mentioned briefly: the account of the life of the Jerusalem church in the Acts of the Apostles; Jewish Christianity; the pre-canonical gospel tradition as a source for our knowledge of Christianity apart from Paul; Stephen and the Hellenists; and the church in Antioch.

In dealing with the church in Jerusalem we have to rely almost exclusively on the material in the early chapters of the Acts of the Apostles. This has been the subject of considerable disagreement among historians of early Christianity,[2] for there is a substantial body of opinion which argues that we cannot rely on the material in Acts for knowledge of the life and beliefs of the primitive community in Jerusalem. We shall have something to say later about the ecclesiastical organization and life of the primitive community. For the present I want to comment briefly on the pattern of Christian belief, which emerges in the opening chapters of Acts.

Detailed examination of the speeches in Acts suggests that we may be in possession of some early material,[3] even if we attribute the present composition of the speeches to the author of the work. Of other information which is particularly worthy of note is the fact that there is no evidence of a developed doctrine of the atonement (though this is largely absent from Luke–Acts generally; the one exception being in Acts 20.28).[4] Jesus is the one unjustly put to death, yet vindicated by God, who will come again when the times of refreshment come from the presence of God (3.17ff.).

198

Sophisticated christological doctrine is also absent. Jesus is spoken of with Jewish titles, several of which have few parallels elsewhere in the New Testament.[5] The account in Acts leaves us in the dark about the beliefs and practices of the disciples of Jesus elsewhere in Palestine. Luke–Acts concentrates on Jerusalem; it says nothing, for example, about resurrection appearances in Galilee (unlike Mark, Matthew and John 21). We can conjecture what may have been the situation in Galilee, supposing that some of the gospel material reflects Galilean ideas, but this is a hazardous enterprise.[6] Likewise, apart from Acts 8 and the hints we can glean from John 4, we are no better placed with regard to Samaritan Christianity, which in the light of what we know of later Samaritan tradition was probably a potent source of theological innovation.[7]

When we do hear about the Jerusalem church later in Acts, it is apparent that it contained elements which disapproved of some of the developments which had taken place in the early Christian movement. The account of the Apostolic Council in Acts 15 (which, some argue, is reflected in Gal. 2.1–10)[8] and the statement of James in 21.20 indicate a wide divergence of views on the issue of the condition whereby Gentiles were to be admitted to the messianic community. The acceptance of the Gentiles without circumcision, which, according to Acts 10–11, had already been accepted both by Peter and the elders of the church in Jerusalem, was quite understandably viewed with considerable suspicion by the Jewish Christians, for whom the rite of circumcision had always been the prescribed mark of entry into the covenant people. What we find in the account of Acts 15 is a compromise between the radicals, represented by Paul and Barnabas, and the more conservative Jewish Christians. Gentile converts were to be accepted without circumcision, but only on condition that they accepted the basic requirements sufficient to satisfy the susceptibilities of the stricter Jews.

We know from other early Christian sources that Jewish Christianity had a significant life of its own for a considerable period.[9] Even within the New Testament we see evidence of it in the letter of James,[10] Jude[11] and possibly 1 Peter[12] (or at the very least traditions incorporated in them), and of course, Hebrews.[13] With some justification it has been argued that the Gospel of Matthew reflects in its choice and ordering of the Jesus tradition the outlook of a Jewish community.[14] For example, the infancy narratives in Matthew indicate a concern to reject polemic against Jesus.[15] Elsewhere in the Gospel there is ample evidence of specifically Jewish Christian concerns (e.g., Matt. 17.24ff.).[16] Also, recent study of the Gospel of John has stressed its Jewish Christian setting,[17] and there have been those who have considered that such a setting is most appropriate for the Gospel of Mark.[18] Outside the New Testament information from early Christian writers shows that there was a continuing and vital Jewish Christianity of a somewhat conservative kind, in which the developing Christology of the mainstream was rejected, as well as one which had a more sophisticated doctrinal outlook. So-called 'heresiarchs' repudiated by the later Church, like Cerinthus and Elchesai (about whom, unfortunately, far too little is known), indicate the ongoing importance and doctrinal ingenuity of Jewish Christianity.

Study of the Gospels in recent years has concentrated on redaction criticism: the concern with the use of the traditions by, and the creative capabilities of, the authors of the Gospels.[19] This has meant also that there has been a concern to explore the character of the communities from which the Evangelists wrote and to which the Gospels were addressed. In exploring this dimension of the Gospels there has been a need to lay bare the situations in which the Jesus tradition was handled and used.

Two issues in particular should be mentioned. First of all, there has been a widespread belief that the material which is designated as the Q source (sayings and stories common in one form or other to Matthew and Luke alone) represents the religious outlook of a particular Palestinian Jewish group, whose beliefs centred on the returning Son of Man.[20] Secondly, there have been those who have been prepared to conjecture that behind the Gospel of Mark there lies a concern to repudiate a view of Christ which concentrated on his mighty works as the paradigm for true discipleship, at the expense of other parts of the gospel proclamation.[21] If this was in fact the case, there may be some justification for supposing that Paul's opponents also, particularly those in 2 Corinthians 10–13,[22] may have had similar christological beliefs, which the author of the Gospel of Mark seeks to correct.

Mention of Paul's opponents in 2 Corinthians should remind us that the reconstruction of the problems dealt with by Paul in his letters will enable us to catch a glimpse of the kind of Christianity which the extant documents left largely unrecorded.[23] The opponents of Paul in Galatia and Colossae, for example, show the kind of spiritual and ethical ideas which were current in the Pauline churches (and we may expect elsewhere also in the early Christian movement).[24] Colossians in particular, with its stress on certain Jewish practices and angelic beliefs (2.18), indicates the kind of Jewish Christian beliefs and practices which may have been widely held in Asia Minor. Elsewhere in the New Testament 1 John gives evidence of a Jewish Christian false teaching (2.22f.; cf. 4.2), which had its effects on Christology and against which there were polemics, using Jewish typology (3.12).[25] This letter indicates that, in common with many religious movements, the consequences of disagreement and separation led to vitriolic attacks and hatred against those who dared to disagree and separate themselves (e.g., 2.19ff.).

While the Acts of the Apostles tends to play down the extent of division in the early Church, its record does, as has already been noted in the case of the issue of circumcision, include hints of significant disagreement. The earliest example of such a disagreement is that described in Acts 6 between the Hellenists and the Hebrews, which is followed by the account of the martyrdom of Stephen. There has been much dispute over the identity of the Hellenists.[26] What is clear is that we are dealing with a movement whose outlook included much more radical ideas than was probably the case elsewhere in the Jerusalem church. Some appreciation of this fact may be gleaned from Stephen's speech in Acts 7, where the continuous rebellion of Israel against God and the hostility against the Temple (6.13) seem to mark him off from other Christians (even allowing for the idealization of Luke's portrait of early Christian support for the Temple and its worship: Acts 2.46). Concentration on the Lucan composition of Stephen's speech should not blind us to the distinctive elements in it, which call for detailed examination and note as evidence of early Christian thought. Apart from those issues already mentioned, the description of the martyrdom and of the vision of the son of man (7.56) deserves to be considered as evidence of a distinctive early Christian doctrine and not merely the rounded creation of an inventive writer.[27] What the Stephen material indicates is the probability that Paul was not the first radical within the primitive Church,[28] and that there was already, long before his missionary work, a tradition of thought which was both innovative and productive of a significant degree of tension within the earliest Christian communities.

But where was the focus of this radical thought? Paul in his own letters and the Acts of the Apostles explicitly points to Antioch as one centre (Gal. 2.11ff.; Acts 11.19ff.).[29] According to Acts 11.26, Antioch was the place where the people of the Way were first called Christians. In other words, their beliefs and practices had become so distinctive that there was need to attribute to them a separate label to distinguish them from others of a Jewish persuasion. The fact that it was the community in Antioch which commissioned Paul and Barnabas to embark on the first missionary journey (13.1ff.) indicates that the concept of a Gentile mission was already firmly rooted in this particular Christian community. According to Paul's own testimony, table-fellowship between Jews and Gentiles was already firmly established, even if (for reasons now unknown to us) it was necessary for James the brother of Jesus to persuade Jewish Christians to desist (Gal. 2.12).[30] What is also significant about this passage in Galatians 2 is the fact that we do not seem to be dealing here with a development which was totally at odds with the original founders of the Christian community in Jerusalem. According to Paul's own testimony, the apostle Peter himself was wont to share table-fellowship with Gentiles (a fact which would have offended against some Jewish scruples), thus indicating that the differences between Peter and Paul were not as great as some would suppose (as Acts itself makes clear). The information about the Christian community in Antioch in the earliest period is not easy to come by. We have to rely on the sparse information of Paul's letters and the occasional remarks in Acts. What is clear is that it was, in the first phase of the Christian mission, a centre of progressive thought and developments, which in all probability had anticipated the main thrust of Paul's missionary strategy, at least in outline.

Later we may find further hints of its belief and practice in the Gospel of Matthew, if the conjecture of those who consider that the Gospel emanates from Syria, and Antioch in particular, is right.[31] At the beginning of the second century we find that Ignatius, Bishop of Antioch, has left us the legacy of letters written en route to martyrdom in Rome.[32] They evince a confident and sophisticated understanding of ecclesiastical order and of the right of the bishop to speak with authority to those communities through which he was travelling. Even at the beginning of the second century AD the church in Antioch still had to be listened to, even if its ecclesiastical practice was not immediately obeyed.

The story of non-Pauline Christianity demands a book by itself. Arguably, we all attach too much weight to the work of Paul and pretend that his influence was greater than it was. It is easy to suppose that the place of Paul in the New Testament reflects the central place that he had in the development of Christian origins. But while his influence may have been less extensive than we suppose,[33] even in succeeding centuries, it would be dangerous to go to the other extreme and suppose that all non-Pauline Christianity differed markedly from the Christianity of Paul. That may have been true of the continued close adherence of parts of Jewish Christianity to the totality of the Law of Moses. There are indications from the New Testament that there were others who were thinking 'Pauline thoughts' both before and contemporary with the apostle to the Gentiles; and Paul himself was more devoted to the Law than many allow.[34] It is tempting to make Hebrews and 1 Peter, as well as the so-called deutero-Paulines (Ephesians and the Pastoral Epistles), part of the Pauline tradition. There are sufficient divergences in both 1 Peter and Hebrews to indicate both the vitality of early Christian thought and the widely held assumptions of the 'Pauline' position.[35] Even within the extreme forms of Jewish Christianity, we may suppose that there was more overlap than is commonly allowed, particularly in the area of Christology, between Paul and those who, on grounds of Torah observance, might have been Paul's bitterest opponents.[36] A comparison of the Christology of Revelation and the Pauline epistles would indicate much common ground, clearly derived from the common Jewish heritage. Revelation is clearly not a document from the Pauline circle, even if it comes from a significant area of the Pauline mission (Rev. 2.14, 20 indicate a substantial divergence from 1 Cor. 8). Thus while it would be wrong to minimize the diversity of primitive Christianity and the bitterness and division which this caused, we must not suppose that this necessarily means that there were irreconcilable and profound differences over *all* areas of doctrine; the Jewish heritage which primitive Christianity has in common ensured a substantial degree of common ground.[37]

3

Situation and System in Paul's Letters

The central importance of Paul for the history of early Christianity, and indeed for Christian history as a whole, has meant that his letters have been subjected to such minute scrutiny over the years, that it has become easy to speak of Paul and his theology. It is testimony to the genius of the apostle to the Gentiles that in these relatively short letters he expressed himself with sufficient coherence for later commentators to construct an outline of his thought. Such a task, however, is not without its difficulties, for the following reasons: (i) the difficulty in deciding on the authenticity of the letters; (ii) the occasional nature of the letters he wrote; (iii) the unwillingness of first-century Jews to write with the coherence which is demanded by the Western reader.[1]

In recent years the outline of Paul's thought has proceeded on the assumption that the heart of Paul's theology is to be found in Romans and Galatians. It is in these two letters that we have the exposition of the doctrine of justification by faith and the wrestling with the problem of the Law. Other letters receive less attention for two reasons: because either they may not manifest the condensed theological exposition found in Romans and Galatians, or there may be doubt over authenticity. Into the latter category come the following: Colossians, Ephesians, 1 Timothy, 2 Timothy, Titus and possibly also 2 Thessalonians.[2]

The exclusion of these letters from the survey of Pauline thought has repercussions on the characterization of the apostle's doctrine. It is in the letter to the Colossians that we find one of the most sophisticated christological expositions in early Christian literature (1.15ff.), parallel in many of its ideas with the Prologue of the Gospel of John.[3] Elsewhere in the letter the use of the dying and rising image to speak of the present life of the believer in Christ is a development from the parallel passage in Romans 6 and is akin to the heretical doctrine found in the gnostic Letter to Rheginos (49.15f.) and condemned in 2 Timothy 2.18 (cf. 1 Cor. 4.8).[4] Certainly the ideas which we find in Colossians represent a development as compared with other letters, but this may well be explained by the need to combat a false teaching, which asserted that visions of the heavenly world could be gained by means other than those offered in Christ (2.18f.).[5]

If the authenticity of Colossians is denied, then the Pauline authorship of

Ephesians probably falls as well. Much of the debate about the authenticity of Ephesians has centred on the relationship of the letter to Colossians. Clearly there are many affinities, and Ephesians 6.21f. and Colossians 4.7 indicate some kind of relationship, as also do the resemblances in vocabulary and content.[6] What we have in this letter is a much more overtly ecclesiological exposition than can be found elsewhere.

It is apparent as soon as one starts to read the Pastoral Epistles that one has moved into a very different religious atmosphere. Admittedly these are personal letters by Paul to his trusted companions, and this could explain some of the differences.[7] But the preoccupation with church order, piety and sober living contrasts with the enthusiasm and charismatic fervour manifest in, say, 1 Corinthians. The detailed arrangements given by Paul to his assistants for the ministry in the Church find few, if any, parallels (cf. 1 Cor. 16.15ff.; Phil. 1.1), in the indisputably authentic Pauline letters. What is more, it has proved singularly difficult to fit the itineraries mentioned in the letters (to Asia Minor and Crete) into what we know of Paul's life in Acts (though one should probably not attach too much weight to that fact, if one doubts the historicity of Acts anyway). One solution to this problem has been to suppose that Paul was released from prison in Rome (Acts 28) and embarked on another series of journeys, including one to the Eastern Mediterranean.[8] Thus the speech to the Ephesian elders at Miletus in Acts 20 reflects the belief of the apostle at that time that he would not see their faces again, rather than the statement of a later writer that this was Paul's last visit to Asia Minor. What is more, it may well be that such a view would tend to support an early date for Acts, which would not be by any means universally accepted, for the story of Paul stops with his sojourn in Rome and makes no mention of other journeys.[9] Certainly the late first-century 1 Clement suggests that Paul was released from prison and travelled to Spain (if that is what the furthest bounds of the west means in chapter 5; cf. Rom. 15.24), though it has to be pointed out that no mention is made in 1 Clement of a journey to the Eastern Mediterranean. The importance of the question of authenticity should not be missed. If the Pastorals could be shown to be Pauline, then the picture of church order which emerges in what were probably later epistles, does represent a definite change of attitude as compared with what we find in Romans and 1 Corinthians.

Acceptance of the authenticity of Ephesians has led one commentator on Paul to the conclusion that it evinces a change of mind on Paul's part with regard to eschatology and should be regarded as the mature reflections of the apostle.[10] If all these letters were thought to be inauthentic, it is likely that Paul's testament would be Romans, which would leave us with the struggle over the fate of Israel as the high point of the apostle's writing career.

The concentration on Romans and Galatians has had the effect of pushing into the background the theologically less replete, but equally suggestive, letters to the Corinthians. It is important that we put Romans and Galatians into perspective. These alone wrestle with the theme of the Law and justification by faith. Such ideas hardly make any appearance in 1 Corinthians, and are found only fleetingly in 2 Corinthians (e.g., 5.21) and 1 Thessalonians. The absence of the theme of justification by faith has rightly led some commentators to question whether in fact we are dealing with the heart of Paul's thought, when we read about justification by faith in Romans and Galatians.[11] Its presence in these letters was probably dictated by the issue of the membership of the people of God by Gentiles without circumcision, rather than being the linchpin of his theology. It would be wrong to play down the significance of this doctrine within the whole gamut of Paul's thought, but it is equally wrong to ignore the way in which Paul deals with the issues which manifest themselves in letters like 1 Corinthians and 1 Thessalonians. These reveal in the most direct way the consequences of belief in the Pauline Gospel, and the kind of problems which faith in Christ presented to the Gentile (and Jewish) converts in the ancient world. The Corinthian correspondence is part of a longer sequence of at least two letters (2 Cor. may contain fragments of several letters, namely, 2 Cor. 6.14–7.1; 10–13 and the rest of the letter).[12] Here we see the social and economic pressures, as well as the religious ferment, which were caused by the belief that Jesus was the Messiah. An opportunity to investigate the background to these problems and the way in which Paul deals with them offers a unique insight into the apostle's thought.[13]

The issue which needs most care and attention in interpreting Paul's letters is the recognition that circumstances dictated the content and approach of each letter. In no case can it be said that Paul is offering a systematic presentation of his views. Even Romans, which comes nearest to being such, seems to have been inspired by Paul's need to vindicate his gospel before his visit to the city, and it, too, manifests the same kind of concern with pressing issues (e.g., ch. 13–15), which characterizes other letters, like 1 Corinthians.[14]

Acceptance of the fact that Paul nowhere sits down to offer a systematic presentation of his views on Christology, the death of Christ, the future hope, the doctrine of the Church and the like, should warn us not to look for answers in Paul's letters to questions that he never set out to answer. Our approach to the letters must at all times be controlled by the context in which the particular ideas are formulated and addressed.[15] We should not be surprised to find that particular themes are absent in a letter, if these themes do not happen to coincide with the apostle's purpose. Recognition of this fact will prevent us from hasty judgements over questions of authorship as well as of the apostle's doctrine. What is more, we shall also see that it is quite understandable that there may be the occasional contradiction, particularly in those letters which are separated by several years.[16] But circumstances themselves will also dictate changes of emphasis which may well explain discrepancies.

A good example of these discrepancies is the supposed development, which is said to have taken place from the early 1 Thessalonians, via 1 Corinthians, to 2 Corinthians on the subject of the resurrection-life of believers. In the earliest letter it is alleged that Paul expected an imminent return of Christ, when the elect would be caught up to meet him as they were in the air (4.15f.). In 1 Corinthians, written probably six or seven years later, the apostle returns again to the theme of the final consummation in the context of persuading certain Corinthians that belief in the future resurrection is an essential item of faith (15.12), and shows them that such a belief does not involve acceptance of a mere resuscitation of the carnal body (15.35ff.). In this passage Paul still looks forward to the return of Christ and the general resurrection. As in 1 Thessalonians, the dead who are asleep in the dust of the earth will be raised, but, unlike 1 Thessalonians, Paul speaks of the transformation of the body of flesh into the glorious body similar to Christ's (cf. Phil. 3.21; 1 John 3.2).

The situation is rather different in 2 Corinthians 5. In a section dealing with the nature of the apostolic ministry, Paul returns to the theme of the resurrection body once again. Here he uses language which he had already used in 1 Corinthians 15 (clothing and undressing 5.2ff; cf. 1 Cor. 15.53), but he now speaks of the resurrection body as an eternal entity waiting in the heavenly world to be put on by the believer. The question is: when does this take place? Is it at the return of Christ, as in 1 Thessalonians 4 and 1 Corinthians 15, or is it at death? There is much dispute over the answer to this question. It is not the purpose of this discussion to offer a solution to this problem; rather, in mentioning it, it is hoped to show that circumstances may well affect the kind of language which the apostle uses.[17] One of the essential differences between 1 Corinthians 15 and 2 Corinthians 5 is the fact that the former is dealing with the totality of humanity at the general resurrection, whereas 2 Corinthians 5 is dealing with the individual. Two different questions are therefore being asked and answered. In 1 Corinthians 15 the issue is, 'How are the dead raised and with what body will they come?', whereas in 2 Corinthians 5 the issue is what happens to the believer at death: 'Is there complete separation between him and Christ until the consummation of all things?', and 'Is it possible that the believer may be with Christ (cf. Phil. 1.23) unclothed (i.e., without his heavenly body) until the consummation of all things, when he would be clothed with the body of glory?'

An answer to these questions could be given by assuming that Paul's thought developed to a significant degree.[18] Such an answer assumes that what we have in these documents are three systematic presentations of Paul's thought at different stages of his career. While it would be wrong to exclude the possibility that the apostle's thought *did* undergo some changes over the years, it would be dangerous to suppose that the differences which can be detected necessarily mean significant shifts in his thought, as it is essential to take full account of the circumstances which led to the formulation within each letter.

4

The Essence of the Gospel

Commentators on Paul over the centuries have sought to locate the essence of Paul's gospel in concepts like 'justification by faith' and 'in Christ'. During this century, there has been a continuing debate between those who have followed the lead of Luther and located the heart of Paul's gospel in Romans and Galatians in the idea of justification by faith, and those who have followed Schweitzer in speaking of Paul's mystical doctrine of incorporation in the body of Christ.[1] It is not my concern here to adjudicate between these two positions. Rather I would like to pick up the themes which have already been enunciated in the introduction of this section, for it seems to me that to understand Paul's thoughts one has to start with the eschatological foundations of Paul's doctrine. At the beginning of Romans Paul sets out the heart of his gospel (Rom. 1.16ff.):

> For I am not ashamed of the gospel: it is the power of God for salvation to every one who has faith, to the Jew first and also to the Greek. For in it the righteousness of God is revealed through faith for faith; as it is written, 'He who through faith is righteous shall live'. For the wrath of God is revealed from heaven against all ungodliness and wickedness of men who by their wickedness suppress the truth.

The good news which Paul proclaims is about the power or saving action of God in the world.[2] This is the manifestation of God's righteous character, the God of the covenant who redeemed his people out of bondage in Egypt and keeps faith with his people by manifesting his righteousness in the eschatological acts of power associated with the life, death and resurrection of Jesus of Nazareth. The manifestation of God's righteousness is ultimately salvation to those who believe and continue in that faith but involves judgement, God's wrath, working against all that stands against God. The language used in this passage indicates that the action about which Paul speaks is not merely concerned with the individual's salvation (though that is certainly included) but also with the demonstration of the power of God in the cosmos as a whole.

This passage is important because it reminds us that Paul saw the effects of the Christ-event in more than individual terms. Christ's death was not just 'for me' (Gal. 2.20); its effects did not merely depend on its appropriation by the individual, for it set in train a sequence of events which would lead to final acknowledgement of the lordship of Christ by the universe as a whole (1 Cor. 15.25f.; Phil. 2.11).

Paul's theology starts with the resurrected Jesus whom he saw on the Damascus road and the experience of the Spirit; as one recent writer has put it:

> At the christophany, which was of the same kind as the visions granted to OT prophets at their call and also to some apocalypists, Paul received the revelation (*apokalypsis*) of the gospel, the good news concerning the salvation in Christ which has been realised in the death and resurrection of Jesus Christ and awaits its consummation at his parousia, and together with it, or as a part of it, the revelation of the 'mystery' (*mysterion*), namely God's plan of salvation embodied in Christ for both Jews and Gentiles.[3]

The resurrection of Jesus marks the beginning of the cosmic process of transformation (1 Cor. 15.20). Meanwhile Christ reigns in heaven with his Father, until the universal sovereignty is acknowledged throughout creation and God can be all in all (15.28). To assert the reality of the resurrection, even of just one person, was to take up the eschatological scheme of Judaism, and, as we have said frequently elsewhere in this study, think in terms of fulfilment of eschatological beliefs rather than merely of promise. Certainly Paul and other New Testament writers somewhat modified the eschatological scheme. With the exception of Matthew 27.52f., which presents peculiar problems to the interpreter, early Christians did not assert that the general resurrection had taken place, but that it had happened only in the case of one man. Therefore, it became necessary to modify the eschatological scheme by regarding the resurrection of Jesus as a proleptic act peculiar to him, which nevertheless was confirmation that the sequence of events associated with the eschaton had already been set in train.

The intensity of Paul's hope should never be lost sight of; it is a theme which occurs throughout his letters (e.g., Rom. 5.2; 8.24f.; 1 Thess. 1.9f.; 2 Cor. 5.10). This hope complements the belief in the resurrection of Jesus. As 1 Corinthians 15.20ff. makes plain, the heart of Christian experience is bipolar in character. It looks back to a decisive event at Calvary and Easter and forward to the completion of that train of events set in action by the cross.[4] Christians are in an 'in-between period', when they groan, longing for the consummation of the divine purposes (Romans 8.18ff.), but assured that the time would come when with the return of Christ the elect would be vindicated (1 Thess. 4.15) and the creation be redeemed into the glorious liberty of the children of God (Rom. 8.21). That in-between stage is marked not by knowledge but by faith and hope (2 Cor. 5.7, Rom. 8.24f.). At present, the believer can only see in a glass darkly (1 Cor. 13.12). Seeing face to face or, in Johannine language equally drawn from Jewish eschatology, 'being like him' (1 John 3.2), is still to come; it is the moment when Christ 'will change our lowly body into the likeness of his glorious body, by the power which enables him even to subject all things to himself' (Phil. 3.21).

But Paul's eschatological belief is not confined to the resurrection of Jesus and its consequences. The present, 'in-between' stage is itself marked as an eschatological time. Paul can tell the Corinthians that they are those 'upon whom the end of the age has come' (1 Cor. 10.11). The sign of this is that believers now taste of the Holy Spirit (1 Cor. 12.13; cf. Heb. 6.4). Picking up a belief, which is to be found in some parts of Judaism (cf. *Tos. Sotah* 13.2), Paul thinks of the Spirit as itself a mark of the presence of the new age. It is 'the firstfruits' (Rom. 8.23), the seal placed in the hearts of believers as a guarantee (Rom. 8.23; cf. Eph. 1.14; 2 Cor. 1.22; Acts 2.17). The return of the Spirit was believed to coincide with an outburst of prophetic activity, and such activity was certainly characteristic of the Pauline communities (1 Cor. 12–14; Rom. 12.6; 1 Thess. 5.19; cf Eph. 4.11; Acts 11.28). Like the book of Revelation, which marks the breaking in of the last things with the presence of the prophetic witness (Rev. 19.10; ch. 10–11) Paul and his churches experience the revival of the gift of prophecy, a sign that the promises of God were being fulfilled. Thus the present is not merely a time of waiting, for the communities can already taste what it is like in the kingdom of God within the fellowship of the Church. Here 'there is neither Jew nor Greek, there is neither slave nor free, there is neither male nor female; for you are all one in Christ Jesus' (Gal. 3.28; cf. Col. 3.11). It is the Spirit, of which all have drunk, which brings about this unity and breaks down divisions (1 Cor. 12.13), so that the community of believers can be compared to the human body, each with its different contribution to make but united to one another and to Christ by the Holy Spirit.

The twin beliefs of resurrection and Spirit are the foundations upon which the whole of Paul's theology is built. He starts with the conviction that Christ is vindicated and raised, and the experience of the Holy Spirit, and from these works back to an understanding of the world without Christ and a world under the Law and the rulers of this darkness. To say this is to indicate that for Paul the concept of the two ages is an important way of characterizing the difference between the past and the present (cf. Gal. 4.1–5). Christ delivers believers 'from the present evil age' (Gal. 1.4) and by implication allows them to participate in a new age (cf. Rom. 12.2; 1 Cor. 2.6ff.; 2 Cor. 4.4). Although Paul does not use the contrast between this age and the age to come (cf. Eph. 1.21) familiar to us from Jewish eschatology, it is difficult to resist the conclusion that he presupposes it.

It is commonplace in rabbinic eschatology to find the contrast between the present age with all its inadequacies and weaknesses and the glorious future when God's kingdom would come, characterized by the contrast, 'this age and the age to come' (*ha- 'olam ha-zeh/ha- 'olam ha-ba'*).[5] Clearly the coming of Christ and the events of his passion and resurrection mark a decisive turning point in God's dealings with man. Until Christ the Law was the custodian; it played its part as a necessary part of the divine economy in demonstrating transgression (Gal. 3.19; Rom. 5.20). It was there to be observed. Until Christ, there was no opportunity for the Gentiles to become heirs of Abraham except through circumcision and the acceptance of the Law.[6] But with the coming of Christ all this has changed. Now the righteousness of God has been manifested apart from the Law, though the latter bears witness to this righteous manifestation of God's power (Rom. 3.21). God himself has shown his righteousness, his faithfulness to the covenant promises, to act in power and to offer salvation. With the coming of Christ, man is faced with the challenge of either accepting the righteousness of God (faith in Christ), or rejecting it and finding himself subject to God's wrath, which is now being revealed against all impiety. The righteousness of God is demonstrated by his willingness to act, despite the impiety of man (Rom. 5.6). The eschatological action of God does not depend on repentance; it is a free gift which man can do nothing to earn, but must either accept in faith and so escape the wrath which is coming (Rom. 5.8), or reject and find himself outside the community of the elect. The way of God's saving act places all without distinction in the realm of sin (Rom. 3.23). All mankind is part of the old aeon of sin and death. The only way of transferring from the old domain to the new is through faith in God's Messiah. He alone can deliver from the evil age (Gal. 1.4), for he has conquered those powers who dominate it and will ultimately demonstrate his triumph over them when they acknowledge his lordship (1 Cor. 2.9; cf. 15.25ff; Phil. 2.11).[7]

The present is a time of both fulfilment and ambiguity for the believer. He waits in hope (Rom. 8.18ff.), though he has the firstfruits of the Spirit (Rom. 8.23). Yet picking up a central theme of Jewish eschatological belief, Paul regards the present as a time of struggle and suffering. We saw in considering Jewish eschatology that a central component of the future hope was the belief that before the age to come finally came, there must be a time of great distress on the earth, when the elect may be expected to suffer. It is a theme which is echoed in the eschatological discourses in the Gospels (Mark 13 and par., esp. vv.7–13). Paul often speaks of tribulations, as, for example, in Romans 2.9, which is probably a reference to the righteous judgement of God against the wicked, Romans 8.35 and in 1 Thessalonians 3.3; 7 (cf. Rev. 2.22; 7.14). Elsewhere Paul speaks about the sufferings of the present time in a context which is dealing explicitly with the eschatological events (Rom. 8.18), and it would appear that the travail and persecution endured by believers is viewed by Paul as their undergoing of that tribulation, which is a necessary prelude to the arrival of the new age.[8] This suffering, however, is not seen as a necessary evil. Christians can rejoice in their present sufferings (Rom. 5.3). Indeed, it is possible for there to be reciprocal support between believers, so that the full quota of suffering is shared by all (2 Cor. 1.3ff.).[9]

In outlining Paul's gospel, nothing has been said so far about the cross. The question must be asked whether the death of Christ plays any *decisive and central* role in Paul's thought; did Paul view Christ's death as a sacrifice needed to reconcile man and God? Certainly it has to be said at the outset that sacrificial terms are not frequent in Paul's thought,[10] and much will depend on the weight that is attached to the passage in Romans 3.21ff., where the word 'expiation/propitiation' makes its only appearance in Paul's letters and the word 'redemption' makes one of its occasional appearances. Many have argued that passages like Romans 3.21ff.; 4.25, which seem to reflect an emphasis on the sacrificial, atoning death of Christ, are relics of earlier formulae taken over by Paul and used in these contexts.[11] Paul does quote these formulae, and, therefore, indicates his acceptance of that understanding of the Christ-event, which gives a primary place to the atoning death of Jesus (e.g., Heb., 1 Cor. 15.3; Mark 10.45; 1 Pet. 1.18f.; 2.21ff.).[12]

Paul accepts that stream of interpretation which finds its classic expression in Hebrews, but for him the significance of the cross does not lie primarily in the significance of a death as an atoning sacrifice.[13] For Paul the death cannot be separated from resurrection. Justification is only complete if both the death *and* resurrection are taken into account, as Romans 4.25 and 1 Corinthians 15 make plain. For Paul the cross is the stumbling-block, which finally puts to an end the wisdom of the world (1 Cor. 1.17ff.). The cruel and ignominious end of the messianic pretender is, in Paul's eyes, the decisive revelation of God's wisdom. In the cross the rulers of this age considered that they had defeated the lord of glory (1 Cor. 2.9), but the cross marked the moment of triumph for Christ, when by putting off the body of flesh, he triumphed over the principalities and powers (Col. 2.14f.).

The issue is made more poignant for Paul the Jew because, as he points out in Galatians 3.13, 'Cursed is everyone who hangs on a tree'. The cross marks in the most decisive way possible the end of the old aeon. The period of the Law had come to an end with the cross, for the crucifixion of the Messiah had effectively shown that the Law was never intended as a means of salvation, but as what it had always been, a witness to the glory to come. The cross is to be understood as the gateway to eschatological glory for Christ and ultimately for the believer. It stands before mankind as an implacable barrier, which is either a means of glory or a stumbling-block. It appears to be folly to man, but in it is revealed the wisdom of God, because God has chosen what is weak and foolish (1 Cor. 1.27). It is only by accepting what is foolish in the eyes of men, 'a stumbling-block to Jews and folly to

Greeks', that man will be able to see that in it God has offered the source of new life in Christ Jesus (1 Cor. 1.20). It is when man can see glory in the cross of Christ, that a path is opened to a new creation where neither circumcision nor uncircumcision, Jew nor Gentile, Law or no Law have any place (Gal. 6.15f.). Just as the resurrection and the bestowal of the Spirit mark the dawn of the new age, so the cross just as decisively marks the end of the old aeon. It is only when the believer dies with Christ, something which takes place in baptism (Rom. 6.5ff.) that he can walk in newness of life (Rom. 6.4) and pass from the present evil age (Gal. 1.4):

> The death and resurrection of Christ mark the discontinuity between the old age and the new because history is broken apart into the era of the old Adam and that of the eschatological Adam (Rom. 5.12–21). The death of Christ does not refer primarily to the death of a martyr, an innocent suffering martyr, which evokes remorse and moral cleansing; it does not mean a new moral beginning for the 'old' person, or primarily the forgiveness of his former transgressions so that he can begin with a clean slate. To the contrary, the death of Christ addresses itself to sin as a cosmic power and slavemaster, that is, to the human condition 'under the power of sin'. It announces the negation of the power of sin that controls the world, and thus it has not only a moral but an ontological meaning. 'The old has passed away… the new has come' (2 Cor. 5.17) and a new creation has been established (*kaine ktisis* 2 Cor. 5.17; Gal. 6.15).[14]

Being in Christ means being part of a new order, therefore, initiated by Christ's resurrection and entered by the believer at baptism, when he receives the Spirit (1 Cor. 12.13). But it is not merely a relationship with an absent Messiah whose parousia is still expected but also a participation with others, who have been baptized in the same Spirit (1 Cor. 12.13). The ideal picture of the new community (for this is what Paul offers in his letters; the reality was often very different) is of a group of different individuals related to Christ through the Spirit (1 Cor. 6.15ff.), each of equal importance in the eyes of God and yet with widely different functions within the community. Paul's most distinctive image for the Church is the body (Rom. 12; 1 Cor. 12).[15] If 1 Corinthians is anything to go by, its common life is characterized by a common meal (11.18ff.), in which the community expresses its unity with its Lord through a repetition of the words and acts of Jesus at the Last Supper (11.23ff.): it is nothing less than a participation in the body and blood of Christ (10.16), an antepast of the messianic banquet.[16] The meeting for worship is characterized by spontaneity: prophecy, visions and revelations and hymns, all contributed by different members of the community (14.26f.). Even women, if properly attired, may participate in the prayer and prophecy of the meeting (11.5, 13).[17]

The community is a holy enclave amidst an age which is passing away. It is a community where the Holy Spirit dwells and is described by Paul as the Temple of God, the location of God's presence on earth (1 Cor. 3.16; 6.19).

Like the righteous enclave in the desert, about which we now know so much as the result of the Dead Sea Scrolls, the early Christian communities were outposts of heaven on earth, a present manifestation of the holiness of God.[18] They are the saints (1 Cor. 1.2), not because they keep the commandments and maintain the degree of purity necessary to be a holy people of God, but because they have been sanctified in Christ Jesus (1 Cor. 1.2); they have been bought with a price (6.19); they were washed, sanctified and justified (6.11). The language of the cult and sacrifice is transferred to the life of the holy community. They offer spiritual sacrifices (Rom. 12.1), and both apostle and community can by their deeds offer a sacrifice, acceptable and pleasing to God (Phil. 4.18; 2 Cor. 2.14f.).

Paul says little about the hierarchy within the community. The Lord is the Spirit (2 Cor. 3.17), and he it is who controls the Church and bestows gifts for edification upon its members (1 Cor. 12.4ff.). Certainly there are some gifts which call for particular mention: apostleship, prophecy, miraculous deeds, teaching, helping, administration, speaking in tongues (1 Cor. 12.28). Rarely does Paul mention ecclesiastical officers; only once is mention made of bishops/overseers and deacons (Phil. 1.1) – a contrast with the Pastoral Epistles, where 'Paul' instructs his helpers to set up church officers in the various communities to carry on the work. In Acts, Paul and Barnabas are represented as those who set up elders in the churches (14.23), though this finds no explicit parallel in the indisputably authentic Pauline letters. Nevertheless mention should be made of the occasional hint which indicates that Paul did not entirely ignore the provision of oversight in his churches. In 1 Corinthians 16.15f. he instructs the Corinthians in the following way:

> Now, brethren, you know that the household of Stephanas were the first converts in Achaia, and they have devoted themselves to the service of the saints; I urge you to be subject to such men and to every fellow-worker and labourer.

Here we have a recognition of pastoral oversight, though without the word overseer (*episkopos*) being used. The basis of it may be related to the list of the gifts of the Spirit in 1 Corinthians 12, though it is not explicitly so stated there; only that as the earliest converts the household of Stephanas have a position of pre-eminence, based not only on the length of their discipleship but also on the quality of their ministry and social position.[19] Care should be taken, therefore, not to suppose that Paul's view of the community was of an entirely charismatic and spontaneously ordered group, free of all trace of hierarchy. The relationship of Paul to his churches itself offers us an example of pastoral oversight of an extensive kind.

As far as Christian living was concerned, Paul refused to allow his communities to adopt an escapist attitude, so that the purity of their life and the ideals of their faith might be translated into practice without hindrance from the world (1 Cor. 5.10). There is an uneasy tension here, which we shall have to explore later, between the idealism, indeed utopianism, of the belief that the life of the age to come can already be experienced and that in Christ all barriers are transcended, and the practical advice given by the apostle. In the latter Paul emerges as essentially socially conservative. He refuses to allow the converts to shake the fabric of society too much (1 Cor. 7.17ff.).[20] Even within the life of the community, contemporary practice intrudes (1 Cor. 14.34).[21] Even if Paul does not challenge the relationship between slave and master in his detailed ethical advice, the harsher realities of that relationship are mitigated (Col. 4.1). Nor should one miss the significance of the advice to Philemon to regard his runaway slave Onesimus as a brother (Philemon 16).

It would appear that a distinction is to be made between conservative attitudes towards society at large and the transformation in the Christian community, probably inspired by the view that the present world order was not much longer to be in existence and would be swept away in the establishment of the kingdom of God on earth (cf. 1 Cor. 7.26: 'In view of the impending distress it is as well for a person to remain as he is', and also v.31). State, slavery and sexual relationships are not greatly challenged by Paul. Yet it would be a mistake to miss the revolutionary concept, for which Paul fought, as far as life in the Church was concerned. His confrontation with Peter at Antioch (Gal. 2.10) indicates that, whatever else may have been the case, those patterns of relationships, which are true of life in the world, cannot now apply to life in the Christian community. The Spirit apportions the gifts as he wishes. While we may expect that, in practice, the more important gifts of oversight may have been linked with the head of the household rather than the humbler members of the household, that pattern is not explicitly supported by Paul. Perhaps the revolution is mainly Jewish, in that it stressed the need for complete communion between Jews and Gentiles within the body of Christ. Nevertheless it seems also to have extended its scope to other relationships even if it has to be said that the implications of such views for patterns of behaviour in society at large were left behind in the security of the holy community. Whether this is the result of Paul's limited historical perspective (cf. 1 Cor. 7.31) or one of the problems of opting for a pattern of existence which eschewed withdrawal from the world and stressed the need for accommodation with the old aeon, it is now impossible to say. What is clear is that the ethical principle of care for the weaker brother enunciated in 1 Corinthians 8 and based on 'the law of Christ' (Gal. 6.2) injected a fresh dimension into the ethical response of the believer, which could not fail to have an impact on the surrounding culture.[22]

5

Apostle to the Gentiles

Why did Paul have the burning conviction that he had been set apart as the apostle to the Gentiles, commissioned by the Messiah himself to preach the good news to the nations (Gal. 1.16)? The answer to that question surely lies in the Jewish traditions. We have already noted that Jesus would have shared the beliefs of many Jews that Jewish outcasts (Isa. 11.12) and some Gentiles would indeed be privileged to participate in the glories of the new age.[1] Such ideas have their origins within the Bible (e.g., Zech. 8.20) and were taken up in later Jewish sources (e.g., 1 Enoch 90.30). In the last-mentioned passage the acceptance by the Gentiles of the way of Israel takes place as one of the components of the eschatological events. This belief, Paul thought, was in the process of fulfilment through him (Rom. 15.16).[2] As we have seen, Paul believed that he and the communities of believers dotted around the Eastern Mediterranean were themselves living in a critical period (1 Cor. 10.11). The belief that a quota of Gentiles would be allowed to participate in the new age was one which was shared by Paul (Rom. 11.25) in common with other Jews. The difference between Paul and most of his Jewish contemporaries with regard to Gentiles was twofold:

(i)   He claimed the right to bring the Gentiles into the covenant himself, since he considered that he was the agent of the divine plan to bring into effect this eschatological event;

(ii)   He considered that it was not necessary for those Gentiles whom he brought into the covenant to practise the totality of the Jewish law, as the Law was part of a past aeon and was now obsolete in the light of Christ. This is central to his argument in Galatians 3. The argument starts from the premise that experience of the Spirit, and therefore of the age to come, does not arise through obedience to the Law but through faith (3.3ff.; cf. Acts 10.47). The fact that Gentiles had tasted of the fruits of the age to come *without the Law* inevitably cast a new light on the position of the Law.

In these two areas we can isolate the fundamental reasons why Paul should have come into conflict not only with his Jewish contemporaries but also with certain of his fellow-believers. In his statements about the Law of Moses and in his claim to have authority to bring the Gentiles into the covenant people, he threatens two well-established principles of Judaism: (i) the validity, indeed centrality, of the Law of Moses; (ii) the pattern of authority which validated teaching by recourse to tradition rather than experience.[3]

None of Paul's claims are inherently impossible as part of the fabric of Jewish belief. Rather they are symptomatic of the overwhelming effect that eschatological convictions can have on established patterns of inherited traditions. To grasp this fact and the concomitant conviction of Paul that it was his task to evangelize the Gentiles, and play his part in bringing in the full number of Gentiles (Rom. 11.25) is to understand the heart of Paul's career as a disciple of Jesus of Nazareth.

Reading through Paul's letters, it is difficult to resist the impression that many of his converts were in fact Gentiles and not Jews. In 1 Thessalonians 1.9 (cf. Gal. 4.8; 1 Cor. 12.2) he speaks of the converts at Thessalonica as those who turned to God from idols to serve a living and true God, and to wait for his son from heaven.[4]

In any assessment of the method of Paul and the make-up of his churches much will depend upon the weight that one gives to the evidence of Acts. There Paul is presented as going to the synagogue first of all (17.2). Of course, there is a wide discrepancy between those who regard the historicity of Acts with considerable suspicion,[5] and those others, who think that it represents, at least in general terms, the outline of early Christian history.[6] The assumption in this study is that Acts is not to be discounted as a reliable record either of Paul's activity or for that matter of the character of early Christian belief. What is more, the evidence of Paul's letters indicates that the picture in Acts may in fact be near the mark. Paul's principle of accommodation set out in 1 Corinthians 9.19ff. indicates that he did not go exclusively to Gentiles (but note Gal. 2.9), though it may well have been the case that, as Acts itself indicates, the greatest response came from Gentiles.[7] The fate which Paul suffered in some of the Diaspora synagogues according to Acts (e.g., 13.50; 18.6), finds few echoes in the letters, but we may suppose that 2 Corinthians 11.24 reflects Paul's concern to maintain his connection with the synagogue in his missionary endeavours.

How does this square with Paul's assertion that he was the apostle to the Gentiles? Why does he go to the synagogues? One answer which may be given is that the synagogues in the first Christian century were not merely a collection of Diaspora Jews. The accounts of Paul's preaching in Acts already indicate that among his hearers were non-Jews: those sympathizers with the Jewish tradition, who took upon themselves some basic require-ments but refused circumcision, and were known as the God-fearers (Acts 13.26).[8] This was probably the group which formed the heart of the Pauline churches.[9] The reasons for this are not too difficult to understand. Paul, the apostle to the Gentiles, was asserting that membership of the people of God did not depend on the rite of circumcision.[10] Like other Jews before him he said that baptism, not circumcision, was the means of entry into the people of God,[11] though as far as Paul was concerned, this was linked to belief in Jesus as the Christ.

It may be argued that Paul's missionary method as set out in Acts conflicts with the account of the agreement between Peter and Paul over their respective spheres of activity (Gal. 2.7ff.). What is not clear is how it would have been possible to maintain a precise demarcation between these different spheres. Indeed, there is evidence from 2 Corinthians 10.14 that there was some dispute over Paul's sphere of activity.[12] 1 Corinthians 1–3 hints that Peter had made an appearance in the church at Corinth. But it is difficult to see how there could have been anything but overlap between Christian missionaries in their activities. The apostle to the circumcision is unlikely to have confined himself only to Christians of Jewish extraction, as in the synagogues he would have preached to Gentile sympathizers. What is more, the synagogue must have been a legitimate sphere of Paul's activity, in so far as there were many Gentiles connected with it who would not hear the gospel otherwise.

Some of the issues which are dealt with in Romans 14f. indicate that there was, at the very least, a strong Jewish influence around (cf. Col. 2.16f.).[13] This suggests that there was either a Jewish minority in the congregations or, more likely, that the persisting influence of Jewish practices is a hangover from the long connection of some of the Christian converts with the life of the synagogue. What is more, the contents of Paul's letters suggest that he was writing to communities who had some familiarity with the Old Testament. The use of the Old Testament, particularly in a letter like Galatians, points to a community which, Paul presumed, would have both considered the Jewish Scriptures as an authoritative source for his argument and also would have known them sufficiently well to have made the most of the allusions, frequently unacknowledged, which he makes. The fact that a relapse into another type of Judaism, by accepting circumcision as a prerequisite of salvation, was an issue in Galatians, indicates the level of Jewish influence in the community. We are not dealing here with a group of Gentiles with no connection with Judaism. Rather it is one which had such reverence for the Jewish traditions that they could easily fall prey to those who suggested that circumcision was necessary. The success of Judaizing is itself testimony to the pervasive influence of Jewish ideas and practices on the Pauline communities.[14]

Paul nowhere says anything about the kind of attitude to the Law which would have been incumbent upon a Diaspora Jew who accepted that Jesus was the Messiah. If his practice in 1 Corinthians 9.19ff. is anything to go by, it would appear that he would not have gone out of his way to suggest either that a Jew should stop obeying the Law or that he should continue to obey the Law (cf. Acts 21.21f.). The point at issue in Galatians (which admittedly is addressed to the issue of Gentile observance of the Law) is the position of the Law in the process of salvation. It may be assumed, therefore, that Paul would have been content to allow a Jew to keep the Law, provided that he did not regard that act as itself constituting the basis of salvation (that is the point made in Gal. 5.2ff.).[15] To keep the Law would have been an optional, though not essential, mark of the believer. Thus the charge levelled against Paul in Acts 21.21 that he encouraged Jews to stop obeying the Law of Moses is not true to Paul's own teaching. What he did do was to reject the idea that the Law was the cornerstone of God's saving purposes, now that the Messiah had come.

If we are to take Paul's principle of being all things to all men (1 Cor. 9.22) seriously,[16] we may suppose that his practice was itself a source of confusion, particularly to Jewish onlookers. If, as we have supposed, Paul went first to the synagogues, then it is likely that he would have observed certain dietary laws while living in Jewish homes and a Jewish environment, but, as his confrontation with Peter in Antioch makes plain, when he was in a situation where Jews and Gentiles met together in the messianic community, then the food laws were suspended and table-fellowship between the two sets of believers was paramount. The need for a certain amount of flexibility in dealing with the Gentiles must have been a perennial problem for Diaspora Jews, and a degree of accommodation was almost certainly reached.[17] The issues with which Paul deals in 1 Corinthians 8 and 10 indicate the kind of problem which would emerge in a Gentile environment, when believers from a Jewish background and non-Jews had to work out a pattern of existence in which their common bond in Christ could be acknowledged.

One of the most pressing questions facing the commentator on Paul is the origin of his belief that the Law of Moses was not a necessary condition of the salvation of the Gentiles. There are two related issues here: (i) what Judaism may have said about the demands laid upon Gentiles who were allowed to participate in the new age; (ii) the status of the Law in the messianic age/age to come.[18] Unfortunately the evidence is sparse and what there is does not allow us to answer the questions with any degree of clarity.

It may be supposed that passages like 1 Enoch 90.30, which speaks of the homage done by the Gentiles, and Zechariah 8.20, where the Gentiles acknowledge that Israel has the true religion, presuppose that those Gentiles submit to the Law of Moses and become proselytes, thus accepting circumcision. Indeed, a passage like Isaiah 56.3ff. might suggest that keeping the Law, including circumcision, was the necessary condition for acceptance into the people of God:

> And the foreigners who join themselves to the Lord, to minister to him, to love the name of the Lord, and to be his servants, every one who keeps the sabbath and does not profane it, and holds fast my covenant – these I will bring to my holy

mountain, and make them joyful in my house of prayer, their burnt offerings and sacrifices will be accepted on my altar; for my house shall be called a house of prayer for all peoples.[19]

There seems to be little doubt that the prophet is not here contemplating the admission of foreigners on grounds any different from those offered to true-born Jews. They are expected to keep the sabbath and to offer the sacrifices prescribed in the Law. But the important point to note is the obligation to 'hold fast the covenant' (56.6). Can it be assumed that the prophet here includes in this obligation maintenance of the rite, which is the sign of the covenant, namely, circumcision (Gen. 17.9ff.)?

It would not be surprising that those Jews and perhaps also Jewish-Christians, who did not object to the idea of a certain number of Gentiles participating in the age to come were nevertheless very suspicious of those, like Paul, who said that circumcision was unnecessary. A legitimate interpretation (and the most likely meaning of the original) of Isaiah 56.6 would have indicated that circumcision *was* necessary for the Gentiles, who became members of the covenant people.

The question is whether Paul might have supposed that passages like Isaiah 56.6f. did not require the circumcision of Gentiles. In terms of precise detail it has to be said that no *explicit* requirement is laid upon the Gentiles in this passage to accept circumcision. Much will depend on what is meant by 'holding fast the covenant'. It could have been argued (though one has to admit that Paul never does so) that a legitimate interpretation of holding fast the covenant might have been the new covenant spoken of by Jeremiah and Ezekiel (Jer. 31.31ff.; Ezek. 36.26ff.). An interpretation of Isaiah 56.6 in the light of the inwardness of the new covenant, of which Jeremiah spoke, could well have yielded a concept of Gentiles' membership of the covenant people, in which the condition was not circumcision but the heart of flesh, the Law written on the heart which will enable each man to know the Lord (Jer. 31.34).[20]

It must be said, of course, that there was room for variety of interpretation in the understanding of these demands. The kind of speculations, which are now extant, concerning the situation in the new age do not allow us to reconstruct with any certainty whether there was any messianic *halakah* at all, never mind specific provision made for those Gentiles who would come into Israel in the last days. Certainly the Temple Scroll has given us evidence that one Jewish group did make extensive provision for the new age,[21] but whether this was a typical feature of the debates taking place in other groups at the time is by no means certain.

In any discussion of the Gentile mission, mention must be made of a scheme which occupied Paul's attention during the later years of his missionary activity, the collection for the saints in Jerusalem.[22] Paul mentions this action on the part of the churches of the Gentile mission in several places in his letters (e.g., Rom. 15.25f.; 1 Cor. 16.1ff.; 2 Cor. 8–9; cf. Acts 24.17). There have been many explanations of this action. Some have compared it with the half-shekel Temple tax paid by all Jews, though the collection for the church in Jerusalem was not a levy but a voluntary contribution. Others feel that Paul regards this act as part of the fulfilment of Old Testament prophecy where Gentiles bring in their gifts to Zion (Ps. 72.10; Isa. 60.6ff.). The problem with this is that Paul says nothing explicit along these lines, however attractive such a theory might be on other grounds, because of its eschatological connections. What is clear is that this journey to Jerusalem was regarded as being very important by Paul, as his worries about it expressed in Romans 15.31f. make plain. Whether he really hoped to provoke the Jews to jealousy and so to repentance by his act must remain unclear (cf. Rom. 11.13f.).

6

Paul and the Law

One thing is obvious from the letters of Paul: Christ is the end of the Law for all who have faith (Rom. 10.4). Much ink has been spilt over the meaning of these words: did the apostle think that Christ in some sense abolished the Law or was it more a case of fulfilment of the Law of Moses in Christ?[1] Most commentators tend to choose the second alternative, and this fits the evidence of the letters themselves. Certainly Paul did not see the Law as something which had no more importance in the divine economy. Despite his impassioned words in Galatians, it is clear that he wants to guarantee the central importance of the Law of Moses, though not as the means of salvation. This is the central thrust of Paul's argument in Galatians 3. In dealing with the issue of whether Gentiles needed to accept the Law of Moses and, with it, circumcision, in order to be members of the people of God, Paul argues on the basis of Scripture that righteousness comes by faith and is open to Gentiles as well as Jews on these terms. The use Paul makes of Scripture in this letter and elsewhere is testimony itself to the apostle's conviction that 'the Law is holy, just and good' (Rom. 7.12).[2] The purpose of the Law must be correctly seen, however. According to Paul, its function was not an end in itself. According to Scripture, it did not exist from the beginning of creation (Rom. 5.13), but only came later to show up sin in its true colours (Rom. 5.20; cf. Gal. 3.19). It was not itself the means of righteousness, though it bore witness to the righteousness of God, which comes through faith in Christ (Rom. 3.21). Its function was not to give life

(Gal. 3.21), for if it had been, then the righteousness, which comes by faith, would have been of no avail. We thus come up against a fact of Pauline theology, which has been rightly pointed out by Sanders, namely, that Paul's theological exposition starts from the fact of the revelation of the eschatological event in Jesus of Nazareth.[3] Paul did not start with problems with the Law or the human plight and work through to a solution of the problem. He started with the fact that God had revealed his son to him (Gal. 1.16), and that this marked the moment of his perception that the old aeon was passing away and a new one had begun.

Working back from this fact and the related insight that the observance of the precepts of the Law was not necessary for salvation, Paul then has to find a place for the Law in the divine economy. That it does have a place Paul has no doubt. The point is made in Galatians 3–4 that the Law should be seen in its proper perspective. When it is viewed, as Paul obviously thought it was, as a part of the process of salvation, then the need was to make the contrast as stark as possible between the old and the new, the imperfect and the perfect. The whole argument in Galatians 4 is based on this overriding necessity. Similarly in Galatians 3.19, where Paul asserts that the Law was given by angels and thus inferior to the subsequent revelation of the Son, which was direct, the purpose is to undermine the position of those who would assert that the Law had any hold on those who had faith. The significance of this language should not be missed. It is not a polemic against the Law as such, but against the use of the Law as a means of salvation. There is no doubt in Paul's mind that God gave the Law, and indeed, if the Law is read properly, Paul believes that it will vindicate his own position (3.6ff., 21). It bears witness to the righteousness which comes by faith and serves as a custodian until the Messiah comes (Gal. 3.23).

If Paul finds himself opposed to the written law as the ultimate embodiment of God's saving purposes (cf. 2 Cor. 3.6ff.), he is in no sense opposed to moral constraints on believers. This is a charge he sets out to answer in Romans 6.1, where he responds to the rhetorical question 'Are we to continue in sin that grace may abound?' (cf. Rom. 3.8). Paul is in no doubt that the new life in Christ will mean that those who participate in it will walk in newness of life (6.4). What is involved in this newness of life is never spelt out in detail, though passages, like Galatians 5.14; 6.2; 1 Corinthians 9.21 and Romans 8.4, all indicate that Christians were under the obligation to fulfil a law, though not *the* Law.[4] Whereas the Law weakened by the flesh could bring only death, the Law of the Spirit could bring life (Rom. 8.2f.). Possession of the Spirit marked the beginning of a new pattern of ethical attitudes (Gal. 5.22ff.). If the letters are anything to go by, it did not consist of many or even any specific regulations, except to fulfil the law of Christ (Gal. 6.2), or the command to love one's neighbour (Gal. 5.14; cf. Rom. 13.9), the latter being the fulfilling of the whole Law. Certainly Paul did not abandon the importance of moral earnestness for the members of the covenant people, though he locates the means by which that is achieved elsewhere: life in the Spirit. Whereas other forms of Judaism maintained distinctiveness by observance of circumcision and dietary requirements, Paul abandoned these in favour of another principle, the Law of Christ. Within the life of the new creation, there was no longer room for the continuation of obligations like dietary laws, which would effectively separate Gentile from Jewish Christians. In accepting the Law of Christ, the Law of the Spirit, the believer was indicating his continuity with the old covenant and its demands to fulfil the Law of God. The difference is that the new demand is not the letter which kills (2 Cor. 3.7f.) but the Spirit. It is the indwelling Spirit, which ensures that the Law's (and God's) requirement that we should be righteous is fulfilled. The act of grace, which characterizes the eschatological revelation of the Son and to which the only response is grateful acceptance (faith), is continued in the way in which the believer fulfils what God requires through the promptings of the indwelling Spirit. To say this is not to deny the evidence of other strands in Paul's letters, which indicate the introduction of a new legalism; believers who are justified by faith alone become subject to moral codes, whose relationship with the fact of salvation in Christ is not always clear. This applies particularly to passages like 1 Corinthians 11.2ff.; 14.34f.; Colossians 3.18ff.[5]

7

Membership of the People of God

The belief that Jesus was the eschatological deliverer, who had introduced a new aeon, poses two problems for the non-believing Jew: the status of the nations and the status of those Jews who did not accept the fact that the Messiah had come. We have already noted that one of the foundations of Paul's understanding of his work is that he had received a direct commission to bring in the Gentiles, whom God had foreordained would participate in the life of the age to come. We can all too easily assume that the problem with which Paul wrestles in Romans 9–11 was not considered to be such a difficulty within other Jewish groups. After all, it might be assumed that when the Messiah came it would be obvious to all concerned. But would it?[1] The hints we have about the nature of Jewish messianism suggests that by no means all Jews agreed with their contemporaries who asserted that the Messiah had come. One is reminded of course of the sardonic comment from one of Akiba's contemporaries, when he said that Bar Kochba was the

Messiah: in effect, that Akiba would be long dead and buried before the Messiah had come (*j. Ta'anith* 68d). In practice, of course, this divergence of opinion was a problem for a Jew, who disagreed with his contemporaries on this point. One can see in Paul's own teaching and career the consequences of this. While he had no doubts in his mind that the decisive eschatological event had begun to take place, he was faced with the fact that his fellow-Jews did not in general accept the messiahship of Jesus. This is the issue which occupies his attention in Romans 9–11 and leads him to formulate an eschatological scheme, in which the Gentile mission is seen as a prelude to the redemption of Israel: a reversal of the usual eschatological order, where the central role of Israel in the events of the last days will gradually lead to the complement of Gentiles being brought into the kingdom (Rom. 11.25ff.).[2]

Until that time, Paul offers an alternative way into the people of God, which in practice excluded those who refused to accept his terms of entry. As far as he was concerned, the rite of circumcision as a badge of membership of the covenant people was no longer necessary. For most Jews the proselyte (the convert to Judaism) would have accepted circumcision and the obligation to keep the Torah,[3] so that he would have become a true member of the covenant people. Once inside the covenant people, he would have maintained his place by avoiding major transgression, and in those instances where he did infringe, there was the possibility of repentance and atonement through the sacrificial system in the Temple and pre-eminently the rite of the Day of Atonement. In all likelihood an observant Jew would have been a member of a sect, which set its own (stricter) entrance requirements, such as we find in the Dead Sea Scrolls or in the obligations laid upon members of the pharisaic fellowships. Refusal to accept the obligations of the sect might lead to exclusion from the sect or various kinds of punishment,[4] but such rigid processes of exclusion would not have applied to the vast majority of Jews.

In the Pauline churches, a similar pattern of entry, maintenance of position and even exclusion is contemplated.[5] For Paul, entry into the community came through baptism, which marked the moment of the receipt of the eschatological Spirit (1 Cor. 12.13). That was the outward identification of a man with the death and resurrection of Christ (Rom. 6), and marked release from the old aeon of Law, sin and death and entry into the new creation of the Law of the spirit of life (Rom. 8.2).

Members of the Church (in theory at least) manifested that law of the Spirit, which exhibited particular characteristics (Gal. 5.22ff.) and certain patterns of behaviour towards one another. While Paul never admits as much, there is a sense in which the logic of his argument is that there was little likelihood of transgression in the community of the new age (Rom. 6.11ff.; 8.4ff.; 1 Cor. 4.8; cf. Heb. 6.1; 1 John 3.4ff.). After all, the community which was the Temple of the Holy Spirit (1 Cor. 3.16; 6.19) was not the place where unrighteousness was to be found.[6] The first letter to the Corinthians sees the apostle dealing with a situation where idealism has begun to give way to pragmatism. The community is guilty of various transgressions, and problems have arisen as the result of their application of the Pauline gospel. In dealing with them, Paul summons the Corinthians back to their position as those who have been made righteous in Christ (6.11) and gives advice concerning the kind of attitudes which are appropriate for those who would aspire to be citizens of the kingdom of God (6.10). In one case he sets out a process which will bring about the expulsion of a notorious sinner from the community (5.3ff.), a pattern similar to expulsion from other sectarian groups for grievous offences.

What emerges in the Pauline letters is a pattern of entry, continuation and, if necessary, expulsion, which indicates that the Pauline churches were developing a self-conscious identity over against those who did not accept this particular view of the saving events in Christ.[7] Like the Qumran sect, which maintained a separate existence over against other Jews, the Pauline communities had begun to separate themselves from those Jews who did not accept the messiahship of Jesus. Synagogues of Satan the latter may not yet have been (cf. Rev. 2.9), but the beginnings of a self-conscious differentiation were there. Because the terms of entry into the people of God did differ from those of other Jewish sects, the strain on relationships between non-messianic Jews and Christians must at times have been very great. Belonging to a sect with highly idiosyncratic beliefs and practices was a feature of first-century Judaism, and in this respect the Pauline communities did not differ from other Jewish sects. The problem would come when the messianic sect met with complete rejection of the validity of its interpretation by a more monolithic religious phenomenon than much of Judaism had become at this stage.[8]

8

Paul and Israel[1]

Paul leaves his readers in no doubt that he is proud of his Jewish ancestry and traditions (Rom. 9.4; Phil. 3.4ff.), and the polemic, which we find dotted around the letters, against the Law and Jews should not be mistaken for anti-Jewish sentiments. The issue which preoccupied several early Christian writers was the problem of the deep difference of opinion between themselves and those Jews who did not share their convictions about Jesus. The question with which they were wrestling was: what happens to the

Jewish traditions now that the Messiah has come?[2] This is particularly true of Paul.

It is in his earliest letters (Galatians),[3] that we find the most outspoken criticisms of Judaism. According to Galatians 3.18, for example, Paul interprets the glorious giving of the Law, attended as it was by the angelic host, as an indication of its inferior status in the divine economy. Later in the letter he speaks (on the only occasion in his letters) explicitly of the Church as the Israel of God (6.16).[4] However great Paul's sectarian mentality may have been, unlike the writers of the Dead Sea Scrolls, he still recognizes in his letters that Israel refers to an entity which is much broader than the household of faith.

In 1 Thessalonians Paul refers briefly to the Jewish nation in a context dealing with the persecution of Jewish-Christians by Jews. In a passage which has proved to be taxing for commentators Paul speaks in an uncompromising way about non-Christian Jews (2.14f.):

> ... for you suffered the same things from your own countrymen as they did from the Jews, who killed both the Lord Jesus and the prophets, and drove us out and displease God and oppose all men by hindering us from speaking to the Gentiles that they may be saved – so as always to fill up the measure of their sins. But God's wrath has come upon them at last!

It is an outburst of almost unparalleled vehemence in the Pauline corpus (but note Phil. 3.2ff.) and contrasts with the much more positive comments elsewhere (e.g., Rom. 9.4f.). Clearly Paul himself suffered at the hands of the Jews (e.g., 2 Cor. 11.24f.), a fate which seems to have accompanied his travels, according to Acts (e.g., 13.45f.). The theme of the Jewish rejection of the envoys of God is one which is taken up in the Synoptic tradition on the lips of Jesus (e.g., Matt. 23.29ff.; Luke 13.34), and it is not impossible that behind the Pauline formulation there lies an echo of the Synoptic saying.[5] If Paul's early ministry was beset with vexing debates and extreme hostility from his fellow-Jews, then it may not cause too much surprise if we find such a violent outburst on the lips of Paul. After all, we know from the Dead Sea Scrolls the vitriolic attitude taken by members of the group towards those Jews outside the sect (see 1 *Qp Hab.*). One may assume, therefore, that the weight of harassment led Paul in 1 Thessalonians to make an outburst, which stands in stark contrast with his more reflected cogitations on the problems of non-messianic Judaism in Romans 9–11. Like the prophets before him, who prophesied judgement on an unrepentant nation, and Jesus also in similar vein, according to Luke 10.13f.; 11.49f., Paul speaks the word of condemnation from the point of view of the minority, whose views are either not accepted or treated with hostility by the majority. When the prophet believes he is right, yet no one listens to him, or he is treated with contempt, this kind of reaction can be expected.[6]

This is where the recognition that the occasional character of the letters has contributed to the specific formulations contained within them is so important. While one does not want to deny the full force of what Paul is saying, no one could regard this brief comment as containing a fully worked-out attitude towards non-Christian Judaism. This remark, made in the heat of the struggle, which characterized Paul's early missionary career, must be seen in the light of the more extended treatment of the subject in Romans 9–11.[7] While one does not want to deny the contacts which exist between these chapters and 1 Thessalonians 2.16 (e.g., Rom. 9.6ff.; 9.22; 11.28, 32), the attitude to non-Christian Jews is more positive in Romans 9–11. In this section Paul meditates on the rejection of the gospel by many Jews. He concludes that the rejection of the gospel by the Jews has opened up the possibility of the Gentile mission (9.22f.). But the opportunity created for the Gentiles to hear and receive the gospel cannot be the end of the matter. All this must be seen within the framework of the totality of the divine purposes. Paul clearly has agonized over the fate of the Jewish nation, which had stumbled over the stone of stumbling (9.33). He does not deny the centrality of the means of salvation, which God has offered through Christ (Rom. 10.4ff.), but is unwilling to regard the rejection of the gospel as an indication that God has abandoned his people (11.1). For one thing, there have been Jews like Paul himself who have responded to the gospel. A tiny remnant they may be, but it is an indication that God has not cast off his people (11.2ff.). Paul's solution to Israel's disobedience is to assert that this disobedience was in fact a necessary part of the divine plan for the gospel, to go to the Gentiles (11.11). The clue to the fate of Israel lies with the hidden purposes of God himself. Just as God offered participation in the people of God through grace alone dependent on faith (11.20), so also this grace and mercy of God will be shown towards his people. Their rejection of the gospel does not mean an irrevocable judgement (11.23ff.); the assessment of 1 Thessalonians 2.16 is shown, therefore, not to be Paul's last word on the subject.

In concluding his discussion in Romans 11.25ff., Paul is not prepared to leave the matter with the hope that somehow the Jews will respond to the gospel. Perhaps Paul did indeed entertain the fond hope that his own ministry to the Gentiles would provoke the Jews to jealousy and repentance, which would usher in the eschaton (11.15).[8] What does seem to emerge from 11.25ff. is the deeply rooted conviction on Paul's part that despite all their rebellion against God, he would not cast off his people (11.28f.). Like the rabbis who coined the doctrine 'All Israel will have a share in the age to come' (in *Mishnah Sanhedrin* 10.1), Paul is unwilling to confine ultimate salvation only to those who belong to the Church. He argues that the hardening of heart, which came upon Israel, was a means whereby the gospel could go to the Gentiles. This hardening would continue until the full number of the Gentiles was gathered in (11.25).[9] It is by this means that Israel will be saved. That is, Paul reveals the mystery that the salvation of Israel will involve the reversal of the usually accepted process: first the Jews, then the Gentiles. In his exposition, the rejection of the gospel by the Jews leads to the Gentile mission, but the achievement of the full quota of Gentile converts will be the means by which the salvation of Israel will come about.

The quotations from Isaiah shed some light on how Paul thought that the salvation would take place. The coming of the deliverer from Zion, which must be a reference to Christ (cf. 1 Thess. 1.10), will effect the removal of Israel's transgressions. In this way will God honour his covenant with his people. Despite the fact that they are, in the present, the enemies of God for the sake of the Gentiles (v.28), the promises made by God to the patriarchs will not be revoked, and at the end God will redeem his people. So by reversing the order of salvation and asserting that the salvation of the Jews must wait for the coming of the redeemer, Paul demonstrates his belief that God has not cast off his people, but that ultimately they will share in the life of the age to come. This is an example of the depth of the riches of God (11.33). For Paul, what lies beyond his mission to the Gentiles is the reconciliation between God and his people when 'all Israel will be saved' (Rom. 11.26). Paul might have some part to play in that (Rom. 11.14), but the certainty of the promise lies in the righteousness of God himself (11.28f.).

9

The Problem of Authority[1]

It could be said with some degree of conviction that the major issue posed by Paul's missionary endeavours was not so much his interpretation of the Jewish Scriptures and his conviction that the age to come had already dawned, but his right to assert this, with all its consequences for the understanding of the Law and the position of the Gentiles. In short, the issue of authority is central to Paul's career as it was in the mission of Jesus. It is a theme to which Paul returns in all his major letters, and even when he is not dealing with it explicitly, as, for example, in Romans, it is clear that it is an issue which is very near the surface.

It is in the letter which is taken to be the earliest of Paul's letters in this study, Galatians, that we have the first evidence of the problem posed by Paul's claim to authority.[2] It should be recalled, in all discussions of the letter to the Galatians, that the issues, with which Paul chooses to start, are not the questions about circumcision and the Law, which only surface at the end of chapter 2, but his claim to be an apostle, along with the account of his visits to Jerusalem.[3] Thus the primary concern of the letter is apostolic authority; it is this which is the foundation of all the teaching, which he justifies elsewhere in the letter. Without demonstrating the validity of his credentials his proof from Scripture in Galatians 3–4 that his interpretation of the gospel was in fact in accord with the plan of God might have been of no avail.

It is when we recall how important the issue of authority was in Judaism that we can understand the fundamental issue at stake in Galatians. We have noted that one of the central pillars of Jewish teaching is the appeal to antiquity and tradition. The priests, who minister in the Temple, have to be able to show by their genealogies (note the importance of genealogies in the Bible) that they are of Aaronic descent.[4] Also the pharisiac-rabbinic tradition rested on the importance of precedent and the authority vouch-safed to current interpreters by virtue of their knowledge of the tradition.[5] Claims to speak and act on the basis of inner conviction were inevitably viewed with suspicion, because they cut across the channels of authority which had evolved over the centuries to guarantee a degree of continuity and stability within the religion. That is not to say that there was no room for what one might term 'charismatic figures',[6] but their role always had to be subordinate to tradition and could never be allowed to usurp the dominant position given to it.

A famous example of the attitude towards claims to authority based on supernatural events and experiences is to be found in a story about the late first-century AD rabbi, Eliezer ben Hyrcanus:

> It has been taught: On that day R. Eliezer brought forward every imaginable argument, but they did not accept them. Said he to them: 'If the halachah [i.e., the correct interpretation of the Jewish law] agrees with me, let this carob-tree prove it'. Thereupon the carob-tree was torn a hundred cubits out of its place ... No proof can be brought from a carob-tree, they retorted. Again he said to them: 'If the halachah agrees with me, let the streams of water prove it'. Whereupon the streams of water flowed backward. 'No proof can be brought from a stream of water,' they rejoined. Again he urged: 'If the halachah agrees with me, let the walls of the school-house prove it', whereupon the walls inclined to fall. But R. Joshua rebuked them saying: 'When scholars are engaged in a halachic dispute, what have ye to interfere?' Hence they did not fall, in honour of R. Joshua, nor did they resume upright, in honour of R. Eliezer; and they are still standing thus inclined. Again he said to them: 'If the halachah agrees with me, let it be proved from heaven'. Whereupon a heavenly voice cried out: 'Why do ye dispute with R. Eliezer, seeing that in all matters the halachah agrees with him?' ... But R. Joshua arose and exclaimed 'it is not in heaven'. What did he mean by this? – Said R. Jeremiah: That the Torah had already been given at Mount Sinai; we pay no attention to a Heavenly Voice, because Thou hast long since written in the Torah at Mount Sinai, After the majority must one incline, (*Babylonian Talmud Baba Metzia* 59a).[7]

It is clear from this story (probably much embellished)[8] that, even in those cases where a particular teacher could claim all kinds of miraculous vindications for the teaching which he adopted (cf. Deut. 13.1), that position must be viewed with considerable scepticism and indeed be rejected, if it did not comply with the opinion of the majority of the rabbis. There are two related issues arising here. First of all, the demands on emerging rabbinic Judaism made it essential to eliminate excessive variation in the positions adopted, to minimize the risk of disruption through false teaching. Secondly, because of the unpredictability and unverifiability of the authenticity of claims to divine revelation, they were to be treated with caution unless they happened to coincide with the views of the majority.

The relevance of this story for Paul's accounts of his conversion and visits to Jerusalem in Galatians 1–2 is clear. Like Eliezer, Paul claims that he has heaven on his side (1.1, 12, 16),[9] and therefore, his words should be heeded and his interpretation given as much, if not more, credence as that of others. The issue here is one which is at the heart of Paul's relationship both with non-messianic Judaism and also those who were Christians before him: who should have the right to interpret the Scriptures and to make claims about a crucified criminal, which would have consequences for the whole of the people of God? Paul considers that the apocalyptic vision, which he mentions in Galatians 1.12 and 1.16, is basis enough for his right to speak and act in the way that he does. Drawing on the language of call-visions in the Old Testament (Isa. 49.1; Jer. 1.5) Paul maintains that, like the prophets before him, God had called him to a specific task: to preach Christ among the Gentiles (1.16). It is an extraordinary claim, involving as it does the denial of the continued validity of the Law of Moses as the means of salvation and, what is more, asserting that the Messiah and the age to come had arrived.

The position is somewhat more complicated than the one in the story of Eliezer and Joshua. Galatians 1–2 indicates that it is not merely a question of Paul's right to be an apostle which is at stake nor the validity of his own experience. Rather, what Galatians 1–2 shows is that, in addition, Paul's own claim to *independent* apostolic authority is being questioned. Hence Paul finds that it is necessary to describe his journeys to Jerusalem, where he met the 'pillar apostles' (Gal. 2.9).

Paul's reason for mentioning the visits to Jerusalem,[10] in addition to his conversion experience, was that these had become a point at issue within the Galatian churches. The problem posed by Paul's visits to Jerusalem was twofold. First, they put in question Paul's claim to be an independent apostle called by God, as they seemed to indicate that the journeys to Jerusalem were part of the briefing necessary for an apostle whose commission was from men (cf. 1.1). Why should Paul need to go up to Jerusalem if he had an independent apostolic office? If he was on the same level as the other apostles, there would have been no need to go there and talk with those who were apostles originally, unless, that is, Paul felt that he needed their support or was in fact their emissary.

Secondly, if, as is supposed in this study, Galatians preceded the apostolic council described in Acts 15, it might have been asked why it was that Paul did not conform to the practice of the Jerusalem church, which accepted circumcision as an indispensable sign of membership of the covenant people?

Clearly, the visits to Jerusalem are an embarrassment for Paul. He does his best to explain away their significance, but it is difficult to resist the conclusion that, probably during the first visit and certainly during the second visit, Paul by his own admission offered his gospel for scrutiny to the Jerusalem apostles and also possibly obtained important information from them.[11] Indeed, in 2.2 he states that he laid before them the gospel which he preached among the Gentiles. Inevitably, the question would have been asked why such an important apostle, as Paul claimed to be, should have felt the need to go up to Jerusalem to have his credentials and his message examined by those who, in his view, were in no way superior to him. Paul's reasons for doing this are not explicitly stated, though he does say, with regard to the second visit, that he went up as the result of a revelation; it was no summons by the authorities but a spontaneous act on his part prompted by the call of God.[12]

Paul's embarrassment would have been complete if the reference in Galatians 2 to the incident with Titus in Jerusalem is to be taken to mean that Paul *did* in fact have Titus circumcised. Much depends on how one interprets 2.5 (some versions of this verse omit the negative, thus indicating that Paul *did* submit in this instance).[13] There have been those who have supported the view that, in this rather tortured syntax of Galatians 2.3ff., we should see the signs of Paul's acute embarrassment at having the circumcision of Titus thrown in his face by the Judaizers in Galatia.[14] As we shall argue in the section on Paul's principle of accommodation, such an act would not have been out of character for Paul. We know that he had Timothy circumcised (Acts 16.3), and his principle of being all things to all men (1 Cor. 9.22) would have necessitated him making compromises, which might have been misunderstood by those who did not grasp the intricacy of Paul's logic.

But this issue should not distract us from our main theme. It can be seen from what has been said that fundamental to Paul's argument about the Law is his right to speak with authority. It is an authority which differs markedly from some other types within Judaism, though it has its parallels in the claims made in the Jewish apocalypses and by the Teacher of Righteousness in 1 QpHab 7 and 1 QH.[15]

In the Corinthian correspondence the issue of apostolic authority is never far from the surface. The opening chapters of 1 Corinthians indicate that

Paul's missionary technique has been held up for comparison with other Christian ministers, and the justification of Paul's approach is one that is found here and in 2 Corinthians. In his digression in the discussion concerning food sacrificed to idols, Paul points out the need to limit the use of one's freedom for the benefit of the majority, by speaking about the way in which he had deliberately refrained from making use of his rights as an apostle (9.1).[16] His deliberate refusal to make use of his rights was in itself a cause of problems for Paul in the Corinthian church. It is already clear from 1 Thessalonians 2.6 that Paul did not as a rule make demands on his churches. This involved him in ignoring a command of Jesus: 'the Lord commanded that those who proclaim the gospel should get their living by the gospel' (1 Cor. 9.14f.).[17] Yet, he goes on, 'I have made no use of any of these rights, nor am I writing to secure any such provision'. This decision by Paul is regarded with suspicion by the Corinthian church (2 Cor. 11.7), presumably because Paul chose to conflict with the command of the Lord for apostolic ministry, and his action seemed to be at odds with other apostles, whom the Corinthians had received into their church.

It is in 2 Corinthians that we have the most systematic treatment of the issue of apostolic authority in the Pauline corpus. The Corinthian church seems to have had a succession of apostolic emissaries other than Paul.[18] In 2 Corinthians 10–13 Paul is faced with other Christian apostles, probably of Jewish extraction, whose activity had caused the Corinthian church to make comparisons between Paul and them, which were unfavourable to Paul: Paul does not have the true marks of an apostle; 'his letters are weighty and strong, but his bodily presence is weak (10.10)'; he lacks skill in speaking (11.6); he has no letters of recommendation (3.1).

We are not in a position to say with any degree of certainty who these apostles were.[19] Whether they were engaged in subverting Paul's authority deliberately, or merely had presented such a different characterization of the apostolic ministry that the Corinthians themselves had made an unfavourable assessment of Paul as a result, is not clear; one suspects that the latter is more likely. In any case Paul in his defence expounds his understanding of the apostolic office, partly by trading in the same coinage as the other apostles and speaking of the marks of his apostleship (e.g., 12.2f., 11f.), but in the main by manifesting a completely different view of the role of an apostle from that which the Corinthians had come to expect.[20]

In the letters written towards the end of Paul's career, the issue of authority looms less large. In Romans we find that there is still the fear that the gospel which Paul preached would not find acceptance, and this is linked with the real fear in Romans 15.31 that the collection for the saints in Jerusalem would not be accepted. Paul was right to suspect that possibly the Christians in Jerusalem and almost certainly many non-Christian Jews there (cf. Acts 21.21ff.) would have been very hostile to Paul's activities.

231

In Philippians there is a much more relaxed attitude towards other Christian missionaries and their activities, though an outburst characteristic of the polemical tone of 2 Corinthians and Galatians is to be found at the beginning of chapter 3.[21] The issue in this section is judaizing, similar to the problem in Galatia, but despite Paul's list of qualifications, the problem here is not one of apostolic authority. Paul recounts his Jewish ancestry and training to show his readers that impressive qualifications 'of the flesh' are of no avail. What really counts is to gain Christ (3.9). When Paul speaks of his rivals in 1.15, he does so with a generous spirit which is unparalleled elsewhere. This may be because the rivals are not themselves a threat to his congregation at Philippi, which is making good progress in the faith (1.5).

In the later (non-Pauline?)[22] Pastoral Epistles the issue of authority emerges again, though this time in the context of the discussion of the authentic tradition after Paul. In the light of threats from false teaching of various kinds (1 Tim. 1.4; 4.7; 2 Tim. 2.16; 4.4; Titus 1.14) there is need to encourage sound teaching (1 Tim. 4.6, 14; 6.20; 2 Tim. 1.14; 3.14ff.; 4.1ff.; Titus 2.1f.) and to appoint sober men as overseers, elders and deacons in the communities (1 Tim. 3; 5.17ff.; Titus 1.5f.). The important thing is to concentrate on the teaching which has been received (1 Tim. 6.20). Inspiration by the Spirit which leads to false teaching is to be repudiated (1 Tim. 4.1; cf. 1 John 4.2). It is through the laying on of hands that the Spirit is passed on which gives the right to teach and preach and guarantees the authenticity of what is said (2 Tim. 1.6; cf. 1 Tim. 4.14). Here we have the first signs of that commissioning which was a feature of rabbinic authority: ordination.[23] That is the means whereby the community guarantees the safe transmission of its doctrines by committing it only to those who have been approved by those who were teachers before them.

10

Paul's Method as an Apostle

Paul has often been portrayed as a missionary with an unambiguous message of justification by faith in Christ alone who presented an uncompromising and clear-cut stance to those he dealt with. A glance at the uncertainties which manifest themselves in some of his more polemical letters like Galatians and 2 Corinthians indicates that the reality was probably far different. Indeed, in 2 Corinthians Paul is charged with inconsistency (1.15ff.). There are indications in his letters that some at least of the problems which he spends time unravelling may in part be of his own making. We are used to thinking of converts receiving a pristine gospel which is then corrupted either by influence from the pagan environment (I Cor.)[1] or the influence of outsiders (Gal. and 2 Cor.), so that Paul has to recall them to their original faith (2 Cor. 11.1ff.; Gal. 1.7). While one does not want to minimize such influences, the contribution of Paul's own impact in his initial proclamation and his subsequent dealings with the Church should not be lost sight of as factors in creating the problems which emerge.

One reason for thinking that this might have been the case is the remarkable passage at the end of I Corinthians 9, where Paul enunciates his principle of accommodation: 'I have become all things to all men' (9.22).[2] Even allowing for a degree of hyperbole in what he says in these verses about his varying stances, it is not too difficult to see how such an approach would have presented problems to those who expected a degree of consistency. If Paul behaved as a Jew when in the company of Jews and had no inhibitions about behaving as a Gentile (within certain limits, of course) when with Gentiles, the resulting impression given of his activities would have been highly confusing to onlookers. For Paul the logic of this position is clear enough: 'I do it all for the sake of the gospel' (9.23).

The principle of accommodation manifests itself in two forms: first, the type of activity which is described in I Corinthians 9.19ff. and secondly, a willingness to compromise on statements and teachings already given or received if circumstances justified it.

If the book of Acts is to be believed, Paul's missionary practice involved him in starting his mission to the Gentiles at the Jewish synagogue.[3] This would inevitably have involved him fulfilling certain requirements of Jewish dietary practice as well as sabbath and liturgical observance. Those who accepted his message, both Jews and Gentiles, would then be faced with the need to relax certain of the obligations of the Law to conform to the image of the Church as one body in Christ. Table-fellowship (Gal. 2.11) would have involved Jews and Gentiles in eating together and undermining dietary rules. Paul did not insist on all converts giving up their practice of the Law. For him it was of secondary importance to the fact of unity between Jew and Gentile in Christ (Gal. 3.28); all else was subordinate to this. The practice of the Jewish law, perhaps including circumcision, was neither here nor there.[4] The pattern of behaviour of the believer should be dictated by the law of love and the needs of the weaker brethren (Rom. 14.1ff.; I Cor. 8.1ff.). Observances of festivals, special diets and sabbaths are only to be condemned if they become part of a pattern of religion which, however subtly, undermines the unique role of Christ as the agent of salvation (Gal. 4.8ff.; Col. 2.16ff.).

On at least one occasion Paul circumcised a Gentile. According to Acts 16.3 he circumcised Timothy, not because he thought that it was necessary for salvation but to avoid any offence because of the confused status of

Timothy as far as the Law was concerned (Timothy is said to be the son of a Jewish woman who was a believer, and of a pagan father). It is possible also that he had Titus circumcised in Jerusalem.[5] If so, this would explain why it was that Paul came under so much pressure in the Galatian churches to conform to practices which he had carried out elsewhere. The issue in both cases was clear for Paul. Neither Timothy nor Titus had to be circumcised as Christians. They were circumcised for the sake of expediency (cf. 1 Cor. 10.23). They had become as those under the Law, not in order to be saved but to win those under the Law.

In his dealings with the churches we may suspect that Paul demonstrated a similar kind of accommodation. In his study of Paul's relations with the Corinthian church, Hurd has pointed out that it is possible that what we have in 1 Corinthians is an example of Paul to some extent retreating from positions which he had once held in the light of problems which had emerged.[6] Some at least of the slogans which are quoted in e.g., 7.1; 8.1, 4 may well be quotations by the Corinthians in their letter of Paul's own views. While we are in the dark concerning the initial preaching of Paul in Corinth and the characterization of the Christian life which he offered, there is much to be said for the view that in 1 Corinthians Paul is dampening an initial enthusiasm created by his own proclamation of the eschatological gospel rather than reacting to the importation of alien views into the community.[7] Of course, we may expect that the eschatological enthusiasm of Paul's message of the resurrection and the gift of the Spirit would have been understood rather differently in the Jewish synagogues of the Diaspora as compared with those in Palestine, and even more differently by those Gentiles whose contact with Judaism was either superficial or negligible.

The genius of Paul, which emerges in the letters, is that he refuses to be tied down to particular patterns of behaviour and practice. The glimpse which we have of his relationships with the Corinthian church shows us a man on the move in his ideas, who allows the changing circumstances to influence his advice, so much so that he can appear to be guilty of the occasional *volte face*. Whatever Paul's relationship with the Jerusalem Council may have been,[8] in 1 Corinthians 8 we see Paul taking a position which would have contravened the agreement of the Council; as a result of this, he would have been bound to come under criticism for breaking that agreement.[9] The same problem emerges in the way in which he quotes, only to ignore, a command of Jesus about provisions for Christian missionaries. Unlike other Christian apostles who exercised their right to take their wives with them and to live off the churches where they stayed (1 Cor. 9.5f., 14f.), Paul makes it a principle of his ministry to work for his living and thus place no financial burden upon his churches.[10] He tells us little about the reasons for this course of action, save that it is an obligation to preach the gospel which characterizes his work, rather than a profession which deserves a reward (1 Cor. 9.16f.).

Paul showed himself to be faithful in passing on the traditions that he received,[11] but inspired by his pharisaic background, the centrality of the demands of the situation for the practice guided by the Spirit dominated his thought. Even a command from the Lord himself had to be subordinated to the appropriate action in the present as the apostle understood it. To those with less flexible attitudes towards tradition, such a cavalier approach would have been offensive, and would at least have provided grounds for misunderstanding Paul's motives.

Thus it has to be said that an important thread running throughout Paul's ministry is the conviction that the demands of the present under the guidance of the Spirit must guide action and conduct, even if that meant that there was a string of apparently inconsistent positions and statements in his writings and preaching. To be all things to all men for the sake of the gospel was a dominant theme of Paul's missionary method. From his point of view the position was an entirely consistent one. Matters of Jewish law and their observance were now secondary to the new life in Christ. That was the guiding principle for ethics.[12] Those who were in Christ know no barrier between them; they have all participated in the same Spirit and anything which keeps them apart must be repudiated (1 Cor. 12.13). There were, of course, certain limits to the freedom which was allowed. Paul did not contemplate any concession to idolatry, as he makes plain in 1 Corinthians 10. It may well be all right to eat meat which has been used in the worship of a pagan temple, but when it comes to participating in the worship of pagan shrines, Paul emphatically rejects that. But once these limits are granted, being under the law of Christ clearly in theory gave the individual a freedom of manoeuvre and the opportunity for stances which could betray a degree of inconsistency to observers. We may suspect that in practice a less liberal approach became the norm as the consequences of enthusiastic excess began to compel a greater degree of conformity.

Section 4

From Messianic Sect to Christian Religion

We have examined the literature in the New Testament connected with two of the major figures in the New Testament's presentation of the origins of Christianity, Jesus and Paul. We have noted that throughout the careers of both there was conflict between themselves and those who disagreed with them. While we cannot suppose that any New Testament writer believed that he was in the process of forming a religious system which was separate from Judaism, in their practice both Jesus and Paul paved the way for such a separation, when the circumstances were ripe. The Christian sect was not completely indistinguishable from other Jewish groups. Its convictions about Jesus, the imminence of the Kingdom and certain distinctive practices marked it off from other Jewish sects and other Jews. Let it be reiterated here that the individual beliefs (doctrine of the Messiah and the new age) and practices (baptism, fellowship meal) were not in themselves unique; there is much evidence to suggest that they were believed and practised by other groups. While there may be a case for saying that *particular combinations* of beliefs and practices which we find in Christianity had few parallels in other Jewish sects, that only allows us to conclude that from the very start the Christian movement had a self-conscious identity with a separate existence and focus within Jewish life. To say this is to say no more than would be true of any other Jewish sect at the time.

In this section three themes will be explored. First of all, the practices of the Church and its beliefs which identified it as a separate group or sect within Judaism. Secondly, the way in which the early Christians learnt to live with their eschatological beginnings, and finally the factors which led to a rupture between church and synagogue. Understanding the way in which the Jewish messianic movement ended up as the Christian Church separate from Judaism demands investigation of both of these factors. Otherwise we shall not be in a position to understand why it was that Christianity had the resources to persist as a religious movement when so much of its ideology seemed to be contrary to the values of established society.

236

1

Early Christian Initiation and Worship

We have noted that already, before the beginning of the Christian era, significant changes had taken place in the pattern of Jewish religious life. While the Temple remained the focal point of the worship of God for all Jews, the emergence of the synagogue and with it, the study of the Torah and the education of the pious, meant that in practice the dominant part of religious observance for most Jews, particularly those in the Diaspora, was the regular meeting to study the Torah on the Sabbath. While this development did not make the cessation of Temple worship any easier to accept after the end of the Roman siege of Jerusalem in AD 70, the fact that there already existed, alongside the worship of the Temple in Jerusalem, a framework of religious observance which could readily fill the vacuum left by the Temple, made its removal from Jewish piety the more easy to deal with; but still Jews longed to see the Temple rebuilt and sacrifice restored (e.g., Shemoneh Esreh; 4 Ezra 9–10; 1 Enoch 90.28ff.; Syr. Bar. 32.2).

A group like the Qumran community, whose priestly origin and cultic inspiration we cannot doubt, found it necessary, because of distaste for the conduct of worship in the Jerusalem Temple, to spiritualize cultic language. In the desert, their common life was itself interpreted in cultic terms.[1]

> It shall be an Everlasting Plantation, a House of Holiness for Israel, an Assembly of Supreme Holiness for Aaron . . . It shall be a Most Holy Dwelling for Aaron, with everlasting knowledge of the covenant of justice, and shall offer up sweet fragrance. It shall be a house of Perfection and Truth in Israel that they may establish a covenant according to the everlasting precepts. And they shall be an agreeable offering atoning for the land . . .[2]

> They shall atone for guilty rebellion and for the sins of unfaithfulness that they may obtain loving kindness for the land without the flesh of holocausts and the fat of sacrifice. And prayer rightly offered shall be as an acceptable fragrance of righteousness, and perfection of way as a delectable free will offering . . .[3]

The situation of the Qumran community finds many parallels in the writings of early Christianity.[4] Here too we find that cultic terminology is transferred to the community: the church is the Temple (1 Cor. 3.16; 6.19) and its members offer spiritual sacrifices to God (Rom. 12.1). The members of the Body of Christ are themselves holy and are a royal priesthood ministering before God (1 Pet. 2.9f.; cf. Rev. 1.6). In its worship, however, it

237

is not apparent that such cultic language was applied to its activities. Its holy meal was not a sacrifice (1 Cor. 10.16; 11.23f.), nor were its ministers priests in the Old Testament sense of those who offered sacrifice (but cf. Rom. 15.16). The Temple and its sacrifices and the ministers who attended to them continued to be in the background of the early Christian movement's understanding (Acts 2.46), but its distinctiveness is to be found elsewhere.

But what then was the pattern of early Christian worship? The New Testament itself gives us very little information about the kind of activity which went on. From the evidence before us two distinct activities are apparent, both of which probably have their origin within Jewish practice.

(a) Baptism[5]

According to the account of Peter's speech in Acts 2 the basis of admission to the life of the new age was acceptance of the message concerning the salvation God had wrought through Christ, repentance, baptism and the receiving of the Holy Spirit. This in turn led to a welcome into a community which practised fellowship and the common meal (Acts 2.38f.; 42; cf. Acts 10.44). There seems to be no reason to dispute the claim of Acts that acceptance into the earliest Christian community was an immediate event and did not depend upon a long probationary period as we find for example practised at Qumran (1 QS and Josephus, BJ 2.137). In this respect early Christian practice differed from the later church,[6] where an extended catechumenate formed an essential part of Christian discipleship,[7] baptism itself being delayed until much later in life (e.g., Hippolytus Apost. Trad. 17).

The origin of the Christian rite of initiation can only be ascertained in the most general terms. Several possible sources have been suggested, the frequent lustrations, practised by various Jewish sects, and proselyte baptism being the favourite Jewish sources. Of these, there is no doubt that the latter, with its emphasis on the passage from the old life to the new, from a life outside the people of God to one inside, provides the most convincing parallel. Doubts have been raised about the date of the introduction of baptism as well as circumcision for proselytes, but it may have been common enough within the first century.[8]

But why did the Christians take up the rite of baptism as the sign of initiation into their sect? While certainty is out of the question, it would appear likely that the origin of Jesus' own mission with the baptizing prophet John provides as convincing an origin as we are likely to find,[9] particularly when we remember that according to the Fourth Gospel, Jesus and his disciples continued to practise baptism, even after they had separated themselves from John (3.22; 4.1f.). The fact that, according to the Gospels, John's baptism was linked with the appearance of an eschatological judge

(Mark 1.7f.; cf. Matt. 3.1ff.; Luke 3.1ff.; John 1.15; 19ff.; cf. Josephus *Ant.* 18.116ff.) makes a link between Christian baptism and John's baptism likely. The eschatological character of Christian baptism is maintained in many of our sources (1 Cor. 12.13; Acts 2.38), though there are passages in Acts where the Spirit does not come until the laying on of hands by the apostles (e.g., 8.17; 19.2ff.). It is the mark of the transfer into the new age (Titus 3.5 – new birth is an eschatological concept; see also John 3.5; Matt. 19.28; 1 Pet. 1.3). Like Christ, who at his death laid aside the body of flesh and took a new body of glory, the believer at baptism puts off the body of flesh with all its influence (Rom. 6). He is buried with Christ in baptism and raised to a new life in the Spirit (cf. Col. 2.11f.). In Colossians Paul can describe baptism as the Christian circumcision (Col. 2.11). In terms of Paul's thought, baptism marks the identification of the believer with the decisive historical events which inaugurated the new age. Baptism gave the believer access to the world above (Col. 3.1; cf. Eph. 1.3) and enabled the believer to sit with Christ in the heavenly places (Eph. 2.6; cf. Rev. 3.21). No longer did the hostile powers have any control over the believer;[10] Christ was the creator of the heavenly powers (Col. 1.16) and their conqueror (Col. 2.14f.; cf. 1 Pet. 3.22; Eph. 1.22).[11] The language about Christian baptism, about release, while having its origin in the Jewish world, readily adapted itself to new circumstances, where the contrast was not between this age and the age to come but between a world dominated by hostile powers and a world where these forces had been overcome; it was entry into this world of light that Christian baptism promised.

(b) The Eucharist[12]

The Acts of the Apostles speaks in general terms about Christian fellowship, in which there was devotion to the apostles' teaching and breaking of bread (2.42; cf. 20.7; 27.35). It is not obvious that what is being referred to is what we would call the Holy Communion or Eucharist; it is probably a typical Jewish fellowship meal celebrated by those who believed that the Messiah had come.[13] Of course, such a meal, like all meals in Judaism, would not have been devoid of religious significance (1 Cor. 10.31; Luke 24.30). In his description of the worship at Troas (20.7) the author of Acts indicates that the meeting took place on the first day of the week (cf. Rev. 1.10: 'on the Lord's Day', the day of the resurrection).[14] Whether Christians continued to worship in synagogues on the sabbath as well as having their own liturgy on the first day of the week, the anniversary of the resurrection (cf. Justin, *Apology* 1.67), is not clear (note John 20.19, 26).

   The contribution of the synagogue to early Christian worship would have been very great.[15] Its emphasis (and deliberately so) on non-cultic activity, to avoid any suggestion of conflict with the Temple as the only shrine prescribed by the Torah (Deut. 12.4f.) meant that its emphasis was on the reading (and if necessary, translation) of Scripture and expositions of it (Acts 13).[16] If the Corinthian church is anything to go by, the characteristic convictions of early Christianity concerning the coming New Age probably affected the pattern of worship. Paul reports that at the meeting for worship, in addition to any reading from the Scriptures (i.e., the Old Testament), individual members of the community came along with their own contributions: prophecies, revelations, and hymns (1 Cor. 14.26). Later on in the middle of the second century AD, when the Gospels had been written, readings from these texts formed part of the worship:

> And on the day which is called the day of the sun there is an assembly of all those who live in the towns or in the country; and the memoirs of the Apostles [probably a reference to one or more of our Gospels] or the writings of the prophets are read, as long as time permits. Then the reader ceases, and the president speaks, admonishing us and exhorting us to imitate these excellent examples (Justin, *Apology* 1.67).

In addition to the Gospels, Paul expected his letters to be read aloud to the churches when they assembled (Col. 4.16). By the time of Justin, the reading and exposition of the Scriptures were united with the eucharistic meal, as the following passage makes plain:

> Then we arise all together and offer prayers; and, as we said before, when we have concluded our prayer, bread is brought, and wine and water, and the president in like manner offers up prayers and thanksgivings with all his might; and the people assent with Amen; and there is the distribution and partaking by all of the eucharistic elements; and to them that are not present they are sent by the hand of the deacons. And they that are prosperous and wish to do so give what they will, each after his choice. What is collected is deposited with the president, who gives aid to the orphans and widows and such as are in want by reason of sickness or other cause; and to those also that are in prison, and to strangers from abroad, and in fact to all that are in need he is a protector.

The evidence from the New Testament does not allow us to conclude with any degree of certainty that the common meal, the Eucharist and the synagogue-type service necessarily coincided at this stage. The indication from Acts 20.7ff. is that they did, but the evidence from 1 Corinthians is less clear on the matter. In the section dealing with the common meal in 1 Corinthians (11.18ff.) Paul mentions the eucharistic words of Jesus (11.23ff.) and the need for all those who participate to share their food, but no mention is made here of the reading of Scripture. Likewise in the account of early Christian worship in 1 Corinthians 14 there is no mention made of the common meal, and the fact that outsiders are welcome at the service is probably an indication that the worship described was not confined to believers (14.22ff.) (cf. Didache 9: 'let none eat or drink of Eucharist, save

such as are baptized'; Apostolic Tradition 26.5).[17] What is clear from
I Corinthians II, however, is that the eucharistic meal is a proper meal,
unlike the meal described by Justin; otherwise it would not be possible to
understand the significance of advice Paul gives to the Corinthians about the
sharing of food (II.21ff.).

The origin of the meal described in I Corinthians II and elsewhere in the
New Testament is to be found in the central importance which meals had
with Judaism. In addition to the Passover meal, when the central facts of
Israel's redemption were recalled during a special meal (and which was the
context of Jesus' own words at the Last Supper),[18] there was the weekly meal
at the beginning of the sabbath.[19] This regular pattern of meals seems to be
what is presupposed in I Corinthians II (cf. Luke 24.30f.). Despite the
language which Paul chooses to use about it (I Cor. 10.16), we are probably
still some way from the cult meal which characterized the celebration of the
Eucharist in the day of Justin.[20] Whether or not this was a regular or even
weekly event is by no means clear. As is well known, the various texts of the
eucharistic words of Jesus (I Cor. II.23ff.; Matt. 26.26ff.; Mark 14.22ff.;
Luke 22.19–22) disagree over the inclusion of the words 'Do this in
remembrance of me'.[21] From I Corinthians one gets the impression that the
regular meeting for the common meal probably included a recollection of
the words of Jesus at some point during the meal, just as year by year the
domestic Passover meal included recollection of the events of redemption
from Egypt.[22]

The eschatological dimension is apparent in the interpretation of the
eucharistic meal (II.26).[23] In the Passover, the past redemption by God was
regarded as a type of the future deliverance of the people of God out of their
present bondage.[24] Consequently, Passover was always a time of heightened
eschatological expectation in Judaism (a fact which needs to be borne in
mind in considering the passion of Jesus, e.g., Luke 22.35ff.). The use of
Exodus typology in referring to the death of Jesus (his death is ransom, Mark
10.45; cf. Rom. 3.25)[25] is an indication of the way in which the death of Jesus
and the deliverance at the Passover were linked by the early Christians. The
eschatological flavour of the common meal is most apparent in the early
church order known as the Didache or the Teaching of the Twelve
Apostles.[26] In the eucharistic prayer contained in this manifestly Jewish-
Christian work the future hope permeates the prayer:

> We give thanks, Holy Father, for thy holy name, which thou hast made to
> tabernacle in our hearts, and for the knowledge, faith and immortality which thou
> hast made known to us through thy servant Jesus. To thee be glory for ever. Thou
> Lord Almighty didst create all things for thy name's sake, and gavest food and
> drink to men for their enjoyment, that they might give thee thanks; and to us thou
> didst grant spiritual food and drink and life eternal, through thy servant. Above all
> we thank thee that thou art mighty. To thee be glory for ever. Remember, Lord,

thy church, to deliver her from all evil and to make her perfect in thy love, and to gather from the four winds her that is sanctified into thy kingdom which thou didst prepare for her; for thine is the power and the glory for ever. Let grace come and let this world pass away. Hosanna to the God of David. If any is holy, let him come; if any is not holy, let him repent. Maranatha. Amen (Didache 10).

The concluding sentences recall parts of the New Testament, particularly Paul's final words in 1 Corinthians 16.22f. (cf. Rev. 22.20), which include the phrase Maranatha ('Come, Lord').[27] The common meal provided a setting not only for recall of God's saving purposes in the past, but also a reminder of the consummation of his saving purposes, which the Church longed to see fulfilled and expressed the fervour of its hope by the Maranatha.[28] It was an occasion when the company at table hailed the longed-for Lord with glad Hosannas.[29]

At the end of the discourse on the Bread of Life in John 6.51ff. (a passage whose eucharistic overtones have long been recognized)[30] resurrection on the last day for the individual believer is linked very closely with eating the flesh and drinking the blood of the Son of Man (6.54). An eschatological dimension is thus preserved. Even in the writings of Ignatius, where the eucharistic meal is described as 'the medicine of immortality' (Ephes. 20) the eschatological element is preserved. Nevertheless, the main thrust of his interpretation is to make the meal a means whereby the individual can maintain and ultimately gain access to heaven. It has become the means of gaining access to another world and has ceased to be the foretaste of that kingdom of God on earth in the present.[31]

While eschatological emphasis still persisted,[32] in the course of time the Eucharist gradually took on the significance of cultic demonstration of communion with the Saviour. The infiltration of the cultic understanding into the worship of the eschatological community led to an increased influence of the Temple-model on the worship of the Christian communities.[33] With this emerging influence the question of presidency became important. Paul had assumed that the Spirit would inspire both men and women in the course of worship (1 Corinthians 11.5), and nothing is said about presidency at the Eucharist. If a Jewish pattern was followed we may expect that the head of the family would normally have presided. Normally this would have been the duty of a man, though we may expect that in some of the more enthusiastic communities and in those households where a woman was the head (e.g., 1 Cor. 1.11), this might have been a woman. One cannot exclude the possibility that it was a female prophet who exercised this role (after all, according to Didache 10 the prophets may give thanks (*eucharistein*) as much as they will). Women prophets formed part of the Montanist movement and there is evidence of them presiding at the Eucharist in Montanist circles (see Cyprian Epistle 75.110).[34] Elsewhere in the later New Testament writings nothing is said in the list of duties of the Christian minister about any function as president at the Eucharist; it is the teaching function which is most important. The situation is very different in the letters of Ignatius of Antioch, however, written while the Bishop of Antioch was travelling to Rome for execution. Writing to communities in situations where false teaching was a particular problem, Ignatius stresses the central role of the bishop in the eucharistic worship of the Church.[35]

> See that you all follow the bishop, as Jesus Christ follows the Father, and the presbytery as if it were the apostles. And reverence the deacons as the command of God. Let no one do anything appertaining to the church without the bishop. Let that be considered a valid eucharist which is celebrated by the bishop, or by one whom he appoints. Wherever the bishop appears let the congregation be present; just as wherever Jesus Christ is there is the Catholic Church. It is not lawful either to baptize or to hold *agape* without the bishop; but whatever he approve, this is also pleasing to God, that everything which you do may be secure and valid (Smyrnaeans 8).

We may suppose that in the light of the repeated emphasis throughout his letters on the centrality of the bishop within the order of the Church, this pattern was by no means universally accepted, and needed the authoritative persuasion of the Bishop of Antioch to guarantee its consideration. In situations where there was schism and false teaching (as is apparent from the letters), the emphasis upon one man as the focus of unity and right teaching was potent remedy against division.

A glance at the roughly contemporary Didache and 1 Clement shows that few churches were prepared to go as far along the road of monarchical episcopacy (one leader/bishop in charge of the Church) as Ignatius. Indeed, in the Didache, prominence is given to the role of the prophets, despite the problems which they were causing in some of the communities (e.g., 11.7ff.; cf. Rev. 2.20; Did. 13.6).[36] Nevertheless what we find here is indicative of a trend which was to gain momentum throughout the second century, particularly as the need to repudiate gnostic heresy increased by the appeal to tradition.

It is often argued that the Letter to the Hebrews marks the start of this process within the New Testament. Nevertheless the argument about the heavenly high priesthood of Christ and his sacrifice, which enabled him to enter the holiest place in heaven behind the veil (Heb. 6.19f.; cf. 9.24), concerns the death of Christ, and no attempt is make to link this with the eucharistic meal of the assembled Christians; nor is there any suggestion that the minister functions as the representative of the heavenly high priest on earth. For the writer to the Hebrews there is no earthly shrine which can compare with the heavenly, and it is to this through the ministry of Christ that believers have been allowed to draw near.

Such questions of order are issues which an eschatologically-oriented community does not appear to have concerned itself with. Participation in the antepast of heaven does not appear to have demanded particular qualifications of the one who presided at the meal. Yet control over those who were allowed in and exernal pressures paved the way for restrictions on presidency. As the Eucharist became more the medicine of immortality, it became more and more important to make sure that the one who dispensed the medicine was in fact suitably qualified to do so.

2

The Emergence of Beliefs about Jesus

(a) The Foundations of Christology[1]

In contrast with the debates of the succeeding centuries the evidence of intense christological debate is absent from the earliest Christian writings. That is not to suggest that the first Christians were uninterested in the person of Christ: the pages of the New Testament themselves affirm unequivocally that Jesus of Nazareth was the key to salvation. What is apparent is that with the exception of the Fourth Gospel, and one or two passages elsewhere in the epistles (e.g., Col. 1.15ff.; Phil. 2.6ff.; Heb. 1.1ff.), there is hardly any extended christological exposition in the New Testament. The reasons for this are not easy to explain. It may be that in the initial stages of the movement little need was felt to explain who Jesus was, either because false pictures of him had not emerged, or because there were other more important factors which governed the development of doctrinal interest. We may suppose that both of these alternatives had their contribution to make. The evidence from the Pauline letters indicates that problems concerning the person of Christ were not the main issues with which Paul was having to contend. It is only in the letter to the Colossians that we have any hint of any uncertainty about the unique status of the person of Christ, though there are hints that within the Johannine community there were problems similar to those which confront us in the false teaching combated by the Church in the centuries to come (e.g., 1 John 4.2).

We have located the main thrust of Jesus' message and work in his proclamation of the imminent reign of God. Thus while it would be true to say that the central place of Jesus in this proclamation is everywhere presupposed, what is dominant is the initiation of this reign of peace and righteousness. Concentration, therefore, is on the gift that is offered by God rather than expositions of the character of the one who gave it. Certainly Jesus is the key to the gift of salvation but all attention is focused on the opportunity of divine salvation that is offered. When uncertainty surrounds the identity of the agent of salvation, then what is offered by the agent is undermined also, and in this respect we may understand some of the essential features of the christological debates of the early Church.

Of course, Christology was no mere afterthought in the growth of Christian doctrine. We have already noted that in the teaching of Jesus himself there are already signs that a Christology of a profound kind is either implied or explicitly outlined.[2] Even if many commentators would not want to assert as much as has been said in this study about Jesus' messianic consciousness, few would deny that there is a link between the affirmations about Jesus found in the earliest Christian confessions and the implicit Christology of the proclamation of the kingdom of God. The proclamation of the kingdom of God by Jesus and his own view of his mission inevitably set the pattern for subsequent christological reflection. There is not space to go into all the vicissitudes of the development of christological titles. All that can be done here is to give some idea of the basis of christological development, and by examining one major christological exposition, the Gospel of John, see how the pattern of christological reflection was set for future centuries.

According to the Acts of the Apostles,[3] the earliest titles which were applied to Jesus were Lord and Christ (Acts 2.36). These two are by far the most common in the Pauline letters and their use indicates why the early Christians thought Jesus of Nazareth so important for their experience of salvation: he was the anointed one, the fulfiller of God's purposes.

We have suggested that already Jesus of Nazareth had identified himself with the Messiah, albeit without the characteristics associated with the Davidic Messiah, who would come at the head of the army of the sons of light and remove by force all defilement from the earth. What was true of Jesus, namely that the messianic issue was bound to be important, was even more true of the first Christians. Their teacher, who had been put to death, had, they believed, been vindicated by God. Jesus was regarded as the key to the coming of the messianic age (Acts 2.33; Rev. 5). Even if he did not correspond exactly to the pattern of some Jewish belief about the Messiah, Jesus of Nazareth was, as far as the Christians were concerned, the one who had been the means whereby God's eschatological promises were being fulfilled. He it was who by his life, death and resurrection was God's means of initiating the fulfilment of his promises: 'God was in *Christ* reconciling the world to himself' (2 Cor. 5.19).[4]

In contrast to the title Christ, Lord[5] (*Kyrios*) as it is used in the New Testament does not have its origins in Jesus' messianic consciousness. It is true that there are examples of Jesus being addressed as such, but in all likelihood it is used as a polite designation reserved for a teacher (e.g., Luke 9.54).[6] Elsewhere in the New Testament, probably in usage derived from

Psalm 110,[7] ('The Lord said to my Lord, Sit at my right hand until I make your enemies a stool for your feet') the title 'Lord' speaks of the divine dominion delegated to the exalted Christ by God (Acts 2.33ff.; 1 Cor. 15.24f.; cf. Matt. 28.18; Dan. 7.13). As Messiah Christ would have his part to play in the final demonstration of God's sovereignty (2 Thess. 2.8f.) and his lordship, delegated to him temporarily by God (1 Cor. 15.28), would finally be manifested over the powers opposed to God when in the end all would worship before him and confess that Jesus Christ is Lord (Phil. 2.11). It is a central feature of early Christian belief that the manifestation of divine sovereignty through God's agent, the Christ, has started but has to be completed. Meanwhile heaven must receive the Christ 'until the time for the establishing of all that God spoke by the mouth of his holy prophets from of old' (Acts 3.20f.). In the Pauline letters (but also note James 5.7) the title Lord or Kyrios is used in contexts dealing with the return of Jesus (e.g., 1 Thess. 4.15; 2 Thess. 2.8) who would come to complete the work started on the cross and Calvary.[8]

With these two titles we are at the heart of the New Testament conviction about the significance of the person of Jesus of Nazareth. In them are expressed the twin affirmations of early Christian belief of the eschatological character of the activity of Christ and the delegation of divine sovereignty and power, which takes place at his exaltation. Jesus is endowed with that power and character of the almighty God as the expression of God's purposes in his person and work and the one will reign, until such time as 'God would be all in all' (1 Cor. 15.28).

Only rarely do we find an example of a detailed exposition of Christology in the New Testament. One such example is to be found in the Gospel of John.[9] Some of the editorial comments interspersed in the text by the writer demonstrate the nature of the issues which are confronting the community. According to the Gospel, the Jews believe that Jesus is arrogating to himself divine power: 'he also called God his Father, making himself equal with God' (5.18). The claims which Jesus makes (e.g., 8.58; 10.30f.) are indications of the kind of belief which appeared to be such a threat to Jewish monotheism. As far as the Fourth Evangelist is concerned, it is now no longer sufficient to say that Jesus is the Messiah and Lord; indeed, opponents believe that the claims which Christians are making about Jesus are such that they threaten the traditional beliefs. The Evangelist sets out to expound in the prologue to his exposition of the life of Jesus the conviction that Jesus of Nazareth was none other than the eternal Word or Logos incarnate. It was no use, in Paul's words, to view Christ merely from a human point of view (cf. 2 Cor. 5.16), for in the Evangelist's estimation Jesus was the one who made known the unseen Father (1.18).

These twin themes dominate the Gospel: the compatibility of belief in Jesus of Nazareth as the unique emissary of the Father with Jewish monotheism; and that in the life of Jesus of Nazareth the character and nature of the invisible God were made known. It has been suggested in recent years that the background to such concerns was the growing tension between non-Christian Jews and Jewish Christians probably towards the end of the first century AD.[10] Thus the Gospel was written to show those who are already believers[11] (John 20.31f.) that their confession of Jesus as the Messiah, the Son of God, was in fact in full accord with the traditions of Judaism (cf. 5.39; 45) and did not involve an abdication of their central tenets. In presenting this case we have in the Fourth Gospel the most explicit and sophisticated Christology in the New Testament, whose importance may be gauged by the enormous influence it has had on subsequent debates about the person of Christ.[12] The essential contours of that christological presentation are set out in the first twelve chapters. Though the intimate discourses of Jesus with his disciples (13–16), the so-called 'High Priestly' prayer in chapter 17[13] and the passion narratives are replete with their own christological themes, they add little to the main weight of the argument in these chapters.

At the heart of the christological presentation of the Fourth Evangelist is the conviction that he who has seen Jesus has seen the Father (14.9); no one has ever seen God at any time (1.18). Even the claims of those who in the past said that they had seen God had to be questioned (5.37). Those seers and prophets, who had been fortunate to glimpse a theophany, had not seen God but the pre-existent Christ[14] (12.41). 'No one has seen God except him who is from God; he has seen the Father' (6.46). The basis of the christological claim made by the Evangelist is that, unlike all other emissaries sent from God, Jesus alone has seen the Father and as a result is the authentic revealer of God. That revelation was not a revelation of propositions about the nature of God, for the Revealer descended from heaven to reveal God in his own person;[15] 'the only Son, who is in the bosom of the Father, he has made him known' (1.18). Drawing on traditions which are now known to us from Jewish apocalyptic angelology, the Fourth Evangelist was able to stand firmly within the Jewish tradition and yet stress that another being with a will of his own who still subordinated that will to the will of him who sent him (cf. 7.16)[16] was able to be the complete embodiment of divine character (cf. Col. 2.9).[17]

Throughout the Gospel there is an emphasis on Jesus as the emissary of the Father. Exploration of the background of this theme in Jewish law has revealed how important the notion of agency is for an understanding of the Christology of our Gospel.[18] The agent is the plenipotentiary of the one who sent him. Those who receive the agent must treat him as if they were receiving the one who sent him. The repeated stress on sending and on the subordination of the will of the agent to the one who sends is a key to the understanding of how it is that Jesus the one sent can function as the perfect fulfilment of the divine purposes. What is stressed throughout the Gospel is the simple fact that Jesus sets out only to do the will of his Father. The unity of will between the Father and the Son, the sender and the agent, is brought out most forcefully in the statement of Jesus which leads to an attempted stoning: 'I and the Father are one' (10.30).

The structure of the Gospel enables us to see a coherent attempt to use the traditions, which the Evangelist had inherited, to expound the relationship of Jesus, the Word made flesh, to the rest of Jewish tradition. The position of the cleansing of the Temple at the beginning of Jesus' ministry makes it likely that the Evangelist regards the locus of divine revelation in the only-begotten son as *the* place where God's presence is located. It is the Son of Man to whom angels descend, not Bethel (1.51).[19] Similarly it is the Risen Christ who after the destruction of the Temple in Jerusalem is the place where the true worshippers will come to find God (cf. 4.23f.).

The one to whom Jewish custom and tradition bear witness has come is Jesus. For Samaritans[20] (ch.4), as well as orthodox Jews like Nicodemus, the revelation of God through Jesus is the way to a new relationship with God, entry into the kingdom of God (3.3). The Jewish festivals[21] (7–8), the experience of Israel in the past and the Torah itself (5.39) all point to the greater reality which is manifest in Jesus. All the ideas and traditions of Judaism could not of themselves be regarded as the ultimate revelation of salvation; God did not intend them as the final revelation of himself. They pointed beyond themselves to that definitive revelation, which now took place in the Son.[23] Any attempt to ignore that revelation and assume that what had been given in the past was of itself the definitive way to God (cf. 9.29) made those traditions serve a purpose for which they had never been intended and those who espoused such a use of them were children of the devil rather than children of God (8.41ff.).

For the Fourth Evangelist there could be no question of his group being guilty of formulating another religion. The issue in the Gospel is one of continuity. The assertion that in some way the christological claim was an offence against one of the prime beliefs of Judaism is to misunderstand the Evangelist's belief in Christ. It is not the case that there are two divine powers in heaven, two independent gods.[24] The application of the sending formula to the exposition of Jesus' relationship with the Father indicates that for the writer there could be no doubt that the relationship of such intimacy was based entirely on the subordination of the one sent to the sender. It was because the Son who came from heaven did not do his own will, but the will of him who sent him and sought not his own glory but the glory of the one who sent him (7.18), that the completeness of the disclosure of the divine nature could be effected. In this exposition, couched as it is in the ideas of contemporary Jewish angelology, we have an exposition of Christology

248

which affirms in the most basic form the essential character of that theology which was to become the distinctive mark of Christian thought. Even if the Spirit in the Fourth Gospel is not yet an area of theological discussion,[25] there is little doubt that the relationship of Jesus with the Father as set out in these pages exhibits all the characteristics of the later trinitarian formulations. To say this, however, is not to assert that the theological speculation went beyond what was available from the resources of the Jewish tradition. But the application of this terminology to Jesus of Nazareth meant a use of these traditions in which the impact of Jesus and his work necessarily played a significant role.

In Jesus the ultimate revelation of the divine character and purpose was being revealed. It has long been recognized that behind the Johannine phrase 'eternal life' there lies the Hebrew concept of the life of the age to come.[26] To enter the kingdom of God is to gain eternal life. Ultimately the uniqueness of the revealer is based on the unique offer of life which he brings. There can be no further offer, because what he brings is the life of the age to come. Even the eschatological Spirit breathed upon the disciples on the first Easter Sunday, bringing a new creative act (20.22), functions not as an agent of new revelation but to remind the disciples of the unique revelation of God in Christ (16.12ff.). To believe in Jesus as the Messiah (20.31) and to taste of the Spirit of God is to know eternal life, the life of the age to come, which new birth by water and spirit has brought about (3.3f.). Possibly the Johannine traditions are in danger of losing sight of that eschatological dimension, as we shall suggest, but the presentation of them in the Fourth Gospel has not completely lost that interest in ultimate salvation which has been offered by God's unique emissary. The Johannine interpretation of the person of Christ, dictated as it is by the church/ synagogue struggles of the early years of the Church's existence, is rooted in the belief that their interpretation of commonly held traditions in the Jewish community represented the definitive understanding of the purposes of God. To grasp this fact is to understand the foundation of christological reflection and the mushrooming superstructure of the Christology of the succeeding centuries.

(b) The Dissolution of the Eschatological Framework of Primitive Christology

It is an interesting fact that much of the energy of students of early Christianity has been devoted to the study of the development of ideas connected with the person of Christ. A glance at a handbook of early Christian doctrine will reveal what a central place the study of Christology has within presentations of early Christianity.[27] The same is also true of the earliest phase of Christian life and thought. If critical scholarship is any guide, the dominant concern of the first Christians was an attempt to answer the question: who was Jesus? Of course, some of the extant literature itself seems to project the early Christian movement as concerned with such beliefs. It is by no means obvious, however, that the bulk of the literary products of Christianity is oriented towards christological ideas. We must regard the literature as part of that attempt to justify and explain the religion to outsiders and to correct misunderstandings by those on the inside. In such endeavours it would be unnecessary to offer a total picture, and it would be a mistake to suppose that the literary remains offered us one.

Thus it is wrong to imagine that we can understand the early Christian movement simply by explaining its Christology. Writing on Christology is mistaken if it thinks that it has spoken comprehensively about early Christianity by concentrating on the emergence of particular christological beliefs.[28] But we cannot begin to understand the significance of Christology, at least in its earliest phase, without acknowledging the eschatological framework within which that christological belief was found. Such an assertion is nothing new; the Schweitzer school had attempted to trace the growth of Christian doctrine within the framework of a treatment of eschatology.[29] Schweitzer did this for Paul and Martin Werner did the same for the emerging Christian doctrine. Martin Werner's work has continued to have great influence,[30] particularly his theory about the Delay of the Parousia (the problem posed by the non-appearance of the kingdom of God).[31] In that regard the eschatological perspective has never totally disappeared from the scene, but whether its implications have been fully appreciated is another matter.

Certainly it would be a mistake to minimize the importance of christological deviations as a pressing reason for precision and theological clarity in christological ideas; there certainly were reasons for suspicion over the Arian christology, for example,[32] as an exposition of the thrust of New Testament christology, though preoccupation with such matters led to distasteful strife and an unhealthy preoccupation with this area of doctrine.[33]

One of the most interesting features of the development of Christology is the way in which the attention of ancient commentators moved from the use of eschatological categories to speak of Christ and his work to rather different ones, which did not bear that distinctive eschatological stamp. The point may well be illustrated by the development of the use of the title Messiah.[34] From the very earliest period of the Christian movement this title offered a way of expressing the first disciples' convictions about Jesus of Nazareth (Mark 8.29; Acts 2.36f.; John 9.22; 20.31; Acts 13.23). He was the one who was to come; there was no need to look for another (Matt. 11.2ff.). In much New Testament usage there is reflected that development known in other Jewish works, where the title 'Messiah' was being linked with an eschatological figure, who would have a part to play in the new age. The whole welter of beliefs and experiences, which characterized the primitive Christian experience, convinced Christians that Jesus of Nazareth was the anointed of God, the agent of the future reign of God. This conviction undergirds much early Christian belief. Even Paul, who often uses the word Christ virtually as a proper name, retains the eschatological dimension in his use (e.g., 2 Cor. 5.19).[35]

We know, however, that early Christians did not rest content with the title 'Messiah' to express their convictions about Jesus. There was a contribution from another theological stream in Judaism which was only loosely related to the eschatological categories like Messiah. When early Christians wanted to explore the relationship between God and Christ they used two streams, one of which has been explored in some detail in New Testament scholarship, the wisdom tradition of Judaism,[36] and the other, about which little has been written, the angelomorphic ideas developing in ancient Judaism.[37] In using these categories early Christians gave a very different twist to Christology.

The origin of the use of wisdom ideas in early Christianity is much debated, though it probably has its origin in some sayings of Jesus (e.g., Matt. 11.28ff.; Luke 11.49).[38] They are apparent in some of Paul's letters (1 Cor. 8.6; Col. 1.15ff.) and were taken up in the prologues to both the Letter to the Hebrews (Heb. 1.1ff.) and to the Fourth Gospel (John 1.1ff.).[39] While this framework certainly did enable early Christians to maintain their monotheistic faith, while speaking of the unity of being and purpose between Jesus and God, the use of the wisdom tradition inevitably had the effect of diminishing the centrality of eschatology. What we have in the Prologue of the Fourth Gospel, for example, is certainly a confession of the unique manifestation of the divine Logos ('the Word became flesh and dwelt among us' (John 1.14)), but also a continuation of a process, which had been at work long before (cf. 1.13). Hitherto people had only glimpsed God in a glass darkly, but in Jesus they had come face to face with him. With this Gospel the heart of the Christian gospel becomes focused on the one who has come from the Father and who brings with him divine light and life. To know the Father is to know Christ and to accept that he is in fact the Word made flesh. Belief in Christ becomes inextricably linked with the need to see God in him and through his actions. It is a unique and definitive disclosure and one that effects a critical division between the children of light and the children of darkness. The use of the wisdom terminology has two effects. First of all, it tends to encapsulate God in a particular person; and as a result makes christological confession the key to a relationship with God. Secondly, wisdom categories tend to play down the radical disjuncture which the messianic belief effects. In the Old Testament wisdom tradition, wisdom is always present in the world, always active and always there to be received by men. What the Fourth Gospel asserts is that in Jesus there is a unique disclosure of God's Word/wisdom, differing only in degree rather than kind, from other manifestations of the immanent wisdom of God. The focus of this Christology is revelation (albeit of a complete kind transcending all previous manifestations of the Logos),[40] knowledge, rather than disruption and transformation. It is interesting to note that, while some traditional eschatological language remains (e.g., 5.24ff.; 6.40), the Fourth Gospel is intensely individualistic in its concerns. The concern is with the salvation of the individual soul.[41] Absent is the concern with the salvation of the cosmos (Rom. 8.22ff.; Rev. 21), which is so characteristic of the eschatological beliefs of Judaism and early Christianity alike. Throughout the Fourth Gospel the world is of little interest as something to be redeemed. The elect themselves are to be taken out of the world when the Lord takes them to himself (14.3; cf. Mark 13.26).[42]

A characteristic feature of the growing wisdom tradition of Judaism is the way in which a pattern of descent and ascent was linked with wisdom (e.g., Ecclus. 24; 1 Enoch 42).[43] The heaven/earth orientation of that wisdom myth has obviously found its way into the christological presentation of the Fourth Gospel (e.g., 3.13; 6.61). Jesus is the one who comes from the realm of light from the Father and goes back there again. That vertical dimension is a dominant pattern in the Gospel.[44] Similar themes can be found in the use of angelomorphic categories.[45] There is evidence of the emergence of beliefs in angelic intermediaries, some of whom were believed to be embodiments of the divine glory. These angels descended from heaven to earth to be the agents of the divine purposes and to bear the divine glory in the world of men. Belief that another figure in heaven could embody divine characteristics was an important framework which could be used for the christological expression of the earliest Christians. Once those traditions, which enabled Jesus to be related closely to God, while maintaining his separate identity, were used, the christological focus centred on the descent of the divine being from heaven and his manifestation in the world of men. Salvation was very much bound up with recognition of this figure and the goal of being where this figure would lead (cf. Heb. 6.19f.). It was only eschatological in the sense that it concerned the ultimate destiny of those individuals who accepted or rejected the divine emissary.

While it would not be accurate to assert that the eschatological dimension of the coming of Christ has been lost in the Fourth Gospel[46] (e.g., John 5.26; 6.53; 6.44; 6.39; cf. 1 John 3.2; 2.28), its importance is not so great as in other New Testament writings. Alongside this the Christology takes a much more central position, and, what is more, concentrates the being and activity of the all-holy God in a single person (1.14) and beyond him the elect group (14.23). The Gospel of John has had a profound influence on both the form of the Christian message and Christology alike in subsequent Christian doctrinal formulation. It is the hidden Christ, calling his own to himself from a naughty world, who has dominated the Christian imagination.

Opposed to him is a world whose nature and character are not expected to change. Into this darkness the light descends and moves about, to be recognized by all who are children of light. This is more the language of the wisdom tradition; it is not the language of messianism, where the arrival of the anointed one of God effects a crisis in the course of this age and starts the inexorable process towards the establishment of the new. To this extent the Christology[47] and eschatology of the two major Johannine writings in the New Testament stand far apart. In the Revelation the exaltation of the Lamb means not only sharing the throne of God in the millennium (20.4; cf. 3.21; Matt. 19.28) but also the start of that process, which will lead to the establishment of the messianic reign on earth and the replacement of the old aeon by the new heavens and the new earth. The importance of Christ (Rev. 5.6), one like a lamb which was slain, is the fact that he it is who alone could start the cosmic process of the fulfilment of God's saving purposes. In the Fourth Gospel the coming of the Christ into the world certainly effects a division between the children of light and the children of darkness;[48] and what is more, brings about judgement (3.17f.). To this extent the Fourth Gospel continues an eschatological theme. Nevertheless the coming of Christ is not intended to change *the world*; that is merely an arena where the shepherd seeks to gather all his sheep into the fold. The difference can be characterized in simple terms as a contrast between a horizontal and vertical outlook with regard to the saving purposes. In the Fourth Gospel the myth of the descent and ascent of the Saviour confirms the orientation of the believer towards heaven as the goal of his aspirations; in Revelation the eyes of the communities are pointed forward to the kingdom of God on earth, where sorrow and sighing will flee away: 'To them that overcome I will make him a pillar in the Temple of my God; never shall he go out of it, and I will write on him the name of my God and the name of the city of my God, the new Jerusalem which comes down from my God out of heaven, and my own new name' (3.12).

Much has been written about the origin of the doctrine of the incarnation.[49] Wherever we locate its entrance into early Christian thought, it is probably no accident that it emerges in its most explicit form in a document where concern with the transformation of the cosmos has all but disappeared. We shall note in Paul's doctrine of ministry a basis for the doctrine of the holy man, centred on inward transformation through identification with Jesus. The doctrine of the incarnation is an example of a similar trend in Christology. God comes to the world not through the complex process of historical events, by putting down the mighty from their seat and exalting the humble and meek, but through the Word made flesh. Those who are his own recognize Jesus for what he truly is, just as those who know what true holiness is see in the life of the suffering apostle the authentic presence of Christ. The hidden Logos amidst the flux of a decaying world becomes a more compelling paradigm in late antiquity than the prophet of the kingdom of God presaging the imminent overthrow of the present order and the establishment of a new one. For Christian spirituality the doctrine of the incarnation offered a model of existence, which meant that Christian discipleship was concerned with bearing witness to the divine Logos, present yet unseen, amidst the vicissitudes of human affairs, and with being the locus of that presence through the indwelling Spirit.[50]

3

Emerging Patterns of Ministry

It is important to be aware of certain trends within first-century Judaism,[1] in order to appreciate the emphasis on the role of the whole people of God in the understanding of ministry, which emerges in the major writings of the New Testament. As we have seen, alongside an elaborate cultic apparatus in the Temple in Jerusalem was the pharisaic movement, whose basic aim was to involve the whole of Israel in taking seriously God's command 'You shall be holy, even as I am holy' (Lev. 19.2). Thus, as far as they were concerned, priestly purity was an obligation laid on every Jew.

In making this emphasis, Pharisaism represents a very significant attempt at understanding the role of the laity, which was to help guarantee the continued influence of Pharisaism and subsequent dominance after the destruction of the Temple and the cessation of the sacrificial system in AD 70. Despite the continued dominance of the cult, we see that within first-century Judaism there was a movement to extend the obligation of purity much more widely. Even within the hierarchical framework of the Qumran sect, we can see a similar trend: all members of the community were part of a holy enclave, an extension of the citizens of heaven on earth.[2]

The main characteristics of the preaching of Jesus offer many parallels to this emphasis of the pharisaic movement. Like the Pharisees, he offered to the people the same access to God irrespective of their social or religious background. The imminence of the reign of God presented all with a challenge to prepare for it. Already there were signs in Jesus' ministry of the eschatological acts of God and his presence with his people. The basis of Jesus' call was his eschatological conviction that God was present in a new and ultimate way.[3] Access to God depended on nothing but the trust and dependence of a child (Mark 10.15). As a result it appealed to many who, while they may have been attracted by the democratizing principles of Pharisaism, found the fulfilment of the pharisaic halakah impossible. Jesus taught his disciples to address God as father (Abba).[4] It was the familiar address of a child to his earthly father (Luke 11.2; cf. Mark 14.36). This was the appropriate address of one whose entry into the kingdom of God depended on the child-like response of acceptance in the face of God's gracious act. It was the fulfilment of the eschatological hope of Judaism, the dwelling of God with man and the realization in full of God's fatherly care for his children (Jubilees 1.24; Rev. 21.3ff.). Being aware of God's presence did not depend on the mediation of the cult, nor did it involve the fulfilment of the detailed requirements of the halakah. Upon the disciples was laid the obligation to continue that message (Luke 10.16). Whatever distinctive role Jesus may have given Peter (Matt. 16.16ff.),[5] the disciples as a whole were those who had the privilege of a reward in the age to come (Mark 10.29f.). Also, even if the Twelve had a significant role within Jesus' thought (Matt. 19.28), there is no reason to suppose that the exercise of ministry was exclusively theirs. Those who left all to follow Jesus knew the joy of the kingdom of God (Matt. 13.45; Mark 10.29ff.; Luke 9.57ff.).

(a) Paul's Letters[6]

Sharing Jesus' relationship with the Father is at the basis of Paul's theology (Gal. 4.6; Rom. 8.15ff.). Those who have faith in Christ have direct access to God without the mediation of Law or cult (Rom. 5.1f.). Divine sonship and brotherhood with Christ by the Spirit are the prerogatives of every Christian (Rom. 8.14; 29). That is not to diminish the great variety of personalities within the Church, but it does mean that in the Church there can be no longer any divisions (Gal. 3.28; 1 Cor. 12.13). As in one body there are many limbs and organs, each in their different ways contributing to the well-being of the whole, so in the Church, in which barriers have been broken down, the gifts given by the Spirit enable the community of believers to grow in love.

The pharisaic vision of the holiness of the whole people of God is captured by Paul too. The means of holiness differ from those set out by pharisaism (1 Cor. 6.11). In Christ all share the same level of holiness; all are saints (*hagioi*), for all together are the Temple, where the Holy Spirit dwells (1 Cor. 3.16). The spiritualizing of cultic language gave the priests no special status in the people of God, and, as we have already noted, Paul has little to say about ecclesiastical offices.[7]

But even if Paul says nothing about ecclesiastical offices, does that mean that he was unconcerned with ministry? The reverse seems to have been true. Paul has much to say about the gifts of the Spirit for the ministry in the Church (Rom. 12; 1 Cor. 12). But it is in connection with his own ministry as an apostle that Paul makes some of the most eloquent comments about ministry in the whole of early Christian literature. There is little here said about function and office, but there is a profound exposition of the intimate relationship which exists between the life and work of the Christian apostle and the living Christ.[8] Despite all the vicissitudes of his career Paul lived with the conviction that he was the minister of a new covenant, which far outweighed in glory the splendour of the covenant given by Moses on Mount Sinai (2 Cor. 3.7f.).[9] This outrageous claim, all the more so because it did not seem to be attended by glory, was linked with the firm conviction that the guarantee of the apostolic ministry of the new covenant was the identification with the crucified Christ. In contrast to those apostolic delegates who had appeared in Corinth and had made much of various indications of their justification for apostolic office – letters of recommendation (2 Cor. 3.1), speaking ability (10.10f.) and fulfilment of the commands of Jesus (1 Cor. 9.14f.; cf. 2 Cor. 11.7) – Paul seems to fall far short (though he is anxious to point out that even he can boast of spectacular experiences (2 Cor. 12.2ff., 12)). In a remarkable contrast between his ministry and that of Moses in 2 Cor. 3, Paul concludes that the ministry of the gospel reflects the glory of God himself in a way which has never been possible before (2 Cor. 3.18; 4.5f.).

The destruction of the outward man amidst sufferings and persecutions is the mark of true apostleship (2 Cor. 4.16f.). It is precisely because the apostle is weak that he can truly reflect the weakness of the suffering Jesus in the cross; that is the means whereby the power of God is manifest (2 Cor. 4.11, 16; cf. 12.8f.). The fact is that the apostle's task is to be an imitator of Christ (1 Cor. 11.1). The true apostles are those who are always bearing in the body the death of Jesus (2 Cor. 4.10). They offer an example of true discipleship to the churches.

But does not this represent the first stage of the emergence of an hierarchical structure? At first sight it would appear so, particularly in the Corinthian correspondence. Is what Paul is saying about the apostles something which is peculiar to their own office or something which can be shared by the rest of the Christians?

When Paul talks about bearing the marks of Jesus' death and his suffering, he does so in letters to churches which are in a rather fragile relationship with himself, primarily because they have questioned his apostolic authority. Indeed, we find that Paul's greatest emphasis on authority and his position as an apostle are to be found in those contexts where the particular church's attitude to himself is most inimical. The attitude of a community like that at Corinth involved questioning of the apostle's credentials, which had the effect of separating the apostle and his work from the community and revealing in the starkest possible way the gap between Paul's understanding of ministry and the church's. Paul envisages the apostle's task to be a living example of the life in Christ, which should be the responsibility of all those who have died with Christ in baptism (Rom. 6), but which is not perceived by the recipients of his letters.

There is also an extra dimension to the work of an apostle, for by his suffering he repairs the lack of costly obedience in those communities where the full implications of the cost of discipleship have not been realized (Col. 1.24). In Corinth, for example, the Corinthian community has, according to Paul's sarcastic remark in 1 Cor. 4.8, 'already come into its kingdom'. Its excessive triumphalism stands in marked contrast to the suffering apostles (1 Cor. 4.10; cf. 2 Cor. 1.5f.; 2.15; Gal. 2.17; 6.14, 17), and Paul offers himself to the church as the type of what life in Christ involves (4.15; 11.1). The church is in need of the apostolic example as a guide back to the fulfilment of what is after all its own calling, to reflect Jesus' obedience to death (Phil. 2.8; cf. 2.5). The apostle's extensive dealings with the church at Corinth show how anxious he was to communicate the ideal of dying with Christ to a church which had not perceived its implications, or for that matter noticed the fulfilment of the ideal in Paul himself.

Paul's emphasis on himself as the type of Christ in the Corinthian correspondence is to be contrasted with what he writes to the Philippians, and to some extent, the Thessalonians.[10] In these two churches the response to Paul and his gospel had been more positive, and Paul's change of attitude is revealing. We still find Paul referring to his own afflictions as an example of Christian service, but many of the references in this letter are merely in order to give information about himself rather than to compare the church with himself (1.13, 20, 24; 2.17; 4.9). Such references should be balanced by those which speak of the Philippians themselves participating in the suffering which elsewhere he had characterized as belonging to the apostle. Now Paul tells them: 'It has been granted to you that for the sake of Christ you should not only believe in him but also suffer for his sake, engaged in the same conflict which you saw and now hear to be mine' (Phil. 1.29; cf. 1.7; 2.4f.; 4.14, 18). That is not to say that Paul's example had no more part to play, as 3.17 makes plain, but that the great gulf between the apostle and the church, which had existed in Paul's relations with the Corinthian church, did not exist in Philippi. The Philippians were beginning to reflect the character of the apostolic ministry in their own lives, for what they do is also characterized as an acceptable offering to God (4.18; cf. 2.17; 2 Cor. 2.15). It is hardly a coincidence that this particular letter offers us one of the few examples of the *imitatio Christi*[11] in the Pauline letters (cf. 1 Pet. 2.21f.). The church is now in a position to follow the example of Christ directly without needing the mediated presence of Christ through the apostle.

Similar ideas are found in 1 Thessalonians. Not only does Paul link this church, which is undergoing suffering on behalf of Christ, with himself (1.6), but also with the churches in Judaea, who are suffering (2.14). In addition, we note that, as in Philippians, the Thessalonian church has attained a position where it can now actively assist in the apostolic ministry through encouraging Paul by their development in the Christian life (3.7f.;

cf. Phil. 4.14f.), whereas in the Corinthian correspondence it is the apostle who, by his suffering, is bringing life to the church (2 Cor. 1.6) and does not feel himself to be in a position to accept any support from a church whose response to Christ is so superficial. Probably the church at Thessalonica, like the church at Philippi, helped with Paul's financial commitments (2 Cor. 11.9; cf. 1 Thess. 1.7).

All this leads to the suggestion that in a church where the response to the gospel had been growing consistently, the role of the apostolic ministry gradually decreases in importance, even if its function never entirely disappears. When a community, by its daily dying with Christ, begins to fulfil the responsibilities of baptism, then it reaches a maturity where the apostolic example is no longer so necessary. The need for his presence and interference in the life of a church comes precisely at those times when there is a failure of the church to live up to its calling. It is Paul's aim as an apostle to enable every member of the body of Christ to fulfil his or her baptismal dying with Christ. A. T. Hanson has admirably summarized this area of Paul's ministerial task in the following way:

> The task of ministry is to serve the church, but to serve it by itself first living out the suffering redeeming life of Christ in the world, in order that the church as a whole may do likewise. There is no suggestion that the ministry can do anything which the church as a whole cannot do.[12]

As we have already noted, we should not neglect those passages, like 1 Corinthians 16.15 and 1 Thessalonians 5.12ff., which indicate that Paul singled out for special consideration those whose labours of ministry demanded respect and honour in the church. Such a ministry is justified on the basis of its proven worth, though the relatively high social status of such Christians should not be ignored as a factor in their assumption of authority.[13]

What is more, in stressing the importance of the totality of the ministry of the body of Christ, we should not ignore the distinctive role the apostle Paul played in the lives of his churches in promoting relationships between them. The focus of unity between those scattered communities around the Eastern Mediterranean was the apostle. He it was who could guarantee a degree of uniformity between those far-flung churches (1 Cor. 11.16; 14.34; cf. 4.17; 7.17). With such a role his task was never done, and the apostle remained indispensable as a focus of unity and means of ensuring catholicity.

So the absence of specific details of ecclesiastical order should not lead us to suppose that Paul was indifferent to such things. He had a clear vision of the equal responsibility before God of all believers, to reflect the heart of discipleship, symbolically represented at baptism in their dying with Christ. How Paul maintained that aim, particularly when there was a possibility that he would be removed from the scene by death, we cannot now answer, unless that is, we consider that the Pastoral Epistles reflect at least in general terms the mind of Paul. If they do, we should have to say that the seeds of order already sown, grow into a pattern of ministry which, whatever its suitability for the peculiar needs of the period, inevitably did quench the prophetic spirit at work within the whole body of Christ.

This development of the understanding of ministry has had significant ramifications for Christian spirituality.[14] The sign of the true apostle is the identification with the crucified Jesus. In stressing this view within the context of his conflict with the Corinthians, Paul has begun to outline the paradigm of the true Christian, and particularly its holy man, concentrating on a particular type of life. Obedience to the Messiah consists of re-presenting him and his obedience to death on a cross in everyday life. In other words, the apostle or holy man himself becomes the locus of the divine presence in the world.[15] This marks the beginning of an understanding of holiness which enabled a religious movement to internalize its radical demand when there seemed little possibility of radical change in the order of this world.[16] The duty of following Jesus could thus concentrate on radical internal change through the identification with the model offered by the Messiah; it need not concern itself with a society whose very complexity seemed to yield few signs of the desired transformation promised by God. The creation of internal holiness becomes a goal in itself rather than the endeavour to create that infinite holy space in the world which the inauguration of the kingdom of God involved. Certainly Paul longed for that to happen, but his own conception of his ministry opened the door for an understanding of spirituality, which need not involve itself too much with the holiness of God's world.

(b) The Johannine Literature[17]

The function of the first two letters of John is not to deal with church order; yet two things stand out in the presentation of his case by the author(s). First, there is an emphasis on tradition. This is most apparent in 1 John. The author sets the scene at the very beginning of the epistle by stressing the importance of continuity with the revelation of which he and the Church are witnesses (1.1). In 2 John 9 there is criticism of those who seek to move on in their doctrine, leaving beind the beliefs previously held. Such claims to subsequent revelation and initiation are firmly repudiated by the author of 1 John (2.27f.). What is all important is that the Church abides in that which they have received from the beginning (2.24).

Secondly, it is clear that the writer of both epistles thinks that he is in a position of authority to address the Church and correct the abuses which have taken place.[18] So much so, that he is quite prepared to categorize those who have left the community as 'antichrists' (2.18) and emissaries of the devil (3.8ff.). At the beginning of 2 John the writer describes himself as the elder, a position which is mentioned elsewhere in the New Testament (e.g., 1 Tim. 5.17; 1 Pet. 5.1). But it is not the reference to an ecclesiastical office which is of most importance; it is the fact that the author sets himself up as the paragon of orthodoxy, with whom it was necessary for all true believers to agree. In a remarkable statement in 1 John 4.6 he sets this out in a most uncompromising fashion:

> We are of God. Whoever knows God listens to us, and he who is not of God does not listen to us. By this we know the spirit of truth and the spirit of error.

Here is one of the most unequivocal claims to orthodoxy and authority in the New Testament.[19] No room is found for any divergence from the interpretation of the tradition offered by the elder.

An ecclesiastical problem seems to lie behind the third letter of John. The doctrinal issues, centring on the reality of Jesus' humanity which had loomed so large in 1 John 4.2; 5.6 and 2 John 7, have now given way to a dispute between the elder and a member of another church, Diotrephes, who refused to accept emissaries from the elder. There is little to suggest that the reason for this rejection by Diotrephes was because of a doctrinal disagreement.[20] Two problems might lie behind this dispute between Diotrephes and the elder: either the suspicion which had begun to attend the activities of wandering missionaries (v.5; cf. Didache 12) or the claim to autonomy by Diotrephes and his companion in the face of the elder's extension of his authority over a wider area. Perhaps it was a mixture of these issues. Diotrephes certainly did not acknowledge the authority of the elder (3 John 9) and as a result did not welcome the brethren who had set out from the elder's community. The problem of wandering prophets and teachers was a continuing difficulty for the primitive Church. It could be argued that some of Paul's problems with the church at Corinth could have been alleviated, if there had not been so much evidence of other Christian missionaries with their varying approaches in the Corinthian church.

The impression with which the Johannine letters leave us is of tightly knit communities,[21] for whom false teaching was something which was a new phenomenon, as also was the idea of any division between the brethren. It has been suggested, with some plausibility, that the Johannine communities were indeed inward-looking groups, who managed to maintain a high degree of cohesion possibly at the expense of any extensive intercourse with the world.[22] Their concept of community life is idealistic, some would say naive. The command to love the brethren is the key to social relationships (1 John 3.11; 4.7ff.; 2 John 5; cf. John 13.34). Nothing is said about any structure, which ensures the fulfilment of this command, and the establishment of right teaching (the references to children, fathers and young men are not references to offices in the Church in 2.12ff.). The tradition functions as a dominant factor in the life of the Church, as we have already seen. It is in the community, where few problems sully the purity of relationships and the harsh realities of the world hardly intrude, that the idealism of the community life can flourish, perhaps with the belief that they lived in complete sinlessness (1 John 3.9; 5.18; cf. 1.8). It is the life of perfection, the life of the kingdom of God on earth (cf. 1 Cor. 4.8), similar in its religious intensity to the holiness of the Qumran community, which ensured thereby its participation with the lot of the holy ones (1 *QS* 11; cf. Col. 1.12).[23]

We have started with the Johannine epistles, because, despite the frequently expressed view that the material in the Gospel of John is merely a reflection of the beliefs, problems and social relationships with the community which produced it,[24] due attention should be given to its claim to repeat tradition and not be merely a mouthpiece for its community views. Nevertheless, what we find there substantially supports what we find in the Epistles. The contrast between light and darkness, the believer and the unbeliever, life and death all confirm that what we have is a clear division between the realm of light and the realm of darkness, the sheep who are in the safety of the fold (chapter 10) and an evil world which is massed against the elect. That is not to say that the world is intrinsically evil, but that man preferred darkness to light (3.19). The traditions which the author has chosen to include in the Gospel themselves reflect this feeling of alienation from the world and the heavenward orientation of the community. Jesus will come again not to transform the cosmos, but in order that the disciples may go to be with him (14.2) and to see his glory (17.24). The pattern of descent and ascent,[25] which forms such a crucial part of the presentation of Johannine Christology, also stresses that it is the vertical, heavenly dimension of existence which is so important rather than the relationship with the world.[26] The disciples are in the world but not of it (17.16). The world is the arena of the saving process, which must go on after Jesus' departure, so that all the sheep may enter the sheepfold (10.16). Jesus prays only for his disciples, not for the world (17.9). It is the community of believers which is the locus of the divine presence (14.23). In its life together the community is characterized by the presence of the Holy Spirit-Paraclete (14–16) whom the world cannot receive (14.17), and the world will know the disciples of Jesus because of the love they have towards each other (13.34f.). In this respect the Gospel confirms the simple acceptance of the perfectionism possible for the disciples of Jesus. Like the Epistles, the Gospel manifests its concern for the past and tradition, both in its historical perspective (1.14; 19.35) and also in its doctrine of the Paraclete, whose function it is to point backwards, to Jesus (16.12ff.).

The charismatic flavour, which we noticed in the Pauline letters, and the lack of evidence of structures apparent in the Johannine Gospel and Epistles is also found in the book of Revelation.[27] While making due allowance for the fact that the author is not setting out to deal with church order but to communicate a disclosure of heavenly mysteries, what comes across is a view of ecclesiastical order which is similar in type to the Pauline churches. That is not to suggest that there is any dependence on Paul's letters. Indeed, we find polemic against certain Pauline injunctions in Revelation 2.14, 20 (cf. 1 Cor. 8). The author, as we might expect of an apocalyptic seer, stresses the importance of prophecy (e.g., 1.3; 10–11; 19.10). His own call is instructive for our understanding of the way in which he approaches the issue of ministry and authority. It is not the claim to have been with Jesus or, for that matter, to be a bearer of tradition, which qualifies the imprisoned John to speak. His authority to speak to the seven churches is based entirely on his conviction that he has had a vision of the risen Lord, who commissioned him directly to write to the seven churches of Asia Minor (1.10). It is those who share this view of divine ministry who are particularly singled out for attention in the book, 'for the testimony of Jesus is the spirit of prophecy' (19.10). There are signs that all God's people are called to be prophets and to share the fate of the prophetic witnesses in hearing their testimony before the world (ch. 11).[28] All are called to be priests and those who suffer like him will reign with him in glory (1.6; 5.10; 20.4).

Whether the belief that the consummation of all things was near affected the approach to church order in the book is not clear. In the light of the central role given to prophets in the early part of the history of the Church, we may suppose that the eschatological expectation had some influence on the prominence given to prophecy.[29] As we have already seen, the return of the spirit and the return of the prophetic voice were both intimately linked with the eschatological realities, which, the members of the primitive Church believed, were being activated in their midst and in the world at large (Acts 2.17ff.). To that extent, it would probably be fair to say that the continued existence of the Church necessitated at least the regulation of prophetic activity, such as we find in Didache 12 and, in some circumstances, the denial of its validity in favour of a more prosaic but safer form of ministry (e.g., Pastorals). The fact that a century later the Montanists in Phrygia[30] claimed that they were the true heirs to the early Christian experience, in emphasizing the importance of prophecy and the activity of the Spirit-Paraclete, is an indication that this form of activity was deeply ingrained within the Christian experience. This was particularly the case in an area like Asia Minor, from which the book of Revelation certainly, and according to tradition, the Gospel of John, emerged.[31]

(c) The Church in Jerusalem[32]

The picture we have of the Jerusalem church from Paul's letters and the Acts of the Apostles is one which converges in certain important respects. The spontaneity which characterized some of the Pauline churches, is not always apparent there after the initial burst of enthusiasm (Acts 2).[33] Despite its dramatic beginnings, it would appear that the Jerusalem church was characterized by a formality, which stressed the importance of tradition and catholicity. According to Acts 8 and 11, the extension of the mission outside the boundaries of Judaism had to be ratified by the Jerusalem church. This is all the more significant in the case of Acts 11, where *Peter* had to justify not only his action, based on his vision of the sail, but also the validity of the conversion of the Gentiles, characterized as that was by an outburst of religious enthusiasm.

Despite the great embarrassment that it caused him, Paul was compelled to admit, however reluctantly, that he went to Jerusalem to receive some kind of legitimization of his role as an apostle to the Gentiles from those who were apostles before him (Gal. 1.18; 2.2). Without much doubt, the authority which the Jerusalem church attemped to wield was a source of friction. This can be seen in the incident at Antioch which Paul recounts in Galatians 2.10f. In this James attempts to assert his influence in the church in Syria by sending envoys to persuade Jews not to eat with Gentiles.[34] In the incident, which Paul relates, Peter bows before the will of James, the person who became the dominant figure in the Jerusalem church.

The account of the Apostolic Council in Acts 15 shows James as the prime figure,[35] conducting a session, which is in stark contrast with the more enthusiastic meeting described in 1 Corinthians 14. The brief account of the decision-making process shows that James' voice and judgement were of central importance (Acts 15.13ff.). The writer of Acts tells us nothing about James' rise to power.[36] He comes on the scene out of the blue in Acts 12.17 and is accepted as one of the 'pillar' apostles by Paul, according to Galatians 1–2. From the early tradition in 1 Corinthians 15, we can glean that he too was the recipient of a resurrection appearance (15.7),[37] which, it is suggested, may have proved a turning point in his relationship with Jesus, which had hitherto been hostile (cf. John 7.5). His position in the Jerusalem church was of such prominence that it attracted the attention of the Jewish historian Josephus (*Ant.* 20.200). This passage is testimony enough to James' reputation for holiness, and, we may suspect, strict observance of the law (cf. Acts 21.20). Nevertheless, it is worthy of note that he too attracted hostility and was put to death by the priestly group. Hostility from certain quarters of Judaism towards the church in Jerusalem is confirmed by Paul himself, when he mentions the persecution which that church had undergone (1 Thess. 2.14f.; cf. Acts 3–12).

The pre-eminence of James in the primitive Church is hardly surprising in a Jewish milieu. We know that in contemporary Jewish sects it was quite common for the leadership of the sect to be kept within the same family. This is true of the Zealots (Josephus, *BJ* 2.433) and also of the Hillelite wing of Pharisaism (e.g., Rabban Gamaliel II).[38] According to Eusebius (*HE* 3.11.1), the see of Jerusalem was kept within Jesus' family after the death of James, an indication that a dynastic principle was the factor which brought James to prominence. Thus the leading role, which James plays in the Council of Jerusalem in Acts 15, probably rests on his blood-relationship with Jesus of Nazareth.

What we can reconstruct of the church in Jerusalem suggests that its officers were more doctrinal authorities and interpreters of the tradition (cf. Acts 6.2[39]), whose main task it was to control the spread and development of the Christian interpretations of the Jewish traditions. Their approach to tradition and authority, if Luke is to be believed, depended much on varying types of relationship with Jesus of Nazareth (Acts 1.21ff.). Such an outlook would naturally have led to suspicion of those who, like Paul, claimed a similar kind of authority on the basis of experience only. The tension between charisma and tradition thus had its origins not in the emerging structures which succeeded the initial enthusiastic communities but in the varied patterns of response, which were to be found in the Jerusalem church and its relationship with other Christian missionaries.

(d) Post-Pauline Developments

(i) EPHESIANS AND THE PASTORAL EPISTLES[40]

Whatever we decide about the authorship of the Pastoral Epistles, there is little doubt that they reflect the needs of the Church after Paul had been (or was about to be) removed from the scene. They certainly do not communicate the vitality of Paul's varying degrees of involvement with his churches, which we find in the indisputably authentic letters. In them we find churches threatened by heresy (1 Tim. 4.1; 2 Tim. 2.17), and there is a strong emphasis on guarding the faith handed down from perversion (2 Tim. 3.14). Throughout these letters we find that the task of Timothy and Titus is to maintain orthodox doctrine in the face of heretical incursions and to appoint suitable men to guarantee the survival of the faith in its pristine form. The guarantors of orthodox teaching are designated by ordination (1 Tim. 4.14; 2 Tim. 1.6), a rite familiar to us from Judaism as the mark of a fully trained rabbi.[41] In Judaism, after AD 70, the rite of ordination (*semikah*) became a means of guaranteeing the passage of orthodox teaching and the tradition handed down from generations past to the future generations. The qualities of the man ordained were that he should be well-equipped with knowledge of what had been said in the past and able to use it in such a way that there would be essential continuity of the faith taught from one generation to another. This is also the main concern of the Pastoral Epistles.

The minister's task is to represent a sober, upright and inoffensive face to the world (1 Tim. 3.1ff.) and to guard the tradition (1 Tim. 4.16). It is this rather than any function in the worship of the Church which is stressed by the Pastorals.

In Ephesians we have a vision of the Church universal existing for a long time to come (cf. 1 Cor. 7.26), with a variety of ministries bestowed upon it by the ascended Christ (4.11) as his departing indispensable gift to the Church. We may note that the ministries mentioned here are much more akin to those outlined in Romans and 1 Corinthians 12. But we should also note that there is emphasis on the maintenance of unity (4.4) and purity of doctrine (4.14), as well as the Church's understanding of the faith. The vision of the Church is still the vision of the body with varying ministries. To this extent Ephesians contrasts with the Pastorals, where the variety of gifts within the Body (an image which does not make its appearance in these letters) is not to be found.

(ii) IGNATIUS[42]

In his letters to the churches en route to martyrdom Ignatius the Bishop of Antioch expounds a view of the ministry which is without parallel in the earliest Christian literature. As with the author of the Pastoral Epistles Ignatius is dealing with situations where there have been considerable incursions by false teaching (Ephes. 7; Magnes. 8; Trall. 6 and 10). He lays great emphasis on the bishop as the focal point of unity and the remedy against schism and heresy (Ephes. 5; Magnes. 7; Trall. 2 and 7). It is the bishop alone who celebrates the valid Eucharist (Philad. 3f.; Smyr. 8), and the sign of belonging to the Church is belonging to the bishop (Philad. 3). Indeed, the bishop is regarded as the Lord himself (Ephes. 6).

In the situations confronting Ignatius, it is not too difficult to understand why he should have wanted to stress the cultic as well as the doctrinal position of the bishop as a remedy against schism and heterodoxy. The confluence of cultic and doctrinal function makes its first explicit appearance in early Christian literature. The 'rabbinic' pattern of ministry is here linked with the cultic in a way which was to be of significance for the development of ministry within the Church in succeeding centuries.

After AD 70 the fissures, which had already begun to appear in relationships between Christians and certain Jewish groups, widened. One feature of early Christian apologetic was to use Old Testament cultic imagery of the saving work of Christ (e.g., in Hebrews) and of life in the Christian Church (e.g., Epistle of Barnabas).[43] One of the most significant developments was the transference of priestly language to the Christian ministry. There is the occasional hint of it in the New Testament (e.g., Rom. 15.16), but largely such language is reserved either for Christ (as in

Hebrews) or the Church as a whole (e.g., 1 Pet. 2.9; Rev. 1.6). There are clear signs of the transference beginning to take place in 1 Clement 40f. and Didache 13.3 (though Justin can still call the Church as a whole a priestly race in his Dialogue with Trypho 116.3).[44] But it is in the early liturgy known as the Apostolic Tradition of Hippolytus that we find language which leaves us in no doubt that Old Testament priestly concepts had been transferred to the office of bishop. We read the following in the prayer for the consecration of a bishop:

> Father, who knowest the hearts of all, grant upon this thy servant whom thou hast chosen for the episcopate to feed thy holy flock and serve as thine high priest, that he may minister blamelessly by night and day, that he may ceaselessly behold and propitiate thy countenance and offer to thee the gifts of thy holy church.[45]

Whilst it would be an oversimplification to argue that the use of priestly language in connection with the Christian ministry was merely the result of the antagonism between church and synagogue, the place which this struggle had within the history of early Christian doctrinal development makes it one of the more obvious factors. We cannot but be aware of the profound significance attached to such a transference of roles. Not least was the implicit abandonment of the trend, which we found in first-century Judaism and taken up in the Pauline churches, where the priesthood of the whole of God's people was being stressed. By adopting such cultic patterns, the Church began to create the kind of divisions between priest and lay within the people of God, which Pharisaism had begun to undermine. With the acceptance of the sacerdotal aspect of Christian ministry the priestly obligation of the people of God is edged out. Spirit-inspired ministry is confined to those who are eligible for it (i.e., men and not women),[46] and would come after the due process of selection had taken place. Just as in the early Church, a long preparation became necessary for reception into the Church (catechumenate), so also ministry in the Church came to be identified with an élite, who exercised a priestly ministry, vicariously, for the whole people of God.

(e) Tradition and Charismatic Authority

One of the features of early Christianity, which continues to receive a considerable amount of comment, is the extent of tensions between different groups within the early Church and those Jews who rejected the messianic claim for Jesus. What has not been explored in enough detail, however, is the extent to which the pattern of authority which operated in Judaism and early Christianity affected the attitudes which were taken by various factions.

It has often been stated that certain groups within Judaism were extremely suspicious of claims to authority, which had their origin outside the normal patterns of authority. Attitudes towards the heavenly voice (*bath qol*), for example, were by no means uniform. In the famous story concerning Eliezer ben Hyrcanus reported in *b. Baba Metzia* 59a,[47] the divine voice's support for the position of Eliezer is not accepted when it conflicts with the decision of the majority. The reasons for the emergence of this attitude are difficult to assess, though it may be partly the result of anti-Christian polemic that led the rabbinic academies to treat such claims with great circumspection. Whatever the reason for the attitude, there can be little doubt that an issue of some controversy within contemporary Judaism concerned the right of an individual to claim to speak of God and for God on the basis of his own inner conviction. That this was also an issue of some importance for early Christianity is indicated by the evidence of the New Testament itself.

In the Acts of the Apostles there are several examples of visions and related experiences proving to be the basis for critically important action.[48] Among these incidents is the report of Peter's vision of the sail containing clean and unclean animals in Acts 10. This, together with the outpouring of the Holy Spirit on Gentiles (10.44f.), manifested in the form of glossolalia, formed the basis for Peter's judgement that the gospel could go to the Gentiles and that they could become inheritors of the promises of God on the basis of faith in Christ. But it is perhaps the most notable of all the visions recounted in Acts, which epitomizes the problem that such claims posed not only for Judaism but also Christianity, namely, the conversion-vision of Paul on the road to Damascus. Of course, this has a central place in the account in Acts, no less than three versions being included in the work.[49] Whatever we make of the historicity of these stories, there can be little doubt that for the author of Acts the event marks a decisive turning point in the history of the early Christian mission. The point is that, as with the case of the conversion of Cornelius, this event was one which was initiated by an experience of a dramatic kind.

We need a brief review of the evidence, which is to be found in the Pauline letters, particularly Galatians, concerning the issue of Paul's claim to authority.[50] Paul claimed that his right to preach the good news concerning Jesus of Nazareth and the particular version of that good news came as the direct result of his commission by Jesus. Indeed, he claimed to have seen Christ (1 Cor. 9.1) and to have received his commission to proclaim the gospel to all nations from him (Gal. 1.16).

It will be seen from this that for Paul the whole basis of his ministry is focused on the conviction that such a commission bears the marks of authenticity. Certainly for Paul the direct commission was primary in his call to be an apostle. The letter to the Galatians is ample testimony of Paul's concern to demonstrate the lack of human contact in this appointment. Even if one believes, as the evidence of Galatians 1.1 would seem to suggest, that Paul's opponents claimed a right to control Paul, because of the superior claim to authority of the other apostles,[51] Paul himself believes that all human contact was entirely secondary to the revelatory character of the call to be an apostle to the Gentiles. Whereas the journeys to Jerusalem could have been regarded by Paul's opponents as evidence of his dependence on the Church in Jerusalem and the need for ratification of the gospel,[52] Paul is clear in his own mind that such excursions formed only a minor part in his preparation. Indeed, if Galatians 2.1ff. is to be believed, they served only to confirm a course of action entered upon some considerable time before the decisive visit. It may, of course, be true that Paul's strong rejection of any human part in his call to the apostolic ministry is the result of an excessive embarrassment on the apostle's part concerning certain events in his life.[53] The fact is that Paul makes extravagant claims for Jesus, for himself as a recipient of the divine Spirit, and concerning the purposes of God, on the basis of his own direct experience of God.

As has already been suggested, here we have the twofold problem of early Christianity. On the one hand it made claims about Jesus which were based, certainly in Paul's case and we may suppose in the case of others too,[54] on the basis of inner conviction. As a result those Jews who rejected the validity of such claims and the corollaries drawn from them found that an important pattern of authority based on tradition and the transmission of authentic information by recognized authorities was subverted. On the other hand, while many Christians would have accepted many, if not all, of Paul's claims about Jesus, it is difficult to see how some of the leading Christians, perhaps including the church in Jerusalem, could have accepted the claims being made by Paul to share *equal* authority with them to expound the Christian message and make provision for its dissemination. Indeed, the more vehemently Paul claims the right to have authority to act as the representative of Christ independently of those who were Christians before him, the more acute the problem which confronts the early Christian movement. It may be true that Paul wanted to assert an essential link between himself and those who had been apostles before him (1 Cor. 15.8),[55] thus separating himself from any similar claims to authority based on the sight of the vision of the Risen Lord. The problem with this, however, is that Paul's position is itself vulnerable, as it cannot easily be shown why the distinctive appearance of Jesus should have stopped with Paul.

That we are dealing here with a real problem in the life of the Church and not just a hypothetical case is shown by the parallel visionary phenomena, which turn up elsewhere, not to mention the excesses of charismatic activity evident in Corinthian Christianity.[56] Treated in isolation they do not appear at all threatening until we realize that they manifest similar kinds of claims to those made by Paul.

One example from within the New Testament itself is the book of Revelation.[57] All the evidence would lead us to suppose that the book is only apostolic in that, like those who had been commissioned before him, John of Patmos considers that he too has been commissioned as an envoy to communicate God's purposes to the seven churches in Asia Minor (1.9ff.). It is the vision of the Risen Christ in 1.13ff. which is the basis of all the authority that is subsequently claimed for the book (Rev. 22.18). We are not in a position to know what the reaction to the book was or what view of it was taken by church leaders at the end of the first century. Information about false teaching in the area after the Pauline period is scanty and has to be gleaned from the few hints which we find in the letters of Ignatius of Antioch to the various churches in the area in the opening decade of the second century.[58] In the light of the uncompromisingly authoritarian message to the churches it is not improbable that there would have been an adverse reaction and a questioning of the authority for making these claims.

If the reaction of the churches in Asia Minor to the book of Revelation at the end of the first century remains an enigma, the fate of the same book a century or so later is not in doubt.[59] We know from later writers that many doubts were expressed about the book, mainly because it became one of the major inspirations of the Montanist movement in the last quarter of the second century. This movement which swept through the churches of Asia Minor and North Africa[60] claimed to have recovered the pristine character of the primitive Church. In the face of a growing institutionalism the Montanists claimed to be inspired by the Spirit (the work of the Paraclete) which plays such an important part in the New Testament writings. While, as far as we can gather, there is little about the Montanist theology, which is gravely suspect, we may suppose that their emphasis on the charismatic ministry, the role of women and the implicit challenge to emerging structures implicit in their claims to authority would have been a threat of intolerable proportions to a Church which was still emerging from the long and painful struggle with gnosticism and its claims to esoteric revelation.

But even if the doctrinal threat from Montanism was not great, the same cannot be said for the teaching of Elchesai and possibly also Cerinthus.[61] If Eusebius is to be believed, the call of Cerinthus to be a teacher of the Christian religion came, like that of John of Patmos and Paul, by means of a divine intermediary. Similarly also Elchesai's teaching came as the result of the appearance of the Son of God, who communicated to him the various doctrines which became characteristic of that sect. Also we find that in the gnostic literature the literary genre of the apocalypse has a place of some prominence.[62] Here the esoteric teaching is communicated direct to the apostle by some intermediary figure and, as a result, the cloak of authority is given to the teaching by its revelatory form. The evidence from the Nag Hammadi texts suggests that there was a significant contribution to gnostic religion from the apocalyptic tradition of Judaism,[63] not only with regard to the literary form of many of the gnostic texts but also in terms of ideas.

269

What this material indicates is that the religious authority claimed for direct experience of God and his world was something which had a continuing history within early Christianity. The evidence does not allow us to assess the effects of these claims to authority based on such experiences nor the reactions of those who did not accept these claims. What we do know is that groups like the Elchesaites and figures like Cerinthus were classed among the false teachers by later Christian writers. In the case of the Montanists, there is little doubt that there was considerable suspicion within early Christianity with regard to the claims to experience made by the Montanist prophets (e.g., Eusebius, *HE* 5. 17.2f.). Those who suppose that there is a fundamental distinction between the ecstasy of the Montanists and similar features recorded in the early Christian texts, fail to do justice to the centrality of these phenomena within earliest Christianity.[64] The problem posed by the Montanists in the second century was exactly like that posed by parts of the early Christian movement in the middle of the first. In the former case we have an increasingly institutionalized religious group being challenged by a group, which claimed an authority for its speech and actions which was to a great degree independent of the institution.

The evidence from the New Testament itself suggests that threats from individuals or groups who claimed to teach on the basis of such authority was a pressing problem within the Church. Already in 1 Corinthians, we find Paul dealing with a church whose members stressed freedom and charismatic inspiration and had to be guided by the apostle into saner channels. It is in the later Pauline tradition, particularly the Pastorals, that we find the first hints of a rebuke to those who would claim to have inspiration from God. In 1 Timothy (4.1) the writer warns his readers against 'giving heed to deceitful spirits and the doctrines of demons' (cf. 2 Pet. 2.1.; Jude 4ff.).[65] Instead there is a stress throughout these letters on sound teaching and the tradition handed down by authorized teachers. Clearly it is a church under threat which is reflected in these documents, a threat countered by a pattern of teaching familiar to us from some areas of contemporary Judaism: the appeal to tradition.[66] That there is a resort to such a means of conveying authority in the Pastoral Epistles is by no means surprising; the dangers of relying on charismatic authority for the defence of a religious tradition is a dangerous exercise.[67] The consequences of allowing such a free rein are hinted at in the first letter of John (2.27; cf. 4.2).[68]

Similar problems also emerge in the Didache.[69] Here we find a stress on the importance of the prophetic office in the life of the Church but also a matching concern with the problems that office presented for individual Christian communities. Congregations are now troubled by prophets who travel around taking advantage of the congregations (16.3). The test of the true prophet is some kind of accord between the life-style of the prophet and his claim to be from God (Didache 11.3ff.). Little is said about the need to test the content of his message. It would appear that if he passes the first test, he is immune from all further criticism. Here the congregations are in danger of allowing themselves to be taken over by men of spiritual power whose teaching can be allowed to pass with virtually no criticism.[70]

At the centre of the New Testament there stand the letters of one whose position for developing Christianity was an ambivalent one. On the one hand, we find in the Corinthian correspondence, and probably more so in the initial preaching,[71] a concern for freedom in the Spirit and little or no hierarchical structure established in the churches of his new converts. It may be true that certain items of traditional teaching were passed on (e.g., 1 Cor. 11.23; 15.3ff.),[72] but there is little evidence of any regularized oversight, except that ordained by the Spirit within the mutual ministry of the Body of Christ. What is more, the transference of the allegiance of Saul from pharisaic Judaism to the early Christian group was of such a kind that it inevitably questioned patterns of authority, which sought to base themselves on tradition and continuity rather than the occasional inspiration of the prophet or visionary. Indeed, there is an ambivalence in the Pauline correspondence on precisely this issue. Freedom, newness and the like are all catchwords which come naturally to a commentator on Paul's letters. Alongside the break with the past (the accent on the new age and particularly the rejection of the Law) there exists a concern for order, tradition and sobriety which, while not totally inconsistent with the stress on innovation is certainly in tension with it. It will not surprise us to find the accounts of Paul's conversion being used at a later time by Mani in his attempt to speak of his own prophetic office[73] nor the Pauline corpus being the centrepiece of Marcion's radical attempt to separate Christianity from its Jewish matrix.[74] The fact is that the letters of Paul, and we may suspect through them the character of the apostle himself, bequeathed to later interpreters an ambiguous and often apparently contradictory attitude towards authority and the role which charisma played in the establishment of the ecclesiastical order.

4

Coming to Terms with the Old Age

(a) The Common Life[1]

According to the Acts of the Apostles, one of the features of the primitive Christian community in Jerusalem was its practice of the community of goods. Doubts have been cast upon the veracity of this account of early Christian practice, because it is regarded as an example of Luke's idealizing the life of the early Church.[2] Such scepticism is not entirely justified, however. According to the Synoptic tradition, it would appear that attitudes to property, either among those who preserved (or created) certain groups of sayings (e.g., Matt. 6.25ff.) or in the immediate circle of Jesus, involved, at the very least, a rejection of most conventional patterns of living.[3] There was probably a common purse (John 12.6; 13.29), and Jesus had nowhere to lay his head (Luke 9.58). The likelihood is, therefore, in the light of the practice of Jesus' circle as recorded in the gospel tradition, that there continued to be a style of life which differed markedly from what was typical in the Pauline churches.

Uncertainty attaches to the precise nature of this practice. Was it a voluntary activity, which was not a prerequisite of discipleship or did the primitive Christian movement demand renunciation of property as a condition of membership of the people of the Way?[4] The emphasis in Acts 2.44 and 4.32 on having all things in common looks like a deliberate pattern of behaviour, which was regarded as normative for the Christian group. But if this was the case, the story of Ananias and Sapphira fits awkwardly into this pattern. According to the statement of Peter, there was no question of Ananias and Sapphira being compelled to sell their property and lay it at the apostle's feet (5.4). At first sight, if this story is anything to go by, we do not have compulsory community of goods as condition of membership.[5] It is likely that there was no compulsory community of goods in the early Church, and what we have in Acts 5.4 is a pattern of behaviour which was voluntary, but while being such, it was so typical that it provided a pattern, which was usually adopted. Thus community of goods was not a condition of entry into the community, but the normal practice of those who became Christians. According to Luke, this practice had the effect of leaving no one in need. But the pattern outlined in the Gospels meant that the risks were great (cf. Matt. 10.40–2). Indeed, all the evidence from the Pauline letters and elsewhere in Acts suggests that this practice did lead to some serious problems for the primitive communities (Acts 11.27ff.; cf. Gal. 2.10). It was such problems which prompted Paul to promote the collection (1 Cor. 16; 2 Cor. 8–9). It is clear from 2 Corinthians 8 that a significant reason for this was the state of the churches in Judaea, which had undergone persecution (1 Thess. 2.14f.) and poverty (Rom. 15.26f.).[6]

As far as we can ascertain, community of goods was not typical of the Pauline churches. Indeed, the kind of injunction which we find in 2 Thessalonians 3.6ff. ('If anyone will not work, let him not eat') suggests that the pattern of behaviour outlined in passages like Matthew 6.28ff. would not have been readily accepted by Paul. What is enjoined here is the continuation of accepted patterns of behaviour only slightly altered to accommodate the demands of the Christian gospel. The common life is now located in the occasional meetings of the Christian fellowship.[7] While the household regulations (e.g., Col. 3–4; Eph. 5–6)[8] were not particularly oppressive for the lower classes, they hardly indicate a radical departure from patterns which would have normally applied.[9] What we find in the Pauline letters is a different social atmosphere from what is reflected in the Synoptic Gospels. Theissen has argued with regard to figures like Paul and Barnabas that they espoused a different type of ministerial activity from that which had operated in Palestine.[10] Unlike the wandering charismatics of Palestine, who had nothing to call their own, Paul and Barnabas worked for their living, not relying on the magnanimity of their local communities (1 Cor. 9.14f.). It was this attitude which caused some of the problems in Corinth, when the Corinthian Christians became aware of another pattern of apostolic activity different from Paul's, in which reliance on the community was paramount (cf. Didache 11).

There were also problems in Corinth related to the social backgrounds of the various members of the church there (e.g., 1 Cor. 11.17ff.), but it is most noticeable that in this church there is little sign of the practice which was so characteristic of Palestinian churches. It is true that enthusiasm of various kinds is not absent from the descriptions of the Corinthian church. Nevertheless the assumption throughout the letter is that the Christians come together for worship with some owning homes of their own (11.34). The exhortation by Paul to share adequately at the Lord's Supper indicates that they are part of a world, where any extensive sharing of resources was not common (11.21ff.).[11] The form of Christianity, which Paul allows to emerge in Corinth (and from what we can gather from the other letters) in other cities as well, tended to stress the *individual's* obligation to live according to the laws of God. There was no dramatic transformation in attitudes about the circumstances in which the Christian discipleship is lived (1 Cor. 7.17ff.), nor was there to be any offence given to outsiders (1 Cor. 14.23; 1 Tim. 3.7; 1 Pet. 3.2; 2.12).

It might be argued that the absence of references to community of goods in the Pauline corpus should be taken as the most important datum for the existence or not of this practice in the Christian churches. Could Luke be guilty of pious fancy in speaking as he does about this issue? The evidence suggests that this practice continued to be important within the early Church. We have already noted that the Didache gives evidence of the kind of religious practice, which differed from Paul's and is more akin to the outline of missionary conduct set out in the gospel tradition (e.g., Luke 10). Throughout early Christian literature this practice seems to have carried on. It was not just Tertullian, who spoke of the practice as common in his day at the beginning of the third century (*Apol.* 39.11).[12] Thus while we may suppose that by and large the Christian communities tended to follow the lead of Paul, there was a significant strand within early Christian practice which reaffirmed the importance of an alternative ideal.

The existence of this practice and the ambivalence with regard to it are of fundamental importance for our understanding of the early Christian movement. The practice of community of goods, though by no means novel in the ancient world,[13] does exhibit a kind of idealism which is entirely comprehensible in a movement with such an intense eschatological dimension. The interesting thing about early Christian literature is that in the Pauline correspondence there is little sign of this ethical idealism. Life goes on very much as before. The changes are at the margins; the fabric of society remains as before. That is not to suppose that Paul did not think that things would change; it is evident that he did (1 Cor. 7.31). Nevertheless he clearly felt that continued existence within the present order, without unnecessary provocation of the powers that be, was the appropriate response. Demonstrative and radically alternative patterns of behaviour and outlook were not repudiated, but certainly attempts were made to modify them. For whatever reason Paul chose to turn his back on community of goods, it is certain that he laid the foundations for the frameworks of the Christian attitudes and response to society in the decades to come.

Even if community of goods finds few echoes in the Pauline letters, the importance of mutual support in almsgiving is not neglected. Almsgiving became a central feature of Christian charitable activity.[14] It is worth noting that even this activity is not regarded as an essential part of discipleship. Thus, for example, in discussing the collection for the saints in Jerusalem in 2 Corinthians 9.6ff. Paul has to plead with the Corinthians. The non-fulfilment of his request did not in Paul's eyes (as far as we can tell) affect the ultimate salvation of the Corinthians. The social and economic cost of discipleship was clearly considerable for Paul; whether it was true of all his converts is by no means so evident.

The Church never lost sight of the idealism of the earliest days as set out in the Acts of the Apostles. We find several protests against the pattern of response initiated by Paul. The 'leaven in the lump' philosophy, which presupposes that by being involved in society and its life one will change it from the inside, inevitably has its effects on the character of discipleship; compromises with the old order are inevitable. From the Montanists to the monastic movement,[15] we find the response which cries 'halt' to the swallowing-up of Christian utopianism by the old aeon. Of these two responses, it is the monastic movement which has left its most indelible mark on the Church. From its very beginning in the deserts of Egypt and the solitary protests of Christian ascetics against contemporary society to the rule of Saint Benedict in the sixth century, we find that same Christian idealism which flourished in the first decades of the Christian movement in Palestine.

(b) The Problem of Ethics in the New Age[1]

One of the most fascinating things about Paul's letters is the way in which they have been claimed by antinomians and traditionalists alike as the basis of their views of religion and society. Already in the second century we find that Paul is looked to as an authority by extreme gnostic antinomians to support their radical views of the Christian tradition.[2] We find that at the Reformation some of the regulations concerning social ethics and the state have been appealed to by those who would seek to maintain the existing order.[3] This varied use of Paul illustrates one of the contradictions, which is most evident in the Pauline corpus. On the one hand, we discover that some of the radical hopes of Jewish eschatology have been taken up by Paul; Christians are in Christ a new creation (Gal. 6.15; cf. 2 Cor. 5.17). On the other hand, as we have seen, the regulations for the Christian household, which are to be found at the end of Colossians and Ephesians and which themselves take up themes already hinted at in 1 Corinthians 7, are hardly disturbing of the existing social order. Slaves are to be obedient to their masters (Col. 3.22f.) or are to remain in whatever state they were in when they became Christians (1 Cor. 7.20f.).[4] This ambivalence in the Pauline ethics is one of the most important features of early Christian tradition and helps us to understand some of the varied features of the Christian religion throughout the centuries. The fact that Thomas Münzer[5] and Martin Luther could have come to such radically different conclusions when reading the same Scriptures is hardly surprising, when in the writings ascribed to one man we find a definite ambivalence towards this problem. The adequate appreciation of this theme in the early Christian literature may go some way towards explaining why it is that the Christian traditions still seem to provide the resources for both radical and conservative groups.[6]

We have already seen that the heart of Jesus' proclamation was the conviction that the kingdom of God was at hand. Even if we are bound to admit that there may well have been a deep reluctance on the part of Jesus to throw in his lot with the Jewish fight for freedom,[7] there can be little doubt that the impression left by his teaching was of considerable reserve towards the maintenance of the existing social order. In the tradition of his sayings there are some radical views of normal patterns of social intercourse: rejection of families and acquaintances (Luke 14.25f.), placing of all human need and provision in the hands of God[8] (Matt. 6.25ff.), and the appearance of Jesus and his disciples as a group of wandering figures stirring up the people. Whatever happened in the desert when Jesus fed the multitudes (Mark 6.30ff.) it is likely that such activity would have attracted the attention of the authorities, afraid as they were of the repetition of the unrest caused by similar messianic pretenders.[9] Two traditions in the Fourth Gospel remind us of the disquiet, which Jesus' activity probably caused. In John 6.14 the attempt by the crowds to take Jesus and make him king is an indication of the popular feeling which was prevalent at the time.

While it may be true that such disquiet on political grounds is not as obvious in the Pauline tradition, we do find that in the reports concerning Paul in Acts, there is the widespread belief that Paul and his friends are the ones whose activities in the synagogues are 'turning the world upside down' (17.6).[10] Throughout Acts there are put on the lips of the opponents of the Christians charges which relate to the subversive activities of the sect. Indeed, it is difficult to believe that this is not a theme, which forms a significant part of the author's purpose.[11] Paul is presented as one whose doctrines and teaching are found to be uncontroversial, at least in the eyes of the authorities (26.31), though the author of Acts is forced to deal with the attempts made on Paul's life and the threat, which he seemed to pose to Judaism, when the apostle arrived in that city with his companions (21.19ff.). Thus we find in Acts that, while the popular impression of Paul's activity was that it was either turning the world upside down or causing a significant Jewish minority within the Empire a great deal of disquiet, the author presents Paul as a conservative figure, a preacher of religion and not of revolution.[12]

As we have already noted, Paul speaks in eschatological categories of the new life which Christian faith brings.[13] Baptism and receiving of the Spirit mean entry into a community in which new values, new patterns and norms of behaviour and relationships are to be expected (1 Cor. 12.13; Col. 3.10; Gal. 3.28).[14] In some cases, like that of the church in Corinth, this brought about some amazing transformations in the lives of individuals and the groups as a whole. In 1 Corinthians Paul is having to deal with a series of serious ethical and social problems, some of which he has heard about from a letter or letters written to him by the Corinthian community and from information which he had received by word of mouth. There is a significant degree of immorality and freedom of action within the community, which has culminated in scandalous behaviour by some individuals (1 Cor. 5.1).

There has been much speculation about the origin of this condition. Suggestions have been made ranging from the proverbial iniquity of the city of Corinth itself to the influence of gnostic teaching on the nascent Christian communities.[15] Whatever weight we give to these various interpretations, it must be said that a certain degree of responsibility for the condition of the church in Corinth must attach to Paul himself.

The character of Paul's relations with the church in Corinth before the writing of 1 Corinthians has been explored on several occasions, most notably by J. C. Hurd.[16] Even if one cannot go all the way with his explanations, he has certainly made a case for regarding the problems of the church in Corinth as being to a significant degree the result of Paul's initial preaching of a gospel, which was marked by eschatological enthusiasm and lack of ethical precision. Thus the Paul who spoke in tongues more than all the rest of the Corinthians is now forced in this letter to put the gift of tongues in the context of the ministry of the Spirit as a whole and to defuse a potentially damaging situation by playing down its importance.

But how could it be that Paul's teaching may have caused such disturbances, when throughout the letter Paul seems to be determined to play down some of the extreme claims which are being made by members of the Corinthian church? The character of Paul's initial preaching to the Corinthians is not easily ascertained. We have to rely on hints from 1 Corinthians itself about its content, as the account in Acts tells us very little about Paul's activity in the city (Acts 18.1ff.). The reconstruction of Paul's initial teaching has depended greatly on the interpretation of certain catchwords and phrases which make their appearance in the response Paul makes to inquiries from the church (e.g., 6.12; 7.1; 8.1; 10.23). It is impossible to be certain what led to the use of these slogans by certain Corinthian Christians, but it is difficult to believe that the Corinthian slogans *all* represent a move away from Paul's initial preaching, a contamination of the pure Pauline gospel by gnostic libertinism. Accordingly it has been suggested with some degree of plausibility that what the Corinthians are saying reflects their beliefs about the content of the Pauline gospel and its implications for life and conduct. Indeed, when we read of Paul's attempt in Romans 6.1ff. to repudiate antinomianism, and the dramatic use of the resurrection imagery of the present experience of Christians in Colossians, 3.1f., it becomes a little easier to see why Corinthian Christians could have interpreted the Pauline message in libertine terms (10.23) and considered that they had already achieved the glory of the kingdom of God (1 Cor. 4.8ff.).

The new life of the Christian meant that he had passed from the old order into the new: 'If any one is in Christ, he is a new creation; the old has passed away, behold, the new has come' (2 Cor. 5.17). Participation in the Spirit meant sharing in the glory of the age to come. In that respect they could taste the glory of the new age (cf. Heb. 6.4); the Messiah had come. There is much to commend the thesis of J. C. Hurd, therefore, that some of the Corinthian ideas were in fact very close to Paul's original proclamation of the gospel. So in 1 Corinthians Paul moves away from the enthusiastic view of the Christian life, which he had preached originally to the Corinthians, and in its place offers a more conservative view of human relationships which was much less controversial than that implied in his original proclamation.[17]

The fact is that in the authentic Pauline letters there is a tension between the eschatological realization of a totally new order and a reluctance to pursue the implications of this theme. Indeed, many have pointed out the contradictions, which can be found even in one letter like 1 Corinthians, particularly over the issue of the role of women in the worship of the community (11.5; cf. 14.34). Such disjunctions can be explained by the growing reserve which Paul had towards the uninhibited expression of the messianic life-style. Of course, the climax of this process is to be found in the Pastoral Epistles, where there is the concern to present a sober face to the outside world (1 Tim. 3.7). Yet what we find in the Pastorals is not confined to these documents alone. There is a fundamental uncertainty about the nature of the Christian response, not only with regard to the State (Rom. 13),[18] but also with regard to issues like the role of women,[19] slavery and wealth.[20] The formula 'in the world but not of the world' may seem to be a trite way of speaking about Christian existence; yet in a very real sense it expresses the fundamental conflict within the Pauline letters between the conviction that already, in some sense, a new order had arrived, which was changing both individuals and groups, and the (ultimately stronger) conviction that there was need for Christians to live within an order, which did not recognize the demands of the new and which may well have regarded them as entirely subversive of the existing order.[21] The fact is that the church began to come to terms with the old order and found itself playing down those aspects of its message, which might seem to threaten the world as it was.[22] That is not to say that the Christian gospel ceased to have an effect on the society of late antiquity. Undoubtedly its uncompromising demand of allegiance to another lord than Caesar was bound to have a gradual undermining effect on the fabric of society, however strongly the Christians protested to the contrary.

It is in the Acts of the Apostles that we see most clearly the way in which the demands of the new and the restraining influence of the old seem to confront each other. The picture, which Luke gives, of primitive Christianity is of a group with distinctive religious and social practices, which certainly threatened the patterns of some other Jewish groups and probably also those outside Judaism as well. Throughout the book we find that Christians are brought face to face with civil authorities on the charge of subversion. Indeed, the charge of 'turning the world upside down' (Acts

17.6) is one which is found on the lips of outsiders or opponents of the Christian movement rather than the Christians themselves. So although the Christians find themselves in very difficult situations, whether facing an angry crowd in Ephesus (19.23) or suspicious Jews in Jerusalem (21.27), the problem is not one which is posed by the religious beliefs of the Christians, which are shown to be relatively harmless (e.g., 18.14), but by the intransigence of Jews (18.12) or the economic interests of pagans (19.27). The Christian message is not seen by the authorities to be one which threatens the well-being of the Empire, despite the fact that its adherents frequently found themselves involved in trouble. Apart from the description of the life of the Christian community in Jerusalem immediately after Pentecost, very little is said about the radical social implications of the Christian faith. Nothing is said in Acts 10 about the ethical demands laid upon the newly converted Cornelius. Luke is perfectly content to record the conversion of a Roman centurion. It would not have suited his purpose to describe Cornelius forsaking all to follow Jesus if that is what did happen. Thus the picture we have does not place an insuperable barrier before those wealthy and influential people, who would become Christians.[23]

It is understandable why the enthusiastic beginnings of Christianity should not be continued, when it became necessary to reach an accommodation with society at large. It is not just a question here of a move away from initial enthusiasm in the face of the delay of the coming of the New Age in all its glory. The fact is that, within Christian experience from the very beginning, there existed the tension between the need to reach a *modus vivendi* with contemporary society and the earnest expectation that God would bring about a new order, in which sorrow and sighing would be no more. But once it had been decided that the Christian groups were to remain *within* non-redeemed society, then it was inevitable that the need would arise to temper some of those ideals, which at times characterize the Christian view of society. Attitudes to women and slaves which cut right across the patterns normally accepted could not be tolerated.[24]

While it would be a gross distortion to say that early Christianity was as a whole a profoundly revolutionary movement, it would be equally perverse to deny that there existed at the heart of its doctrine a subversive strain which meant that an acceptance of the status quo could never entirely satisfy the demands made by its traditions; complacency could never be justified. To be a follower of Jesus meant following the path of one who was regarded as an outcast by certain members of the religious authority in his own day.[25] It also meant looking forward to the establishment of a kingdom which would in due course take the place of Rome. As the book of Revelation so graphically demonstrates, there could be no room for both Caesar and Christ in the New Age. Whatever injunctions may have been given by church leaders about quiet acceptance of the status quo in the present (e.g., in 1 Pet. 2.13ff.; Titus

3.1ff.), the eschatological beliefs of necessity put a question mark against both the loyalty of Christians and the implicit demand that all barriers were to be broken down in Christ.

Another problem, which was never fully resolved in early Christianity, was antinomianism (Rom. 3.8; cf. Rom. 6). The early Christians came to the conclusion that the Law of Moses had been replaced by Christ. As such they accepted the Pauline view, which finds parallels in other parts of the New Testament, particularly the letter to the Hebrews. Clearly this was a long process and one which was not met by universal approval, as the continuation of an alternative view of the Law would seem to suggest. Nevertheless the fact that many of the Christian communities were composed of former Gentiles accelerated the process whereby the Church loosed its ties with the demands made by the Torah.[26]

While at the level of theology it would seem that Paul reconciled his abandonment of the Law of Moses with a continuing demand for a high moral content in Christian ethics as is evident throughout his Epistles,[27] there can be little doubt that his view of the Law as part of a past aeon led to severe difficulties in the articulation of Christian ethics.[28] Paul has no doubts that the law of the Spirit of life has taken the place of the law of sin and death in forming the Christian attitudes towards moral problems (Rom. 8.1f.).[29] The indwelling Spirit, which manifested itself in particular types of behaviour, enabled the Christians to bring forth good works (Gal. 5.22ff.). Of course, the problem, when such an emphasis is placed on the inward promptings of the Spirit, is that it becomes very difficult to ascertain what is and what is not in accord with the demand of God. Thus a corollary of the move away from the Law of Moses, notwithstanding Paul's firm grasp of the centrality of ethical responses for those in Christ, is that precise norms for behaviour disappear, to be replaced by an emphasis on individual freedom (e.g., 1 Cor. 8).[30] It is certainly true that Paul lays great stress on the centrality of the law of love (Rom. 13.10) and indicates that there is a degree of continuity between the old and new covenants in that an ethical response is an essential feature of the new as well as the old; but he fails to articulate the nature of that response. The reason for this is clear. In the community of the new age those who have been baptized with the Spirit will know instinctively what the law of the Spirit of life is (1 Cor. 2.10ff.). Such an idealistic picture of the nature of Christian existence, however defensible it may have been in theory, did not survive in practice, as the Corinthian correspondence, and possibly also 1 Thessalonians, makes plain. It comes as no surprise that in the later Pauline correspondence, particularly Colossians and in the letters which are often ascribed to followers of Paul (namely, Ephesians and the Pastorals), we find the introduction of ethical lists, probably of pagan origin[31] which enable members of the Christian community to regulate their lives in accordance with precepts which inculcate good order and inoffensive behaviour.

While it must be said that Paul, in particular, nowhere intended problems for moral rectitude, it cannot be denied that the *effect* of the Pauline ethical teaching probably meant that this may have been the case in practice.[32] To say this is not to deny the profound link which Paul found between the new life in Christ and the social and moral consequences which would result.[33] Rather the problem is the general nature of the guidance (Rom. 13.11) and the supernatural means for fulfilling it, which initially inhibited the formation of a corpus of moral injunctions, which would enjoy the prestige and authority of the rabbinic laws.[34] Paul himself seems to have had no doubt about the firm link which existed between the fact of salvation and the demands made upon those who participated in it. While this theological connection can be demonstrated, it is more difficult to show why it was that particular ethical principles were taken on by Christians as the corollaries of this theological conviction: how, for example, did Paul relate the belief that all the political powers were ordained by God and had, therefore, to be obeyed, with central features of his theology?[35] While it may be true to say that the New Testament writers nowhere assert the need for revolutionary activity of a violent kind exercised by human beings to overthrow the existing order, such a passive view of an attitude to the State and acceptance of its demands accords ill with some of the stark condemnations in Revelation and the cry of Peter and the apostles in Acts 5.29, 'We must obey God rather than men'.[36] Careful consideration needs to be given, therefore, to the suggestions of those who argue that the teaching about the state in Romans 13 is very much influenced by Paul's knowledge of the political situation in the capital of the Empire in the mid-fifties and should be understood in the light of this and be seen in its appropriate context.[37] The way in which circumstances dictated the character of ethical responses is a theme of considerable importance for our understanding of the New Testament literature.[38] If we take seriously the fact that many of the NT documents are only occasional pieces, we shall have to accept the probability that the advice contained in them will also be dictated by the circumstances of the people addressed and as a result betray varying degrees of inconsistency with other parts of the corpus of writing, stemming from a particular author. Of course, the problem with Romans 13 is that there is very little, if anything, in the Pauline letters with which one may compare this passage, even if we may point to passages like 1 Corinthians 15.24f. as indicative of Paul's conviction that ultimately all the powers in heaven and earth would be subordinated to the rule of God. Nevertheless there does appear, at first sight, to be a certain conflict between Paul's conviction that a new order has come with a new lord and new demands which would replace the old, and a passage like Romans 13, where there seems to be little concern with the transforming power of the eschatological spirit in the attitudes of those in Christ, with regard to what was, in Paul's day, perhaps the most obvious power opposed to the ways of God.

Paul's varying attitudes can be dealt with by various means. Different weight can be attached to passages like Galatians 3.28 as compared with 1 Corinthians 11.2ff.;[39] stress may be put on circumstances as the reason which dictated the particular response, so that Paul is absolved of – what seem to us – some of the more reactionary views. Of course, we may want to find no inconsistency between the various passages and to suppose that the apparent contradiction can be explained by relating the more radical passages like Galatians 3.28 and Colossians 3.10 to the religious realm. It seems to me that we should give full weight to the contradictions as a demonstration of the existence of the struggle between idealism and pragmatism, between the utopian spirit and the need for caution in attempting to realize the eschatological glory in the present.[40] Paul's attitudes are not neatly categorized. There is certainly a sense in which his vision of a new creation does subvert the present order. This is even evident in those passages where his views seem to be most conformed to the old aeon: for example, when he deals with slavery. Thus there is reason to suppose that Paul's views did actually lead to a way of life which was significantly different from the prevailing order (Philemon v.21; 1 Cor. 11.5).[41]

With regard to his ancestral religion, Paul was actively engaged in the subversion of much contemporary practice. The beginnings of the fulfilment of the scriptural promises meant for him that barriers to the participation in the people of God of those Gentiles, who were called, must be removed. He had a vision of Jew and Greek united in Christ, which *had* to become a reality, whatever the practice of the present order might provide. Paul had no scruples in this regard. His career is an example of that outlook which, when translated into reality, tends to shatter, either partially or wholly, the order of things prevailing at the time. Circumcision was denied as a necessary qualification for membership of the people of God; table-fellowship was central and all that hindered it in the Torah must be repudiated. In this area Paul's actions indicate that his ideals definitely influenced his conduct.

The logic of Paul's eschatological position demands that transformation, both inward and outward, is already a present reality: already the new age has dawned; already the eschatological spirit has been poured out (cf. Heb. 6.4), and therefore it is only to be expected that the norms of the new creation will be apparent in the individual lives and in the corporate existence of the new community.[42] But what we find in 1 Corinthians is the beginning of Paul's retreat from the first flush of eschatological enthusiasm to an outlook which admits that in Christ there is a new creation but without this having a disturbing effect on the present order. There is evidence of an attitude, which gradually replaces utopian views. Emphasis on the transforming power of the Spirit is there, but the effects on the present order are marginal. No doubt the circumstances in Corinth needed a careful and considered response. Clearly utopianism can be immature. Nevertheless in 1 Corinthians Paul is in danger of undermining that central utopian element in the Christian experience and outlook, which gave the movement such an initial impetus. In his great contribution to the eschatology of early Christianity Paul had himself been instrumental in allowing a utopianism derived from contemporary Jewish eschatology to disturb the current pattern of relationships between Jews and Gentiles over the issue of their admission into the people of God. In giving effect to this utopianism Paul never wavered, but with regard to its effects on society at large, he remained either ambivalent or positively conservative.[43]

We have noted already that with regard to the community of goods and the missionary practice of the Palestinian church, Paul seems to have taken a very different line, which stressed the obligation of the individual to continue to work as a member of society. In addition, Paul was responsible for disseminating the view in his churches that the true nature of Christian discipleship did not involve complete separation from the world (1 Cor. 5.9; cf. 2 Cor. 6.14; John 17.16). That kind of existence inevitably meant compromises in the way in which the believer related to the old aeon. The question remains, however, whether those compromises, which were made, subtly changed the nature of the earliest Christian idealism. Until we take seriously the way in which early Christian writers came to a compromise between their eschatological convictions, realized and future, and their belief that their obligation to their new lord did not mean separation from the world, we shall not understand a fundamental element of the dynamic of early Christian religion. Inevitably the demands imposed by accommodation require a dilution of the idealistic hopes for transformation and renewal at any but the individual level. Yet, as the repeated attempts to redefine Christian attitudes to society down the centuries in the light of some of the more radical demands from the biblical tradition indicate, the Church has never felt itself able to rest content with an interpretation of its gospel, which tacitly ignores the social and political dimension of the change which its message contains. What we find in the pages of the New Testament are some of the first attempts to live with this tension and the resulting imbalances, which were inevitable in such a situation.

Elsewhere in the New Testament similar developments call for consideration. Even in that text which offers the principal evidence in the New Testament for the transformation of the cosmos, we find that the *presentation* of the material has initiated a subtle shift in its significance. The process, whereby the kingdom of God is established, is described in the book of Revelation within the framework of the letters to the seven churches. The dominant concern of these letters is directed to ecclesiastical and individual renewal and strengthening. Inaugurated eschatology is at a minimum in the letters. Certainly, already, followers of Christ are priests (Rev. 1.6) and witnesses to a dramatic change, which will remove (ultimately) the Roman order, though in the present all they can expect is to suffer (11.7ff.; cf. Luke 11.49). By placing the vision of the coming of the kingdom of God within the epistolary framework, we find that this vision has become a means of challenging the individual to greater piety. It makes the concern for the individual paramount; it is for him or her to be equipped to enter the Paradise of God rather than extensively reflecting the values of the new order. Patient waiting and suffering is all that is offered in Revelation 2–3; changing the world order is not a concern.

In the Fourth Gospel we find that concern with the renewal of the cosmos has all but disappeared. Even when eschatological language makes its appearance, it is directed towards the individual (5.21; 6.39; 6.53; 14.1ff.). The document is preoccupied with Christ coming to a world which is full of darkness. It reflects the concerns of an inward-looking sect, alienated from the world.[44]

Much has been written about world-views or ideologies and their origins and functions. There is an ideology, which starts life as a reflection of the socio-economic circumstances; yet this ideology begins to have a retroactive force and an influence on the nature of the very circumstances from which it had its origin.[45] There is another, which offers a contrast with the present order but whose fulfilment is transposed into the future, so that an individual can have an idealism, which acts as a spur to gain a future goal. Thirdly, there is the ideology which functions as a legitimation of the present order, by offering a justification for its continued presence within the divine purposes. All these ideological types may be found in early Christian literature. Probably the origin of early Christian utopianism is to be understood under the first head. Secondly, we have the ideological type which predominates in the New Testament: looking forward to a new order but doing little to bring about change in the present. Of course, that outlook cannot help but change the present, however much ancient Christians may have argued that they were not so doing. As many ancient and modern writers have pointed out, Christians presented an alternative to the state.[46] They were not indistinguishable from other citizens; they refused to acknowledge the gods of the state and to do military service.[47] They looked forward to another order. Even when this hope was becoming totally other-worldly, it still meant that it posed a subversive threat to the traditional values of society. Finally, there was the outlook which comes closest of all to a complete legitimation of the present order. Of course, early Christians could not do this completely, because of antipathy to certain Roman beliefs and customs. Nevertheless in a passage like Romans 13 the apocalyptic framework enables Paul to legitimate the powers that be as part of the divinely ordained nature of things.

(c) The Delay of the Parousia[1]

Much has been made in this study of the centrality of the eschatological convictions for the understanding of the primitive Christian movement. This is in line with the bulk of recent scholarship on the New Testament since the beginning of this century. It will come as no surprise, therefore, that the question must arise: if a belief in the imminent arrival of the new age was so central to the early Christians, how did they cope with a situation in which that hope did not seem to materialize? After the work of Weiss and Schweitzer on Jesus, attention was given to this subject by, among others, Schweitzer himself and Martin Werner. It was Martin Werner in his substantial examination of early Christian doctrine, who set forth the central importance of eschatology as the underlying influence for doctrinal development. His thesis is quite simply this: that the early Christian soteriology and Christology was, in part at least, a reaction to the failure of the Parousia hope to materialize. It is a bold thesis and one which has had immeasurable influence on the study of early Christian thought.[2] From the Gospel of Matthew to the book of Revelation we can find studies, which argue that the influence of the delay of the Parousia stands below the surface of the writer's concerns. The thesis itself has its attractions. If we assume on the basis of sayings like Mark 9.1 that Jesus expected the kingdom of God to be established on earth within a very short time, we may expect that the concerns which normally dominate the world-views of those who do not share such a belief would not be so important. Jesus tells his disciples not to be anxious about their needs and to assume that God will provide for them (Matt. 6.25ff.). What is more, his dispositions for his disciples after his death are scanty, and in the view of some, non-existent. All in all, the Gospels (with the exception of the Farewell Discourses in John) may leave us with the impression that since Jesus expected the consummation of history in the near future, he showed no interest whatsoever in establishing an organization to carry on his work.

Likewise the picture of the charismatic community in 1 Corinthians may be a reflection of the kind of idealism which feels that it does not have to accept the problems posed by the real world. Paul himself is full of urgency in his mission, convinced that his task may itself be the very fulcrum on which the final consummation hinges. His role as apostle to the Gentiles is the essential prelude to the establishment of God's kingdom (Rom. 11.25ff.; cf. Mark 13.10). Once that is completed, the short interval before the return of Christ will be over and the events of the last days will take their course (2 Thess. 2.5ff.).

It certainly is a remarkable fact that the earliest New Testament documents have very little to say about church order. All are imbued with an enthusiasm which carries along the community with little or no need for structures to ensure continuity.³ It is only in those later New Testament documents like the Pastoral Epistles that we begin to find attempts to deal with deviant teachings by means of the establishment of authoritative church officers. In documents like these, it is suggested, we are to find the first signs of that need to ensure the continuity of the faith in the face of the growing uncertainty about the imminence of the return of Christ. Once there are doubts about this, inevitably the freedom from anxiety, which carried the initial communities along, would disappear and be replaced with the need to consolidate. That does not mean that the Parousia hope disappears; what it does mean is that the intimate link, which existed between the events of Jesus' life on earth and his return again in glory, has been dissolved, so that eschatology can become a part of doctrine, one belief among many which are important for Christians, instead of the underlying framework of all early Christian convictions.

We have noted that in the New Testament there is an indissoluble link between resurrection-faith, experience of the Spirit and the imminent return of Christ.⁴ If Jesus is raised, it can only mean that the new age has dawned and that final deliverance will not be delayed. When this hope was not fulfilled, the character of the original resurrection-faith subtly changed. Instead of its being a sign of the coming of the new age, it becomes a sign of hope for the individual,⁵ so that just as Jesus has gone into new life with God, so also those who follow him will do the same (cf. John 14.2ff.). The close ties, which bind the Parousia expectation and the resurrection-faith, are loosed. Instead of living in the expectation that at any point the age to come would arrive and regarding all that is experienced as a mark of that arrival, the present becomes, not the overlap of the ages, but a period of pilgrimage through an alien world waiting for something better in the next.

The enormous influence of this thesis should not blind us to the fact that the New Testament itself does not actually give us much explicit evidence that it was a problem. Indeed, there is a danger of our assuming that what *we* consider to be a problem must also have been one for the early Christians. The clearest evidence that it was a problem emerges in what is by common consent the latest document in the New Testament, 2 Peter. Here we have the clearest indication possible that the community addressed was having to wrestle with the issue:

> This is now the second letter that I have written to you, beloved, and in both of them I have aroused your sincere mind by way of reminder; that you should remember the predictions of the holy prophets and the commandments of the Lord and Saviour through your apostles. First of all, you must understand this, that scoffers will come in the last days with scoffing, following their own passions,

and saying, Where is now the promise of his coming? For ever since the fathers fell asleep, all things have continued as they were from the beginning of creation (2 Peter 3.1ff.).[6]

But lack of explicit evidence has not prevented commentators from finding other, less obvious, examples within the New Testament. We can categorize the bulk of the evidence of the problem of the delay of the Parousia as *implicit* evidence, unlike the passage just quoted from 2 Peter, which is explicit evidence. The implicit evidence can itself be divided into two sub-divisions: material which deals with the delay of the Parousia by re-emphasizing the Parousia hope (much in the way that 2 Peter does); and material which tends to play down an imminent expectation, either by omitting mention of the hope, or by subtly altering the character of the history of salvation.

Of the documents with the most pronounced eschatological expectation in the New Testament, the book of Revelation is a case in point; it is a document with the belief in an imminent expectation, which is clearly directed to communities that are going through a period of moral and spiritual laxity and some persecution.[7] The first of the letters to the seven churches is to Christians who 'have lost their first love' (2.4); the last is to Christians who think much of their spiritual status but in the eyes of Christ are spiritually poor (3.17). In Matthew's Gospel the theme of the disciples of Jesus endeavouring to ensure that their righteousness exceeds that of the Scribes and the Pharisees is a constant preoccupation (5.20). Linked to this we find that some of the Parousia parables stress the fact that there has been a delay and urge readiness for the coming of Christ at a time which disciples may not expect (24.45ff.; 25.1ff.; 25.14ff.). It is not those who say 'Lord, Lord', who will enter the kingdom of heaven, but those who do the will of God (Matt. 7.21). The theme of uncertainty pervades the Gospel. The believers do not know precisely when the end will come, nor can they be sure who will be saved, e.g., 13.24ff. The wheat and the tares grow together until the harvest; it is only then that they will be separated. So also within the Church, there is a mixed community of righteous and unrighteous, and the separation between the sheep and the goats will take place at the end (cf. Matt. 25.31ff.). Meanwhile it is necessary for the Christians to endeavour to enter by the narrow way (7.13).[8]

The problem of the non-appearance of the Parousia manifests itself in a slightly different form in Paul's early letters to the Thessalonians. In both letters eschatological issues are dominant concerns. In the first it is apparent that there has been a question about the death of Christians before the Parousia (4.13ff.). It would appear that the Thessalonians thought that those who died before the arrival of Christ would have been at a disadvantage and would not participate in the life of the age to come. Such a belief is consistent with Jewish eschatology where, generally speaking, only those who were alive when the Messiah came would be fortunate enough to participate in the life of the messianic kingdom (Syr. Bar 29; cf. Syr. Bar. 51f.).[9] Paul deals with this problem by asserting that those who have died will in fact *precede* those left alive, in being united with the returning Christ (4.16). The advice given concerning the arrival of the kingdom in 5.1ff. suggests that the community was in a state of expectancy and was perplexed about its non-arrival.

In 2 Thessalonians a different issue emerges. Already in 1 Thessalonians Paul had advised the Christians to live as children of the new age (5.4ff.) and to work with their hands to avoid giving offence to those outside the Church (4.11f.). A more specific problem emerges in 2 Thessalonians. It seems that some of the Christians had decided that, with the imminence of the coming of Christ, there was no need to live a normal life in the world (3.6ff.). Such people are rebuked by the apostle. In order to dampen eschatological enthusiasm, which had emerged in the community, Paul sets out an eschatological programme, which is intended to *diminish* the intensity of expectation (2.3ff.). Certain things have to take place before Christ will return. Until they do, there is no point in idleness; Christians should carry on with their normal lives and not be carried away with their enthusiasm.

The Gospel of Mark is not an easy document to interpret as far as its eschatology is concerned. One of the most influential studies of the Gospel argued that it was shot through with an imminent eschatological expectation,[10] being written during the Jewish war amidst an expectation that the Lord would return to gather his elect in Galilee (13.26; cf. 16.7). Such an interpretation is not now widely held. Indeed, it is difficult to understand why a gospel should have been written, including such a diversity of material extraneous to the main theme, when the end was in sight. What is more, Mark 13.10 may indicate that, far from being written when the end was in sight, there was still a significant period of time which had to elapse before Christ would vindicate the elect. Indeed, it could be argued that the eschatological material in Mark 13 serves the purpose of encouraging those undergoing persecution or persuading them that discipleship involves them in suffering rather than glory, with vindication coming, as it did for Christ, only after suffering.

Among those New Testament documents which are regarded as marking a move away from the primitive eschatological expectation, pride of place must go to the Gospel of Luke and the companion volume, the Acts of the Apostles. In an important study Hans Conzelmann argued that the Lucan presentation of Christian history marked a move away from the earliest Christian proclamation, in the light of the delay of the Parousia.[11] This is not the place to go into all the details of Conzelmann's thesis, but the following general points may be made:

(i) Luke presents a picture of salvation history in which there are clear divisions between three epochs of God's activity. Also, whereas the primitive preaching presupposed that there was an intimate link between the events of Easter and the establishment of the kingdom of God and the return of Christ, Luke dissolves this link by inserting an extended period between the departure of Christ and his return in glory: the era of the Church.

(ii) The centrality of the ascension is the means whereby Luke injects the third period into his salvation of history. The departure of Christ at the end of the Gospel and the beginning of Acts leaves the stage clear for the era of the Church/Spirit, which has to take its course until the return of Christ.

(iii) Luke is writing after the fall of Jerusalem and, as a result, dissolves the link between that event and the return of Christ which seems to be found in Mark 13.[12]

As a result, Conzelmann suggests the following scheme for Luke's understanding of history:

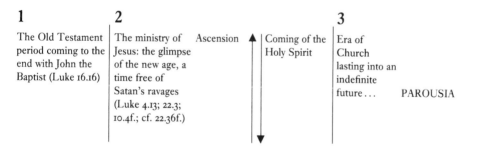

1	2		3
The Old Testament period coming to the end with John the Baptist (Luke 16.16)	The ministry of Jesus: the glimpse of the new age, a time free of Satan's ravages (Luke 4.13; 22.3; 10.4f.; cf. 22.36f.)	Ascension ▲ Coming of the Holy Spirit	Era of Church lasting into an indefinite future ... PAROUSIA

Three other pieces of evidence are pointed to to indicate that Luke was writing in a period when the Parousia hope had faded. First, the Lucan rewriting of Mark 13 indicates that an attempt is being made to 'update' this tradition in the light of history:

(i) The abomination of desolation is equated with the fall of Jerusalem (21.20);

(ii) The times of the Gentiles have to be fulfilled before there can be a change in Jerusalem's fortunes (21.24);

(iii) There is omission of the references to messianic pretenders in Mark 13.21ff.;

(iv) There is a dissolution of the links between the fall of Jerusalem and the coming of the Son of Man; and, finally,

(v) There is an emphasis on the suddenness of the coming (cf. Luke 17.24 but note Mark 13.36).

Secondly, in Acts there is an interest in both church history and church order, both of which, it is suggested, manifest those concerns of the later Church, when it had to come to terms with the need to continue its existence in the world. The writing of a defence of Christianity for Theophilus comes when the need arises to establish the religion and its continued existence in the eyes of the world. Signs of church order can be found in Acts in the emphasis on apostolic ordering of events (Acts 8 and 11), the mention of *episkopoi* in Acts 20.28, the organized apostolic council in Acts 15, and the uniformity in belief and practice which Luke presents as the ideal for church life.

Thirdly, as we have seen, it has been argued that the Lucan concept of ethics is one which tones down the radicalism of Jesus and the primitive Church. Certainly Luke includes the rigorous demands of Jesus and the portrait of the Jerusalem church practising communism but, at the same time, he makes response to Jesus a more manageable exercise: Zacchaeus is said to have given away only half his goods (Luke 19.8; cf. 18.24f.); Ananias and Sapphira are judged not because they refused to lay all their wealth at the apostles' feet but because they deceived the Holy Spirit (Acts 5.4), and, finally, the picture of the relationship between Christians and Romans indicates a wish to come to some kind of accommodation with the state by showing that Roman leaders found nothing wrong with the Christian religion.

Whereas Luke still retains those traditions which speak about the coming of Christ but has used them, it is argued, in such a way that he has subtly played down the centrality of the eschatological expectation, there are other New Testament documents where the Parousia hope in its classic form has faded into the background. Prime among these is the Gospel of John. Here the emphasis is on the new life which can be experienced *now* through belief in Jesus (5.24). The references to the future consummation are there, but are not numerous.[13] The tenor of the Gospel is the relationship which the believer can enjoy with Christ and, through him, with the Father (14.23).[14] Similarly, in the letter to the Ephesians the hope for the future consummation, while certainly present (e.g., 1.10) has moved to the periphery in favour of the present relationship of believers with the exalted Christ (1.23).[15] In Hebrews the heavenly world is the focus of salvation and the orientation of believers. Christ has gone into the heavens, behind the veil, and is there a sure anchor of hope for those who follow him (6.19f.). The hope for a future establishment of the reign of God on earth has not entirely disappeared (12.26), but has moved into the background.[16]

All this evidence has led scholars to argue that already within the New Testament we can find evidence of the disappointment at the failure of the Parousia hope and the need to come to terms with a situation where the

Church might be expected to exist far into the future. The consequence of this was the emergence of what is called 'primitive catholicism' (*Frühkatholizismus*).[17] It has the following characteristics:

(i) A move away from the belief that the goal of the salvation of God is the manifestation of God's righteousness in the world to be replaced by an emphasis on the salvation of the individual and his union with the exalted Christ (e.g., John 14.2; 17.24);

(ii) The need for an ecclesiastical structure to preserve the faith of the apostles from distortions;

(iii) Consequently, the need for a pattern of ministry, which is such that it would act as the prime defence against attack and the main instrument of propaganda;

(iv) The emergence of church life, worship and doctrine as the means of keeping the faithful within the scope of the divine saving activity. This would involve clarity in the delineation of boundaries between true and false religion, those inside and those outside, by initiation and confirmatory rites and actions and a pattern of life, which would be the minimum acceptable for those who joined the community.

That there was a diminution in the hope of the establishment of God's kingdom on earth and the emphasis on the transcendent realm as the goal of the Christian soul can be seen from the evidence of the early Christian texts. We note with interest, for example, the condescending attitude of the early church historian Eusebius of Caesarea (fourth century) who poured scorn on Papias of Hierapolis (early second century) because of his view that the kingdom of God would be set up on earth (*EH* 3.39.11: cf. Cerinthus in Eusebius *EH* 3.28.2). But to speak of the move of eschatology to the margin does not necessarily mean that the delay of the Parousia was a *problem*. It is likely that the failure to see the realization at an early date of the hopes for the coming of the kingdom of God would have caused some embarrassment, *but we must beware that we do not read into the texts an assumption that it was the non-appearance of Christ which necessarily led to a radical rethinking of early Christian thought, away from eschatology to other doctrinal concerns.*[18]

The number of documents from early Christianity covered in the survey of implicit evidence of the delay of the Parousia is a reflection of the way in which this issue has dominated interpretation of the New Testament. Nevertheless one should recognize that such an approach to these documents is not universally accepted. Study of Luke/Acts has not been unanimous in affirming that the dominant concern was the delay of the Parousia, and – what is more – the periodization of history, which we find in these documents, has been considered by other commentators as typical of the New Testament as a whole.[19] Certainly other explanations may be offered of those differences which exist between Luke and Mark, particularly in Luke 21.5ff., which has been regarded as an alternative form of the eschatological discourse rather than a rewriting of it by Luke.[20] What is evident in Luke/Acts (and for that matter the Pastorals also) is the concern to come to terms with the world and present a view of the Christian religion which will enable it to find acceptance by society at large. The need to do this and to tell the story of its origin may *in part* indicate the perspective of one who now feels that an accommodation is needed with the world, because of the problem of having to accept continued existence in it. As such we would be talking about subtle changes in the world view of the Christians rather than a conscious attempt to answer the problem of the delay of the Parousia.

This need to consider the change of emphasis is an important one and corresponds to aspects of Jewish eschatology, which we have examined already.[21] We noted earlier that in the Dead Sea Scrolls there was a clear emphasis on the way in which the holy community could share the lot of heaven, even eschatological bliss, in the present. To be a member of the holy enclave enabled the elect to share the lot of the angels and the joy of the age to come.[22] Jewish apocalyptic has an important vertical dimension to its thought. Thus the apocalyptic seer can already see the glory of the age to come, which is stored up in the treasure-house of heaven.[23] Such a vertical dimension of apocalyptic cosmology may well lie behind the description of the saving process within the letter to the Hebrews. It is not the case, therefore, that the eschatological hope has been abandoned or transferred. Rather, there is concentration in the vertical dimension of that hope, always inherent in Jewish texts, rather than the fulfilment in history. The fact that God's kingdom already exists with God in heaven before it is realized on earth means that to participate in it now means to enjoy the bliss of heaven, which will in due course be manifest on earth. When the letter to the Ephesians speaks of the Church being 'in the heavenly places in Christ' (1.20; 2.6; 3.10; 6.12),[24] and the Jewish-Christian Odes of Solomon depict life within the Christian community as the life of Paradise, we are seeing the switch from the horizontal eschatological expectation to the vertical, from the hope for the realization in history to the experience of that salvation which already exists with God in the realm above. The two positions are not mutually exclusive.

It has been the contention of this study that at the heart of the early Christian message was the belief that in Christ God had acted decisively in history to introduce his promised new age, which would ultimately be manifested in the affairs of men. The central characteristic of New Testament eschatology, therefore, was the tension between the 'now' and the 'not yet'. Already the Christians believed that 'they had tasted the goodness of the word of God and the powers of the age to come' (Heb. 6.5), but that the final completion of God's saving purposes still had to take place.

We have noted that within the apocalyptic framework adopted by the early Christians there lies the resource to cope with the delay in the fulfilment of the promise. As Paul writes to the Colossians, 'your life is hid with Christ in God. When Christ who is our life appears, then you also will appear with him in glory' (3.3f.). Christ was enthroned in heaven, waiting to come to bring to completion the work which had been started in his ministry, at Calvary and in the resurrection (1 Cor. 15.22ff.; Rev. 19.11).[25] Meanwhile it was possible to enjoy the benefits of that heavenly dimension to earthly existence, that inheritance of the saints in light (Col. 1.12) in the old aeon. When fulfilment is delayed and little sign of it is to be seen, an adequate compensation can be found in the present communion with the exalted Christ in heaven (Eph. 1.21). In addition, when believers died and it became imperative to decide their fate in the time which had to pass before Christ came again, the belief in the presence of the soul with Christ gradually emerged, already hinted at in a fragmentary way by Paul himself (Phil. 1.23; 2 Cor. 5).[26] Thus the temporary relationship with the exalted Christ, while the Parousia was awaited, readily became of central importance in itself. What was sought was that reward which was laid up in heaven: freedom from this world and union with Christ in his presence and that of the Father for ever. The heavenly eschatological dimension took over from the earthly eschatology as a more meaningful doctrine for the believer and his pilgrimage.

There emerged an understanding of Christian discipleship which speaks of an earthly pilgrimage and a heavenly destination (1 Pet. 1.4; 2.11; 1.9; 1.17).[27] The use of this language, however, immediately transfers the focus of interest of the believer from his present world to the joys of heaven. This world is not to be changed in the present; it is a place of pilgrimage, even, at times, a snare which might prevent the elect from reaching their true home. Such an outlook contrasts with the bulk of New Testament eschatology and the way in which the apocalyptic cosmology functions in Revelation. There is no question in Revelation that the present tension between heaven and earth, the life of the age to come and this age, is any other than a *temporary* phenomenon and cannot be considered a fact which is accepted as a permanent theological datum.

In the opening chapter of the vision John reaffirms the cosmological dualism, which we find elsewhere in the New Testament. God is enthroned in glory and praised by living creatures and elders. He is hymned as creator of the whole universe, the all holy-God (Rev. 4.11, 8). There is an implicit contrast in this chapter between the dwelling of the holy God in heaven, where God's name is acknowledged and glorified, and the earth below where the ways of God are rejected.[28] The references to the unwillingness of mankind to repent later in the vision indicate that the world below did not share the beliefs of the heavenly hosts as they sang the praises of God (e.g., 9.20f.). This is also confirmed when we look at Revelation 5. Here the seer is shown a scroll which no one had been found worthy to open (5.3). As we soon learn, the scroll's opening is of great importance because it inaugurates the eschatological woes, which must precede the setting up of the kingdom of God (6. 8–9, 16). The seer weeps because no one has been found who can open the scroll. Once again the implication is that the purposes of God in the world are not being carried out, and the grief of the seer indicates the longing for that day of righteousness (cf. 6.9). The coming of a lamb who bore the marks of slaughter to God to receive and open the scroll is the essential initiative, which marks the beginning of the fulfilment of the purposes of God.

What must be noted is the contrast between these two chapters and the consummation of God's purposes in chapter 21. At the climax of the book John sees a new heaven and a new earth; but the significant thing about the new creation is that it does not retain the cosmological dualism of the old creation; heaven is no longer the dwelling place of the holy God separated from men who dwell on earth. Now the tabernacle of God is with men (Rev. 21.3). A situation, in which there existed a contrast between the world of light and the world of darkness, heaven and earth, above and below, is not maintained. It is contrary to the divine purpose, whose sole direction is towards the abolition of that dichotomy which exists between the kingdom of God in heaven and its absence on earth. What the book of Revelation sets out to show is how the petition of the Lord's Prayer is fulfilled; how God's kingdom comes on earth as it is in heaven. In so doing, it refuses to allow the possibility of a fixed cosmology, in which earth and heaven are eternally polarized. Heaven cannot be seen as an escape from things on earth, at least as a permanent solution to the problems of humanity and theology. The controlling vision is the new creation; in it the dichotomy is swept away and the tension resolved.

A religious outlook which fossilizes the present contrast between heaven and earth as being of the essence of things is guilty of transforming the visionary idealism into mystical escapism. To make the pilgrimage to heaven the goal of the Christian discipleship is to accept the cosmos as it is, with its principalities and powers intact, and to treat the realm above as a haven from the world, whose end is destruction and nature evil. The end of this interpretative road is Gnosticism.

(d) The Rise of Gnosticism[1]

The heavenly dimension to earthly existence is found in its most acute form in Gnosticism, a religious outlook whose main feature is its claim to radical otherworldliness. From the second century onwards we have documentary evidence of religious systems, which purport to offer explanations of the origin of the world and of evil, together with the means whereby the individual can achieve salvation in a world beyond. The key to this process of salvation is 'gnosis', knowledge. Gnosticism is salvation by knowledge, 'knowing whence one has come and whither one will go' (Pirke Aboth. 3.1).[2]

Apart from their claim to offer salvation by knowledge the gnostic systems of the second century and later are characterized by the rigid separation of the cosmos into two separate realms, of darkness and light, of spirit and matter. This separation manifests itself in gnostic texts in two ways: first of all, a separation between the created world and a higher realm, the former being the creation of an inferior divinity, usually identified with the God of Israel; secondly, theological dualism, the division between a supreme being and an inferior being, the product of a mistake in the cosmic process. In the developed systems much is made of the reasons why this lesser being was created and all that emanates from this mistake, as well as of the relationship between man and the highest divine being. Humanity is the result of the creation of the lower being (demiurge) but is also the result of some knowledge of the character of the highest beings. Thus in the gnostic work, the Hypostasis of the Archons,[3] man is said to have been created in the image of a reflection in the waters of something greater, glimpsed by the inferior divine being. The fact that man has the spark of divinity within himself indicates why it is that some men have the glimpse of eternity and by their knowledge of their origin and destiny are enabled to see creation for what it really is and seek their true origin in the highest celestial spheres.

The consequences of this kind of theology were manifold. First, it led to a disparagement of this world as part of a lower order. Such views owed much to popular philosophical ideas, influenced by Platonism.[4] This rejection of the world finds its classic expression in the religion of the Manichees,[5] to which Augustine for a time gave his allegiance.[6] Secondly, it led to a conflicting attitude towards ethical behaviour. On the one hand, there were those who argued that because the world and the flesh were the creations of an inferior being and that the essential nature of man had nothing to do with this world, it mattered little how he behaved.[7] On the other hand, there were those whose behaviour can be characterized as ascetic. For them it was necessary to eschew the things of this world as tainted by the flesh and to pursue only the things of the spirit. Abstinence from sexual activity and from certain kinds of food and drink as well as the avoidance of too much contact with society at large are all features of this kind of attitude.[8]

The major problem for the student of primitive Christianity is the issue of gnostic origins. It is clear that by the middle of the second century AD, Gnosticism was a series of major religious systems, and was probably the dominant form of Christianity espoused by several religious communities.[9] There are wide differences of opinion among scholars about the extent to which the New Testament writings themselves exhibit the influence of gnostic religion.[10] Some would argue that Gnosticism is essentially a

Christian heresy. While there may be hints in the New Testament that ideas similar to those found in the later gnostic texts may have been in the air at the time, it is suggested that Christianity was the catalyst, which led to the formation of these ideas into the coherent religious systems, which we find in fully fledged Gnosticism.[11] For these scholars there can be no suggestion that Gnosticism as we know it in the second century was a major factor in the development of Christian doctrine, at least in the most formative period of its development.

The evidence adduced in support of this position is quite substantial. It is pointed out that the documentary evidence for Gnosticism comes from a period well *after* the emergence of Christianity. The great gnostic systems of Marcion, Basilides and Valentinus emerged during a period well into the second century AD. What is more, many of the gnostic texts from Nag Hammadi in Egypt, which have been discovered over recent years, exhibit Christian influence either explicitly or implicitly. The fact that the documentary evidence comes from a period later than the time of writing of the bulk of the New Testament has persuaded many that we should not assume that Gnosticism was a significant religious movement at the time of the emergence of Christianity.

On the other side, there are those who refuse to accept that Gnosticism is only a deviant form of Christianity and argue that the Christian elements are merely an alien accretion to an otherwise coherent religious system, which evinces the major characteristics of the spirit of the late Hellenistic age. The discovery of a library of gnostic texts at Nag Hammadi in Upper Egypt has set study of Gnosticism on a completely new footing. Certainly the texts as they stand were written much later than the first century, but there are signs that they may contain systems which have little or no Christian influence. Of course, this is still a matter for debate, and we still await a much more systematic evaluation of the evidence from Nag Hammadi. While it may be true that the systems of Basilides *et al.* do not themselves seem to have influenced early Christian writers in the first century AD, there are indications from the Nag Hammadi texts that a pre- (and therefore non-) Christian Gnosticism looks much more likely.

It has to be stressed that the essential features of fully fledged Gnosticism are not without doubt pre-Christian. That characteristic of Gnosticism, metaphysical dualism, cannot be shown to have existed before the first century AD. But there are indications that suggest that several religious currents may have been well on the way to what was later to emerge as Gnosticism. This is even true of Judaism,[12] which may be a very surprising assertion, in the light of the fact that several of the gnostic texts are explicitly anti-Jewish in character. In Marcion's system, for example, the God of the Jews is relegated to a subordinate position as creator of the world, the God of the Old Testament, opposed to the God revealed by Jesus and his apostle

Paul, the supreme being unknown to the OT writers. The ridicule attached to the God of the Jews seems to indicate that Gnosticism emerged in an environment separated from Judaism. Much evidence suggests that the reverse may at least sometimes have been the case.[13] There are many Jewish elements in the gnostic texts, which could not have been assimilated from the Old Testament alone and indicate influence from extra-canonical Jewish material.[14] Certainly by the time we reach the second-century systems, we have viewpoints which are clearly anti-Jewish. What we have to ask ourselves is whether in the process, which led to this position, we may not have evidence of the theological ideas of certain groups on the fringe of Judaism. There are signs that certain parts of Jewish theology had made a distinction between the appearance of God and his indefinable essence.[15] Dualism of quite a significant kind can be found in several documents from pre-Christian Judaism. The connection between this dualistic language and the abandonment of the God of Israel is tenuous and the links in the chain are at present obscure. The hints are that some kind of link does indeed exist, even if we cannot at present be entirely sure what led to the conclusions of the second-century Gnostics.[16]

(e) Odium Humani Generis

It is commonly assumed that there was a consistent harassment of Christians by the state during the first three hundred years of the existence of Christianity. That the early Christians did from time to time meet with disapproval and penalties from administrators is not in doubt, but it would be false to suppose that there was a coherent policy laid down by the emperors, which was ruthlessly prosecuted throughout the various territories under Roman jurisdiction.[1]

It should be noted that martyrdom was not something which was unfamiliar to the religious tradition in which the early Christians grew up.[2] Ancient Judaism had given much weight to the vicarious significance of martyrdom, and similar themes are to be found in most early Christian works, stemming, of course, from what Christians regarded as the ultimate example of martyrdom, the death of Jesus of Nazareth.[3] The letters of Ignatius show the intense preoccupation with death which gripped the Bishop of Antioch as he journeyed to Rome. To follow in the steps of his master was a calling greater than any which could be offered, and he is anxious to avoid any hindrance to the fulfilment of this goal. Similar examples can be found in the martyrologies of the early Christian period.

But surely we cannot lay the blame for martyrdom solely at the feet of the Christian infatuation with self-sacrifice? The answer to that is almost certainly, No. Tertullian (*Apology* 40.2) makes the point that when things were going wrong in city, or Empire, scapegoats were needed and the

Christians proved to be eminently suitable candidates.[4] Why should this have been so? Almost certainly the reason for this was the unpatriotic nature of Christian belief. Like the Jews Christians steadfastly refused to worship the gods of the Romans or to show allegiance to the Empire by burning a pinch of incense to the genius of the Emperor.

The incident which is described during the last moments of the venerable bishop of Smyrna, Polycarp, graphically illustrates this (Martyrdom of Polycarp 9.2). In this story the aged Christian refuses the plea of the Roman officer to save himself by buring incense to the genius of the Emperor. The problem posed by the Christians was quite simply this: when it came to the crunch, could they really be trusted as loyal citizens? Were they not after all subversives who were not ultimately interested in the well-being of the Empire? Did they not despise the local and imperial gods by refusing to worship them? When things went wrong, the fault was laid at the door of those who had been guilty of angering the gods. This may already have happened in the case of the fire of Rome in the early sixties when Nero laid the blame on the Christians and, so Tacitus tells us (*Annals* 15.44), many suffered as a result. But it is also true that at other times Christians proved to be scapegoats because of their ambivalence with regard to the state.

This hostility towards Christians did not always manifest itself in the form of *official* opprobrium. The Martyrdom of Polycarp indicates that proceedings against Polycarp were set in action as the result of the initiative taken by the local populace. Certainly there is evidence to indicate that Emperors and administrators did from time to time take the initiative in proceedings against the Christians. Usually, however, the fears of the majority with regard to deviants in their society were the main cause of hostility and persecution. Despite all the protestations of the Christian apologists, nothing could be said which could remove the stigma of disloyalty to the Empire, which manifested itself in what to early Christians seemed to be entirely religious scruples, the wholehearted devotion to the God of Israel and his Messiah. That was regarded by non-Christians as a profoundly political statement and the rejection of the ultimate position of Rome in the lives and affections of believers. Indeed, when we come to the major persecutions, it is probable that one of the principal reasons for taking this kind of action was the subversion of traditional Roman values, which was believed to have taken place as the result of the growing influence of Christianity throughout the Empire.[5] The religion of the state was rigorously eschewed by the Christians. Those who were adherents of the new religion rejected the pattern of practices which were at the heart of the traditional religion. This applied just as much to the position of Christians within the local city-states. Their attitude towards the local tutelary gods was equally uncompromising. We may compare the attitude of local people towards Christians at the beginning of the Christian era with the severe bouts of anti-

Catholic fever which spread through the populace of England at times of greatest political threat. A threat to the religion of the established Church was a threat to the monarchy and the constitution. Catholics owed their allegiance not to the crown but to the Bishop of Rome, who was himself supported by *catholic* monarchs. It is only by understanding this political dimension to the refusal of Christians to acknowledge Roman and local deities in the customary way that we can understand why it was that at times so much hostility was generated against early Christians throughout the Empire, more by local pressure than the edicts of the Roman administrators.

Yet in the earliest period the strongest pressure on Christians came from elsewhere, and it is to this we must turn.

(f) The Separation of Church and Synagogue

It is important for any understanding of Jewish and Christian origins that proper consideration is given to the impact of the fall of Jerusalem in AD 70 on both Christians as well as Jews and its consequences. According to rabbinic tradition, in the wake of the fall of Jerusalem a group of Jewish sages and Pharisees met at Jamnia (Yavneh) and set about picking up the pieces of Judaism.

Much has been written in recent years of the council (if such it was) of rabbis, which met at Jamnia (Yavneh) and which was largely responsible for setting Judaism on its feet after the débâcle of AD 70.[1] Clearly this had important implications for the nascent Christian sect as well as for later rabbinic Judaism, as it helped to define, at least in part, the conditions in which it would be possible for an individual or groups to relate to the religious reorganization, which had gone on at Jamnia. While there is still much uncertainty about the various resolutions which were carried during the years when the rabbis met to reorganize Judaism, several matters do seem to have been decided upon during those years.[2] One of the most important decisions, and the one which was to affect the Christians most of all, was the reformulation of the *'amidah* or *tefillah*, the major synagogue prayer to form the *Shemoneh Esreh*.[3] The Eighteen Benedictions included one (the twelfth), which effectively excluded all significantly deviant religious groups from participating in the religious life of the synagogues under the jurisdiction of the council of Jamnia. The *birkath ha-minim* (the 'blessing' = curse of the heretics), as it is euphemistically referred to, makes it difficult for those who rejected the rabbinic interpretation to participate in the synagogue liturgy. There has been much debate whether the earliest version of this benediction also included a specific reference to the Christians. Certainly one of the earliest versions of the benediction does indeed explicitly mention the Christians (*Notzrim*):

For the renegades let there be no hope, and may the arrogant kingdom soon be rooted out in our days, and the Nazarenes (*notzrim*) and the *minim* perish as in a moment and be blotted out from the book of life and with the righteous may they not be inscribed. Blessed art thou, O Lord, who humblest the arrogant.[4]

If Justin is to be believed, we may suppose that by his day (the second or third decade of the second century AD at the latest), a curse on the Christians did form part of the regular pattern of synagogue worship.

According to Jewish tradition, therefore, the council meeting at Jamnia took steps to exclude heretics from the life of the synagogue. In other words, the opportunity was taken at this time to formalize what amounted to a ban on the use of synagogues under the influence of the Jamnian authorities, by those whose adherence to certain interpretations of the Jewish traditions was suspect; though whether a specific indictment on Christians formed part of the *earliest* prayer is still uncertain.[5]

The reasons which led to this formula are not easy to ascertain. It would, of course, be wrong to suppose that it was only after the destruction of the Temple that a need was felt to discipline those suspected of wayward beliefs. The evidence from the New Testament itself, which can be dated before AD 70, suggests that, long before this time, various groups had disciplinary measures, which allowed them to punish, and ultimately to exclude, those who deviated to any great degree from the pattern of religion which the group found acceptable.[6] In 2 Corinthians 11.24f. Paul talks of punishment from fellow-Jews, and, even if we are to date Acts after the fall of Jerusalem, it is difficult to ignore the evidence that we find there, of official harassment of Christians (4.5ff.; 5.27ff.; 6.12ff.), exclusion from synagogues (13.45f.), and Jewish suspicion (17.5f.; 18.12ff.; 20.3; 21.27; 23.20; cf. 28.21). Nevertheless the picture, as it emerges in Acts, is hardly of the situation where members of the Christian sect find themselves excluded from the Jewish synagogues on a regular basis. Indeed, according to Acts 17.1ff. (cf. 21.21) Paul is presented as being able to go into the various synagogues to dispute with those who attended. Thus it would appear that the situation, as it is portrayed in Acts, is much more fluid than was the case in Justin's day.

In a sense, this is exactly what we should expect within the Judaism which existed before AD 70. While it may be true that the Sanhedrin which met in Jerusalem exercised a significant role within Jewish life by regulating religious practice,[7] the possibility of making this formal control a reality in practice must have been extremely limited. From what we know of Jewish religion before the fall of Jerusalem, the very variety made strict control of belief and practice impossible. After a terrible war when many had been killed and the future looked bleak, the chances of a small group taking the initiative and directing the course of a religious tradition was much more possible than when there existed various sects, with varying degrees of difference, which asserted their right to interpret the common religious tradition. What struggles went on before this group eventually triumphed, we have no means of knowing; after all, the Jewish traditions which have come down to us are in the main the property of the triumphant party, or at least have been subject to later reflection by that party. With the exception of the Christian texts, which, at least explicitly, are silent on this issue, the tensions felt by those who could not wholeheartedly subscribe to the Hillelite position cannot now be known. That Sadducees, Essenes and more closely related groups like Shammaite Pharisaism did experience great heart-searching cannot be in doubt,[8] for the long cherished beliefs of a sect are never easily subordinated to the interpretations of an opponent. Ultimately, however, that was the crisis which faced Jews of all persuasions after the fall of Jerusalem, and the emergence of pharisaic-rabbinic Judaism as the dominant religious force. The group which took the initiative at Jamnia dictated the terms which covered the ways in which those who wished to affirm their allegiance to the interpretation of the Jewish tradition would have to accept.

The disentanglement of the relationship between the Christians and the rabbis of Jamnia is a task which still awaits completion, though, of course, the paucity of information at our disposal makes the completion of it a very difficult enterprise. The fact remains that, however strained relationships may have been between Christians and certain Jews before the fall of Jerusalem and with the rabbis at Jamnia afterwards, there is little doubt that the early Christians still endeavoured to maintain the belief that their convictions about Jesus made them a legitimate, indeed *the* legitimate, continuation of the biblical traditions. The point at issue between Jews and Christians, therefore, was the legitimacy of a certain form of interpretation of the ancestral traditions which, because of its claim to have ascertained the ultimate reality in the life of the new age and through the ministry of Jesus of Nazareth, had the effect of rendering other interpretations at best inadequate and at worst redundant. The exclusivism of early Christianity should not blind us, however, to the grasp, which many of the Christian writers had, of the essential nature of their continuity with the Jewish tradition.

(g) You are his Disciples but we are Disciples of Moses

While recognizing that the Pauline corpus offers us important insights into the debates which were going on between one part of the Christian movement and other Jews, the most extended discussions of relations with other Jews who do not accept the authority and mission of Jesus, is to be found in the Fourth Gospel. Throughout the first twelve chapters it is *Jewish* issues (festivals, practices, authority) which are examined in the light of the claim made right at the start of the Gospel that in Jesus of Nazareth 'the

Word became flesh and dwelt among us'. Stress on the Jewishness of the Fourth Gospel may cause some surprise.[1] After all, for years it has been said that the Fourth Gospel is the most Hellenized book in the New Testament. But apart from the dangers of driving too large a wedge between Judaism and Christianity, it is difficult to offer an interpretation of the Fourth Gospel, which does not take full account of the intense debates about Jews and Judaism in the first part of the Gospel. As many scholars have pointed out, particularly in the last two decades, but some long before, there is evidence of knowledge of a vast range of Jewish traditions barely beneath the surface of the Gospel. Indeed, without recourse to the knowledge which we have of contemporary Judaism, it becomes impossible to see the force of the argument of the Evangelist.

Of course, it has been since the discovery of the Dead Sea Scrolls that we have had what may be called 'the New Look' at the Fourth Gospel.[2] In dramatic fashion various parts of the Scrolls have confirmed not that the Dead Sea Scrolls provided the *origin* of the Johannine imagery but that the kind of ideas which we find in the Gospel would have been entirely at home within Palestinian Judaism. Thus since the Second World War we have witnessed a complete change in the character of Johannine scholarship as more and more scholars have sought to utilize Jewish material to illuminate the ideas of this Gospel.

Even the most ardent supporter of the Jewish approach to the theology of the New Testament cannot fail to note the very polemical statement, which we find from time to time in the Fourth Gospel. In it the hostility between Jesus and his Jewish opponents reaches such a level that in 8.44 Jesus accuses the Jews of having the Devil as their father. This anti-Jewish tone should not be mistaken for a rejection of the Jewish heritage or even an incipient anti-Semitism. As Professor Wayne Meeks has rightly suggested, 'the Fourth Gospel is most anti-Jewish just at the points it is most Jewish'.[3] Virulent polemic against the Jews is a reflection of the rejection not of the insights and traditions of Judaism, but the use which was made of them which led some Jews to reject Jesus of Nazareth. Indeed, throughout the Gospel we find an evident concern to demonstrate that the very traditions which, other Jews assert, point in the direction of *their* particular interpretation, should rather be seen as vindicating the Jewish-Christian position. Thus Moses is summoned as a witness to Jesus (5.45) as also is Abraham (8.56). Scripture itself points forward to Jesus (5.39f.), and the prophet Isaiah himself saw the glory of the pre-existent one (12.41). What is going on in the Fourth Gospel, therefore, is an attempt to harness those same traditions, which also formed the basis of the rival group's interpretation of religion, in favour of the Christian position.

No doubt the result of all this, as we find it in the Fourth Gospel, is the subordination of the Torah to the revelation of God in Jesus (1.17). But the antithesis between the Law, which came through Moses, and the grace and truth, which came through Jesus Christ, does not mean that there is an implicit denial that *any* grace and truth was manifested in the Law. Rather, as Pancaro has asserted,[4] 1.17 should be seen as a perspective on the Law in the light of the coming of Christ. As we have noted, the Fourth Evangelist is anxious to have the Scriptures on his side of the argument. Thus, although it is clear that he still wants to appeal to the Law, the disparaging references to the Law, as if it was something alien from the Christians (8.17; 10.34; 15.25), are best explained as references to the way in which the Law was interpreted by emerging orthodox Judaism, or, if the Gospel was written before the fall of Jerusalem,[5] the Jewish opponents with whom the Fourth Evangelist is interacting. Thus with the advent of the Word made flesh, the Law had to be seen in a completely new light. It was not a means by which the whole of existence could be organized as if it alone were the definitive revelation of God, but something which pointed forward to the revelation of the way, the truth and the life of Christ (14.6).

Study of the Fourth Gospel over the last two decades has moved in the direction of considering the Gospel and the related Epistles as the products of a Jewish-Christian community engaged in the struggle to justify their existence over against Jews who disagree profoundly about the relationship of Jesus to Jewish traditions. Thus we are faced with a struggle not so much between two religions as between rival interpretations by two (possibly more) mutually antagonistic groups.[6] Of course, we are in possession of only one side of this debate, and we have to face the fact that the position of the opponents, as it is reflected in the Fourth Gospel, may be something of a caricature. What we can do at present, however, is to see how, in one important episode, the Fourth Evangelist characterizes the relationship between the opponents and his own group as evidence of the feelings of the Christian side with regard to their opponents, if not the actual position of the opponents themselves.

In John 9 we have the account of the healing of a blind man by Jesus, which took place on the sabbath day (9.14).[7] In performing the healing, Jesus actually engaged in work by making clay with which he anointed the man's eyes (v.6), after which the man went to bathe in the pool of Siloam. The blind man is denounced to the Pharisees and an inquiry is initiated by the Pharisees as to the nature of the healing (v.15f.). In this process Jesus plays no part and is only mentioned in the discussion; he appears finally to receive the confession of faith of the blind man at the end of the chapter (vv.35ff.). Throughout the ensuing interrogation the blind man steadfastly maintains his belief that Jesus must be a man sent from God (v.33), even a prophet (v.17). The miracle is differently interpreted by the Jewish opponents. Some refuse to believe that a man who broke the sabbath could be from God (v.16), whereas others emphasize the importance of the miracle as a sign of the divine commission (v.16b). Ultimately the man born blind is faced with a test: 'Give God the praise; we know that this man is a sinner' (v.24). In the following verses it becomes apparent that there will be no going back by the blind man on his conviction that the man who wrought such a wonderful deed on his behalf must be from God (v.33). The issue is then polarized by the Jewish opponents, between the discipleship which can trace its origin back to Moses and the new-fangled interpretations, whose authority stems only from 'this man' (v.28f.). The unwillingness of the man born blind to deny that Jesus was sent from God leads to his expulsion from the synagogue (it may be assumed in the light of v.22 that this was from the synagogue, though this is not stated in v.34). After this he meets Jesus and confesses his faith in Jesus as the Son of Man (v.38).

In the light of the editorial addition in v.22, it is difficult to resist the conclusion that an issue is being considered in this chapter, which has direct relevance to the life of the Johannine community and its relationship with Jews, who did not accept Jesus as Messiah. The fear of the parents of the man born blind is indicative of a fear of overt Christian profession in the light of a formal decision to exclude Christians from the synagogue (7.13; 12.42; 20.19). The word *aposynagogos* is used three times in the Gospel, and only in this work in the whole of the New Testament (9.22; 12.42; 16.2; cf. Luke 6.22).[8] Most commentators are agreed that it refers to one of the major problems confronting the Johannine community, as it seeks to understand its position over against other Jews.[9] As part of this process of self-understanding, the story of the man born blind plays a significant part. He it is who is on trial as an unrepentant adherent to the authenticity of the mission of Jesus. With some justification it has been pointed out that the story of the healing itself contains some fairly explicit christological and ecclesiological features. Most obvious of all is the interpretative gloss on the meaning of Siloam (v.7). The identification of bathing in Siloam with the one who is sent picks up one of the dominant christological themes in the Gospel. The obvious implication of v.7, therefore, is that bathing in the pool of Siloam is seen by the Evangelist as a type of Christian baptism, a belief which seems to be confirmed, when we note that language about anointing and enlightening (vv.6 and 39) are also used, both of which have baptismal overtones.[10] The man born blind, whose healing leads him to affirm that Jesus is a prophet sent from God, finds himself put in the position of being on trial for his conviction. At last he is brought before the Pharisees and commanded, 'Give God the praise; we know that this man is a sinner' (v.24).[11] This formula, familiar to us from the Old Testament, is a means whereby an individual is asked to confess his sin, in this case his conviction that a man who, by his healing on the *sabbath*, has shown himself to be a sinner (Jos. 7.19; 1 Sam. 6.5; cf. *M. San.* 6.2). The purpose of this demand is to persuade the man to withdraw his earlier support for Jesus (v.17), by indicating to him that in the eyes of the Pharisees what Jesus has done rather suggests that he is a sinner inspired by the Devil (cf. Luke 11.15). Thus any one who sides with a man like this puts himself in an incriminating position also.[12] The refusal of the man born blind to accept the position of the Pharisees and instead to affirm that such a miracle must indicate a divine origin for Jesus' authority (cf. 8.48; *b. San.* 90a; *b. Berak.* 58a)[13] can only lead to his rejection by the Pharisees as the disciple of a charlatan whose authority and office have not been authenticated (v.29).

This story has been the starting point for several discussions of the provenance of the Fourth Gospel. The formal decision by the Jews to eject from the synagogue any who confessed Jesus as the Messiah, is said to be particularly connected with the *birkath ha-minim*. So in John 9 we find an example of the Christian response to this bar on Jewish-Christian participation in the liturgy of the synagogue. Commentators, therefore, tend to see the chapter as a skilful projection onto the life of Jesus of the debate between Jews and Christians going on in the Evangelist's day.[14] The assumption has been that the bulk of the story of the encounter between the man born blind and the Jewish authorities is considered to be the work of the Evangelist. Nevertheless the importance of the *birkath ha-minim* should not blind us to the fact that regulations for heresy were in force long before the fall of Jerusalem. To say that the story may have an appositeness for the situation of Jewish-Christians agonizing over their relationship with the synagogue after the promulgation of the *birkath ha-minim*, need not necessarily lead to the conclusion that the investigation, which follows the healing miracle, is merely the invention of the Evangelist. It seems that there could well have been traditions of Christians facing various forms of exclusion from the synagogue circulating before AD 70, whose appropriateness was seen in a completely new light after that date.[15] It is the gloss added by the Evangelist in v.22, which makes the story particularly related to the messiahship of Jesus and appears to give the exclusion a fairly permanent quality.[16] Whatever the history of the tradition of this incident may have been, there can be no doubt that as far as the Fourth Evangelist is concerned, the story is working on two different levels. The incident dealing with the exclusion of a man, whose blindness is healed by Jesus on the sabbath, has become a paradigm of the way of true discipleship for the Church of his own day. For him the Pharisees and Jews, who range themselves against the blind man and resolve to exclude those who confess Jesus as the Messiah from their synagogue, are typical of the hostility of Jews in his day, whose determination to rid themselves of the Christian interpretation of the Torah has led them to take the extreme course of excluding Christians from their synagogues.

It is when we begin to interpret the Johannine traditions (some of which may well have a long history in the community, going back to the very

305

beginnings of its existence)[17] in the light of the pressing need of Christians to explain their beliefs about Jesus over against the rival interpretations of non-Christian Judaism, that we shall understand the way in which the polemic is directed in the Gospel. Indeed, at many points it is not too difficult to find echoes of charges levelled against Jesus, which make their appearance from time to time within the Jewish traditions. For example, Jesus' role as a magician and deceiver (*b. San.* 43a; cf. 89a, 107b; *b. Sotah.* 47a; Justin *Dial.* 69; Origen, *Contra Cels.* 3.4)[18] is hinted at in various places (7.14ff.; 7.45ff.; 9.24ff.; 18.19ff.; cf. Deut. 13, 18.20–2).[19] What is more, the origin of Jesus in heaven and his authority is an issue which provokes much discussion (7.15ff.; 8.23ff.). The claim to exclusive revelation and the validity of the descent and ascent to heaven is maintained not only in the face of rejection of the validity of such claims in some quarters (*b. Sukkah* 5a; *j. Ta'anith* 65b) but also the frequency of the belief that others as well as Jesus had ascended into the world above and had ascertained the divine secrets (3.13). What we have in the Fourth Gospel, therefore, is an attempt to present Jesus' origin and authority in the light of the conviction that he has descended from heaven, direct from the Father's side as the authentic revelation of the Father and the speaker of his words (6.46; cf. 1.18). Thus those interpretations of Jesus, which view his claims as contumacious, his miracles as diabolically inspired, and his activity generally as indicative of heresy rather than divine vocation, are rejected as stemming from an inadequate view of the divine origin of his person and work.

This feature of the theology of the Fourth Gospel raises an issue of considerable importance in the discussions between Jesus and his opponents in the Gospel. The quotation from John 9 which heads this section indicates not only a polarization of opinions, but also a contrast in the different understandings of authority which exist between the two sets of disciples. The question of authority is one which we have had reason to mention already in this study.[20] It runs throughout the Gospel, and is particularly prominent in the opening twelve chapters.

When Jesus cleanses the Temple in Jerusalem, this act is taken as a sign of prophetic authority, and the opponents ask Jesus to justify the basis of this authority (2.18f.).[21] In the discourse with Nicodemus, Jesus, for the first time, indicates his importance by telling Nicodemus of his heavenly knowledge (3.11ff.), a theme taken up in the strange soliloquy of the Baptist in 3.31ff. The link between authority and the one who sent Jesus makes its first appearance on the lips of Jesus in 4.34 and it is a theme which is taken up on many occasions throughout the Gospel: Jesus is the one who is sent by the Father to do his works and speak his words.[22]

The point is rammed home with a repetitious regularity. Little justification is offered for this claim, apart from Jesus' own testimony that he has been with the Father and heard directly from him and seen his face (6.46;

3.13). The fact that Jesus is of the world above is basis enough for the claim he makes to speak directly of the things of God (8.23). The proof of Jesus' authority, however, is something which falls short of full demonstration. The reason for this is that the claim comes independently of the accepted channels of authority in other Jewish circles. Indeed the claim is made more problematical by virtue of the fact that it involves the claimant in acts which seem to be flagrant denials of the validity of the usual patterns of authority and prescriptions for action (9.16). This is an issue which touches on one of the most sensitive areas of early Christian faith and practice.

Thus the Gospel presents us with the most consistent attempt to focus on the important issue of authority within Judaism and the implications for faith in Jesus, arguing the claim that he spoke the things of God. It reminds us that the early Christian movement did present a significant threat to some patterns of interpretation and authority in Judaism. It would, however, be a mistake to suppose that such a threat was in any way unique. There was not something so peculiar about Christianity which made it without parallel among the Jewish groups of the period. The fact is that Christianity presented approaches to the Jewish traditions which raised problems of an acute kind, not without parallel but posing the question in the starkest possible form. What we see in the Fourth Gospel is a literary reflection of one issue which was to help precipitate the parting of the ways between some Jewish Christians (though not all)[23] and those Jews who did not accept the messiahship of Jesus and may have had its part to play in the formation of rabbinic Judaism. It indicates, too, that the major tensions were located in an internal Jewish dispute over the Jewish tradition and the authority which should guide the interpretation of that tradition.

Elsewhere in the New Testament there is a similar setting for these disputes. In Hebrews, for example, discussion focuses on the cult in an argument which stresses the inferiority of present cultic practice and its religious efficacy, as compared with the priestly offering of Jesus (Heb. 7–10).[24] Christ has entered the heavenly shrine, where God dwells.[25] There is nothing un-Jewish about the ideas used here, but the circumstances have demanded that contrasts be made between the use of tradition by Christians, in particular their eschatological framework (e.g., Heb. 1.2) and non-Christian Jews. Opponents had played down the significance of Christ (Heb. 1–2) and the recipients of the letter were in danger of relapsing into a pattern of Jewish interpretation, which did not allow for the messiahship of Jesus (6.5f.; 10.26; 10.32f.; 12.25ff.; 13.10f.).[26] Accordingly, the writer finds it necessary to define the boundaries anew and thereby affirms the ultimate character of the Christ-event and its consequences for the interpretation of the Jewish tradition. In Matthew discussion over righteousness[27] involves a recognition of both positive and negative features of contemporary Jewish practice (Matt. 23.2f.) and a demand that the Christian response should

307

exceed that of the Scribes (Matt. 5.22). In this Gospel we can detect an attempt to define where the boundaries are to be drawn between Christian and non-Christian Jews,[28] possibly in the light of the debates at Jamnia. It represents another testimony to that necessity felt by some Jewish-Christians to crystallize the differences between their interpretation and that of those who disagreed with them.

EPILOGUE

At the end of my book on apocalyptic, I suggested that an exploration of the wider hermeneutical issues arising out of my study would have to be left for another occasion. One friend pointed out (quite rightly) that the interpretative process had been going on all the way through the book. In this book, I think I have been more conscious from the very start of the inevitably complex process of interpretation, which goes on in any attempt to write on Christian origins. The choice and the presentation of the material and the methodological assumptions tell as much about the interpreter and his view of reality as the character of the ideas and the movements which he or she is examining. For some this might be a fatal chink in the armour of academic objectivity; but I do not think that the fact that we can begin to recognize the factors, which dispose us to particular interpretative positions, is a matter for which to apologize. I have little doubt that a greater understanding of the world in which I live and work and my own place within it has helped and not hindered my understanding of Christian origins, though the final judgement on that must be left to others.

The perceptive reader will have noted, without too much difficulty, the theological struggle which has been going on in the foregoing pages. It is one which has beset Christians in every generation, namely the conflicting claims of a utopian message and the pragmatic approach needed to deal with an unregenerate world. I hope that what I have written, particularly in the last part of the book, is not merely a projection of a present problem for Christians, though I recognize that it is a concern which has catalysed the presentation of the issues. Some may consider that it is wrong to suppose that the 'cognitive dissonance' suffered by millenarian or utopian groups is common to groups and individuals in different ages. It may be that I have been guilty of causing the divide between the strange world of Christian origins and our own to collapse; that is a risk that all interpreters have to run.

The present is a difficult time for those whose inclinations lead them to sympathize with the utopian wing of the primitive Church. It is probably because liberal views have become so widely accepted that not enough thinking has gone on in support of such positions. It is not my concern in this book to answer twentieth-century problems via first-century texts and ideas. Nevertheless I believe that it has been possible to isolate a recurring issue for Christians of all shades of opinion: the resolution of the tension (if that is the appropriate goal) between the vision of the new creation and the life of the old. It has been a central thesis of this book that a fundamental feature of early Christian literature, particularly the Pauline corpus of writings, is dealing with this eschatological inheritance.

Exegetes tend to be suspicious of those of their number who transgress the boundaries of their specialisms. I am aware that I have done this all the way through this book, and there will be many occasions when I have shown my ignorance not only of particular fields of Judaism and Christianity but also of other theological disciplines, ancient history and the social sciences. Perhaps I should have stayed with the apocalypses. Yet I am aware that the future of exegesis lies with the attempt to say more than what actually happened. Some of the most stimulating exegesis has come from the pens of those who have had a profound interest in wider theological and social issues. One only has to mention the name of Rudolf Bultmann to be reminded how exegesis and theology can come together in a creative and provocative way. It may be argued that it was precisely because Bultmann allowed his exegesis to be clouded with other assumptions that his work has not stood the test of time. For all the shortcomings of his interpretation, the stimulating exposition of central New Testament themes, dependent as it is on a debt to contemporary philosophy, has yielded many profound insights, which, arguably, would not have been forthcoming without that creative interaction. There are other contemporary exegetes, who find in the biblical writings issues which may indirectly at least have an impact on the contemporary Church. Perhaps they are guilty of causing the gulf which exists between the New Testament and ourselves to collapse. One who stresses the unbridgeability of the gap is just as much open to criticism, in denying the common features which exist in various areas of human experience and ignoring the rich possibilities of interpretative approaches other than the historical-critical method. Assertion of common ground should not be taken as a datum, but should always be open to the criticism of further information of the world of late antiquity and the different perspectives on common problems which that world offered.

Today, in our concern about nuclear weapons and poverty in the Third World, we still find ourselves, sometimes reluctantly, driven back into dialogue with the Jesus tradition. Of course, this is nothing new; the apostle Paul found himself doing the same thing within a couple of decades of the crucifixion (see 1 Cor. 9.14f.). The wider ramifications of the tensions between the needs of 'the real world' and the utopian dream of Jesus have been a theme of this story of Christian origins. We, like Paul, are seeking to do justice to that new vision, which was manifest in the Jesus tradition and the totality of the Christ event. The recognition of cultural and ideological diversity within the New Testament is an important contribution to the understanding of the struggle which was going on in the Church and of the developments which led to the formation of Christendom. It was the struggle between the prayer 'Thy kingdom come; thy will be done on earth as it is in heaven' and the spiritualization of that hope. That is at the heart of the history of Christian discipleship: the temptation to follow the path which leads away from the Jesus tradition and the proclamation of the kingdom of God is as real today as it was for those who first of all, however reluctantly, found it necessary to turn their backs on the reign of God and its inauguration on earth as in heaven.

APPENDIX   THE SOURCES

Introduction

Recognition of the great importance of Jewish literature for our understanding of Christian origins has meant that in the last decade or so there has been a considerable amount of scholarly energy devoted to the study of what is loosely described as the intertestamental literature. This is a blanket term (and an inaccurate one) used to describe those works which failed to get into the Hebrew canon and yet were written by non-Christian Jews. In fact, the term is stretched to include works which were written *after* the bulk of the New Testament (e.g., 4 Ezra and Syr. Baruch), as well as the rabbinic literature. It would be wrong to confine the term 'intertestamental literature' to those works which can with certainty be dated before the rise of Christianity or, for that matter, to drive too sharp a wedge between those books which do not form part of the canon of the Old Testament, and the later portions of the OT canon, with which the intertestamental works often have a great deal of affinity. Doubts are expressed about the use of this material only when we want to use portions of works, which were written after the rise of Christianity, for the detailed exegesis of the New Testament. Thus we should not feel the need to limit the scope of our consideration of Jewish literature, which can shed light on the character of early Judaism, only to that group of texts which can with certainty be dated before the first century AD.[1]

The literature, which we could include in this category, is enormous and of great variety. On the one hand, we have the vast corpus of rabbinic literature, which includes legal pronouncements, stories of rabbis, parables and legends, as well as scriptural exposition of various kinds. On the other hand, we have what are loosely described as the pseudepigrapha, so-called because the various works are often attributed to figures of Israel's past, such as Enoch, Abraham, Isaiah, Ezra, etc. Then we have the great historical works of Flavius Josephus and the interpretative treatises of Philo of Alexandria. Finally, of course, there are the discoveries, which have been made in the desert of Judaea over the past thirty years or so, the Dead Sea Scrolls, many of which fall outside the scope of any of the categories so far mentioned, although several works known hitherto have also turned up there.

313

1

Jewish Literature

(a) Josephus² and Philo³

Flavius Josephus is the best known of all the Jewish historical writers, but it should be recognized that there was a considerable tradition of historiography before him.[4] Best known, because of their place in the Apocrypha, are the books of the Maccabees, which speak in various ways about the Maccabean crisis in the middle of the second century BC. Of greatest importance from the point of view of authenticity is 1 Maccabees. The rest are of less value as works of history, and indeed 4 Maccabees takes the form of a martyrology, with a long eulogy in the form of a history of the martyr's fate.

Josephus' most extended works are the *Antiquities of the Jews* and the *Jewish War*. The former is an attempt to tell the story of Judaism from the Creation down to the Jewish Revolt. It is quite clear from his introduction to the *Antiquities* that Josephus' purpose is mainly apologetic. In the wake of the violent war waged by the Romans against the Jews in Palestine, there was obviously a need to clear the air somewhat and remove misapprehensions, by showing the greatness of the Jewish religious past. In addition, there is, according to Josephus, a religious reason for writing, for he wants to show that 'the main lesson to be learned from this history by anyone who comes to peruse it, is that men, who conform to the will of God and do not venture to transgress the laws that have been laid down, prosper in all things beyond belief, and for their reward, are offered by God felicity' (*Ant.* 1.14).

In his retelling of the scriptural stories, Josephus frequently amplifies the original and thereby betrays evidence of his knowledge of current interpretations. A good example is his rendering of the sacrifice of Isaac (Gen. 22; cf. *Ant.* 1.224ff.). Josephus clearly identifies the mountain with the Temple Mount (226f.) and also has much to say about the glad acceptance by Isaac of his fate, a feature of the story, which was to gain importance in later Jewish tradition.[5] This long work (it runs to twenty books) is a mine of information to the student of the character of early Jewish exegesis, as well as to the historian.

Historically speaking, the *Jewish War* (*Bellum Judaicum*, frequently abbreviated as *BJ*) is of greater value, as it describes (sometimes in considerable detail) the events which led up to the outbreak of the war of the

Jews against Rome, in which Josephus himself was deeply involved, as well as the course of the war itself. There is some overlap between the *Antiquities* and the *BJ*, particularly over matters like the Jewish sects (*BJ* 2.119ff.), and Josephus himself is apt to offer cross-references to his other work. Josephus provides an account of the events leading up to the war, partly to correct any misapprehensions, which the Hellenistic world may have had. Indeed, it is worth reflecting that he was completing the *Antiquities* at the time that Domitian was intensifying the prosecution of the Jewish tax,[6] which was inevitably having severe repercussions on those with Jewish connections. There can be little doubt about Josephus' pro-Roman sympathies and his disdain for the fanatics, 'the tyrants and band of marauders' (*BJ* 1.11), who brought Judaea and Jerusalem to destruction. What is more, his admiration for his masters, the Flavian dynasty, which had given such a warm reception to the Jewish traitor, is evident, particularly in his prophecy that Vespasian would be Emperor (*BJ* 3.398); he is in no doubt that God was behind the Jewish defeat (*BJ* 3.293f.). Even allowing for all his hostility to many of his coreligionists, Josephus makes no sycophantic attempt to place all the blame on the Jews, for he insists that appalling behaviour by a succession of Roman procurators must also be partly to blame. Josephus was writing for a world which was unfamiliar with Judaism, was suspicious of many of its customs and habits and was particularly hostile to the Jews after the war. His presentation is therefore an attempt to rehabilitate the Jews and their traditions and to make this strange group more comprehensible (for an example of misinformation about the Jews see Tacitus, *Hist.* 5). Often we find him translating the details of Jewish belief into a Hellenistic garb, in order to enable his readers to comprehend what the Jews believed (e.g., *BJ* 2.162f., where Josephus speaks of the pharisaic belief in the resurrection from the dead, which he calls 'the immortality of the soul').

Mention may also be made of Josephus' apologetic account of his life, in which he defends his conduct during the Jewish war, and also of the *Contra Apionem*, essentially an apology for Judaism, which reflects some of the common anti-Jewish prejudices of the period.

Like Josephus, Philo was attempting to make sense of Judaism for a sophisticated audience, but, this time, one which had been schooled in the philosophical climate of Alexandria. His method differs markedly from that of Josephus in the *Antiquities*. Whereas the latter was content merely to retell the story of the Pentateuch and later Jewish traditions, Philo uses the allegorical method, in order to draw an incredible amount of meaning from the text. His commentaries on the Pentateuch, which are usually referred to by their Latin titles (e.g., *De Opificio Mundi*, *De Legum Allegoria*, etc.), by no means represent the whole of Philo's literary production. In addition to his commentaries in Greek, we have further works, now extant only in an Armenian version, *The Questions and Answers on Genesis and Exodus*, as well as fragments of an apology for Judaism. Mention must also be made of Philo's polemical tracts, *De Legatione ad Gaium* and *In Flaccum*, both of which focus on the potentially explosive issue of Jewish rights and the relationship of Jews with their pagan neighbours.[7] The former is an invective against Gaius and his proposal to erect a statue of himself in the Temple in Jerusalem, whereas *In Flaccum* is a polemic against Flaccus, the Roman prefect in Egypt (*c.* AD 32), who indulged in cruel actions against the Jews.[8]

(b) The Pseudepigrapha/Non-Rabbinic Writings[9]

This heading covers a large number of works, some of which are falsely attributed to writers of Israelite antiquity (e.g., the book of Daniel in the OT), others not so. For convenience this group has been divided into sections as follows: (i) Apocalypses; (ii) Non-apocalyptic Testaments; (iii) Miscellaneous works. Mention cannot be made here of all the works, which might conceivably fall under the category of pseudepigrapha. A complete list may be found in J. H. Charlesworth's survey of Jewish Pseudepigrapha in *Aufstieg und Niedergang der römischen Welt*, ed. W. Haase.

(i) APOCALYPSES[10]

This is a fairly distinctive literary genre, in which a writer purports to give revelations or disclosures from God or his angel. All claim to offer information about a wide range of subjects, including eschatology, the reason for human suffering, uranology and astronomy. Their common feature is that they claim to reveal things, which are normally hidden from human perception, to give encouragement and warning to the recipients. In an era when the living voice of prophecy had ceased, this was the means whereby direct communication between the world and beyond could be asserted. Characteristic of all these Jewish texts is pseudonymity, namely, the attribution of the revelations to a great figure of Israel's past history, like Abraham, Daniel, Isaiah or Ezra. This was a means of gaining authority and respectability for these disclosures.[11]

The form of the various apocalypses differs enormously. In some (e.g., the Enochic literature), the seer is said to have ascended to heaven[12] to be shown the secrets, whereas in others, the seer communicates with an angel who appears to him (4 Ezra, Syr. Baruch). A popular setting for such disclosures is before the death of a righteous man, when he is allowed to glimpse into heaven and communicate what he sees to his children (Test. Levi, Test. Abraham, Slav. Enoch).

There has been much dispute over which works should or should not be categorized as apocalyptic. The list which follows corresponds to that which I have given elsewhere:[13] 1 Enoch, Daniel, Revelation, Slav. Enoch,

Jubilees, Syr. Baruch, Greek Baruch, 4 Ezra, Apoc. Abraham, Test. Abraham, Test. Levi and Naphtali (from Test. Twelve Patriarchs), Ascension of Isaiah, Shepherd of Hermas and the apocalypses from the later Jewish mystical tradition, like Hebrew Enoch (3 Enoch).

(ii) NON-APOCALYPTIC TESTAMENTS[14]

Into the second category fall those testaments attributed to biblical figures like Moses and Job, which diverge from the apocalyptic type by virtue of the fact that they do not purport to offer visions of divine secrets, but merely the pronouncements of a dying patriarch, without any claim that they derive directly from God. Among such works we should include the Assumption of Moses, the bulk of the Testaments of the Twelve Patriarchs, the Testament of Job and the Life of Adam and Eve.

Whether there is any justification for separating this small category from the variety of works which we have included below under the category miscellaneous, is difficult to assess. Certainly this latter group contains such a diversity of works that it is very difficult to divide them up with any precision. It does seem possible, however, to distinguish these testaments from the related apocalyptic testaments noted above, which are much more explicitly revelatory in content.

(iii) MISCELLANEOUS WORKS

The Odes and Psalms of Solomon: there has been considerable debate whether in fact the former should be classed with the Jewish pseudepigrapha. In their present form the Odes are probably Jewish-Christian in inspiration but are the end-product of a literary tradition, which includes Qoheleth and the Wisdom of Solomon. The latter have many resemblances to the biblical psalms and are particularly important for their messianic beliefs found in Psalms 17 and 18.

Sibylline Oracles: as their name implies, these are a series of prophetic oracles ascribed to a sibyl, a pagan prophetess. In their present form this collection is Jewish and, in part, Christian in its inspiration. Whilst the predictions are put into the mouth of a pagan prophetess, this is merely a device to show that even pagan divines had to acknowledge the supremacy of Judaism and the ultimate vindication of her hopes.

Joseph and Asenath: this is a remarkable work. Essentially it is a form of story, which describes the courtship and marriage of an Egyptian princess to Joseph. Once again, it is not too difficult to detect an apologetic motive in it, namely, the conversion of the pagan Asenath from idolatry. Opinion has been divided over the extent of Christian influence in this work, particularly in those sections which seem to reflect early Christian sacramentalism.

The Letter of Aristeas: this work purports to show the circumstances in which the LXX version was written in the time of Ptolemy Philadelphus of Egypt (285–247 BC).

The Life of Adam and Eve: this work is a strange mixture of legend, exhortation and vision. It tells of the circumstances of the Fall and its aftermath and includes advice to Seth, Adam's son.

Apocrypha: one group of writings must be mentioned, as it formed part of the OT canon of the Christian Church for centuries, as a result of its inclusion in the Vulgate by Jerome. This is the Apocrypha, that group of writings which is in the Vulgate but not in the Hebrew Bible: 1 and 2 Maccabees, 1 and 2 Esdras, Tobit, Judith, Additions to Esther, Wisdom of Solomon, Ecclesiasticus (or Wisdom of Jesus ben Sirach), Baruch, Epistle of Jeremiah, Song of the Three Children, Susanna, Bel and the Dragon, and the Prayer of Manasseh.[15]

(c) Rabbinic Literature[16]

(i) CHARACTER AND CATEGORIZATION OF MATERIAL

By far the most extensive collection of material relating to Jewish life and thought in the period covering the rise and consolidation of the Christian Church are the various collections of sayings and pronouncements of rabbis from Palestine and Babylon, the corpus of rabbinic literature. The volume of this literature, its complexity of thought and argument, as well as the linguistic barrier, make it a formidable proposition for most Christian scholars. Nevertheless, thanks to the labours of Jewish scholars, it is becoming much more accessible to non-specialists, and the great value of it for our understanding of the origin of Christianity cannot be overestimated.

With the gradual emergence of a canon of Scripture, finally ratified by the rabbinic group at Jamnia after AD 70, there inevitably arose the need to interpret the sacred writings for subsequent generations and to ascertain how these offered advice concerning the conduct of life of the individual, the cult and the state, either from the exposition of the various parts of the sacred writings themselves or by means of new rules specifically formulated for the occasion. It is this kind of procedure which is the basis of much of the rabbinic tradition: the ongoing interpretation of Scripture and later reinterpretations of those earlier attempts for subsequent generations. The rabbinic corpus contains material of great antiquity, among a much greater amount of more recent commentary. In referring to the date of the rabbis who are mentioned in the rabbinic literature, their place within two groups is normally used. The earliest group of all – the one which specifically relates to the earliest Christian communities – is referred to as the *tannaim*; the second group (from the third century AD onwards) are *amoraim*. The material which we find in the two Talmuds is tannaitic and amoraic. The earliest collections of rabbinic tradition were handed on by word of mouth and were designated the Oral Torah.[17] Some of the various types of material in the rabbinic literature may be categorized as follows:

Halakah is the normative doctrinal statement transmitted by word of mouth and often without any obvious relationship with Scripture. It is the pronouncement of an authorized teacher on some matter concerned with Jewish praxis. The Mishnah is full of halakah (halakoth).

Midrash is the exposition of a text of Scripture. This is done for a variety of purposes: (i) the attempt to explain what the text means; (ii) to use the text as a means of extracting information concerning the nature of the divine demand upon God's people. A halakic midrash, therefore, is the use of Scripture to offer some kind of insight on a matter relating to conduct.

Haggadah is the term used to denote all non-halakic elements in rabbinic literature, whether it is non-legalistic exegesis, parable or stories concerning the various teachers.

Mishnah is frequently used as a collective term for the corpus of halakic statements codified by R. Judah ha-Nasi (*c.* AD 200), but can be used as another way of speaking of halakah.

Gemara is the word used to describe the mass of additional material which is to be found in the Talmuds and which has been added as a way of interpreting the earlier pronouncements contained in the Mishnah and other collections.

(ii) TYPES OF LITERATURE

Mishnah[18]

At the heart of the rabbinic corpus stands the Mishnah, which, as its name implies, is mainly a collection of halakoth relating to the central areas of Jewish life. A glance at the table of contents in Danby's translation will show that it is divided into six orders corresponding to the main categories of Jewish religious practice (seeds, set feasts, women, damages, hallowed things, and cleannesses). In its present form, it is the result of the redaction of R. Judah ha-Nasi in *c.* AD 200, but it is quite clear that attempts at codification had been made much earlier than this. Most of the material is tannaitic, though the proportion of it stemming from teachers who flourished before the fall of Jerusalem is quite small. It is a witness, therefore, to the debates in the second-century academies, concerning the nature of religious practice. Whilst some of the material in this collection probably reflects real problems facing Jews in deciding how to practise their religion, it cannot be doubted that some of the issues were merely hypothetical situations for debate and discussion within the *scholarly circles*. In addition to the halakic material, the Mishnah contains two tractates, which stand apart from the rest: Pirke Aboth and Middoth. The former is a collection of aphorisms of Sages from the tannaitic period, with little or no halakic content, and the latter is a description of the measurements (middoth) of the temple in Jerusalem.

The means of referring to the Mishnah is through the designation M(ishnah), followed by the tractate (e.g., Berakoth), the chapter and the section.

Parallel with the collection of halakoth in the Mishnah is the additional collection in the Tosefta. In many places it parallels what is contained in the Mishnah, but includes other material, some of which is non-halakic. A translation of the Tosefta is in process of appearing.[19] There are editions of the Hebrew.[20]

The Talmudim[21]

These are to be found in two recensions, the longer one stemming from Babylon (Babli) and the shorter from Palestine (Yerushalmi). The writing down of the Talmudim marks a later stage in the process of the interpretation and understanding of the received tradition than was reached in the Mishnah and Tosefta. The form of the Talmudim shows that clearly, for, with one or two exceptions, the order of the Mishnah is followed, the halakah is quoted, and the additional material, which follows, serves as a commentary on it. While much of this material comes from later commentators, it would be wrong to suppose that the comments which are appended to the Mishnah are all later. Indeed, frequently we find that extraneous tannaitic material has been included, some of which has been paralleled in other collections. As we might expect, the different provenances of the two Talmuds help to explain the concentration of Babylonian scholars and Palestinian scholars in Babli and Yerushalmi respectively. Of course, the process of commenting on the tradition has not stopped with the Talmuds, and some examples of the continuation of this process can be seen in the exegetical notes, which surround the Talmudic text and were written by great medieval commentators, like Rashi.

Reference to the Talmudim is usually quite straightforward. A passage in the Babylonian Talmud is designated by b or TB, followed by the name of the tractate and the folio number. One figure is used to designate one folio, with front and back being designated by the letters a and b respectively. Thus the front of folio 57 in tractate Berakoth would be b. Berakoth 57a. As far as the Jerusalem Talmud is concerned, there is less standardization. References are sometimes given to the Mishnah and at others, as with the Babylonian Talmud, to the page and column number, for example, j.

Hagigah 2.1 and j. Hag. 77b (the columns are numbered a–d).

One of the greatest problems in using the rabbinic material concerns the date of particular traditions, though this problem should not be seen as an excuse for Christian scholars to neglect this material. In addition to the fact that many of the traditions in the rabbinic corpus come from a date after the writing of the NT documents and cannot therefore be used with certainty to illustrate first-century material, we now have to face the fact that traditio-historical criticism has been used with great effect by Jacob Neusner and his pupils on the rabbinic traditions.[22] Thus it is not possible simply to look at the attribution of a particular saying or tradition and assume that it necessarily stems from the rabbi, whose name is attached to the tradition. In this respect, contemporary rabbinic scholarship has derived many insights from the way in which the traditio-historical method has been employed on the Gospels in the New Testament.

Tannaitic Midrashim[23]

As the name implies, these are collections of scriptural exposition, stemming from the tannaitic period and consist of verse by verse commentaries on Exodus (Mekilta), Leviticus (Sifra) and Numbers and Deuteronomy (Sifre). As a rule, the material contained in these commentaries is halakic and shows how doctrinal formulations were linked with the text of Scripture.

Midrash Rabbah[24]

This important collection consists of verse by verse commentaries on the Torah and Megilloth (Song of Songs, Ruth, Esther, Qoheleth and Lamentations). There is much illustrative and, particularly, parabolic material. References to these works usually take the form of the English or Hebrew title to the book, followed by a capital R(abbah), with a reference to the chapter, within the commentary itself rather than the chapter of the biblical book.

Aboth de Rabbi Nathan[25]

Mention has already been made of the collection Pirke Aboth now contained within the Mishnah. A later collection, mainly of material relating to tannaim, is the Aboth according to Rabbi Nathan. In addition to a greater number of sayings of the tannaim than had been included in Aboth, there are other stories, some of a legendary character, which throw light on the rabbis of this period.

Pirke de R. Eliezer

This is a very late collection, but is of great interest, in that it sheds light on the speculative interest within the rabbinic tradition. As a work, it differs quite markedly from those that we have just mentioned and has the appearance of an anthology. It follows the order of various events in the early part of the book of Genesis, with special attention being paid to the process of creation. In speaking of these matters, it unlocks various doors on subjects of interest to Jewish mystics, such as the creation of the world, cosmology and the throne of God. It forms a link with the more extreme speculation which confronts us in the pages of the Kabbalah, as well as reaching back to the beginnings of the earliest rabbinic mysticism. There is a translation of the Pirke de Rabbi Eliezer by G. Friedlander.

The Targumim[26]

Other important repositories of Jewish ideas, which have been given considerable prominence in recent years as a significant source for the character of early Jewish interpretation of Scripture, are the Aramaic targumim. When Hebrew ceased to be the dominant spoken language of Palestine, there was clearly the need for some kind of translation within the liturgy, so that people could understand the Hebrew Scriptures. This process was the beginning of the targumic interpretation, in which a verse by verse translation into Aramaic was given by a member of the synagogue (*methurgeman*), after the reading from the Hebrew Scriptures. As with any translation, of course, the problems of expressing the ideas inevitably led to changes and amplifications to the original. But in the targumim we are faced with much more than this, namely the inclusion of a vast amount of material expanding the details of stories, having little or no warrant in the original and also giving interpretations of obscure passages.

There are targumim on most parts of the Hebrew Bible, but of most importance are those on the Pentateuch, for these contain some of the oldest elements. These targumim have come down to us in various versions. The official version which, on the whole, keeps closest to the Hebrew text (even though it occasionally reflects the expansions to be found in other versions), is called Onkelos. By far the longest of the targumim on the Pentateuch is Pseudo-Jonathan. This has extensive additions and rewritings of biblical stories, with material from a great range of dates, right down to the time of the rise of Islam (Targum Ps. Jonathan on Gen. 15.14). Despite the late date of its final form, it contains many interpretations, which have been either suppressed or forgotten in other areas of Jewish tradition and is therefore a repository of great value for the kind of Jewish interpretation current at the beginning of the Christian era. A variety of other versions are loosely referred to as the Fragment Targum, because we possess only fragments of it from a variety of sources; this targum is not continuous over the course of the whole Pentateuch. Finally, mention should be made of the so-called Targum Neophyti 1, discovered in Codex Neophyti in the Vatican Library by A. Diez Macho. The bulk of the Pentateuch of this targum has now been published. Ps. Jonathan (or TJ1), the Fragment Targum (TJ2) and Neophyti 1 are all believed to preserve the Palestinian targumim in various recensions and can all be used as a repository of the way in which various passages were read and understood at the beginning of the Christian era. Nevertheless, as far as the use of targumic material for the interpretation of the New Testament is concerned, there has been much discussion about the problems facing the dating of various traditions stemming from different ages and the difficulty in isolating early material.[27] In short, all that can be safely said on the matter is that each tradition needs to be treated in isolation, and a conclusion with regard to one piece of tradition cannot necessarily apply to another section.

(d) The Dead Sea Scrolls[28]

Since their discovery just after the Second World War and their gradual publication ever since, the Dead Sea Scrolls have attracted a great deal of attention. It would not be going too far to say that they have revolutionized our understanding of first-century Judaism; they have enabled a shift in perspective, which has made it understandable why a group like the early Christians could have existed under the umbrella of Judaism for so long.

The variety of material discovered at Qumran is well-known. As far as the reconstruction of the sect's beliefs is concerned, the Manual of Discipline (1QS) and the Damascus Document (CD), known already from a version in the Cairo Geniza, are the most important.[29] The distinctive biblical interpretation of the sect is well demonstrated by the commentary on Habakkuk (1QpHab).[30] This is a verse by verse commentary that includes exegesis, which relates scriptural prophecies to events which have taken place in the life of the community. This method of exegesis is designated Pesher exegesis. Other texts of importance are the moving and intensely personal Thanksgiving Hymns (1QH),[31] the precise details of the War Scroll (1QM),[32] which sets out the story of the final struggle of the sons of light against the sons of darkness and has affinities with Zealot beliefs. Other texts, which are of interest to the student of early Christianity, are the messianic collections (4QFlor and 4QTest) and the angelic liturgies (4Q sirot olat ha-sabat).

The usual abbreviations for the most important texts are as follows:

1QS	The Manual of Discipline
1QSa	The messianic addition to the Manual
1QH	The Thanksgiving Hymns
1QM	The War Scroll
CD	The Damascus Document

4QFlor	The Blessing of Jacob
4QTest	The Collection of messianic Proof Texts
4Q sirot olat ha-sabat	The Angelic Liturgy and the description of the Throne Chariot
11QMelch	The Fragment concerning the Heavenly Melchizedek

These abbreviations begin with a number, which identifies the cave in which the scroll was found, a letter identifying the area and an abbreviation denoting the character of the document concerned.

2

Early Christian Literature

Unlike the Jewish literature of the period, the early Christian literature is well-known and studied in great detail, though it is a measure of the influence of the canon that concentration on the NT texts has eclipsed the importance of other literature, which was written during the first two centuries AD. Study of the text[33] and canon[34] of the New Testament does not receive the attention that it deserves, but it is the documents, which do not form part of the canon, which have suffered worst of all. It is true that the collection of writers referred to loosely as the Apostolic Fathers (all derive from the sub-apostolic age or soon after), namely, 1 Clement, 2 Clement, the Letters of Ignatius, the Shepherd of Hermas, the Letter of Diognetus, the Epistle of Barnabas and the Didache, is well-known.[35] Indeed, in the case of the Shepherd of Hermas, its inclusion in the Codex Sinaiticus indicated that by some parts of the Church and for a considerable period, it was regarded as a writing of some authority. Yet with the Apostolic Fathers, conveniently collected in the Loeb edition, we are only beginning to cover the vast penumbra of early Christian literature outside the New Testament, which is all too little known and even less well researched by students of early Christianity. Much of the important literature is described and some of it is translated either in whole or in part in the edition of the NT apocrypha of Hennecke-Schneemelcher.[36] There is so much of this literature that only a few items can be touched on here.

Particular mention should be made of the extra-canonical sayings of Jesus, which are to be found in the patristic literature, Islamic texts and among the Nag Hammadi texts and other papyri finds. This collection of material has been reasonably well researched, and scholars like Jeremias have attempted to evaluate the different items which have come down to us.[37] Even if some of the material may not have any great value for a reconstruction of the teaching of Jesus, it certainly allows us to glimpse the ideas of the various communities that produced it. Similarly, the Jewish-Christian gospels, like the Gospel of the Hebrews, the Gospel of the Ebionites and the Gospel of the Nazarenes, which are quoted by later Christian writers, cast light on the beliefs and practices of those who maintained the centrality of Jesus, but whose christological doctrine fell short of the norms which were gradually being accepted within the Church. The strange world of early Jewish Christianity is one which one enters as if into a mine-field, aware of the many dangers which confront an evaluation of the various literary monuments to this tradition. Many of the important texts have now been collected.[38]

As far as the earliest phase of Christian thought and history is concerned, we are inevitably thrown back on the New Testament.[39] Here the problem is not so much knowledge and lack of critical texts as evaluation and the problems of use. Nowhere is this better illustrated than in the case of gospel study over the last hundred years or so. No longer can the student of the New Testament treat the Gospels as if they were simple chronological histories of the life of Jesus of Nazareth.[40] It has become apparent as the result of what might be all-embracingly described as the traditio-historical method,[41] that they are made up of isolated units of tradition (stories, sayings, etc.), which have been put together in their present form either by the Evangelist or by the transmitters of the tradition, who precede the Gospels. Few would argue that the order of the sayings, as they confront us in the Gospels, actually reflects the order in which they were uttered by Jesus.

Also, comparison of the same saying in different Gospels has led to the conclusion that changes were made during the transmission of the saying and, on occasion, in its final redaction, either deliberately or through the vicissitudes of oral tradition. These changes, which have been made to the content of a saying or a story, either by changes in wording or in the order in which it is placed in a particular Gospel, have been the concern of redaction-criticism,[42] whereas the developments or literary forms and the changes in the oral period have been placed under the heading of the form-critical study of the Gospels.

Alongside the study of the development of the tradition, mention must be made of the continuing interest in source-critical evaluation. The close relationship between the first three Gospels (hence their title 'Synoptic Gospels', because they can be placed together in a synopsis) has persuaded many that there is some form of literary relationship between them.[43] For many years scholars were persuaded of the substantial accuracy of the Two-Document theory, which maintains that Matthew and Luke were dependent in the writing of their Gospels on Mark and another source common to them both, designated *Q*. This theory is the basis of much of the work done on the Gospels since the Second World War. Indeed, it is probably fair to say that most redaction-critical studies of Matthew and Luke start from the premise that the Two-Document hypothesis is correct, so that variations between a particular Gospel and Mark are taken to signify a change of some doctrinal import for the writer. Recently, however, the assumptions, which have been made about the validity of the Two-Document hypothesis, have come under severe pressure from several quarters. Consequently, that assured result of NT criticism, the priority of the Gospel of Mark and the dependence of Matthew and Luke upon it, has now come under suspicion. Suggestions made long ago by Augustine (Mark is dependent on Matthew) and two hundred years ago by Griesbach (Mark is dependent on both Matthew and Luke) have been revived. Such doubts as have been expressed have by no means persuaded all, and all that can be said at present is that simple acceptance of the Two-Document hypothesis would no longer seem to explain the complexity of the relationship between the first three Gospels in the New Testament.

In all these discussions of the relationship between the Synoptic Gospels little mention has been made of the Gospel of John.[44] Few would deny that in its present form and style the Gospel of John stands apart from the others. It has been dubbed the 'spiritual Gospel', and many have been convinced that we have in this text a sophisticated theological exposition of the significance of Jesus of Nazareth, in which the reporting of the incidents of Jesus' life takes second place to theological exposition. For a long time, it was considered that the lack of concern for historical reporting in the Gospel meant that the Evangelist had simply taken over incidents and sayings from one or more of the other Gospels and used them in his presentation of the impact of Jesus. While no one will doubt the sophistication of Johannine theology, it represents a strange reversal of fortunes that the 'spiritual Gospel' has been rehabilitated as a document of some worth for the historian, whereas its companion Gospels have suffered the fate of having doubts cast upon their historical reliability. Nearly fifty years ago, Percy Gardner-Smith challenged the assumption of many of his contemporaries that the Gospel of John was dependent on the Synoptic Gospels. While there are still some who maintain that it is dependent on one or more of the other Gospels, the studies of C. H. Dodd[45] have indicated that the basis for such a belief does not exist. Consequently, we find that today most commentators believe that the Gospel depends for its sources on material which is independent of the Synoptic Gospels, even if it may ultimately link with it further back in the period of oral tradition.

The other New Testament documents present their own problems. With the exception of the Acts of the Apostles, which alone purports to give a history of the expansion of Christianity, all the other NT documents are documents whose main purpose is the doctrinal and ethical instruction of the recipients. As such, any information that they may give us about the history and chronology of early Christianity or, for that matter, the particular doctrinal standpoint of the community addressed, is only incidental. Thus the problem of reconstructing, say, the outline of Paul's apostolic ministry is a task of great difficulty, should we depend on the letters of Paul alone. Certainly, passages like Galatians 1–2 give us a certain amount of information about Paul's activities, but such items of information are infrequent. As a result, resort is usually made to the Acts of the Apostles, where some account of Christian history is attempted. The value of this text for the reconstruction of early Christian history has been hotly disputed,[46] and there are some who prefer to ignore Acts entirely as a source of early Christian history, believing that its perspective is so conditioned by the concerns of the writer that the amount of accurate historical information is extremely limited. Certainly, there are problems with Acts, as a comparison of the accounts of Paul's visits to Jerusalem (Acts 9.11, 15; Gal. 1–2) will reveal.[47]

The major problem confronting us with the other documents is their authorship and date and the situation which provoked the writers to respond in the way that they did. The authorship and date are important,[48] because answers to these questions enable us to have some indication of the particular place which they take in the development of Christian thought. Dispute over the authorship of the Pauline letters is by no means resolved. It can probably be said that there are four documents, which many would consider to be inauthentic, namely, Ephesians, 1 Timothy, 2 Timothy and Titus, and two others, about which doubt is often expressed, Colossians and 2 Thessalonians (Hebrews is always assumed to be non-Pauline).

NOTES

Preface
1 J. Robinson and H. Koester, *Trajectories.*

PART I
Introduction

1 *The Rock Whence Ye Were Hewn*

1 On Jesus in Jewish tradition, see Herford, *Christianity;* Bammel, *Christian Origins;* Maier, *Jesus von Nazareth;* S. Krauss, *Das Leben Jesu.*

2 See 'Nostra Aetate' in *Documents of Vatican II*, pp. 743ff.; U. Simon, *A Theology of Auschwitz.*

3 On Jewish background of the Christian liturgy, see Levertoff in *Liturgy and Worship*, ed. Lowther Clarke; P. Bradshaw, *Daily Prayer;* Oesterley, *The Jewish Background;* Dugmore, *The Influence of the Synagogue;* Wainwright and Jones, *The Study of Liturgy;* Le Déaut, *Message.*

4 On the kingdom of God, see Perrin, *The Kingdom of God,* and below, pp. 133ff.

5 Concisely stated in English by Brandon, *Fall.*

6 On the Tübingen school, see Harris, *The Tübingen School,* and for its continued influence, see Brandon, *Fall;* Munck, *Paul.*

7 See Brandon, *Fall,* pp. 54ff.; *Religion in Ancient History*, p. 310; cf. H. D. Betz, *Galatians,* p. 64.

8 de Lange, *Origen;* Kelly, *Jerome.* On Justin, see E. Osborne, *Justin;* L. W. Barnard, *Justin;* Harnack, *Judentum und Judenchristentum.*

9 For a survey of this polemic see Maier, *Auseinandersetzung,* and also A. L. Williams, *Adversus Judaeos;* J. Parkes, *Conflict.*

10 On the Dialogue, see Barnard and Harnack, op. cit.

11 See the McMaster project, under the supervision of E. P. Sanders, *Jewish and Christian Self-Definition* (3 vols); Wilken, *Judaism.*

12 On the canon, see von Campenhausen, *Formation;* Moule, *Birth.* Note also the salutary remarks of Stone, *Scriptures,* p. 53.

13 See the excellent survey by Vermes, *The Dead Sea Scrolls;* P. R. Davies, *Qumran.*

14 See Stone, *Scriptures.*

15 The Dead Sea Scrolls may offer something of an exception. The position of the Teacher of Righteousness has some affinities with the central position of Jesus. See G. Jeremias, *Lehrer* and Carmignac, *Christ and the Teacher of Righteousness.*

16 See de Ste Croix, 'Why were the early Christians persecuted?'; Frend, *Martyrdom.*

17 On the variety of early Christian belief see Bauer, *Orthodoxy;* Dunn, *Unity.*

329

18 Moore, *Judaism*; Urbach, *Sages*; Neusner, 'Formation'.

19 Sevenster, *Anti-Semitism*; Stern, *Greek and Latin Writers*; Smallwood, *Jews*.

20 On Celsus, see Beaker in ANRW 2.23.2, pp. 1055ff. Celsus criticized the Christians for undermining the strength of the state and its powers of resistance (*Contra Celsum* Bk. 8.66).

2   An Approach to Ancient Judaism

1 Moore, *Judaism*; Urbach, *Sages*; but note the comments of Neusner, 'Formation'.

2 Classically in Bousset, *Religion*. See Moore, *Judaism* 1, pp. 128ff.

3 Still found in the influential book by Rössler, *Gesetz*, but note the criticisms of Nissen, 'Tora'.

4 Neusner, 'Formation' cf. Rivkin, *Hidden Revolution*.

5 Bousset, *Religion*.

6 Knibb in Knibb, Coggins and Philips, *Israel's Prophetic Tradition*; Knibb, 'Apocalyptic'.

7 See Rowland in Carson ed., *From Sabbath to Sunday*.

8 See below, pp. 39ff. and *SVM History* 2, pp. 237ff.

9 *SVM History* 2, pp. 260ff., 292ff.

10 See below and also Moore, *Judaism* 2, pp. 40ff.

11 On the cult at Leontopolis, see below, p. 39. On the Samaritans see Coggins, *Samaritans and Jews*.

12 Moore, *Judaism* 2, pp. 3ff.; Freyne, *Galilee*, pp. 259ff.

13 See below, pp. 87ff and *SVM History* 2, 488ff.; Moore, *Judaism* 2, pp. 323ff.; Urbach, *Sages* 1, pp. 649ff.

3   The Jews After the Exile

1 For the history see *SVM History*, Hayes and Miller, *Israelite and Judean History*; later history in Safrai and Stern, *Jewish People*; Rhoads, *Israel in Revolution*; Baron, *Social and Religious History*; Smallwood, *Jews*; Aberbach, *War*. Summaries in Ackroyd, *Israel*; Russell, *Jews*; Reicke, *NT Era*; Koester, *Introduction*. See also Sandmel, *The First Christian Century* and id. *Judaism and Christian Beginnings*.

2 Note the way in which Nehemiah, Ezra and Daniel speak of Jews holding positions of authority in pagan courts (Neh. 2; Ezra 7; Dan. 1ff.).

3 See the Letter of Aristeas. On Egyptian Judaism, see Collins, *Athens*; Tcherikover, *Hellenistic Civilisation*.

4 Tcherikover, op. cit. On Antiochus, see Morkholm, *Antiochus IV*.

5 In addition to Tcherikover, see Hengel, *Judaism* and *Jews*; Momigliano, *Alien Wisdom*.

6 Farmer, *Maccabees*; Hengel, *Zeloten*; Rhoads, *Israel*.

7 Freyne, *Galilee*, pp. 68ff.; Hoehner, *Herod*; *SVM History* 1, pp. 330ff.; A. H. M. Jones, *Herods*.

8 *SVM History* 1, p. 386f.

9 On this troubled period for Rome, see K. Wellesley, *The Longest Year*.

10 Yadin, *Bar Kochba*; Bowersock, 'A Roman Perspective'; Schäfer, 'Akiba'; *Aufstand*.

11 Hengel, *Judaism* and *Jews*.

12 See below, pp. 8off.

13   Mantel, *Sanhedrin*; *SVM History* 2, 199ff.

14   The Temple inscription reads as follows: 'No man of another nation is to enter within the fence and enclosure round the Temple. And whosoever is caught will have himself to blame that his death ensues.' See Barrett, *NT Background*, p. 50; *SVM History* 2, p. 284.

15   *SVM History* 2, p. 312.

16   Neusner, *Traditions about the Pharisees*; *Politics*, cf. Rivkin, *Hidden Revolution*. See further, *SVM History* 2, pp. 314ff., 381ff.

17   *SVM History* 1, p. 379; Josephus, *Ant.* 18.95; 15.403ff.; Jeremias, *Jerusalem*, especially pp. 230ff.

18   On Galilee, see Freyne, *Galilee*, pp. 55ff. Rhoads, *Israel*; Vermes, *Jesus*, pp. 42ff.; Meyers, 'Cultural Setting'; Klausner, *Jesus*, pp. 175ff. For an attempt to ascertain the views of the Jewish rebels via numismatic study, see L. Kadman, *Coins*.

19   Kautsky, *Foundations*; Kreissig, *Sozialen Zusammenhänge*; Malherbe, *Social Aspects*; Aberbach, *War*; Riches, *Jesus*; Jeremias, *Jerusalem*; Belo, *Materialist Reading*; Pixley, *God's Kingdom*; Derrett, *Jesus' Audience*. On the wider issues, Rostovtzeff, *Social and Economic History*; Macmullen, *Roman Social Relations*; de Ste Croix, *Class Struggle*. Earlier periods are discussed in Gottwald, *Tribes* (origins of Israel); Kippenberg, *Religion und Klassenbildung*. On early Christianity, see Gager, *Kingdom*; Malherbe, *Social Aspects*; Meeks, *Urban Christians; Jews and Christians*; Malina, *NT World*; Theissen, *First Followers; Social Setting*.

20   *Marxist*, p. 22.

21   See Geertz, 'Religion as a Cultural System'; 'Religion is both the model for social order, at once reflecting the existing order and shaping it to the really real world, to which its own symbolic system refers.'

22   Freyne, *Galilee*, p. 228.

23   Caution is required in linking the apocalypses too closely only with eschatologically oriented groups. It is apparent that they also exhibit another strand, which sought answers to life's perplexities. See below, pp. 56ff.

24   See Safrai and Stern, *Jewish People* 1, p. 637.

25   ibid.; Freyne, *Galilee*, pp. 194ff.

26   In Safrai and Stern, *Jewish People* 1, p.657. On seizure of property and the impoverishment of the people, see Josephus, *Ant.* 15.6; 121; 299ff.; *BJ* 1.370.

27   Kreissig, *Zusammenhänge*, pp. 36ff.; Safrai and Stern, *Jewish People*, 1, p. 662; Riches, *Jesus*, pp. 77ff.; Rhoads, *Israel*.

28   *BJ* 1.401f.; 2.404; 407; *Ant.* 16.136ff.; 149ff.; 17.302ff.; Safrai and Stern, *Jewish People* 1, pp. 330ff., 661ff.; Tacitus, *Annals* 2.42.

29   On the debt records, see Kreissig, op. cit., pp. 127ff., especially p. 132. For other evidence of attempts at social justice, see Josephus, *BJ* 7.261; 4.507ff.; 5.439ff.; also the maltreatment of the aristocracy: Josephus, *BJ* 4.138ff.; 354ff.; 2.425ff. See also Goodman, 'First Jewish Revolt' and Rajak, *Josephus*.

30   Note the reference to Simeon b. Giora in *BJ* 2.652 and references in 37n below; Rhoads, *Israel*, p. 80.

31   On the industry connected with the Temple, see Jeremias, *Jerusalem*.

32   On *Fiscus Judaicus*, see also *Ant.* 18.313; *BJ* 5.187; 7.218; Dio Cassius 66.7; Philo, *Spec. Leg.* 1.76ff.; also Smallwood, *Jews*, pp. 345ff.; Falk, *Introduction* 1, pp. 67ff.

33 Safrai and Stern, *Jewish People*, p. 691f.

34 cf. Kreissig, *Sozialen Zusammenhänge*, p. 92, who has protested against the tendency of many scholars to find an exclusively religious explanation for unrest in Palestine. See also Aberbach, *War*. For an attempt to examine earlier periods of Israelite history from this perspective, see Gottwald, *Tribes*.

35 On Galilee, see Freyne, *Galilee* and below, pp. 117ff.

36 See below, pp. 8off.

37 Neusner, *Jews in Babylon*; Tcherikover, *Hellenistic Civilisation*; Leon, *Jews*; Magie, *Roman Rule*; Kraabel, *Judaism in Asia Minor*.

38 On the proscription of cults see Smallwood, op. cit., pp. 133ff.

39 Safrai and Stern, *Jewish People* 2.701ff.; 1.117f; 420ff. See also Sevenster, *Anti-Semitism*; Smallwood, *Jews*; Stern, *Greek and Latin Authors*.

40 On citizenship see Safrai and Stern, *Jewish People* 1, pp. 440ff.

41 On Jewish rights, see pp. 8off.

42 On synagogues, see below, pp. 43ff.

43 Archaeological evidence, see Safrai and Stern, *Jewish People* 2, pp. 908ff.; Gutmann, *Ancient Synagogues*.

44 On God-fearers, see Moore, *Judaism* 1, pp. 325f., 340; TDNT 9, pp. 207f.; 8, 615, 618; and Siegert, 'Gottesfürchtige'.

45 Strack-Billerbeck 2, pp. 715ff.

46 On problems posed by circumcision, see TDNT 6, pp. 72ff.; Martial, *Epigr.* 7, and 11.

47 Theissen, *Social Setting; First Followers*.

48 Malherbe, *Social Aspects*; Deissmann, *Light*; and particularly Meeks, *Urban Christians*. See also S. J. Case, *Social Origins*.

PART II
Jewish Life and Thought at the Beginning of the Christian Era

1 *God and his Covenant with Israel*

1 Sanders, *Paul*, exposes some of the caricatures of Judaism by Christian writers.

2 Le Déaut, *La Nuit*.

3 Sanders, *Paul*, pp. 1ff. and 33ff.

4 Sanders, op. cit., pp. 233ff.

5 On the covenant, see Eichrodt, *Theology*; Baltzer, *Covenant Formulary*; Mendenhall, *Law and Covenant*; McCarthy, *Old Testament Covenant*; Buchanan, *Consequences*; TDNT 2, pp. 106ff. On continuing importance in the NT, see Mark 14.24 and par.; 2 Cor. 3; Gal. 4; M. D. Hooker in ed. Hooker, *Paul and Paulinism*, pp. 47ff.

6 On this see Nicholson, 'Interpretation'.

7 Vermes, *Dead Sea Scrolls in English*, pp. 25ff.; *Dead Sea Scrolls*, pp. 163ff.; Jeremias, *Eucharistic Words*.

8 On attitudes to circumcision, see McKelvey, 'Conversion' and Nolland, 'Uncircumcised Proselytes?'

9   See below, pp. 87ff.

10 On halakah in the OT, see Weingreen, *From Bible to Mishnah*.

11 On the land, see Davies, *Gospel and Land*.

12 On this subject, see Clements, *God and Temple; Abraham and David*; Sawyer, *Moses*.

2   The God of the Covenant

1   Urbach, *Sages* 1, pp. 525ff.; Moore, *Judaism* 1, p. 537; 2, pp. 16ff.; von Rad, *OT Theology* 1, pp. 12, 308. On the social and political origins of the people of Israel, see Gottwald, *Tribes*.

2   Note the development of theological reflection in Jewish mysticism and Kabbalah; see Scholem 'Kabbalah' and below, pp. 60ff.

3   On this passage see von Rad, *OT Theology* 1, pp. 122f.; id., *Problem of the Hexateuch*.

4   On the wisdom tradition, see von Rad, *Wisdom*. Note how Exodus and the wisdom tradition converge in Wisd. 11, 16f.

5   On the Deuteronomistic history, see Ackroyd, *Exile*, pp. 62ff.

6   But note the strains on this view in 4 Ezra. See Sanders, *Paul*, pp. 409f.; A. L. Thompson, *Problem of Evil*.

7   Jeremias, *Jesus' Promise*, pp. 60f.

8   Cross, *Canaanite Myth*.

9   Cross, 'Council of Yahweh'.

10 Urbach, *Sages* 1, pp. 138ff., but note the comments of Carr, *Angels*, pp. 30ff.

11 Brown, *World*, pp. 45ff.; Dodds, *Pagan*; Nock, *Conversion*.

12 Eliade, *Shamanism*; Bloch, *Hoffnung*; Davis, *Utopia*; Mandel, *Utopian Thought*.

13 Clements, *Prophecy*.

14 Lindblom, *Prophecy*; Blenkinsopp, *History of Prophecy*.

15 cf. the comments of Bowker, *Religious Imagination*, on the problem of theology in the ancient world.

16 Goldberg, *Schekhinah*; Urbach, *Sages* 1, pp. 37ff.; Moore, *Judaism* 1, pp. 414ff.

17 Mack, *Logos*; Ringgren, *Word*; Wolfson, *Philo*; Nickelsburg and Stone, *Faith and Piety*, pp. 203ff.; Strack-Billerbeck 2, pp. 303ff., but note the cautionary remarks of Moore, 'Intermediaries'; 'Christian Writers'.

18 Schäfer, *Heilige Geist*; TDNT 6, pp. 332ff.

19 Kadushin, *The Rabbinic Mind*; Sanders, *Paul*, pp. 217ff.

20 See Rowland, 'Visions'; Chernus, 'Visions of God'.

21 Goodenough, *Jewish Symbols*.

22 Scholem, *Major Trends*.

23 See below, pp. 60ff. On Jewish cosmology, see Bietenhard, *Himmlische Welt*; Séd, *La mystique cosmologique juive*.

3   The Heavenly Host

1   Urbach, *Sages* 1, pp. 135ff.; Moore, *Judaism* 1, pp. 401ff.

2   Cross, *Canaanite Myth*; Day, *OT Utilisation*.

3 Schäfer, *Rivalität*; Carr, *Angels*.

4 Eichrodt, *Theology* 2, pp. 23f. and Stier, *Gott und sein Engel*.

5 On Gnosticism, see Yamauchi, *Pre-Christian Gnosticism*; Grant, *Gnosticism*; Wilson, *Gnosis*; Foerster, *Gnosis* and below, pp. 294ff.

6 See TDNT 7, pp. 151ff.

7 This development should probably be linked with the wider escalation of beliefs in hostile supernatural powers and the growth of magic. See Smith, *Jesus*; Guthrie, *Greeks*, pp. 270ff.

8 On the significance of this tradition as a reflection of an alternative theological stream in Judaism, see Barker, 'Reflections'.

9 Greene, *Moira*; Brown, *World*.

10 Dodds, *Greeks and the Irrational*.

4 Angelic Mediators

1 Summary in Dunn, *Christology*; Schillebeeckx, *Jesus* and *Christ*.

2 Mack, *Logos*; Dunn, *Christology*.

3 Dunn, *Christology*.

4 Casey, *Son of Man* and see below, pp. 95ff.

5 Collins, *Apocalyptic Vision*.

6 Theisohn, *Der auserwählte Richter*; Collins in *Ideal Figures*, ed. Nickelsburg.

7 Rowland, *Open Heaven*, pp. 94ff.; Segal, *Two Powers*; Kim, *Origin*.

8 Rowland, 'Vision of the Risen Christ'.

9 Dunn, *Christology*.

10 Bietenhard, *Himmlische Welt*, pp. 255f.; Segal, op. cit. But note the comments of Moore in 'Intermediaries' and 'Christian Writers'.

11 See Vermes, *Dead Sea Scrolls*, pp. 174f. and Kuhn, *Enderwartung*.

12 Dunn, *Christology*, pp. 19ff.

13 On Enoch, see TDNT 2, pp. 556ff.

14 Van der Woude and de Jonge, 'Melchizedek and the NT', but note Dunn's cautionary remarks, *Christology*, pp. 152f. and see now Kobelski, *Melchizedek*.

15 On Abel in Test. Abr., see Rowland, *Open Heaven*, p. 107; Kim, *Origin*, p. 211.

16 On the Prayer of Joseph, see J. Z. Smith in *Religions in Antiquity*, ed. J. Neusner; Dunn, *Christology*, pp. 153ff. and Hengel, *Son of God*, p. 47.

17 On Moses, see TDNT 4, pp. 848f.; Goodenough, *By Light*; Meeks, *Prophet King*; in *Religions in Antiquity*, ed. Neusner; Schillebeeckx, *Christ*, pp. 309ff.; Gager, *Moses*.

18 On this see Meeks, *Prophet King*, and now van der Horst, 'Moses' Throne Vision' and Jacobson, *Exagoge*.

19 cf. Dunn, *Christology*.

20 Segal, *Two Powers*.

5 The Temple

1 *SVM History* 2, pp. 237ff.; *Enc. Jud.* 15, col. 955–84; Safrai and Stern, *Jewish People* 2, pp. 561ff.; 865ff.; Jeremias, *Jerusalem*, 21; pp. 147ff.; Falk, *Introduction* 1, pp. 63ff.;

Nickelsburg and Stone, *Faith*, pp. 51ff.

2　On the relationship of the tractate Middoth in the Mishnah to Josephus' description of the Temple (*BJ* 5.184ff.), see O. Holtzmann, *Middoth*, and the plan of the Temple in *JE* 12, pp. 94f.

3　Benediction 14: 'And to Jerusalem thy city, return with mercy and dwell in its midst as thou hast spoken; and build it soon in our days to be an everlasting building'.

4　Clements, *God and Temple*.

5　Plöger, *Theocracy*; Hanson, *Dawn*.

6　On Leontopolis, see Baron, *Social and Religious History* 1, p. 394; Hirsch in *Jews College Jubilee Volume*, pp. 39ff.; F. Petrie, *Hyksos*; Hayward in *JJS* (1982), and Delcor in *Études Bibliques*; on Elephantine, see Porten, *Archives*.

7　See below, pp. 41f.

8　On Temple-tax, see *SVM History* 2, p. 273 and above, p. 19.

9　On Fiscus Judaicus, see Smallwood, *Jews*.

10　See Horbury in *Jesus and the Politics of his Day*, ed. Bammel.

11　On priestly dues, see *SVM History* 2, pp. 257ff.; de Vaux, *Ancient Israel*.

12　On the people of the land (*'am ha-aretz*), see Oppenheimer, *Am Ha-Aretz*; Urbach, *Sages* 1, pp. 584ff.; 632ff.

13　See below pp. 69ff.

14　See Freyne, *Galilee*, pp. 259ff.

15　See the Temple Scroll (German translation by Maier) and on the cultic language in the Scrolls, see Gärtner, *Temple*.

16　McKelvey, *New Temple*.

6　Jewish Festivals

1　Moore, *Judaism* 2, 40ff.; Safrai and Stern, *Jewish People*, 2 pp. 561ff., 793ff. and Elbogen, *Gottesdienst*.

2　On the origins, see de Vaux, *Ancient Israel*.

3　On Passover, see J. B. Segal, *Passover*; Le Déaut, *La Nuit Pascale*; TDNT 5, pp. 896ff.

4　See Le Déaut, op. cit., and the Passover Haggadah ed. Roth.

5　See TDNT 6, pp. 44ff.; *EJ*, vol. 14, col. 1319f.; *JE*, vol. 9, p. 592.

6　See Halperin, *Merkabah*, pp. 55ff.; Strack-Billerbeck 2, pp. 603ff. Strack-Billerbeck 2, pp. 597ff.

7　TDNT 7, p. 390.

8　Guilding, *Fourth Gospel*; Strack-Billerbeck 2, p. 490.

9　Daniélou, *Theology of Jewish-Christianity*, pp. 343ff.; Draper in Horbury and Rowland, *Essays*.

10　Moore, *Judaism*, 2, p. 55.

11　Jeremias, *Jerusalem*, pp. 58ff.; Strack-Billerbeck 2, pp. 604ff.

7　The Synagogue

1　*SVM History* 2, pp. 423ff.; Safrai and Stern, *Jewish People* 2, pp. 908ff.; *Ancient Synagogues*, ed. Gutmann; Kraabel, 'Diaspora Synagogue'; Hengel, 'Proseuche'; TDNT 7, pp. 798ff.

2   On the subject of origins, see Gutmann, op. cit.

3   Dugmore, *Influence* but note Bradshaw *Daily Prayer*. A convenient collection of Jewish synagogue prayers may be found in *Authorized Daily Prayer Book*, ed. Singer.

4   On Dura, see Kraeling, *The Synagogue*; Smallwood, *Jews*, pp. 507ff.; Goodenough, *Jewish Symbols*; J. Gutmann (ed.), *The Dura-Europos Synagogue*.

5   See Goodenough, *Jewish Symbols*.

6   See *SVM History* 1, pp. 508ff.; 2, p. 454 and Heinemann and Petuchowski, *Literature of the Synagogue*.

7   Mann, *Bible as Read and Preached*.

8   Guilding, *Fourth Gospel*; Goulder, *Midrash; Evangelists' Calendar*; Bowker, 'Proem'.

9   Sevenster, *Do you know Greek?*

10 For an introduction to the targums, see Bowker, *Targums*; Vermes, *Scripture*; Vermes in *Cambridge History*, vol. 1, ed. Ackroyd and Evans; on links with NT, Le Déaut, *Message of NT*, Chilton, *Glory of Israel*; bibliography by Grossfeld. On translations into Greek, see below, pp. 8off.

11 Alexander, 'Rabbinic Lists'.

12 See below, pp. 300ff. and Horbury, 'Blessing'; and Kimelman in *Jewish and Christian self-definition*, vol. 2, ed. Sanders.

13 Kilpatrick, *Origin*; Martyn, *History*.

14 Collins, *Sibylline Oracles*; *Athens*; Jeremias, *Jesus' Promise*; Hahn, *Mission*; Harnack, *Mission and Expansion*.

8   The Torah

1   *SVM History* 2, pp. 314ff.; Falk, *Introduction*; Urbach, *Sages* 1, pp. 286ff.; Neusner, *Foundations*.

2   *Cambridge History*, ed. Ackroyd and Evans 1, pp. 113ff.; Blenkinsopp, *Prophecy*; Leiman, *Canonisation*; Sundberg, *Old Testament*; Beckwith, *Old Testament Canon of the New Testament Church*.

3   On Sadducean scribal tradition see Jeremias, *Jerusalem*, pp. 147ff. and 222ff.

4   Freyne, *Galilee*, p. 322.

5   Ackroyd, *Exile*.

6   Blenkinsopp, *Prophecy and Canon*. id. *History of Prophecy*.

7   Hanson, *Dawn* and Plöger, *Theocracy*.

8   Jeremias, *Jerusalem*, pp. 233ff.

9   Weingreen, *From Bible to Mishna*.

10 Evidence set out in Gerhardsson, *Memory*, 71ff.

11 On the Sanhedrin and its competence, see Mantel, *Sanhedrin*; Safrai and Stern, *Jewish People* 1; 377ff.; *SVM History*, 2, 199ff.; Sherwin-White, *Roman Society*.

9   The Interpretation of Scripture

1   *SVM History*, 2, pp. 314ff.; Vermes, *Scripture*; Longenecker, *Biblical Exegesis*; Bowker, *Targums*; Gerhardsson, *Memory*; Urbach, *Sages* 1, pp. 286ff.; Porton, 'Midrash'; Neusner, *Foundations*; Patte, *Hermeneutic*; Horgan, *Pesharim*.

2   See the conflict over the altar of incense in Tos. Yoma 1.8 (quoted in Bowker, *Jesus*, p. 118).

3   On the influence of custom and society on halakah, see Finkelstein, *Pharisees*.

4   See Neusner, *Traditions*.

5   See Bowker, *Targums*, p. 41 and Appendix II.

6   For biblical interpretation at Qumran, see Bruce, *Biblical Exegesis*; Vermes, *Dead Sea Scrolls*, pp. 66, 164ff.; O. Betz, *Offenbarung*; Horgan, *Pesharim*.

7   On this passage, see Gruenwald in *ANRW* 2.19.1; 'Knowledge and Vision'.

8   See Talmon in *Script. Hieros.* 4.

9   See Stendahl, *School*, particularly the second edition.

10 On the use of Scripture in the NT, see Lindars, *NT Apologetic*; Dodd, *According to the Scriptures*; Gundry, *Use*; Reim, *Studien*; E. Ellis, *Paul's Use of OT*; Longenecker, *Biblical Exegesis*.

11 On collections of Scriptural citations, see Rendel Harris, *Testimonia*.

12 A vast array of this interpretative material is collected in Ginzberg, *Legends*.

13 For a brief introduction to the targumim, see Bowker, *Targums*. On their relationship with the NT, see McNamara, *New Testament and Palestinian Targums*, but note the cautionary remarks of Sanders, *Paul* pp. 25ff. and see, below pp. 322ff.

14 e.g. Targum, Ps. Jon. on Gen. 15.14 mentions Muhammad's wives.

15 On the targum of Job, see van der Ploeg and van der Woude, *Le Targum de Job*.

16 One example is the Akedah, the account of Abraham's journey to sacrifice Isaac in Gen. 22. There has been considerable dispute over the relevance of the targums on this passage for the interpretation of NT passages dealing with the death of Christ; see Schoeps, *Paul*; Vermes, *Scripture*; Hayward, 'Sacrifice'; Swetnam, *Jesus*. For the targum of Isaiah, see Chilton, *Glory of Israel*.

17 See e.g., Wilcox, 'Peter and the Rock'.

18 Vermes, *Scripture*.

10   Apocalyptic: Scripture and the Disclosure of Heavenly Knowledge

1   See the discussions in Hennecke-Schneemelcher, *NT Apocrypha* 2, pp. 608ff.; further, D. Hellholm, *Apocalypticism*; Hanson, *Visionaries*.

2   'Apocalypticism' in *IDB Supplement*.

3   See further, Plöger, *Theocracy*; Hanson, *Dawn*.

4   So also Stone, 'Lists',.

5   See Stone, 'Lists', p. 451, 78n.

6   See further, Rowland, *The Open Heaven*.

7   Stone, 'Lists' and *Scriptures*.

8   See Milik, *Books of Enoch*; Greenfield and Stone, 'Books of Enoch'.

9   On 4 Ezra, see Thompson, *Evil*.

10 On this theme, see Nickelsburg, *Resurrection*.

11 So Stone, 'Lists', p. 443.

12 On pseudepigraphy, see the essays by Hengel and Smith in von Fritz, *Pseudepigrapha*.

13 Stone, 'Paradise'.

14 See Hengel, *Judaism* 1, pp. 210ff.; Dodds, *Greeks*; Segal, 'Heavenly Ascents'.

15 *Method*, p. 166; see futher, Rowland, *Open Heaven*, pp. 214ff.

16 e.g., Rössler, *Gesetz*; cf. W. D. Davies, 'Apocalyptic and Pharisaism' in *Christian Origins and Judaism*.

17 Jeremias, *Jerusalem*, pp. 233ff.

18 On the origins of Jewish mysticism, see Gruenwald, *Apocalyptic*; Scholem, *Major Trends; Jewish Gnosticism*; Urbach, in *Studies in Mysticism and Religion for G. Scholem*; Wewers, *Geheimnis*; Halperin, *Merkabah*; Chernus, 'Visions of God' and *Mysticism*.

19 See Gruenwald, *Apocalyptic*, pp. 213ff.

20 This matter is explored in Rowland, *The Open Heaven*; 'Visions of God', but cf. Halperin, *Merkabah*.

21 On 4QSerek, see now Schiffman, 'Merkavah Speculation'.

22 See further, Hartmann, *Prophecy Interpreted* and Gruenwald, *Apocalyptic*, pp. 3ff.

23 For a discussion of these passages, see Gruenwald, *Apocalyptic*, pp. 99ff.; Rowland, *The Open Heaven*, pp. 228ff.

24 See further, C. Jeremias, *Nachtgesichte*.

25 In addition to the works of Stone and Gruenwald already cited, see von Rad, *OT Theology* 2, p. 301f., but note the points made by von der Osten-Sacken, *Apokalyptik*.

26 See Müller, 'Mantische Weisheit'.

27 See Gruenwald, *Apocalyptic*, p. 4f.; Stone, 'Lists', p. 421; Knibb, 'Apocalyptic'.

28 See Rowland, *The Open Heaven*, pp. 358ff.

11 Jewish Sectarianism

1 Weber, *Protestant Ethic*, pp. 144f.; surveys in Giddens, *Capitalism*; Hill, *Sociology*. See also Troeltsch, *Social Teaching*; Wilson, *Religion*; *Sects*; *Magic*; Elliott, *Home for the Homeless*.

2 See Sanders, *Paul*, pp. 152ff. On Jewish sects generally see Smith, *Palestinian Parties*; 'Palestinian Judaism'; Vermes, *Jesus*; Simon, *Jewish Sects*; Nickelsburg and Stone, *Faith and Piety*, pp. 11ff.

3 The outlook of Matthew's Gospel, if the parable of the wheat and the tares in chapter 13 is anything to go by, is an example of the view which regards the community as a mixture of righteous and sinners. See Barth in Bornkamm *et al.*, *Tradition*, pp. 38ff. and further, on the early Church, Gager, *Kingdom*; Meeks, *Urban Christians*.

4 *Paul*, p. 424.

5 This may have taken place in the post-Exilic community; see Hanson, *Dawn*.

6 On the concerns of the rabbis at Yavneh, see Neusner, 'Formation'; Davies, *Setting*; Podro, *Pharisee*; Neusner, *Eliezer*; *Development*; *A Life*; and Guttmann, *Judaism*.

7 Note the different exegetical approaches from Akiba and Ishmael. See Marmorstein, *Old Rabbinic Doctrine* 2, pp. 29ff.

8 Neusner, *Traditions about the Pharisees*.

9 On the importance of Eliezer b. Hyrcanus, see Neusner, 'Formation'.

10 See McKeleney, 'Orthodoxy'; Aune, 'Orthodoxy'; Sanders, *Jewish and Christian Self-Definition*, vol. 2.

11 On the importance of geographical considerations, see Freyne, *Galilee*; Vermes, *Jesus*; de Ste Croix, *Class Struggle*, pp. 427ff.

12 On social stratification, see Jeremias, *Jerusalem*; Kreissig, *Sozialen Zusammenhänge*.

13 On the Samaritans, see Coggins, *Samaritans*; Purvis, *Samaritan Pentatecuh*; Macdonald, *Theology*; Nickelsburg and Stone, *Faith and Piety*, pp. 13f.

14 On the attitude to the Temple in the Dead Sea Scrolls, see Vermes, *Dead Sea Scrolls*, pp. 180f.

15 See *SVM History* 2, pp. 199ff., Mantel, *Studies*.

16 See further, Falk, *Introduction*.

17 On the infiltration of social customs into the halakah, see Finkelstein, *Pharisees*.

12 An Outline of Jewish Groups in the First Century AD

1 TDNT 7, pp. 35ff.; Jeremias, *Jerusalem* pp. 147ff. and 222ff., and Le Moyne, *Les Sadducéens*.

2 See Tcherikover, *Hellenistic Civilisation* and Hengel, *Judaism*.

3 Note Freyne's judgement about Galilee in *Galilee*, pp. 293ff.

4 Jeremias, *Jerusalem*, pp. 233ff.; Neusner, 'Formation', and Strack-Billerbeck 4.334ff. and above, p. 336.

5 See Bowker, *Jesus and the Pharisees*.

6 On the Pharisees see Neusner, *Traditions; Politics to Piety*, 'Making'; Jeremias, *Jerusalem*, cf. Rivkin, *Hidden Revolution*. There has been much debate in recent years over the extent of the continuity between the Pharisees and the later rabbis. The refusal of the rabbinic traditions to label their religious ancestors 'pharisees' seems to make a simple identification of the Pharisees with the later rabbinic tradition difficult.

7 The rabbinic evidence is considered in Bowker, *Jesus*; Rivkin, in *Hidden Revolution*; and 'Pharisees' in *IDB Supp*.

8 See Finkel, *Pharisees*, for an unsophisticated attempt to relate Jesus to a particular pharisaic outlook.

9 See Freyne, *Galilee*, pp. 306ff. According to him, Pharisaism was an extension of cultic holiness and thus offered a new understanding of God to meet the needs of the Jew in an urban context of the Hellenistic age.

10 Jeremias, *Jerusalem*, p. 257.

11 See Neusner, *The Idea of Purity*.

12 On sectarian boundaries, see Forkman, *Limits*.

13 On the oral tradition, see Gerhardsson, *Memory*.

14 For the sources, see below, pp. 313ff.

15 On the synagogue, see pp. 43f.

16 See Goldberg, *Schekhinah*.

17 On Yohanan's escape, see Saldarini, 'Johanan ben Zakkai's Escape'; Schäfer, 'Flucht'.

18 Neusner, 'Formation'; Davies, *Setting*; and Schäfer, 'Synode'; 'Flucht'.

19 Neusner, *Eliezer*.

20 On the birkath ha-minim, see Justin, *Dial.* 16; 47; 93; 95f.; 108; 117; 133 and 137; Horbury, 'Benediction'; *SVM History* 2, 462 and Kimelman 'Birkat' in Sanders, *Jewish and Christian Self-Definition*, vol. 2 and below, pp. 299ff.

21 Finkel, *Pharisees*.

22 Yadin, *Masada*; on the Zealots, see Farmer, *Maccabees*; Hengel, *Zeloten*; *Victory over Violence*; *Was Jesus a Revolutionist?*; Freyne, *Galilee*; Brandon, *Jesus the Zealot*; Eisler, *Messiah Jesus*; Bammel and Moule (ed.), *Jesus*; Hayward in *SVM History* 2, 595ff.; Rhoads, *Israel*; Aberbach, *Roman Jewish War*.

23 On Judas, see Freyne, *Galilee*, pp. 216ff.; Rhoads, *Israel*, pp. 47ff.

24 See Rhoads, *Israel*.

25 On the Dead Sea Scrolls, see Vermes, *Dead Sea Scrolls in English; Dead Sea Scrolls*; Milik, *Ten Years*; Cross, *Ancient Library*; Dupont-Sommer, *Essene Writings*; Driver, *Judaean Scrolls* and Davies, *Qumran*. There is a bibliography by Fitzmyer, *The Dead Sea Scrolls*.

26 Evidence on Philo and Pliny in Milik, *Ten Years*, p. 44.

27 On different suggestions with regard to background see Vermes, *Dead Sea Scrolls*. On the Zealot link, see Driver, *Judean Scrolls*.

28 On possible links with the NT, see Stendahl, *Scrolls*; Braun, *Qumran*; Black, *Scrolls*; *Paul and Qumran*, ed. Murphy O'Connor; and *John and Qumran*, ed. Charlesworth.

29 On this dimension, see Kuhn, *Enderwartung*; Aune, *Cultic Aspect*.

30 On the links with Paul, see Hodayoth, e.g., 1QH 4 (Vermes, p. 164); ed. Murphy O'Connor, op. cit.

31 On the calendar, see Jaubert, *Date*; Goudoever, *Calendars*; Safrai and Stern, *Jewish People* 2, pp. 834ff.

32 On the spiritualizing of the cult at Qumran, see Gärtner, *Temple*; McKelvey, *New Temple*; Klinzing, *Umdeutung*; Vermes, *Dead Sea Scrolls in English*, p. 46.

33 On the War Scroll, see Davies, *1QM*; Yadin, *War*.

34 On Jewish and Christian self-definition, see the publications of the McMaster project, ed. E. P. Sanders. On early Christian sectarianism, see Scroggs, 'Earliest Christian Communities'; Elliott, *Home for the Homeless*, pp. 73ff.

35 The use of 'Israel' terminology is an interesting example of the New Testament writers' self-understanding. On the lack of evidence for a 'New Israel' doctrine in earliest Christianity, see P. Richardson, *Israel*.

36 On the centrality of eschatology for earliest Christianity, see below, pp. 113ff.

37 But note the different explanation of the inconsistencies in O'Neill, *Romans*.

38 On Paul and Israel, see Munck, *Paul*; Davies, 'Paul and Israel'.

39 Examples of gnostic treatment of Paul may be found in Pagels, *Gnostic Paul*; Harnack, *Marcion*.

40 On Paul's espousal of a different type of Judaism from that commonly found in Palestine, see Sandmel, *Genius*; Schoeps, *Paul*. See also D. Hagner on the treatment of Paul in Jewish scholarship.

41 See McKeleney, 'Orthodoxy'; Aune, 'Orthodoxy'; and on this issue see also Sanders, *Paul*; *Paul the Law*.

42 On Jewish sectarian boundaries, see Forkman, *Limits*; Derrett, 'Cursing Jesus'. According to Acts 26.11, Paul seems to have applied a test to Christians, when he persecuted the Church.

43 On pagan attitudes, see Sevenster, *Anti-Semitism*.

44 See Safrai and Stern, *Jewish People* 2, pp. 1161ff.

45 See the discussions in *Sabbath to Sunday*, ed. Carson.

46 The letter is quoted in *A New Eusebius*, ed. J. Stevenson.

47 See Finkelstein, *Akiba*; Schäfer, *Aufstand*.

48 The comparisons with the messianic movement in the seventeenth century, centred on Sabbatai Sevi, are most interesting. See Scholem, *Sabbatai Sevi*; Davies, 'From Schweitzer to Scholem'.

49 On the importance of this chapter for Judaism and early Christianity, see Horbury, 'I Thess.'.

50 Reflections of this may be found in the New Testament; see Pancaro, *Law*.

51 See Bowker, *Targums*, p. 41.

13 Diaspora Judaism

1 On Jews in Babylonia, see Neusner, *Jews in Babylonia*. Note the fascinating incident concerning the conversion to Judaism of Izates, king of Adiabene, in Josephus, *Ant.* 20.34.

2 See Stone, *Scriptures*, p. 78; Cowley, *Papyri*; Porten, *Archives*.

3 On Hellenism, see Tarn, *Hellenistic Civilisation*, especially pp. 181ff.; Tcherikover, *Hellenistic Civilisation*; Cumont, *Oriental Religions*; Festugière, *Personal Religion*; Guthrie, *Greeks*; Nock, *Conversion*; Dodds, *Greeks*.

4 Jones, *Greek City*. On Alexandria, see Fraser, *Ptolemaic Alexandria*.

5 See Jaeger, *Paideia*.

6 See Tarn, op. cit., pp. 129, 191; and Safrai and Stern, *Jewish People* I, pp. 440ff.

7 Jeremias, *Jerusalem*, p. 77.

8 On Onias' Temple, see p. 335.

9 See Kraabel, *Judaism in Asia Minor*; Johnson, 'Early Christianity and Asia Minor'; Magie, *Roman Rule*; cf. Yamauchi, *Archaeology*.

10 See Smallwood, *Jews*, especially pp. 378ff.

11 Safrai and Stern, *Jewish People* I, p. 443.

12 See Kraabel, op. cit.

13 Safrai and Stern, *Jewish People* I, p. 460.

14 On Sardis see Kraabel, op. cit.; Johnson, 'Asia Minor' and Yamauchi, *Archaeology*.

15 Safrai and Stern, *Jewish People* I, p. 449.

16 Safrai and Stern, *Jewish People* I, p. 452. On anti-Jewish feeling, see Sevenster, *Anti-Semitism*; Sherwin-White, *Racial Prejudice*; Musurillo, *Acts*.

17 See Kraabel, op. cit.

18 On the LXX, see Dodd, *Bible*; Jellicoe, *Septuagint*; 'Septuagint' in *IDB Supp.*, *Studies*, ed. Jellicoe; Gooding, 'Aristeas'; Walters, *Text*.

19 On Gen. 1.1 of LXX, see Schmidt in *ZAW* 86: Dodd, *Bible*, pp. 111f.

20 On the order of the books, see Sawyer, *Moses*, pp. 2ff. and further, Childs, *Introduction*.

21 e.g., Codex Vaticanus (B) and Origen's *Hexapla*; see Vermes, *Jesus*, pp. 109ff.

22 See Gooding, *Tabernacle*.

23 Williamson, *Israel*.

24 On the use of the LXX in the NT, see the survey in *Cambridge History of the Bible* I, ed.

Ackroyd and Evans, p. 377.

25 On Colossian teaching, see Meeks and Francis, *Conflict*, and see p. 341, 9n.

26 On Wisd., see Reese, *Hellenistic Influence*; Winston, *Wisd. Sol.*; the extensive survey by Larcher in *Études*.

27 On the Sibylline oracles, see Collins, *Sibylline Oracles*.

28 See Sänger, *Antikes Judentum*; Burchard, *Untersuchungen*.

29 Collins, *Athens*.

30 On Philo, see Goodenough, *Introduction; By Light; Politics of Philo*; Sandmel, *Philo*; Wolfson, *Philo*. See the art. 'Philo', in *The Cambridge History of Later Greek Philosophy*.

31 On Philo and Gnosticism, see Wilson, *Gnostic Problem*.

32 On Stoicism, see Rist, *Stoic Philosophy*; Macmullen, *Enemies*, ch. 2.

33 On Philo's doctrine, see Wolfson, *Philo*. On the possible influence of this passage on Pauline Christology, see Cullmann, *Christology*.

34 On the mysticism of Philo, see Winston, 'Was Philo a Mystic?' in *Studies in Jewish Mysticism*.

35 See Smallwood, *Legatio*.

36 On Clement, see Osborne, *Clement*; Bigg, *Platonists*; H. Chadwick, *Early Christianity*.

37 On Alexandrian Christianity in the earliest period, see the suggestions by Bauer, *Orthodoxy*.

38 Wilson, *Gnostic Problem* and further, below, pp. 294ff.

14   The Expression of Hope

1 Summary of material in *SVM History* 2, pp. 488ff.; Charles, *Eschatology*; Klausner, *Messianic Idea*; Mowinckel, *He that Cometh*; Volz, *Eschatologie*; Bousset, *Religion*; Fischer, *Eschatologie*; Cavallin, *Life after Death*; Neusner, *Foundations*; Nickelsburg and Stone, *Faith and Piety*.

2 On messianic woes, see *SVM History* 2, pp. 514ff.

3 On the Apocalypse of Weeks, see Dexinger, *Zehnwochenapokalypse*.

4 See the discussion in Harnisch, *Verhängnis*.

5 See Schlatter, *Theologie*; de Jonge in *Josephus Studien*, ed. Betz *et al.*

6 See W. D. Davies, *Gospel and the Land*.

7 See further, W. D. Davies, *Torah*; Schäfer 'Torah'.

8 On the origins of the resurrection belief, see Nickelsburg, *Resurrection*; Martin-Achard, *Death*; Cavallin, *Life after Death*.

9 See Sawyer, 'Hebrew Words'.

10 On resurrection in the Dead Sea Scrolls, see Vermes, *Dead Sea Scrolls*, pp. 186ff.; Laurin, 'Question of Immortality'.

11 See Nickelsburg and Cavallin, op. cit.; Cullmann, *Resurrection*. On life after death in Greek religion, see the studies of Charles, Cavallin and Nilsson, *A History of Greek Religion*. On Paul, see M. Harris, *Raised Immortal*.

12 Hengel, *Judaism*.

13 Summary in Vermes, *Jesus*; also *SVM History* 2, pp. 517ff.; TDNT 9, pp. 493ff.; Mowinckel, *He that Cometh*; on the Dead Sea Scrolls, see van der Woude, *Vorstellungen*.

14 On the background of Christology, see e.g., Cullmann, *Christology*; Dunn, *Christology*.

15 On Son of David, see Hahn, *Titles*; TDNT 9, pp. 478ff.

16 Urbach, *Sages* 1, pp. 672ff.

17 The literature on this subject is vast. Mention may be made of the following: Casey, *Son of Man*; Cullmann, *Christology*; Tödt, *Son of Man*; Dunn, *Christology*; Collins, *Apocalyptic Vision*; Colpe, TDNT 8; Theisohn, *Der auserwählte Richter*; Lindars, *Jesus the Son of Man*.

18 So, e.g., Casey, op. cit.

19 See e.g., Collins, *Apocalyptic Vision*; also in *Ideal Figures*, ed. Nickelsburg; also Nickelsburg and Stone, *Faith and Piety*, pp. 177f.

20 See Stone in *Religions in Antiquity*, ed. Neusner.

21 Theisohn, *Der auserwählte Richter*.

22 e.g., Leivestad, 'Exit'; Milik, *Books of Enoch*.

23 See above, p. 35ff.; Horton, *Melchizedek*; Kobelski, *Melchizedek*.

24 G. Jeremias, *Lehrer*, pp. 284ff.

25 See Teeple, *Eschatological Prophet*; Meeks, *Prophet-King*; Schillebeeckx, *Christ*, pp. 300ff.

26 See TDNT 2, pp. 928ff.; 6, pp. 781ff. Also Urbach, *Sages* 1, p. 661; *SVM History* 2, pp. 515ff.

27 For Moses in Samaritan material, see Meeks, *The Prophet-King*; Macdonald, *Theology*.

15   Pragmatism and Utopianism in Ancient Judaism

1 See Farmer, *Maccabees*, pp. 177f.

2 On the ban, see Deut. 20.16f.; Josh. 6–8; 1 Sam. 15; Num. 31.14f.; von Rad, *Studies*, pp. 45ff.

3 See Hanson, *Dawn*; Cross, *Canaanite Myth*; Miller, *Divine Warrier*.

4 On this, see Childs, *Isaiah*.

5 See Farmer, *Maccabees*.

6 *SVM History* 1, pp. 330ff.

7 See Hayward in *SVM History* 2, pp. 598ff.; Freyne, *Galilee*, pp. 208ff.; Rhoads, *Israel*.

8 *SVM History* 2, p. 603.

9 Urbach, *Sages* 1, pp. 668f.

10 On this, see Saldarini, 'Escape' and above, p. 339.

11 On the links of Simeon ben Gamaliel with John of Gischala, a leading figure in the Revolt, see Josephus, *Vita*, 190ff., and further, Rhoads, *Israel* pp. 150ff.

12 See e.g., Rössler, *Gesetz*; Herford, *Talmud*.

13 So Hanson, *Dawn*; Plöger, *Theocracy*.

14 Neusner, *Politics*; Rivkin, 'Pharisaism and Crisis'.

15 See Philo, *Embassy* (Smallwood, *Legatio*).

16 On relations of Jews with Romans, see Smallwood, *Jews*.

17 Aune, *Cultic Aspect* drawing on Kuhn, *Enderwartung*.

18 Hengel, *Zeloten*; *Was Jesus a Revolutionist?*; W. D. Davies, *The Gospel and the Land*.

19 On Roman policy, see *SVM History* 1, pp. 376ff.

20 de Ste Croix, *Class Struggle*, pp. 441f.

21 On this passage, see e.g., Cullmann, *State*.

22 Cf. the War Scroll (see Yadin, *Scroll*; Davies *1QM*).

23 On the infiltration of eschatological beliefs into the scribal schools, see Urbach, *Sages* 1, p. 651.

24 See e.g., Barrett, *Judaism*, but note the comments below, pp. 285ff.

25 Rowland, *Open Heaven*, pp. 269ff.

26 On Bar Kochba, see Yadin, *Bar Kochba; SVM History* 2, pp. 534ff.; Schäfer, *Aufstand*.

27 See above, pp. 60ff.

28 See the comments of Neusner in *Life*, pp. 140f.

29 On shekinah, see above, pp. 32 and 71.

30 See Rowland, *Open Heaven*, pp. 113ff.

31 See Vermes, *Dead Sea Scrolls*, p. 174f. Of course, communion with the holy God was possible in the worship of the Temple.

32 On this material, see Aune, *Cultic Aspect*.

33 In *Gnosticism*, and see below, pp. 294ff.

34 Noted by Barrett in 'New Testament Eschatology', pp. 138f.

PART III
The Emergence of a Messianic Sect

SECTION 1   INTRODUCTION

1 Early Christianity: What Kind of Religious Movement?

1   On the study of the social world of the early Christians, see Gager, *Kingdom*; Kee, *Christian Origins*; Derrett, *Jesus' Audience*; Malherbe, *Social Aspects*; Theissen, *First Followers; Social Setting*; Meeks, *Urban Christians*.

2   So Gager, *Kingdom*, but cf. Judge, *Social Pattern*; Meeks, *Urban Christians*.

3   On Jesus and his disciples, see Hengel, *Charismatic Leader*; Theissen, *First Followers*.

4   See Gager, *Kingdom*; Cohn, *Pursuit*; Wilson, *Magic*.

5   On early Christian asceticism, see Strathmann, *Geschichte*; TDNT 1, pp. 492f.

6   See Theissen, *Social Setting*.

7   See Dodds, *Pagan*, pp. 112ff.

8   On this, see Jones, *Constantine*; A. Kee, *Constantine*.

9   On this and the problem of cognitive dissonance, see Gager, *Kingdom*; cf. Carroll, *When Prophecy Failed*.

2 The Centrality of Eschatology in Primitive Christian Belief

1   See Schweitzer, *Quest; Mysticism*; Beker, *Paul the Apostle; Apocalyptic Gospel*; Vögtle, *Zukunft*.

2   See, e.g., Moltmann, *Theology of Hope*; Pannenberg, *Jesus*; Bloch, *Atheism*; and on the influence of Ernst Bloch, Hudson, *Marxist Philosophy*.

3 For alternative approaches to the subject of eschatology, see Carmignac, *Mirage*; Glasson, *Jesus*; Marshall, 'Eschatology'.

4 See Caird, *Language and Imagery*.

5 See further, Moltmann, *The Crucified God*.

6 See, e.g., Cullmann, *Salvation in History*.

7 On the meaning of resurrection, see Selby, *Look for the Living*.

8 See the works of Cullmann, e.g., *Christ and Time; Salvation in History*.

9 Dunn, *Jesus*.

10 See further, TDNT 6, pp. 332ff.

11 See Schäfer, *Heilige Geist*. It should be noted that the Holy Spirit plays an important role in the religion of the Dead Sea Scrolls, though it is not clear that the Scrolls interpret the Spirit eschatologically.

12 See further, Jeremias, *NTT* pp. 76ff.

13 On the doctrine of the incarnation see Dunn, *Christology* and Hengel, *Son of God*.

14 On messianic expectation see above, pp. 92ff. and *SVM History* 2, pp. 517ff.

15 See Hengel in *Paul and Paulinism*, ed. Hooker and Wilson.

16 See Rowland, *Open Heaven*, pp. 423ff.

3 The World of Jesus and the First Christians

1 Freyne, *Galilee*. See also Meyers, 'Cultural Setting'; Theissen, *First Followers*, esp. pp. 31ff.

2 On this, see de Ste Croix, *Class Struggle*, pp. 9ff., 427.

3 Freyne, op. cit., p. 91.

4 Freyne, op. cit., p. 194ff.

5 Freyne, op. cit., pp. 221ff.; Green, 'Palestinian Holy Men'; Vermes, *Jesus*.

6 See Theissen, *First Followers*, pp. 17ff., and Freyne, *Galilee* pp. 356ff.

7 For the socio-economic explanation, see Kautsky, *Foundations* and note also Kreissig, *Sozialen Zusammenhänge*.

8 On the change of environment, see Theissen, *First Followers; Social Setting*; Malherbe, *Social Aspects*; de Ste Croix, *Class Struggle*; Meeks, *Urban Christians*. On the setting of non-Palestinian Christianity in Asia Minor, see Kraabel, *Judaism*; Yamauchi, *Archaeology*.

9 e.g., Meeks and Wilken, *Jews and Christians*; Meeks, *Urban Christians*.

10 In his *Social Setting*.

11 So also Judge, *Social Pattern*; cf. Deissmann, *Light*.

12 See Meeks, *Urban Christians* and on social relations see Macmullen, *Roman Social Relations*.

SECTION 2 JESUS

1 The Quest for the Historical Jesus

1 Surveys and literature in Schweitzer, *Quest*; Anderson, *Jesus*; Käsemann in *New Testament Questions*; J. M. Robinson, *A New Quest*; Schillebeeckx, *Jesus*; Dodd, *Founder*;

Tatum, *In Quest*; Farmer, *Jesus*.

2 Strauss, *Life*, p. 88.

3 On the Marcan hypothesis, see Streeter, *Four Gospels*; Farmer, *Synoptic Problem*; Tuckett, *Revival*; Stoldt, *Marcan Hypothesis*.

4 See Harnack, *What is Christianity?*, p. 36.

5 From *Christianity at the Crossroads*, p. 49.

6 Weiss, *Jesus' Proclamation*.

7 From *Quest*, p. 397.

8 For an introduction to Barth's theology, see Hartwell, *Theology of Karl Barth*.

9 See Bultmann, *History of the Synoptic Tradition*. Another pioneering form-critical work is Dibelius, *From Tradition to Gospel*.

10 Bultmann, *Theology* 1, p. 3: 'the message of Jesus is a presupposition for the theology of the New Testament rather than a part of that theology itself.'

11 cf. Jeremias, *Problem*.

12 See Bultmann, *Jesus and the Word*.

13 e.g., Jeremias, *Eucharistic Words*; *Parables*.

14 Stauffer, *Jesus and his Story*.

15 See Käsemann, 'Problem' in *Essays*; 'Blind Alleys' in *Questions*, pp. 23ff.

16 Bornkamm, *Jesus of Nazareth*.

17 On eye-witness tradition, see Taylor, *Formation*, pp. 41ff.; Dodd, 'Framework'; Nineham, 'Eye-Witness Testimony'.

18 cf. Cadbury, *Perils*.

2 *Using the Gospels to Establish the Character of Jesus' Life and Message*

1 For a necessary reminder of the importance of the epistemological issues, see Meyer, *Aims*; Downing, *Church*.

2 See Catchpole in *NT Interpretation*, ed. Marshall; Barbour, *Traditio-Historical Criticism*. There is a good survey in Reumann, *Jesus and the Church's Gospels*; also Perrin, *Rediscovering*; Hayes and Holladay, *Biblical Exegesis*; Henry, *New Directions*; Nickle, *Synoptic Gospels*.

3 e.g., Dodd, *Historical Tradition*.

4 See pp. 299ff.

5 For an introduction to this method, see Perrin, *What is Redaction Criticism?*; Rohde, *Rediscovering*; Marshall, *Luke*; Martin, *Mark*; Nineham, *St Mark*; Hooker, *Message*. For a very different approach to Mark, see Belo, *Materialist Reading*.

6 Survey in Cadbury, *Making*, pp.299ff.; further, Maddox, *Purpose*.

7 See Nineham in *Studies in the Gospels*, ed. Nineham.

8 See Barbour, *Traditio-Historical Criticism*,; Jeremias, *Parables*, Part 2.

9 On form criticism, see Bultmann and Kundsin, *Form Criticism*.

10 There is a concise introduction to the practice of redaction criticism in Perrin, *What is Redaction Criticism?* and Rohde, *Rediscovering*.

11 Perrin, *Rediscovering*, p. 39; Conzelman, quoted in Perrin, op. cit., p. 42: 'we may accept as authentic material which fits in with neither Jewish thinking nor the conception of the

primitive community'. On the application of this method, see Downing, *Church and Jesus*; Hooker, 'On the Wrong Use of a Tool'; Barbour, *Traditio-Historical Criticism*.

12 On the parable of the wedding feast, see Jeremias, *Parables*, pp. 176ff.

13 On the possibility of the Matthaean conclusion being a separate parable added to the originally different parable of the wedding feast, see Jeremias, *Parables*, pp. 187ff.

14 See Bultmann, *History* pp. 11ff.; Taylor, *Formation*, pp. 63ff.

15 On the use of the oral tradition from Judaism as a means of illustrating the transmission of tradition in early Christianity, see Gerhardsson, *Memory*; *Tradition and Transmission*; *Gospel Tradition*. But note the comments of Barrett, *Jesus*; W. D. Davies, 'Reflections' in *Setting*; Sanders, *Tendencies*. Further, on the relationship between the gospel tradition and early Christian preaching, Stanton, *Jesus of Nazareth*; McDonald, *Kerygma*; Dodd, *Apostolic Preaching*.

16 See the form-critical method (better described as traditio-historical method) applied to rabbinic material by Jacob Neusner, e.g., in *Development of a Legend* and his study of the mishnaic laws of purity.

17 On the possibility of sayings of the risen Lord through the mouths of Christian prophets being included in the gospel tradition, see Dunn, 'Prophetic "I" Sayings'; Boring, *Sayings*.

18 See Dungan, *Sayings of Jesus*.

3 John the Baptist

1 On John the Baptist, see Scobie, *John*; Wink, *John*; Kraeling, *John*; Hollenbach, 'Social Aspects'. O'Neill, *Messiah*, puts the case for a recognition by the Baptist that Jesus was the 'one to come'.

2 Vermes, *Jesus*, p. 197.

3 See the survey in Scobie, *John*.

4 Vermes, *Jesus*, p. 75.

5 See Barrett, *NT Background*, p. 196; Freyne, *Galilee*, pp. 216ff.

6 On this material, see Wink, op. cit., and on Elijah, see TDNT 2, pp. 928ff.

7 Summary in Dodd, *Fourth Gospel*, pp. 115ff.

8 On this, see Käsemann, in *Essays*.

9 See Brown, *John*, I, LXVII.

10 On this saying, see Suggs, *Wisdom*; Hamerton-Kelly, *Pre-Existence*.

11 On this, see McNeile, *Matthew*, p. 154.

4 The Proclamation of the Kingdom of God

1 Literature on this subject is extensive. Mention may be made of the following: Dalman, *Words*; Kümmel, *Promise*; and *Theology*, pp. 27ff.; TDNT 1, pp. 579ff.; Perrin, *Kingdom of God*; *Rediscovering*; *Jesus and the Language of the Kingdom*; Minear, *And Great Shall Be Your Reward*; Harvey, *Jesus*; Schnackenburg, *God's Rule*; Glasson, *Jesus*; Ladd, *Jesus and the Kingdom*; Riches, *Jesus*; Chilton, *God in Strength*; Schillebeeckx, *Jesus*, pp. 140ff.; Jeremias, *NTT*; Schweitzer, *Quest*; Weiss, *Jesus' Proclamation*; Manson, *Sayings; Teaching*; Meyer, *Aims*; O'Neill, *Messiah*; and Pixley, *God's Kingdom*. Summary in Chilton, *The Kingdom of God*.

2 See Perrin, *Kingdom of God*.

3 See Dodd, *Fourth Gospel*, pp. 144f.

4   See pp. 87ff.

5   Weiss, *Jesus' Proclamation*, pp. 129f.

6   On realized eschatology, see Dodd, *Parables*; Robinson, *Jesus and his Coming*; Glasson, *Second Advent; Jesus.* cf. Kümmel, *Promise.*

7   Manson, *Teaching*, pp. 120ff.

8   On the future dimension, see Hiers, *Kingdom of God*; O'Neill, *Messiah*; Fuller, *Mission.* cf. Glasson, *Jesus.*

9   For a description of the character of inaugurated eschatology, see Cullman, *Salvation in History*, pp. 193ff.; Jeremias, *Parables*, p. 230; Kümmel, *Promise.*

10 But note the interpretation of Luke 11.20 and 17.21b offered by O'Neill in *Messiah.*

11 See Weiss, *Jesus' Proclamation*, p. 129.

5   The Parables

1   See Jeremias, *Parables*; Perrin, *Rediscovering*; Linnemann, *Parables*; Perrin, *Jesus and the Language of the Kingdom*; and Lambrecht, *Once More.*

2   On allegorization, see Jeremias, *Parables*, pp. 66ff. Note the importance of the gnostic Gospel of Thomas for study of the parables. See Turner and Montefiore, *Thomas and the Evangelists.*

3   Jeremias, *NTT* p. 29: *Parables*, pp. 113f.; Perrin, *Rediscovering* but cf. Moule, *Birth*, pp. 115ff.; and *Essays.*

4   See further, Derrett, *Jesus' Audience.*

5   Jeremias, *Parables*, p. 56.

6   Ibid., p. 150.

7   See Urbach, *Sages* i. p. 668f.

8   The similarity between Jesus and Paul in this regard should not be ignored: Jesus calls Jewish sinners; Paul calls Gentiles.

9   Sanders, 'Jesus, Sinners and the Am Ha-Aretz' in (ed.) Horbury and Rowland, *Essays*; Schillebeeckx, *Jesus*, pp. 206f.

10 On covenantal nomism, see Sanders, *Paul*, pp. 44ff.

6   Other Teaching

1   On the life-style of Jesus, see Hengel, *Charismatic Leader*; Mealand, *Poverty*; Theissen, *First Followers*; Freyne, *Galilee.*

2   On the issue of property and early Christian attitudes to it, see de Ste Croix, *Class Struggle*; Grant, *Early Christianity and Society*; Hengel, *Property and Riches.*

3   On the importance of this passage, see Yoder, *Politics.*

4   On this parable, see Perrin, *Rediscovering*, pp. 122ff.; on the love command, see Furnish, *Love Command*; Piper, *Love Your Enemies.*

5   On Samaritans, see Coggins, *Samaritans.*

6   On the meaning of brethren in the Johannine corpus, see Montefiore in *Jesus.*

7   On the vexed issue of the eschatological Torah in Judaism, see Davies, *Torah in the Messianic Age*; Schäfer, 'Torah'.

8   On Jesus and the law see below, pp. 156ff., and O'Neill, *Messiah.*

9   Harvey, *Jesus*, p. 64.

10 Hengel, *Charismatic Leader.*

11 Cullmann, *State*, p. 51. See also Brandon, *Jesus* p. 87.

12 Cullmann, *State*, p. 50.

13 See Jeremias, *NTT*, p. 294; Mealand, *Poverty*, p. 69.

14 See Mealand, op. cit., p. 70: 'it is better to conclude that in a time of great danger, the rules about poverty, trust and defencelessness were revised.' On the changing social circumstances of the early Christian movement, see Theissen, *First Followers*; de Ste Croix, *Class Struggle*, pp. 427f.

15 See Brandon, *Jesus.*

16 cf. Schweitzer, *Quest*; Barrett, *Jesus.*

7 The Signs of the Coming Kingdom

1 See Harvey, *Jesus*; McCasland, *By the Finger of God*; Jeremias, *NTT*, pp. 85ff.; Vermes, *Jesus*, 58ff.; Dunn, *Jesus*, 69ff.; Fuller, *Interpreting*; Hull, *Hellenistic Magic*; van der Loos, *Miracles*; M. Smith, *Jesus the Magician*; W. S. Green, 'Palestinian Holy Men'; Theissen, *Miracle Stories* (which has a full bibliography), and Kee, *Miracle.*

2 On the infancy narratives, see Brown, *Birth.*

3 On Jewish parallels, see Vermes, *Jesus*, pp. 58ff.; Freyne, *Galilee*, pp. 329ff.; Green, 'Palestinian Holy Men'.

4 For a concise introduction, see Schillebeeckx, *Jesus*, pp. 179ff. and Meyer, *Aims.*

5 cf. Petzke, *Apollonius.* There have been several attempts to explore the possibility that Jesus was being presented as a wonder-worker in the early Church; see e.g., Weeden, *Traditions*; and Koester in Robinson and Koester, *Trajectories.* On the much discussed concept of the *theios aner* or divine man in antiquity, see the recent critical survey by Holladay.

6 See Smith, *Jesus the Magician.*

7 But see Harvey, *Jesus.*

8 See further, Hull, *Hellenistic Magic.*

9 On Matt. 17, see Horbury in *Jesus and the Politics of his Day*, ed. Bammel.

10 See the apocryphal gospels in Hennecke-Schneemelcher, *NT Apocrypha*, for examples of the growth of miraculous legends about Jesus' life.

11 See Brown, *World*, pp. 51ff.

12 See Jeremias, *NTT*. pp. 85ff.

13 See e.g., O'Neill, *Messiah*, pp. 14ff.

14 On Balaam see Vermes, *Scripture and Tradition.*

15 On false prophecy, see Horbury, '1 Thess. 2.3'; Bauckham, *Jude*, pp. 236f.

8 Jesus and the Future

1 On this, see Kümmel, *Promise*, 'Eschatological Expectation'; Perrin, *Rediscovering*, pp. 154ff.; Beasley-Murray, *Jesus and the Future*; Robinson, *Jesus and his Coming*; Harvey, *Jesus*; Meyer, *Aims*; Jeremias, *NTT*, pp. 138ff.

2 Kümmel, *Promise*, p. 149; Jeremias, *NTT*, p. 139.

3 Dodd, *Parables*; see also Chilton, *God in Strength* on Mark 9.1; cf. Kümmel, *Promise*, pp. 25ff.

4 Bultmann, *History*, pp. 151f.; Riches, *Jesus*, p. 176.

5 e.g., Hooker, *Son of Man*; Robinson, *Jesus and his Coming*; Glasson, *Second Advent*.

6 See pp. 182ff.

7 On the Beatitudes, see Dupont, *Beatitudes*; Wrege, *Überlieferung*; Schnackenburg, *Moral Teaching*; Jeremias, *NTT*, pp. 203ff.; Schweizer in *NTS* 19, pp. 121ff.

8 See Wainwright, *Eucharist*.

9 On the Lord's Prayer, see J. Carmignac, *Recherches*; Petuchowski, *Lord's Prayer*; Lohmeyer, *Vater-Unser*; Evans, *The Lord's Prayer*; Wainwright, *Eucharist*. Jeremias, *NTT*, p. 248 spiritualizes Jesus' view of the consummation. He suggests that the kingdom is stripped of materialistic and nationalistic features, and argues that Jesus 'speaks of a transfigured world only in the images of symbolic language'. Of the sayings in the gospel tradition only Mark 12.25 would tend to support Jeremias' hypothesis.

10 On Jesus and the Gentile mission, see Jeremias, *Jesus' Promise*; see further, Hahn, *Mission*; Harnack, *Mission and Expansion*.

11 Vermes, *Jesus*.

12 See Caird, *Jesus and the Jewish Nation*.

13 Bousset, *Religion*, pp. 233f.

14 Jeremias, *Jesus' Promise*.

15 See above, pp. 140f. and Riches, *Jesus*, pp. 176ff.

16 Flew, *Jesus and his Church*; von Campenhausen, *Ecclesiastical Authority*, pp. 1ff.; Schweizer, *Church Order*, pp. 20ff.

17 Loisy, *The Gospel and the Church*, p. 166.

18 For a recent restatement of a Schweitzerian position, see Barrett, *Jesus*, p.48 but note the comments of Glasson in *Jesus*.

19 Jeremias, *Eucharistic Words*, pp. 237ff.

20 On Holy Spirit in Gospels, see Barrett, *Holy Spirit*; Dunn, *Jesus*.

21 Theissen, *First Followers*.

22 Hengel, *Charismatic Leader*. On evidence of Jesus teaching his disciples, see Gerhardsson, *Memory*; Riesner, *Jesus als Lehrer*; also Daube, 'Responsibilities'; Derrett, *Jesus' Audience*, pp. 101ff.

23 On sending formula, see Borgen, 'God's Agent'.

24 See Kümmel, *Promise*, p. 147. On Jesus and Community, see Lohfink.

25 See TDNT 3, p. 520; Emerton in *JTS* 13 (1962), Wilcox in *NTS* 22; Meyer, *Aims*, pp. 185ff. and O'Neill, *Messiah*, pp. 90ff.

26 See O'Neill, *Messiah*, pp. 92f.

27 On 'EDAH and related terms in Dead Sea Scrolls, see *SVM History* 2, pp. 575ff.; TDNT 3, p. 524; Vermes, *Dead Sea Scrolls*.

28 On Peter, see Cullmann, *Peter*; Brown and Donfried, *Peter*.

9 Jesus and Contemporary Judaism

1 An enormous amount of literature has grown up around this theme. Mention may be made of Vermes, *Jesus*; Finkel, *Pharisees*; Klausner, *Jesus of Nazareth*; Flusser, *Jesus*; Harvey, *Jesus*; Riches, *Jesus*; Betz, *What do we Know?*; Westerholm, *Jesus and Scribal Authority*.

2   For Jewish polemic, see Herford, *Christianity*; Klausner, *Jesus of Nazareth*; Maier, *Jesus von Nazareth*; Bammel, 'Christian Origins'.

3   See Neusner, *Politics* and above, pp. 69ff., though note the remarks of Freyne, *Galilee*, pp. 305ff.

4   Westerholm, *Jesus and Scribal Authority*.

5   On 'I' Sayings, see Jeremias, *NTT*, p. 250 and Arens, *ELTHON Sayings*.

6   On Jesus' baptism, see Rowland, *Open Heaven*, pp. 358ff.; Lentzen-Deis, *Die Taufe Jesu*; further, Bruegemann, *Prophetic Imagination*.

7   Goldberg, *Schekhinah*, pp. 109ff.

8   cf. Bowker, *Religious Imagination*, pp. 121ff.

9   See Pancaro, *Law*, 87ff.

10 On Jesus and the Torah, see Banks, *Jesus and the Law*; Berger, *Gesetzauslegung*; Harvey, *Jesus*, ch. 3; Derrett, *Law*; Freyne, *Galilee*, pp. 309ff.; Schillebeeckx, *Jesus*, pp. 229ff.

11 See *Sabbath to Sunday*, ed. Carson.

12 See Rowland in *Sabbath to Sunday*, ed. Carson.

13 See Finkel, *Pharisees*.

14 See Daube, 'Responsibilities'; Derrett, *Jesus' Audience*, pp. 142ff.

15 cf. M. Smith, *Clement of Alexandria*, pp. 254ff.

16 See *Sabbath to Sunday*, ed. Carson, p. 84.

17 There may be a reflection of Jesus' attitude to Sabbath-breaking in the saying preserved in Codex Bezae (D) at Luke 6.4. See Jeremias, *Unknown Sayings*, p. 49.

18 Bousset, *Religion*, pp. 283ff.

19 cf. Jeremias, *NTT*, pp. 205ff.

20 On authenticity, cf. Jeremias, *NTT*, p. 210.

21 On Jesus' attitude to the dietary laws, see Vermes, *Jesus*, p.80; Westerholm, *Jesus*, p. 90.

22 Vermes, *Jesus*, p. 28.

23 Harvey, *Jesus*, p. 50.

24 Surveys in Vermes, *Jesus*; Jeremias, *Jerusalem*; *SVM History* 2, pp. 404ff.; Lauterbach, *Rabbinic Essays* 2, pp. 3ff.; TDNT 7, pp. 35ff.; Lescynsky, *Sadduzäer* and le Moyne, *Sadducéens*.

25 See Jeremias, *Jerusalem*, pp. 233ff; *SVM History* 2, pp. 381ff; TDNT 9, pp. 11ff; Bowker, *Jesus*; Jeremias, *NTT*, pp. 142ff and above, pp. 68ff.

26 On Zealots, see above, pp. 73ff. and also G. L. Edwards, *Jesus and the Politics of Violence*; Yoder, *Politics*; Hengel, *Was Jesus a Revolutionist?*; *Victory*; Riches, *Jesus*.

27 See further Belo, *Materialist Reading*.

28 See Derrett, *Jesus' Audience*, p. 187.

29 e.g., Brandon, *Jesus; Trial*; Eisler, *Messiah Jesus*.

30 On this see Hengel, *Die Zeloten*.

31 See TDNT 7, p. 51.

32 See Freyne, *Galilee*, pp. 259ff.

33 See Jeremias, *Jerusalem*, p. 148; Josephus, *Ant.* 18.90ff.; 20.6ff.; Rhoads, *Israel*, p. 41.

34 See above, p. 68.

35 On the cleansing in the Fourth Gospel, see Brown, *John* 1, pp. 115ff.; Schnackenburg, *John* 1, p. 356; McKelvey, *New Temple*, pp. 75ff.

36 On the cleansing, see Harvey, *Jesus*, pp. 129ff.; Meyer, *Aims*, pp. 197ff.; on Mark, see Telford, *Barren Fig-Tree*. Further, on the Temple, see Gaston, *No Stone*.

37 Jeremias, *Jerusalem*, p. 145.

38 See Black, *Scrolls*; Jeremias, *Eucharistic Words*.

39 See McKelvey, *New Temple*, pp. 58ff.; Gaston, *No Stone*.

40 On John 2.19, see Schnackenburg, *John*, 1, p. 349.

10   The Arrest and Trial of Jesus

1 Literature: Blinzler, *Trial*; Winter, *On the Trial*; Brandon, *Trial; Jesus*; Harvey, *Jesus*, ch. 2; *Trial*, ed. Bammel; *Jesus and the Politics of his Day*; Hoehner, *Herod*; Carmichael, *Death of Jesus*; Catchpole, *Trial*; Mantel, *Sanhedrin*; Sherwin-White, *Roman Society*.

2 On earlier investigations of Jesus' activity, see Stauffer, *Jesus and his Story*; Harvey, *Jesus on Trial*; Bammel in *Trial*, ed. Bammel.

3 On the Pharisees and Jesus' death, see Winter, *Trial*; Finkel, *Pharisees*.

4 On the Lucan Passion Narrative, see Catchpole, *Trial*; Taylor, *Passion Narrative*; Stanton, *Jesus of Nazareth*.

5 See Dodd, *Historical Tradition*.

6 On 23.2, see *Jesus and the Politics of his Day*, ed. Bammel, pp. 403ff.

7 On the date of the Last Supper, see Jeremias, *Eucharistic Words*; Jaubert, *Date*.

8 On Jesus' reply to the High Priest, see Catchpole, 'Answer'.

9 See Catchpole, *Trial*.

10 On John 18.31, see *SVM History* 2, pp. 221f. Further, on the rights of Jewish authorities, see Mantel, *Sanhedrin*; Catchpole, *Trial*; Winter, *On the Trial*.

11 *SVM History* 2, p. 220.

12 See Blinzler, *Trial*.

13 On the Roman execution, see Brandon, *Trial* and the review by de Ste Croix in *Eng. Hist. Rev.* 86 (1971), pp. 149f.

14 See Marshall, *Luke*, p. 158.

15 On mishnaic regulations and their history, see Mantel, *Sanhedrin*; Catchpole, *Trial*.

16 Of course, it could be argued that M. Sanhedrin represents the views of the Sages, not the Pharisees. On the relationship see Neusner, 'Formation'.

17 Vermes, *Jesus*, p. 234, 159n.

18 See Stauffer, *Jesus and His Story*.

19 See Segal, *Two Powers*; Catchpole, *Trial*, p. 141, but note the critical comment of Vermes, *Jesus*, p. 258, 34n. It is not easy to decide whether Jesus' sayings against the Temple could be construed as blasphemy (cf. Josephus *BJ* 6.301); it may well be that in Jesus' day blasphemy covered a variety of offences (see Mark 2.7).

20 Bowker, *Jesus*, p. 45.

21 On the silence of Jesus, cf. O'Neill, *Messiah*, and id. *NTS* 15 (1968–9); cf. Flusser, *Jesus*.

22 See 10n.

23 On Megillat Ta'anith, see Dalman, *Dialektproben*; TDNT 7, pp. 41ff.; Jeremias in *ZNW*

43, pp. 145ff.

24 On date of the execution of the High Priest's daughter, see Catchpole, 'Historicity'.

25 See Harvey, *Jesus*, pp. 17ff., 30f.

26 Though it should be noted that such actions may have increased as the political situation deteriorated (Rhoads, *Israel* p. 77). See further now, *Jesus and the Politics of his Day*, ed. Bammel, p. 427.

27 Bowker, *Jesus*, p. 49; *Trial*, ed. Bammel, pp. 21ff; Harvey, *Jesus*, pp. 17ff.

28 Rhoads, *Israel*, pp. 62, 68f.

29 See Cullmann, *State*, pp. 8ff.; Yoder, *Politics*; but cf. now (ed.) Bammel, *Jesus and the Politics of his Day*.

11 Jesus' Personal Claim

1 There is a vast amount of literature relating to this theme. Books which refer to a wide amount of secondary material as well as offering detailed discussion of the sources include: Cullmann, *Christology*; Dunn, *Jesus*; *Christology*; Hahn, *Titles*; Fuller, *Mission*; Harvey, *Jesus*; Lampe, *God as Spirit*; Moule, *Origin*.

2 Conzelmann, *Outline*, p. 140.

3 Borgen, 'God's Agent'; Bühner, *Gesandte*.

4 See Harvey, *Jesus*, p. 57ff.; TDNT 6, pp. 781ff.; Lampe, *God as Spirit*, pp. 63ff. On Luke 4.14ff. see Yoder, *Politics*.

5 Bowker, *Jesus*, p. 44.

6 Rowland, *The Open Heaven*, pp. 358ff., but cf. O'Neill, *Messiah*.

7 Barrett, *Holy Spirit*.

8 See Dunn, *Jesus*; Jeremias, *NTT*, pp. 61ff.

9 See Stanton, *Jesus of Nazareth*, pp. 67ff.

10 On the testing of the prophet's vocation, see Bultmann, *History*, pp. 253f.; on Luke 4.16, see Yoder, *Politics*.

11 Bowker, *Jesus*, p. 50: 'the only justification for a claim to be receiving direct authority from God would have been a manifest return of the Spirit which inspired the prophets.'

12 On the importance of the geographical setting of Jesus' ministry, see de Ste Croix, *Class Struggle*, pp. 427ff.; Freyne, *Galilee*, pp. 221, 332; Theissen, *First Followers*.

13 cf. Casey, *Son of Man* and Lindars, *Jesus the Son of Man*, on the origin of the sayings.

14 On the origins of the Eucharist, see Jeremias, *Eucharistic Words*; O'Neill, *Messiah*; Lietzmann, *Mass*.

15 On Isa. 53 in the gospel tradition, see Cullmann, *Christology*; Jeremias, *NTT*, pp. 276ff.; cf. Hooker, *Jesus*.

16 On Jewish martyrology, see Frend, *Martyrdom*; Lohse, *Märtyrer*; Lampe, *God as Spirit*, pp. 93f.

17 On the suffering Messiah, see Jeremias in Zimmerli and Jeremias, *The Servant of God*; Hegermann, *Jesaja 53*.

18 *Theology*, p. 94.

19 See above, 3n, on the agency motif.

20 On false prophecy, see TDNT 6, pp. 807f.; Horbury, '1 Thess. 2.3' and above, pp. 155f.

21 On Son of God, see Dunn, *Jesus*; *Christology*; van Iersel, *Sohn*; Vermes, *Jesus*, p. 192; Jeremias, *Prayers*; Harvey, *Jesus*.

22 Jeremias, *NTT*, pp. 61ff.

23 cf. Vermes, *Gospel* also in id. *Jesus and the World of Judaism*.

24 Vermes, *Jesus the Jew*, pp. 192ff.

25 Used by Jesus: Matt. 11.27 (par. Luke 10.22); Mark 13.32; John 3.35; 5.19f.; 8.35f. Used of Jesus: Matt. 2.15; 4.3f.; 8.29; 17.5 and par.; 27.40; Mark 1.11. Presupposed: Mark 12.6; 14.36; Luke 11.2, par.; Matt. 6.9f.

26 Jeremias, *Prayers*, p. 51; on Matt. 11.25ff., see Arvedson, *Mysterium*; Dalman, *Words*, pp. 268ff.

27 See TDNT 8, p. 373.

28 Dalman, *Words*, pp. 282f.

29 On the background, see Arvedson, *Mysterium*.

30 On the Messiah, see Cullmann, *Christology*, pp. 111ff.; Harvey, *Jesus*, ch. 6; Vermes, *Jesus*, pp. 129ff.; TDNT 9, pp. 493ff.

31 See above, p. 87ff.

32 For variant messianic expectations, see e.g., Meeks, *Prophet King*.

33 It seems to be the case in Mark 14.62 (and par.; see Catchpole, 'Answer'). It is discussed at Mark 9.41 and 12.35 and attributed to Jesus by others at Matt. 16.16; cf. Mark 8.27; 15.32, Matt. 27.17; Luke 23.2; John 4.25f.; 7.41; 10.28; 11.27.

34 On Peter's confession, see Cullmann, *Peter*; *Christology*; O'Neill, *Messiah*, pp. 92f.; Meyer, *Aims*, pp.185ff.

35 For a suggestion with regard to the composition of this section, see Haenchen, *Weg Jesu*, pp. 292ff.

36 Recently, on the Triumphal Entry, see Harvey, *Jesus*, pp. 120ff.

37 See Catchpole, *Trial*.

38 Harvey, *Jesus*, pp. 140ff.

39 On the Son of Man, see e.g., TDNT 8, pp. 400ff.; Tödt, *Son of Man*; Hooker, *Son of Man*; Leivestad, 'Exit'; Casey, *Son of Man*; Moule, 'Neglected Features' in *Essays*; Lindars, *Jesus the Son of Man*; Dalman, *Words*, pp. 234ff.; Vermes, *Jesus*, pp. 160ff.

40 See Moule, 'Neglected Features'.

41 Dodd, *Fourth Gospel*, p. 247, and on the Johannine Son of Man note the study of Moloney (*The Johannine Son of Man*).

42 On the Greek of the Son of Man sayings, see the comments by Moule and Casey, op. cit., and O'Neill, *Messiah*, pp. 107f., who argues that 'the first article could easily have been used to translate an indefinite expression that bore a particular force'.

43 Survey of OT material in Dalman, *Words*, 234f.

44 Vermes, pp. 160ff.; cf. Fitzmyer in *Wandering Aramean*; Black, *Aramaic Approach*, pp. 310ff. Note the amplification of this position by Bowker, 'Son of Man'.

45 On 'one like a son of man' in Dan. 7.13 as a heavenly being, see Collins, *Apocalyptic Vision*; Colpe in TDNT 8, pp. 420ff.; cf. Casey, *Son of Man*, pp. 7ff.

46 See e.g., Bultmann, *History*, e.g., pp. 121f.; Riches, *Jesus*, pp. 161ff.

47 See Jeremias, *NTT*, pp. 257ff.; Fuller, *Mission*, pp. 95ff.

48 Vermes, *Jesus*, pp. 163ff.; cf. Casey, *Son of Man*, pp. 224ff.

49 The criticisms of the Vermes theory by Jeremias may be found in *NTT*, p. 261; cf. O'Neill, *Messiah*.

50 Note the comments of Casey on Vermes' position in *Son of Man*, p. 224 and also O'Neill, *Messiah*, pp. 103ff. and Lindars, *Jesus the Son of Man*.

51 Vermes, *Jesus*, p. 183; Casey, *Son of Man*, pp. 165ff. and now Lindars, *Jesus the Son of Man* and Vermes, *Jesus and the Jewish World*.

52 cf. Glasson, *Second Advent*; Robinson, *Jesus and his Coming*; Perrin, *Rediscovering*, pp. 154ff.

53 See Casey, *Son of Man*, for a summary of this interpretation.

54 See Moule, 'Neglected Features'; Hooker, *Son of Man*.

55 e.g., Collins in *Apocalyptic Vision*; and in *Ideal Figures*, ed. Nickelsburg, pp. 111ff.

56 Fuller, *Mission*, pp. 107f.

57 cf. Casey's conclusion on New Testament scholarship's preoccupation with discussion of the Son of Man, op. cit., p. 239.

58 See Jeremias, *NTT*, p. 276.

12 The Resurrection Narratives

1 Literature: *Significance*, ed. Moule; Moule, *Phenomenon*; Fuller, *Formation*; Schillebeeckx, *Jesus* 381ff.; Selby, *Look for the Living*; Pannenberg, *Jesus*; Moltmann, *Theology of Hope*; Williams, *Resurrection*; Alsup, *Post-Resurrection Appearances*; Evans, *Resurrection*; Marxsen, *Resurrection*; Dunn, *Jesus*, pp. 95ff.

2 On the importance of the resurrection for christological reflection, see Pannenberg, *Jesus*.

3 Nickelsburg, *Resurrection*; Martin-Achard, *From Death to Life*; and above, pp. 91f.

4 See Selby, *Look for the Living*.

5 See Fuller, *Formation*; Alsup, *Post-Resurrection Appearances*; Dunn, *Jesus*, pp. 95ff.

6 On the empty tomb, see Wilckens in *Significance*, ed. Moule, pp. 51ff.

7 O'Neill in Sykes and Clayton, *Christian History*.

8 See Berger, *Auferstehung*, on the theme of exaltation. For Moses, see Josephus, *Ant.* 4.326.

9 See Marxsen, in *Significance*, ed. Moule; pp. 30ff.

10 On *ektroma*, see Dunn, *Jesus*, pp. 101f.

11 On the material, see Fuller and Alsup, op. cit.; Perrin, *Resurrection Narratives*.

12 See Jeremias, *Jerusalem*, pp. 374f.

13 On transfiguration, see Alsup, *Post Resurrection Appearances*, pp. 141ff.; Chilton, 'Transfiguration'.

14 On the form and character of the resurrection appearances see Dodd in *Studies in the Gospels*, ed. Nineham; (also in his *More New Testament Studies*).

15 For the materialist eschatological beliefs attributed to Cerinthus, see Klijn and Reinink, *Patristic Evidence*.

16 So also Dunn, *Jesus*, p. 122.

17 R. D. Williams, *Resurrection*, pp. 106f.

18   Vermes, *Jesus*, p. 41.

SECTION 3   PAUL

1   Introduction

1   See Stendahl, *Paul*. Further on Paul, see Bruce, *Paul Apostle of Free Spirit*; Bornkamm, *Paul*; Ridderbos, *Paul*; Whiteley, *Theology*; Ramsay, *Paul, Traveller*; Grollenberg, *Paul*; Knox, *St Paul and the Church of Jerusalem*, and *St Paul and the Church of the Gentiles*; Sanders, *Paul*, and *Paul the Law*; Davies, *Paul*. On the social setting of Pauline Christianity, see particularly Meeks, *Urban Christians*; Theissen, *Social Setting*.

2   See Dunn, *Unity*; Bauer, *Orthodoxy*; cf. Turner, *Pattern*.

3   See Harris, *Tübingen School*, and the restatement of that position in Brandon, *Fall*.

4   See e.g., Hunter, *Paul and his Predecessors*; Dungan, *Sayings*.

5   On justification, see Käsemann, 'Righteousness' in Käsemann, *Essays*; *Romans*. Also Sanders, *Paul*, pp. 523ff.

6   See Brandon, *Fall*.

7   See Betz, *Galatians*, p. 64: 'Strictly speaking we cannot speak at all of a conversion of Paul... he changed parties within Judaism from Pharisaism to Jewish Christianity.'

8   Cf. Josephus' account of sectarian transfer in *Vita*, pp. 9ff.

9   On the importance of his 'conversion-experience', for his theology see Kim, *Origin*.

10   Cf. Sanders, *Paul the Law*, who would not want to attach such significance to these words (e.g. pp. 25f.).

11   See Kim, *Origin*, pp. 269ff.

12   Views are divided on the continued messianic significance of this title; see Krämer, *Christ*, pp. 203ff. and Hengel in Hooker and Wilson, *Paul and Paulinism* (now in English in *Between Jesus and Paul*).

13   On Paul's use of Scripture, see Ellis, *Paul's Use*; Sanders, *Paul the Law*; Hübner, *Law*.

14   See Davies, *Paul*.

15   Some have recognized the importance of the continued debt to Jewish thought in Paul's writing as a Christian, but think that it derives largely from the Hellenistic Jewish world. See Sandmel, *Genius*; Schoeps, *Paul*.

16   But note the way in which Sanders has indicated the continuing influence of the Law in the Pauline communities. See *Paul the Law*, pp. 93ff.

17   See Davies, *Paul*, pp. 147ff.

18   Davies rightly recognized the importance of this issue for the study of early Christianity. See his study, *Torah in the Messianic Age*, but note also the comments of Schäfer, 'Torah'.

2   The Gospel Before and Apart from Paul

1   On Rome, see Leon, *Jews*; Cullmann, *Peter*.

2   For a variety of approaches to Acts, see Haenchen, *Acts*; Hengel, *Acts*; *Between Jesus and Paul*; Keck and Martyn, *Studies*; Gasque, *History*.

3   On the speeches, see, e.g., Cadbury, *Making*; Wilckens, *Missionsrede*; Moule in Keck and Martyn, *Studies*.

4   On the subject of the atonement, see Hengel, *Atonement*; Williams, *Jesus' Death as Saving Event*.

5   On the early Jewish Christology, see Longenecker, *Christology*.

6   For a hypothesis along these lines, see W. Marxsen, *The Evangelist Mark*; and see also Freyne, *Galilee*.

7   See further, Scobie, 'Samaritan Christianity'; Freyne, *Galilee*; Goulder in Hick, *Myth*; Macdonald, *Theology*.

8   On the Council, see Catchpole, 'Apostolic Council'.

9   On Jewish Christianity, see Hort, *Judaistic Christianity*; Schoeps, *Theologie*; Cullmann, *Roman Pseudo-Clémentin*; Strecker's appendix to Bauer, *Orthodoxy*; Kraft, 'Search'; 'Heritage'; Daniélou, *Theology*; Longenecker, *Christology*; Dunn, *Unity*, pp. 235ff.; Klijn and Reinink, *Patristic Evidence*.

10 On James, see the most recent commentary by Laws and the English translation of Dibelius' commentary.

11 There is a full consideration of recent scholarship on Jude and 2 Peter in the commentary by Bauckham.

12 See, e.g., Reicke, *Disobedient Spirits*; Dalton, *Christ's Proclamation*. For further recent work on 1 Peter, see Elliott, *Elect*; id., *Home*.

13 The Jewish character of Hebrews is well brought out in Hofius' monographs, *Katapausis* and *Vorhang*.

14 See Kilpatrick, *Origin*; Davies, *Setting*; and a summary of recent scholarship in Stanton, *Interpretation*.

15 For the Jewish material see Krauss, *Leben*; Herford, *Christianity*. On the infancy narratives, see most recently Brown, *Birth*.

16 See Horbury in Bammel, *Jesus and the Politics of his Day*.

17 e.g., Martyn's *History*.

18 e.g., Marxsen, *The Evangelist Mark*. For other work on Mark see Telford's forthcoming collection of essays; Hooker, *Message*; Kee, *Community*; and Tuckett, *Messianic Secret*.

19 Generally on redaction criticism see Rohde, *Rediscovering*; Perrin, *What is Redaction Criticism?*; also see 14 and 18nn.

20 On the setting of the *Q* source, see Tödt, *Son of Man*; Edwards, *The Sign of Jonah*; Schillebeeckx, *Jesus*, pp. 403ff.; Hamerton-Kelly, *Pre-Existence*; Suggs, *Wisdom*; Stanton in Lindars and Smalley, *Christ and Spirit*.

21 See Weeden, *Mark: Traditions in Conflict*; Martin, *Mark*; Koester, 'One Jesus and Four Primitive Gospels', in *Trajectories* and Schillebeeckx, *Jesus*, pp. 424ff.

22 On 2 Cor. and Paul's opponents, see Georgi, *Gegner*; Barrett, *Essays on Paul*.

23 Generally on the Jewish background of Paul's opponents, see Gunther, *Opponents*.

24 e.g., Howard, *Crisis*; on Colossians, see Francis and Meeks, *Conflict* and Rowland in Horbury and Rowland, *Essays*.

25 For a survey of the material on the Johannine false teaching, see the commentaries of Brown and Marshall.

26 See Simon, *St Stephen*; Cullmann, *The Johannine Circle*; and Scroggs; 'The Earliest Hellenistic Christianity'. On Stephen, see Scharlemann, *Stephen*; Bihler, *Stephanusgeschichte*; Hengel, *Between Jesus and Paul*; and Rowland, *Open Heaven*, pp. 369f.

27 On the speeches in Acts, see 3n and also the comments of Stanton in *Jesus of Nazareth*, pp. 19ff.

28 On Paul's relation to earlier Christian traditions see the admirable summary in Hunter, *Paul and his Predecessors*.

29 On Antioch, see Marshall, 'Palestinian and Hellenistic Christianity'; Meeks and Wilken, *Jews and Christians*; Dunn, in JSNT 18, pp. 3ff.

30 For a discussion of this incident, see Schmithals, *Paul and James*.

31 See the books mentioned in 14n.

32 On Ignatius, see below, pp. 265f.

33 See the comments of Brandon, *Fall*; Stendahl, *Paul*.

34 See Sanders, *Paul the Law*, pp. 93ff.

35 For a survey of Jewish Christian beliefs, see Daniélou, *Theology*.

36 See Rowland, 'Vision'; Kim, *Origin*.

37 On this theme see Dunn, *Unity*; Bauer, *Orthodoxy*; Turner, *Pattern*.

3 Situation and System in Paul's Letters

1 But note the important statement of the contrary position by O'Neill (e.g., *Romans*, *Galatians*), and 'Glosses'. He poses the question whether we are right to assume that the versions of Paul's letters in our possession are substantially as they left the Apostle's hand. In the light of the vicissitudes of textual transmission, he asks whether we can assume that inconsistencies between various letters and within a single letter are best explained by stressing the occasional character of each letter, which led Paul to formulate differing positions. He thinks that inconsistencies should be regarded as evidence of the works of glossators. This is an alternative approach with little support in the scholarly world, but it is a thesis not without some cogency and deserves more consideration than it is given. For a recent study along similar lines see Munro, *Authority*.

2 Kümmel, *Introduction*, pp. 268ff., considers that Col. and 2 Thess. are authentic; Ephesians and the Pastorals are not.

3 See Dunn, *Christology*, who treats it as authentic. For the opposite, see Lohse, *Colossians*.

4 On this theme, see Tannehill, *Dying*. On the Letter to Rheginos see Peel, *Rheginos*.

5 See Francis and Meeks, *Conflict*.

6 There is an exhaustive survey in van Roon, *Authenticity*. See also *Studies*, ed. F. L. Cross.

7 The comparison between the indisputably authentic Philemon and the Pastorals is instructive. The former, while a personal letter, breathes so much more of the spirit of the Paul of Rom. and 1 Cor. For a way of explaining the differences between the Pastorals and the authentic letters see Moule in *Essays*; cf. Wilson, *Luke and the Pastorals*.

8 See Guthrie, *Introduction*, pp. 584ff. (on pseudepigraphy, pp. 671ff.); cf. Robinson, *Redating*, pp. 67ff.

9 See Robinson, *Redating*; Reicke, *Luke*; Kümmel, *Introduction*, pp. 122ff.

10 See Dodd, 'Mind of Paul' in *New Testament Studies*.

11 See further, Schweitzer, *Mysticism*; Sanders, *Paul*; Stendahl, *Paul*; and Davies, *Paul*.

12 On the critical problems see Kümmel, *Introduction*, p. 287, Barrett on 2 Cor. and Gnilka in *Paul and Qumran*, ed. Murphy O'Connor, pp. 48f.

13 See Theissen, *Social Setting*.

14 See further, Minear, *Obedience*; Beker, *Paul the Apostle*; Sanders, *Paul the Law*.

15   See Beker, *Paul the Apostle*, pp. 23ff.

16   But see O'Neill's work mentioned in 1n above.

17   See Moule, 'Paul and Dualism', in *Essays*; Lincoln, *Paradise*, pp. 55ff.; Harris, *Raised Immortal.*

18   See Dodd, 'Mind of Paul'; Lowe, 'Examination'; Moule, 'Influence' in *Essays.*

4   The Essence of the Gospel

1.   On justification, see above, p. 356, 5n. On the centrality of eschatology, see Beker, *Paul the Apostle*; id. *Paul's Apocalyptic Gospel*; Munck, *Paul*; Baumgarten, *Paulus*; Ziesler, *Meaning.*

2   See Käsemann, 'Righteousness' in *Essays*; Beker, op. cit.

3   See Kim, *Origin*, p. 330.

4   See Cullmann, *Salvation*, pp. 166ff.

5   On the contrast between the two ages, see Davies, *Torah.*

6   On proselytes, see *Beginnings* 5, ed. Jackson and Lake, pp. 74ff. TDNT 6, p. 727; Bamberger, *Proselytism*; Braude, *Jewish Proselytising*; and above, p. 21.

7   Concise survey in Bornkamm, *Paul*; Bruce, *Paul*. On the powers see Caird, *Principalities*; Carr, *Angels.*

8   On the idea of tribulation (*thlipsis*), see TDNT 3, pp. 139ff.

9   See also Col. 1.24: Moule, *Colossians*, p. 76; Lohse, *Colossians*, pp. 70f.

10   On the sacrificial terminology and its application to the death of Christ in Paul's writings, see Morris, *Apostolic Preaching*; *Cross*; Hill, *Greek Words*; Whiteley, *Theology*; Hengel, *Atonement*; S. Williams, *Jesus' Death*; Anderson Scott, *Christianity.*

11   On the possibility of relics of a pre-Pauline formula in the Pauline corpus, see Bultmann, *Theology* 1, p. 46; Käsemann, *Romans*, p. 92; Hunter, *Paul and his Predecessors.*

12   On sacrificial understanding of the death of Christ in NT generally, see Morris, *Cross.*

13   On Hebrews, see Nairne, *Epistle of Priesthood*; Young, *Sacrifice.*

14   Beker, *Paul the Apostle*, p. 191.

15   See TDNT 7, p. 1024; Best, *One Body*; Gundry, *Sōma.*

16   See Wainwright, *Eucharist.*

17   See Fiorenza, *In Memory of Her*; cf. Clark, *Man and Woman.*

18   McKelvey, *New Temple.*

19   See Theissen, *Social Setting*; Meeks, *Urban Christians.*

20   Beker, *Paul the Apostle*, pp. 323f.

21   On the possibility of 1 Cor. 14.34 being a later gloss, see Barrett, *1 Corinthians*, pp. 330f.

22   See Dodds, *Pagan*; Theissen, *Social Setting*; Meeks, *Urban Christians.*

5   Apostle to the Gentiles

1   Jeremias, *Jesus' Promise*; SVM *History* 2, p. 533.

2   Munck, *Paul*; Hahn, *Mission*; Zeller, *Juden.*

3   On the place of religious experience in dealing with halakic matters, see Falk, *Introduction* 1, p. 13; Davies, *Setting*, p. 284; and below, pp. 227ff.

4   Repudiation of idolatry was part of the Jewish propaganda; see Wisd. 13ff., Sib. Or. On

Jewish apologetic literature, see, e.g., Collins, *Athens to Jerusalem*; *Sibylline Oracles*.

5 See the discussions of Knox, *Chapters*; Haenchen, *Acts*. O'Neill, *Theology*, thinks that Acts is a second-century work, but uses earlier material.

6 See Hengel, *Acts*. History of scholarship in Gasque, *History*.

7 cf. Sanders, *Paul the Law*.

8 On God-fearers, see TDNT 6, pp. 727ff. and Gager, *Kingdom*, p. 128, 138; Meeks, *Urban Christians*, pp. 25, 207, 175n on the factors conditioning the spread of Christianity; and above, pp. 21 and 45.

9 cf. Sanders, *Paul the Law*.

10 Note Gager's comments on circumcision in *Kingdom*, p. 135. On pagan attitudes, see Safrai and Stern, *Jewish People*, 2, p. 1101.

11 See McKeleney, 'Conversion', but cf. Nolland, 'Uncircumcised Proselytes'.

12 On 2 Cor. 10.14, see Barrett, *2 Corinthians*, pp. 296f.

13 See Munck, *Paul*; and Sanders, *Paul the Law*.

14 On judaizing, see Munck, *Paul*; on Galatians, see Howard, *Crisis*. The letter to the Hebrews is also an example of the pervasive Jewish influence.

15 On Gal. 5.2ff., see Betz, *Galatians*, pp. 258f.

16 See below, pp. 232ff.

17 See Kraabel, *Judaism in Asia Minor*. On attitudes to the Law in the Diaspora, see the suggestions of Schoeps, *Paul*.

18 See Davies, *Torah in the Messianic Age*; cf. Schäfer, 'Torah'.

19 On Isa. 56.3ff. see Westermann, *Isaiah*, 40–66, p. 312; '... obviously a designation for a proselyte current at the time'.

20 In his discussion of circumcision Paul does not choose to base his arguments on Isa., but on the figure of Abraham (Gal. 3; Rom. 4). That covenant-ideas undergird this is pointed out by Hooker in *Paul and Paulinism*, ed. Hooker and Wilson. See further Deidun, *New Covenant Morality*.

21 For the Temple Scroll, see Maier, *Tempelrolle*.

22 On the collection, see Nickle, *Collection*; Georgi, *Kollekte*; Meeks, *Urban Christians*, e.g., pp. 65f.

6 Paul and the Law

1 See Cranfield, *Romans*, pp. 2, 515ff., Käsemann, *Romans*, pp. 281f.; Campbell, 'Christ the End of the Law'.

2 On Paul and Law, see Sanders, *Paul the Law*; Hübner, *Law*.

3 On the starting point of Paul's theological reflection, see Sanders, *Paul*, pp. 442f.; Beker, *Paul the Apostle*, pp. 238f.

4 cf. Sanders, *Paul the Law*.

5 On the household regulations (*Haustafeln*), see Crouch, *Colossian Haustafeln*; Munro, *Authority*; on the continued influence of the Law of Moses, see Sanders, *Paul the Law*.

7 Membership of the People of God

1 Note the interesting parallels in the career of Sabbatai Sevi (see Scholem, *Sabbatai Sevi*).

2 See Munck, *Paul*.

3 See Nolland, 'Uncircumcised Proselytes'.

4 Forkman, *Limits*; Meeks, *Urban Christians*, pp.75ff.

5 See Sanders, *Paul the Law*, pp. 93ff.

6 On perfectionism, see Bogart, *Orthodoxy*; Peterson, *Hebrews* and *Perfectionism*.

7 See Forkman, *Limits*.

8 On the post AD 70 situation, see below, pp. 299ff.

8 Paul and Israel

1 See Munck, *Paul*; Zeller, *Juden*; Luz, *Geschichtsverständnis*; Käsemann, *Romans*, pp. 313f.; ed. de Lorenzi, *Die Israelfrage*; Sanders, *Paul the Law*.

2 See Bowker, 'Origin and Purpose of John's Gospel' in *NTS* 11.

3 A later date is given for Gal. in Kümmel, *Introduction*, p. 304; see the discussions in Guthrie, *Introduction*, p. 457 but note Robinson, *Redating*, pp. 55ff.

4 See Richardson, *Israel*, but cf. Sanders, *Paul the Law*.

5 See, e.g., Best, *1 Thess.*, pp. 119f.

6 Best, *1 Thess.*, p. 122.

7 On these chapters, see Munck, *Paul*; Käsemann, *Romans*, pp. 313ff.; Hanson, *Pioneer Ministry*.

8 See Munck, op. cit., pp. 47f.

9 For a different approach, see Hahn in Hooker and Wilson, *Paul and Paulinism*.

9 The Problem of Authority

1 See von Campenhausen, *Ecclesiastical Authority*; Schütz, *Anatomy*; Holmberg, *Power*; Dunn, *Jesus*, pp. 271ff.; Widengren, *Ascension of the Apostle*; Shaw, *Authority*; Meeks, *Urban Christians*, pp. 111ff., 171ff.

2 There are hints also in 1 Thess. 2.4ff., on which see Best, *1 Thess.*, pp. 93ff. On the issue of false prophecy, see Horbury '1 Thess. 2.3'.

3 On the problems in Galatia, see Howard, *Crisis*; Meeks, *Urban Christians*, pp. 95f.

4 See *SVM History* 2, p. 240 on the priestly genealogies and note Josephus, *Vita*, 1, 4f.

5 On rabbinic authority, see Urbach, *Sages* 1, pp. 593ff.

6 See Büchler, *Types*; Vermes, *Jesus*; Freyne, *Galilee*, pp. 330ff.; Green, 'Palestinian Holy Men'.

7 On this passage, see Davies, *Setting*, p. 284; Falk, *Introduction* 1, pp. 13, 161.

8 cf. Neusner, *Eliezer*, 2, pp. 410ff., who does not regard it as one of the most reliable historical reminiscences of Eliezer.

9 On Gal. 1.12ff., see Betz, *Galatians*, pp. 62ff.; Kertelge, 'Apokalypsis'; Rowland, *Open Heaven*, pp. 376f.; Kim, *Origin*, pp. 67ff.; Meeks, *Urban Christians*, pp. 171ff.

10 Paul's visits to Jerusalem have occasioned much scholarly debate. See Jackson and Lake, *Beginnings*, 2, pp. 271ff.; Knox, *Chapters*; Jewett, *Dating*; Robinson, *Redating*; Kümmel, *Introduction*, pp. 252ff.

11 On Gal. 1.18, see Kilpatrick in *Studies in the Gospels*, ed. Nineham.

12 Acts 15.2 in D (Codex Bezae) has a different version, where reference is made to compulsion (see *Beginnings* 3, ed. Jackson and Lake, p. 183).

13 On the text of Gal. 2.5, see Lightfoot, *Galatians*, p. 121.

14 Burkitt, quoted in Bruce, *Paul*, p. 158.

15 On the authority of the Teacher of Righteousness, see Jeremias, *Lehrer*.

16 See Theissen, *Social Setting*; Hock, *Social Context*; Meeks, *Urban Christians*.

17 See Dungan, *Sayings*.

18 On the Corinthian opponents, see Schmithals, *Gnosticism*; Hurd, *Origin*; Munck, *Paul*; Georgi, *Gegner*; Barrett, *Essays on Paul*.

19 See the surveys in Barrett, *Essays on Paul*.

20 On differing views of the apostolic ministry, see the outline by Koester in Koester and Robinson, *Trajectories*, pp. 187ff.; Barrett, *Signs*; Meeks, *Urban Christians*, pp. 131ff., and see below, pp. 254ff.

21 On this sudden change of mood, see Kümmel, *Introduction*, p. 332.

22 On the Pastorals, see the commentaries of Kelly and Dibelius and also Harrison, *Problems*, and Wilson, *Luke and the Pastorals*, and below, pp. 264ff.

23 On ordination, see von Campenhausen, *Authority*, pp. 115, 157ff.; Lohse, *Ordination*.

10 Paul's Method as an Apostle

1 For suggestive comments on the problems posed by Paul's message and its reception, see Robinson in Koester and Robinson, *Trajectories*, pp. 20ff.

2 See Chadwick, 'All Things'.

3 cf. Sanders, *Paul the Law*.

4 Gal. 5.3 refers to the one who undertakes the rite as a necessary part of the process of salvation and does not, therefore, refer to an acceptance of circumcision as a rite which might be expedient in certain circumstances, e.g., Gal. 6.15.

5 See above, pp. 230ff.

6 Hurd, *Origin of 1 Cor.*, but note the comments of Barrett, *1 Cor.*, pp. 7f.

7 cf. Schmithals, *Gnosticism*.

8 On the relationship between Acts 15 and 21.23, see *Beginnings*, ed. Jackson and Lake 5, pp. 195ff., add. n. 16. On Paul and Council, see also Hurd, *Origin*.

9 See Catchpole, 'Apostolic Council'; *Beginnings*, 5, pp. 195ff.

10 See Hock, *Social Context*; Meeks, *Urban Christians*, pp. 27ff.

11 Further, Hunter, *Paul and his Predecessors*; Gerhardsson, *Memory*.

12 See Dodd, *Gospel and Law*; Sanders, *Paul the Law*. On the basis of Paul's ethic, see Furnish, *Theology and Ethics*.

SECTION 4
FROM MESSIANIC SECT TO CHRISTIAN RELIGION

1 Early Christian Initiation and Worship

1 On the views contained in the Dead Sea Scrolls, see pp. 73ff.

2 Translation from Vermes, *Dead Sea Scrolls in English*, p. 85.

3 Translation from Vermes, op. cit., p. 87.

4 For the use of the Temple imagery, see McKelvey, *New Temple*; Gärtner, *Temple*.

5 On baptism in the NT, see Cullman, *Baptism*; Beasley-Murray, *Baptism*; Wagner,

Pauline Baptism; Tannehill, *Dying and Rising*; and on its social setting, Meeks, *Urban Christians*, pp. 150ff.

6 See Dunn, *Baptism in the Holy Spirit*, pp. 90ff.

7 On the catechumenate, see Dujarier, *Parrainage*.

8 On proselyte baptism, see TDNT 6, 738f.

9 On John the Baptist, see above, pp. 131ff.

10 On the hostile powers in the ancient world-view, see Brown, *World*, pp. 53ff.; *Making*, p. 10; Caird, *Principalities*; Meeks, *Urban Christians*, pp. 155f.

11 On Col. 2.14f., see Anderson Scott, *Christianity*, p. 34f.

12 On the Eucharist and its origins, see Lietzmann, *Mass* (together with a new essay by Richardson); Jeremias, *Eucharistic Words*; Cullmann, *Worship*; Moule, *Worship*; Delling, *Worship*; Higgins, *Lord's Supper*; and more generally in Meeks, *Urban Christians*, pp. 140ff.

13 Detailed discussion in Lietzmann and Richardson, *Mass*.

14 See *Sabbath to Sunday*, ed. Carson.

15 On the difficulties of a proper assessment, see Bradshaw, *Daily Prayer*.

16 See Bowker, 'Proem and Yelammedenu Forms'.

17 It may well be that the particular issues which primarily concern Paul in 1 Cor. 11 and 14 (sharing the common meal and speaking with tongues) have dictated the way in which the issues have been presented. Thus the separation of the worship described in ch. 14 from the Eucharist described in ch. 11 need not indicate that they took place on separate occasions in the life of the Church.

18 See Jeremias, *Eucharistic Words*.

19 On the significance of the meal at Qumran see Vermes, *Dead Sea Scrolls*, pp. 95f., 125f.

20 On this, see Lietzmann, *Mass*.

21 On this phrase, see Jeremias, *Eucharistic Words*, pp. 237ff.

22 See above, pp. 176ff. and for the Passover Haggadah, see e.g., *Haggadah for Passover*, ed. Roth.

23 See Wainwright, *Eucharist*.

24 Further, Le Déaut, *La Nuit*.

25 On this imagery, see Hill, *Greek Words*, pp. 49ff.

26 On the Didache, see Audet, *Didache*; Vokes, *Riddle of the Didache*; and now Draper, *Didache* Diss., Cambridge.

27 On 1 Cor. 16.22, see Robinson in *Twelve NT Studies*; Moule, *Worship*, p. 43.

28 On Maranatha, see Moule, *Worship*, pp. 70f.; Bornkamm in *Early Christian Experience*, pp. 123ff.; 161ff.; TDNT 4, pp. 466f.

29 See Lietzmann, *Mass*, p. 204.

30 On John 6, see Cullmann, *Worship*; cf. Bultmann, *John*; Brown, *John* 1, pp. 272ff. Schnackenburg, *John* 2, pp. 56ff.

31 On Ignatius' eucharistic thought, see Lietzmann, *Mass*, pp. 210, 242, 421, 684.

32 See Wainwright, *Eucharist*.

33 On the link between the cult and realized eschatology, see Aune, *Cultic Aspect*.

34 On Montanism see Labriolle, *Crise*; von Campenhausen, *Ecclesiastical Authority*, pp. 178f. For an important contribution to the history of the role of women in primitive Christianity see Fiorenza, *In Memory of Her*.

35 On Ignatius, see Schweizer, *Church Order*, pp. 150ff.; von Campenhausen, *Ecclesiastical Authority*, pp. 97ff.; Corwin, *St Ignatius*; Richardson, *Christology* and Barnard, *Studies*.

36 See below, pp. 270f., and on false prophecy see above, pp. 147f.

2 The Emergence of Beliefs about Jesus

1 Literature may be found in Bousset, *Kyrios Christos*; Dunn, *Christology*; Cullmann, *Christology*; Moule, *Origin*; Hahn, *Titles*; Fuller, *Foundations*; Schillebeeckx, *Jesus*; *Christ*.

2 On christological titles in the Gospels, see above, pp. 174ff.

3 On the Christology of Acts, see Moule in *Studies*, ed. Keck and Martyn; Robinson, 'Earliest Christology' in his *Twelve NT Studies*; Longenecker, *Christology*.

4 On Christ as a messianic title in Paul, see Hengel in *Paul and Paulinism*, ed. Hooker and Wilson (in English in *Between Jesus and Paul*).

5 See Vermes, *Jesus*; Cullmann, *Christology*; Fitzmyer in *Wandering Aramean*.

6 See Moule in Keck and Martyn, *Studies*.

7 On the use of Ps. 110, see Hay, *Glory*.

8 On Kyrios in Paul, see Krämer, *Christ*, pp. 151ff.

9 On Johannine Christology, see Dunn, *Christology*, pp. 213ff. and on the christological heresy in 1 John see Wengst, *Häresie*.

10 See Martyn, *History*.

11 See Brown, *John 2*, pp. 1060; Barrett, *John and Judaism*, p. 17; *Gospel of John*, pp. 134ff.; 575.

12 Wiles, *Spiritual Gospel*.

13 See Käsemann, *The Testament of Jesus*; Pascal, *John 17*, Diss., Cambridge.

14 See Hanson, *New Testament Interpretation*.

15 See Bultmann, *John*, pp. 83, 145.

16 On subordination in John, see Barrett in his *Essays on John*.

17 On the Jewish background see Borgen, 'God's Agent'; Dahl, 'Johannine Church'; Bühner, *Gesandte*; Segal, *Two Powers*; Odeberg, *Fourth Gospel*; Pascal, *John 17*.

18 See Borgen, 'God's Agent'.

19 On this verse, see Rowland, 'John 1.51'.

20 On John and the Samaritans, see Freyne, *Galilee*, pp. 367ff.; Meeks, *Prophet-King*; Cullmann, *The Johannine Circle*; Scobie, 'Samaritan Christianity'; and Goulder in *Myth*, ed. Hick.

21 On John and the Jewish festivals, see, e.g., Guilding, *Fourth Gospel*.

22 On John 6 see Borgen, *Bread from Heaven*.

23 For a consideration of the Law in the Fourth Gospel, see Pancaro, *Law*.

24 See Segal, *Two Powers*.

25 For a discussion of the Spirit-Paraclete passages, see Johnston, *Spirit-Paraclete*; Betz, *Der Paraklet*; TDNT 5, pp. 800ff.

26 On the phrase 'eternal life', see Dodd, *Fourth Gospel*, pp. 144f.; Hill, *Greek Words*, pp.

175ff.; also TDNT 2, pp. 832ff.

27 See, e.g., Kelly, *Early Christian Doctrines*; Grillmeier, *Christ.*

28 It should be noted also that study of early Christianity is incomplete without an attempt to investigate the social setting of its ideas, whether christological or eschatological. See Meeks, *Urban Christians*, for a preliminary attempt to carry out this task.

29 Schweitzer, *Quest*; *Mysticism.*

30 See Werner, *Formation* (abridged version of *Entstehung*).

31 On the influence of the Delay of the Parousia, see below, pp. 285ff.

32 On the Arian controversy, see Grillmeier, *Christ*, pp. 219ff.; Lorenz, *Arius Ioudaizans.*

33 de Ste Croix, *Class Struggle*, p. 452.

34 See TDNT 9, pp. 493ff.

35 On Christ in Paul, see Preiss, *Life*; Bouttier, *Christianity*; Krämer, *Christ*; Hengel, *Paul and Paulinism*, ed. Hooker and Wilson. (In English in *Between Jesus and Paul*.)

36 See Dunn, *Christology*, pp. 163ff. Also on John, Schillebeeckx, *Christ*, pp. 303ff.

37 On angelomorphic Christology, see Rowland, *Open Heaven*, pp. 98ff.; Bühner, *Gesandte*; Berger, *Auferstehung*; Segal, *Two Powers*; cf. Dunn, *Christology.*

38 See Suggs, *Wisdom*; Hamerton-Kelly, *Pre-Existence.*

39 On these passages, see Sanders, *NT Christological Hymns*; Dunn, *Christology.*

40 On the theophanic material in the OT, see Jeremias, *Theophanie.*

41 On the individualism of the Fourth Gospel, see Moule, *Essays*. Note the different approach in Miranda, *Being and Messiah.*

42 See below, pp. 284ff.

43 See Schnackenburg, *John* I, pp. 543ff.; Talbert, *What is a Gospel?*, pp. 53ff.

44 See Meeks, 'Man from Heaven'; Segal, 'Heavenly Ascents'.

45 Talbert, loc. cit., and above 37n.

46 See Dodd, *Fourth Gospel*, pp. 144ff.

47 On the Christology of Rev., see Holtz, *Christologie.*

48 On Johannine dualism, see Charlesworth in *John and Qumran*, ed. Charlesworth, pp. 76ff.; also Böcher, *Johanneische Dualismus*; Schottroff, *Welt.*

49 Dunn, *Christology*, offers a suggested development leading to the doctrine of the incarnation; cf. Hengel, *Son of God.*

50 See Brown, *Making*; Williams, 'The Prophetic and the Mystical'.

3   Emerging Patterns of Ministry

1 On trends in Judaism, see pp. 65ff.

2 See above, pp. 73ff., and Vermes, *Dead Sea Scrolls*, pp. 174ff.

3 See Bowker, *Religious Imagination*, pp. 121ff.; Williams, *Eucharistic Sacrifice*, p. 17; Brown, *Making*, pp. 56ff.

4 Jeremias, *Prayers*; Dunn, *Jesus*, pp. 21ff., cf. Vermes, *Gospel.*

5 See above, p. 178ff., and the summary on Jesus in von Campenhausen, *Ecclesiastical Authority*, pp. 1ff.

6 On Pauline ecclesiology, see Schweizer, *Church Order*; von Campenhausen, *Ecclesiastical Authority*; Meeks, *Urban Christians*, pp. 111ff.; Banks, *Paul's Idea of Community.*

7   On the use of cultic language, see McKelvey, *New Temple*; Gärtner, *Temple*. There is one
     example of the use of priestly language in connection with the apostolic ministry in Rom.
     15.16.

8   On apostleship, see TDNT 1, pp. 398ff.; Barrett, *Signs*.

9   On 2 Cor. 3 and 4, see Barrett, *2 Corinthians*, pp. 111ff.; McNamara, *NT and Palestinian
     Targums*; Kim, *Origin*.

10   On Paul's example, see von Campenhausen, *Ecclesiastical Authority*, pp. 30ff.

11   On the motif of the *Imitatio Christi*, see Tinsley, *Imitation*, and on Phil. 2.6ff., see Martin,
     Carmen Christi.

12   *Pioneer Ministry*, p. 62 and note p. 82. See also Hooker, 'Interchange'.

13   Theissen, *Social Setting*, p. 83.

14   See Williams, 'The Prophetic and the Mystical'; *The Wound of Knowledge*.

15   On *en Christo*, see Deissmann, *Formel*; Neugebauer, *En Christus*; Moule, *Origin*.

16   cf. Brown, *Making*. Also note Rivkin, 'Pharisaism', for a not dissimilar development in
     Pharisaism.

17   On Johannine literature, see Schweizer, *Church Order*, pp. 117f.; von Campenhausen,
     Ecclesiastical Authority, pp. 138ff.; Brown, *Community*; *Johannine Epistles*; Aune, *Cultic
     Aspect*; Woll, *Johannine Christianity*.

18   See von Campenhausen, *Ecclesiastical Authority*, pp. 141f.

19   On this, see Bauer, *Orthodoxy*.

20   See von Campenhausen, *Ecclesiastical Authority*, p. 141.

21   For an attempt to describe the history of the Johannine community, see Brown,
     Community; Woll, *Johannine Christianity*.

22   On the ideological world of the Johannine community, see Meeks, 'Man from Heaven'.

23   On perfectionism, see Bogart, *Orthodox and Heretical Perfectionism*; Peterson, *Hebrews*; on
     the Scrolls, see Vermes, *Dead Sea Scrolls*, pp. 163ff. On links of 1 John with Judaism, see
     O'Neill, *Puzzle*.

24   See Martyn, *History*; Brown, *Community*.

25   See Meeks, 'Man from Heaven'; Talbert, *What is a Gospel?*; Segal, 'Heavenly Ascents',
     for the pattern of descent and ascent.

26   cf. Lincoln, *Paradise*; Aune, *Cultic Aspect*.

27   On church order in Rev., see Satake, *Gemeindeordnung*.

28   See further, Satake, op. cit.; Trites, *Witness*.

29   See Dunn, *Unity*; Werner, *Formation*, pp. 269ff.

30   See von Campenhausen, *Ecclesiastical Authority*, pp. 181ff.

31   On Asia Minor, see Calder, 'Philadelphia'; Ramsay, *Letters*; *Cities and Bishoprics*;
     Johnson, 'Asia Minor and Early Christianity'; Müller, *Theologiegeschichte*.

32   On the primitive Church, see Goguel, *The Primitive Church*; Brandon, *Fall*; Fitzmyer,
     Wandering Aramean, pp. 271ff.; *Scrolls and NT*, ed. Stendahl.

33   On sources and redaction, see Haenchen, *Acts*; cf. Hengel, *Acts* and *Between Paul and
     Jesus*.

34   See Schmithals, *Paul and James*.

35   On the Council, see above, p. 199.

36 On James, see Lightfoot, *Galatians*, pp. 252ff., 292ff.

37 On this tradition, see the summary in Dunn, *Jesus*, pp. 97ff. On the resurrection appearance to James, see Gospel of Hebrews (Hennecke, *NT Apocrypha*, p. 165).

38 On dynastic succession, see Stauffer, 'Kalifat'; Lightfoot, *Galatians*, pp. 241ff.

39 On the apostles as doctrinal authorities, see the suggestion of Gerhardsson, *Memory*, pp. 220ff.

40 On authorship, see Kümmel, *Introduction*. On the church order, see Schweizer, *Church Order*, pp. 105ff., 77ff.

41 On ordination, see Lohse, *Ordination*, and on the importance of tradition in the early Church, see Hanson, *Tradition*.

42 For a concise summary of the spirituality of Ignatius, see Williams, *Wound*; also Richardson, *Christology of Ignatius*; Barnard, *Studies*; Paulsen, *Studien*; and on Antioch, see Meeks, *Jews and Christians*.

43 On Barnabas, see Barnard, op. cit.; Windisch in *HNT* and Wengst, *Tradition*.

44 On the transference of cultic language to Christian ministers, see Schweizer, *Church Order*, pp. 172ff.

45 On the apostolic tradition, see the edition of Dix.

46 Note the way in which menstruation affects religious attitudes in apostolic tradition (see Dix, op. cit., p. 32).

47 See above, pp. 228f.

48 See Rowland, *Open Heaven*, pp. 368ff.; Meeks, *Urban Christians*, pp. 171ff.

49 On the accounts of Paul's conversion, see Kim, *Origin*; Munck, *Paul*; Burchard, *Dreizehnte Zeuge*. For attempts to separate the Damascus experience from other visions in Paul's career, see Dunn, *Jesus*, pp. 97ff.

50 See Holmberg, *Power*; Schütz, *Anatomy*; Theissen, *Social Setting*, pp. 40ff.

51 cf. Betz, *Galatians*, p. 39.

52 On the issue of Paul's journey to Jerusalem, see above, pp. 199; 220f.

53 On circumcision, see TDNT 6, pp. 72ff.; Borgen in *Paul and Paulinism*, ed. Hooker and Wilson.

54 von Campenhausen, *Ecclesiastical Authority*; Meeks, *Urban Christians*.

55 On Paul and tradition, see Hunter, *Paul and his Predecessors*.

56 See Hurd, *Origin*; Rowland, *Open Heaven*, pp. 368ff.

57 On the importance of the prophetic ministry, see Satake, *Gemeindeordnung* and Fiorenza, *In Memory of Her*.

58 See Bauer, *Orthodoxy*.

59 Doubts about the canonicity of the book of Rev. were often expressed; see von Campenhausen, *Formation*, pp. 215ff., 235ff.

60 On Montanism, see Labriolle, *Crise*; Daniélou, *Origin of Latin Christianity*, on Tertullian; also Knox, *Enthusiasm*; von Campenhausen, *Ecclesiastical Authority*, pp. 181ff.

61 On Elchesai, see Hennecke-Schneemelcher, *NT Apoc.* 2, pp. 745ff. and also Henrichs and Koenen in *ZPE* 5. On Cerinthus, see Bardy, 'Cerinthe'. For the sources, see Klijn and Reinink, *Patristic Evidence*.

62 See now *The Nag Hammadi Library*, ed. Robinson.

63 See Gruenwald, 'Knowledge and Vision' and his essay in *Studies in Jewish Mysticism*, ed. Dan and Talmage.

64 See Knox, *Enthusiasm*; von Campenhausen, *Ecclesiastical Authority*, p. 189.

65 See the survey of this material and relevant literature in Bauckham, *Jude and 2 Peter*, e.g., pp. 236ff.

66 On the growing importance of tradition, see Prestige, *Fathers and Heretics*; Hanson, *Tradition*; von Campenhausen, *Tradition and Life*; *Ecclesiastical Authority*, pp. 149ff; Turner, *Pattern*; Cullmann, *Early Church*.

67 Note the parallels with the Jewish messiah Sabbatai Sevi; see Scholem, op. cit.

68 See the commentaries by Brown and Marshall.

69 On the Didache, see Audet, *La Didache* and Draper, *Didache*.

70 Note Lucian of Samosata, *De Morte Peregr.* 13; Grant, *Early Christianity and Society*, p. 161.

71 See Hurd, *Origin*, on the character of the initial preaching at Corinth.

72 See 66n.

73 See the Cologne Mani texts, ed. by Henrichs and Koenen, in *ZPE* 5.

74 On Marcion, see Harnack, *Marcion*; Blackman, *Marcion*.

4 Coming to Terms with the Old Age
(a) The Common Life

1 On this, see von Campenhausen, *Tradition*, pp. 90ff., 141ff.; de Ste Croix, *Class Struggle*; Grant, *Early Christianity and Society*, pp. 96ff. J. P. Miranda attempts to make out a case for the 'communist' outlook in the Bible generally in *Communism in the Bible*.

2 See further Haenchen, *Acts*, pp. 230ff.; Hengel, *Property and Riches*.

3 Theissen, *First Followers*; Mealand, *Poverty*.

4 See Capper in *Essays*, ed. Horbury and Rowland.

5 See *Beginnings*, ed. Jackson and Lake, 5, pp. 140ff.; Dunn, *Jesus*, pp. 182ff.; Cadbury, *Making*, pp. 251, 261.

6 The problem with the practice of the primitive community in Jerusalem was that it was not productive; it depended on a regular influx of capital for its survival; (cf. Luke 8.3). As far as we can ascertain, its practice did not include the common ownership of the means of production, even within the narrow confines of the Christian community. This left it open to the vicissitudes of the extent of the membership and the viability of the economy of society at large. The viability of Essene practice may well have been its concern to do something about common ownership of the means of production, so that it functioned as a kind of co-operative venture in which the benefits of economic activity, at least within the religious group, were shared by all.

7 But note the possibility that some kind of monastic life lies behind 1 Cor. 7. On this, see Barrett, *1 Corr.*, pp. 153ff.; Hurd, *Origin*, pp. 154ff.

8 See Crouch, *Origin*; Munro, *Authority*.

9 See the remarks in de Ste Croix, *Class Struggle*, pp. 419ff.

10 See Theissen, *Social Setting*, pp. 69ff.; *First Followers*.

11 cf. the attitude in the Pastorals and see Dibelius, *Pastorals*, pp. 39f., and further, von Campenhausen, *Tradition*, p. 155.

12 But note de Ste Croix's questioning of the value of this comment on Tertullian in *Class Struggle*, p. 433 (on Tert. *Apol.* 39.11; Justin, *Apol.* 14.2).

13 See Capper, op. cit.

14 See Grant, *Early Christianity*, pp. 96ff.; 124f.; cf. de Ste Croix, *Class Struggle*, pp. 436f.

15 On monasticism, see Knowles, *Pachomius to Ignatius*; Chitty, *Desert*; Vööbus, *History of Asceticism*; Brown, *Making*. On Syriac-speaking Christianity see Murray, *Symbols of Church and Kingdom*.

(b) The Problem of Ethics in the New Age

1 On Ethics in the NT, see Sanders, *Ethics*; Houlden, *Ethics*; Schnackenburg, *Moral Teaching*; Troeltsch, *Social Teaching*; Grant, *Early Christianity*; and generally Meeks, *Urban Christians*; Gager, *Kingdom*; on the ethical teaching of the early Fathers, see Osborne, *Ethical Patterns*.

2 For hints of libertine ideas, see 1 Cor. 5.1ff.; Rom. 3.8; Basilides Fragment 4, Irenaeus, *Haer.* 1.6.4; *Excerpta Theod.* 52, Hippolytus, *Ref.* 5.8.33, 9ff.; and further, Smith, *Clement*, pp. 254ff.

3 See, e.g., Bettenson, *Documents*, 193, 197.

4 Whether this acceptance of the status quo extended to Christian participation in the Roman army is uncertain (cf. Acts 10). On Christians and military service, see Hornus, *It Is Not Lawful*; von Campenhausen, *Tradition*, pp. 160ff.; Harnack, *Militia Christi*; Cunningham, *Early Church*; Jones, 'Christianity and the Roman Imperial Cult'.

5 On Münzer, see Bloch, *Thomas Münzer*; Williams, *Radical Reformation*; Gritsch, *Reformer*.

6 Some discussion of this theme in Glasswell, in *Paul and Paulinism*, ed. Hooker and Wilson; de Ste Croix, *Class Stuggle*, p. 116; Clark, *Man and Woman*; Meeks, *Urban Christians*, pp. 88, 155, and note Pixley, *God's Kingdom*, pp. 92f.

7 See above, pp. 160f.

8 See Theissen, *Social Setting*, and above, pp. 141ff.

9 See Montefiore in *Jesus Across the Centuries* and 'Revolt'; but cf. *Jesus and the Politics of his Day*, ed. Bammel and Moule.

10 On Acts 17.6, see Haenchen, *Acts*, p. 510.

11 On the 'political' purpose of Acts as an apology for the political innocence of the early Christian movement, see Cadbury, *Making*, pp. 308ff.; Haenchen, *Acts*, pp. 106ff.; Walaskay, *And So We Came to Rome*; Maddox, *Purpose*, pp. 91ff.

12 For a textual history of church-state relations see Coleman-Norton, *Roman State*; also Cunningham, *Early Church*.

13 See Beker, *Paul*; Baumgarten, *Paulus*.

14 On Col. 3.10, etc., see Bouttier, 'Complexio Oppositorum' and note 6, above.

15 See Schmithals, *Gnosticism*.

16 See Hurd, *Origin*.

17 See, e.g., pp. 287f.

18 But cf. Rev. 13. On the state in the NT, see Cullmann, *State*; Morrison, *The Powers that Be*; Käsemann in *NT Questions*; Carr, *Angels*; Borg, 'New Context'; Osborne, *Ethical Patterns*. On Rev., see the commentaries of Sweet and Prigent.

19 See Clark, *Man and Woman*; but cf. Fiorenza, *In Memory of Her*.

20 On wealth and property, see de Ste Croix, *Class Struggle*, pp. 425ff.

21 On threats to the Roman order, see Macmullen, *Enemies*.

22 Note the perceptive comment of Grant, *Early Christianity and Society*, p. 21: 'what took the place of the primitive Christian concern for the Kingdom of God was a double concern for the Christian Church and for the State as the sphere of the Church's life.'

23 On the conversion of Cornelius, see Haenchen, *Acts*, p. 360 and further, on the political theme of Acts Walaskay, *And So We Came to Rome*.

24 One point should be made with regard to 1 Cor. 11.2ff.: why should Paul go to such great lengths to justify the subordination of woman to man, when this would have been widely accepted in the ancient world? Could it be that rejection of such subordination was becoming a cause of embarrassment in Corinth? This issue is dealt with in Clark, *Man and Woman* (who comes to fairly conservative conclusions), but with little grasp of the dynamic of Paul's relationship with the church in Corinth or of the eschatological consequences for ethics arising from the gospel; see now Fiorenza, op. cit., 19n.

25 There are many pertinent comments in Selby, *Look for the Living*.

26 On antinomianism see above, 2n and note Origen, *Contra Celsum*, 6, 24ff.

27 On the theological basis of Pauline ethics, see Furnish, *Theology and Ethics*.

28 See Sanders, *Paul the Law*.

29 On this verse, see Käsemann, *Romans*, p. 215, and Cranfield, *Law*, pp. 166f.

30 cf. Fletcher, *Situation Ethics*; for a survey, see Hebblethwaite, *Christian Ethics*.

31 See above, p. 368.

32 cf. Knox, *Ethic of Jesus*.

33 See Moule in *Christian History*, ed. Farmer, Moule and Niebuhr; Dodd, *Gospel and Law*.

34 On early Christian ethical teaching, see Osborne, *Ethical Patterns*.

35 For an attempt, see Cullmann, *State*. For more radical treatment, which considers the section to be a later interpolation, see O'Neill, *Romans*, p. 220; Kallas in NTS 11.

36 On early Christian attitudes to the state, see Osborne, *Ethical Patterns*; Grant, *Early Christianity and Society*; Cunningham, *The Early Church*.

37 See Borg, 'New Context'; Bammel, 'Beitrag'.

38 On the influence of circumstances on early Christian doctrinal formulations, see Moule in his *Essays*.

39 cf. Glasswell in *Paul and Paulinism*, ed. Hooker and Wilson. On Gal.3.28, see Beker, *Paul, the Apostle*, pp. 318f., 323: 'indirectly the existence of the Church provided models for a different life style in society'. See also Schüssler-Fiorenza, *In Memory of Her*, pp. 205ff.

40 The contrast offered by Mannheim between ideology and utopia is relevant for a discussion of the early Christian outlook: 'ideologies are the situationally transcendent ideas, which never succeed *de facto* in the realization of their projected contents, though many often become the good intentioned motives for the subjective conduct of the individual. When they are actually embodied in practice their meanings are most frequently distorted' (*Ideology and Utopia*, p. 175) and 'a state of mind is utopian when it is incongruous with the state of reality within which it occurs … However, we should not regard as utopian every state of mind which is incongruous with and transcends the immediate situation … only those orientations transcending reality will be referred to as utopian which, when they pass over into conduct, tend to shatter, either partially or

wholly, the order of things prevailing at the time' (op. cit., p. 173). On the later utopian spirit, see Davis, *Utopia*. Further discussion of ideology in Seliger, *Ideology*; Ricoeur, 'Ideology'; Lash, *Matter of Hope*.

41 On slavery, see de Ste Croix, *Class Struggle*, especially pp. 419ff.; Beker, *Paul the Apostle*, pp. 318ff.

42 See 1 Cor. 4.8; Barrett, *1 Corinthians.*, p. 108; Hurd, *Origin*, p. 111; Meeks, *Urban Christians*, pp. 177f.

43 See Beker, *Paul*, pp. 318ff. and note the attitude to Rome found in the writings of Josephus.

44 On the inward-looking character of the Fourth Gospel, see Meeks, 'Man from Heaven', and above, pp. 260ff.

45 See Geertz, in *Religion as a Cultural System*, ed. Banton.

46 See the discussion by Theissen, *Social Setting*; Dodds, *Pagan*; Brown, *Making*; Meeks, *Urban Christians*, pp. 164ff.

47 See above, p. 369.

(c) The Delay of the Parousia

1 On this, see Werner, *Formation*; *Enstehung*; Grässer, *Parusieverzögerung*; Stroebel, *Untersuchungen*; Schweitzer, *Mysticism*; Moore, *Parousia*; Hiers, 'Delay'; Bauckham, 'Delay'; Gager, *Kingdom*. Interesting comments on a parallel OT theme may be found in Carroll, *When Prophecy Failed*.

2 e.g., Conzelmann on Luke; Dodd, 'Mind of Paul'; Brown, *John* 1. LXV.

3 On early Christianity as a quasi-millenarian movement, see Gager, *Kingdom*; Bloch, *Atheism*; cf. Festinger, *When Prophecy Fails*; Cohn, *Pursuit*; TDNT 9, p. 466.

4 See Werner, *Formation*, pp. 31ff.

5 On differing types of eschatology, see Caird, *Language*, pp. 243ff.

6 On 2 Peter, see Käsemann in his *Essays*; Fornberg, *An Early Church*; Bauckham's commentary.

7 On the background to Rev., see Ramsay, *Letters*; Hemer, *Letters*; Sweet, *Revelation*.

8 See Bornkamm in *Tradition*, ed. Bornkamm *et al.*

9 On this see Cavallin, *Life*; Charles, *Eschatology*; and above, pp. 87ff.

10 See Marxsen, *Mark*; Rohde, *Rediscovering*.

11 Conzelmann, *Theology*; Rohde, *Rediscovering*; Barrett, *Luke*; and summary in Dunn, *Unity*, pp. 344ff.

12 Note the doubts expressed by Robinson, *Redating*, pp. 27ff. about the suggested Lucan rewriting of Mark 13.

13 For an attempt to attribute these passages to a later redactor, see Bultmann, *John*, p. 261.

14 On the individualism of the Fourth Gospel, see Moule in his *Essays*.

15 But note Dunn, *Unity*, p. 346 on the relics of future hope in Eph.

16 On this see Lincoln, *Paradise*; Hofius, *Katapausis*; *Vorhang*.

17 On primitive catholicism see Dunn, *Jesus*, pp. 345ff.; *Unity*, pp. 341ff.; Hengel, *Acts*; Bauckham, *Jude*, p. 8.

18 Bauckham, 'Delay', has argued that Jewish apocalyptic literature had already paved the way for a change in perspective. See further his commentary on 2 Peter and Jude.

19   See Cullmann, *Salvation; Christ and Time*.

20   See Dodd in *More NT Studies*; Robinson, *Redating*, pp. 13ff. on Luke 21.

21   See above, pp. 104ff.

22   See above, pp. 73ff.

23   See Rowland, *Open Heaven*, pp. 113ff.

24   See Lincoln, *Paradise*.

25   See Cullmann, *Salvation*, pp. 166ff.

26   On 2 Cor. 5, see Lincoln, *Paradise*, pp. 55ff.; and see further, Harris, *Raised Immortal*.

27   On 1 Peter, see now Elliott, *Home for the Homeless*.

28   On the contrast between Rev. 4 and 5, see Rowland, *Open Heaven*, pp. 425f.

(d) The Rise of Gnosticism

1   Summaries and discussions of this vexed subject may be found in *Le Origini*, ed. Bianchi; Wilson, *Problem*; *Gnosis*; Yamauchi, *Pre-Christian Gnosticism*; Grant, *Gnosticism*; Doresse, *Secret Books*; Logan, *The New Testament and Gnosis*. Texts in Foerster, *Gnosis*; Robinson, *Nag Hammadi Library*; Layton, *The Rediscovery of Gnosticism*.

2   See Davies in *Christian History and Interpretation*, ed. Farmer, Moule and Niebuhr.

3   Translation in *The Nag Hammadi Library*, pp. 152ff.

4   On the influence of Platonism, see *Le Origini*, ed. Bianchi.

5   See Burkitt, *Religion of Manichees*; Henrichs and Koenen in *ZPE* 5.

6   On Augustine, see Brown, *Augustine of Hippo*; *Religion and Society*.

7   See Schmithals, *Gnosticism*, and above, pp. 157; 221f.; 275.

8   See Gunther, *Opponents*, for a collection of materials relating to these themes.

9   See Bauer, *Orthodoxy*, pp. 44ff.

10   Concise survey in Yamauchi, *Pre-Christian Gnosticism*, though he minimizes the extent of the possibility of pre-Christian Gnosticism.

11   See, e.g., Dunn, *Christology*; Wilson, *Gnosis*.

12   On the Jewish background, see Quispel in *The Bible in Modern Scholarship*, ed. Hyatt; Fallon, *Enthronement*; Grant, *Gnosticism*; see also Macrae, 'Sophia' and *Le Origini*, ed. Bianchi.

13   Segal, *Two Powers*.

14   Cf. Gruenwald in Dan and Talmage, *Studies in Jewish Mysticism*, and Fallon, op. cit.

15   See Scholem, *Major Trends*; *Jewish Gnosticism*; Yamauchi, op. cit., p. 158.

16   See Grant, *Gnosticism*.

(e) Odium Humani Generis

1   On the subject of persecution, see Frend, *Martyrdom*; de Ste Croix, 'Why were the Early Christians persecuted?' On Roman attitudes, see R. Wilken, *The Christians as the Romans Saw Them*.

2   On martyrdom, see Frend, op. cit.; Lohse, *Märtyrer*.

3   Trites, *Witness*; TDNT 4, pp. 474ff.

4   See Brown, *Making*, pp. 37f.

5   On Decius and Diocletian, see summary in Brown, *World*, pp. 33, 86; cf. the career of

Julian the Apostate.

(f) The Separation of Church and Synagogue

1. On Jamnia, see Neusner, 'Formation'; Schäfer, 'Flucht' and in *Studien*; Davies, *Setting*, pp. 284ff.; *SVM History* 1, pp. 508ff. and above, p. 339. On the post-70 situation, see Büchler, *Economic Conditions*; Smallwood, *Jews*, pp. 331ff.
2. See Schäfer, op. cit.
3. See Horbury, 'Benediction'; *SVM History*, 2, p. 454; Kuhn, *Achtzehngebet*; Kimelman in Sanders, *Jewish and Christian Self-Definition*, vol. 2.
4. Barrett, *NT Background*; p. 167.
5. On the textual problems, see Horbury, op. cit.
6. Forkman, *Limits*.
7. On the Sanhedrin, see *SVM History*, 2, pp. 199ff.; Mantel, *Sanhedrin*; Safrai and Stern, *Jewish People*, 2, pp. 377ff.
8. See Neusner, *Eliezer*; Bokser, *Pharisaic Judaism*; Podro, *The Last Pharisee*; Neusner, *Yohanan*; *Development of a Legend*.

(g) You are his Disciples but we are Disciples of Moses

1. For the Jewish background to the Fourth Gospel, see Martyn, *History*; Meeks, *Prophet-King*; Smalley, *John*; Bowker, 'Origin'; Schillebeeckx, *Christ*, pp. 307ff.; Barrett, *The Gospel of John and Judaism*; and Dunn 'Let John be John'.
2. Robinson, *Redating*, pp. 254ff.; *John and Qumran*, ed. Charlesworth.
3. See Meeks, 'Am I a Jew?, p. 172.
4. See Pancaro, *Law*, pp. 489ff.
5. For a pre-70 date, see Robinson, *Redating*, pp. 254ff.
6. For the hypothesis that the Fourth Gospel reflects differing attitudes towards Jesus, see Brown, *Community* and further, Woll, *Johannine Christianity*.
7. See Martyn, *History*; Pancaro, *Law*.
8. On the term *aposynagogos*, see Martyn, *History*; TDNT 7, p. 852.
9. See Barrett, *The Gospel of John and Judaism*, pp. 47, 70; Brown, *John* 1. LXXIII and Lindars *John*, pp. 35ff. cf. Robinson, *Redating*, pp. 272ff.
10. Brown, *John* 1, p. 381 and Schnackenburg, *John* 2, pp. 257f.
11. Cf. Dodd, *Fourth Gospel*, p. 81 and further Strack-Billerbeck 2. p. 535.
12. See Schnackenburg, *John* 2, p. 251.
13. Strack-Billerbeck 2, p. 534; 1, p. 465.
14. Brown, *John* 1, p. 378; Schnackenburg, *John*, 2, p. 243; Strack-Billerbeck 4, pp. 293ff.; Forkman, *Limits*.
15. Stauffer, *Jerusalem*, pp. 113ff.; Derrett, 'Cursing Jesus'.
16. Schnackenburg, *John*, 2, p. 250.
17. On the history of the Johannine traditions, see, e.g., Dodd, *Historical Tradition*; Brown, *John*, 1, XLI.
18. On Jesus as a deceiver, see Smith, *Jesus the Magician*; Pancaro, *Law*, pp. 87ff.
19. See Bammel, 'Christian Origins'.
20. See above, pp. 174ff.; 266ff.

21 On the obsolescence of the Temple in John, see Schnackenburg, *John*, 1, p. 356.

22 List of references to the sending of Jesus: (*pempo*) 4.34; 5.23f.; 5.30; 5.37; 6.38f.; 6.44; 7.16; 7.18; 7.28; 7.33; 8.16; 8.18; 8.26; 8.29; 9.4; 12.44; 12.49; 13.16; 13.20; 14.24; 15.21; 16.5; cf. 20.21; (*apostello*) 3.17; 3.34; 5.36; 5.38; 6.29; 6.57; 7.29; 8.42; 9.7; 10.36; 11.42; 17.3; 17.8; 17.18; 17.21; 17.23; 18.25; 20.21.

23 On the importance of the Bar Kochba revolt as a significant moment in the separation of church and synagogue, see Eusebius, *Chron.*; Justin, *Apol.* 31.6; *SVM History* 1, p. 545.

24 Summary in Schillebeeckx, *Christ*, pp. 237ff. On the Jewish background, see Williamson, *Philo*; Hofius, *Katapausis*; *Vorhang*; Lincoln, *Paradise*.

25 See McKelvey, *New Temple*; Barrett, 'Eschatology of Hebrews'.

26 On the situation of Hebrews, see Kümmel, *Introduction*, p. 398; Schillebeeckx, *Christ*, pp. 242ff.

27 See Bornkamm *et al.*, *Tradition*; Przybylski, *Righteousness*; Stanton, *Interpretation*.

28 See Davies, *Setting*; Kilpatrick, *Origin*.

APPENDIX
The Sources

1 Though this approach to the Jewish material is not shared by all students of the New Testament; note the consideration of Jewish material in Dunn, *Christology*.

1 Jewish Literature

2 On Josephus, see Betz *et al.*, *Josephus-Studien*; Schlatter, *Theologie*; Rhoads, *Israel*; Attridge, *Interpretation*; Thackeray, *Josephus* and Rajak, *Josephus*.

3 On Philo, see Goodenough, *Introduction*; Wolfson, *Philo*; Sandmel, *Philo*; Smallwood, *Legatio*.

4 See *SVM History* 1; Denis, *Fragmenta*.

5 On the interpretation of Gen. 22, see Vermes, *Scripture*; Hayward in *JJS* 32; Bowker, *Targums*.

6 On this, see Smallwood, *Jews*, pp. 377f.

7 Smallwood, *Jews*; Safrai and Stern, *Jewish People* 1, pp. 420ff.; Kraabel, *Judaism*; Goodenough, *Politics*.

8 Mention should be made of a work attributed to Philo, the *Biblical Antiquities*, which is an account of Israel's history from Adam to the death of Saul. There are editions by Kisch (with ET) and Harrington *et al.* See also Wadsworth, *Liber Antiquitatum Biblicarum*.

9 For an introduction and survey of this literature, see Nickelsburg, *Jewish Literature*; Denis, *Introduction*; Charlesworth, *Pseudepigrapha*; Rost, *Judaism*; Sanders, *Paul*; Eissfeldt, *Old Testament Introduction*. Some of the religious ideas in these works can be found in Stone and Nickelsburg, *Faith and Piety*.

10 On the apocalyptic literature, see Gruenwald, 'Apocalyptic Literature'; Collins, *Apocalypse*; Hanson, *Visionaries*; Stone, *Scriptures* and id. in Safrai and Stern, *Jewish People*, 2, p. 2. The literature is collected in Charles, *Pseudepigrapha* and Charlesworth, *OT Pseudepigrapha*, vol 1.

11 On pseudonymity, see von Fritz, *Pseudepigrapha*; Brox, *Pseudepigraphie*.

12 Segal, 'Heavenly Ascents'.

13 *Open Heaven*; cf. Collins, *Apocalypse*; Koch, *Rediscovery*.

14 On the role of the testament, see von Nordheim, *Lehre*; on the Testaments of the Twelve Patriarchs, see Slingerland, *Testaments*.

15 For introductions to the Apocrypha, see Eissfeldt, *Old Testament Introduction*; Brockington, *Critical Introduction*; Metzger, *Introduction*; Pfeiffer, *Introduction*; Rost, *Judaism*.

16 For concise introduction, see Bowker, *Targums*; Strack, *Introduction* (rev. ed. of German ed. G. Stemberger); Neusner, *Study*; Horbury 'Rabbinics' and Sanders, *Paul*. There is a systematic presentation of rabbinic (and other Jewish) thought in Urbach, *Sages*.

17 See Gerhardsson, *Memory*; Neusner, 'Problem of Oral Tradition'.

18 Neusner, *Modern Study*; 'Formation'; and his history of the mishnaic laws.

19 See Neusner, *The Tosefta*, tr. from the Hebrew.

20 Editions of the Tosefta by Zuckermandel and Lieberman.

21 Tr. in the Soncino version; anthology in Cohen, *Everyman's Talmud*; French tr. of the Jerusalem Talmud by Schwab; one in English by Neusner is in progress. For general introductions, see Neusner, *The Formation of the Babylonian Talmud*; *Invitation*; *Judaism: The Evidence of Yerushalmi*.

22 e.g., Neusner's studies on the Pharisees and the mishnaic purity laws.

23 English tr. of the Mekilta of Rabbi Ishmael by Lauterbach.

24 English tr. of the Midrash Rabbah in the Soncino version.

25 Tr. in the Soncino series and by Judah Goldin.

26 Tr. of Ps. Jonathan and Onkelos by Etheridge and of Neophyti I by Diez-Macho. Editions: Ps. Jonathan and the Fragmentary Targum by Ginsburger; Onkelos: Sperber, *Bible*; Targum on Isaiah: Stenning. For the Cairo Genizah material, see Kahle, *Geniza*. Bibliography in Grossfeld, *Bibliography*.

27 On the question of dating, see York 'Dating'; McNamara, *The New Testament and the Palestinian Targum to the Pentateuch*; Sanders, *Paul*, pp. 5ff.

28 Of the writers of books and articles on the Dead Sea Scrolls, mention may be made in particular of Vermes, *Dead Sea Scrolls*; Milik, *Ten Years*; Dupont-Sommer, *Essene Writings*; Cross, *Ancient Library*; Davies, *Qumran*; Mansoor, *Dead Sea Scrolls*. The best Hebrew text with German translation is in Lohse, *Texte*. For bibliographical information see Fitzmyer, *Dead Sea Scrolls*.

29 On this important text, see Wernberg-Møller, *Manual*; Leaney, *Rule of Qumran*; see also Davies, *The Damascus Covenant*.

30 On biblical exegesis in the Dead Sea Scrolls, see Horgan, *Pesharim*; Bruce, *Biblical Exegesis*; Betz, *Offenbarung*.

31 On the hymns, see Mansoor, *Thanksgiving Hymns*; Holm-Nielsen, *Hodayot*.

32 On the War Scroll, see Yadin, *Scroll*; Davies, *1QM*.

2 Early Christian Literature

33 For an introduction, see Metzger, *Text*.

34 von Campenhausen, *Formation*; Moule, *Birth*. On the Old Testament canon, see Anderson in *The Cambridge History of the Bible*, vol. I, ed. Ackroyd and Evans; and above, pp. 46f.

35 Jackson and Lake, *Apostolic Fathers*, in Loeb edition.

36 Collected in Hennecke, *New Testament Apocrypha*. On the extra-canonical material see

Jeremias, *Unknown Sayings* and Bruce, *Christian Origins.*

37 On the Gospel of Thomas, see Gärtner, *Theology*. Tr. of the Nag Hammadi texts in *Nag Hammadi Library*, ed. Robinson.

38 On Jewish Christianity, see Daniélou, *Theology*; Schoeps, *Theologie*; Longenecker, *Christology*; texts also in Klijn and Reinink, *Patristic Evidence.*

39 For introductions to the New Testament writings, see Kümmel, *Introduction*; Guthrie, *New Testament Introduction*; Lohse, *Formation*; Perrin, *New Testament Introduction*; Bornkamm, *New Testament*; Fuller, *Critical Introduction*; and Koester, *Introduction*; Franklin, *How the Critics can Help*. A useful introduction to the apostolic age may be found in Caird, *Apostolic Age*. On the history of New Testament times, see Bruce, *New Testament History*; Filson, *New Testament History*; Conzelmann, *History*; Lietzmann, *History*; Harnack, *Mission*; Conzelmann, *History*; Reicke, *New Testament Era* and Pfeiffer, *Introduction.*

40 On the history of research, see Kümmel, *New Testament*; Schweitzer, *Quest.*

41 There is an introduction to this method in Barbour, *Traditio-Historical Criticism*. See also Bultmann and Kundsin, *Form Criticism*; on the methodological problems, see Güttgemanns, *Candid Questions.*

42 See Rohde, *Rediscovering* and on the individual gospels, see Bornkamm *et al.*, *Tradition*; *Interpretation*, ed. Stanton; *Messianic Secret*, ed. Tuckett; Martin, *Mark*; *Interpretation of Mark*, ed. Telford, and Marshall, *Luke.*

43 The classic exposition of the Two-(Four) Document hypothesis, which asserts the priority of Mark and dependence of Matt. and Luke on Mark and another source *Q*, is set out by Streeter in *The Four Gospels*. For criticism of this, see Farmer, *The Synoptic Problem*; Rist, *Independence*. For an assessment of recent study, see Stoldt, *History and Criticism*; Tuckett, *Revival.*

44 See Howard, *Fourth Gospel*; Smalley, *John.*

45 The best example of this in English is Dodd, *Historical Tradition*, and, most recently, Robinson, *Redating* and his 1984 Bampton Lectures on John.

46 On the historicity of Acts, see Barrett, *Luke the Historian*; Ramsay, *Paul*; Harnack, *Luke the Physician*; Marshall, *Luke*; Haenchen, *Acts of the Apostles*; Hengel, *Acts* and *Between Jesus and Paul*. For a history of the study of Acts, see Gasque. On the problems of chronology in the early Christian movement, see Ogg, 'Chronology of Paul', in Peake's *Commentary*, id. *The Chronology of Paul's Life* and Jewett, *Dating Paul's Life.*

47 There is a survey of critical opinion in Kümmel, *Introduction*. Among recent important studies in English on the less studied New Testament documents, see Marshall and Brown on the Johannine epistles, Laws on James and Bauckham and Fornberg on 2 Peter (and Bauckham on Jude).

48 See Kümmel, *Introduction.*

BIBLIOGRAPHY

Aberbach, M., *The Roman Jewish War*, London 1966 [= *War*].

Ackroyd, P. R., *Exile and Restoration*. London 1968 [= *Exile*].

—*Israel under Babylon and Persia*. Oxford 1970 [= *Israel*].

Ackroyd, P. R. and Evans, C. F., *The Cambridge History of the Bible*, I. Cambridge 1970 [= *Cambridge History*].

Alexander, P. S., 'Rabbinic Lists of Forbidden Targumim', *JJS* 27 (1976), pp. 177ff.

Alsup, J. E., *The Post-Resurrection Appearances of the Gospels*. London 1975 [= *Post Resurrection Appearances*].

Altaner, B., *Patrology*, London 1960.

Anderson, H., *Jesus and Christian Origins*. Oxford 1964 [= *Jesus*].

Arens, E., *The HΛΘON-Sayings in the Synoptic Tradition*. Göttingen 1976 [= *HΛΘON Sayings*].

Arvedson, T., *Das Mysterium Christi: eine Studie zu Matt. 11.25-30*. Leipzig and Uppsala 1937 [= *Mysterium*].

Attridge, H. W., *The Interpretation of Biblical History in Antiquitates Judaicae*. Missoula 1976 [= *Interpretation*].

Audet, J. P., *La Didache*. Paris 1958.

Aulén, G., *Christus Victor*. London 1931.

Aune, D. E., 'Orthodoxy in First Century Judaism?', *JSJ* 7 (1976), 1ff. [= 'Orthodoxy'].

—*The Cultic Aspect of Realised Eschatology in Early Christianity*. Leiden 1972 [= *Cultic Aspect*].

Avineri, S., *The Social and Political Thought of Karl Marx*. Cambridge 1968.

Bacher, W., *Die Agada der Tannaiten*. Strasbourg 1903.

Bacon, B. W., *Studies in Matthew*. London 1930.

Baltzer, K., *The Covenant Formulary*. Philadelphia 1972.

Balz, H. R., *Heilsvertrauen und Welterfahrung*. Munich 1971.

Bamberger, B. J., *Proselytism in the Talmudic Period*. Cincinnati 1939 [= *Proselytism*].

Bammel, E., *The Trial of Jesus*. London 1970 [= *Trial*].

—'Ein Beitrag zur paulinischen Staatsanschauung', *TLZ* 11 (1960), col. 837ff. [= 'Beitrag'].

—'Erwägungen zur Eschatologie Jesu', *Studia Evangelica* III (*TU* 88). Berlin 1964, pp. 3ff.

—'Christian Origins in Jewish Tradition', *NTS* 13 (1967), pp. 317ff. [= 'Christian Origins'].

—and Moule, C. F. D. (ed.), *Jesus and the Politics of his Day*. Cambridge 1984.

Banks, R., *Jesus and the Law in the Synoptic Tradition*. Cambridge 1975 [= *Jesus and the Law*].

—*Paul's Idea of Community*. Exeter 1980.

Barbel, J., *Christos Angelos*. Bonn 1941.

Barbour, R. S., *Traditio-Historical Criticism of the Gospels*. London 1972 [= *Traditio-*

Historical Criticism].

Bardy, G., 'Cérinthe', *RB* 30 (1921), pp. 344ff.

Barker, M., 'Reflections on the Enoch Myth', *JSOT* 15 (1980), pp. 7ff.

Barnard, L. W., *Justin Martyr*. Cambridge 1967 [= *Justin*].

—*Studies in the Apostolic Fathers and their Background*. Cambridge 1967 [= *Studies*].

Baron, S. W., *A Social and Religious History of the Jews*. Philadelphia 1952 [= *Social and Religious History*].

Barrett, C. K., *The Holy Spirit and the Gospel Tradition*. London 1947 [= *Holy Spirit*].

—'New Testament Eschatology', *SJT* 6 (1953), pp. 136ff.

—*The New Testament Background: Selected Documents*. London 1961.

—*Luke the Historian in Recent Study*. London 1961 [= *Luke*].

—*A Commentary on the Epistle to the Romans*. London 1962.

—'The Eschatology of Hebrews', in Daube and Davies, *The Background of the New Testament and its Eschatology*.

—*The Gospel according to St John*. London 1982.

—*A Commentary on the First Epistle to the Corinthians*. London 1968 [= *1 Cor.*].

—*A Commentary on the Second Epistle to the Corinthians*. London 1973 [= *2 Cor.*].

—*Jesus and the Gospel Tradition*. London 1967 [= *Jesus*].

—*Signs of an Apostle*. London 1970 [= *Signs*].

—*The Gospel of John and Judaism*. London 1975 [= *Judaism*].

—*Essays on John*. London 1982.

—*Essays on Paul*. London 1982.

Bauckham, R. J., 'The Delay of the Parousia', *Tyndale Bulletin* 31 (1980), pp. 3ff.

—*Jude: 2 Peter*. World Biblical Commentary. Waco, Texas 1983 [= *Jude*].

Bauer, W., *Orthodoxy and Heresy in Earliest Christianity*. London 1971 [= *Orthodoxy*].

—*Das Leben Jesu*. Tübingen 1909.

Baumgarten, W., *Paulus und die Apokalyptik*. Neukirchen 1975 [= *Paulus*].

Beaker, S., 'Pagan Criticism of Christianity during the First Two Centuries', ANRW 2.23.2. Berlin 1980, pp. 105ff.

Beasley-Murray, G. R., *Jesus and the Future*. London 1954.

—*A Commentary on Mark 13*. London 1957.

—*Baptism in the New Testament*. London 1963 [= *Baptism*].

—*The Book of Revelation*. London 1974.

Beckwith, R., *The Old Testament Canon of the New Testament Church*. London 1985.

Beker, J. C., *Paul the Apostle. The Triumph of God in Life and Thought*. Edinburgh 1980 [= *Paul*].

—*Paul's Apocalyptic Gospel*. Philadelphia 1982 [= *Gospel*].

Belo, F., *A Materialist Reading of the Gospel of Mark*. Maryknoll N.Y. 1981 [= *Materialist Reading*].

Berger, K., *Die Gesetzauslegung Jesu*. Neukirchen 1972 [= *Gesetzauslegung*].

—*Die Auferstehung des Propheten und die Erhöhung des Menschensohnes*. Göttingen 1976 [= *Auferstehung*].

Best, E., *One Body in Christ*. London 1955 [= *One Body*].

—*A Commentary on the First and Second Epistles to the Thessalonians*. London 1972 [= *1 Thess.*].

Bettenson, H., *Documents of the Christian Church*. Oxford 1963 [= *Documents*].

Betz, H. D., *Galatians*. Philadelphia 1979.

Betz, O., *Offenbarung und Schriftforschung in der Qumransekte*. Tübingen 1960 [= *Offenbarung*].

—*Der Paraklet*. Leiden 1963.

—*What do we know about Jesus?* London 1968 [= *What do we know?*].

—*et al.*, *Josephus-Studien*. Göttingen 1974.

Bianchi, U. (ed.), *Le Origini dello Gnosticismo*. (Supp. to *Numen* 12). Leiden 1967 [= *Origini*].

Bickerman, E., *From Ezra to the Last of the Maccabees*. New York 1962.

—*The God of the Maccabees*. Leiden 1979.

Bietenhard, H., *Die himmlische Welt im Urchristentum und Spätjudentum*. Tübingen 1951 [= *Himmlische Welt*].

—'The Millennial Hope in the Early Church', *SJT* 6 (1953), pp. 12ff.

Bigg, C., *The Christian Platonists of Alexandria*. Oxford 1913 [= *Platonists*].

Bihler, J., *Die Stephanusgeschichte im Zusammenhang der Apostelgeschichte*. Munich 1963.

Billerbeck, P., with Strack, H. L., *Kommentar zum Neuen Testament aus Talmud und Midrasch*. Munich 1922–6 [= Strack-Billerbeck].

Black, M., *An Aramaic Approach to the Gospels and Acts*. Oxford 1967.

—*The Scrolls and Christian Origins*. London 1961 [= *Scrolls*].

Blackman, E. C., *Marcion and his Influence*. London 1948 [= *Marcion*].

Blenkinsopp, J., *Prophecy and Canon*. Notre Dame, Indiana, 1976 [= *Prophecy*].

—*A History of Prophecy in Israel*. London 1984.

Blinzler, J., *The Trial of Jesus*. Westminster, Md, 1959 [= *Trial*].

Bloch, E., *Das Prinzip Hoffnung*. Berlin 1955 [= *Hoffnung*].

—*Thomas Münzer als Theolog der Revolution*. Frankfurt 1962 [= *Thomas Münzer*].

—*Atheism in Christianity: the Religion of the Exodus and the Kingdom*. London 1972 [= *Atheism*].

Böcher, O., *Der johanneische Dualismus im Zusammenhang des nachbiblischen Judentums*. Gütersloh 1965 [= *Johanneische Dualismus*].

Boff, L., *Jesus Christ the Liberator*. London 1980.

Bogart, J., *Orthodox and Heretical Perfectionism in John*. Missoula 1977 [= *Orthodoxy*].

Bokser, B. Z., *Pharisaic Judaism in Transition*. New York 1935 [= *Pharisaic Judaism*].

Borg, M., 'A New Context for Ro. xiii', *NTS* 19 (1972–3), pp. 205ff. [= 'New Context'].

Borgen, P., 'God's Agent in the Fourth Gospel', in *Religions in Antiquity*, ed. J. Neusner [= 'God's Agent'].

—*Bread from Heaven*. Leiden 1965.

Boring, M. E., *Sayings of the Risen Jesus*. Cambridge 1982 [= *Sayings*].

Bornkamm, G., *Jesus of Nazareth*. London 1960.

—*Early Christian Experience*. London 1969.

—*Paul*. London 1971.

—*The New Testament: a Guide to its Writings*. London 1974.

—*et al.*, *Tradition and Interpretation in Matthew*. London 1963 [= *Tradition*].

Bousset, W., *Die Religion des Judentums*. Tübingen 1966 [= *Religion*].

—*Kyrios Christos*. Abingdon, Tenn. 1970.

Bouttier, M., *Christianity according to Paul*. London 1966.

Bowersock, G. W., 'A Roman Perspective on the Bar Kochba War', in *Approaches to Ancient Judaism*, ed. W. S. Greene [= 'Roman Perspective'].

Bowker, J. W., 'The Origin and Purpose of St John's Gospel', *NTS* 11 (1964–5), pp. 398ff.

—'The Speeches in Acts: A Study in Proem and Yelammedenu Forms', *NTS* 14 (1967), pp. 96ff. [= 'Proem'].

—*The Religious Imagination and the Sense of God.* Oxford 1978 [= *Religious Imagination*].

—*The Targums and Rabbinic Literature.* Cambridge 1969 [= *Targums*].

—*Jesus and the Pharisees.* Cambridge 1973 [= *Jesus*].

—'The Son of Man', *JTS* 28 (1977), pp. 19ff.

Bradshaw, P., *Daily Prayer in the Early Church.* London 1981 [= *Daily Prayer*].

Brandon, S. G. F., *The Fall of Jerusalem and the Christian Church.* London 1957 [= *Fall*].

—*Jesus and the Zealots.* Manchester 1967 [= *Jesus*].

—*The Trial of Jesus of Nazareth.* London 1968 [= *Trial*].

—*Religion in Ancient History.* London 1969.

Braude, W. G., *Jewish Proselytising in the First Five Centuries of the Common Era.* Providence 1940 [= *Jewish Proselytising*].

Braun, H., *Spätjudisch-häretischer und frühchristlicher Radikalismus.* Tübingen 1969.

—*Qumran und das Neue Testament.* Tübingen 1966 [= *Qumran*].

Bright, J., *A History of Israel.* London 1972.

Brockington, L. H., *A Critical Introduction to the Apocrypha.* London 1961 [= *Introduction*].

Brown, P. R. L., *Augustine of Hippo.* London 1967.

—*The World of Late Antiquity.* London 1971. [= *World*].

—*Religion and Society in the Age of St Augustine.* London 1972 [= *Religion and Society*].

—*The Making of Late Antiquity.* Cambridge, Mass., 1978 [= *Making*].

Brown, R. E., *The Birth of the Messiah.* London 1977 [= *Birth*].

—*The Semitic Background of the Term 'Mystery' in the New Testament.* Philadelphia 1968.

—*The Gospel according to John.* London 1971 [= *John*].

—*The Community of the Beloved Disciple.* London 1979 [= Community].

—*The Epistles of John.* London 1982 [= *Johannine Epistles*].

—with Donfried, K. P. and Reumann, J., *Peter in the New Testament.* Minneapolis 1973 [= *Peter*].

Brox, N., *Pseudepigraphie in der heidnischen und jüdisch-christlichen Antike.* Darmstadt 1977 [= *Pseudepigraphie*].

Bruce, F. F., *Biblical Exegesis in the Qumran Scrolls.* London 1959 [= *Biblical Exegesis*].

—*New Testament History.* London 1969.

—*Jesus and Christian Origins outside the New Testament.* London 1974 [= *Christian Origins*].

—*Paul, Apostle of the Free Spirit.* Exeter 1977 [= *Paul*].

Brueggemann, W., *The Prophetic Imagination.* Philadelphia 1978.

Buchanan, G. W., *The Consequences of the Covenant.* Leiden 1970 [= *Covenant*].

Büchler, A., *The Economic Conditions of Judea after the Destruction of the Second Temple.*

London 1912 [= *Economic Conditions*].

—*Types of Jewish Palestinian Piety*. London 1922 [= *Types*].

—*Studies in Sin and Atonement*. London 1928.

Bühner, J. A., *Der Gesandte und sein Weg in 4en Evangelium*. Tübingen 1977 [= *Gesandte*].

Bultmann, R., *The Theology of the New Testament*. London 1952 [= *Theology*].

—*Primitive Christianity in its Contemporary Setting*. London 1956.

—*Jesus and the Word*. London 1958.

—*The History of the Synoptic Tradition*. Oxford 1963 [= *History*].

—*The Gospel of John*. Oxford 1971 [= *John*].

—with Kundsin, K., *Form Criticism*. New York 1962.

Burchard, C., *Untersuchungen zu Joseph und Aseneth*. Tübingen 1965 [= *Untersuchungen*].

—*Der dreizehnte Zeuge*. Göttingen 1970.

Burkitt, F. C., *The Gospel History and its Transmission*. Edinburgh 1920.

—*The Religion of the Manichees*. Cambridge 1925.

—*Church and Gnosis*. Cambridge 1932.

Cadbury, H. J., *The Peril of Modernising Jesus*. London 1937 [= *Peril*].

—*The Making of Luke-Acts*. London 1968 [= *Making*].

Caird, G. B., *Principalities and Powers*. Oxford 1956 [= *Principalities*].

—*Jesus and the Jewish Nation*. The Ethel M. Wood Lecture. London 1965.

—*The Revelation of Saint John*. London 1966.

—*The Language and Imagery of the Bible*. London 1980 [= *Language and Imagery*].

Calder, W., 'Philadelphia and Montanism', *BJRL* 7 (1923), pp. 309ff. [= 'Philadelphia'].

Campbell, J. Y., 'The Origin and Meaning of the Term Son of Man', in *Three New Testament Studies*. Leiden 1965.

Campbell, W. S., 'Christ the End of the Law: Romans 10:4', *Studia Biblica* 3 Sheffield (1978), ed. E. A. Livingstone.

Campenhausen, H. von, *Tradition and Life in the Church*. London 1968 [= *Tradition*].

—*Ecclesiastical Authority and Spiritual Power in the Church of the First Three Centuries*. London 1969 [= *Ecclesiastical Authority*].

—*The Formation of the Christian Bible*. London 1972 [= *Formation*].

Carmichael, J., *The Death of Jesus*. London 1961.

Carmignac, J., *Christ and the Teacher of Righteousness*. Baltimore 1962.

—*Recherches sur le 'Notre Père'*. Paris 1969 [= *Recherches*].

—*La Mirage de l'Eschatologie*. Paris 1979 [= *Mirage*].

Carr, W., *Angels and Principalities*. Cambridge 1981 [= *Angels*].

Carroll, R. P., *When Prophecy Failed*. London 1979.

Carson, D. A., (ed.), *From Sabbath to Sunday*. Grand Rapids 1982.

Case, S. J., *The Social Origins of Christianity*. Chicago 1923 [= *Social Origins*].

Casey, P. M., *The Son of Man*. London 1979.

Catchpole, D. R., 'The Trial of Jesus', *IDB Supplement* (1962).

—'The Historicity of the Sanhedrin Trial', in E. Bammel, *The Trial of Jesus*. London 1970.

—*The Trial of Jesus*. Leiden 1971 [= *Trial*].

—'The Answer of Jesus to Caiaphas', *NTS* 17 (1971), pp. 226ff. [= 'Answer'].
—'Paul, James and the Apostolic Council', *NTS* 23 (1976–7), pp. 428ff.
Chadwick, H., *Early Christianity and the Classical Tradition.* Oxford 1966 [= *Early Christianity*].
—'All Things to All Men'. *NTS* 1 (1965), pp. 261ff. [= 'All Things'].
—*Priscillian of Avila.* Oxford 1976.
Charles, R. H., *Eschatology: the Doctrine of a Future Life.* repr. New York 1963 [= *Eschatology*].
—(ed.), *The Apocrypha and Pseudepigrapha of the Old Testament.* Oxford 1913.
Charlesworth, J. H., *The Odes of Solomon.* Oxford 1973.
—*The Pseudepigrapha and Modern Research.* Missoula 1977 [= *Pseudepigrapha*].
—'The History of Pseudepigrapha Research' in *ANRW* 2.19.1, ed. W. Haase, Berlin 1979, pp. 54ff.
—*The Old Testament Pseudepigrapha*, 1, Apocalyptic Literature and Testaments. London 1983 [= *OT Pseudepigrapha*].
—(ed.), *John and Qumran.* London 1972.
Chernus, I., 'Visions of God in Merkabah Mysticism', *JSJ* 13 (1982), pp. 123ff. [= 'Visions'].
—*Mysticism in Rabbinic Judaism.* Berlin 1982.
Childs, B., *Isaiah and the Assyrian Crisis.* London 1967 [= *Isaiah*].
—*Exodus.* London 1974.
—*Introduction to the Old Testament as Scripture.* London 1979 [= *Introduction*].
Chilton, B., *God in Strength.* Freistadt 1979.
—'The Transfiguration: Dominical Assurance and Apocalyptic Vision', *NTS* 27 (1980), pp. 115ff. [= 'Transfiguration'].
—*The Glory of Israel.* Sheffield 1983.
—*The Kingdom of God.* London 1984.
Chitty, D. W., *The Desert a City.* Oxford 1966 [= *Desert*].
Clark, S., *Man and Woman in Christ.* Ann Arbor 1980 [= *Man and Woman*].
Clements, R. E., *Prophecy and Covenant.* London 1965 [= *Prophecy*].
—*God and Temple.* Oxford 1965.
—*Prophecy and Tradition.* Oxford 1965.
Coggins, R., *Samaritans and Jews.* Oxford 1975 [= *Samaritans*].
Cohn, N., *The Pursuit of the Millennium.* London 1957 [= *Pursuit*].
Coleman-Norton, P., *Roman State and Christian Church.* London 1966.
Collins, J. J., *The Sibylline Oracles of Egyptian Judaism.* Missoula 1974 [= *Sibylline Oracles*].
—*The Apocalyptic Vision of the Book of Daniel.* Missoula 1977 [= *Apocalyptic Vision*].
—*Between Athens and Jerusalem.* New York 1983 [= *Athens*].
—(ed.), *Apocalypse: Morphology of a Genre.* Semeia 14. 1979 [= *Apocalypse*].
—(ed.), *Ideal Figures in Ancient Judaism.* Chico 1980.
Conzelmann, H., *The Theology of Saint Luke.* London 1961.
—*An Outline of the Theology of the New Testament.* London 1969 [= *Outline*].
—*History of Primitive Christianity.* London 1973.
Corwin, V., *St Ignatius and Christianity in Antioch.* New Haven 1960.
Cowley, A. E., *Aramaic Papyri of the Fifth Century.* Oxford 1923 [= *Papyri*].
Cranfield, C. E. B., *A Critical and Exegetical Commentary on the Epistle to the Romans.*

Edinburgh 1975–9.

Cross, F. L., (ed.), *Studies in Ephesians*. London 1956 [= *Studies*].

Cross, F. M. and Talmon, S., 'The Council of Yahweh in Second Isaiah', *JNES* 12 (1953), pp. 273ff. [= 'Council of Yahweh'].

—*The Ancient Library of Qumran*. New York 1961 [= *Ancient Library*].

—with Talmon, S., *Qumran and the History of the Biblical Text*. Cambridge, Mass., 1975.

—*Canaanite Myth and Hebrew Epic*. Harvard 1973 [= *Canaanite Myth*].

—*Magnalia Dei*. New York 1976.

Crouch, J. E., *The Origin of the Colossian Haustafeln*. Göttingen 1972 [= *Colossian Haustafeln*].

Cullmann, O., *Le problème littéraire et historique du roman pseudo-clémentin*. Paris 1930.

—*Baptism in the New Testament*. London 1950 [= *Baptism*].

—*Early Christian Worship*. London 1953 [= *Worship*].

—*Immortality of the Soul or Resurrection from the Dead?* London 1958 [= *Resurrection*].

—*The State in the New Testament*. London 1957 [= *State*].

—*The Christology of the New Testament*. London 1963 [= *Christology*].

—*Peter: Disciple, Apostle and Martyr*. London 1966 [= *Peter*].

—*Salvation in History*. London 1967.

—*The Johannine Circle*. London 1976.

Cumont, F., *Oriental Religions in Roman Paganism*. Chicago 1911 [= *Oriental Religions*].

Cunningham, A., *The Early Church and the State*. Philadelphia 1982 [= *Early Church*].

Dahl, N. A., 'The Johannine Church and History', in W. Klassen and G. L. Snyder, *Current Issues in New Testament Interpretation*. New York 1962 [= 'Johannine Church'].

Dalman, G., *The Words of Jesus*. Edinburgh 1902 [= *Words*].

—*Aramäische Dialektproben*. Darmstadt 1960 [= *Dialektproben*].

Dalton, W. J., *Christ's Proclamation to the Spirits*. Rome 1965.

Dan, J. and Talmage, F.(ed.), *Studies in Jewish Mysticism*. Cambridge, Mass. 1982.

Danby, H., *The Mishnah*. Oxford 1933.

Dancy, J. C., *1 and 2 Maccabees*. Oxford 1954.

Daniélou, J., *Origen*. London 1955.

—*The Theology of Jewish Christianity*. London 1964.

—*The Gospel Message and Hellenistic Culture*. London 1973.

—*The Origins of Latin Christianity*. London 1977.

Daube, D., *The New Testament and Rabbinic Judaism*. London 1956.

—*Collaboration with Tyranny in Rabbinic Law*. Oxford 1965.

—'Responsibilities of Master and Disciples in the Gospels', *NTS* 19 (1972); pp. 1ff. [= 'Responsibilities'].

—with Davies, W. D., *The Background of the New Testament and its Eschatology*. Cambridge 1956.

Davies, W. D., *Torah in the Messianic Age and/or Age to Come*. Philadelphia 1952 [= *Torah*].

—*Christian Origins and Judaism*. London 1962.

—*Paul and Rabbinic Judaism*. London 1965 [= *Paul*].
—*The Setting of the Sermon on the Mount*. Cambridge 1966 [= *Setting*].
—*The Gospel and the Land*. Berkeley 1974.
—'From Schweitzer to Scholem: Reflections on Sabbatai Svi' *JBL* 95 (1976), pp.
  529ff. [= 'Schweitzer'].
—'Paul and the People of Israel', *NTS* 24 (1977), pp. 4ff. [= 'Paul and Israel'].
—and Finkelstein, L., *The Cambridge History of Judaism*. Cambridge 1983– .
Davis, J. C., *Utopia and the Ideal Society*. Cambridge 1983 [= *Utopia*].
Davis, P. R., 1*QM: The War Scroll from Qumran*. Rome 1977 [=1 *QM*].
—*Qumran*. London 1982.
—*The Damascus Covenant*. Sheffield 1983.
Day, J., *The OT Utilisation of Language and Imagery Having Parallels in the Baal
  Mythology of the Ugaritic Texts*. Diss: Cambridge 1976 [= *OT Utilisation*].
Déaut, R. Le, *La Nuit Pascale*. Rome 1963.
—*The Message of the New Testament and the Aramaic Bible*. Rome 1982 [= *Message*].
Deidun, T. J., *New Covenant Morality in Paul*. Rome 1981 [= *New Covenant
  Morality*].
Deissmann, A., *Die neutestamentliche Formel 'in Christo Jesu'*. Marburg 1892 [=
  Formel].
—*Paul: a Study in Social and Religious History*. London 1912.
—*Light from the Ancient East*. London 1910 [= *Light*].
Delcor, M., *Études bibliques et orientales de religions comparées*. Leiden 1979 [= *Études
  bibliques*].
Delling, G., *Worship in the New Testament*. London 1962 [= *Worship*].
—*Bibliographie zur jüdisch-hellenistischen und intertestamentarischen Literatur 1900–
  70*. Berlin 1975.
Denis, A. M., *Introduction aux pseudépigraphes grecs d'Ancien Testament*. Leiden 1970
  [= *Introduction*].
—*Fragmenta pseudepigraphorum quae supersunt Graece*. Leiden 1970 [= *Fragmenta*].
Derrett, J. D. M., *Law in the New Testament*. London 1970.
—*Jesus' Audience*. London 1973.
—'Cursing Jesus (1 Cor. xii.3): the Jews as Religious Persecutors', *NTS* 21 (1975),
  pp. 544ff. [= 'Cursing Jesus'].
Dexinger, F., *Henochszehnwochenapokalypse und offene Probleme der Apokalyptikfor-
  schung*. Leiden 1977 [= *Zehnwochenapokalypse*].
Dibelius, M., *Jesus*. London 1963.
—*From Tradition to Gospel*. London 1971.
—*James*. Philadelphia 1976.
Diez-Macho, A., *Neophyti I*. Madrid 1968.
Dix, G., *The Shape of the Liturgy*. London 1945.
—*Jew and Greek*. London 1953.
—rev. Chadwick, H., *The Apostolic Tradition*. London 1968.
Dodd, C. H., *The Bible and the Greeks*. London 1935 [= *Bible*].
—*The Parables of the Kingdom*. London 1935 [= *Parables*].
—*Gospel and Law*. Cambridge 1951.
—*New Testament Studies*. Manchester 1953.
—*Historical Tradition in the Fourth Gospel*. Cambridge 1963 [= *Historical Tradition*].

—*According to the Scriptures*. London 1965.

—*The Interpretation of the Fourth Gospel*. Cambridge 1968 [= *Fourth Gospel*].

—*More New Testament Studies*. Manchester 1968.

—*The Founder of Christianity*. London 1970 [= *Founder*].

Dodds, E. R., *The Greeks and the Irrational*. Berkeley 1951 [= *Greeks*].

—*Pagan and Christian in an Age of Anxiety*. Cambridge 1965 [= *Pagan*].

Doeve, J. W., *Jewish Hermeneutics in the Synoptic Gospels and Acts*. Assen 1954.

Doresse, J., *The Secret Book of the Egyptian Gnostics*. London 1960.

Downing, F. G., *The Church and Jesus*. London 1968 [= *Church*].

Draper, J., *A Commentary on the Didache in the Light of the Dead Sea Scrolls and Related Documents*. Diss., Cambridge 1983.

Driver, G. R., *The Judean Scrolls*. Oxford 1965.

Dugmore, C. W., *The Influence of the Synagogue on the Divine Office*. London 1964 [= *The Influence of the Synagogue*].

Dujarier, M., *Le Parrainage des Adultes aux trois premiers siècles de l'Église*. Paris 1962 [= *Parrainage*].

Dungan, D., *The Sayings of Jesus in the Churches of Paul*. Oxford 1971 [= *Sayings of Jesus*].

—'Mark: the Abridgement of Matthew and Luke', in *Jesus and Man's Hope*, ed. D. Miller, Pittsburgh 1970–1.

Dunn, J. D. G., *Baptism in the Holy Spirit*. London 1970.

—*Jesus and the Spirit*. London 1975 [= *Jesus*].

—*Unity and Diversity in the New Testament*. London 1977 [= *Unity*].

—'Prophetic "I" Sayings and the Jesus Tradition' *NTS* 24 (1977–8), pp. 175ff.

—*Christology in the Making*. London 1980 [= *Christology*].

—'The Incident at Antioch', *JSNT* 18 (1983), pp. 3ff.

—'Let John be John', in *Das Evangelium und die Evangelien*, ed. P. Stuhlmacher, Tübingen 1983.

Dupont, J. *The Sources of Acts*. London 1964.

—*Les Béatitudes*. Paris 1969.

Dupont-Sommer, A., *The Essene Writings from Qumran*. Oxford 1961 [= *Essene Writings*].

Edwards, G. L., *Jesus and the Politics of Violence*. New York 1972.

Edwards, R. A., *The Sign of Jonah*. London 1971.

Eichrodt, W., *The Theology of the Old Testament*. London 1967 [= *Theology*].

Eisler, R., *The Messiah Jesus and John the Baptist*. London 1931 [= *Messiah Jesus*].

Eissfeldt, O., *The Old Testament: An Introduction*. Oxford 1965.

Elbogen, I., *Der jüdische Gottesdienst in seiner geschichtlichen Entwicklung*. Frankfurt 1931 [= *Gottesdienst*].

Eliade, M., *Shamanism*. London 1964.

—*Myths, Dreams and Mysteries*. London 1968.

Elliott, J. H., *The Elect and the Holy*. Leiden 1966.

—*A Home for the Homeless*. London 1982 [= *Home*].

Ellis, E., *Paul's Use of the Old Testament*. Edinburgh 1957.

—*Prophecy and Hermeneutic in Early Christianity*. Tübingen 1978.

Emerton, J. A., 'Binding and Loosing—Forgiving and Retaining', *JTS* 13 (1962), pp. 325ff.

Epp, E. J., *The Theological Tendency of Codex Bezae Cantabrigiensis*. Cambridge 1966.

Etheridge, J., *The Targum of Onkelos and Jonathan ben Uzziel on the Pentateuch with the Fragments of the Jerusalem Targum*, translated from the Chaldee. New York 1968.

Evans, C. F., *The Lord's Prayer*. London 1963.

—*Resurrection and the New Testament*. London 1970 [= *Resurrection*].

Falk, Z. W., *Introduction to the Jewish Law of the Second Commonwealth*. Leiden 1978 [= *Introduction*].

Fallon, F. T., *The Enthronement of Sabaoth*. Leiden 1978 [= *Enthronement*].

Farmer, W. R., *Maccabees, Zealots and Josephus*. New York 1956 [= *Maccabees*].

—*The Synoptic Problem*. New York 1964.

—*Jesus and the Gospel*. Philadelphia 1982.

—with Moule, C. F. D. and Niebuhr, R., *Christian History and Interpretation*. Cambridge 1967 [= *Christian History*].

Festinger, L., *When Prophecy Fails*. New York 1964.

Festugière, A. M., *Personal Religion among the Greeks*. Berkeley 1954 [= *Personal Religion*].

Feuer, L. S. (ed.), *Marx and Engels: Basic Writings on Politics and Philosophy*. London 1969.

Filson, F. V., *New Testament History*. London 1965.

—*Yesterday: A Study of the Epistle to the Hebrews in the Light of Heb. 13*. London 1967.

Finkel, A., *The Pharisees and the Teacher of Nazareth*. Leiden 1964 [= *Pharisees*].

Finkelstein, L., *Akiba; Scholar, Saint and Martyr*. New York 1936 [= *Akiba*].

—*The Pharisees*. Philadelphia 1946.

Fiorenza, E. S., *In Memory of Her*. London 1983.

Fischer, U., *Eschatologie und Jenseitserwartung im hellenistischen Diasporajudentum*. Berlin 1978 [= *Eschatologie*].

Fitzmyer, J., *Essays on the Semitic Background of the New Testament*. London 1971.

—*The Genesis Apocryphon*. Rome 1971.

—*The Dead Sea Scrolls*. Missoula 1977.

—*A Wandering Aramean: Collected Essays*. Missoula 1979.

Flemington, W. F., *The New Testament Doctrine of Baptism*. London 1948.

Fletcher, J., *Situation Ethics*. London 1966.

Flew, R. N., *Jesus and his Church*. London 1943.

Flusser, D., 'The Dead Sea Scrolls and Pre-Pauline Christianity', *Scripta Hierosolymitana*. 4 (1958), pp. 215ff.

—*Jesus*. New York 1969.

Foerster, W. (ed.), *Gnosis*. Oxford 1972–4. (2 vols.).

Forkman, L., *The Limits of the Religious Community*. Lund 1972 [= *Limits*].

Fornberg, T., *An Early Church in a Pluralist Society*. Lund 1977.

Francis, F. O., and Meeks, W. (ed.), *Conflict at Colossáe*. Missoula 1975 [= *Conflict*].

Franklin, E., *How the Critics Can Help*. London 1982.

Fraser, P., *Ptolemaic Alexandria*. Oxford 1972.

Frend, W. H. C., *Martyrdom and Persecution in the Early Church*. Oxford 1955 [= *Martyrdom*].

—*The Early Church*. London 1965.

Freyne, S., *Galilee from Alexander the Great to Hadrian 323 BCE to 135 CE*, Notre Dame, Indiana, 1980 [= *Galilee*].

Friedlander, G., *Pirke de Rabbi Eliezer*. New York 1965.
Fritz, K. von, *Pseudepigrapha I: Pseudopythagorica, Lettres de Platon, Littérature pseudépigraphe juive*. Geneva 1972.
Fuller, R. H., *Interpreting the Miracles*. London 1963 [= *Interpreting*].
—*A Critical Introduction to the New Testament*. London 1966.
—*The Mission and Achievement of Jesus*. London 1967 [= *Mission*].
—*The Formation of the Resurrection Narratives*. London 1972 [= *Formation*].
—*The Foundation of New Testament Christology*. London 1965 [= *Foundations*].
Furnish, V. P., *Theology and Ethics in Paul*. Nashville 1968 [= *Theology*].
—*The Love Command in the New Testament*. London 1973 [= *Love Command*].
Gager, J., *Moses in Greco-Roman Paganism*. Missoula 1972 [= *Moses*].
—*Kingdom and Community*. Prentice-Hall 1975 [= *Kingdom*].
Gärtner, B., *The Theology of the Gospel of Thomas*. London 1961 [= *Theology*].
—*The Temple and the Community in Qumran and the New Testament*. Cambridge 1965 [= *Temple*].
Gasque, W., *A History of the Criticism of the Acts of the Apostles*. Tübingen 1975 [= *History*].
Gaston, L., *No Stone On Another*. Leiden 1970 [= *No Stone*].
Geertz, C., 'Religion as a Cultural System' in *Anthropological Approaches to the Study of Religion*, ed. M. Banton. London 1966, pp. 1ff.
Georgi, D., *Die Gegner des Paulus im 2 Korintherbrief*. Neukirchen 1964 [= *Gegner*].
—*Die Geschichte der Kollekte des Paulus für Jerusalem*. Hamburg 1965 [= *Kollekte*].
Gerhardsson, B., *Memory and Manuscript*. Lund 1961 [= *Memory*].
—*Tradition and Transmission in Early Christianity*. Lund 1964 [= *Tradition and Transmission*].
—*The Gospel Tradition*. London 1977.
Gibbs, J., *Creation and Redemption*. Leiden 1971.
Giddens, A., *Capitalism and Modern Social Theory*. Cambridge 1971 [= *Capitalism*].
Ginsburger, M. (ed.), *Das Fragmentthargum*. Berlin 1899.
—(ed.), *Thargum Jonathan ben Uzziel zum Pentateuch*. Berlin 1903.
Ginzberg, L., *The Legends of the Jews*. Philadelphia 1938 [= *Legends*].
Glasson, T. F., *The Second Advent*. London 1963.
—*Jesus and the End of the World*. London 1980 [= *Jesus*].
Glover, T. R., *The Conflict of Religions in the Early Roman Empire*. London 1909.
—*Paul of Tarsus*. London 1925.
—*The Influence of Christ in the Ancient World*. London 1929.
Goguel, M., *The Primitive Church*. London 1963.
Goldberg, A., *Untersuchungen über die Vorstellung von der Schekhinah in der frühen rabbinischen Literatur*. Berlin 1969 [= *Schekhinah*].
Goldin, J., *The Fathers according to Rabbi Nathan*. New Haven 1955.
Goldstein, J. A., *1 Maccabees*. New York 1976.
Goodenough, E. R., *By Light Light: the Mystic Gospel of Hellenistic Judaism*. New Haven 1935 [= *By Light*].
—*The Politics of Philo Judaeus*. New Haven 1938 [= *Politics*].
—*An Introduction to Philo Judaeus*. Oxford 1962 [= *Introduction*].
—*Jewish Symbols in the Greco-Roman Period* (13 vols.). New Haven 1953–65 [= *Jewish Symbols*].

387

Gooding, D. W., *The Account of the Tabernacle*. Cambridge 1959 [= *Tabernacle*].
—'Aristeas and Septuagint Origins', *VT* 13 (1963), pp. 357ff. [= 'Aristeas'].
Goodman, M., Review of S. Freyne, *Galilee* in *JJS* 32 (1981), p. 204.
—'The First Jewish Revolt: Social Conflict and the Problem of Debt', *JJS* 33 (1982), pp. 417ff. [= 'First Jewish Revolt'].
Goodwin, B., and Taylor, K., *The Politics of Utopia*. London 1982.
Gottwald, N. K., *The Tribes of Yahweh*. London 1980 [= *Tribes*].
Goudoever, J., *Biblical Calendars*. Leiden 1959 [= *Calendars*].
Goulder, M. D., *Midrash and Lection in Matthew's Gospel*. London 1974 [= *Midrash*].
—*The Evangelists' Calendar*. London 1978.
Grant, M., *The Jews in the Roman World*. London 1973.
—*Paul*. London 1976.
—*Jesus*. London 1977.
Grant, R. M., *Second Century Christianity*. London 1957.
—*Gnosticism and Early Christianity*. London 1959 [= *Gnosticism*].
—*Early Christianity and Society*. London 1977 [= *Early Christianity*].
Grässer, E., *Das Problem der Parusieverzögerung in den synoptischen Evangelien und in der Apostelgeschichte*. Berlin 1960.
Green, W. S., *Approaches to Ancient Judaism*. Missoula 1978– .
—'Palestinian Holy Men', in ANRW 2.19.2, ed. W. Haase. Berlin 1979, pp. 619ff.
—*Traditions of Rabbi Joshua ben Hananyah*. Leiden 1981.
Greene, W. C., *Moira: Fate, Good and Evil in Greek Thought*. 1944 [= *Moira*].
Greenfield, J., and Stone, M. E., 'The Books of Enoch and the Traditions of Enoch, *Numen* 26 (1979), pp. 81ff. [= 'Books of Enoch'].
Grillmeier, A., *Christ in Christian Tradition*. London 1975 [= *Christ*].
Gritsch, E. W., *Reformer without a Church*. Philadelphia 1967 [= *Reformer*].
Grollenberg, L., *Paul*. London 1978.
—*Jesus*. London 1978.
Grossfeld, B., *A Bibliography of Targum Literature*. Cincinnati 1972 [= *Bibliography*].
Gruenwald, I., 'Knowledge and Vision', *Israel Oriental Studies* 3 (1975), pp. 63ff.
—*Apocalyptic and Merkavah Mysticism*, Leiden 1978 [= *Apocalyptic*].
—'Jewish Apocalyptic Literature', ANRW 2.19.1, Berlin 1979, pp. 89ff.
Guignebert, C., *The Jewish World in the Time of Jesus*. London 1939.
Guilding, A., *The Fourth Gospel and Jewish Worship*. Oxford 1960 [= *Fourth Gospel*].
Guillaume, A., *Prophecy and Divination among the Hebrews and Other Semites*. London 1938.
Gundry, R. H., *The Use of the Old Testament in St Matthew's Gospel*. Leiden 1967 [= *Use*].
—*Sōma in Biblical Theology*. Cambridge 1976 [= *Sōma*].
Gunther, J. J., *St Paul's Opponents and their Background*. Leiden 1973 [= *Opponents*].
Guthrie, D., *New Testament Introduction*. London 1970 [= *Introduction*].
Guthrie, W. K. C., *The Greeks and their Gods*. London 1950 [= *Greeks*].
Gutmann, J. (ed.), *The Dura-Europos Synagogue: a Re-Evaluation* (1932–72). Missoula 1973 [= *Dura-Europos*].
—(ed.), *Ancient Synagogues*. Chico 1981.
Güttgemanns, E., *Candid Questions concerning Gospel Form Criticism*. Pittsburgh 1979

[= *Candid Questions*].

Guttmann, A., 'The Significance of Miracles for Talmudic Judaism', *HUCA* 20 (1947), pp. 363ff.

—*Rabbinic Judaism in the Making*. Detroit 1970 [= *Judaism*].

Haenchen, E., *Der Weg Jesu*. Berlin 1966.

—*The Acts of the Apostles*. Oxford 1971.

Hagner, D., 'Paul in Modern Jewish Thought', in *Pauline Studies*, ed. Hagner. Exeter 1980 [= 'Paul'].

Hahn, F., *Mission in the New Testament*, London 1965 [= *Mission*].

—*The Titles of Jesus in Christology*. London 1969 [= *Titles*].

—*The Worship of the Early Church*. Philadelphia 1973.

Halperin, D., *The Merkabah in Rabbinic Literature*. New Haven 1980 [= *Merkabah*].

Hamerton-Kelly, R., *Pre-Existence Wisdom and the Son of Man*. Cambridge 1973 [= *Pre-Existence*].

Hanson, A. T., *Jesus in the Old Testament*. London 1965.

—*The Wrath of the Lamb*. London 1957.

—*Studies in Paul's Technique and Theology*. London 1974.

—*Grace and Truth*. London 1975.

—*The New Testament Interpretation of Scripture*. London 1980.

—*The Living Utterances of God*. London 1983.

Hanson, P. D., *The Dawn of Apocalyptic*. Philadelphia 1975 [= *Dawn*].

—'Apocalypticism' *IDB Supplement*.

—(ed.), *Visionaries and their Apocalypses*. London 1983 [= *Visionaries*].

Hanson, R. P. C., *Tradition in the Early Church*. London 1962 [= *Tradition*].

Harnack, A. von, *Militia Christi*. repr. Philadelphia 1981.

—*What is Christianity?*. London 1901.

—*The Mission and Expansion of Christianity in the First Three Centuries*. London 1908 [= *Mission*].

—*Marcion*. Berlin 1921.

—*Judentum und Judenchristentum in Justins Dialog mit Trypho*. Leipzig 1913 [= *Judentum*].

Harnisch, W., *Verhängnis und Verheissung der Geschichte*. Göttingen 1969 [= *Verhängnis*].

—*Eschatologische Existenz*. Göttingen 1973.

Harrington, D. J., *et al.*, *Pseudo-Philo. Les Antiquités bibliques*. Paris 1976.

Harris, H., *The Tübingen School*. Oxford 1975.

Harris, M., *Raised Immortal*. London 1983.

Harris, R., *Testimonies*. Cambridge 1916.

Harrisson, P., *The Problem of the Pastoral Epistles*. London 1921 [= *Problems*].

Hartmann, L., *Prophecy Interpreted*. Lund 1966.

Hartwell, H., *The Theology of Karl Barth: an Introduction*. London 1964 [= *Theology of Karl Barth*].

Harvey, A. E., *Jesus on Trial*. London 1976.

—*Jesus and the Constraints of History*. London 1982 [= *Jesus*].

Hay, D. M., *Glory at the Right Hand*. Abingdon, Tenn. 1973 [= *Glory*].

Hayes, J. H., and Holladay, C. H., *Biblical Exegesis*. London 1982.

—and Miller, J. M., *Israelite and Judean History*. London 1977.

Hayward, C. T. R., 'The Present State of Research into the Targumic Account of the Sacrifice of Isaac', *JJS* 32 (1981), pp. 127ff. [= *Sacrifice*].

—'The Jewish Temple at Leontopolis: a Reconsideration', *JJS* 33 (1982), pp. 429ff. [= 'Jewish Temple'].

Hegermann, H., *Jesaja 53 in Hexapla Targum und Peshitta*. Gütersloh 1954 [= *Jesaja 53*].

Heinemann, J., and Petuchowski, J., *The Literature of the Synagogue*. London 1978 [= *Literature*].

Hellholm, D. (ed.), *Apocalypticism in the Mediterranean World and the Near East*. Tübingen 1982 [= *Apocalypticism*].

Hengel, M., *Was Jesus a Revolutionist?* Philadelphia 1971.

—*Judaism and Hellenism*. London 1974 [= *Judaism*].

—*Property and Riches in the Early Church*. London 1974 [= *Property and Riches*].

—'Proseuche und Synagoge', in *Tradition und Glaube*, ed. G. Jeremias *et al.* Göttingen 1975 [= 'Proseuche'].

—*Victory over Violence*. London 1975 [= *Victory*].

—*The Son of God*. London 1976.

—*Die Zeloten*. Leiden 1976.

—*Crucifixion*. London 1977.

—*Acts and the History of Earliest Christianity*. London 1979.

—*Jews, Greeks and Barbarians*. London 1980. [= *Jews*].

—*The Atonement*. London 1981.

—*The Charismatic Leader and his Followers*. Edinburgh 1981 [= *Charismatic Leader*].

—*Between Paul and Jesus*. London 1983.

Hennecke, W., and Schneelmecher, W., *New Testament Apocrypha*. London 1965.

Henrichs, A., and Koenen, L., 'Ein griechischer Mani-Codex', *Zeitschrift für Papyrologie und Epigraphik* 5 (1970), pp. 97ff.

Henry, P. *New Directions in New Testament Study*. London 1980 [= *New Directions*].

Herford, R. T., *Christianity in Talmud and Midrash*. London 1903 [= *Christianity*].

—*Talmud and Apocrypha*. London 1933 [= *Talmud*].

Hick, J. (ed.), *The Myth of God Incarnate*. London 1977 [= *Myth*].

Hiers, R. H., *The Kingdom of God in the Synoptic Tradition*. Gainesville 1970 [= *Kingdom of God*].

—'The Delay of the Parousia in Luke-Acts', *NTS* 20 (1973–4), pp. 145ff.

Higgins, A. J. B., *The Lord's Supper in the New Testament*. London 1952 [= *Lord's Supper*].

Hill, D., *Greek Words and Hebrew Meanings*. Cambridge 1967 [= *Greek Words*].

Hill, M., *A Sociology of Religion*. London 1973 [= *Sociology*].

Hinchliff, P., *Holiness and Politics*. London 1982.

Hock, R. F. *The Social Context of Paul's Ministry*. Philadelphia 1980 [= *Social Context*].

Hoehner, H., *Herod Antipas*, Cambridge 1972 [= *Herod*].

Hofius, O., *Katapausis*. Tübingen 1970.

—*Der Vorhang vor dem Thron Gottes*. Tübingen 1972 [= *Vorhang*].

Holladay, C. H., *Theios Aner in Hellenistic Judaism*. Missoula 1977.

Hollenbach, P., 'Social Aspects of John the Baptiser's Preaching Mission in the context of Palestinian Judaism', in ANRW 2.19.2, ed. W. Haase. Berlin 1979, pp.

850ff. [= 'Social Aspects'].

Holm-Nielsen, S., *Hodayoth*. Copenhagen and Aarhus 1960.

Holmberg, B., *Paul and Power*. Philadelphia 1978 [= *Power*].

Holtz, T., *Die Christologie der Apokalypse des Johannes*. Berlin 1962 [= *Christologie*].

Holtzmann, O., *Die Mischna: Middot*. Giessen 1913.

Hooker, M. D., *Jesus and the Servant*. London 1959.

—*The Son of Man in Mark*. London 1967 [= *Son of Man*].

—'Using the Wrong Tool', *Theology* 3 (1972), pp. 590ff.

—'Interchange in Christ', *JTS* 22 (1971), pp. 349ff. [= 'Interchange'].

—*Pauline Pieces*. London 1979.

—*The Message of Mark*. London 1983.

—and Wilson, S. G., *Paul and Paulinism*. London 1982.

Horbury, W., 'Keeping Up with Recent Studies: V Rabbinics' *Exp T* 91 (1980), pp. 233ff. [= 'Rabbinics'].

—'The Benediction of the Minim and Early Jewish Christian Controversy', *JTS* 33 (1982), pp. 19ff. [= 'Benediction'].

—'i Thess. ii.3 as Rebutting the Charge of False Prophecy', *JTS* 33 (1982), p. 492ff. [= '1 Thess.'].

—and Rowland, C. C., ed., *Essays for Ernst Bammel JSNT* 19 (1983).

Horgan, P. P., *Pesharim: Qumran Interpretations of Biblical Books*. Washington 1979 [= *Pesharim*].

Hornus, J. M., *It Is Not Lawful For Me To Fight*. Scottdale 1980 [= *It is Not Lawful*].

Horst, P. van der, 'Moses' Throne Vision in Ezekiel the Dramatist', *JJS* 34 (1983), pp. 21ff. [= 'Moses' Throne Vision'].

Hort, F. J. A., *Judaistic Christianity*. London 1898.

Horton, F. L., *The Melchizedek Tradition*. Cambridge 1976 [= *Melchizedek*].

Houlden, J. L., *Paul's Letters from Prison*. Harmondsworth 1970.

—*Ethics and the New Testament*. Harmondsworth 1973 [= *Ethics*].

—*A Commentary on the Johannine Epistles*. London 1973.

Howard, G., *Crisis in Galatia*. Cambridge 1979 [= *Crisis*].

—'The Letter of Aristeas and Diaspora Judaism', *JTS* (1971), pp. 337ff.

Howard, W. F., *The Fourth Gospel in Recent Study*. London 1955.

Hübner, H., *Law in Paul's Thought*. Edinburgh 1983 [= *Law*].

Hudson, W., *The Marxist Philosophy of Ernst Bloch*. London 1982 [= *Marxist Philosophy*].

Hughes, G. R., *Hebrews and Hermeneutics*. Cambridge 1979.

Hull, J. M., *Hellenistic Magic and the Synoptic Tradition*. London 1971 [= *Hellenistic Magic*].

Hunter, A. M., *Paul and his Predecessors*. London 1961.

Hurd, J. C., *The Origin of 1 Corinthians*. London 1965 [= *Origin*].

Iersel, B. M. F. van, *Der Sohn in der synoptischen Jesusworten*. Leiden 1964 [= *Sohn*].

Jackson, F. J. Foakes, and Lake, K., *The Beginnings of Christianity*. London 1939 [= *Beginnings*].

Jacobson, H., *The Exagoge of Ezekiel*. Cambridge 1983.

Jaeger, W., *Paideia: the Ideals of Greek Culture*. Oxford 1939.

—*Early Christianity and Greek Paideia*. Oxford 1962.

James, M. R., *The Biblical Antiquities of Pseudo-Philo*. London 1917.

—*The Apocryphal New Testament*. Oxford 1924.

James, W. R., *The Varieties of Religious Experience*. London 1960.

Jaubert, A., *The Date of the Last Supper*. New York 1965 [= *Date*].

Jellicoe, S., *The Septuagint and Modern Study*. Oxford 1968 [= *Septuagint*].

—(ed.), *Studies in the Septuagint: Origins, Recensions, Interpretations*. New York 1974 [= *Studies*].

Jeremias, C., *Die Nachtgesichte des Sacharjas*. Göttingen 1977 [= *Nachtgesichte*].

Jeremias, G., *Der Lehrer der Gerechtigkeit*. Göttingen 1963 [= *Lehrer*].

Jeremias, J., *Theophanie*. Neukirchen 1965.

Jeremias, Joachim, *Jesus' Promise to the Nations*. London 1958 [= *Jesus' Promise*].

—*Unknown Sayings of Jesus*. London 1958 [= *Unknown Sayings*].

—*The Parables of Jesus*. London 1963 [= *Parables*].

—*The Problem of the Historical Jesus*. Philadelphia 1964 [= *Problem*].

—*The Eucharistic Words of Jesus*. London 1966 [= *Eucharistic Words*].

—*The Prayers of Jesus*. London 1967 [= *Prayers*].

—*Jerusalem in the Time of Jesus*. London 1969 [= *Jerusalem*].

—*New Testament Theology 1: the Proclamation of Jesus*. London 1971 [= *NTT*].

Jewett, R., *Paul's Anthropological Terms*. Leiden 1971.

—*A Chronology of Paul's Life*. Philadelphia 1979 [= *Chronology*].

Johnson, S., 'Asia Minor and Early Christianity', in *Christianity, Judaism and Other Greco-Roman Cults*, ed. J. Neusner. Leiden 1975, pp. 74ff. [= 'Asia Minor'].

Johnston, G., *The Spirit-Paraclete in the Fourth Gospel*. Cambridge 1970 [= *Spirit-Paraclete*].

Jones, A. H. M., *The Herods of Judaea*. Oxford 1938 [= *Herods*].

—*The Greek City from Alexander to Justinian*. Oxford 1940 [= *Greek City*].

—*Constantine and the Conversion of Europe*. London 1965 [= *Constantine*].

—*The Cities of the Eastern Roman Provinces*. Oxford 1971.

—*The Decline of the Ancient World*. London 1975.

Jones, D. L., 'Christianity and the Roman Imperial Cult', in *ANRW* 2.23.2, ed. W. Haase. Berlin 1980, pp. 1023ff.

Judge, E. A., *The Social Pattern of Christian Groups in the First Century*. London 1960 [= *Social Pattern*].

Kadman, L., *The Coins of the Jewish War of 66–73*. Tel Aviv 1960 [= *Coins*].

Kadushin, M., *The Rabbinic Mind*. New York 1965.

Kahle, P., *Masoreten des Östens*. Leipzig 1913.

—*Masoreten des Westens*. Stuttgart 1927.

—*The Cairo Geniza*. London 1947.

Kanter, S., *Rabban Gamaliel II*. Chicago 1980.

Käsemann, E., *Essays on New Testament Themes*. London 1964 [= *Essays*].

—*The Testament of Jesus*. London 1968.

—*New Testament Questions of Today*. London 1969 [= *NT Questions*].

—*Commentary on Romans*. London 1980 [= *Romans*].

Kautsky, K., *The Foundations of Christianity*. London 1925 [= *Foundations*].

Keck, L. E., and Martyn, J. L., *Studies in Luke-Acts*. London 1968 [= *Studies*].

Kee, A., *Constantine versus Christ*. London 1982 [= *Constantine*].

Kee, H. C., *The Community of the New Age*. London 1977.

—*Christian Origins in Sociological Perspective*. London 1980 [= *Christian Origins*].

—*The Origins of Christianity: Sources and Documents*. London 1980.
—*Miracle in the Early Christian World*. New Haven 1983.
—and Young, F. W., *The Living World of the New Testament*. London 1960.
Kelly, J. N. D., *A Commentary on the Letters to Timothy and Titus*. London 1963.
—*Early Christian Doctrines*. London 1968.
—*Jerome*. London 1975.
—*Early Christian Creeds*. London 1981.
Kemmler, D., *Faith and Reason*. Leiden 1975.
Kermode, F., *The Sense of an Ending*. Oxford 1966.
—*The Genesis of Secrecy*. Cambridge, Mass., 1979.
Kertelge, K., 'Apokalypsis Iesou Christou' in *Neues Testament und Kirche*, ed. J. Gnilka. Freiburg i/Br. 1974 [= 'Apokalypsis'].
Kilpatrick, G. D., *The Origin of the Gospel according to Saint Matthew*. Oxford 1946 [= *Origin*].
Kim, S., *The Origin of Paul's Gospel*. Tübingen 1981 [= *Origin*].
Kimelman, R., 'Birkat ha-Minim and the Lack of Evidence for an Anti-Christian Prayer' in *Jewish and Christian Self-Definition*, ed. E. P. Sanders.
Kippenberg, H., *Religion und Klassenbildung im antiken Judäa*. Göttingen 1978 [= *Religion und Klassenbildung*].
Kittel, G., and Friedrich, G. (ed.), *Theological Dictionary of the New Testament*. Grand Rapids 1964– [= *TDNT*].
Klausner, J., *Jesus of Nazareth*. London 1925 [= *Jesus*].
—*The Messianic Idea in Israel*. London 1956 [= *Messianic Idea*].
—*From Jesus to Paul*. London 1942.
Klein, C., *Anti-Judaism in Christian Theology*. London 1978.
Klijn, A. F. J., and Reinink, G. S., *Patristic Evidence for Jewish Christian Sects*. Leiden 1973 [= *Patristic Evidence*].
Klinzing, G., *Die Umdeutung des Kultus in der Qumrangemeinde und im NT*. Göttingen 1971 [= *Umdeutung*].
Knibb, M. A., *The Ethiopic Books of Enoch*. Oxford 1978.
—'Apocalyptic and Wisdom in 4 Ezra', *JSJ* 13 (1982), pp. 56ff. [= 'Apocalyptic'].
—(ed.) *Israel's Prophetic Tradition*. Cambridge 1982.
Knowles, D. A., *From Pachomius to Ignatius*. Oxford 1966.
Knox, J., *Marcion and the New Testament*. Chicago 1942.
—*Chapters in a Life of Paul*. London 1954.
—*The Ethic of Jesus and the Teaching of the Church*. London 1962 [= *Ethic*].
—*The Humanity and Divinity of Christ*. Cambridge 1967.
Knox, R. A., *Enthusiasm: a Chapter in the History of Religion*. Oxford 1950.
Knox, W. L., *St Paul and the Church of Jerusalem*. Cambridge 1925.
—*St Paul and the Church of the Gentiles*. Cambridge 1932.
Kobelski, P. J., *Melchizedek and Melchireša*. Washington 1981 [= *Melchizedek*].
Koch, K., *The Rediscovery of Apocalyptic*. London 1970 [= *Rediscovery*].
—*The Prophets*. London 1982.
Koester, H., *Introduction to the New Testament*. Philadelphia 1982 [= *Introduction*].
Kraabel, A. T., *Judaism in Asia Minor in the Imperial Period*, Diss. Harvard 1968 [= *Judaism in Asia Minor*].
—'The Diaspora Synagogue' in *ANRW* 2.19.1, ed. W. Haase. Berlin 1979, pp.

477ff. [= 'Diaspora Synagogue'].

Kraeling, C. H., *John the Baptist*. New York 1951 [= *John*].

—*The Synagogue*. New Haven 1956.

—*The Christian Building*. New Haven 1967.

Kraft, R. A., 'In Search of Jewish Christianity and its Theology', *RSR* 60 (1972), pp. 81ff. [= 'Search'].

—(ed.), 'The Multiform Heritage of Early Christianity', in *Christianity, Judaism and Other Greco-Roman Cults*. ed. J. Neusner, Leiden 1975 [= 'Heritage'].

—and Nickelsburg, G., *Early Judaism and its Modern Interpreters*. Philadelphia (forthcoming).

Kramer, H., *Christ, Lord, Son of God*. London 1966 [= *Christ*].

Krauss, S., *Das Leben Jesu nach jüdischen Quellen*. Berlin 1902 [= *Das Leben Jesu*].

Kreissig, H., *Die sozialen Zusammenhänge des judäischen Krieges*. Leipzig 1970 [= *Sozialen Zusammenhänge*].

Kuhn, H. W., *Enderwartung und gegenwärtiges Heil*. Göttingen 1966 [= *Enderwartung*].

Kuhn, K. G., *Achtzehngebet und Vaterunser und der Reim*. Tübingen 1950 [= *Achtzehngebet*].

Kümmel, W. G., *Promise and Fulfilment*. London 1957 [= *Promise*].

—'Eschatological Expectation in the Proclamation of Jesus' in *The Future of Our Religious Past*, ed. J. M. Robinson. London 1971 [= 'Eschatological Expectation'].

—*The New Testament: the History of the Investigation of its Problems*. London 1973 [= *The New Testament*].

—*The Theology of the New Testament*. London 1974 [= *Theology*].

—*Introduction to the New Testament*. London 1975 [= *Introduction*].

Künneth, W., *The Theology of the Resurrection*. London 1965.

Labriolle, P. de, *La Crise Montaniste*. Paris 1913.

—*Les Sources de l'Histoire du Montanisme*. Paris 1913 [= *Crise*].

Ladd, G. E., *Jesus and the Kingdom*. New York 1964.

Lake, K., *The Apostolic Fathers*. London 1912.

Lambrecht, J., *Die Redaktion der Markus-Apokalypse*. Rome 1967.

—*Once More Astonished*. New York 1978 [= *Once More*].

Lampe, G. W. H., *God as Spirit*. Oxford 1977.

Lange, N. de, *Origen and the Jews*. Cambrige 1976 [= *Origen*].

—'Jewish Attitudes to the Roman Empire' in *Imperialism in the Ancient World*. ed. P. D. A. Garnsey and C. R. Whittaker. Cambridge 1978 [= 'Jewish Attitudes'].

Larcher, C., *Études sur le Livre de la Sagesse*. Paris 1969 [= *Sagesse*].

Lash, N., *A Matter of Hope*. London 1982.

Laurin, R. B., 'The Question of Immortality in the Qumran Hodayot', *JSS* 3 (1958), pp. 344ff. [= 'Question of Immortality'].

Lauterbach, J. Z., *Rabbinic Essays*. Cincinnati 1959.

—*Mekilta*. Philadelphia 1956.

Laws, S., *A Commentary on the Epistle of James*. London 1980.

Layton, B. (ed.), *The Rediscovery of Gnosticism*. Leiden 1980.

Leaney, A. R. C., *The Rule of Qumran and its Meaning*. London 1966.

—*The Jewish and Christian World, 200 BC to AD 200*. Cambridge 1983.

Leiman, S. Z., *The Canonisation of Hebrew Scripture*. New York 1974 [= *Canonisation*].

Leivestad, R., 'Exit the Apocalyptic Son of Man', *NTS* 18 (1971–2), pp. 243ff. [= 'Exit'].

Lentzen-Deis, F., *Die Taufe Jesu nach den Synoptikern*. Frankfurt 1970 [= *Taufe Jesu*].

Leon, H. J., *The Jews of Ancient Rome*. Rome 1960 [= *Jews*].

Lescynsky, R., *Die Sadduzäer*. Berlin 1912.

Levertoff, P., 'Synagogue Worship in the First Century', in *Liturgy and Worship*, ed. W. K. Lowther Clarke. London 1959, pp. 60ff.

Lietzmann, H., *History of the Early Church* (4 vols.). London 1937–44.

—with Richardson, R., *Mass and Lord's Supper*. Leiden 1979 [= *Mass*].

Lightfoot, J. B., *The Epistles of St. Paul: Galatians*. London 1865 [= *Galatians*].

—*The Apostolic Fathers*. London 1898.

Lincoln, A. T., *Paradise Now and Not Yet*. Cambridge 1981 [= *Paradise*].

Lindars, B., *New Testament Apologetic*. London 1961.

—*The Gospel of John*. London 1972 [= *John*].

—*Jesus, the Son of Man*. London 1983.

—with Smalley, S. S., *Christ and Spirit in the New Testament*. Cambridge 1973 [= *Christ and Spirit*].

Lindblom, J., *Prophecy in Ancient Israel*. Oxford 1967 [=*Prophecy*].

—*Gesichte und Offenbarungen*. Lund 1968.

Linnemann, E., *The Parables of Jesus*. London 1966 [= *Parables*].

Logan, A. H. B. and Wedderburn, A. J. M., *The New Testament and Gnosis*. Edinburgh 1983.

Lohmeyer, E., *The Lord's Prayer*. London 1965 [= *Lord's Prayer*].

Lohse, E., *Die Ordination im Spätjudentum und im Neuen Testament*. Göttingen 1951 [= *Ordination*].

—*Märtyrer und Gottesknecht*. Göttingen 1955 [= *Märtyrer*].

—*Die Texte aus Qumran*. Munich 1971.

—*Colossians and Philemon*. Philadelphia 1971 [= *Colossians*].

—*The Formation of the New Testament*. Abingdon, Tenn. 1981.

Loisy, A., *The Gospel and the Church*. London 1903.

Longenecker, R. N., *The Christology of Early Jewish Christianity*. London 1970 [= *Christology*].

—*Biblical Exegesis in the Apostolic Period*. Grand Rapids 1975 [= *Biblical Exegesis*].

Loos, H. van der, *The Miracles of Jesus*. Leiden 1965 [= *Miracles*].

Lorenz, R., *Arius Judaizans?* Göttingen 1980.

Lorenzi, L. de, *Die Israelfrage nach Römer 9–11*. Rome 1977 [= *Israelfrage*].

Lowe, J., 'An Examination of Attempts to Detect Developments in St Paul's Theology', *JTS* 42 (1941), pp. 129ff. [= 'Examination'].

Löwenstamm, A., 'The Samaritans', *Enc. Jud.* 14. Jerusalem 1971, col. 738ff.

Lührmann, D., *Das Offenbarungsverständnis bei Paulus und in der paulinischen Gemeinden*. Neukirchen 1965.

Luz, U., *Das Geschichtsverständnis des Paulus*. Munich 1968 [= *Geschichtsverständnis*].

McCarthy, D. J., *Old Testament Covenant*. Oxford 1972.

McCasland, S. V., *By the Finger of God*. New York 1951.

Macdonald, J., *The Theology of the Samaritans*. London 1964 [= *Theology*].

Macdonald, J. H., *Kerygma and Didache*. Cambridge 1980.

—'The Concept of Reward in the Teaching of Jesus', *ExpT* 89 (1978), pp. 269ff.

Machoveč, M., *A Marxist Looks at Jesus*. London 1976 [= *Marxist*].

Mack, B. L., *Logos und Sophia*. Göttingen 1973 [= *Logos*].

McKeleney, N., 'Orthodoxy in Judaism of the First Christian Century', *JSJ* 4 (1973), pp. 19ff. [= 'Orthodoxy'].

—'Conversion, Circumcision and the Law', *NTS* 20 (1974), pp. 328ff. [= 'Conversion'].

McKelvey, R. J., *The New Temple*. Oxford 1969.

Macmullen, R., *Enemies of the Roman Order*. Cambridge, Mass., 1967 [= *Enemies*].

—*Roman Social Relations*. New Haven 1974.

—*The Roman Government's Response to Crisis*. New Haven 1976.

McNamara, M., *The New Testament and the Palestinian Targum to the Pentateuch*. Rome 1966.

McNeile, A., *The Gospel according to Saint Matthew*. Cambridge 1915.

MacRae, G., 'The Jewish Background of the Gnostic Sophia Myth', *NovT* 12 (1970), pp. 86ff. [= 'Sophia'].

Maddox, R., *The Purpose of Luke-Acts*. Göttingen 1982 [= *Purpose*].

Magie, D., *Roman Rule in Asia Minor to the End of the Third Century after Christ*. Princeton 1950 [= *Roman Rule*].

Maier, J., *Vom Kultus zu Gnosis*. Salzburg 1964.

—*Jesus von Nazareth in der talmudischen Überlieferung*. Darmstadt 1978 [= *Jesus von Nazareth*].

—*Die Tempelrolle vom Toten Meer*. Munich 1978 [= *Tempelrolle*].

—*Jüdische Auseinandersetzung mit dem Christentum im Altertum*. Darmstadt 1981 [= *Auseinandersetzung*].

Malherbe, A., *Social Aspects of Early Christianity*. Baton-Rouge 1977 [= *Social Aspects*].

Malina, B. J., *The New Testament World*. London 1983 [= *NT World*].

Mann, J., *The Bible as Read and Preached in the Old Synagogue*. Cincinnati 1940.

Mannheim, K., *Ideology and Utopia*. London 1960.

Manson, T. W., *The Teaching of Jesus*. London 1935 [= *Teaching*].

—*The Sayings of Jesus*. London 1949 [= *Sayings*].

Mansoor, M., *The Thanksgiving Hymns*. Leiden 1961.

—*The Dead Sea Scrolls: A College Text Book*. Leiden 1964.

Mantel, H., *Studies in the History of the Sanhedrin*. Cambridge, Mass., 1961 [= *Sanhedrin*].

Manuel, F. P., and Manuel, F. G., *Utopian Thought in the Western World*. Oxford 1979 [= *Utopian Thought*].

Marmorstein, A., *The Old Rabbinic Doctrine of God*. Oxford 1927. [= *Old Rabbinic Doctrine*].

Marshall, I. H., *Luke, Historian and Theologian*. Exeter 1970 [= *Luke*].

—'Palestinian and Hellenistic Christianity: Some Critical Comments', *NTS* 19 (1973), pp. 271ff.

—(ed.), *New Testament Interpretation*. Exeter 1977.

—*The Gospel of Luke*. Exeter 1978.

—'Slippery Words: Eschatology', *ExpT* 89 (1978), pp. 264ff.

Martin, R. P., *Carmen Christi*. Cambridge 1967.

—*Mark Evangelist and Theologian.* Exeter 1972 [= *Mark*].
—*New Testament Foundations.* Exeter 1975–8.
Martin-Achard, R., *From Death to Life.* Edinburgh 1960 [= *Death*].
Martini, R., *Pugio Fidei.* Leipzig 1687.
Martyn, J. L., *History and Theology in the Fourth Gospel.* New York 1968 [= *History*].
Marxsen, W., *The Evangelist Mark.* Nashville 1969.
—*The Resurrection of Jesus of Nazareth.* London 1970 [= *Resurrection*].
Mealand, D. L., *Poverty and Expectation in the Gospels.* London 1980 [= *Poverty*].
Meeks, W. A., *The Prophet King.* Leiden 1967.
—'Moses as God and King', in *Religions in Antiquity*, ed. J. Neusner, Leiden 1968, pp. 354ff.
—'The Man from Heaven in Johannine Sectarianism', *JBL* 91 (1972), pp. 44ff. [= 'Man from Heaven'].
—'Am I a Jew?' in *Christianity, Judaism and Other Greco-Roman Cults*, ed. J. Neusner, Leiden 1975.
—*Jews and Christians in Antioch.* Missoula 1978 [= *Jews and Christians*].
—*The First Urban Christians.* New Haven 1983 [= *Urban Christians*].
Mendenhall, G. E., *Law and Covenant in the Ancient Near East.* New York 1970 [= *Law and Covenant*].
Meshorer, Y., *Jewish Coins of the Second Temple Period.* Tel Aviv 1967.
Metzger, B. M., *An Introduction to the Apocrypha.* New York 1957 [= *Introduction*].
—*The Text of the New Testament.* Oxford 1968 [= *Text*].
—*A Textual Commentary on the Greek New Testament.* London 1971.
Meyer, B. F., *The Aims of Jesus.* London 1979 [= *Aims*].
Meyers, E. M., 'The Cultural Setting of Galilee', in *ANRW* 2.19.1, ed. W. Haase. Berlin 1979, pp. 686ff. [= 'Cultural Setting'].
Milik, J. T., *Ten Years of Discovery in the Wilderness of Judea.* London 1959 [= *Ten Years*].
—*The Books of Enoch.* Oxford 1976.
Millar, F., *A Study of Dio Cassius.* Oxford 1964.
—*The Emperor in the Roman World.* London 1977.
Millar, W. R., *Isaiah 24–27 and the Origin of Apocalyptic.* Missoula 1976.
Miller, D. (ed.), *Jesus and Man's Hope.* Pittsburgh 1970.
Minear, P. S., *And Great Shall be your Reward.* New York 1941.
—*And I Saw a New Earth.* Washington 1968.
—*The Obedience of Faith.* London 1971 [= *Obedience*].
—*To Heal and to Reveal: a Prophetic Vocation according to Luke.* New York 1976.
Miranda, J. P., *Marx and the Bible.* New York 1974.
—*Being and the Messiah.* New York 1977.
—*Communism in the Bible.* London 1982.
Moloney, F. J., *The Johannine Son of Man.* Rome 1976.
Moltmann, J., *The Theology of Hope.* London 1967.
—*The Crucified God.* London 1974.
Momigliano, A., (ed.), *The Conflict between Christianity and Paganism in the Fourth Century.* Oxford 1963.
—*Alien Wisdom.* Cambridge 1975.
Montefiore, H., 'Revolt in the Desert?', *NTS* 8 (1962), pp. 135ff.

—*A Commentary on the Epistle to the Hebrews.* London 1964.
—*Jesus across the Centuries.* London 1983 [= *Jesus*].
Moore, A. L., *The Parousia in the New Testament.* Leiden 1966.
Moore, G. F., 'Christian Writers on Judaism', *HTR* 14 (1921), pp. 197ff. [= 'Christian Writers'].
—'Intermediaries in Jewish Theology', *HTR* 15 (1922), pp. 41ff. [= 'Intermediaries'].
—*Judaism in the First Centuries of the Christian Era.* Cambridge, Mass., 1927 [= *Judaism*].
Mørkholm, O., *Antiochus IV of Syria.* Copenhagen 1966.
Morris, L., *The Cross in the New Testament.* Exeter 1965 [= *Cross*].
—*The Apostolic Preaching of the Cross.* London 1965 [= *Apostolic Preaching*].
Morrison, C. D., *The Powers That Be.* London 1960.
Moule, C. F. D., *Worship in the New Testament.* London 1961 [= *Worship*].
—*The Epistles of Paul the Apostle to the Colossians and Philemon.* Cambridge 1962 [= *Colossians*].
—'The Individualism of the Fourth Gospel', *NovT* 5 (1962), pp. 171ff.
—'The Problem of the Pastoral Epistles', *BJRL* 47 (1964–5), pp. 430ff.
—*The Phenomenon of the New Testament.* London 1968 [= *Phenomenon*].
—*The Origin of Christology.* Cambridge 1977 [= *Origin*].
—*The Birth of the New Testament.* London 1981 [= *Birth*].
—*Essays in New Testament Interpretation.* Cambridge 1982 [= *Essays*].
—(ed.), *The Significance of the Message of the Resurrection for Faith in Jesus Christ.* London 1968 [= *Significance*].
Mowinckel, S., *He That Cometh.* Oxford 1956.
Moyne, J. Le, *Les Sadducéens.* Paris 1972.
Müller, H. P., 'Mantische Weisheit und Apokalyptik', in *Supplements to VT* 22. Leiden 1972, pp. 268ff. [= 'Mantische Weisheit'].
Müller, U., *Zur frühchristlichen Theologiegeschichte.* Gütersloh 1976.
Munck, J., *Paul and the Salvation of Mankind.* London 1959 [= *Paul*].
Munro, W., *Authority in Paul and Peter.* Cambridge 1981 [= *Authority*].
Murray, R., *Symbols of Church and Kingdom.* Cambridge 1975.
Musurillo, H. A. (ed.), *The Acts of the Pagan Martyrs.* Oxford 1954 [= *Acts*].
Nairne, A., *The Epistle of Priesthood.* London 1913.
Neugebauer, F., *En Christus.* Göttingen 1961.
Neusner, J., *The History of the Jews in Babylonia.* Leiden 1965 [= *Jews in Babylon*].
—*A Life of Rabban Yohanan ben Zakkai.* Leiden 1970 [= *Life*].
—*The Development of a Legend.* Leiden 1970 [= *Development*].
—*The Formation of the Babylonian Talmud.* Leiden 1970.
—*The Rabbinic Traditions about the Pharisees.* Leiden 1971 [= *Traditions*].
—'The Problem of Oral Tradition', *JJS* 22 (1971), pp. 1ff.
—*Aphrahat and Judaism.* Leiden 1971.
—*Eliezer ben Hyrcanus.* Leiden 1973 [= *Eliezer*].
—*The Modern Study of the Mishnah.* Leiden 1973 [= *Modern Study*].
—*From Politics to Piety.* Englewood Cliffs 1973 [= *Politics*].
—*The Idea of Purity in Ancient Judaism.* Leiden 1973 [= *Idea*].
—*Ths Mishnaic Laws of Purity.* Leiden 1974.

—*First Century Judaism in Crisis*. New York 1975.
—*Invitation to the Talmud*. New York 1975.
—'The Formation of Rabbinic Judaism', in *ANRW* 2.19.2, ed. W. Haase. Berlin 1978 [= 'Formation'].
—*The Study of Ancient Judaism*. New York 1981 [= *Study*].
—*The Tosefta*. New York 1981.
—*The Foundations of Judaism: Method, Teleology, Doctrine*. Philadelphia 1983 [= *Foundations*].
—*Judaism: the Evidence of Yerushalmi*. Chicago 1983.
—(ed.), *Religions in Antiquity*. Supplements to Numen 14. Leiden 1968.
—(ed.), *Christianity, Judaism and Other Greco-Roman Cults*. Leiden 1975.
Nicholson, E. W., 'The Interpretation of Ex. 24.9–11', *VT* 24 (1974), pp. 77ff. [= 'Interpretation'].
Nickelsburg, G. W., *Resurrection, Immortality, and Eternal Life*. Cambridge, Mass., 1972 [= *Resurrection*].
—*The Jewish Literature between the Bible and the Mishnah*. London 1981 [= *Jewish Literature*].
—(ed.), *Ideal Figures in Ancient Judaism*. Chicago 1980 [= *Ideal Figures*].
Nickelsburg, G. W., and Stone, M. E., *Faith and Piety in Early Judaism*. Philadelphia 1983 [= *Faith*].
Nickle, K. F., *The Collection*. London 1966.
—*The Synoptic Gospels*. London 1982.
Niebuhr, R., *The Nature and Destiny of Man*. London 1941–3.
Nilsson, M. P., *A History of Greek Religion*. Oxford 1925.
Nineham, D. E., 'Eye Witness Testimony and the Gospel Tradition', *JTS* 9 (1958), pp. 13ff., 243ff.; 11 (1960), pp. 253ff. [= 'Eye Witness Testimony'].
—*Saint Mark*. Harmondsworth 1963.
—(ed.), *Studies in the Gospels*. Oxford 1955.
—(ed.), *Historicity and Chronology in the New Testament*. London 1965.
Nissen, A., 'Tora und Geschichte im Spätjudentum', *NovT* 9 (1967), pp. 241ff. [= 'Tora'].
Nock, A. D., *Conversion*. Oxford 1933.
Nolland, J., 'Uncircumcised Proselytes', *JSJ* 12 (1981), pp. 173ff.
Nordheim, A. von, *Die Lehre der Alten*. Leiden 1980 [= *Lehre*].
Noth, M., *A History of Israel*. London 1960.
O'Connor, J. Murphy, (ed.), *Paul and Qumran*. London 1968.
Odeberg, H., *The Fourth Gospel*. Uppsala 1929.
—*3 Enoch*. Cambridge 1928.
Oesterley, W. O. E., *The Jewish Background of the Christian Liturgy*. Oxford 1925 [= *The Jewish Background*].
—*An Introduction to the Books of the Apocrypha*. London 1958.
—and Robinson, T. H., *Hebrew Religion: its Origin and Development*. London 1937.
Ogg, G., *The Chronology of the Life of Paul*. London 1968.
O'Neill, J. C., *The Theology of Acts*. London 1970 [= *Theology*].
—*The Recovery of Paul's Letter to the Galatians*. London 1972 [= *Recovery*].
—*Paul's Letter to the Romans*. Harmondsworth 1975 [= *Romans*].
—*The Messiah*. Cambridge 1980.

—'Glosses and Interpolations in the Letters of Paul', in *Studia Evangelica* 7, ed. E. Livingstone. Berlin 1982, pp. 379ff. [= 'Glosses'].

—*The Puzzle of 1 John*. London 1966 [= *Puzzle*].

Oppenheimer, A., *The 'Am ha-Aretz*. Leiden 1977.

Osborne, E. E., *The Philosophy of Clement of Alexandria*. Cambridge 1957 [= *Clement*].

—*Justin Martyr*. Tübingen 1973 [= *Justin*].

—*Ethical Patterns in Early Christianity*. Cambridge 1976.

Östen Sacken, P. von der, *Die Apokalyptik in ihrem Verhältnis zu Prophetie und Weisheit*. Munich 1969 [= *Apokalyptik*].

—*Römer 8 als Beispiel paulinischer Soteriologie*. Göttingen 1975.

Pagels, E., *The Johannine Gospel in Gnostic Exegesis*. Nashville 1973.

—*The Gnostic Paul*. Philadelphia 1975 [= *Gnostic Paul*].

—*Gnostic Gospels*. Harmondsworth 1982.

Pancaro, S., *The Law in the Fourth Gospel*. Leiden 1975 [= *Law*].

Pannenberg, W., *Jesus, God and Man*. London 1968 [= *Jesus*].

Parkes, J., *The Conflict of the Church and the Synagogue*. London 1934 [= *Conflict*].

Pascal, W., 'The Farewell Prayer of Jesus: a Study of the Gattung and the Religious Background of John 17'. Diss. Cambridge 1982 [= John 17].

Patte, D., *Early Jewish Hermeneutic in Palestine*. Missoula 1975 [= *Hermeneutic*].

—*The Faith of the Apostle to the Gentiles: a Structural Introduction to Paul's Letters*. Philadelphia 1983.

Paulsen, H., *Studien zur Theologie des Ignatius von Antiochen*. Göttingen 1978 [= *Studien*].

Pearson, B. A., *The Pneumatikos-Psychikos Terminology in 1 Corinthians*. Missoula 1973.

Peel, M. L., *The Letter to Rheginos*. London 1969 [= *Rheginos*].

Perrin, N., *The Kingdom of God in the Teaching of Jesus*. London 1963 [= *The Kingdom of God*].

—*Rediscovering the Teaching of Jesus*. London 1967 [= *Rediscovering*].

—*Jesus and the Language of the Kingdom*. London 1976 [= *Jesus*].

—*The Resurrection Narratives*. London 1977.

Pesch, R., *Der Lohngedanke in der Lehre Jesu*. Munich 1955.

Peterson, D., *Hebrews and Perfection*. Cambridge 1982 [= *Hebrews*].

Petuchowski, J. J., and Brocke, M., *The Lord's Prayer and Jewish Liturgy*. New York 1978 [= *Lord's Prayer*].

Petzke, G., *Die Traditionen über Apollonius von Tyana und das Neue Testament*. Leiden 1970 [= *Apollonius*].

Pfeiffer, R. H., *History of New Testament Times with an Introduction to the Apocrypha*. New York 1949 [= *Introduction*].

Philonenko, M., *Joseph et Aséneth*. Leiden 1968.

Piper, J., *'Love Your Enemies'*. Cambridge 1979.

Pixley, G., *God's Kingdom*. London 1981.

Ploeg, J. van der, and Woude, A. S. van der, *Le Targum de Job de la Grotte II de Qumran*. Amsterdam 1962.

Plöger, O., *Theocracy and Eschatology*. Oxford 1968 [= *Theocracy*].

Podro, J., *The Last Pharisee: the Life and Times of Rabbi Joshua ben Hananyah*. London

1959 [= *Pharisee*].

Porten, B., *The Archives from Elephantine: the Life of an Ancient Jewish Military Colony*. Berkeley 1968 [= *Archives*].

Porton, G., *The Traditions of R. Ishmael*. Leiden 1976.

—'Midrash: Palestinian Jews and the Hebrew Bible in the Greco-Roman Period', in *ANRW* 2.19.2, ed. W. Haase. Berlin 1979, pp. 103ff. [= 'Midrash'].

Preiss, T., *Life in Christ*. London 1954 [= *Life*].

Prestige, G. L., *God in Patristic Thought*. London 1936.

—*Fathers and Heretics*. London 1940.

Prigent, P., *L'Apocalypse de Saint Jean*. Paris 1981.

Przybylski, B., *Righteousness in Matthew and his World of Thought*. Cambridge 1980 [= *Righteousness*].

Purvis, J., *The Samaritan Pentateuch and the Origins of the Samaritan Sect*. Cambridge, Mass., 1958 [= *Samaritan Pentateuch*].

Quispel, G., 'Gnosticism and the New Testament' in *The Bible in Modern Scholarship*, ed. J. P. Hyatt. New York 1965.

Rad, G. von, *Studies in Deuteronomy*. London 1961 [= *Studies*].

—*Old Testament Theology*. Edinburgh 1962.

—*The Problem of the Hexateuch and Other Essays*. Edinburgh 1966.

—*Wisdom in Israel*. London 1972.

Rajak, T., *Josephus*. London 1983 [= *Josephus*].

Ramsay, W. M., *The Cities and Bishoprics of Phrygia*. Oxford 1895 [= *Cities*].

—*St Paul the Traveller and Roman Citizen*. London 1896 [= *Paul the Traveller*].

—*The Letters to the Seven Churches*. London 1904 [= *Letters*].

Reese, J. M., *Hellenistic Influence on the Book of Wisdom and its Consequences*. Rome 1970 [= *Hellenistic Influences*].

Reicke, B., *The Disobedient Spirits and Christian Baptism*. Lund 1946.

—*Diakonie, Festfreude und Zelos*. Uppsala 1951.

—*The Gospel of Luke*. London 1965.

—*The New Testament Era*. London 1969 [= *NT Era*].

Reim, G., *Studien zum alttestamentlichen Hintergrund des Johannesevangeliums*. Cambridge 1974.

Reumann, J., *Jesus in the Church's Gospel*. London 1970.

Rhoads, D. M., *Israel in Revolution 6–74 CE: a Political History based on the Writings of Josephus*. Philadelphia 1976 [= *Israel*].

Richardson, A., *The Miracle Stories in the Gospel*. London 1941.

—*An Introduction to the Theology of the New Testament*. London 1958.

—*The Political Christ*. London 1973.

Richardson, C. C., *The Christology of Ignatius of Antioch*. New York 1935 [= *Christology*].

Richardson, P., *Israel in the Apostolic Church*. Cambridge 1969 [= *Israel*].

Riches, J., *Jesus and the Transformation of Judaism*. London 1980 [= *Jesus*].

Ricoeur, P., 'Ideology and Utopia as Cultural Imagination', *Philosophic Exchange* 2 (1976), pp. 171ff. [= 'Ideology'].

—*Essays on Biblical Interpretation*. London 1981.

Ridderbos, H., *Paul*. Grand Rapids 1975.

Riesner, R., *Jesus als Lehrer*. Tübingen 1981.

Ringgren, H., *Word and Wisdom*, Lund 1947 [= *Word*].
—*The Messiah in the Old Testament*. London 1956.
—*Israelite Religion*. London 1966.
Rist, J. M., *Stoic Philosophy*. Cambridge 1969.
—*The Stoics*. Berkeley 1970.
—*On the Independence of Matthew and Mark*. Cambridge 1978 [= *Independence*].
Rivkin, E., 'The Pharisees' in *IDB Supplement*.
—'Defining the Pharisees: the Tannaitic Sources', *HUCA* 40 (1969–70), pp. 234ff.
—'The Pharisees and the Crisis of the Individual in the Greco-Roman World', *JQR* 61 (1970), pp. 27ff.
—*The Hidden Revolution*. London 1975.
Roberts, B. J., *The Old Testament Text and Versions*. Cardiff 1951.
Robinson, J. A. T., *The Body*. London 1952.
—*Jesus and his Coming*. London 1957.
—*Twelve New Testament Studies*. London 1962.
—*Redating the New Testament*. London 1975 [= *Redating*].
Robinson, J. M., *The Problem of History in Mark*. London 1957.
—*A New Quest for the Historical Jesus*. London 1959 [= *New Quest*].
—with Koester, H., *Trajectories through Early Christianity*. Philadelphia 1971 [= *Trajectories*].
—(ed.), *The Nag Hammadi Library*. Leiden 1978.
Rohde, J., *Rediscovering the Teaching of the Evangelists*. London 1968 [= *Rediscovering*].
Roon, A. van, *The Authenticity of Ephesians*. Leiden 1975 [= *Authenticity*].
Rose, H. J., *Ancient Greek Religion*. London 1948.
—*Ancient Roman Religion*. London 1949.
Rössler, D., *Gesetz und Geschichte*. Neukirchen 1960 [= *Gesetz*].
Rost, L., *Judaism outside the Hebrew Canon*. Abingdon, Tenn. 1976 [= *Judaism*].
Rostovtzeff, M., *The Social and Economic History of the Roman Empire*. Oxford 1957 [= *Social and Economic History*].
Roth, C. (ed.), *Haggadah for Passover*. London 1965.
Rowland, C. C., 'The Visions of God in Apocalyptic Literature' *JSJ* 10 (1979), pp. 138ff. [= 'Visions'].
—'The Vision of the Risen Christ', *JTS* 31 (1980), pp. 1ff.
—*The Open Heaven: a Study of Apocalyptic in Judaism and Early Christianity*. London 1982.
—'John 1.51 and the Targumic Tradition', *NTS* 1984.
Russell, D. S., *Between the Testaments*. London 1960.
—*The Method and Message of Jewish Apocalyptic*. London 1964 [= *Method*].
—*The Jews from Alexander to Herod*. Oxford 1967 [= *Jews*].
Safrai, S., and Stern, M., *The Jewish People in the First Christian Century*. Assen 1974–6 [= *Jewish People*].
Sainte Croix, G. E. M. de, 'Why were the Early Christians Persecuted?' *Past and Present* 26 (1963), pp. 6ff.
—*The Class Struggle in the Ancient Greek World*. London 1981 [= *Class Struggle*].
Saldarini, A. J., 'Johanan ben Zakkai's Escape from Jerusalem', *JSJ* 6 (1975), pp. 189ff. [= 'Escape'].

Sanders, E. P., *Tendencies in the Synoptic Tradition*. Cambridge 1969 [= *Tendencies*].
—*Paul and Palestinian Judaism*. London 1977 [= *Paul*].
—*Paul, the Law and the Jewish People*. Philadelphia 1983 [= *Paul the Law*].
—'Jesus, the Sinners and the Am ha-Aretz' in Horbury and Rowland, *Essays for Ernst Bammel*.
—(ed.), *Jewish and Christian Self-Definition*. 3 vols. London 1981–3.
Sanders, J. A., *The Psalms Scroll from Qumran Cave II*. Oxford 1965.
Sanders, J. T., *The New Testament Christological Hymns*. Cambridge 1971.
—*Ethics in the New Testament*. London 1975 [= *Ethics*].
Sandmel, S., *The First Christian Century in Judaism and Christianity*. Oxford 1969.
—*Judaism and Christian Beginnings*. Oxford 1978.
—*The Genius of Paul*. New York 1958 [= *Genius*].
—*Philo's Place in Judaism*. New York 1971 [= *Philo*].
—*A Jewish Understanding of the New Testament*. London 1974.
Sänger, D., *Antikes Judentum und die Mysterien*. Tübingen 1980 [= *Antikes Judentum*].
Sarasa, R. S. (ed.), *The Modern Study of the Midrash*.
Satake, A., *Die Gemeindeordnung in der Johannesapokalypse*. Neukirchen 1966 [= *Gemeindeordnung*].
Sawyer, J. F. A., 'Hebrew Words for the Resurrection of the Dead', *VT* 23 (1973), pp. 218ff. [= 'Hebrew Words'].
—*From Moses to Patmos*. London 1977 [= *Moses*].
Schäfer, P., *Die Vorstellung von heiligen Geist in der rabbinischen Literatur*. Munich 1972 [= *Heiligen Geist*].
—*Rivalität zwischen Engeln und Menschen*. Berlin 1975 [= *Rivalität*].
—*Studien zur Geschichte und Theologie des rabbinischen Judentums*. Leiden 1978.
—'Akiba and Bar Kochba', in W. S. Greene, *Approaches to Ancient Judaism*. Missoula 1978 [= 'Akiba'].
—'Die sogenannte Synode von Jabne', in *Studien* [= 'Synode'].
—'Die Torah der messianischen Zeit', in *Studien* [= 'Torah'].
—'Die messianischen Hoffnungen des rabbinischen Judentums zwischen Naher-wartung und religiösen Pragmatismus', in *Studien*.
—'Die Flucht Johanan b. Zakkais aus Jerusalem', in *ANRW* 2.19.2, ed. W. Haase. Berlin 1979, pp. 43ff. [= 'Flucht'].
—*Der Bar Kochba-Aufstand*. Tübingen 1981 [= *Aufstand*].
Schaller, J. B., 'Genesis 1 und 2 im antiken Judentum'. Diss. Göttingen 1961.
Scharlemann, M. H., *Stephen: a Singular Saint*. Rome 1968 [= *Stephen*].
Schechter, S., *Aboth de Rabbi Nathan*. Vienna 1887.
Schepelern, W., *Der Montanismus und die phrygischen Kulte*. Tübingen 1929.
Schiffman, L., *The Halakah at Qumran*. Leiden 1975.
—'Merkavah Speculation at Qumran', in *Mystics, Philosophers and Politicians*, ed. J. Reinharz and D. Swatchinski. Durham, N.C., 1982 [= 'Merkavah Speculation'].
Schillebeeckx, E., *Jesus: an Experiment in Christology*. London 1979.
—*Christ: the Christian Experience in the Modern World*. London 1980.
Schlatter, A., *Die Theologie des Judentums nach dem Bericht des Josefus*. Gütersloh 1932 [= *Theologie*].

Schmithals, W., *Paul and James*. London 1963.
—*Gnosticism at Corinth*. New York 1963 [=*Gnosticism*].
—*The Apocalyptic Movement*. Abingdon, Tenn. 1975.
Schnackenburg, R., *God's Rule and Kingdom*. London 1963 [= *God's Rule*].
—*The Gospel according to Saint John*. London 1968– [=*John*].
—*The Moral Teaching of the New Testament*. London 1965 [=*Moral Teaching*].
Schoeps, H. J., *Die Theologie und Geschichte des Judenchristentums*. Tübingen 1949 [= *Theologie*].
—*Paul: the Theology of the Apostle in the Light of Jewish Religious History*. London 1961 [= *Paul*].
Scholem, G., *Major Trends in Jewish Mysticism*. London 1955 [=*Major Trends*].
—*Jewish Gnosticism, Merkabah Mysticism and Talmudic Tradition*. New York 1965 [= *Jewish Gnosticism*].
—article 'Kabbalah', *Enc. Jud.* 10, col. 489ff.
—*Sabbatai Sevi*. London 1973.
Schottroff, L., *Der Glaubende und die feindliche Welt*. Neukirchen 1970.
Schürer, E., *The Jewish People in the Age of Jesus Christ*. Rev. ed. by G. Vermes and F. Millar. 2 vols. Edinburgh 1973– [= *SVM History*].
Schütz, J. H., *Paul and the Anatomy of Apostolic Authority*. Cambridge 1974 [=*Anatomy*].
Schweitzer, A., *Paul and his Interpreters*. London 1912.
—*The Quest for the Historical Jesus*. London 1931 [= *Quest*].
—*The Mysticism of Paul the Apostle*. London 1931 [= *Mysticism*].
Schweizer, E., *Church Order in the New Testament*. London 1961 [= *Church Order*].
—'Formgeschichtliches zu den Seligpreisungen Jesu', *NTS* 19 (1972–3), pp. 21ff.
Scobie, C. H. H., *John the Baptist*. London 1964. [=*John*].
—'The Origins and Development of Samaritan Christianity', *NTS* 19 (1973) [= 'Samaritan Christianity'].
Scott, C. A. Anderson, *Christianity according to St Paul*. Cambridge 1927 [= *Christianity*].
Scroggs, R., 'The Earliest Christian Communities as Sectarian Movement' in *Christianity, Judaism and Other Greco-Roman Cults*, ed. J. Neusner. Leiden 1975, Part 2, pp. 1ff. [= 'The Earliest Communities'].
—'The Earliest Hellenistic Christianity' in *Religions in Antiquity*, ed. J. Neusner.
—*The Last Adam*. Oxford 1966.
—'Paul and the Eschatological Woman' *JAAR* 40 (1972), pp. 283ff.
Séd, N., *La Mystique cosmologique juive*. Paris 1981.
Segal, A. F., *Two Powers in Heaven*. Leiden 1978 [= *Two Powers*].
—'Heavenly Ascent in Hellenistic Judaism, Early Christianity and their Environments', *ANRW* ed. W. Haase, 2.23.2. Berlin 1980. [= 'Heavenly Ascents'].
Segal, J. B., *The Hebrew Passover*. London 1963 [= *Passover*].
Selby, P. S. M., *Look for the Living*. London 1976.
Seliger, A., *The Marxist Conception of Ideology*. Cambridge 1977 [= *Ideology*].
Sevenster, J. N., *The Roots of Pagan Anti-Semitism in the Ancient World*. Leiden 1975 [=*Anti-Semitism*].
Shaw, G., *The Cost of Authority*. London 1982 [=*Authority*].
Sherwin White, A. N., *Roman Society and Roman Law in the New Testament*. Oxford

1963 [= *Roman Society*].

—*Racial Prejudice in Imperial Rome*. Cambridge 1967 [= *Racial Prejudice*].

Siegert, F., 'Gottesfürchtige und Sympathisanten', *JSJ* 4 (1973), pp. 109ff. [= 'Gottesfürchtige'].

Simon, M., *St Stephen and the Hellenists in the Primitive Church*. London 1958.

—*Verus Israel*. Paris 1948.

—*Jewish Sects at the Time of Jesus*. Philadelphia 1976 [= *Jewish Sects*].

Simon, U., *A Theology of Auschwitz*. London 1967.

Singer, S. L., *Authorised Daily Prayer Book*. London 1962.

Slingerland, J. D., *The Testaments of the Twelve Patriarchs*. Missoula 1977 [= *Testaments*].

Smalley, S. S., *John Evangelist and Interpreter*. Exeter 1978 [= *John*].

Smallwood, E. M., *Documents illustrating the Principates of Gaius, Claudius and Nero*. Cambridge 1966 [= *Documents*].

—*Legatio ad Gaium*. Leiden 1970. [= *Legatio*].

—*The Jews under Roman Rule*. Leiden 1976 [= *Jews*].

Smith, D. M., *The Composition and Order of the Fourth Gospel*. New Haven 1964.

—and Spivey, E., *The Anatomy of the New Testament*. New York 1974.

Smith, J. Z., *Map is Not Territory*. Leiden 1978.

Smith, M., 'Palestinian Judaism in the First Century', *Israel: Its Rôle in Civilisation*, ed. M. David. New York 1956 [= 'Palestinian Judaism'].

—*Palestinian Parties and Politics that Shaped the Old Testament*. New York 1971 [= *Palestinian Parties*].

—*Clement of Alexandria and a Secret Gospel of Mark*. Cambridge, Mass. 1971 [= *Clement of Alexandria*].

—*Jesus the Magician*. London 1978 [= *Jesus*].

Sperber, A., *The Bible in Aramaic*. Leiden 1959.

Stanton, G. N., *Jesus of Nazareth in New Testament Preaching*. Cambridge 1974 [= *Jesus of Nazareth*]

—*The Interpretation of Matthew*. London 1983 [= *Interpretation*].

Stauffer, E., *Christ and the Caesars*. London 1955.

—*New Testament Theology*. London 1955.

—*Jerusalem und Rom in Zeitalter Jesu Christi*. Berne 1957.

—*Jesus and his Story*. London 1960.

—'Zum Kalifat des Jacobus', *ZRGG* 4 (1952), pp. 1ff.

Stendahl, K., *The School of Saint Matthew*. Uppsala 1954 [= *School*].

—*Paul among Jews and Gentiles*. London 1976 [= *Paul*].

—(ed.), *The Scrolls and the New Testament*. New York 1957 [= *Scrolls*].

Stern, M., *Greek and Latin Writers on Jews and Judaism*. Jerusalem 1974 [= *Greek and Latin Writers*].

—'The Jews in Greek and Latin Literature', in *The Jewish People in the First Christian Century*, ed. Safrai and Stern. Assen 1974–6 [= *Jewish People*].

Stevenson, J., *A New Eusebius*. London 1965.

Stier, F., *Gott und sein Engel im AT*. Münster 1934 [= *Gott*].

Stoldt, H. H., *History and Criticism of the Marcan Hypothesis*. Edinburgh 1983 [= *Marcan Hypothesis*].

Stone, M. E., 'Paradise in 4 Ezra', *JJS* 17 (1966), pp. 85ff. [= 'Paradise'].

—'The Messiah in 4 Ezra' in *Religions in Antiquity*, ed. J. Neusner. Leiden 1968.

—'Lists of Revealed Things in Apocalyptic Literature' in *Magnalia Dei*, ed. F. M. Cross. New York 1976 [= 'Lists'].

—*Scriptures, Sects and Visions*. Oxford 1982 [= *Scriptures*].

Strack, H. L., *Einleitung in Talmud und Midrash*, ed. G. Stemberger. Munich 1982; (E. T.) *Introduction to the Talmud in Midrash*. New York 1980 [= *Introduction*].

Strathmann, H., *Geschichte der frühchristlichen Askese*. Leipzig 1914 [= *Geschichte*].

Strauss, D. F., *The Life of Jesus Critically Examined*. London 1973 [= *Life*].

Streeter, B. H., *The Four Gospels*. London 1961.

Strobel, A., *Untersuchungen zum eschatologischen Verzögerungsproblem auf Grund der spätjudisch–urchristlichen Geschichte von Habakkuk 2.2ff.* Leiden 1961.

Strugnell, J., 'The Angelic Liturgy from Qumran', *Supp. to VT* 7. Leiden 1960, pp. 318ff.

Suggs, M. J., *Wisdom Christology and Law in Matthew's Gospel*. Cambridge, Mass., 1970 [= *Wisdom*].

Sundberg, A. C., *The Old Testament of the Early Church*. Cambridge, Mass., 1964 [= *Old Testament*].

Sweet, J. P. M., *Revelation*. London 1979.

Swetnam, J., *Jesus and Isaac*. Rome 1981.

Sykes, S. W., and Clayton, J. P. (ed.), *Christ, Faith and History*. Cambridge 1972 [= *Christ*].

Talbert, C. H., *What is a Gospel?* London 1977.

Talmon, S., 'The Calendar Reckoning of the Sect from the Judean Desert' *Scripta Hierosolymitana* 4 (1958), pp. 162ff.

—*Qumran and the History of the Biblical Text*. Cambridge, Mass., 1976.

Tannehill, R. C., *Dying and Rising with Christ*. Berlin 1967 [= *Dying*].

Tarn, W. W., *Hellenistic Civilisation*. London 1930.

Tatum, W.B., *In Quest of Jesus*. London 1983 [= *In Quest*].

Taylor, V., *The Formation of the Gospel Tradition*. London 1933 [= *Formation*].

—*Behind the Third Gospel*. Oxford 1926.

—*The Passion Narrative of Saint Luke*. Cambridge 1972 [= *Passion Narrative*].

Tcherikover, V., *Hellenistic Civilisation and the Jews*. New York 1970 [= *Hellenistic Civilisation*].

Teeple, H. M., *The Mosaic Eschatological Prophet*. Philadelphia 1957 [= *Prophet*].

Telford, W., *The Barren Fig-Tree*. Sheffield 1980.

—*The Interpretation of Mark*. London 1985.

Thackeray, H. S. J., *Josephus: the Man and the Historian*. New York 1929 [= *Josephus*].

Theisohn, J., *Der auserwählte Richter*. Göttingen 1975.

Theissen, G., *The First Followers of Jesus*. London 1978 [= *First Followers*].

—*The Social Setting of Pauline Christianity*. Edinburgh 1982 [= *Social Setting*].

—*The Miracle Stories of the Early Christian Tradition*. Edinburgh 1983 [= *Miracle Stories*].

Thompson, A. L., *Responsibility for Evil in the Theodicy of 4 Ezra*. Missoula 1977 [= *Evil*].

Tinsley, E. J., *The Imitation of God in Christ*. London 1960 [= *Imitation*].

Tödt, H. E., *The Son of Man in the Synoptic Tradition*. London 1965 [= *Son of Man*].

Trachtenberg, J., *Jewish Magic and Superstition*. New York 1939.

Trites, A. A., *The Concept of Witness in the New Testament*. Cambridge 1977 [= *Witness*].

Troeltsch, E., *The Social Teaching of the Christian Churches*. London 1931 [= *Social Teaching*].

Tuckett, C. M., *The Revival of the Griesbach Hypothesis*. Cambridge 1983 [= *Revival*].

—*The Messianic Secret*. London 1983.

Turner, H. E. W., *The Pattern of Christian Truth*. London 1954 [= *Pattern*].

Turner, H. E. W., and Montefiore, H., *Thomas and the Evangelists*. London 1962.

Tyrrell, G., *Christianity at the Crossroads*. London 1909.

Unnik, W. C. van (ed.), *La Littérature juive entre Tenach et Mischna*. Leiden 1974.

Urbach, E. E., *The Sages: their Concepts and Beliefs*. Jerusalem 1975 [= *Sages*].

—'The Traditions about Esoteric Teaching in the Tannaitic Period' (in Hebrew) in *Studies in Mysticism and Religion for G. G. Scholem*. Jerusalem 1967, pp. 1ff.

Vaux, R. de, *Ancient Israel: its Life and Customs*. London 1965.

Vermes, G., *Scripture and Tradition*. Leiden 1973 [= *Scripture*].

—*Jesus the Jew*. London 1975 [= *Jesus*].

—*The Dead Sea Scrolls in English*. Harmondsworth 1975.

—*The Dead Sea Scrolls: Qumran in Perspective*. London 1975.

—*The Gospel of Jesus the Jew*. Newcastle upon Tyne 1981 [= *Gospel*].

—*Jesus and the World of Judaism*. London 1983.

Vögtle, A., *Das Neue Testament und die Zukunft des Kosmos*. Düsseldorf 1971 [= *Zukunft*].

Vokes, F. E., *The Riddle of the Didache*. London 1938.

Volz, P., *Die Eschatologie der jüdischen Gemeinde im neutestamentlischen Zeitalter*. Tübingen 1934 [= *Eschatologie*].

Voöbus, A., *History of Asceticism in the Syrian Orient*. Paris 1958–60 [= *Asceticism*].

Wadsworth, M. P., 'The Liber Antiquitatum Biblicarum of Pseudo Philo'. Diss. Oxford 1975.

Wagner, G., *Pauline Baptism and Pagan Mysteries*. Edinburgh 1967 [= *Pauline Baptism*].

Wainwright, G., *Eucharist and Eschatology*. London 1971 [= *Eucharist*].

—*et al.*, *The Study of Liturgy*. London 1978.

Walaskay, P. W., *And So We Came to Rome*. Cambridge 1983.

Walters, P. (ed. D. W. Gooding), *The Text of the Septuagint*. Cambridge 1973 [= *Text*].

Weber, M., *The Protestant Ethic and the Spirit of Capitalism*. London 1930 [= *Protestant Ethic*].

Weeden, T. J., *Mark: Traditions in Conflict*. Philadelphia 1971.

Weingreen, J., *From Bible to Mishna*. Manchester 1976.

Weiss, J., *Jesus' Proclamation of the Kingdom of God*. London 1971 [= *Jesus, Proclamation*].

Wellesley, K., *The Long Year*. London 1975.

Wengst, K., *Tradition und Theologie des Barnabasbriefes*. Berlin 1971 [= *Tradition*].

—*Häresie und Orthodoxie im Spiegel des ersten Johannesbriefes*. Gütersloh 1976 [= *Häresie*].

Wernberg-Møller, P., *The Manual of Discipline*. Leiden 1957 [= *Manual*].

Werner, M., *Die Entstehung des christlichen Dogmas*. Tübingen 1954 [= *Enstehung*].
—*The Formation of Christian Dogma*. London 1957 [= *Formation*].
Westerholm, C., *Jesus and Scribal Authority*. Lund 1978.
Wewers, G. A., *Geheimnis und Geheimhaltung in rabbinischen Judentum*. Berlin 1975 [= *Geheimnis*].
Whiteley, D. E. H., *The Theology of Saint Paul*. Oxford 1962 [= *Theology*].
Widengren, G., *The Ascension of the Apostle and the Heavenly Book*. Uppsala 1950 [= *Ascension of the Apostle*].
Wilckens, U., *Die Missionsrede im Apostelgeschichte*. Neukirchen 1961.
Wilcox, M., *The Semitisms of Acts*. Oxford 1965.
—'Peter and the Rock', *NTS* 22 (1975), pp. 73ff.
Wiles, M. F., *The Spiritual Gospel*. Cambridge 1960.
—*The Making of Christian Doctrine*. Cambridge 1967.
Wilken, R. L., *Judaism and the Early Christian Mind*. New Haven 1971 [= *Judaism*].
—*The Christians as the Romans Saw Them*. New Haven 1984.
Williams, A. L., *Adversus Judaeos: a Bird's Eye View of Christian Apologiae until the Renaissance*. Cambridge 1935.
Williams, G. H., *The Radical Reformation*. Philadelphia 1962.
Williams, R. D., *The Wound of Knowledge*. London 1979.
—*Resurrection*. London 1982.
—*Eucharistic Sacrifice: the Roots of a Metaphor*. Nottingham 1982 [= *Eucharistic Sacrifice*].
—'The Prophetic and the Mystical', *New Blackfriars* 69 (1983), pp. 330ff.
Williams, S. K., *Jesus' Death as Saving Event*. Missoula 1975.
Williamson, H. G. M., *Israel in the Books of Chronicles*. Cambridge 1977 [= *Israel*].
—*1 and 2 Chronicles*. London 1982.
Williamson, R. *Philo and the Epistle to the Hebrews*. Leiden 1970 [= *Philo*].
Wilson, B., *Sects and Society*. Berkeley 1961 [= *Sects*].
—*Magic and the Millennium*. New York 1973 [= *Magic*].
—*Religion in Sociological Perspective*. Oxford 1982 [= *Religion*].
Wilson, R. McL., *The Gnostic Problem*. London 1958 [= *Problem*].
—*Studies in the Gospel of Thomas*. London 1960.
—*Gnosis and the New Testament*. Oxford 1968 [= *Gnosis*].
Wilson, S. G., *Luke and the Pastoral Epistles*. London 1979.
—*Luke and the Law*. Cambridge 1983.
Wink, W., *John the Baptist in the Gospel Tradition*. Cambridge 1968 [= *John*].
Winston, D., *The Wisdom of Solomon*. Garden City, New York 1978 [= *Wisd. Sol.*].
—'Was Philo a Mystic?', in *Studies in Jewish Mysticism*, ed. J. Dan and F. Talmage. Cambridge, Mass., 1982.
Winter, P., *On the Trial of Jesus*. Berlin 1961 [= *On the Trial*].
Wolfson, H. A., *Philo: Foundation of Religious Philosophy in Judaism*. Cambridge, Mass., 1947 [= *Philo*].
Woll, D. B., *Johannine Christianity in Conflict*. Chico 1981.
Woude, A. S. van der, *Die messianischen Vorstellungen der Gemeinde von Qumran*. Assen 1957 [= *Vorstellungen*].
—and Jonge, M. de, 'Melchizedek and the New Testament', *NTS* 12 (1965), pp. 301ff.

Wrege, H. T., *Die Überlieferungsgeschichte der Bergpredigt*. Tübingen 1968 [= *Überlieferung*].

Yadin, Y., *The Scroll of the War of the Sons of Light against the Sons of Darkness*. London 1962 [= *War*].

—*The Ben Sira Scroll*. Jerusalem 1965.

—*Masada*. London 1966.

—*Bar Kochba*. London 1971.

Yamauchi, E., *Pre-Christian Gnosticism*. London 1973.

—*The Archaeology of New Testament Cities in Western Asia Minor*. Glasgow 1980 [= *Archaeology*].

Yoder, J. H., *The Politics of Jesus*. Grand Rapids 1972 [= *Politics*].

York, A. D., 'The Dating of Targumic Literature', *JSJ* 5 (1974), pp. 49ff. [='Dating'].

Young, F., *Sacrifice and the Death of Christ*. London 1975 [= *Sacrifice*].

—*From Nicaea to Chalcedon*. London 1983.

Zahn, T., *Introduction to the New Testament*. Edinburgh 1909.

Zeller, D., *Juden und Heiden*. Stuttgart 1976 [= *Juden*].

Ziesler, J., *The Meaning of Righteousness in Paul*. Cambridge 1972.

Zimmerli, W., and Jeremias, J., *The Servant of God*. London 1957.

INDEX OF ANCIENT SOURCES

OLD TESTAMENT

APOCRYPHA AND PSEUDEPIGRAPHA

JOSEPHUS AND PHILO

418

Colossians (contd.)
3.22ff 275
4.1 214
4.7 204
4.16 240

1 Thessalonians
1.6 257
1.7 258
1.9 31, 208, 216
1.10 227
2.3f 361
2.6 231
2.14f 225, 257, 263, 273
2.16 77, 226
3.3 210
3.7f 210, 257
4.11 287
4.13ff 112, 287
4.15f 91, 206, 208, 246, 287
5.1 115, 287
5.12ff 258
5.19 209

2 Thessalonians
2.2f 115, 287
2.5ff 285
2.8f 246
3.6 112, 273, 287

1 Timothy
1.4 232
2.1ff 20
3.1ff 232, 264
3.7 273, 278
4.1 232, 264, 270
4.6 232
4.7 232
4.14 232, 264
4.16 264
5.17ff 232, 260
6.20 232

2 Timothy
1.6 232, 264
1.14 232
2.16 232
2.17 264
2.18 203
3.14 232, 264

4.1ff 232
4.4 232

Titus
1.5ff 232
1.14 232
2.1ff 232
3.1ff 279
3.5 239

Philemon
.16 214
.21 282

Hebrews
1.1ff 244, 251, 307
1.14 31
6.1 223
6.4 114, 209, 278, 282
6.5 116, 292, 307
6.19f 243, 252, 290
7—10 307
7.1ff 54
8.7ff 26
9.— 43
9.24 243
10.26 307
10.32f 307
11.27f 29
12.25f 290, 307
13.10f 307

James
5.7 246

1 Peter
1.3 239
1.4 293
1.7 115
1.9 293
1.10f 53
1.17 293
1.18f 211
2.9 237, 266
2.11 293
2.12 273
2.13ff 279
2.21 211
2.24f 176
3.2 273

3.21ff 34, 54, 239
5.1 260

2 Peter
2.1 148, 270
3.1ff 286f
3.13 90

1 John
1.1 259
1.8 261
2.12ff 260
2.18 259
2.19ff 200
2.22 148, 200
2.24 259
2.27f 259, 270
2.28 252
3.2 114, 206, 209, 252
3.4ff 223
3.8ff 260, 261
3.11 260
3.12 200
4.2 200, 244, 260, 270
4.6 260
4.7ff 260
5.6 260
5.18 261

2 John
.5 260
.7 260
.9 259

3 John
.5 260
.9 260

Jude
.4ff 270

Revelation
1—3 31
1.1 64
1.3 262
1.5 189
1.6 237, 262, 266, 284
1.9ff 239, 262, 269
1.13ff 36, 192, 269
2—3 284
2.4 287

2.7 107
2.9 78, 224
2.14 202, 262
2.20 202, 243, 262
2.22 210
3.12 253
3.17 287
3.21 239, 253
4.— 32, 58, 62, 64
4.8 293
4.11 293
5.— 117, 187, 245
5.3 294
5.6 253
5.9 29
5.10 262
6.— 88, 294
6.9 92, 294
7.— 42
7.9f 150
7.14 210
8.— 88, 294
9.— 88, 294
9.20f 293
10—11 188, 209, 262
11.— 262
11.7ff 284
12.7 33
12.9f 34
13.— 62, 90, 279, 369
14.— 101
15.— 29
16.— 88, 294
17.— 90
19.10 209, 262
19.11ff 56, 293
20.— 149, 253
20.4 91, 262
20.10f 137
20.12 91
21—22 90, 252, 294
21.1ff 28, 188
21.3 255, 294
21.4 150
21.24f 150
21.25 30
22.15 64
22.18 269
22.20 56, 115, 242

Index of Ancient Sources

EARLY CHRISTIAN LITERATURE

Ascension of Isaiah
6ff 58
9.8ff 92

Barnabas 265, 367

Basilides 369

Clement of Alexandria:
Excerpta ex Theodoto
52 369

1 Clement
5 204
40 266

Cyprian
Epistle 75.110 242

Didache
9 240f
10 241f
11.3ff 148, 270, 273
11.7f 243, 273
12 260, 262
13.3 266
13.6 243
16.3 148, 270

Eusebius
Chron. 374
Hist. Eccl. (EH)
1.7 119
2.23 168
3.11 264
3.28 149, 291
3.39 291
4.6 15
5.17 270
Praep. Evang. 37

Hippolytus
— 266
Apostolic Tradition
17 238
26 241
Refutations
5.8.33 369

Ignatius
Ephesians
5 265
6 265
7 265
20 242
Magnesians
7 265

8 265
Philadelphians
3 265
Smyrnaeans
8 243, 265
Trallians
2 265
6 265
7 265
10 265

Irenaeus
Heresies (Adv. Haer.)
1.6.4 369
5.33.3f 149

Justin
Apology
39 369
67 239
Dialogue with Trypho
7 148
16 5, 339
47 5, 339
69 306
93 5, 339
95 5, 339

108 5, 339
116 266
117 5, 339
133 5, 339
137 5, 339

Martyrdom of Polycarp
9 297
13 78

Odes of Solomon
11.16f 107
20.7 107

Origen
Contra Celsum
3.4 306
6.24ff 370

Peter, Gospel of
10 192

Tertullian
Apology
21 81
39 274, 369
40 297f

OTHER SOURCES

GNOSTIC TEXTS
Hypostasis of the Archons
141.23ff 295

Letter to Rheginos
49.15f 203

GREEK & LATIN AUTHORS
Dio Cassius
Histories
66.7 81, 331
69.12ff 15

Martial
Epigr. 7 & 11 332

Pliny
Letters 10.96f 78

Tacitus
Annals
2.42 331
15.44 298
Histories
5 14, 315

422

INDEX OF SUBJECTS